The Ministers Manual

By the same editor

Best Sermons (seven annual volumes)
Biblical Preaching: An Expositor's Treasury
God's Inescapable Nearness (coauthor with Eduard Schweizer)
A Guide to Biblical Preaching
A Handbook of Themes for Preaching
Learning to Speak Effectively
Minister's Worship Manual (coeditor with Ernest A. Payne and Stephen
    F. Winward)
Preaching: A Comprehensive Approach to the Design and Delivery of
    Sermons
Surprised by God
The Twentieth Century Pulpit, Vols. I and II

SEVENTY-FOURTH ANNUAL ISSUE

THE MINISTERS MANUAL

1999 EDITION

Edited by

JAMES W. COX

Jossey-Bass Publishers • San Francisco

Editors of THE MINISTERS MANUAL

G. B. F. Hallock, D.D., 1926–1958
M. K. W. Heicher, Ph.D., 1943–1968
Charles L. Wallis, M.A., M.Div., 1969–1983
James W. Cox, M.Div., Ph.D.

Substantial discounts on bulk quantities of Jossey-Bass books are available to corporations, professional associations, and other organizations. For details and discount information, contact the special sales department at Jossey-Bass Inc., Publishers (415) 433–1740; Fax (800) 605–2665.

For sales outside the United States, please contact your local Simon & Schuster International Office.

Jossey-Bass Web address: http://www.josseybass.com

 Manufactured in the United States of America on Lyons Falls Turin Book. This paper is acid-free and 100 percent totally chlorine-free.

Library of Congress Cataloging Card Number

25-21658
ISSN 0738-5323
ISBN 0-7879-4205-7

FIRST EDITION
HB Printing   10 9 8 7 6 5 4 3 2 1

CONTENTS

PREFACE

The value of *The Ministers Manual* can best be described by first noting what it can do for the preacher, but its use extends to other ministers—musicians, directors of Christian Education, teachers, youth workers, discussion group leaders, evangelists, and missionaries. As well, many others find the *Manual* useful for private devotional reading.

For preachers, it can get the creative processes going and can provide a nudge toward discovering potential variety in the treatment of texts and themes. At the same time, it can serve as a kind of checklist to determine if one is neglecting or overlooking important texts and themes. Also, it often provides the needed illustration to make the sermon memorable and impressive.

For musicians and sometimes for preachers, it can suggest the appropriate hymn for choir or congregation—music that complements the lectionary selections for the day or that highlights the season in the church year.

For children's workers, it provides a talk for each Sunday of the year.

Two special sections in the *Manual* deserve particular notice. Eduard Schweizer has written two Bible Studies that take us verse by verse through extended passages from the Bible. Dr. Schweizer is former professor of New Testament and Rektor (president) of the University of Zurich in Switzerland. Clayton K. Harrop has written six sermons on faith. Dr. Harrop is former professor of New Testament and Dean of the Golden Gate Theological Seminary in California.

Many contributors—from many different denominational backgrounds—have made this volume possible. They share our common faith and enrich our personal understanding and devotion. The Southern Baptist Theological Seminary, where I have taught since 1959, has provided valuable secretarial assistance in producing the manuscript. The current volume was word-processed by Linda Durkin, with the assistance of Ja-Rhonda Staples and Bev V. Tillman. I wish to thank all of these people and the authors and publishers from whose works I have quoted. I am again deeply grateful.

James W. Cox
The Southern Baptist Theological Seminary
2825 Lexington Road
Louisville, Kentucky 40280

SECTION I.
General Aids and Resources
Civil Year Calendars for 1999 and 2000

1999

January						
S	M	T	W	T	F	S
					1	2
3	4	5	6	7	8	9
10	11	12	13	14	15	16
17	18	19	20	21	22	23
24	25	26	27	28	29	30
31						

February						
S	M	T	W	T	F	S
	1	2	3	4	5	6
7	8	9	10	11	12	13
14	15	16	17	18	19	20
21	22	23	24	25	26	27
28						

March						
S	M	T	W	T	F	S
	1	2	3	4	5	6
7	8	9	10	11	12	13
14	15	16	17	18	19	20
21	22	23	24	25	26	27
28	29	30	31			

April						
S	M	T	W	T	F	S
				1	2	3
4	5	6	7	8	9	10
11	12	13	14	15	16	17
18	19	20	21	22	23	24
25	26	27	28	29	30	

May						
S	M	T	W	T	F	S
						1
2	3	4	5	6	7	8
9	10	11	12	13	14	15
16	17	18	19	20	21	22
23	24	25	26	27	28	29
30	31					

June						
S	M	T	W	T	F	S
		1	2	3	4	5
6	7	8	9	10	11	12
13	14	15	16	17	18	19
20	21	22	23	24	25	26
27	28	29	30			

July						
S	M	T	W	T	F	S
				1	2	3
4	5	6	7	8	9	10
11	12	13	14	15	16	17
18	19	20	21	22	23	24
25	26	27	28	29	30	31

August						
S	M	T	W	T	F	S
1	2	3	4	5	6	7
8	9	10	11	12	13	
15	16	17	18	19	20	
21	22	23	24	25	26	27
28	29	30				

September						
S	M	T	W	T	F	S
			1	2	3	4
5	6	7	8	9	10	11
12	13	14	15	16	17	18
19	20	21	22	23	24	25
26	27	28	29	30		

October						
S	M	T	W	T	F	S
					1	2
3	4	5	6	7	8	9
10	11	12	13	14	15	16
17	18	19	20	21	22	23
24	25	26	27	28	29	30
31						

November						
S	M	T	W	T	F	S
	1	2	3	4	5	6
7	8	9	10	11	12	13
14	15	16	17	18	19	20
21	22	23	24	25	26	27
28	29	30				

December						
S	M	T	W	T	F	S
		1	2	3	4	
5	6	7	8	9	10	11
12	13	14	15	16	17	18
19	20	21	22	23	24	25
26	27	28	29	30	31	

2000

January						
S	M	T	W	T	F	S
						1
2	3	4	5	6	7	8
9	10	11	12	13	14	15
16	17	18	19	20	21	22
23	24	25	26	27	28	29
30	31					

February						
S	M	T	W	T	F	S
		1	2	3	4	5
6	7	8	9	10	11	12
13	14	15	16	17	18	19
20	21	22	23	24	25	26
27	28	29				

March						
S	M	T	W	T	F	S
			1	2	3	4
5	6	7	8	9	10	11
12	13	14	15	16	17	18
19	20	21	22	23	24	25
26	27	28	29	30	31	

April						
S	M	T	W	T	F	S
						1
2	3	4	5	6	7	8
9	10	11	12	13	14	15
16	17	18	19	20	21	22
23	24	25	26	27	28	29
30						

May						
S	M	T	W	T	F	S
	1	2	3	4	5	6
7	8	9	10	11	12	13
14	15	16	17	18	19	20
21	22	23	24	25	26	27
28	29	30	31			

June						
S	M	T	W	T	F	S
				1	2	3
4	5	6	7	8	9	10
11	12	13	14	15	16	17
18	19	20	21	22	23	24
25	26	27	28	29	30	

July						
S	M	T	W	T	F	S
						1
2	3	4	5	6	7	8
9	10	11	12	13	14	15
16	17	18	19	20	21	22
23	24	25	26	27	28	29
30	31					

August						
S	M	T	W	T	F	S
		1	2	3	4	5
6	7	8	9	10	11	12
13	14	15	16	17	18	19
20	21	22	23	24	25	26
27	28	29	30	31		

September						
S	M	T	W	T	F	S
					1	2
3	4	5	6	7	8	9
10	11	12	13	14	15	16
17	18	19	20	21	22	23
24	25	26	27	28	29	30

October						
S	M	T	W	T	F	S
1	2	3	4	5	6	7
8	9	10	11	12	13	14
15	16	17	18	19	20	21
22	23	24	24	26	27	28
29	30	31				

November						
S	M	T	W	T	F	S
		1	2	3	4	
5	6	7	8	9	10	11
12	13	14	15	16	17	18
19	20	21	22	23	24	25
26	27	28	29	30		

December						
S	M	T	W	T	F	S
					1	2
3	4	5	6	7	8	9
10	11	12	13	14	15	16
17	18	19	20	21	22	23
24	25	26	27	28	29	30
31						

Church and Civic Calendar for 1999

JANUARY

1 New Year's Day
   The Name of Jesus
5 Twelfth Night
6 Epiphany
   Armenian Christmas
18 Martin Luther King Jr. Day
    Confession of St. Peter
25 Conversion of St. Paul

FEBRUARY

1 National Freedom Day
2 Presentation of Jesus in the
   Temple
   Groundhog Day
3 Four Chaplains Memorial Day
12 Lincoln's Birthday
14 St. Valentine's Day
15 Presidents' Day
17 Ash Wednesday
21 First Sunday in Lent
22 Washington's Birthday
24 St. Mathias, Apostle
28 Second Sunday in Lent

MARCH

2 Purim
7 Third Sunday in Lent
14 Fourth Sunday in Lent
17 St. Patrick's Day
19 Joseph, Husband of Mary
21 Fifth Sunday in Lent
25 The Annunciation
28 Palm/Passion Sunday
28-April 3 Holy Week

APRIL

1 Maundy Thursday
1-8 Passover
2 Good Friday
4 Easter
   Daylight saving time begins
11 Orthodox Easter
14 Pan-American Day
25 St. Mark, Evangelist

MAY

1 Law Day
   Loyalty Day
   May Day
   St. Philip and St. James, Apostles
1-5 Cinco de Mayo Celebration
9 Mother's Day
13 Ascension Day
21 First Day of Shavuot
23 Pentecost
30 Trinity Sunday
31 Memorial Day
    The Visitation of Mary

JUNE

11 St. Barnabas, Apostle
13 Children's Sunday
20 Father's Day
24 The Nativity of St. John the
    Baptist
29 St. Peter and St. Paul, Apostles

JULY

1 Canada Day
4 Independence Day
22 St. Mary Magdalene
25 St. James, Apostle

AUGUST

1 Civic Holiday (Canada)
6 The Transfiguration
14 Atlantic Charter Day
15 Mary, Mother of Jesus
24 St. Bartholomew, Apostle
26 Women's Equality Day

SEPTEMBER

5 Labor Sunday
6 Labor Day
11 First Day of Rosh Hashanah
12 National Grandparents' Day
    Rally Day
21 St. Matthew, Apostle and
    Evangelist
25 First Day of Sukkoth
29 St. Michael and All Angels

OCTOBER

3 World Communion Sunday
10 Laity Sunday

11 Columbus Day (observed)
Thanksgiving Day (Canada)
16 World Food Day
18 St. Luke, Evangelist
23 St. James, Brother of Jesus
24 United Nations Day
31 Daylight saving time ends
National UNICEF Day
Reformation Day
Halloween

NOVEMBER

1 All Saints' Day
2 All Souls' Day
11 Armistice Day
Veterans Day
Remembrance Day (Canada)
14 Stewardship Sunday
25 Thanksgiving Day

28 First Sunday of Advent
Bible Sunday
30 St. Andrew, Apostle

DECEMBER

4 First Day of Hanukkah
5 Second Sunday of Advent
12 Third Sunday of Advent
19 Fourth Sunday of Advent
21 Forefathers' Day
St. Thomas, Apostle
24 Christmas Eve
25 Christmas
26 Boxing Day (Canada)
St. Stephen, Deacon
27 St. John, Apostle and Evangelist
28 The Holy Innocents
31 New Year's Eve
Watch Night

The Revised Common Lectionary for 1999

The following Scripture lessons are commended for use in public worship by various Protestant churches and the Roman Catholic Church and include first, second, and Gospel readings, and Psalms, according to Cycle A from January 3 to November 21 and according to Cycle B from November 28 to December 26. (Copyright 1992 Consultation on Common Texts.)

Jan. 3: Jer. 31:7–14; Ps. 147:12–20; Eph. 1:3–14; John 1:(1–9) 10–18

EPIPHANY SEASON

Jan. 10 (Epiphany Sunday): Isa. 60:1–6; Ps. 72:1–7, 10–14; Eph. 3:1–12; Matt. 2:1–12
Jan. 17: Isa. 49:1–7; Ps. 40:1–11; 1 Cor. 1:1–9; John 1:29–42
Jan. 24: Isa. 9:1–4; Ps. 27:1, 4–9; 1 Cor. 1:10–18; Matt. 4:12–23
Jan. 31: Mic. 6:1–8; Ps. 15; 1 Cor. 1:18–31; Matt. 5:1–12
Feb. 7: Isa. 58:1–9a (9b–12); Ps. 112:1–9 (10); 1 Cor. 2:1–12 (13–16)
Feb. 14: Deut. 30:15–20; Ps. 119:1–8; 1 Cor. 3:1–9; Matt. 5:21–37

LENTEN SEASON

Feb. 17 (Ash Wednesday): Joel 2:1–2, 12–17; Ps. 51:1–17; 2 Cor. 5:20b–6:10; Matt. 6:1–6, 16–21

Feb. 21: Gen. 2:15–17; 3:1–7; Ps. 32; Rom. 5:12–19; Matt. 4:1–11
Feb. 28: Gen. 12:1–4a; Ps. 121; Rom. 4:1–5, 13–17; John 3:1–17
Mar. 7: Exod. 17:1–7; Ps. 95; Rom. 5:1–11; John 4:5–42
Mar. 14: 1 Sam. 16:1–13; Ps. 23; Eph. 5:8–14; John 9:1–41
Mar. 21: Ezek. 37:1–14; Ps. 130; Rom. 8:6–11; John 11:1–45

HOLY WEEK

Mar. 28 (Passion/Palm Sunday): Liturgy of the Palms: Matt. 21:1–11; Ps. 118:1–2, 19–29; Liturgy of the Passion: Isa. 50:4–9a; Ps. 31:9–16; Phil. 2:5–11; Matt. 26:14–27:66
Mar. 29 (Monday): Isa. 42:1–9; Ps. 36:5–11; Heb. 9:11–15; John 12:1–11
Mar. 30 (Tuesday): Isa. 49:1–7; Ps. 71:1–14; 1 Cor. 1:18–31; John 12:20–36
Mar. 31 (Wednesday): Isa. 50:4–9a; Ps. 70; Heb. 12:1–3; John 13:21–32
Apr. 1 (Holy Thursday): Exod. 12:1–4 (5–10), 11–14; Ps. 116:1–2, 12–19; 1 Cor. 11:23–26; John 13:1–7, 31b–35
Apr. 2 (Good Friday): Isa. 52:–53:12; Ps. 22; Heb. 10:15–25; John 18:1–19:42
Apr. 3 (Holy Saturday): Job 14:1–14; Ps. 31:1–4, 15–16; 1 Pet. 4:1–8; Matt. 27:57–66
Apr. 3–4 (Easter Vigil): Gen. 1:1–2:4a; Ps.

136:1–9, 23–26; Gen. 7:1–5, 11–18; 8:6–18, 9:8–13; Ps. 46; Gen. 22:1–18; Ps. 16; Exod. 14:10–31; 15:20–21; Exod. 15:1b–13, 17–18 (resp.); Isa. 55:1–11; Isa. 12:2–6 (resp.); Bar. 3:9–15, 32; 4:4 (alt.); Prov. 8:1–8, 19–21; 9:4–6 (alt.); Ps. 19; Ezek. 36:24–28; Pss. 42–43; Ezek. 37:1–14; Ps. 143; Zeph. 3:14–20; Ps. 98; Rom. 6:3–11; Ps. 114; Luke 24:1–12

Apr. 4 (Easter): Acts 10:34–43; Ps. 118:1–2, 14–24; Col. 3:1–4; John 20:1–18 or Isa. 25:6–9; Ps. 114; 1 Cor. 5:6b–8; Luke 24:13–49

Apr. 11: Acts 2:14a, 22–32; Ps. 16; 1 Pet. 1:3–9; John 20:19–31

Apr. 18: Acts 2:14a, 36–41; Ps. 116:1–4, 12–19; 1 Pet. 1:17–23; Luke 24:13–35

Apr. 25: Acts 2:42–47; Ps. 23; 1 Pet. 19–25; John 10:1–10

May 2: Acts 7:55–60; Ps. 31:1–5, 15–16; 1 Pet. 2:2–10; John 14:1–14

May 9: Acts 17:22–31; Ps. 66:8–20; 1 Pet. 3:13–22; John 14:15–21

May 16: Acts 1:6–14; Ps. 68:1–10, 32–35; 1 Pet. 4:12–14, 5:6–11; John 17:1–11

SEASON OF PENTECOST

May 23 (Pentecost): Num. 11:24–30; Ps. 104:24–34, 35b; Acts 2:1–21 or 1 Cor. 12:3b–13; John 20:19–23 or John 7:37–39

May 30 (Trinity): Gen. 1:1–2:4a; Ps. 8; 2 Cor. 13:11–13; Matt. 28:16–20

June 6: Gen. 12:1–9; Ps. 33:1–12; Rom. 4:13–25; Matt. 9:9–13, 18–26

June 13: Gen. 18:1–15 (21:1–7); Ps. 116:1–2, 12–19; Rom. 5:1–8; Matt. 9:35–10:8

June 20: Gen. 21:8–21; Ps. 86:1–10, 16–17; Rom. 6:1b–11; Matt. 10:24–39

June 27: Gen. 22:1–14; Ps. 13; Rom. 6:12–23; Matt. 10:40–42

July 4: Gen. 24:34–38, 42–49, 58–67; Ps. 45:10–17; Rom. 7:15–25a; Matt. 11:16–19, 25–30

July 11: Gen. 25:19–34; Ps. 119:105–112; Rom. 8:1–11; Matt. 13:1–9, 18–23

July 18: Gen. 28:10–19a; Ps. 139:1–12, 23–24; Rom. 8:12–25; Matt. 13:24–30, 36–43

July 25: Gen. 29:15–28; Ps. 105:1–11, 45b; Rom. 8:26–39; Matt. 13:31–33, 44–52

Aug. 1: Gen. 32:22–31; Ps. 17:1–7, 15; Rom. 9:1–5; Matt. 14:13–21

Aug. 8: Gen. 37:1–4, 12–28; Ps. 105:1–16, 16–22, 45b; Rom. 10:5–15; Matt. 14:22–33

Aug. 15: Gen. 45:1–15; Ps. 133; Rom. 11:1–2a, 29–32; Matt. 15:(10–20), 21–28

Aug. 22: Exod. 1:8–2:10; Ps. 124; Rom. 12:1–8; Matt. 16:13–20

Aug. 29: Exod. 3:1–15; Ps. 105:1–6, 23–26, 45b; Rom. 12:9–21; Matt. 16:21–28

Sept. 5: Exod. 12:1–14; Ps. 149; Rom. 13:8–14; Matt. 18:15–20

Sept. 12: Exod. 14:19–31; Ps. 114; Rom. 14:1–12; Matt. 18:21–35

Sept. 19: Exod. 16:2–15; Ps. 105:1–6, 37–45; Phil. 1:21–30; Matt. 20:1–16

Sept. 26: Exod. 17:1–7; Ps. 78:1–4, 12–16; Phil. 2:1–13; Matt. 21:23–32

Oct. 3: Exod. 20:1–4, 7–9, 12–20; Ps. 19; Phil. 3:4b–14; Matt. 21:33–46

Oct. 10: Exod. 32:1–14; Ps. 106:11–6, 19–23; Phil. 4:1–9; Matt. 22:1–14

Oct. 17: Exod. 33:12–23; Ps. 99; 1 Thess. 1:1–10; Matt. 22:15–22

Oct. 24: Deut. 34:1–12; Ps. 90:1–6, 13–17; 1 Thess. 2:1–8; Matt. 22:34–46

Oct. 31: Josh. 3:7–17; Ps. 107:1–7, 33–37; 1 Thess. 2:9–13; Matt. 23:1–12

Nov. 7: Josh. 24:1–3a, 14–25; Ps. 78:1–7; 1 Thess. 4:13–18; Matt. 25:1–13

Nov. 14: Judges 4:1–7; Ps. 123; 1 Thess. 5:1–11; Matt. 25:14–30

Nov. 21: Ezek. 34:11–16, 20–24; Ps. 100; Eph. 1:15–23; Matt. 25:31–46

ADVENT AND CHRISTMAS SEASON

Nov. 28 (Advent): Isa. 64:1–9; Ps. 80:1–7, 17–19; 1 Cor. 1:3–9; Mark 13:24–37

Dec. 5: Isa. 40:1–11; Ps. 85:1–2, 8–13; 2 Pet. 3:8–15a; Mark 1:1–8

Dec. 12: Isa. 61:1–4, 8–11; Ps. 126; 1 Thess. 5:16–24; John 1:6–8, 19–28

Dec. 19: 2 Sam. 7:1–11, 16; Luke 1:47–55; Rom. 16:25–27; Luke 1:26–38

Dec. 25 (Christmas Day): Isa. 9:2–7; Ps. 96; Titus 2:11–14; Luke 2:1–14 (15–20) or Isa. 62:6–12; Ps. 97; Titus 3:4–7; Luke 3:(1–7), 8–20 or Isa. 52:7–10; Ps. 98; Heb. 1:1–4 (5–12); John 1:1–14

Dec. 26: Isa. 61:10–62:3; Ps. 148; Gal. 4:4–7; Luke 2:22–40

Four-Year Church Calendar

	1999	2000	2001	2002
Ash Wednesday	February 17	March 8	February 28	February 13
Palm Sunday	March 28	April 16	April 8	March 24
Good Friday	April 2	April 21	April 13	March 29
Easter	April 4	April 23	April 15	March 31
Ascension Day	May 13	June 1	May 24	May 9
Pentecost	May 23	June 11	June 3	May 19
Trinity Sunday	May 30	June 18	June 10	May 26
Thanksgiving	November 25	November 23	November 22	November 28
Advent Sunday	November 28	December 3	December 2	December 1

Forty-Year Easter Calendar

1999 April 4	2009 April 12	2019 April 21	2029 April 1
2000 April 23	2010 April 4	2020 April 12	2030 April 21
2001 April 18	2011 April 24	2021 April 4	2031 April 13
2002 March 31	2012 April 8	2022 April 17	2032 March 28
2003 April 20	2013 March 31	2023 April 9	2033 April 17
2004 April 11	2014 April 20	2024 March 31	2034 April 9
2005 March 27	2015 April 5	2025 April 20	2035 March 25
2006 April 16	2016 March 27	2026 April 5	2036 April 13
2007 April 8	2017 April 16	2027 March 28	2037 April 5
2008 March 23	2018 April 1	2028 April 16	2038 April 25

Traditional Wedding Anniversary Identifications

1 Paper	7 Wool	13 Lace	35 Coral
2 Cotton	8 Bronze	14 Ivory	40 Ruby
3 Leather	9 Pottery	15 Crystal	45 Sapphire
4 Linen	10 Tin	20 China	50 Gold
5 Wood	11 Steel	25 Silver	55 Emerald
6 Iron	12 Silk	30 Pearl	60 Diamond

Colors Appropriate for Days and Seasons

White. Symbolizes purity, perfection, and joy, and identifies festivals marking events in the life of Jesus, except Good Friday: Christmas, Epiphany, Easter, Eastertide, Ascension Day; also Trinity Sunday, All Saints' Day, weddings, funerals. Gold also may be used.

Red. Symbolizes the Holy Spirit, martyrdom, and the love of God: Good Friday, Pentecost, and Sundays following.

Violet. Symbolizes penitence: Advent, Lent.

Green. Symbolizes mission to the world, hope, regeneration, nurturance, and growth: Epiphany season, Kingdomtide, Rural Life Sunday, Labor Sunday, Thanksgiving Sunday.

Blue. Advent, in some churches.

Flowers in Season Appropriate for Church Use

January: carnation or snowdrop
February: violet or primrose
March: jonquil or daffodil
April: lily, sweet pea, or daisy
May: lily of the valley or hawthorn
June: rose or honeysuckle

July: larkspur or water lily
August: gladiolus poppy
September: aster or morning star
October: calendula or cosmos
November: chrysanthemum
December: narcissus, holly, or poinsettia

Historical, Cultural, and Religious Anniversaries in 1999

Compiled by Kenneth M. Cox

10 years (1989). *Jan. 16:* Police shooting of an unarmed black man sparks three days of rioting in Miami. *Mar. 24:* The oil tanker *Exxon Valdez* runs aground on a reef in Prince William Sound, Alaska, spilling more than 200,000 barrels of crude oil. *Apr. 17:* A Warsaw court restores the legal status of Poland's Solidarity Party. *May 4:* Retired marine lieutenant colonel Oliver North is convicted on charges related to the Iran-Contra affair, and later receives a suspended sentence. *June 3:* Ayatollah Ruholla Khomeini dies in Iran. *July 3:* The U.S. Supreme Court upholds individual states' ability to impose certain restrictions on abortion rights. *Oct. 5:* Television evangelist Jim Bakker is convicted on all counts of fraud and conspiracy in connection with his Praise The Lord ministry in Charlotte, North Carolina, and later receives a forty-five–year prison sentence. *Dec. 1:* Mikhail Gorbachev becomes the first Soviet leader to meet with the head of the Roman Catholic Church, conferring with Pope John Paul II in the Vatican. *Dec. 22:* Romanian president Nicolae Ceausescu is overthrown, and executed three days later for genocide and abuse of power.

25 years (1974). *Feb. 2:* China launches its Cultural Revolution in a war against capitalism and imperialism. *Feb. 4:* Patricia Hearst is kidnapped in Berkeley, California, by a group connected with the radical Symbionese Liberation Army. *Apr. 8:* Hank Aaron of baseball's Atlanta Braves hits his 715th career home run, surpassing Babe Ruth's lifetime total. *Aug. 9:* Richard Nixon resigns the U.S. presidency and Vice President Gerald Ford is sworn in to succeed him. *Sept. 8:* Ford grants Nixon a full pardon for all federal crimes he "committed or may have committed or taken part in" while in office.

50 years (1949). *Apr. 4:* The North Atlantic Treaty Organization (NATO) is created by a treaty signed by the United States, Belgium, Britain, Canada, Denmark, France, Iceland, Italy, Luxembourg, the Netherlands, Norway, and Portugal—a pledge of cooperation and mutual assistance in resisting aggression in the area. *Oct. 1:* The People's Republic of China is proclaimed, with Mao Tse-tung as chairman and Chou En-lai as premier, and Chiang Kai-shek's power ends. *Debuts:* George Orwell's *Nineteen Eighty-Four;* Silly Putty; Pillsbury Bake-offs.

75 years (1924). The Leopold-Loeb murder case makes national headlines. *Jan. 21:* Vladimir Ilyich Lenin dies, leading to a struggle between Joseph Stalin and Leon Trotsky for power in Russia. *Debuts:* IBM; *Little Orphan Annie;* Wheaties; Macy's Thanksgiving Day Parade.

100 years (1899). Thorstein Bunde Veblen's *The Theory of the Leisure Class* introduces the terms *conspicuous consumption* and *conspicuous waste. Apr. 10:* Theodore Roosevelt, then governor of New York, says in a speech, "I wish to preach, not the doctrine of ignoble ease, but the doctrine of the strenuous life." *Oct. 12:* The Boer War begins in South Africa. *Debuts:* Mount Rainer National Park; Oysters Rockefeller.

150 years (1849). Henry David Thoreau's essay "Resistance to Civil Government" (later republished under the title "On the Duty of Civil Disobedience") advocates citizens' duty to oppose bad government by acts of passive resistance and says "that government is best which governs least." Tens of thousands of "Forty-Niners" flock to California to search for gold. Maryland slave Harriet Tubman escapes to the North and begins work on the Underground Railway, ultimately freeing

hundreds from slavery in the South. *Debuts:* U.S. Department of the Interior; Bowler hat (derby); Moscow's Kremlin Palace.

200 years (1799). A large, black basalt block bearing hieroglyphics and demotic and Greek characters, which will become known as the Rosetta stone, is discovered in Egypt. *Dec. 14:* George Washington dies at 67; he is remembered in a funeral oration as "first in war, first in peace and first in the hearts of his countrymen." *Debuts:* American smallpox vaccination; U.S. Executive Mansion (later called the White House); gas lighting.

Quotable Quotations

1. Thou shalt ever joy at eventide if thou spend the day fruitfully.—Thomas à Kempis, *The Imitation of Christ*

2. A miracle has never yet brought anyone to faith, since it is always open to other interpretations.—Helmut Thielicke, *The Silence of God*

3. We need to be reminded that at its heart Christianity is joy and that laughter and freedom and the reaching out of arms are the essence of it.—Frederick Buechner, *The Hungering Dark*

4. Religion is full of difficulties, but if we are often puzzled what to think, we need seldom be in doubt what to do.—John Lubbock, *Pleasures of Life*

5. Just as every natural event is the manifestation at a particular place and moment of Nature's total character, so every particular Christian miracle manifests at a particular place and moment the character and significance of the Incarnation.—C. S. Lewis, *Miracles*

6. Conversions are to be known by their fruits, not by their tendrils and blossoms.—Theodore Bovet, *That They May Have Life*

7. The problem of life is the problem of controlling and directing aggressions.—Karl Menninger, *Love Against Hate*

8. God guides more of His servants in the paths of obscurity than He guides in the floodlit way.—W. E. Sangster, *God Does Guide Us*

9. Christ is God's Forgiveness.—George MacDonald, *Creation in Christ*

10. God is the "beyond" in the midst of our life.—Dietrich Bonhoeffer, *Letters and Papers from Prison*

11. For each individual soul there is a vocation as real as if that soul were alone upon the planet.—Mark Rutherford, *The Deliverance of Mark Rutherford*

12. It is unfortunate that some Christians, exulting in the gospel of grace, can overlook the vital necessity of being gracious.—John N. Gladstone, *Living with Style*

13. The resurrection life of Christ is actualized wherever man takes up the cross of Christ, which means that he refuses to cling to this-worldly realities, that he lets them slide in order that God may bestow upon him the life of the transcendent world of the spirit.—Rudolf Bultmann, *This World and the Beyond*

14. The blazing evidence of immortality is our dissatisfaction with any other solution.—Ralph Waldo Emerson, *Journal*

15. Really satisfactory life is not inherent in our human condition. It is a gift of grace from beyond the human being. Simply the fact that we do find this grace, even now and then, in our present, earth-bound lives is one reason for believing in a God who wants us to go on to a new level of life in this universe of his.—Morton T. Kelsey, *Afterlife*

16. The tragedy that threatens to break man's spirit and destroy his world is a constant reminder of Love's weakness. But faith also apprehends Love's strength and gives to hope a logic of its own.—Peter Baelz, *Prayer and Providence*

17. It is through obedience, yes, even through our misguided actions, that we find ever greater light.—Paul Tournier, *To Resist or to Surrender*

18. Christ died to save us, not from suffering, but from ourselves; not from injustice, far less from justice, but from being unjust.—George MacDonald, *Creation in Christ*

19. Holiness is the toughest, most demanding, vocation in the world.—Charles Colson, *Loving God*

20. My father considered a walk among the mountains as the equivalent of churchgoing.—Aldous Huxley, *Those Barren Leaves*

21. If God did not exist we should have to invent him.—Voltaire

22. If we look beyond ourselves at that which is greater than we, then we can feel called to help others in just the moment when we ourselves need help most urgently—and astonishingly.—Paul Tillich, *The Eternal Now*

23. I find only one way to ease the weight of my own cross, and that is the way of Simon of Cyrene: Carry another's cross, help another Christ struggle to Calvary.—Walter J. Burghardt, S.J., *Still Proclaiming Your Wonders*

24. The intrinsic greatness of Christianity is revealed in this capacity of development by which it advances with the advancing life of humanity.—George Galloway, *The Philosophy of Religion*

25. Whatever we say about God and His ways can only be half-truths, expressed haltingly in our poor, human language.—D. M. Baillie, *Faith in God*

26. If we want each Christian to live out his faith in a concrete way in his personal life, how can we not want all Christians to do so in a collective way?—Jacques Ellul, *The New Demons*

27. If we encounter in a personality fear of divine punishment as the sole sanction for right doing, we can be sure we are dealing with a childish conscience, with a case of arrested development.—Gordon Wallport, *Becoming*

28. When a man loathes himself, he has begun to be saved.—George MacDonald, *Creation in Christ*

29. To be a leader, means, especially, having the opportunity to make a meaningful difference in the lives of those who permit leaders to lead.—Max DePree, *Leadership Is an Art*

30. When I become certain that Jesus Christ is with me—then, and then alone, am I armed against evil.—Emil Brunner, *I Believe in the Living God*

31. Thou wast with me, and I was not with thee.—St. Augustine, *Confessions*

32. What can only be taught by the rod and with blows will not lead to much good; they will not remain pious any longer than the rod is behind them.—Martin Luther, *The Great Catechism, Second Command*

33. Even the most puzzling or bitter thing that happens to us can be accepted in such a way that it is transmuted into something of value to ourselves, to others and to God.—Leslie J. Tizard, *Facing Life and Death*

34. The mind which demands, "Prove it to me," is not a mind: it is an IBM machine totting up pros and cons. A live mind, like any other living creature, must make its ventures. Prayer is man's most amazing and shining venture.—George A. Buttrick, *The Power of Prayer Today*

35. Ambition is a very dangerous thing; without it, in some degree a man would soon grow weary, and with it he is likely to be led away.—Francois Fenelon, *Spiritual Letters*

36. We do not know in what ways or in what scale of time God is bringing future good out of present evil; but that He is doing so, and that we can therefore commit ourselves wholly to His providence, is the practical outcome of faith in God's love and sovereignty seen in the life, death and resurrection of the Christ.—John Hick, *Evil and the God of Love*

37. If we ask, What is Man? Then the answer above all others which we must give again and again for all men to hear is this:

Man is God's creature
Man is God's partner
Man is God's beloved child
He is one to whom God speaks
He is one whose sins have all been taken away by God's Son
He is one who has been made partaker of God's Holy Spirit
—Theodore Bovet, *That They May Have Life*

38. Usually a person with an unswerving belief in a God of justice and goodness is one who was blessed with a loving incorruptible parent.—Karl Menninger, *Love Against Hate*

39. If the redeeming death and resurrection reveal a "love divine, all loves excelling," they reveal also a divine determination which nothing in earth or hell shall prevail to break, and a Christ who is marching from the green hill where He died to the throne of all the world.—James S. Stewart, *A Man in Christ*

40. "Faith" . . . seems to carry a warmer glow of affection than does bare "belief." It suggests that though the risk may be greater, still the commitment is stronger and the outcome of the wager more precious.—Gordon W. Allport, *The Individual and His Religion*

41. There never was a good war, or a bad peace.—Benjamin Franklin

42. When thou prayest, rather let thy heart be without words than thy words without heart.—John Bunyan

43. Revelation is event plus interpretation, where the event and interpretation are mutually interactive. When the interpretation is under constraint, above all when it is compulsive, there can be no revelation; there is then only some form of totalitarian dictatorship.—Paul Scherer, *The Word God Sent*

44. We draw near to Christ by following him even on clumsy and reluctant feet and without knowing more than two cents' worth at first about what is involved in following him—into the seventy-five-mile-per-hour, neon-lit pain of our world.—Frederick Buechner, *The Hungering Dark*

45. An act of faith is an act of a finite being who is grasped by and turned to the infinite.—Paul Tillich, *Dynamics of Faith*

46. Life is lent to be spent.—Douglas V. Steere, *On Beginning from Within*

47. The doctor who has experienced in his own life the effect of grace knows that, without excluding medicines, advice, and psychological analyses, grace is more precious than all these.—Paul Tournier, *The Person Reborn*

48. Only as we jointly seek to unmask the principalities of this age and to reclaim a biblical vision can we offer the world a compelling hope.—Tom Sine, *Wild Hope*

49. Man is that being who has invented the gas chambers of Auschwitz; however, he is also that being who has entered those gas chambers upright, with the Lord's Prayer or the Shema Yisrael on his lips.—Viktor Frankl, *Man's Search for Meaning*

50. It is religion's peculiar secret that it brings to the individual a solemn assurance unlike anything else in life, a tranquillity, an ever-present help in trouble, that makes next steps easier no matter what mesh of circumstances may entangle the life.—Gordon W. Allport, *The Individual and His Religion*

51. He who lives with Jesus Christ not only has light but also becomes a light—and were it only a modest little candlelight for others.—Emil Brunner, *I Believe in the Living God*

52. God is perfect love and perfect wisdom. We do not pray in order to change His Will, but to bring our wills into harmony with His.—William Temple

Questions of Life and Religion

These questions may be useful to prime homiletic pumps, as discussion starters, or for study and youth groups.

1. How should the sanctity of human life influence one's views on abortion?

2. Is God really absent during the "dark night of the soul"?

3. Do addictions have a spiritual cure?

4. What are the positive and compensating potentials in aging?

5. Is there any good in anger?

6. What does baptism do for the person baptized?

7. In what ways can we experience blessing?

8. Are there effective alternatives to capital punishment?

9. How can young people have human and Christian values instilled in them?

10. What constitutes a church?

11. Is absolute separation of church and state possible?

12. What creates true community?

13. Is confession to God alone enough?

14. What are the marks of a good conscience?

15. Is conversion once-and-for-all or is it a continuing process?

16. How does God make a covenant with his people?

17. Why do we call God creator?

18. In what ways is the cross of Christ a vital part of the Christian faith?

19. How does one prepare for death?

20. What are the basic ingredients of sound decision making?

21. How do Christians help one another deal with depression?

22. What does true discipleship look like today?

23. Are strict disciplines only for the monastic life or for the life of all Christians?

24. Is disease a matter of spiritual import?

25. How must divorce and remarriage be related to God's loving and redemptive purpose?

26. Does doubt, in some cases, play a

positive and creative role in intellectual and spiritual growth?

27. What are the responsibilities of Christian leaders in providing religious education for children and for new believers?

28. What is the purpose of God's election?

29. Is the "end time" a threat or a promise?

30. Why is protection of the environment a humanitarian and Christian duty?

31. How can we handle our envy and jealousy?

32. Which inequalities among us should be accepted and which should be contested?

33. What is "eternal life"?

34. To what extent and in what ways are biblical ethical teachings relevant now?

35. Why is the Lord's Supper (Communion, Eucharist) essential?

36. Should we send Christian missionaries to devout people of other faiths?

37. How can we define and characterize evil?

38. What is faith?

39. How is the church like a family?

40. Is fear good or bad or both?

41. What makes it possible to forgive those who have deliberately done us wrong?

42. How can God be defined and described?

43. Why is "grace" important in Christian faith and life?

44. How can we help those who are experiencing grief?

45. How can we find God's guidance for our decision making?

46. When is a person guilty before God?

47. What and where is "heaven"?

48. What are the several roles of the Holy Spirit in human experience?

49. Can people be truly and consistently honest in our kind of world?

50. Is "hope" more than wishful thinking?

51. Is humility a virtue or a weakness?

52. How widespread is idolatry in Western civilization today?

53. What is the meaning and significance of "the image of God" in human beings?

(These questions were suggested by and treated extensively in *Handbook of Themes for Preaching*, edited by James W. Cox, Westminster/John Knox Press, 1991.)

Biblical Benedictions and Blessings

The Lord watch between me and thee when we are absent from one another.—Gen. 31:49

The Lord our God be with us, as he was with our Fathers; let him not leave us nor forsake us; that he may incline our hearts unto him, to walk in all his ways and to keep his commandments and his statues and his judgments, which he commanded our fathers.—1 Kings 8:57–58

Let the words of my mouth and the meditation of my heart be acceptable in thy sight, O Lord, my strength and my redeemer.—Ps. 19:14

Now the God of patience and consolation grant you to be like-minded one toward another according to Christ Jesus; that ye may with one mind and one mouth glorify God, even the Father of our Lord Jesus Christ. Now the God of hope fill you with all joy and peace in believing, that ye may abound in hope, through the power of the Holy Ghost. Now the God of peace be with you.—Rom. 15:5–6, 13, 33

Now to him that is of power to establish you according to my gospel and the teaching of Jesus Christ, according to the revelation of the mystery, which was kept secret since the world began, but now is manifest, and by the scriptures of the prophets, according to the commandments of the everlasting God, made known to all nations for the glory through Jesus Christ for ever.—Rom. 16:25–27

Grace be unto you, and peace, from God our Father, and from the Lord Jesus Christ.—1 Cor. 1:3

The grace of the Lord Jesus Christ and the love of God and the communion of the Holy Ghost be with you all.—2 Cor. 13:14

Peace be to the brethren, and love with faith, from God the Father and the Lord Jesus

Christ. Grace be with all them that love our Lord Jesus Christ in sincerity.—Eph. 6:23–24

And the peace of God, which passeth all understanding, shall keep your hearts and minds though Christ Jesus. Finally, brethren, whatsoever things are true, whatsoever things are honest, whatsoever things are just, whatsoever things are pure, whatsoever things are lovely, whatsoever things are of good report; if there be any virtue, and if there be any praise, think on these things. Those things which ye have both learned and received, and heard and seen in me, do; and the God of peace shall be with you.—Phil. 4:7–9

Wherefore also we pray always for you, that our God would count you worthy of this calling and fulfill all the good pleasure of this goodness, and the work of faith with power; that the name of our Lord Jesus Christ may be glorified in you, and ye in him, according to the grace of our God and the Lord Jesus Christ.—2 Thess. 1:11–12

Now the Lord of peace himself give you peace always by all means. The Lord be with you all. The grace of our Lord Jesus Christ be with you all.—2 Thess. 3:16–18

Grace, mercy, and peace, from God our Father and Jesus Christ our Lord.—1 Tim. 1:2

Now the God of peace, that brought again from the dead our Lord Jesus, that great shepherd of the sheep, through the blood of the everlasting covenant, make you perfect in every good work to do his will, working in you that which is well-pleasing in his sight, through Jesus Christ, to whom be glory for ever and ever.—Heb. 13:20–21

The God of all grace, who hath called us unto his eternal glory by Christ Jesus, after that ye have suffered a while, make you perfect, establish, strengthen, settle you. To him be glory and dominion for ever and ever. Greet ye one another with a kiss of charity. Peace be with you all that are in Christ Jesus.—1 Pet. 3:10–14

Grace be with you, mercy, and peace from God the Father, and from the Lord Jesus Christ, the Son of the Father, in truth and love.—2 John 3

Now unto him that is able to keep you from falling, and to present you faultless before the presence of his glory with exceeding joy, to the only wise God our Savior, be glory and majesty, dominion and power, both now and ever.—Jude 24–25

Grace be unto you, and peace, from him which was, and which is to come; and from the seven Spirits which are before his throne; and from Jesus Christ, who is the faithful witness, and the first begotten of the dead, and the prince of the kings of the earth. Unto him that loved us, and washed us from our sins in his own blood, and hath made us kings and priests unto God and his Father, to him be glory and dominion for ever and ever.—Rev. 1:4–6

SECTION II.
Sermons and Homiletic and
Worship Aids for Fifty-Two Sundays

SUNDAY: JANUARY THIRD

LECTIONARY MESSAGE

Topic: The Gospel in a Nutshell
TEXT: John 1:1–18
Other Readings: Jer. 31:7–14; Ps. 147:12–20; Eph. 1:3–14

Stained glass church windows often picture the Gospel of John as an eagle, because an eagle can look straight into the sun without blinking, and for many the fourth Gospel looks deepest into the heart of Christ. Nowhere is this more striking than in John's introduction. He forecasts in compressed theological prose what he says later in narrative style so he can give us the gospel in a nutshell.

At first glance, John seems to address the unevangelized, with as wide a cross-cultural message as possible. For those with a Jewish background, he uses many Old Testament references, and he reminds the followers of John the Baptist that the Baptist came to prepare the way for Jesus. He uses terminology that both Jews and Gentiles can understand when he describes Jesus as the Word of God. For the Jews, "the Word" means God's active involvement in the world, and for the Gentiles it means the divine mind. That is why his opening words are "In the beginning was the Word, and the Word was with God, and the Word was God" (1:1).

A closer look, however, shows us that John is also addressing believers. He knows that carrying out the Great Commission of Christ depends on a thoroughly converted church. He aims to clarify the church's vision, mature its faith, and correct false doctrine that threatens to destroy it.

The key to this passage is understanding his use of the term *word*. Here it means God's revelation of himself and his will in Jesus. The gospel is not only the good news about Jesus; the gospel *is* Jesus.

John has a twofold purpose in the introduction to his gospel.

I. *He wrote to convince us that Jesus of Nazareth is the in-flesh revelation of God.* In his magnificent series of claims about Jesus, John shows us how good the good news really is.

a. Christ existed in the beginning with God, long before he came to earth in human flesh. "He was with God in the beginning" (1:2).

b. Jesus is co-creator of the universe. "Through him all things were made; without him nothing was made that was made" (1:3). He was not part of creation, he created it. This text echoes Genesis 1:1, "In the beginning God created the heavens and the earth." Christ was there.

c. Jesus is the only source of life, and the life he gives is eternal (1:4). Eternal life begins now in this life and goes on forever. It is both here and hereafter, now and not yet.

d. Jesus is the light that penetrates the darkness of sin, and the darkness cannot overpower him (1:5).

e. Jesus is the object of John the Baptist's ministry. God sent the Baptist, the greatest preacher-prophet of his day, to prepare the way for Jesus' coming. John made it clear that he was not the light but was sent to bear witness to the light (1:6–8). "Behold the Lamb of God," he declared, "who takes away the sin of the world" (1:29).

13

f. Jesus is God incarnate—God in human flesh. "The Word became flesh and lived for a while among us" (1:14). He became like us for a little while so that we could be like him forever.

g. Jesus is greater than Moses, the greatest leader in the Old Testament. The law came through Moses, but grace and truth came through Jesus Christ (1:17). He is the one for whom Moses prepared the way.

h. Jesus is the one and only Son of God. His glory is the glory of "the one and only Son, who came from the Father," and he is the only one who has seen God: "God the only Son, who is at the Father's side, has made him known" (1:14, 18). John stacks claim upon claim about Jesus to convince us that Jesus is the in-flesh revelation of God.

II. *He also wrote to tell us the gospel message that Jesus brought from the Father.*

a. John warns us that many will refuse Christ's offer of eternal life and choose to stay in darkness.

1. Some do not understand it (1:5). The darkness of their sinful life has blotted out the light so they are blind to it.

2. Others do not recognize or accept him when he comes even though the evidence tells us that we can trust him. His own people had been expecting him for centuries, but when he got there, many turned their backs on him.

b. But John promises everyone who chooses to receive Jesus and believe in him (trusting and obeying Christ for salvation) that Christ will give us the power to become the children of God. Look at what John says Jesus offers us.

1. Christ offers his light for our darkness—light to guide us in this life and light for the darkness of death (1:9).

2. Christ offers us the opportunity to be born again—to start all over with a clean slate. Nicodemus is the classic biblical example of what Christ means by the new birth (3:3, 5).

3. Christ offers us our finest window on the character and glory of God (1:14). If you want to know what God is like, look at how Jesus treated people, listen to what he said, observe how he lived—and you have seen God in action.

4. Christ offers us blessing after blessing from the fullness of his grace (1:16).

5. Christ offers us his truth filled with grace, instead of the condemnation of the law (1:17).

Conclusion. John also wants us to know that Jesus is not only the one and only Son of God, but he is also the one and only way to God. "No one," Jesus says, "comes to the Father except through me" (14:6). No universalism here! And he wants everyone to know him and be saved (John. 3:16).— Wayne E. Shaw

Illustrations

INCARNATION.   My Hebrew professor in seminary was born in Japan and grew up without knowledge of anything Christian. Two things made the difference in his conversion. One was the humble, godly life of the missionary, and the other was the life of Christ. "When I realized God became man for me," he said, "I could not resist him."— Wayne E. Shaw

GOD IN JESUS.   It was only when Jesus came that men saw fully and completely what God has *always* been like. It is told that a little girl was once confronted with some of the more bloodthirsty and savage parts of the Old Testament. Her comment was: "But that happened before God became a Christian!" If we may put it so with all reverence, when John says that the Word was always there, before the beginning of things, he is saying that God was always a Christian. He is telling us that God was and is and ever shall be always like Jesus; but men could never know and realise that until Jesus came.—William Barclay[1]

SERMON SUGGESTIONS

Topic: The Faith That Defies Defeat
TEXT: Dan. 3:16–18
(1) Two contemporary attitudes—complacency and despair. (2) The attitudes of Daniel's friends—neither complacency nor despair. (3) The secret of their victory: (a) providence; (b) prayer; (c) the divine presence.—James S. Stewart[2]

[1] *The Gospel of John, Vol. 1*
[2] *River of Life*

Topic: The Master Passes By

TEXT: Luke 5:27–28

(1) Matthew (Levi) must have been haunted by the challenge of Jesus in an earlier meeting. (2) Jesus' attitude toward Matthew was different—based not on outward appearance but on the depths of Matthew's heart. (3) When Matthew answered the call of Christ, his character underwent transformation.—John Sutherland Bonnell[3]

Hymn Suggestions

1. "We Thy People Praise Thee," Kate Stearnes (1932); ST. ANTHONY'S CHORALE, Franz Joseph Haydn (c. 1780)

This twentieth-century hymn, set to a famous tune, gathers up the themes of praise and thanksgiving for the blessings of God expressed in the Scriptures from both the psalmist and the prophet Jeremiah.

2. "You Satisfy the Hungry Heart," Omer Westendorf (1976); FINEST WHEAT, Robert E. Kreutz (1976)

This recently popular hymn for use at Holy Communion has for its refrain the thought set forth in Psalm 147:14b.

3. "My Tribute," Andraé Crouch (1971); MY TRIBUTE, Crouch (1971)

Reflecting the apostle Paul's refrain in the Ephesian passage, "to the praise of his glory," this praise song can serve as the people's response to the Epistle reading.

4. "Christ, Whose Glory Fills the Skies," Charles Wesley (1740); RATISBON, J. G. Werner's *Choralbuch* (1815); harm. William H. Havergal (1861)

Wesley, master of the biblical mosaic, incorporates ideas from the prologue to John's Gospel: "The true light that enlightens everyone, was coming into the world" (1:9) and "we have believed his glory as of the only Son from the Father" (John 1:14b), combining them with messianic metaphors for Christ drawn from Isaiah and Malachi as well as Luke and 2 Peter. This is one of the finest of morning hymns.—Hugh T. McElrath

[3] *What Are You Living for?*

Worship Aids

CALL TO WORSHIP. "Praise the Lord, O Jerusalem; praise thy God, O Zion. For he hath strengthened the bars of thy gates; he hath blessed thy children within thee" (Ps. 147:12–13).

INVOCATION. Eternal God, who knows us as we are but who has made us for finer things, may our encounter with thee today set our sights upon new levels of worship and service. Banish from our minds every wrong desire that competes with thy love for a place to reign. Claim us solely to be thine own, and being possessed by thee may we be transformed from common flesh into children of strength and light. In thy holy name we pray.—Donald Macleod

OFFERTORY SENTENCE. "And Moses spake unto all the congregation of the children of Israel, saying, 'This is the thing which the Lord commanded,' saying, 'take ye from among you an offering unto the Lord: whosoever is of a willing heart, let him bring it, an offering of the Lord'" (Exod. 35:4–5a).

OFFERTORY PRAYER. We thank you, O God, for your generous gifts to us. Your love has placed within our hearts the desire to bring an offering to you. We know that there are many gifts we can bring besides money, and you will receive, bless, and use them all for your kingdom. Help us, first of all, to offer our very selves.

PRAYER. O God, whoever else you are in the mystery and greatness of your being, you are *love*. Looking into the face of Jesus, we see something we have never seen before: a light—your love—an everlasting love; a love that will not let us go; a love so big that it embraces the whole world—you've got the whole world in your nail-scarred hands—yet a love so intimate, so immanent, to include every person; a love that gives and gives even to dying on a cross.

With what love you are loving us here and now that we should be called your children, and with what promise you are loving us in our every tomorrow, for it does not yet appear what we shall be.

You are the fountain of all love: "We love

because you first loved us." In creation, your love called the worlds into being and created us little lower than the angels. You are here calling us each by name. But the destiny of each one of us is embraced in your love purpose for all.

O God, so often we come with our hidden agendas—with ulterior motives—we are not really there for the other; we are there for ourselves. Help us to learn to love, that we can identify with the other according to his or her need, permitting him or her to write the agenda of our meeting. Love is a risky business. It makes us vulnerable to all kinds of hurt. Love costs. It gives and gives until there is nothing more to give. How we need the grace of our Lord Jesus Christ, that we may be faithful to the highest that we know in him—to be a true neighbor to others—to all others.—John Thompson

Sermon: God, Gideon, and Gumption

TEXT: Judges 6:14–16, 7:2–8, 16–21

Life consists in how you see it, and the most important decisions you and I ever make are the ones in which we decide whether to believe in ourselves and in a God we cannot see.

I. First, God wants you and me to do well. In the beginning Gideon didn't see it that way, however. When the angel came to Gideon that day, the Midianites had been oppressing the Hebrews for seven years. Every time the Hebrews harvested a crop, the Midianites would swoop down and steal it or destroy it. So when the angel came to him, Gideon was down in the bottom of the winepressing vat, threshing his wheat down there so the Midianites wouldn't see him working and steal it. God's angel climbed down into that winepress where Gideon was working and said, "The Lord is with you, you mighty warrior." Who says God doesn't have a sense of humor? Gideon didn't think it was funny, though. He heard the plan and said, in effect, "Are you crazy, God? I'm from the smallest family in Israel and I'm the smallest one in my family. What am I possibly going to be able to do for you?"

There is a little bit of Gideon in most of us, I think. Some of you children may think you're never going to be big enough or good enough to make the team. You adults may be going through some personal struggle. You think you know what God wants for you. You even want it yourself. But with Gideon you and I turn to the Lord and say, "I can't, Lord!"

It's not that we wouldn't like it. We just don't really believe we can make it happen. That's what Gideon thought, you see. And the Lord answered: "But I will be with you. This is my plan for you and I will be with you while you carry it out. Trust me and I will do great things through you."

"God loves you and has a wonderful plan for your life." Back in the sixties that sentence was Law 1 in the Campus Crusade tract titled "The Four Spiritual Laws." For Christian students it became a kind of joke after a while. Whenever someone failed a test or broke up with a steady, you slapped them on the back and said brightly, "Well, God loves you and has a wonderful plan for your life!" What we forgot then, what you and I forget too often now, is that those words may be simplistic and subject to all kinds of abuses, but there is also a sense in which they are profoundly true. God does love us. God does want the very best for you and for me. Whether that will happen doesn't depend on your strength or your skill or your bank account or mine. It depends on whether you and I are willing to trust God to see us through. God wants God's best for you and me.

II. Second, God will lead us at each step of the way. Notice how God worked with Gideon. God didn't expect Gideon to trust completely from the beginning. Instead God brought Gideon along step by step. Gideon didn't really want to do anything, so he put a sheepskin outside on the ground and said, "OK God, if you really want me to do this, let the fleece be wet in the morning and all the ground around it be dry." He got up next morning and the fleece was wet and all the ground around it was dry. So Gideon started to sweat a little and he said, "OK God, if you really, really want me to do this, tomorrow morning let the fleece be dry and all the ground around it be wet." It was, and he was stuck. So Gideon decided if he had to do this he might as well get plenty of help. He gathered the biggest army he could find—32,000 men. And step by step God cut Gideon's army down from 32,000 to 300—the 300 who got down on their knees and lapped up their water like dogs. (God really does have a sense of humor.) Then God led Gideon and his 300 lappers into battle against the Midianite hordes. Most of the time, Gideon had no idea what he was going to do in the long run. God only told him what he was to do next. God brought Gideon along step by step, until Gideon could see 300 troops as enough.

III. I believe that God will lead us to win if you and I follow him in the days ahead. This is the third thing we learn from the story of Gideon, you see. God will give us the victory if we follow. So Gideon did the crazy thing God suggested. He gave his 300 men torches, which they lit and covered with pottery pitchers so they could not be seen until the pitchers were broken. And he gave each of them a jazz trumpet lesson in blowing hot, loud, and nasty. And those three hundred fools for God sneaked up on the thousands of Midianites in the middle of the night and yelled "Boo!" and scared the bejeebers out of them, and pulled off the biggest surprise ambush of all time. They did God's plan God's way and it worked!

Notice that that wasn't as easy as it sounds. The danger of failure was real. Each one still had to do his part. Too often you and I try to claim God's promises as if they have nothing to do with our response. Christ promises to forgive, we say, and I love to sin, so that means everything is admirably arranged. God promises an abundant life, so all I have to do is sit back and rake in the profits. Nothing could be further from the truth. God asks nothing less than obedience. God demands nothing less than that you and I follow.

You see, it is still possible for you and me to fail in the good plan God has for our lives. All that has to happen for us to fail is to turn away from God's leadership day by day, to try to carry out a different plan than God's plan. Or just to be indifferent to what God is doing and try to do life on our own. God will allow us to experience the consequences of the choices we have made. God will fulfill God's promise to make your life and my life and the life of this church all God intends them to be. If you haven't already, I ask you right now to begin to pray for God's direction for your life in the days ahead. I promise you, if you ask, the Lord will show you the way. Church members, I ask you to pray for our church and to be ready to serve as we dis-

cover together what needs to be done. Life consists in how you see it, you see. You can hold back, refuse commitment, do nothing. Or you can decide with Gideon to cast your lot with God and trust that God can see you through. This is what God has done since the days of Gideon. That is what God will do again.—Ronald D. Sisk

Illustrations

A COLONY OF HEAVEN. Do you remember what Paul called them in his letter to the Philippians? *"We are a colony of heaven,"* he said. The Philippian Christians would understand that figure, for their city of Philippi was a Roman colony. When Rome wanted to Romanize a new province, it took Roman people and planted them as a colony in the midst of it. There, as a powerful minority, they stood for Roman law, Roman justice, Roman faith, and Roman custom—leaven in the lump of the province, until the whole province was leavened. Rome understood the art of government. When, therefore, Paul said to that little group of Philippian Christians, "We are a colony of heaven," they understood. They were a minority thrown out, as pioneers, in the midst of an unchristian world to represent the ideals, faiths, and way of living of a nobler realm until the earth should be the Lord's and the fullness thereof.—Harry Emerson Fosdick[4]

A GOD OF DELIVERANCES. When God ceases to become a God of Deliverances for us, prayer immediately loses its power. It becomes a bit of spiritual whistling in the dark instead of a dialogue with God; a piece of wishful thinking instead of a struggle to understand His purposes and the means to release His power. What a profound difference there is in the mood and outlook of the person who is convinced that God cares and that He can do something about the complex situations we are in.—Elam Davies[5]

[4] *The Hope of the World*
[5] *This Side of Eden*

SUNDAY: JANUARY TENTH

LECTIONARY MESSAGE

Topic: Responding Wisely to the Appearance of the King

TEXT: Matt. 2:1–12

Other Readings: Isa. 60:1–6; Ps. 72:1–7, 10–14; Eph. 3:1–12

Today is Epiphany Sunday. The word *epiphany* means appearance. It signifies something that was already there—something hidden—that suddenly makes its appearance, like the sun hidden by clouds that suddenly appears in blazing brightness. In their Gospels, both Matthew and John tell us that Jesus already existed with God the Father before he made his appearance in human flesh and revealed God to us. Matthew says that an angel spoke to Joseph in a dream, telling him that what was conceived in Mary was of the Holy Spirit and that "the virgin will be with child and will give birth to a son, and they will call him Immanuel—which means 'God with us.'" (1:20–23). Joseph had no union with Mary until after Jesus was born. Jesus had already existed with God the Father before he came to Bethlehem's manger.

John put the same thing in different language when he wrote, "In the beginning was the Word, and the Word was with God, and the Word was God" and "The Word became flesh and lived for a while among us. We have seen his glory, the glory of the one and only Son, who came from the Father, full of grace and truth" (1:1, 14). Epiphany is a marvelous truth of the Christian faith.

I. *The appearance of the King.* Matthew's scenario is this: wise men called Magi journeyed from the East to bring him gifts and to worship him. They had seen his star and followed it to Jerusalem to ask where they could find the newborn king of the Jews.

The news of their arrival spread quickly to King Herod and it terrified him. He brought all of the high priests and religious scholars together as soon as he could and asked them, "Where is the Messiah supposed to be born?"

"In Bethlehem in Judah," they told him, "for this is what Micah prophesied many years ago" (5:2).

Pretending to be as devout as they, Herod set up a secret meeting with the wise men. He got them to tell him exactly when the star had appeared, then he shared the location in the prophecy with them and told them to bring him word once they had found the child so that he too could worship him.

The wise men set off immediately, following the star, until it led them to the place where the child was. They were so overjoyed that they could hardly contain themselves. When they entered the house, they saw the child with his mother and knelt and worshiped him. They opened their bags and presented him with gifts of gold, frankincense, and myrrh. Later, while they slept, God warned them in a dream not to report back to Herod, so they went back to their country by a different route.

II. *Those who denigrate the appearance of the King.*

a. There have always been Herods around who trust in earthly might rather than in the living God, and there have been religious people who trust in their religious activity, their superior knowledge of holy things, and their prominent religious positions instead of in the living God.

b. Herod used all of his power to do away with the newborn Son of God, ordering the murder of all boys under two years old; but God protected Jesus by sending his family to Egypt (2:13–18). All of the forces of evil combined could not defeat God's plan.

c. The chief priests and teachers of the law knew their Bibles thoroughly, and when its central figure came into their midst they could pinpoint exactly where he would be born, but they would not follow him. It is not enough to know all about him; we must know him personally and obey him. Religious practices without a heart for God are never, ever enough.

d. There are other ways to denigrate his appearance besides seeking to destroy him. Some of us try to deny him, as if that will make him go away. Others merely ignore him, as if "out of sight, out of mind" will make him go away. But the King has made his appearance, and he will never go away. We cannot escape him, and we have to deal with him. Every knee will bow and every tongue will confess that Jesus Christ is Lord, to the glory of God the Father (Phil. 2:10, 11). We can denigrate him like Herod and the Jewish religious leaders, but we will pay a terrible price for doing so.

III. *Those who celebrate the appearance of the King.* We know so little about them. They were scholars from the East, probably Persia, who came seeking the newborn king. One tradition says that there were twelve of them. We tend to think there were three because they brought three gifts to Jesus; but whatever their number, the contrast is striking. The Gentile Magi came a great distance to celebrate the birth of Jesus while the Jewish scholars who lived close by refused to worship him. It is never enough to know about him; we must know him personally, and we have to bow before him in surrender. Like the Magi, many of us have come a long way from where we were to worship Christ.

The three gifts remind us of who he is. Gold is the king of metals, and a gift for a king—a king who rules from a cross. Frankincense is a gift for a priest—for use as sweet perfume in the temple sacrifices. Myrrh is a gift for one who is to die—for use in embalming the body of the dead.

Conclusion. The greatest gift we can bring him is our surrendered lives. Wise men still worship him, they still bring him gifts, and they still serve him.—Wayne E. Shaw

Illustrations

HEEDING THE STARS. Can you imagine a mariner setting off to sail the seas in a sailing vessel and saying to himself, "I am not going to take any notice of this conventional chart, or this compass, or indeed of the stars in heaven. I am free of them all. I am going to do what I like. I am going to sail my vessel as I like and where I like. These old, conventional, stuffy rules about navigation, what are they to me?"

How grimly the stormy seas would laugh at him and how soon he and his ship would find the bottom of the ocean! It is when he accepts the discipline of the chart, the advice of the compass, the tyranny—if you like—of the eternal stars, that he finds at last the harbor. Let me remind you of that old proverb which says: "He who will not

heed the stars, shall heed the rocks."—Leslie D. Weatherhead[6]

AFRAID TO SURRENDER. A rich woman said, "I was afraid to surrender to God, for I was afraid He would drive my last cow out of the pasture." But when she surrendered, she found God's will was not only perfect love, but perfect reasonableness. The cows were all there, only she and God were partners in raising them, and partners in their disposal. Life was a partnership, with God as senior Partner. She was released and free and effective. She was relieved that she was no longer God.—E. Stanley Jones[7]

SERMON SUGGESTIONS

Topic: The Coming of Light
TEXT: Isa. 60:1
(1) God's people shine as light in the world. (2) God is the source of this light. (3) The light encounters darkness in various designs and depths. (4) Always the bearers of light can rely on the promises of God for help along the way and for final victory of the light over darkness.

Topic: Now We Know
TEXT: Eph. 3:8–12
(1) God has always been revealing himself to humankind (Rom. 1:20; Heb. 1:1–2). (2) In Christ, God broke the mystery wide open. Therefore: (a) we are in touch with God's eternal purpose; (b) we are enfolded in God's love through faith in Christ Jesus our Lord.

Hymn Suggestions

1. "Hail to the Lord's Anointed," James Montgomery (1821); ELLACOMBE, *Gesangbuch der h, w, K. Hofkapelle* (1784)

This free paraphrase of Psalm 72 is considered by many to be Montgomery's finest hymn. While absorbing the essential intent of the psalmist, it breathes a Christian passion for justice, righteousness, and social reform.

2. "Shine, Jesus, Shine," Graham Kendrick (1987); SHINE, Kendrick (1987)

---

[6] *Key Next Door*
[7] *The Way*

Made popular in recent years by use in youth evangelistic circles, this song voices the Epiphany theme that the light of Christ and of the gospel must shine forth into a world of darkness.

3. "We Three Kings of Orient Are," John H. Hopkins (1857); KINGS OF ORIENT, Hopkins (1857)

In highly dramatic fashion both textually and musically, the author-composer depicts the relentless search of the kings from the East for the "perfect light" of the Christ Child as related in the Gospel reading. Often effective is the use of three male soloists for the minor key stanzas, singling out the offerings of each king, followed by the congregation joining on the refrain in a major key.

4. "Arise, Your Light Is Come," Ruth Duck (1974); FESTAL SONG, William H. Walker (1894)

Quoting the first phrase of the Isaiah 60 passage for its theme, this fairly recent hymn, with its rousing tune, can set the appropriate tone for Epiphany Sunday.—Hugh T. McElrath

Worship Aids

CALL TO WORSHIP.   "God is our refuge and strength, a very present help in trouble" (Ps. 46:1).

INVOCATION.   O God, you are our first and last resort in time of trouble. We need you just as much in time of success and joy. Grant us the desire to rely on you for wisdom and the courage to obey you, as well as the desire for your comfort and help. We pray that you will come to us, so that we may turn to you.

OFFERTORY SENTENCE.   "And when they were come into the house, they saw the young child with Mary his mother, and fell down, and worshiped him: and when they had opened their treasures, they presented unto him gifts; gold, frankincense, and myrrh" (Matt. 2:11).

OFFERTORY PRAYER.   We do not come, gracious Lord, with treasure chests, as did the wise men of old, but such as we have we open to you and pay *our* homage. Let our tithes and offerings be used as witnesses of our love and yours to all people everywhere.

PRAYER.   We adore thy name and bless thee, O Lord most high and holy. We draw near to thee to give thanks. We draw near to thee to render thee tokens of love. We draw near to confess our sin and unworthiness, and to lay hold, by faith, upon all thy promises, and upon thy help. Vouchsafe thy blessing to everyone in thy presence that seeks thee; and if there be any in error, let not the error be their destruction. If there are any in partial truth, let the truth that they have, though it be in fragments, be mighty through thy blessing. Grant, we pray thee, that those who seek thee ignorantly and afar off may be very graciously guided. Are there not some souls here that are like a stranger in a great city seeking a friend, who, ignorant of where that friend is, inquires of one and another? O! Are there not those who inquire of the watchman tonight, "Where is my beloved?" Grant that they may find the way, and find him whom their souls need. Are there not those in thy presence that are wavering; that are tempted; that find themselves shaken as the reeds by the wind? O Lord! Thou canst give them strength, and cause them to stand, who have no strength in themselves.—Henry Ward Beecher

Sermon: Ministry—The Minister's Mandate
TEXT: 2 Tim. 1:1–12

We are accustomed to such phrases as "call to the ministry," "enter the ministry," and "surrender to the ministry." Normally these phrases come from preachers and are applied to preachers. Our message today relates to the biblical truth that all of you can receive a call to the ministry.

Today I am issuing to you a call to the ministry. Many of you are already in the ministry. You are already doing ministry in various forms. Yet some of you are not doing ministry; some are merely doing a job. Many of you are ministering as you worship with your offerings, but others among you are simply paying admission—paying your fair share of the church's program. There is a vast difference. I long for the day when every member is a minister.

I have found in 2 Timothy 1:1–12 a brief treatise on the ministry. Paul was rehearsing with a young preacher boy what it meant to be in the ministry. I find in the first few verses the *foundation* for the ministry: faith.

Then I find in the seventh verse the *formula* for the ministry: that we renounce the spirit of fear and take on the spirit of power, of love, and of a sound mind. Finally, I see in the last five verses the *fruit* of the ministry: replacing shame with suffering for the gospel's sake.

I. *The foundation for the ministry.* Knowing that God has equipped me to do what he has called me to do is a function of faith. God has not called me to do something for which he has not equipped me. He has not called you to do something for which he has not equipped you.

In verses 1 to 6 we see the *foundation* for the ministry. Paul identified himself by saying, "Paul, an apostle of Jesus Christ by the will of God, according to the promise of life in Christ Jesus" (v. 1). The faith demonstrated here illustrates what it can mean to be a Christian.

a. *Through faith, one can be obedient to the will of God.* In essence, Paul was saying, "I've been called to be an apostle, to be a preacher. I've been called into the ministry. By faith I've been obedient to the will of God."

It is apparent that many have been called to the ministry, not vocationally but called nonetheless, and have not been obedient to the will of God.

b. *By faith one can be a recipient of the grace, mercy, and peace of God.* The Scriptures always record them in that order: grace and then peace. The reason is that the grace of God must be accepted before one can know the peace of God. The fifth chapter of Romans says, "Where sin abounded, grace did much more abound" (v. 20). Every time we wander away in sin there is ample grace to cover our sin; there is plenty of grace if we will but accept that grace. Then we can know the peace of God. By faith we are recipients of the grace, mercy, and peace of God.

c. *By faith one can be an advocate for brothers and sisters.* In verse 3, Paul said, "I thank God, whom I serve from my forefathers with pure conscience, that without ceasing I have remembrance of thee in my prayers night and day." Paul engaged in intercessory prayer for a brother in the faith.

d. *By faith one can keep alive the gift of God that dwells in one.* Paul reminded Timothy to stir up the gift of God, to rekindle it. He called on Timothy, and calls on us, to stir the embers and blow the bellows on it to make it flame up again. Some of our people need that stirring. They need that rekindling of the gifts that are within so that all might enter the ministry.

II. *The formula for the ministry.* Verse 7 says, "God hath not given us the spirit of fear." Fear is the opposite of faith. God has not caused us to be overcome by fear. Satan has caused that. God has given us the spirit of power, the spirit of love, and the spirit of a sound mind. Freed from fear, protected by power, launched by love, and settled in by a sound mind is the formula for the ministry.

I wish we could be freed from fear. If I know myself and my relationship with Jesus Christ, I can honestly say that I do not mind standing completely open before God. I don't mind saying anything to God, and I do. I don't mind telling him all of my troubles, all of my inner fears, all of my insecurities, all of my guilts, all of my frustrations and anxieties. I'm often afraid to do this with his people. I'm afraid they won't understand.

Not only are we freed from fear and protected by his power, but in the ministry we are launched by his love. Our ministry must be an extension of Jesus' ministry, which was a ministry of love.

III. *The fruits of the ministry.* In verses 8 to 12 you will find the fruit of the ministry. This is what happens when God moves in among his people and works with them. First of all, they are not ashamed of him or his work. Second, they are willing to suffer if need be in order for his work to be done. Paul said, "Be not thou therefore ashamed of the testimony of our Lord."

Paul asked also that we not be ashamed of him as the prisoner of the Lord. It was a potentially embarrassing position for Paul. But Paul was not ashamed to be a prisoner for the Lord and asked his followers not to be ashamed of him.

We are not to be ashamed of the testimony of the Lord or his servants. When we become Christians, a change occurs. All of a sudden we realize that we are not ashamed of Jesus Christ. We are no longer ashamed of the church or the work of the church. We are not ashamed of the weaker brother or sister. The Bible teaches us that if one among us is weak, it is the responsibility of the stronger ones to sustain him. All shame is dispelled. What comes in its place is the willingness to minister to one another for the sake of the gospel of Christ.

Paul put it this way: "Be thou partaker of the afflictions of the gospel according to the power of God." Suffering may be a part of the ministering life. It may come in the form of attack from Satan or in the unkindly attack of men. But the promises of God remain sure.

Freed from fear, no longer ashamed, standing unified in the fellowship, and empowered by his grace—that's what happens when we enter the ministry.—Greg Clements[8]

Illustrations

A PORTION OF YOURSELF. When the wealthy society women of Paris came to help Vincent de Paul they were shocked at the indifference and lack of appreciation from the poor. He counseled them, "You should not be shocked that they do not appreciate your good deeds, but grateful if they do not hate you." The drug addict does not want a keeper; he seeks a brother who is willing to enter into his pain and suffering with compassion. This will arise in the heart of a Christian as a gift of God, but only as he stands beside his brother.— George W. Webber[9]

GOD ALIVE IN US. Read Paul's letter, and the power of the Spirit takes on fresh flesh and flavor. Here is a thrilling theology of the Spirit. The Holy Spirit lives in you as in a shrine, frees you from sin and death, makes you sons and daughters of God, helps you in your weakness, intercedes for you with the Father. Only in the power of the Spirit can you believe the unbelievable, hope for the grace beyond your grasp, the glory beyond the grave, love with God's own love poured into your hearts. If you walk by the Spirit, Paul insists, you will be kind and good, grow gentle and prove faithful, experience incomparable peace, a joy the world cannot give.

The examples are legion, the needs endless. Right now, the need I see beneath all needs is for each of you to simply realize how powerful you are. Rediscover where and how you can make things happen—from a smile on a careworn face, through legislation for the afflicted, to peace in some corner of your world. Link your power in the world to the Power within you, the Spirit of light and of life and of love. Shake that Spirit loose! In a nutshell, let God come alive in you!—Walter J. Burghardt, S.J.[10]

SUNDAY: JANUARY SEVENTEENTH

LECTIONARY MESSAGE

Topic: How to Approach Our Problems in the Church
TEXT: 1 Cor. 1:1–9
Other Readings: Isa. 49:1–7; Ps. 40:1–11; John 1:29–42

The simple fact is that every church has problems. There are problems if we change, and there are problems if we do not change. Problems exist across generational lines; for example, builders, baby boomers, and busters serving Christ together in the same congregation can create tensions. In addition, many people are confused about Christian doctrine and struggle to practice Christian morality.

Our problems sound a lot like those at Corinth. They had divided over their leaders, and at least one of their members was practicing sexual immorality. They were arguing over the proper way to worship. They were quarreling about their God-given gifts. And they were confused about the difference between the Christian teaching on the Resurrection and the Greek philosophy of immortality.

The Corinthian church shows us a church with problems, and some of those problems seem overwhelming. In fact, it is hard to imagine a congregation with more problems than the church at Corinth. But the real question is not "Does our church have problems?" but "How are we approaching our

---

[8]*Award Winning Sermons,* vol. 4, ed. by James Barry (Nashville: Broadman Press, 1980), 125–132.

[9]*The Congregation in Mission*
[10]*Lovely in Eyes Not His*

problems?" Notice how Paul approaches the church's problems. He teaches us three great principles about how to tackle problems in the church.

I. *Treat the members as part of God's family.*

a. *Treat them as brothers and sisters in Christ.* We did not choose our brothers and sisters in Christ; we are brothers and sisters because we have the same Father. And our family goes beyond the borders of our congregation. It includes all the Sosthenes around the world that have God as their father and Christ as their savior. We were born into the family by the birth from above, and God gives us all of our Christian family on earth. Paul does not name the Corinthians the Church of Corinth; he calls them the Church of God because they are a part of all of God's people.

b. *Treat them as sanctified by Christ.* Christ's family in every community is to live his lifestyle and carry out his mission. That is why he puts us here. He describes us as "sanctified in Christ Jesus" and "called to be holy." God's people in the Old Testament were called "the holy people," and they understood themselves to be different from others because they belonged to God in a special way. A saint (one who is holy) has been dedicated to the Lord for his possession and service.

Many are confused about what it means to live a holy life. For some it means living a life of total perfection, so they give up on ever achieving it. For others it means a life of personal devotion, regular public worship, and moral behavior; but that also falls short of the holiness to which God has called us. Our holy God has called us into a holy fellowship known as the Church to glorify him before the eyes of a watching world by our Christian conduct and ministry.

II. *Pray for God's richest blessing on them (1:1–3).* Paul prays a powerful benediction of grace and peace from God the Father and the Lord Jesus Christ as he greets them.

a. *Grace is the noblest blessing a Greek could give a person,* and when Paul relates grace to God in Christ, he encompasses its sweeping range—God's unmerited favor that saved us from our sin, that sustains us every day, and that will finally lead us home to him. We cannot save ourselves, we cannot sustain ourselves, and we cannot get to heaven by ourselves. " 'Tis grace has brought me safe thus far, and grace will lead me home." Espe-

cially appropriate for a divided church, God's grace is the only thing that can bring them together again. They will treat each other graciously when they allow God's grace to work effectively in them.

b. *Peace is the noblest blessing a Hebrew could give anyone.* It is a rich word in the Bible. For us today it means the cessation of hostilities, but for them it meant wholeness, salvation, health, and all that is blessed and beautiful in life. The human heart yearns for peace with a deep hunger, and it can only be found in Christ as a gift of God's grace. If we have grace for our sins and peace for our souls, we have the core of everything else we need in life.

III. *Keep on thanking God for them (1:4–9).*

a. Thank him because the promises of the gospel are coming true in our lives. What has happened to us is beyond human speech and human knowledge. The evidence of Christ has clearly been seen in our changed lives (1:4–6).

b. Thank him because your gifts are adequate for the needs of the Church. Our gifts are not to be used selfishly but for the glory of God and the good of men and women.

c. Thank him because he promised to keep you secure to the end. When the ultimate judgment comes, we who are in Christ can meet it unafraid because we will be clothed in the merits of Christ and none can impeach us (1:8, 9).

Conclusion. Paul could have chosen to bless or to blast; he chose to bless. Later he will blast away at sinful shortcomings, but only in the context of a pastoral heart, and he wants to make sure we hear that up front. We are to treat all Christians as part of God's family, to pray God's richest blessings on them, and to keep on thanking God for them.

But notice this: all of these blessings are based on what God has done, not on our merit. The Corinthian Christians had messed up miserably, but they were still his Church and recipients of his grace. It is all God's doing! When you come to Christ, you come to his Church and you come to him.—Wayne E. Shaw

Illustrations

ILL-TEMPERED. The peculiarity of ill-temper is that it is the vice of the virtuous. It is often the one blot on an otherwise noble character. You know men who are all but perfect and women who would be entirely perfect but for an easily ruffled, quick-tempered, or "touchy" disposition. This compatibility of ill-temper with high moral character is one of the strangest and saddest problems of ethics.—Henry Drummond[11]

PRAYING FOR OTHERS.   Intercessory prayer can best be understood as God's release of his Spirit and healing, creative forces within a law-abiding world, such release being dependent in part upon our willingness to work with him for the furtherance of other persons' good. This means that God does not automatically bestow all the good gifts he is waiting to impart, but the outpouring of his Spirit comes in greater measure when we pray. It comes not in defiance of law but within it. We ought not to suppose that prayers for the safety of a son in war or for the recovery of a loved one from mortal illness will bring about this result when conditions prevail which in a law-abiding world must lead to another outcome. But neither ought we to stop praying for them, as if everything in God's world were mechanically determined. There may be what is sometimes referred to as a "law of prayer," though since its course cannot be precisely charted we would better call it a power of prayer, through which God acts to express purposes which he shares with us. If this is true, then our intercession matters greatly, not only to God but to the total social situation.—Georgia Harkness[12]

SERMON SUGGESTIONS

Topic: Patience in Prayer
TEXT: Ps. 40
(1) Puts an end to depressed spirits (v. 2). (2) Shares God's goodness with joy and praise (vv. 3, 9–10). (3) Looks to God with confidence for the future (v. 11).

Topic: The Lamb of God
TEXT: John 1:29
(1) The sacrificial Lamb in Israel's worship (Lev. 1:1–4). (2) The atoning Lamb in the

[11] *The Greatest Thing in the World*
[12] *Prayer and the Common Life*

fullness of time (1 Cor. 5:7; 1 Peter 1:18–19). (3) The eternal Lamb (Rev. 13:8).

Hymn Suggestions

1. "Great Is Thy Faithfulness," Thomas O. Chisholm (1923); FAITHFULNESS, William M. Runyan (1923)
Although this song is based primarily on Lamentations 3:22–23, it is also suitable for use with the Epistle reading in 1 Corinthians as well as with the Isaiah passage (Isa. 49:7), in both of which God is declared as faithful.
2. "Behold the Lamb," words and music, Dottie Rambo (1980); BEHOLD THE LAMB, arranged by Lee Herrington (1980)
A new Scripture song based on John 1:29, this can serve appropriately as a response to the gospel reading for the day.
3. "He Keeps Me Singing," Luther B. Bridgers (1910); SWEETEST NAME, Bridgers (1910)
This familiar gospel song reflects the spirit of Psalm 40:3 with its exuberant melody—a testimony to God's power through Jesus to put a melody in the heart.
4. "O Splendor of God's Glory Bright," Ambrose of Milan (339–397); WAREHAM, William Knapp (1738)
Carrying the Epiphany theme and metaphor of light, this venerable hymn would be appropriate sung in response to the reading from prophecy (Isa. 49:1–7).—Hugh T. McElrath

Worship Aids

CALL TO WORSHIP.   "I waited patiently for the Lord; and he inclined unto me, and heard my cry" (Ps. 40:1).

INVOCATION.   We come to worship today with many needs, many longings, and some disappointments, as well as with many things for which we are grateful and for which we praise your name. Keep us thankful for what we have and patient for what we do not yet have. To those ends may this service of worship strengthen our faith and courage.

OFFERTORY SENTENCE.   "Each of us will be accountable to God" (Rom. 14:12 NRSV).

OFFERTORY PRAYER. Help us, gracious Lord, to love being accountable to you, for that further assures us that there are things we can do, possessions we can share, prayers we can pray, and offerings we can bring. We are indeed your servants. You have trusted us beyond our merit. And now we again join together in placing in your treasury a part of ourselves for your glory and use.

PRAYER. God, thou great Redeemer of mankind, our hearts are tender in the thought of thee, for in all the afflictions of our race thou hast been afflicted, and in the sufferings of thy people it was thy body that was crucified. Thou hast been wounded by our transgressions and bruised by our iniquities, and all our sins are laid at last on thee. Amid the groaning of creation we behold thy spirit in travail till the sons of God shall be born in freedom and holiness.

We pray thee, O Lord, for the graces of a pure and holy life, that we may no longer add to the dark weight of the world's sin that is laid upon thee, but may share with thee in thy redemptive work. As we have thirsted with evil passions to the destruction of men, do thou fill us now with hunger and thirst for justice that we may bear glad tidings to the poor and set at liberty all who are in the prison house of want and sin.

Lay thy spirit upon us and inspire us with a passion of Christlike love, that we may join our lives to the weak and oppressed and strengthen their cause by bearing their sorrows. And if the evil that is threatened turns to smite us, and if we must learn the dark malignity of sinful power, comfort us by the thought that thus we are bearing in our body the marks of Jesus, and that only those who share in his free sacrifice shall feel the plenitude of thy life. Help us in patience to carry forward the eternal cross of thy Christ, counting it joy if we, too, are sown as grains of heat in the furrows of the world, for only by the agony of the righteous comes redemption.—Walter Rauschenbusch, *Prayers of the Social Awakening*

Sermon: Stick to the Knitting

TEXT: 1 Cor. 4:1–5; John 1:43–51

"Stick to the knitting" is a phrase I came across in a book by Peters and Waterman, *In Search of Excellence.* They outlined some successful businesses that emerged in this country following the Second World War. One of the characteristics they said successful businesses had in common was that they focused on what they did best. Peters and Waterman called that "stick to the knitting."

I. *We have a mission.* The first mission statement of the Church is "The Great Commission." It was given by Jesus to the apostles at the end of the Gospel of Matthew:

Go make disciples of all nations, baptizing them in the name of the Father, and of the Son and of the Holy Spirit, teaching them to observe all that I have commanded you.

The second statement, I suggest, is the one proposed by Paul to the Corinthians in the passage just read:

This is how one should regard us, as servants of Christ and stewards of the mysteries of God.

Paul is saying to the Corinthians, this is what I think the Church ought to look like. It is about as tidy and succinct a mission statement as you could ever find. It "sticks to the knitting."

This is how one should regard us, as servants of Christ and stewards of the mysteries of God.

Let's start with the phrase, "stewards of the mysteries of God." Ironically, it is the scientists in our time, and not so much the theologians, who are using the word *mystery*. I heard this beautiful phrase somewhere, "The greater the shoreline of knowledge, the vaster the sea of mystery."

Mystery in that sense refers to the creation, that part of the creation that eludes our reason.

But there is another kind of mystery. It is the kind of mystery that Paul is talking about to the Corinthians. It does not refer to gaps in our knowledge. It's the news that confounds and contradicts our knowledge. That is why Paul, in the same chapter to the Corinthians, says it sounds like "foolishness to the Greeks and a scandal to the Jews," because it contradicts their understanding of who God is.

II. This is the mystery he is talking about: God loves us so much that he came to us to be with us. The theological word for that is *incarnation*. Incarnation means "in the flesh." That is how God came to us, as one of us. "Scandalous," that is what the Jews said. "Foolishness," that is what the Greeks said. Do you know what Paul said? "Then I am a fool for Christ, because I am compelled, commissioned, to preach the news that God has come to be with us, and to love us as we are." We are stewards of that mystery about God. In the Second Letter to the Corinthians, Paul said, "God was in Christ reconciling the world unto himself."

It was "foolishness to the Greeks" because the Greeks believed the gods are detached, removed, and distant from us.

It was "a scandal to the Jews" because the Jews believed that God was holy, and to be holy means to be pure. So God could have nothing to do with human life, because human life was sinful and the earth is corrupted. God, in Jewish thought, was removed from human life as well.

Not aloof, not indifferent, not separated from us because of his holiness. He did not come only to us and remain apart from those people who are sinners in this world. He ate with the sinners. He invited them to be with him. He touched and embraced the unclean of this world. He was crucified with thieves, and told the one thief, "Today you will be with me in paradise."

III. That is the mystery of God that Paul is talking about. We are stewards of that mystery, because we believe that God is what the world is waiting for. The love with which he loves us, in the words of Dante, is "the love that moves the sun and stars."

Part of that mystery, also, is that we proclaim that while God was fully in Christ, Jesus was fully human. Therefore Jesus is the pattern for our life. That's why the second part of Paul's formula is, we are "servants of Christ."

Notice that in our day there are still people who think like the ancient Greeks—religious people, who say that if you are going to be religious, then don't get involved in the world.

He comes to us as he came to his disciples, and says to us, "Follow me." To "follow me" means identifying with the poor and the oppressed, loving the sinner, and living sacrificially for others in this world, taking up your cross. That is the sole qualification for everybody to be his disciple, that you take up your cross.

Martin Luther King Jr. understood that, I think, probably better than anybody else in our time. Like all historical figures, he will be interpreted from different perspectives. But the way he would want to be interpreted is that he was a "servant of Christ."

As "servants of Christ," that is how you are to regard us, and as "stewards of the mysteries of God." Not a bad mission statement.— Mark Trotter

Illustrations

CHANGE.   I remember a story about a woman who brought home a plaque that said, "Prayer changes things." She put it in her kitchen, above her sink. Her husband came home and said, "Take that down, please." She said, "Why? Don't you believe in prayer?" He said, "Yes. But I don't believe in change."—Mark Trotter

THE PROPER SUBJECT.   There is an old story about a church in Ystad, Sweden. It seems that in 1716, King Charles XII of Sweden announced to that little town that he was going to come and visit them, and that he would worship in the village church. The pastor of the church got all excited about the presence of the king in his congregation. He decided he would put aside the prescribed text for that Sunday, and he would deliver a sermon in the form of a eulogy on the greatness of the royal family. He did that.

Three months later, a gift arrived at the church, a big box. The pastor opened it up. It was a present from the king. Inside was a life-size crucifix, a lifelike statue of Jesus on the cross, with this instruction: "Place this on the pillar opposite the pulpit, so that the one who stands there will always be reminded of his proper subject."—Mark Trotter

SUNDAY: JANUARY TWENTY-FOURTH

LECTIONARY MESSAGE

Topic: How to Relate to One Another as Christians in a Church with Tensions
TEXT: 1 Cor. 1:10–18
Other Readings: Isa. 8:1–4; Ps. 27:1, 4–9; Matt. 4:12–23

Tensions can be either healthy or unhealthy. The Church will always have tensions: tension with the world, tension between what we are and what we can be, and tension between the now and the not yet of God's future for us. Tensions can even be healthy if they lead us to resolve them in a godly way that causes us to stretch and grow.

But tensions can also tear the heart out of a church when they are unhealthy and destructive. They often lead to divided relationships if they are not resolved. New Christians are especially vulnerable and easily disillusioned. Relationships between members of God's family often become strained, and consequently the whole church is robbed of the joy it could have. One of our problems is that we often forget who the enemy is. "For our struggle is not against flesh and blood," says Ephesians 6:12, "but against the rulers, against the authorities, against the powers of this dark world and against the spiritual forces of evil in the heavenly realms."

How are Christians to relate to one another in a church filled with division-breeding tension? You may not be able to control the tension brought on by other people, but you can control your own attitude about how you relate to those people. Paul tells us how in three admonitions.

I. *Be agreeable with one another.* "I appeal to you, brothers," Paul writes, "in the name of our Lord Jesus Christ, that all of you agree with one another so that there may be no divisions among you and that you may be perfectly united in mind and thought" (1:10). He did not mean that we have to agree on every fine point of doctrine or every personal opinion. No marriage could survive that, and no church could hold together if that were a requirement. We must agree on the basic Christian truths of the gospel in order to be the people of God, but on all other matters we can agree to disagree with-

out causing a tear in the body of Christ. Paul's list in Ephesians 6:4–6 does not exhaust everything Christians are to believe, but Christians are to agree on these seven great unities: "There is one body and one Spirit—just as you were called to one hope when you were called—one Lord, one faith, one baptism; one God and Father of all, who is over all and through all and in all." But notice that he precedes this statement of doctrinal unity with a statement of relational unity: "Be completely humble and gentle; be patient, bearing with one another in love. Make every effort to keep the unity of the spirit through the bond of peace" (1:2, 3). A fine old slogan captures the idea: "In essentials unity, in nonessentials liberty, in all things love."

II. *Be loyal to your leaders.*
a. The problem: Paul had heard from the family of Chloe that the Corinthian Christians were quarreling over their leaders and were causing divisions: "One of you says, 'I follow Paul,' another, 'I follow Apollos,' another, 'I follow Cephas,' still another, I follow Christ" (1:12). Paul had started the church and spent eighteen months there; Apollos had had a fruitful ministry there (Acts 18:24–19:1); Peter was the favorite among the Jewish Christians; and those who followed Christ either set an example for the others by their attitude or were extremely sectarian. The text is not clear; it could mean either. Perhaps it is not clear for a reason. We need to be pointed to Christ as the only solution to divisions in the Church, and we need to be warned that we can misuse the name of Christ to give biblical warrant to a terribly unChristlike, divisive behavior.

b. The solution: follow your leaders. They are not divisive. They are all committed to Christ and to one another as fellow servants. They taught you the gospel faithfully. They love the Lord, they love you, and they love the Church. Follow their lead: love Christ and love one another.

III. *Remember your conversion to Christ.* "Is Christ divided?" he asks. "Was Paul crucified for you? Were you baptized into the name of Paul?" (1:13). The only cure for division in the Church is to remember whose you are and what brought you into Christ in the first place.

a. *Remember your baptism.* "Don't you know," Paul writes to the Romans, "that all of us who were baptized into Christ Jesus were baptized into his death? We were therefore buried with him through baptism into death in order that, just as Christ was raised up from the dead through the glory of the Father, we too may live a new life" (6:3, 4). We must not misunderstand Paul's point here. He is not belittling baptism when he says, "For Christ did not send me to baptize, but to preach the gospel." He wants them to know that they were baptized into the name of Christ, not into Paul. Baptized into the name of Christ means that we are Christ's absolute and utter possession, and if he is not divided, neither are we to be divided from one another in his body.

b. *Remember the cross.* The cross of Christ must not "be emptied of its power" (1:17). If what brought you into Christ in the first place won't bring you together, then Christian unity doesn't have a chance. If the memory of the supreme sacrifice of Jesus doesn't bring us to our knees again and cause us to lose our selfishness, arrogance, and party spirit, nothing will.

How should we deal with tensions in the Church? By being agreeable with one another, by being loyal to our leaders, and by remembering what brought us into Christ. Then we can become a part of the Church's solution instead of the problem.—Wayne E. Shaw

Illustrations

THE RIGHT OF WAYS.   Yielding the right-of-way is the secret of success in our homes. After I perform a marriage, I usually say to the couple: "Now, remember, it's no longer *yours* or *mine:* it's *ours.*" The husband who decides to do what he wants to do, regardless of what his wife wants, is heading for a collision. The wife who intends to continue her independence even after marriage is asking for an accident. A happy home is the result of two people willing to yield the right-of-way, first to the Lord and then to each other.

This is the secret of a successful church. Church members who insist on having their own way (or else they'll resign from the board or leave the church) are helping to cause tragic accidents, and the result could be the breaking up of a testimony for God.— Warren W. Wiersbe[13]

TURN THE FOXES LOOSE.   A man had some prized foxhounds. One day they got into a fight. The man saw his prized dogs literally chewing up one another. Unable to stop the fight, he remembered that he had a fox in a pen. When he loosed the fox, the dogs forgot their differences as together they took out after the fox. Fighting dogs do not hunt, and hunting dogs do not fight.

Transfer the figure to people, and the meaning is the same. We need to turn loose more *foxes* in our churches and denomination.—Herschel H. Hobbs[14]

THE ANGRY-AFRAID.   The person who fears his own feelings of anger more than likely has been offered some very poor models as expressers of anger. One of the enduring messages of early childhood is passed on by parents who are so afraid of their own feelings of anger that they stifle or attempt to erase its evidence. If the Christian home could learn to distinguish between destructive display of anger and appropriate expression, much of this unnecessary dread and inappropriate teaching would disappear.— Daniel G. Bagby[15]

SERMON SUGGESTIONS

Topic: When God Moves In
    TEXT: Isa. 9:1–4
    (1) There is light. (2) There is joy. (3) There is freedom.

Topic: Because of the Kingdom of Heaven
    TEXT: Matt. 4:12–23
    (1) Get your thinking straight. (2) Follow God's designated leader. (3) Join in the sharing of the good news you have received.

Hymn Suggestions

    1. "God Is My Strong Salvation," James Montgomery (1822); WEDLOCK, American

---

[13] *Turning Mountains into Molehills*
[14] *My Favorite Illustrations*
[15] *Understanding Anger in the Church*

folk tune (nineteenth century); CHRISTUS,
DER IST MEIN LEBEN, Melchoir Vulpius
(1609)

Based on the first verses of Psalm 27, this
paraphrase by the masterful Montgomery
expresses the strong note of confidence in
God's protection in time of stress and trouble
that permeates the psalm. Both tunes, each
in its own style, adequately support this forti-
fying text.

2. "Break Forth, O Beauteous Heavenly
Light," Johann Rist (1641), tr. John Trout-
beck (1873); ERMUNTRE DICH, Johann
Schop (1641); harm. J. S. Bach (1734)

This majestic chorale, if broadly sung, provides a magnificent response to the prophecy
of Isaiah that those in darkness shall see
(have seen) a great light.

3. "At the Cross," Isaac Watts (1707),
refrain, Ralph Hudson (1885); HUDSON,
Ralph E. Hudson (1885), refrain melody,
John H. Hewitt (1864)

Reflecting especially the truth of 1 Corinthians 1:18, this familiar setting of Watts's
great hymn on the Atonement should be
sung deliberately and meditatively to focus
attention on the profundity of its text.

4. "Dear Lord and Father of Mankind,"
John G. Whittier (1872); REST, Frederick C.
Maker (1887)

Especially stanza 2 of this fine hymn,
penned by the poet laureate of American
hymnists, relates to Jesus' calling of the first
disciples beside the sea of Galilee. To sing
certain stanzas in four parts unaccompanied
would be meaningful and effective.—Hugh
T. McElrath

Worship Aids

CALL TO WORSHIP. "The Lord is my light
and my salvation; whom shall I fear? The
Lord is the strength of my life; of whom shall
I be afraid?" (Ps. 27:1).

INVOCATION. Do mighty things in us, O
God; stir us to our depths, motivate us to
serve in the name of Jesus, because we
paused to worship and pray and commit our
lives to God's service.—E. Lee Phillips

OFFERTORY SENTENCE. "But seek ye first
the kingdom of God, and his righteousness;

and all these things shall be added unto you"
(Matt. 6:33).

OFFERTORY PRAYER. Gracious Lord, help
us to see what are the truly important things
in life and to bring all that we are and do into
line with your purposes, assured that this is
all to our good and the good of others. So
may we, in this spirit, bring our offerings and
commit ourselves anew to the work of your
kingdom.

PRAYER. Father, you have promised that
if we seek you with all our heart, we shall ever
surely find you. With seeking hearts we come
to this time of prayer, knowing that you seek
us with a longing far greater than we can ever
experience.

We thank you this morning that your seeking has been translated into goodness when
we have been found and have chosen to follow you along life's journey. May we try more
consistently to deserve your goodness. We
thank you, Father, for treating us better than
we deserve. Our sincere prayer is that we may
be empowered to treat others as we have
been treated by you.

We know that we need your forgiveness.
We have done many things we ought not to
have done. We cannot plead ignorance to our
overt sins. We knew what was right and we did
what we knew was wrong. We stand our moral
shabbiness beside your holiness and we are
ashamed. Create in us a clean heart and mind
and imagination this morning, we pray. What
in us is dark, illumine with the light of your
truth. What is base and low in us, enable us to
turn from it and be raised to a higher plateau
of thought, action, and life.

We pray for your reinforcement. We do
not ask to escape the sorrows that are part of
our human lot. We ask only assurance that in
your divine economy nothing good is lost
and that what is excellent as God lives is permanent. We do not ask to be relieved of our
share of life's burdens. We humbly ask for
strength to bear them without faltering. Neither do we ask for exemption from exacting
tasks. We only ask for wisdom and skill to do
them right.

Grant us your peace. We need that kind of
peace that the world cannot bestow but that
can be found only in you. Help us to handle
tough economic times peacefully. Help us to

manage hard health times from a peaceful spirit. Help us to be peace bringers in strife-torn situations, even as was our Lord, in whose name we pray.—Henry Fields

Sermon: Honesty Is the Best Policy in Prayer (Nice Prayers Finish Last)

TEXT: Pss. 10:1; 22:1; 137:8–9; 32:3–5; 55:6

I have come to believe that too many of us are concerned about the words of our prayers. We want to use the correct words, the religious words, the good-sounding words, the lofty-sounding words. Too many of us are concerned about how to pray nice prayers. But I believe in the truth of the subtitle of this sermon: nice prayers finish last!

How do I know that? I take my model from the Psalms, which constitute not only the hymn book of ancient Israel but also her prayer book. When you note the kind of praying that the psalmists did, you come to the conclusion that "nice, sweet prayers" would be the last way you would characterize what they wrote. I believe that the first rule of thumb in their dialogue with God was honesty. They may not have told it like it was but they certainly told it like they saw it. Honesty was their policy in prayer; it is the best policy in prayer.

I. *When we are dishonest in prayer, we are fooling no one except ourselves.* An Ashleigh Brilliant cartoon depicts a woman with a rather puzzled look on her face. The caption reads: "To be perfectly honest, I sometimes find it difficult to be perfectly honest." Don't we all! For something that sounds so easy, it is usually extremely difficult. In some situations it is more difficult than others. The late Samuel Goldwyn was quoted as saying: "I don't want any yes-men around me. I want everybody to tell me the truth even if it costs them their jobs."

Question: Is the God we have come to know in Jesus Christ anything like Sam Goldwyn? Madeleine L'Engle writes: "Do we dare less than God's people in Scripture? What has happened to us? Don't we trust the Lord enough to tell our Maker how we really feel?" Many are shocked to read the words Keith Miller prayed one morning: "God, I don't like you, I'm sick of Christianity, and I'd like to fly away to Mexico and hide." We shouldn't be taken aback by this prayer. It is simply a modern version of the psalmists prayer

(55:6–7): "*O that I had wings like a dove! I would fly away and be at rest; truly, I would flee far away; I would lodge in the wilderness.*"

The people who wrote the psalms were the original "honest to God" folks. They knew they could not hide their true feelings and thoughts from God. Psalm 139 tells us what we all must confess: "*O Lord, you have searched me and known me. You discern my thoughts from far away. Even before a word is on my tongue, O Lord, you know it completely*" (1, 2b, 4). When we are not honest in our prayers, we are fooling no one except ourselves.

II. *Honesty in prayer simply means praying how we feel and what we think.* My advice to anyone who is struggling with "how to pray" and "what to say" is simply to imagine God asking, "How are things going?" And in your prayer you tell him. This means, of course, that you will never run out of things to say! Just say what is on the top of your mind, what you are concerned about. Begin your prayer where you are, not where you think you ought to be. If you can't come to God as you are, if you can't tell God how you really feel and what you really think, how in the world can you pray?

Genesis 2:25 tells us that Adam and Eve walked in the garden where God walked; they were naked and were not ashamed. I agree with the writer who maintains that the meaning of this is that they were hiding nothing from each other or from God. And then he says: "They were intimate. God evidently made us for open, no-hiding relationships with each other, and with him. Imagine the peace of being fully known by God and each other—and being loved anyway. It would be paradise." We can recapture a little bit of that paradise every time we pray openly and honestly.—Keith Miller[16]

Madeleine L'Engle writes about the very difficult time she had following an automobile accident. After telling about her many troubles, she says: "So what's the Good News? It is that God loves me, even when I am outraged!" That's right. He does. It was true for her. It was true for the psalmists. It is true for us. So when you pray, "let 'er rip!"—Madeleine L'Engle[17]

[16] *The Scent of Love*
[17] *The Rock That Is Higher*

III. *And in this kind of honest praying, you can expect prayer to bring about change.* The psalmist (probably David) declares: *"While I kept silence my body wasted away through my groaning all day long. . . . Then I acknowledged my sin to you, and did not hide my iniquity . . . and you forgave the guilt of my sin"* (32:3, 5). The psalmist discovered what we all know: to deal with things, you have to get them out on the table. Only then can things begin to change. And perhaps the biggest changes of all will be changes that happen inside us.

Have you ever wondered why that awful passage in Psalm 137:8–9 is a part of Scripture? The old Moffatt translation captures the plain meaning: *"And, you, Babylonians, you who plundered us, a blessing on him who deals to you all that you dealt to us! A blessing on him who snatches your babes and dashes them down on the rocks!"* Awful? No, wonderful! Where else should we pour out our anger and wrath against those who have injured us than before God? Where else should we pour out exactly how we feel about those who have done us in? Once we get these feelings out on the table, then God can help us deal with them. Then God can deal with us.

I do believe that prayer changes things. I do believe that prayer changes people. I do believe that my honest praying will change me.

But I want to remind you that all of this honesty does not have to do with simply the sharing of negative feelings and raw emotions. While the writers of the psalms were honest with God in sharing their feelings, they were also honest with God in terms of praise and rejoicing. The psalms are full of joy and praise and thanksgiving. What you discover when honesty becomes your policy in prayer is not just a door that opens into a dark basement full of anger and resentment. What you finally discover is that this open-door policy in prayer is the policy that leads to light and love and fellowship and healing and joy. That is why I say: honesty *is* the best policy in prayer.—Ronald Higdon

Illustrations

CRYING OUT.   In the last century, the laments of Negro spirituals expressed "one continual cry" against oppressive pharaohs, and more recently a similar sense of frustration has found expression in the folk songs of young "prophets with guitars." The psalmists' cry for vindication may be closer to our lives than we realize. Man cries out for justice in the social structures of human society—a justice which would somehow give corporate expression to love.—Bernhard W. Anderson[18]

PRAYER AS THANKSGIVING.   Whether downcast or lighthearted, we ought to thank God for such great blessings as homes, friends, health, enough to eat and to wear, freedom, the beauty of the world and its nourishing sustenance, the chance to work and to play and to enjoy many things. Until something happens to withdraw for a time one or more of these great gifts, we are altogether too prone to take them for granted.—Georgia Harkness[19]

SUNDAY: JANUARY THIRTY-FIRST

LECTIONARY MESSAGE

Topic: How to Gain the Best That Life Has to Offer

TEXT: 1 Cor. 1:18–31

Other Readings: Mic. 6:1–8; Ps. 15; Matt. 5:1–12

Both the Old and New Testaments tell us how to gain the best that life has to offer. Solomon lays it out plainly in Ecclesiastes. Beginning his reign at the summit of Israel's power, he pursued every conceivable promise his opulent world had to offer. He tried learn-ing, and God granted his prayer for wisdom to rule his people wisely. After a brief time in his presence, testing his keen insight and wisdom, the Queen of Sheba declared, "The half has never yet been told." He tried luxury. The Temple was magnificent, and his palace, treasury, granaries, stables, and retinue were the envy of the world. He tried lust, but he discovered that all his wives and concubines did

[18] *Out of the Depths*
[19] *Prayer and the Common Life*

not make him happy. He tried liquor, and learned that it looked appealing in the cup but mocked him when he swallowed it. Finally he tried the Lord. "This is the end of the matter," he said. "Fear God and keep his commandments."

Though it may not seem like it on the surface, the apostle Paul addresses how to gain the best life has to offer at a deeper level than Solomon. He knows that *the best* must be defined in terms of the long haul. This is the only way to make sense out of his claim that to obey the message of the cross leads to the best life has to offer. Otherwise, the cost is too high and what the world has to offer is too appealing. Why obey the challenge of the cross to yield your life completely to Christ in order to find the greatest happiness life has to offer? We are as anxious to find the answer to that question as the Corinthian Christians were. The reasons implied in the text can have a profound impact on our lives.

I. *For one thing, it throws us in with life's winners.*

a. It throws us in with those who trust in God's surpassing strength. Admittedly, it does not look like it. Power politics and armed might have always appeared to win the day, but "the weakness of God is stronger than men" (1:25) and "the message of the cross is foolishness to those who are perishing, but to us who are being saved it is the power of God" (1:18).

b. It throws us in with those who trust in God's magnificent wisdom. To go against the philosophies of the world's greatest secular minds, especially with the influence of the universities and the power of the secular press behind them, has always appeared to be stark foolishness. But God has promised to destroy the wisdom of the wise, to frustrate the intelligence of the intelligent, and to save those who believe because of their obedience to the message of the cross (1:19–21).

II. Another reason is that it answers two of life's biggest demands on God.

a. *Do something about evil; act decisively against it.* What the Jews wanted was a miraculous sign from God, for him to bear his arm and demonstrate his power. Paul's response: he did this once for all on the cross. The cross is the only saving response that God is ever going to make, and it is sufficient.

b. *Tell us the solution to the mystery of meaning.* Give us the central clue to the ultimate purpose of life. Tell us how to wring the best out of our existence. The Greeks were always searching for the missing piece to the jigsaw puzzle of life. They had gone as far as human wisdom by itself could take them. Paul's response: God's one and only saving Word is the message of the cross, and it is sufficient.

III. *The final reason is that it witnesses to the transforming power of Jesus Christ.*

a. *He transforms common people into sons and daughters of God.* The point of the passage is that most of the Christians at Corinth did not have impressive credentials that placed them among the elite. Christ took people of humble origin, many of them slaves, changed them by his grace, and transformed the world with them.

b. *He transforms everyone who is willing to surrender his or her life to him.* The essential requirement is that we are willing to crucify our selfish wills to his perfect will for our lives. We have our Gethsemane and Calvary as he had his. He transforms us because of who he is.

1. *He is our wisdom.* The only right way is to follow him who is the way, the truth, and the life.

2. *He is our righteousness.* We can never be righteous enough for God on our own merit. He alone can put us in a right relationship with God because of his death in our place on the cross.

3. *He is our holiness.* We can never be clean enough or accomplish enough on our own, but he who never sinned can wash us clean and make us whole.

4. *He is our redemption.* Paul means here that Christ sets us free from our own kind of slavery. He can deliver us from our past sins, our present helplessness, and our future fears.

Jesus said, "The person who seeks to save his life will lose it, but the person who loses his life for my sake will find it." He will not only gain his reward in the life to come, he will also receive in this life a hundredfold for anything he gives up for Christ's sake. The way of the cross is still the only way to gain the best that life has to offer, and he offers it to us today.—Wayne E. Shaw

Illustrations

LOOK BACK AND LAUGH.   A man and his wife had been quarreling: she, in the throes of hurt pride, was weeping and accusative;

he, with wounded masculinism, stood glowering. Suddenly their small son, aged four, entered the room. He carried a large hair brush, his solemn eyes fixed on them in reproof. The long minute was finally broken by his lisping voice, "I don't know which one needs to be spanked."

His nonplused pose was too much for them. The shamed parents broke into the relief of laughter. Within a few moments they saw their recent storm as tragically ridiculous. It has been brought about by their hypercritical attitude toward each other and hyper-criticality is, after all, a rather feeble-minded stand. Creation is not perfect. No day is flawless, no human without fault. To require of your intimates a virtue that even Nature seldom exemplifies is pettiness personified. Perfectionism is against life and leads inevitably to misery.—David Seabury[20]

A FORMULA FOR JOY.   *The Westminster Confession* presents a formula for joy in these words: "The chief end of man is to glorify God and to enjoy Him forever." Write this formula indelibly in your mind and heart. It is the secret for true and lasting joy. The psalmist expressed it well as he prayed to God, "In thy presence is fullness of joy: at thy right hand there are pleasures for evermore" (Ps. 16:11).

This formula for the enjoyment of life is confirmed in both the Old and New Testaments. Note these verses:

"I have created him for my glory" (Isa. 43:7).

"Whether therefore ye eat, or drink, or whatsoever ye do, do all to the glory of God" (1 Cor. 10:31).

"For ye are bought with a price; therefore glorify God in your body, and in your spirit, which are God's" (1 Cor. 6:20).

Too many people have the mistaken idea that Christianity takes all the joy out of life, but the Bible teaches that living for the glory of God puts joy into life.—Carlton Myers[21]

JESUS—THE REVELATION.   It is of supreme importance that He wrote no book. It is of even greater advantage that there is no single deed or saying of which we can be perfectly sure that He said or did precisely this or that. Indeed, of His sayings we have no exact reproduction, for presumably He spoke in Aramaic, and our records are in Greek, and all translation makes some difference. But the revelation is not in His teaching nor in His acts; it is Himself.—William Temple[22]

SERMON SUGGESTIONS

Topic: Hear What the Lord Says
TEXT: Mic. 6:1–8
(1) Remember what God has done for you. (2) Do what God requires of you.

Topic: A Different Kind of Happiness
TEXT: Matt. 5:1–12
(1) It contradicts our usual expectations. (2) It surpasses our usual expectations.

Hymn Suggestions

1. "When I Survey the Wondrous Cross," Isaac Watts (1707); HAMBURG, arr. Lowell Mason (1825)
The singing of Watts's greatest hymn about the cross could effectively follow the Scripture reading from 1 Corinthians. Putting stanza 3 in the parallel minor key can enhance the pathos of that poignant section of the hymn before returning to the major key for the climaxing final stanza.

2. "What Does the Lord Require," Albert F. Bayly (1949); SHARPTHORNE, Erik Routley (1968)
Created in contemporary terms, both words and music, this hymn has for its refrain God's requirements for righteous living set forth in Micah 6:8. As such it would be an admirable introduction to the Old Testament reading.

3. "Lord, Who May Dwell Within Your House," Christopher Webber; CHESHIRE, Este's *Psalmes* (1592)
This contemporary paraphrase of Psalm 15 set to a well-known metrical psalm tune could well be sung in place of the Psalter reading for the day. Alternately, the appropriate verses of the psalm could be read before the singing of each of the three stanzas.

[20] *Help Yourself to Happiness*
[21] *It's Your Life—Enjoy It!*

[22] *Revelation*

4. "O How Blest Are the Poor in Spirit," Richard Avery and Donald Marsh (1979); BEATITUDES, Avery and Marsh

Of several modern paraphrases of the Beatitudes in Matthew 5, that of Avery and Marsh is probably the most accessible. Once the congregation has become familiar with the easily learned tune, their singing could replace the traditional scripture reading.— Hugh T. McElrath

Worship Aids

CALL TO WORSHIP.   "O Lord, who may abide in your tent? Who may dwell on your holy hill? Those who walk blamelessly, and do what is right, and speak the truth from their heart" (Ps. 15:1–2 NRSV).

INVOCATION.   Gathered in this hallowed place we join together this morning to sing joyful praise to your name, Father. We know that the Lord is God indeed, that you made us and not we ourselves. We know that you care for us and claim us as your own. Thus we can enter into your presence with praise, for we have found you indeed to be good and your mercy to be everlastingly sure. So we ask that we be met by your empowering Spirit, that we be transformed by the renewing of our minds, and that our lives be guided into service.—Henry Fields

OFFERTORY SENTENCE.   "The children of Israel brought a willing offering unto the Lord, every man and woman, whose heart made them willing to bring for all manner of work, which the Lord had commanded to be made by Moses" (Exod. 35:29).

OFFERTORY PRAYER.   We join together, O Lord, for the support of your work, and our hearts rejoice to share in what you do. Guide us in our decision making, so that real needs may be met in the spirit of your own love.

PRAYER.   Accept, O Lord, our thanks and praise for all that you have done for us. We thank you for the splendor of the whole creation, for the beauty of this world, for the wonder of life, and for the mystery of love.

We thank you for the blessing of family and friends, and for the loving care that surrounds us on every side.

We thank you for setting us at tasks that demand our best efforts, and for leading us to accomplishments that satisfy and delight us.

We thank you also for the disappointments and failures that lead us to acknowledge our dependence on you alone.

Above all, we thank you for your Son, Jesus Christ; for the truth of his Word and the example of his life; for his steadfast obedience, by which he overcame temptation; for his dying, through which he overcame death; and for his rising to life again, in which we are raised to the life of your kingdom.

Grant us the gift of your Spirit, that we may know him and make him known; and through him, at all times and in all places, may we give thanks to you in all things.—*The Book of Common Prayer*

Sermon: A Surprise Answer

TEXT: Mark 1:40–45, *Revised English Bible*

Part of my job, as interpreter of the Bible, is to get you to hear what it really says instead of what you think it ought to say. It's my job to get you to tune in suddenly, like a parent hearing a real cry of pain instead of the sounds of children at play, and to hear something different. And there are some different things in this story. Let's start with Jesus' attitude toward this man with the skin condition. "A leper came to him begging him, and falling down before him, said, 'If you want to, you can make me clean.'" The Sunday School Jesus we've all grown up with smiles sweetly, looks at the man with genuine concern in his eyes, says, "Of course I'll make you clean," and cures him with a touch. So it comes as something of a surprise that this Jesus, Mark's Jesus, is angered, and heals the man with a touch and a four-word reply, "I will. Be clean." Where's the love, man?

I. *Why would Jesus be angry about a request to heal a man?* It isn't because of the way the man asked. Someone may ask Jesus for something for a less-than-honorable motive, Mark tells us—the Pharisees ask him for a miracle to test him, for example. But in this case, Mark is careful to use "nice" words for how the leper approaches Jesus: he begs or beseeches him, he prostrates himself on the ground in front of Jesus. Whatever is wrong is from Jesus' end, not from the leper's.

I think we get a clue when we look at how this first chapter develops. Jesus heals a man in the synagogue; he goes to dinner with Peter and while at Peter's house, heals Peter's mother-in-law; then when he finally gets to his own house, he finds all the sick of the city gathered around his door, waiting for some free medical help. He tries to slip away the next morning, but his good buddies the disciples track him down. He decides to leave home for a while to go on to other towns, and it looks for a second like it might work, until this leper shows up. You know what I think? I think Jesus was tired. I think Jesus had a notion about what he should be doing, and this leper was slowing him up. I believe Jesus thought he ought to be doing more teaching and less healing, and this guy popping up was taking him off-track. So Jesus is a bit perturbed, let's say, when he has made plans to do one thing and this leper comes and puts him on the spot about doing something else.

II. *OK, so he gets a little angry.* Surprising? Maybe a little. But there's more. Jesus touches the leper and heals him, and then, the Scripture says, "And angrily glaring at him, Jesus immediately cast him out and said to him, 'Don't you speak one word of this to anyone; just go and get yourself examined by the priest so you can go on about your life.'" Not only is Jesus unhappy about healing him, Jesus is anxious to end the encounter quickly and to stop any spread of the news. Why so stern a Jesus? Why the concern about keeping this a secret? After all, the word is already out! This leper not only knew of Jesus' reputation, he also knew him by sight. But Jesus is trying to limit the spread of the news; he wants damage control. He wants to be able to go where he wants, when he wants, and teach, and he's worried about more and more people stopping him on the road like this leper did.

And that, of course, is the way it turns out. Jesus' anxieties turn out to be valid, because the man goes out and spreads the word all around. In the end, Jesus isn't just pestered, he's besieged, he's surrounded, he's inundated with folks wanting healing. He gives up his plan to carry out a teaching tour and just plunks down in a rural area, and people flock to him from every community in the region.

Is it surprising that Jesus gets angry with the leper? Maybe, particularly if the Jesus we know best is so god-like that we can't imagine him having normal human emotions like anger. But if we can think of a human Jesus, a Jesus who is put together the same way we

are, then no, it isn't too surprising that he gets angry. We certainly do, especially if we are tired, especially if we are being held back from what we really believe we should be doing.

Is it surprising that Jesus would limit the spread of the word about him? Maybe, especially from our point of view. We know how much good Jesus can do for people, and we want everybody in the story to be able to get to him and receive what they need. Jesus is the miracle cure, the polio vaccine that, if we had our way, would be given free of charge to every child in the world. But we get to see things from above the story. We know how it ends, with the empty tomb, and the spread of the gospel, and the millions and millions of lives changed. What if Jesus were, like us, in the middle of his life's story, unable to see all the way to the end? What if Jesus were, like us, having to rely on his sense of God's will? Can we identify with the feeling of wanting to slow things down long enough to figure them out, with wanting to get away from the pressure just long enough to catch our breath and think about where God wants us to go? You bet we can.

Is it surprising that the leper tells what Jesus orders him to keep secret? No, that's just human nature; in fact, that's the only part of the story that is completely predictable. The surprising turn to that part of the story is this: things don't go the way Jesus wants them to go. He wants the leper to keep quiet, but the leper spreads the word. He wants to be able to continue with his teaching mission, but instead he has to camp out in the boonies and keep on healing lepers and demoniacs, and fevers and other assorted diseases. Do we imagine a Jesus for whom the world always went the way he wanted it to go? A Jesus who, if he were hungry, made stones from bread; a Jesus whose friends never misunderstood him or left him in the lurch; a Jesus who had no enemies; a Jesus who carried out his mission until he was ready to retire, at which point he went off to his home by the lake and wrote his memoirs? Of course we know *that* Jesus never lived.

III. *But look at this:* after the long day of healing in Capernaum, and before he met the leper on the road, Jesus went off by himself to pray. Don't you figure that he prayed for support, for guidance, for wisdom, for strength to do what God wanted him to do? And then he tried to do what he thought God wanted him to do—teach—but folks kept getting in his way with all these healing requests. Perhaps God was answering Jesus' prayer, only not in the way Jesus was expecting. Maybe Jesus was figuring that God would sort of clear a path for him and make it easier for him to teach. Instead, God sent him this leper, who went out and drummed up even more healing business for Jesus. Can you relate? Do you ever pray for God's help, and have a certain kind of help in mind, which doesn't happen; but then, maybe years later, you think back on it and realize that God did help you, only in a surprising kind of way.

Mark's Jesus is one of us. He gets tired, he gets angry, he weeps, he scolds, he yells at his thick-headed disciples. Even for a man who can tame a storm, life gets pretty hard sometimes. So he prays for God's help and guidance, and he tries to do what he believes is God's will; but because he's in the middle of the story and not above it, maybe he can't see all the way to the end. So God helps him. God sends him people who keep him on track.

I don't know about you, but that makes me feel better. I can't find much help in the story of a Jesus who never struggles. But I can be comforted by the story of a Jesus who might not have known what kind of help he needed but got it anyway. That's called grace—God's love: merciful, undeserved, and surprising answers to our heartfelt needs; that's grace, and that's the gospel, brothers and sisters.—Richard B. Vinson

Illustrations

JESUS' ANGER.   Jesus' anger (the ancient reading is "was angry" and not "was filled with pity") applies to the horror of the misery which accompanied the disease (cf. John 11:33–38), which is just as contrary to God's plan of creation as is the action of the demons in 1:24 f. If this is true, then Jesus' pity is not the reason for this healing. The reason is to be found in the far more comprehensive campaign which is waged against every ungodly thing and in which the special authority of Jesus is revealed. The healing is accomplished by a word. Nevertheless, not only is the sovereign "I will" (RSV) mentioned explicitly, but also the fact that Jesus touched him (in contrast to 2 Kings 5:10). God's power lives, almost sacramentally, in the bodily nature of Jesus and will lay hold of the bodily nature of man also. As is true of the "snorting" of Yahweh in the Old Testament, the "speaking harshly" (literally "snorting") on the part of Jesus is because of the blindness of man who praises the miracle-worker, to be sure, but wants nothing to do with his cross (cf. 3:5 and Matt. 9:30).—Edward Schweizer[23]

GOD IS GOOD.   The parental heart of God has no desire to hurt us. But he understands that we must get our priorities straight. We cry. We pout. We sigh and groan. We say unkind things about God. He does not intervene. He lets us continue through the process. And we are saved. A little grief has saved us from a much greater sorrow. We can only conclude that God is good, that he is tender and compassionate even when we feel that we have a right to complain that he is unkind.—Fénelon[24]

SUNDAY: FEBRUARY SEVENTH

LECTIONARY MESSAGE

Topic: Understanding God's Wisdom
   TEXT: 1 Cor. 2:1–12
   Other Readings: Isa. 58:1–9; Matt. 5:13–20
   A frustrated friend has said, "I want to be for the good guys, it is just so hard to figure out who they are." As much as we want clear lines of right and wrong, life is often too ambiguous to provide such clarity. Of course, there are some things that are easy to judge:

murder, thievery, and lying, for example, are clearly prohibited and are clearly wrong. Even these lines, however, can be blurred by extenuating circumstances—wartime, the necessity of survival, protection of the weak. Discerning right and wrong, good and bad, is not always easy.

[23] *The Good News According to Mark*
[24] Quoted in Bernard Barrgely, *Spiritual Treasure*

I. *Not lofty words.* Paul writes to the church of Corinth, reminding them that he came to them not in "lofty words or wisdom." Rather, he came speaking in clear simple speech about the profound mysteries of God. He came speaking to them of Christ crucified. He came with a story, a powerful story about Jesus Christ and about Christ crucified. Paul declares that at the simplest and most significant level, he has committed to know only Jesus Christ and Christ crucified among the Corinthians. The fullness of whatever wisdom Paul brings is in this story, this saying, this knowledge that he brings to Corinth.

Granted, there may be other ways to talk, and in fact Paul acknowledges that among certain circles the talk can and does get a little rarefied, a little lofty. Even then, it is not of the order of the wisdom of the world or the rulers of the age. It is not the world's wisdom but God's wisdom that is the subject of Paul's and Corinth's and every faithful church's speech. God's wisdom is what it is all about.

II. *It is finally God's wisdom that we are after.* For surely, if we can be wise in the ways of God, we will do what is right and avoid what is wrong. So there it is; we need only discover the wisdom of God. How do we do such a thing? Are we not merely human? Are not the ways of God beyond our capacity to grasp? Are not God's ways and God's wisdom greater than ours? There is the rub. We are not God, but to do what is right we need to discover, ferret out, find and follow God's wisdom. How can we do it? For Paul it is done by knowing one thing: Jesus Christ and Christ crucified. The wisdom of God is in this one knowledge, the knowledge of Christ and of Christ crucified.

III. *Discerning wisdom.* Early in this same letter, Paul tells the reader that the cross is a stumbling block. To what extent the cross is a stumbling block for the modern reader is unclear. What is clear is that the cross is at the very least enigmatic. We of course have heard, either directly or indirectly, about the great sacrifice Christ made for us. We have heard about the saving action of Christ on our behalf, through his spilled blood. And these things matter to us, even if sometimes they confuse us.

In this portion of Paul's letter, however, he is not speaking simply of the sacrifice of Christ. He is instead speaking of the absurdity of Christ's crucifixion. Paul writes: "None of the rulers of this age understood this; for if they had they would not have crucified the Lord of glory" (v. 8). Christ was murdered, hung from a cross, because the "rulers of this age" didn't understand the wisdom of God. Had they known, so Paul proposes, they would not have killed the Lord of glory. But kill him they did. And this Paul will not forget or abandon or overlook. Instead, it will become the foundation of his preaching. It is the one truth with which he will seek to discern the wisdom of God. If wisdom, as a human comes to understand it, leads to crucifying the Lord of glory, it is surely *not* God's wisdom.

Embedded deep in this passage is a logic both simple and profound. If one's discernment of God's wisdom leads finally to the crucifixion of the Lord of glory, it is a misperception. Test discernment of right and wrong against this one standard: Does it lead to the agony of the cross? If so, it is not God's wisdom but the flawed and treacherous wisdom of the age.

IV. *Wisdom leads to life.* The agony of the cross is, on the one hand, most certainly the dying of Jesus of Nazareth. In his cross, however, there is also every other wrongful dying. There is the dying of children by starvation, of races eliminated in genocide, of the homeless poor frozen on our city streets. The wisdom of God known in the crucified Lord is a wisdom that abhors the agony of the cross, wherever the cross manifests itself today. About the wisdom of God, a wisdom beyond our reaching, we at least know this: that it leads not to the death of the Lord of glory but to his life, and with him and in him to the life of all.—David Greenhaw

Illustrations

MATERIAL, PHYSICAL, AND SPIRITUAL. In verse 14, Paul speaks of the man who is *psuchikos.* He is the man who lives as if there were nothing beyond physical life, as if there were no needs other than physical and material needs; whose values are all physical and material values, who judges everything from purely physical and material standards. A man like that cannot understand spiritual things. A man who thinks that nothing is more important than the satisfaction of the sexual urge cannot understand the meaning of chastity; a man who ranks the amassing of material things as the supreme end of life cannot understand generosity; a man who thinks his appetite is the last word cannot understand purity; and a man who has never thought beyond this world cannot understand the things of God. To him they look like mere foolishness. No man needs to be like this; but if he forever stifles "the immortal longings" that are in his soul, he may make himself like this, and if he does, the Spirit of God will speak and he will not hear.—William Barclay[25]

REFLECTIONS.   We all reflecting as a mirror the character of Christ are transformed into the same image from character to character—from a poor character to a better one, from a better one to one a little better still, from that to one still more complete, until by slow degrees the Perfect Image is attained. Here the solution of the problem of sanctification is compressed into a sentence: Reflect the character of Christ, and you will become like Christ.—Henry Drummond[26]

SERMON SUGGESTIONS

Topic: When Illusions Break
    TEXT: Isa. 29:8
    We all discover that anticipation is often better than realization. (1) Some things are illusions and it is healthy to find them out: (a) the illusion that material things in themselves can bring happiness; (b) the idea that life must always be good to us; (c) a strange habit of expecting others to be better than they are; (d) it may be that in our estimate of ourselves we are living in illusion. (2) There are other hopes that we are sometimes tempted to call illusions—the hopes that Christ kindles.—James Reid[27]

Topic: Love's Wastefulness
    TEXT: Matt. 26:8
    I can never rest till I have found traces of that love in all I see of God: (1) in nature; (2)

in providence; (3) in grace.—George H. Morrison[28]

Hymn Suggestions

    1. "Ask Ye What Great Thing I Know," Johann Schwedler; HENDON, Henri A. Cesar Malan; tr. Benjamin Kennedy
    This fine hymn, which echoes the statement of the apostle Paul (1 Cor. 2:2) to know nothing except Jesus Christ and him crucified, would be suitable for use with the reading of the Epistle for this day. A soloist or choir could sing the questions of the first three stanzas, with the congregation responding on the refrain: "Jesus Christ, the Crucified."
    2. "God Is So Good," words and music, anonymous; GOD IS SO GOOD
    God's grace and mercy toward those who seek the right—the theme of both the Isaiah and the Psalter selections—can be celebrated in this simple chorus that could be used to alternate with the stanzas of a praise hymn, such as "Praise to the Lord, the Almighty."
    3. "Renew Your Church, Her Ministries Restore," Kenneth Cober (1960); ALL IS WELL, trad. melody (the Sacred Harp) (1844)
    This contemporary prayer for the church to be salt and light in the world can aptly accompany the Gospel reading from the Sermon on the Mount (Matt. 5:13–26). It can be performed antiphonally with soloist or choir singing the first part of the first, second, and fourth phrases and the congregation joining on the last part.
    4. "Let Your Heart Be Broken," Bryan Jeffery Leech (1975); WYE VALLEY, James Mountain (1876)
    As a response to the plea of the prophet Isaiah for justice to the oppressed, this call to tender caring and love in action would be appropriate. Antiphonal singing phrase by phrase between sections of the congregation would enhance its meanings.—Hugh T. McElrath

Worship Aids

CALL TO WORSHIP.   "Praise the Lord! Happy are those who fear the Lord, who

---

[25] *Letters to the Corinthians*
[26] *The Changed Life*
[27] *Making Friends with Life*

[28] *The Greatest Sermons of George H. Morrison*

greatly delight in his commandments" (Ps. 112:1 NRSV).

INVOCATION.   Lord, our maker, by the power of the Holy Spirit, usher us into holy precincts, where matters of the soul are addressed, and God is worshiped, and life is prioritized around the cross of Christ. Then leave us not the same.—E. Lee Phillips

OFFERTORY SENTENCE.   "All shall give as they are able, according to the blessing of the Lord your God that he has given you" (Deut. 16:17 NRSV).

OFFERTORY PRAYER.   We thank you, O Lord, for the blessing of giving, of having a part in what you are doing in the world. Grant that we may never despise the small gifts that we can give or be filled with pride over some large gift.

PRAYER.   Eternal God, we speak to you from the secret places of our own souls. Hear our aches; hear our joys. Touch our fears; touch our hopes. See our sorrows and sense our happiness. Taste our remorse and inspire our confidence.

Deep calls to deep within us. Walk beside us with your presence and uphold us with your strong arm. May we be guided with a sense of your direction.

We pray that you will forgive us for not listening, for jumping to conclusions, for criticizing others so quickly, for not trying to understand. O God, we want to care and to help. Teach us your way.

We celebrate the assurance of your love, the abiding joy of your presence, and the wonder of your redemption. Because we have received so much, teach us by the example of Christ how to live lovingly, generously, faithfully, joyfully, and sacrificially. As we pray through Jesus Christ our living Lord.— William Powell Tuck

Sermon: Pushy People
TEXT: Mark 2:1–12

I. In the first part of Mark's gospel, *Jesus wanted to teach but he kept getting coerced into healing*. He tried to leave Capernaum for other towns, but a leper met him on the road, asked for healing, and then, against Jesus' orders, went out and spread the word about the healing all over the region. So, for a while Jesus was out in the country, and people were coming at him from all sides, wanting healing.

He decided to go back home, and returned to Capernaum, to his own house, and was immediately hemmed in by a mass of people who wanted to get close to him. The people filled up the house and spilled over into the street, gathered so thickly that there wasn't room for even one more. That sounds like the scene we've already read, in chapter 1, where all the sick of Capernaum were pressed in on him, and he healed them and then tried to slip out of town. House and street full of people? Sounds like a nightmare for Jesus. But in this scene he's finally getting to teach. He was "speaking the Word to them." He's finally getting to do what he wants and what he believes God wants him to do—and then these five pushy people make their entrance.

We know there were five; there was a paralyzed man on a pallet and four others, says the text. But there are lots of ways to imagine how it all came about. Was this man's injury something he had lived with for a long time, or was it a recent injury that left him paralyzed? Don't know. The four friends: were they all guys, maybe neighbors or old school buddies? Or were the four friends really two couples who were friends with the paralyzed man and his family? Don't know.

Whose idea was it to go to Jesus for healing? Maybe we should read this story like the one of the woman in chapter 5, who had been sick for quite a while, had given up hope in conventional medicine, and was pinning all her hopes on Jesus. Maybe the paralyzed man was like that. Maybe it was his idea to find Jesus, and maybe he had convinced his four friends to take a chance on having Jesus heal him.

Or maybe the four friends were the pushy ones; maybe they told the man that he had nothing to lose, and that they had heard that this guy Jesus had healed a man who lived down the road from them, and that they were taking him to see Jesus that very day, and that they weren't going to listen to any backtalk about it either. We don't know. The fact is, it could have happened in any of these ways: two couples or four guys, a friend who asked for help, or four friends who insisted that he get help, or some combination of all of those scenarios. There are lots of ways that these things happen in real life, right? Sometimes we ask for help; sometimes our friends just notice what we need and offer, then insist.

II. There's lots we don't know, but what we do know, because the story points it out, is that *these folks didn't quit when the plan ran into some complications.* When they got to the street where Jesus lived and saw the huge crowds, they could have decided to try again another day. But they didn't; they weren't that kind of folks. They were pushy, as I've been saying. The text implies that they tried to move the crowds aside but couldn't. So they figured out a way to get the guy up to the top of Jesus' house, which would have had a flat roof just like everybody else's. Then, without asking first, they dug a hole in Jesus' roof big enough to let this guy through.

Now, granted, houses were roofed with thatch and mud, and so it wasn't quite the same as if they had sawed a hole through shingles, roof decking, and rafters. But all the same, somebody was going to have to fix it. Imagine Jesus, standing in the front room of his own house, trying to talk loudly enough to be heard by all the crowds, enjoying his chance at teaching, figuring that no leper is going to be able to push through this crowd, and then dirt and dust falls out of the ceiling. And then they hack a hole out of his roof and—without explanation—they let this fellow down in front of Jesus.

Now, a story in chapter 1 showed Jesus angry with a man who asked for healing nicely, but these four friends didn't worry about that. They just worked hard to get the man in front of Jesus, believing that if they did, all would be well. And so it was. However Jesus may have felt about the hole in his roof, and however he may have felt about being interrupted from teaching one more time, when he saw their faith, he did what they wanted.

III. *How many friends does it take to bring someone to Jesus?* I can't even count all the folks responsible for putting me in front of the Lord. Start with my parents, who regularly brought me to church. Then add in at least one and sometimes two Sunday School teachers for every year of my life until I was sixteen and started teaching a class myself. These weren't professional clergy, they weren't seminary trained; they were salespeople, farmer's wives, schoolteachers, a foreman of a shipyard crew, a policeman. They were faithful to come and ride herd on a bunch of squirmy boys and tell us about Jesus.

How many people brought you to Jesus? I expect that while the details of our stories will differ, you could talk about the people who made the effort, who saw the need, who kept after you, and who brought you into a community of faith. Because of their faith—because of their tenacious, steady, consistent presentation of what they knew about Jesus, and because they really believed that putting you in front of Jesus would make a difference, and sometimes because they were pushy enough to insist that you come and give it a try, you and I are here.

The man on the pallet needed his friends to get to Jesus; they needed him to give them an opportunity for developing their faith. We need them to grow closer to Jesus; they need us for the same reason. Let's be deliberate, even insistent, maybe even a little pushy in our efforts to bring our friends to Jesus. If we believe, and I think we do, that Jesus really can help them, and if we believe, and I think we do, that this is a good place in which to meet Jesus, then let's bring them. How many friends does it take to bring someone to Jesus? Who knows—maybe you're the one extra friend who is needed.—Richard B. Vinson

Illustrations

TERRIBLE AND WONDERFUL.   The cross of Christ says something terrible about us, but something wonderful about God. It symbolizes not only the triumph in defeat of a good man. It also represents the merciful action of a loving Father: "For God was in Christ, reconciling the world unto himself" (2 Cor. 5:19).—William Sloan Coffin[29]

FAILURE AND SUCCESS.   Who knows what is best and what is worst? How can we tell for sure what has been our failure and what has been our success? In this regard I have

[29]*Living the Truth in a World of Illusions*

learned something which is still too easy for me to forget. It is that when God closes a door He always opens another. It is not always the one we had in mind, and it may not seem quite as good as the one we hoped to go through. But there have been so many times when disappointments were blessings in disguise, that we ought to be chary in proclaiming any event an essential defeat.—Gerald Kennedy[30]

SUNDAY: FEBRUARY FOURTEENTH

LECTIONARY MESSAGE

Topic: Choosing Life

TEXT: Deut. 30:15–20

Other Readings: 1 Cor. 3:1–9; Matt. 5:21–37

The faith community of early Israel, at least as we have access to it in the book of Deuteronomy, knew that there were important and difficult choices to make. In these texts the community recounts God's setting before them a choice between life and death, prosperity and adversity. Although we may not know it as well or as clearly in our faith communities, we too have difficult choices to make, and they too concern life and death, prosperity and adversity. As we stand at a crossroads, at a decision point like those facing early Israel, we surely will be helped by listening carefully to the counsel of this text.

I. *Recognizing the choice.* This particular section of Deuteronomy begins with a call to see: "*See,* I have set before you today life and prosperity, death and adversity" (v. 15). Indeed, we are more than halfway there if we are able to observe that there is a decision to make. Often we believe there is no other choice, assuming that the way it has always been done, or the way everyone else does something, is the only way to do it. Nearly every action we take represents a choice. Will we accept this job or not? Will we spend our money in this way or another? Will we help those in need? Will we be faithful in our loving relationships? What may seem like certainties are often results of choices we make, or fail to make. So, seeing that a choice is to be made is fundamental.

II. *Obeying and hearing.* The English translation of the Hebrew text of Deuteronomy obscures a parallelism in language. In verse 16, the Hebrew word *shama* is translated as "obey." In verse 17, *shama* is translated as "hear." The translations are accurate: the word can and does refer to hearing and to obeying. However, in ancient Israel there was little difference between the two. For us, obedience is often associated with unquestionably doing what we are told. As in the way a soldier is to follow orders, or a child is to do what he or she is told, obedience connotes following orders. Although obedience is a virtue in our common life, it is not one associated with freedom of choice. In this text, however, to obey is to make a choice.

Even more significantly, obedience involves hearing. Failure to hear is failure to obey. The book of Deuteronomy is filled with recitations of what God has done for Israel. It tells and retells the story of enslavement in Egypt and deliverance to the shores of the promised land. By hearing the story of what God has done, the ways in which God has been faithful, the community of faith is called to a path of obedience, led to a choice of fidelity.

The choices we make are affected by the narratives and voices we have heard. If we have not heard stories of God's care, compassion, and deliverance, it should not be surprising that we choose selfish and self-serving ways. If we have not heard of God's abundance, it should not be surprising that we choose to hoard and acquire all we can, in the fear that there may not be enough for us. Hearing and obeying are inextricably bound together. What we hear and who we hear profoundly affects the choices we make. And the choices we make are life and death choices.

III. *Openness to voices previously unheard.* Recently the metaphor of "voice" has been used to describe the inclusion of women and underrepresented minorities in decision making. Phrases like "at last women's voices are being heard," or "the Latino voice has too long been silenced in urban life" proliferate in our contemporary discourse. It may be possible to go overboard in trying to be

[30] *Witness of the Spirit*

"politically correct" and include every possible voice, but this text teaches that it is worthwhile to go out of our way to hear voices not often heard. What we hear has much to do with the choices we make and our level of obedience. Can we respond in obedience to those sisters and brothers from whom we have not heard? Can we attend to them with sufficient care that we do not make decisions that deprive them of their life or their prosperity? When the community of ancient Israel stood at the edge of the promised land, they had difficult choices to make. They had to decide whether they would listen to the voices of the dominant community, the community that already held the land, or whether they would listen to the voice of the one who had led them from slavery to freedom. As they recount the choice, it involved nothing short of life and death.

IV. *Choice of the generations.* When the choices were made between life and death, they were not simply choices for individuals. Choosing between life and death is a communal choice. That is, how the community decides concerning faithfulness ultimately affects more than the decision makers—it affects generations to come. We too would be well served if we made our choices considering that they affect future generations.—David Greenhaw

Illustrations

STANDING TO BE COUNTED.   Just as the speaker began a young man jumped up in the congregation and began to shout: "You don't mean a word of it! You sang, 'All to Jesus I surrender,' 'Where he leads me I will follow,' 'Jesus, I my cross have taken.' How many of us have done or would really do that?" The audience sat stunned and unresponsive. It was a preplanned act on the part of a group of young people at their annual fall student convention. But its impact was felt by everyone there. The question lingers even now in my mind, "Do we really mean that we will follow Jesus anywhere, even into persecution or death?"—William Powell Tuck[31]

vows.   I urged a certain man to accept an important responsibility. He listened attentively while I stated the case. Then he said, "Brother Wagner, I am this kind of a man; if I take a job I do it." He swelled, visibly. He said, "If I accept a responsibility, I throw myself headlong into it. If I make a promise, I keep it. I have yet to take a job that I haven't fulfilled." A great record, that. I blinked, to be sure he was real. Here, I thought, was a man in a thousand. A little shy on modesty, perhaps, but that was more than compensated for by dependability.

"Fine," I said. "You are a man after my own heart. Now will you take this job?"

And the man said, "No."

That is the easiest way I know of to make a record of no failures. Just don't do anything. That is a splendid way to compile a record of no broken promises. Don't promise anything. Personally, I prefer Peter. I think Jesus did, too.—Hughes Wagner[32]

SERMON SUGGESTIONS

Topic: The Responsibilities of Memory
TEXT: Deut. 8:2
(1) To cherish those recollections that tend to deepen recurrence and gratitude. (2) To recall the lessons that teach practical wisdom. (3) To furnish ideals of loftier endeavor. (4) To help one who would nurse one's own moral courage and faith.—Frederick K. Stamm[33]

Topic: The Sin Bearer
TEXT: 1 Pet. 2:24–25
The text speaks of three things: (1) the bearing of our sins by our Lord, (2) the changing of our conditions, (3) the healing of our spiritual diseases.—Charles Haddon Spurgeon[34]

Hymn Suggestions

1. "Praise the Lord! O Heavens, Adore Him," *The Foundling Hospital Collection* (1796); AUSTRIAN HYMN, Franz Joseph Haydn (1707)

---

[31] *The Way for All Seasons*
[32] *The Word in Season*
[33] *One Man's Religion*
[34] *Great Pulpit Masters: Charles H. Spurgeon*

Psalm 199, with its recurring emphasis on the laws, the commandments, the ordinances of God, is appropriately echoed in this anonymous eighteenth-century hymn that calls on all creation to praise the Lord whose laws "never shall be broken."

2. "I Want a Principle Within," Charles Wesley (1749); GERALD, Louis Spohr (1834)

Jesus' requirements of personal purity and integrity laid out in the Sermon on the Mount (Matt. 5:21–37) can find suitable response in this Wesleyan hymn on personal holiness.

3. "Not Far Beyond the Sea," George B. Caird (1945); GANGES, folk melody from *Wyeth's Repository, Part II* (1813)

This contemporary hymn—especially in its second stanza—focuses on the truth that babes in Christ can be fed only with milk until they mature to the extent they can digest the strong meat of the Word, as set forth in the Corinthian passage for today's reading.

4. "I Have Decided to Follow Jesus," words and music, anonymous

The Deuteronomic lesson for today's reading sets forth God's call for his children to choose life by walking in his ways. This little song, which may have originated among the Garo Christians in India, voices in simple terms the decision to choose life by resolutely following Jesus.—Hugh T. McElrath

Worship Aids

CALL TO WORSHIP.   "Blessed are they whose ways are blameless, who walk according to the law of the Lord. Blessed are they who keep his statutes and seek him with all their heart" (Ps. 119:1–2 NIV).

INVOCATION.   Today, O God, help us to make right choices and to stay by those right choices we have already made. We need your guidance and your empowerment.

OFFERTORY SENTENCE.   "If you are eager to give, God will accept your gift on the basis of what you have to give, not on what you don't have" (2 Cor. 8:12 TEV).

OFFERTORY PRAYER.   Owner of the cattle upon a thousand hills and the wealth in every mine, we could not seek to meet any need

that you might have, for we are too lowly and weak. We give because of our need to worship you in the giving way. So we bring our gifts and offer them in Jesus' name.—Henry Fields

PRAYER.   O God, at whose commanding word light first sprang from darkness, we pray for the spreading of that light till the day breaks and the shadows flee away.

Send light unto our inmost souls, we pray, lest some cherished iniquity shut thine ears to our prayers. Let the sunshine of thy love stir our sterile natures into fruitfulness, and win from our stubborn soil a plenteous harvest of heavenly grain. Illumine the unknown tracts of our natures, that hidden powers may come to light and yield their service to thy kingdom.

Shed light upon the dark places of the earth, that the habitations of violence may be destroyed: let human misery melt away before the rising of the Sun of Righteousness.

Grant light upon the problems that perplex the mind of man, dispel the night of doubt and fear, and for the eyes that wait may morning dawn.—W. E. Orchard[35]

Sermon: Halfway up the Mountain

TEXT: Mark 9:2–9, 14:29

The mountain of inspiration and the valley of service belong together. There is hardly a greater contrast in the Gospels than of our text and the verses that follow—the open heavens and the glory on the mount, and the valley of tears and failure below.

The disciples were standing on the threshold of a new era in service. In a few more days they would follow Jesus to Golgotha and beyond, where the expansion of the Kingdom would be thrust into their hands.

The church needs just such an inspiration again. She must not be content to stay on some mountain peak of glorious and necessary experience. She must walk with Christ into the valley. We do well to join Peter, James, and John halfway up their mountain, that we may discover the inspiration and strength that transformed their ultimate service.

For the first and only time in history, it was

[35] *The Temple*

permitted to sinful men to see a perfect spirit illumine a tabernacle of flesh. While the disciples looked, Jesus was transfigured before them. As the disciples looked, though mere bystanders they might have been, their faith in Christ was undergirded and confirmed.

Christ's deity was ratified for them there. Peter gave such a significance to the experience (2 Pet. 1:17–19). Peter had just confessed, "Thou art the Christ, the Son of the living God" (Matt. 16:16), and now he knew he was right. The prophets had spoken of the Messiah, and Jesus had boldly stated that he was the fulfillment of their words. Now God had burst through the heavens to confirm it. Indeed, Jesus was God's Son, and proclaimed so by God himself.

But his purpose was also approved. The most difficult thing for these men to grasp about the ministry of Jesus was the fact that he was to die. A cross was a thing to be rejected and despised. No messiah could go to a cross. His place was on a throne! Thus had Peter spoken his protest against Jesus' prediction of his forthcoming death. It was only six days after Jesus had so talked with them about his death that he was transfigured before them. Now he fell into conversation with Moses and Elijah, both of whom had made their exodus from life under some special providence of God, and the topic of their conversation was Jesus' death (Luke 9:31). It was at this moment that God spoke to confirm his Son. "This is my beloved Son." Just as there could be no Christ without a cross, and no salvation without a cross, so there can be no Christian discipleship without a cross.

It is little wonder that Peter wanted to stay on the mountain. Such wonderful hours are always worthy of continuation. But Jesus felt the pull of the valley. To continue that incarnation, Jesus once again put aside the glory of his divine prerogatives to return to the valley of identification with needy humanity. What is it that pulls us there? The needs of our valley are the same as those of Christ's.

There is opposition in the valley. Jesus found it to be so. The scribes had seized upon the failure of the disciples to cast out a demon as an occasion to wrangle with them. Any service for Christ that is worthy will be accompanied by stinging opposition and doubt. The valley in which we work is full of opposition. It must not discourage us.

There is human need and suffering in the valley. Jesus found a terribly afflicted lad there. A Christ who had just heard his own Father say "This is my beloved Son" now heard another father say "This is my son. If you can, help him." And Jesus was moved!

So must every person who would follow Jesus be moved by the suffering masses of the valley. God has concern for this needy humanity, and the people of God must not stand unmoved in such a presence. But the most terrible suffering that is found in man's valley is the suffering of soul that is the result of man's sin. If we have been with Christ on the mount of personal experience, if we have beheld his glory, if we have shouldered his cross, we cannot be unmoved by the lost humanity of the valley. World need, soul need, is in the valley!

And with it there is despair. Jesus found it in a father who had been disappointed in the followers of Jesus and so now despaired even of Jesus' ability to heal. His plea to Jesus was full of doubt: "If thou canst do any thing, have compassion on us, and help us" (Mark 9:22). Jesus met the despair of failure also in his disciples. They had failed. In utter despair, they asked, "Why could not we cast him out?"

How like the valley today! Men despair for fear, for failure, for suffering, for sin. The mysteries of life challenge their souls. The failures of life rob them of courage and expectation. And often it is the Church herself that is most defeated; wrapped in her shrouds of doubt, failure, and ineffectiveness, she can do nothing for a dying world.

When the father ventured to pray the most honest prayer of human experience, "Lord I believe; help thou mine unbelief," Jesus rushed to bring his little, imperfect faith to magnificent consummation. Christ always honors and rewards the smallest sincere faith. He was likewise sufficient for the suffering lad. Jesus is always sufficient for the great hungers and needs. He is adequate to save people from sin, to release them from the defeats of life, and to transform their suffering into an avenue of glory. But Jesus was also sufficient for his faltering disciples. He knew and shared with them the secret of success in the valley, of demanding, challenging service: prayer was at the center of the entire transfiguration experience.—H. Gordon Clinard

Illustrations

THE SYMBOL WE GO BY. G. K. Chesterton one time remarked that the gospel is the good news of original sin. He had a point, and it is necessary for us to keep clear in our minds that we believe in something that certainly does not shut its eyes to the tragedy and pain of living. We must not forget that the symbol we go by is the cross which means crucifixion and suffering. But the rejoicing comes when we understand that it was this cross that brought to us the knowledge of the love of God and of His concern for all men forever.—Gerald Kennedy[36]

THE VICTOR. Walter de la Mare has a ballad in which he describes how the ghosts of the three traitors, Pilate, Herod, and Judas, riding by, silver-white in the moonlight, are smitten through with sorrow for the foul play meted out to Jesus, who is now enthroned in heaven as Lord of salvation, and "He shall smile their steeds to see," so futile and disconsolate do they seem. It is the smile of One who is grateful to see the regret of former foes and who knows that the future of His cause is safe. All are riding on a vain quest who seek to destroy Jesus Christ, for "He shewed Himself alive after His passion," as victor on the frontier of human vision.—Arthur A. Cowan[37]

SUNDAY: FEBRUARY TWENTY-FIRST

LECTIONARY MESSAGE

Topic: A Down-to-Earth God
TEXT: Matt. 4:1–11
Other Readings: Gen. 2:15–17, 3:1–7, Rom. 5:12–19

The story of Jesus' temptation in the wilderness says almost as much in structure as in content. That is, the action and interchanges of the story are only a part of what it says. A careful look at the structure reveals a message not immediately apparent. Whereas the content of the story shows a challenge of Jesus by Satan and resistance to temptation on the part of Jesus, the structure reinforces an earlier claim that the Spirit of God descended to the earth. Together, content and structure proclaim that God's power, although lofty and great, is not aloof or distant.

I. *Jesus prevails.* The story of Jesus' temptation is straightforward. Jesus is led into the wilderness by the Spirit of God for the purpose of being tempted by the devil. After a period of fasting (forty days and forty nights—the same period observed by the church during Lent), Jesus is challenged by the tempter to demonstrate his power by commanding stones to become bread. Jesus refuses by answering with a quote from Scripture. Then the devil takes Jesus to the top of the Temple and challenges him to demonstrate invincibility by casting himself off the Temple. Again

Jesus refuses by answering with a quote from Scripture. The third time the devil takes Jesus to a very high mountain and challenges him to claim authority over all below. One last time Jesus refuses, and again it is by quoting Scripture. Finally the devil leaves, and Jesus is ministered to by angels.

The first audience for this story, as would a contemporary audience, expects Jesus to prevail over the temptation. There are no disappointments here: Jesus prevails. He resists temptation, and the devil's efforts are thwarted. Because the story begins with the Spirit of God leading Jesus into the wilderness expressly for the purpose of temptation, the reader is clear that this is a necessary step in Jesus' preparation for what is to come. As is the baptism story in the preceding chapter, this temptation is something Jesus must pass through.

This is a story of preparation. In part it functions to establish the credibility of Jesus. As the old song says, "Jesus walked that lonesome valley." The story tells us that having faced and prevailed over temptation, Jesus is able to address our most difficult situation—after all, he has been there himself.

II. *Scripture is quoted.* In each of the exchanges with the devil, Jesus responds by quoting a text out of the religious tradition. The repeated phrase, "it is written," (vv. 4, 7, 10) highlights Jesus' response to the devil.

[36] *For Laymen and Other Martyrs*

[37] *Crisis on the Frontier*

Not only is Jesus able to resist the tempter's power out of his own inner strength, but also, and perhaps more important, it is his reliance on the strength of tradition that enables him to resist. With each effort of the devil to lead Jesus to the abuse of power, Jesus is instructed in its proper use by the tradition's Scriptures.

Interestingly, however, Jesus is not the only one to use Scripture. After the first exchange with the devil, in which Jesus answers the challenge with Scripture, the devil himself begins to quote Scripture. The devil says, "If you are the Son of God, throw yourself down, for it is written, 'He will command his angels concerning you,' and 'On their hands they will bear you up, so that you will not dash your foot against a stone'" (v. 6). Clearly, simply quoting scripture is not the answer to all woes.

III. *Higher and higher.* This text follows immediately the baptism of Jesus, when the Spirit of God descended like a dove. The descent of the Spirit in the preceding verses contrasts with the movement of ascent in the temptation story. The story begins with Jesus in the wilderness. The first exchange between the devil and Jesus takes place there. Each successive exchange, however, takes place at a higher location. First on the pinnacle of the Temple, and then atop a "very high mountain," Jesus and the devil face off. The text is structured in such a way that each temptation takes place on higher ground. Each involves getting farther away from the God who has descended in the form of the Spirit. A clear contrast exists between the attempted ascent of the devil and the deliberate descent of God.

IV. *Down to Earth.* Although the power exists to be high and lifted up, the place of God as communicated in this text is "down to earth." It is in very human form, a form tempted, hungry and yet strong, that God comes. The God who is made known in Jesus is unquestionably powerful. The force and wiles of the devil cannot prevail. At the same time, this powerful God elects to exercise that power with restraint and care.—David Greenhaw

Illustrations

PROLOGUE IN HEAVEN. Jesus' entire ministry is preceded by a kind of "Prologue in Heaven." According to Mark, when Jesus is baptized he alone sees the heavens open and he alone hears the voice of God, calling him to be God's Son (1:9–11). The temptation, too, involves only Jesus, Satan, and God's angels (1:12–13). Thus from the very outset the reader is shown clearly the dimension in which everything takes place. Therefore only he will understand correctly who will hear that in Jesus God himself seeks to speak and act on earth.—Edward Schweizer[38]

TEMPTATION OR TESTING. What we call temptation is not meant to make us sin; it is meant to enable us to conquer sin. It is not meant to make us bad, it is meant to make us good. It is not meant to weaken us, it is meant to make us emerge stronger and finer and purer from the ordeal. Temptation is not the penalty of being a man, temptation is the glory of being a man. It is the test which comes to a man whom God wishes to use. So, then, we must think of this whole incident and experience, not so much as the *tempting,* as the *testing* of Jesus.—William Barclay[39]

SERMON SUGGESTIONS

Topic: Make a Friend of Your Fear
TEXT: Prov. 1:7
(1) The problem of fear. (2) The constructive use of fear: (a) as a spur to knowledge, (b) as a healthy stimulus to faith, (c) as a spur to righteousness and a healthy stimulus to love.—J. Wallace Hamilton[40]

Topic: Surprise Capture by the Cross
TEXT: 1 Cor. 1:23–24
(1) There are mixed feelings about the cross—its weakness and its power. (2) Our Lord commanded the situation on the cross: "Verily this was the Son of God." (3) Our Lord broke the power of evil on the cross.—Arthur A. Cowan[41]

HYMN SUGGESTIONS
1. "O Love How Deep, How Broad," anon. Latin (fifteenth century), tr. Benjamin

---

[38] *Jesus*
[39] *The Gospel of Matthew*
[40] *Ride the Wild Horses*
[41] *Bright Is the Shaken Torch*

Webb (1845); PUER NOBIS, Trier Ms. (fifteenth century); adapt. Michael Praetorius (1609); harm. George Woodward (1910)

In its grand sweeping embrace of the central purpose of Christ's coming to earth, this hymn includes the reference to Jesus' temptations (Matt. 4:1–11) in its second stanza. This venerable hymn should be sung in its entirety in order to follow the narrative progression that is climaxed by a trinitarian doxology.

2. "How Blest Are the People," Barbara Woollett (1985); LOVE TO CHRIST, *Ingall's Christian Harmony* (1805)

A poetic meditation on Psalm 32 from a Christian perspective, this song could appropriately be sung after reading the verses of the psalm as follows: vv. 1–5, stanza 1; vv. 6–7, stanza 2; vv. 8–9, stanza 3; vv. 10–11, stanza 4.

"How Blest Are Those," Fred A. Anderson (1986); ES FLOG KLEINS WALDVÖGELEIN, German song (seventeenth century); harm. George R. Woodward (1904)

This more closely paraphrased version of Psalm 32 could actually be sung in place of the psalm's conventional reading.

3. "Rescue the Perishing," Fanny J. Crosby (1869); RESCUE, William Howard Doane (1870)

Fanny Crosby's familiar gospel song can be used as a response to the apostle Paul's teaching that although sin came into the world through the transgression of Adam, grace and salvation came into the world from God through Jesus Christ.

4. "Lord, Who Throughout These Forty Days," Claudia Hernaman (1873); LAND OF REST, Amer. folk melody; harm. Annable Morris Buchanan (1938)

Referring directly to the Lenten season with its theme of Jesus' forty days of temptation in the desert, the singing of this hymn naturally follows or precedes the gospel lesson for this first Sunday of Lent.—Hugh T. McElrath

Worship Aids

CALL TO WORSHIP. "Happy are those who follow his commands, who obey him with all their heart" (Ps. 119:2 TEV). Holy God, whose face we seek, whose will we desire, whose love embraces us, hear our prayer of praise, and challenge us through worship to respond bravely to the deep needs of the

world, a world for which Christ died.—E. Lee Phillips

OFFERTORY SENTENCE. "Each of you must give as you have made up your mind, not reluctantly or under compulsion, for God loves a cheerful giver" (2 Cor. 9:7 NRSV).

OFFERTORY PRAYER. We thank you, O God, loving Father, for providing for us channels of service, even beyond our knowledge, through our giving. Let each gift go from our hearts and hands with your blessing, even to the ends of the earth.

PRAYER. God, we need wisdom from you to know where and how Jesus fits into life today. We do not want abuses of his name to prevent the right uses of his name. We sense that his ministry belongs as much among us as it did among our forebears in Galilee.

Open our lives to Jesus that he may come to us—by the seashore, in the marketplace, around the dinner table.

Strengthen our attentiveness to Jesus, that we may incorporate into our lives his teachings about love, grace, and service.

Set before our consciences Jesus' convictions about personal worth, human equality, and the necessity of integrity, forgiveness, and compassion in all interpersonal relationships.

Create within us a boldness and loyalty that keep us from trying to push Jesus out of our world by crucifying him afresh.

Grant to us the abandonment that comes from true trust in Jesus, that we may race to the risen Lord, dance in his presence, and then embrace his love and power forever.

O God, we pledge allegiance to Jesus, the pioneer in faith, the pathfinder whose way we follow and in whose name we pray.—C. Welton Gaddy[42]

Sermon: Anticipation!
TEXT: Luke 22:39–46
In the midst of a rocking, Pacific Coast earthquake that snapped like a rifle going off, a man was jarred out of slumber and instinctively reached for his service revolver. "Honey," said his wife calmly, "not even you can stop an earthquake with a gun." We often

[42]*Prayers: From Adoration to Zeal*

try to do something similar with our anxieties, trying to stop them by ignoring them, or numbing ourselves with alcohol, or running away. We can't stop stress with these kinds of revolvers either. Stress eats away at everyone like acid. Our self-confidence is demoralized. Our motivation is often churned into frustration, nightmares, an endless rushing about, confronted by a ceaseless refusal of inner peace to return with an end to our distress.

As stress is part of the human equation, so Jesus demonstrates that in the midst of the turmoil there is an oasis of hope. It was not Gethsemane, that lush garden on the slopes of the Mount of Olives, that was the Lord's oasis of calm, although Jesus sought solitude there often. There were other mountains in Galilee and elsewhere where he retreated when stressed and weary, emotionally drained, and in need of spiritual refreshment. Jesus' oasis of hope, you see, was not a certain place. It was something he carried with him, something you and I possess as well. It was an action. It was prayer.

Jesus' stress was more intense than any experienced by us. The sacrifice that he was about to make was for the sins of the world. The burden was heavier than for us and our personal guilt. Here we see plainly the humanity of the Son of God. He was "born in human likeness"—"being found in human form," writes Paul. "He humbled himself and became obedient to the point of death—even death on a cross" (Phil. 2:7c–8). But there was natural anxiety even for the Son of God.

Jesus knew where to go, however. His stress was not the master, nor his distress a roadblock. The Lord went to his Father. He prayed as he had many times before. In the process, "an angel from heaven appeared to him and gave him strength," writes Luke. Jesus had asked that the cup of sacrifice might be removed. "Yet," prayed our Lord, "not *my* will but *yours* be done."

Jesus experienced the greatest stress any human being can know. He faced the gravest anxiety on earth that was ever confronted. With an angel strengthening him, his internal turbulence came to a climax. He sweat those great drops of blood as his anguish peaked, and then "he got up from prayer." He went and awakened the sleeping disciples and warned them a second time to "pray that you may not come into the time of trial." Immediately he gave encouragement to his followers—and within minutes the Temple police and the mob arrived to arrest him.

But Jesus is now a different person. He is not immobilized by anxiety. The stress is relieved; the tension is diminished. He seizes the moment and speaks directly to Judas, the disciple who betrayed him, and then to Peter, who sought to defend him by cutting off the ear of a slave, and finally to the officials who come to arrest him—but he speaks with impressive calm. He is no longer anxiously troubled, although he faces the troublers of anxiety before him.

Prayer turned his anxiety into anticipation. He said to the crowd gathering around him, "When I was with you day after day in the Temple, you did not lay hands on me. But this is your hour, and the power of darkness." He knew what was before him, but he neither ran from it nor tried to negotiate an "easy out."

In other words, Jesus not only accepted the role he was to fulfill, but the evil these men plotted—for he knew that the end of the story was not in their treachery but in the Father's triumph. He was reassured of the strength needed, and he anticipated its might winning the ultimate battle.

Thus it is that you and I also meet life's tensions. We cannot ignore the stresses, although we try. We can't evade the anxiety, albeit we would like to. But we can spend time in prayer, and in the process discover the God and Father of our Lord Jesus Christ sending us something like angels to strengthen us. It is insight. It is hope. It is faith. It is the strength of encouragement. It is a new understanding of not only who we are but of whose we have become. It is anticipation that God is in charge and that, whatever happens, he will be glorified as we remain confident in him.

As we cannot stop an earthquake with a gun, so we cannot end stress and tension by shouting at it. Therefore I celebrate the value of Christian prayer as a gift to calm the inner being so that it can master the outer struggles, anticipating God's total triumph. So may you.—Richard Andersen

Illustrations

WHY WE PRAY.   We hear in these days of scientific enlightenment a great deal of discussion about the efficacy of *Prayer*. . . . Very little is said of the reason we do pray. The reason is simple: We pray because we cannot help praying.—William James[43]

PHYSICIANS AND PRAYER.   The exercise of prayer, in those who habitually exert it, must be regarded by us doctors as the most adequate and normal of all the pacifiers of the mind and calmers of the nerves.—William James[44]

SUNDAY: FEBRUARY TWENTY-EIGHTH

LECTIONARY MESSAGE

Topic: Night Vision
TEXT: John 3:1–17
Other Readings: Gen. 12:1–41; Rom. 4:1–5, 13–17

Apart from the twenty-third psalm, no text of scripture is as well know by its number as is John 3:16. The contemporary interpreter's temptation is to separate the text from its context and consequently to distort its meaning. That "God so loved the world that he gave his only Son, so that everyone who believes in him may not perish but may have eternal life" (v. 16) is best understood in the context of a community struggling with belief when the last of the eyewitnesses to Jesus' earthly ministry have died. For the generation of believers that the Gospel of John addresses, seeing and believing are no longer a piece. Now the believer must see with eyes different than those of the first generation eyewitnesses. It is in the context of this challenge of believing that the story of Nicodemus is told and in which the concluding remarks concerning what God opens to believers are made.

I. *A preoccupation with seeing.* The Gospel of John is frequently described as the most spiritual Gospel. There are actually very few episodes from the life of Jesus depicted in it. There is no birth narrative or a Last Supper, and although miracles and healings are performed, their number pales in contrast to the Synoptic Gospels. The narratives that are shared are embedded in lengthy descriptions and longer interchanges between parties than in the other Gospels. In contrast to the fast-paced action common to the MTV generation, this Gospel moves at a pace more commonly associated with PBS.

Several strong themes emerge in these longer episodes. There are long discussions on water and bread—consider the wedding at Cana, the woman at the well, the feeding of the five thousand. And in almost every chapter there is strong concern for seeing.

II. *Nicodemus at night.* The story of Nicodemus takes place at night. At night it is difficult to see; the light is dim and figures are hard to make out. Nicodemus comes to Jesus at night. There is every indication that Nicodemus comes earnestly, wanting to understand the signs he has seen Jesus do. Jesus, however, tells Nicodemus that it is not possible to see the kingdom of God without being born anew. Then there is a series of exchanges about what that means and how it is possible to be born anew. In the exchanges it becomes clear to the listener/reader that although Nicodemus may be earnest in his desire to understand Jesus and his signs, he is failing. Jesus speaks of a birth that Nicodemus cannot grasp. Nicodemus can see only in the categories with which he is familiar. Jesus breaks through those categories. Although Nicodemus has seen Jesus, he does not understand. He is not only literally in the dark, he is also figuratively in the dark.

For a community that has not literally seen Jesus in their midst, the message of this text is that the privilege of literally seeing Jesus is not all that it is cracked up to be. There are those who have seen and still do not see. To see the Kingdom of God, one does not have to be standing on the banks of the Jordan in the first century. Instead one needs to be born anew to see this Kingdom. It is a sight beyond the categories of regular sight. It is the result of a birth beyond the categories of regular birth. And it leads to a life beyond the categories of regular life, It leads, as John 3:16 makes clear, to eternal life.

III. *A world saved.* The gift of the believing

community is the promise of eternal life, a life distinct from that which we know daily. Our daily life is marked by a countdown to its end. Each day we get closer to our last day. But eternal life is life lived not in a descending spiral to demise but toward a horizon of hopefulness.

The concluding verse of this portion of scripture, verse 17, states clearly that the purpose of the sending of the Son was so that the world might be saved, not condemned. When all we see is what is right before our eyes, we can be led to despair. However, if we receive the gift of the believing community, the gift of eternal life, we are born anew, with eyes that see not a downward spiral to total demise but toward the hopeful horizon of the world's salvation. We see not a permanent "underclass" but a possibility for equitable distribution of God's good gifts. We see not endless wars and rumors of wars but the birthing of God's *shalom*. With the gift of eternal life we are given eyes to see, a new night vision that makes it possible for us to look beyond the categories that constrain us to the salvation that is promised us.—David Greenhaw.

Illustrations

DRAMA NIGHT.   The indication that the stage setting for this drama was by night suggests (1) that Nicodemus had come to talk theology with Jesus, because the evening was the time set aside for busy men to study the law after the day's work was done; (2) that the visit of so prestigious a leader to one who had recently cleansed the Temple might best be kept confidential because of the controversy that had aroused the populace; (3) that in visiting Jesus Nicodemus was coming out of spiritual darkness into light (cf. 13:30).—William E. Hull[45]

OUR RELIGION.   Our religion is not a system of ideas about Christ. It is Christ. To believe in him is what? To say a creed? To join a church? *No;* but it is to have a great, strong, divine Master, whom we perfectly love, whom we perfectly trust, whom we will follow anywhere, and who, as we follow Him or walk by His side, is always drawing out in us our true nature and making us determined to be true to it through everything, is always compelling us to see through falsehood and find the deepest truth, which is, in one great utterance of it, that we are the sons of God, who is thus always "leading us to the Father."

The hope of the world is in the ever richer naturalness of the highest life. "The earth shall be full of the knowledge of God as the waters cover the sea."—Phillips Brooks[46]

SERMON SUGGESTIONS

Topic: Because God Is Not Man
TEXT: Hos. 11:9
(1) Because God is God and not man, he is changeless. (2) Because God is God and not man, he has infinite faith in people. (3) Because God is God and not man, he is uncompromising in his hatred of sin. (4) Because God is God and not man, his love and patient forbearance are exhaustless.—William M. Elliott Jr.[47]

Topic: Dollars for Christ
TEXT: Matt. 6:19–21
(1) See if you have any of these dollars: (a) the destructive dollar, (b) the delinquent dollar, (c) the disinherited dollar, (d) the dissolute dollar. (2) What about dollars for Jesus Christ: (a) the delegated dollar, (b) the dedicated dollar.—J. Alfred Smith Jr.[48]

Hymn Suggestions

1. "My Faith Has Found a Resting Place," Liddie H. Edmunds (1890); LANDAS, Norwegian folk melody (c. 1890); arr. William J. Kirkpatrick

This witness song of faith and hope can be an effective response to the story of Abraham related in both the Genesis and Romans readings.

2. "Unto the Hills Will I Lift Mine Eyes," *The Psalter* (1912); DUNDEE, *Scottish Psalter* (1615)

A fairly strict paraphrase of Psalm 121, this hymn would be effective sung without instru-

---

[45] *The Broadman Bible Commentary*
[46] *The Light of the World*
[47] *Coming to Terms with Life*
[48] *The Overflowing Heart*

mental accompaniment on at least some of its stanzas. Alternation of Psalter reading and singing of the parallel stanzas would also be meaningful.

3. "Ye Must Be Born Again," William T. Sleeper (1878); BORN AGAIN, George C. Stebbins (1878)

With its chorus reiterating the answer of Jesus to Nicodemus's question about eternal life, this gospel song could be sung as an appropriate response to the Gospel reading for this day.

4. "I Lift My Eyes to the Quiet Hills," Timothy Dudley-Smith (1968); UPLIFTED EYES, M. Baughen and Elizabeth Crocker (1970)

This modern, free paraphrase of Psalm 121 has become popular in recent years. The unison tune, easily learned, lends itself to informal singing by a group or soloist.—Hugh T. McElrath

Worship Aids

CALL TO WORSHIP.   "I lift up my eyes to the hills—where does my help come from? My help comes from the Lord, the Maker of heaven and earth" (Ps. 121 NIV).

INVOCATION.   Majestic and almighty God, before whom we humbly bow and pray; allow our lips to sing your praise, direct our steps into pathways of service, lead our hearts to biblical insight, that worship and witness may combine into a wholeness filled with the power and love of God.—E. Lee Phillips

OFFERTORY SENTENCE.   "And the King shall answer and say unto them, 'Verily I say unto you, inasmuch as ye have done it unto one of the least of these my brethren, ye have done it unto me'" (Matt. 25:40).

OFFERTORY PRAYER.   Open our eyes, O Lord, and let us see the good that our gifts may do. Help us to minister to the hidden Christ in everyone. To that end, bless us with increasing awareness and openness of heart.

PRAYER.   Almighty God whom we do praise on high because the highest hast come to us through the highest, even our Lord, to us and to the highest within us, making appeal to that which is loftiest, so that we cry out in prayer and sing rejoicing this morn-ing, "Holy, Holy, Holy, Lord God Almighty," we bring to Thee from all the lower experiences of our lives the prayers expressed and unexpressed of our very souls, knowing that Thou on high hast proven to us the highness and loftiness of thy divine nature by reaching down to us. Now the weakest of us comes and the weariest and the saddest, the most mistaken, and the most sinful, crying—the lowliest and the highest—"O God of Jesus Christ forgive us our sins in the Name of our Lord and Savior, Jesus Christ. Amen."—Frank W. Gunsaulus[49]

Sermon: Trepidation!

TEXT: Matt. 8:23–27

I. *Jesus stepped into one of the small fishing boats docked at Capernaum. His disciples got on board as well, and they began sailing on the quiet waters of the Sea of Galilee.*

That small freshwater lake is but thirteen miles long by seven-and-a-half miles wide. It is, nevertheless, seven hundred feet below sea level, and it is rimmed with steep hills that reach up to three hundred feet high, making the lake somewhat like a teacup that is easily troubled by swirling windstorms.

On my first visit there, we sailed across the Sea of Galilee in complete calm. A colleague of mine came only a few minutes later and his boat was caught in the turbulence of a violent windstorm similar to the one Matthew describes. The winds arose quickly and with devastating force. Though Jesus and the Twelve began their voyage on becalmed waters, so they also were struck by the fierceness of the wind a few moments later.

Fear swept all on board. It was a small boat. There were no life vests. The waves were swamping the boat. The water was coming in faster than twelve men could bail it out. Jesus slept untroubled. It was merely a rolling water bed to him. He had no fear—none whatsoever. The disciples awakened Jesus with a plea: "Lord, save us! We are perishing!"

Here we see two vital signs: the depth of fear and a quest for assurance. They knew where to turn in their stormy crisis. Although the Lord asked them a salient question, "Why are you afraid, you of little faith?" it is evident

[49]*Prayers*

that he recognized that faith, small as it was, did exist. Small as it was, it was enough.

For the Lord Christ to quiet the raging storms that often assault us, it is only necessary to trust him to command the winds and the rain to cease. Until calm returns, hang on to faith. Hang on to the assurance that Jesus rides with you, awake or asleep, and that you can trust him to respond to your needs.

Your storm may be a nagging illness, or job security, or a course in school in which you fear failure. Your troublesome winds may be stirring fear due to marital problems, or financial matters, or death itself. Have faith, even a little, in the Christ who saves.

Here is the assurance every Christian carries with him or her: Christ does not abandon ship. He knows how to ride out the storm; but more than that, he knows how to quiet its surge and defuse its power, taming its waves by silencing its winds.

II. *The trouble oftentimes is not the storm, but the panic the storm arouses.* Jesus reminds us that there is a better way than letting panic get hold of us to begin with. Although we are initially frightened, it is essential that we remain calm and faithful, trusting God not only to see us through the ordeal but also to enable us to use the gifts he has given us— our own intelligence and wisdom—to deal positively with the conditions that are beginning to become dangerous. God's assurances are often already in place within the faithful Christian. We need only to employ them.

More and more, crises arise within the workplace as well as at home. The security of a job is no longer what it once was. The security of marriage has eroded for many. Advancing old age, debilitating disease, the fear of death, the fear of loneliness when a spouse dies—all of these are genuine issues. Riding the waves when downsizing occurs or when retrenchment in expansion hits or drastic changes take place often means that storms have engulfed us. Calm planning beforehand, including divine counsel, is always wise. What does God want you to gain from the experience? Is it possible to repair the problem before it is shattered by the pursuing storm? Is it a situation that God can heal?

Of course it is. Even before the Galilean storm died naturally for lack of further energy, Jesus quieted it with a word. He healed the turbulence of nature as well as the terror of men.

Mark tells us that Jesus arose from sleep in the stern of the boat and rebuked the wind. "Peace," He said to the sea. "Be still!" And it was. "The wind ceased, and there was a dead calm," writes the evangelist (4:39). If Jesus is capable of silencing winds and taming seas, he can master the storms that surround us or that well up within us.

III. *The problem we all face when storms attack us is not that the Savior is incapable of rescuing us but that we are incapable of believing that we can accomplish what we've set out to do.* The impediments become greater than the perceived accomplishments in our minds. That, however, is the devil's trickery. Discard him, and let Christ captain you to the goal set before you.

If we can only remember Jesus responding to the fearful in the pages of Scripture, we will be assured of moving ahead fearlessly ourselves. If only we can remember to pray as did that father of the epileptic boy, "I believe; help my unbelief!" Then we too will hear the resounding words of Jesus to assure him, "All things can be done for the one who believes" (Mark 9:24, 23).

Friend, fear is normal and natural, but it is neither normal nor natural to let it destroy faith or dominate life or let you drown. Hang on to faith. There is no need for trepidation that catapults you to defeat. Let God the Holy Spirit encourage you to use the gifts given to you to conquer the storms that can rage about you.

There's no need for a fear that will drown you when you can have a faith that will save you.—Richard Andersen

Illustrations

"DON'T BE AFRAID!"   A friend of mine, Wilfred Bockleman, was about three years of age and was being pulled by his mother in a sled when it began to tip. The frightened child began to cry out, when his mother said, "Don't be afraid!" while simultaneously steadying the sled with her hand. He never forgot that experience and said, "That was probably the first time I heard the Gospel in a meaningful way. I was afraid, and someone said to me, 'Don't be afraid.'" And reached out to me at the same time. That is what Jesus did to Peter, and what He offered the twelve in that storm-tossed boat, and gives to you and me. It is the assurance, that He "is with us always, to the end of the age" (Matt. 28:20).—R. A. Andersen[50]

MORE BEYOND.   In the Middle Ages it was the custom of countries and cities to adopt a motto or slogan that revealed or clarified that city. Portugal stood at the zenith of its glory. It was superior in business, banking, education, and culture. It extended farthest west on the continent. It thought it was the last port. To sail farther west would be to drop into oblivion. Portugal adopted the motto *Ne Plus Ultra,* nothing more beyond. Then one man doubted. With the news of the discovery by Columbus, the new world emerged. A conference of the city fathers was called. The motto was changed to *Plus Ultra,* more beyond.—Joseph R. Sizoo

SUNDAY: MARCH SEVENTH

LECTIONARY MESSAGE

Topic: Thirsty
TEXT: John 4:5–42
Other Readings: Exod. 17:1–7; Ps. 45; Rom. 5:1–11

The Old Testament lesson and the Epistle parallel the Gospel for today. One asks whether God can give water to the thirsty people in the desert, the other declares reconciling grace as miraculous as water flowing from a rock. Which is the greater miracle, that Moses strikes the stone of Meribah and water gushes out, or that being justified by faith we have "peace with God through our Lord Jesus Christ?" Psalm 95, appointed for the day, remembers Meribah and calls us to make a joyful noise to "the rock of our salvation."

These motifs combine in the story of the Samaritan woman's conversation with Jesus at Jacob's well. Some of the fourth Gospel's characteristic themes are here. The evangelist is especially interested in worship: What is it to worship God in spirit and in truth, from the heart as opposed to a more pharisaical understanding? The fourth Gospel's miracles are signs of the new life that is present in the world in Jesus: this thirsty man is in fact the water of life, and at his hand the salvation of God is given like a cup of cold water to the famished soul. Also, the Word shines through very human events, as at a village wedding in Cana of Galilee where Jesus' presence changes everything. And of course there are those who cannot see what is before their very eyes. Even the disciples, so long with him, can be obtuse.

If we take this narrative as John tells it, as a story of a thirsty man meeting a woman whose coming to draw water becomes a metaphor for her unquenched thirst for God, then we can make three quite simple points that add up to what the preacher ought to be saying on almost any Sunday.

I. *People are thirsty.* The Samaritan woman lives, as do Jesus and his people, in an arid land. The need for water was the order of the day, and going to the well or seeking out a spring or other source of water was a daily necessity. It would be most instructive for those of us who take clean running water for granted to read through the Bible with an eye for the references to thirst and shortage of water. Is there a more poignant description of the longing for God than the image of a thirsty deer seeking the brook?

The woman's physical thirst is obvious, as she comes in the heat of the day with her water jug. Jesus, the weary traveler, is quick to announce his thirst and to ask for a drink, and no less quick to recognize that human thirst that is not met by wells and buckets.

What does the thirst for God look like in our cities and suburbs? In what guise do we see the Samaritan coming with her jug seeking refreshment? Is there in many air-conditioned homes set in green-lawned suburbs a great and terrible thirst? New York City gets its water—some of the best in the world— from deep lakes in the Catskill Mountains, and there must be ten thousand bars in the city. Is New York still thirsty? The United States has abundant water, and most people can turn on the tap and drink from the public supply, but is our country thirsty? We can be sure that men and women everywhere are thirsty for what Jesus calls "living water."

II. *The thirst cannot be ignored.* Like Israel in the desert, the deer seeking a stream, or the

[50]*Don't Be Afraid!*

woman coming with her jug, the thirsty person will seek some source for assuaging this thirst. We may be able to live for weeks without food, but without water it is only a matter of days. The body's insistent and constant demand for water makes thirst the most compelling metaphor for spiritual longing. "As the deer longs for flowing streams, so my soul cries for you, O God" (Psalm 42).

Jesus at the well recognizes in the woman a thirst greater than that which brings her to draw water. This thirst might be more easily disguised than a parched throat and cracked lips, and not so quick to debilitate as dehydration, but it is no less persistent than the body's absolute dependence upon water.

One could go to a bar, where everything centers on having something to drink. It is often the case that people at their thirstiest are here, trying to find a way out of loneliness or to escape from a disappointing world. The thirst that Jesus spots in the woman at the well cannot, finally, be ignored.

III. *Only God can quench this thirst.* Jesus says to the woman: "Everyone who drinks of this water will thirst again, but whoever drinks of the water that I shall give him will never thirst."

The woman has raised the conventional questions about which is the right place to worship, as if religion were a matter of options and choices. Jesus gets down to what is essential: only God meets the heart's need.

With friends in Italy in high summer, we simply could not get enough to drink. Constantly thirsty, we drank bottled water incessantly and remained thirsty. Those two weeks have remained for me a metaphor of life without God, constantly unsatisfied and without peace.

In the town where I live, across the street from our church is a railroad trestle. Many commuters pass that way each day, on their way to Manhattan's offices and shops. Scrawled in blue paint across the trestle is a single word—perhaps the protest or prayer of some harried commuter who, for all the scurrying and hurrying couldn't "get no 'Satisfaction'."
—Charles L. Rice

Illustrations

THE WILL TO MEANING.   A poll of public opinion was conducted a few years ago in France. The results showed that 89 percent of the people polled admitted that man needs "something" for the sake of which to live. Moreover, 61 percent conceded there was something, or someone, in their own lives for whose sake they were even ready to die. I repeated this poll at my clinic in Vienna among both the patients and the personnel, and the outcome was practically the same as among the thousands of people screened in France; the difference was only 2 percent. In other words, the will to meaning is in most people *fact,* not *faith.*—Victor E. Frankl[51]

RESPONSE TO GOD.   The genuine ethical action is a *response* to God. It is that action which is motivated not by our egocentric desires but rather by the structure of life which makes demands that we cannot refuse. The grace that comes from God when we respond to his commands, far from diminishing our efforts, lends new energy and new power for the social action whose values will be lasting. The religiously healthy person realizes that God, simply in that he *is,* presents demands upon the soul to which we turn a deaf ear only at peril of destroying ourselves.—Rollo May[52]

SERMON SUGGESTIONS

Topic: The Unchanging God
TEXT: Mal. 3, 6
(1) His person never changes. (2) His purpose does not change. (3) His promise never changes. (4) His power does not change. (5) The God who never changes is ever effecting changes.—Montague Goodman[53]

Topic: Worldliness
TEXT: 1 John 2:15–17
(1) The nature of the forbidden world. (2) The reason for which it is forbidden.—Frederick W. Robertson[54]

Hymn Suggestions

1. "Come, Christians, Join to Sing," Christian H. Bateman (1843); MADRID, trad. Spanish melody; arr. David Evans (1927)

[51] *Man's Search for Meaning*
[52] *The Springs of Creative Living*
[53] In *My Way of Preaching,* ed. by Robert J. Smithson
[54] *Sermons Preached at Brighton*

In keeping with the invitation to sing in Psalm 95, this exuberant hymn can serve aptly as a call to worship. Its "Alleluia! Amen!" refrain naturally suggests antiphonal treatment, with the congregation only taking the refrain and choir or choirs singing all the other text.

2. "And Can It Be That I Should Gain," Charles Wesley (1738); SAGINA, Thomas Campbell (1825)

This well-liked hymn of testimony to Christ's saving work reflects the message of Romans 5:8b: "while we were yet sinners, Christ died for us."

3. "O Come and Sing Unto the Lord," *The Psalter* (1912); IRISH, *A Collection of Hymns and Sacred Poems* (1749)

Instead of the traditional Psalter reading for the day, this paraphrase of Psalm 95 could be sung antiphonally by choir and congregation.

4. "People Need the Lord," Greg Nelson and Phill McHugh (1983); PEOPLE NEED THE LORD, Nelson and McHugh (1983)

This popular mini-hymn echoes the call of Jesus (John 4:35) to "look on the fields, ripe for harvest."—Hugh T. McElrath

Worship Aids

CALL TO WORSHIP. "O come, let us sing unto the Lord: let us make a joyful noise to the rock of our salvation" (Ps. 95:1).

INVOCATION. Gracious God, our yearnings are deep and our needs may be great but our hearts are ready to praise you and rejoice in your goodness. Let this entire service of worship glorify you as we witness to our faith in song, prayer, and sermon.

OFFERTORY SENTENCE. "I am crucified with Christ: nevertheless I live; yet not I, but Christ liveth in me: and the life which I now live in the flesh I live by the faith of the Son of God, who loved me, and gave himself for me" (Gal. 2:20).

OFFERTORY PRAYER. Our Father and our God, as Christ lives in us, our hearts go out in care and compassion for the lost of this world, for those in the grip of destructive habits and paralyzing guilt, for those in doubt and bewilderment, for those in hunger and want. Bless, then, our offerings, that they may alleviate needs both physical and spiritual.

PRAYER. We beseech of thee, O Lord our God, that thou wilt fill us this day with a sense of thy graciousness and goodness. May a sense of God banish our doubts and needless fears. May we feel that thou dost know how to sustain thyself and thine administration, and yet take care of guilty and sinful creatures, that their faults may not be their ruin. May we rejoice in believing, though our transgressions have been many, and though our offenses may have been heinous. May we stand in the full faith of that wondrous divine wisdom which knows how to rescue us without jeopardy to any other interests. We do not understand how. What do we understand of thee, or of anything which is a part of thine infinity? But we believe that thou art, and that thou canst have mercy on whom thou wilt. Thou art not hedged in by our prejudices, nor by our restrictions, nor by any necessities of thy government; but thou takest counsel from thine own royalty, thou askest the generosity of thy heart; and by that love which is infinite in all its directions and attributes—by that, thou dost take counsel, and then do as seemest best to thee. Thus we stand surrounded by all the transcendent grandeur of divine love.—Henry Ward Beecher[55]

Sermon: The Realm of Grace
TEXT: Luke 15:20

The father made no effort to find the boy, perhaps because he was not in a position to leave home, perhaps because he had no idea where to begin to look. But it may have been because he knew that unless the boy came back of his own free will, it wouldn't make any difference until he wanted to come. But he never gave up hope, he was always waiting and watching.

One day he saw him coming. In spite of the distance, in spite of his own failing eyesight, in spite of the boy's dilapidated condition, he recognized him at once. (If you love someone, you can spot him anywhere—in a crowd or in the dark, no matter how great the distance, no matter how disfigured he may be.) He ran to him and kissed him. Be-

[55] *Prayers from Plymouth Pulpit*

fore the boy had a chance to make his carefully planned speech, he stopped him. The boy got as far as this: "Father, I have sinned against heaven, and in thy sight, and am no more worthy to be called thy son." He had meant to go on and say, "Make me as one of thy hired servants." But before he had a chance to make the last statement, the father said to his servants, "Bring forth the best robe and put it on him; put a ring on his hand and shoes on his feet: and bring hither the fatted calf, and kill it; and let us eat and be merry: For this my son was dead and is alive again; he was lost and is found."

I. Today the action of the Father leads us into the realm of grace. It is a realm of mystery so vast that anyone who presumes to enter it with full knowledge and understanding is a fool. This is one of the times, and I suppose the times are many, that one must take off his shoes before he steps upon this holy ground. *Grace* is a word that we use to describe *something done,* favorable to us, unforeseen, and usually undeserved. For instance, a senior in college does very little work in his last term and fails all his final examinations. Yet the college's president, for reasons of his own, known only to himself, decides to give him his degree in spite of his failure. The act of the president, unforeseen, particularly by the student, and certainly undeserved, might be called by the students an act of presidential grace.

Very few of us have ever had an experience like that: something wonderful, coming out of the blue, unexpected, unforeseen, certainly undeserved. Grace is always free, always given gladly. It is spontaneous, unsolicited, an act of pure unselfishness. Sometimes the cost to the giver is only slight, if any at all; sometimes it is enormous. I used to wonder what the cost to the father was when he took back the wayward son, and only in recent years have I come to see that the cost was that he lost the love, at least temporarily, of his other son, who would not join in the celebration but stayed outside and pouted, a sour note in a day of great rejoicing.

The important thing to notice is that because what is done is done so freely and so gladly, and because it often costs so much, it sometimes touches your heart as nothing else ever does. This we call the grace of God. It is present everywhere, and it has been present always, and no one is excluded from it.

II. There was one particular time when this sort of thing happened in an unprecedented way, with an unsurpassed intensity, and with unimaginable results.

There was a man who went about doing good. He came from an undistinguished family, and he lived in an unpopular part of the world. He was strong, and yet in a strange way tender and gentle. He had no weapons of any kind, and no thirst for power, yet there was something imperious about him. He was the friend of sinners; he was the implacable enemy of the self-righteous.

From the beginning those close to him felt that there was something about him that was different. They didn't know how to express it in words but when they tried to this is what they said: There is something about him that makes us think of God. They stood in awe of him, yet they couldn't keep away from him. He was beyond their understanding, yet they kept on following him. He asked of them things they couldn't possibly do; yet they never gave up. He got into trouble with the authorities, as you would expect. The people didn't have the courage to stand by him, and his friends were frightened and fled. Yet he went right on, quietly and steadily. In the end he was killed. He could have gotten out of it so easily, if he had wanted to, but it almost seemed as though he walked right straight into it, deliberately, willingly—gladly, shall we say? And as they saw him die—even though it was from a safe distance—and as they thought about it later, it dawned on them that he did it for them! The more they thought about it, the more they realized that God was in him, and that God was doing this for them. And when they tried to put it into words, they said, "God was in him, drawing us to himself."

I am reassured when I remember that I am heir to this one sublime deed of pure unselfish love. I do not therefore take my sin more lightly. Because God takes it so seriously, I take it more seriously, but I hope, less anxiously, more positively, more confidently. I come to myself and I say, "I will arise and go to my Father," but I can say it because I know that in my deepest need my Father came to me.

This is at least a part of what St. Paul meant when he said, "Where sin abounded, grace did much more abound." This is our hope, this is our glory, and this is the meaning of our lives—to let the grace flow through us to draw other people into the realm of its influence, and to help and heal those who are yet outside.—Theodore Parker Ferris[56]

Illustrations

"GOD ALONE" FAITH.   Ask a Luther, a Zwingli, a Calvin whether this "God alone" faith made them lazy! Examine the lives of others who have really received this "God alone" faith in all of its depth and magnificence, and inquire whether it has made them morally indifferent or lazy. It is the great mystery of God that men do not become strong until they know their weakness, and expect all things from the power of God. The strong, the real "doers" in Christendom have been those who relied solely on the work of God, and not those who

trusted much in human activity. For God's power is made perfect in weakness, and only when a man knows how weak he is can God become mighty in him. It is precisely the truly good that is done "by faith alone."—Emil Brunner[57]

OUR HOPE.   The true spirituality of John Wesley is revealed not by his teaching that perfection is possible in the Christian life but in the fact that he never claimed perfection for himself. Integrity is possible not because we can be altogether what we ought to be, but because we can participate in the working of God whose grace includes forgiveness for what we are. Justification by faith in God's grace is the ultimate relationship within which such moral achievement as is possible for us will always have its rightful place.—Daniel Day Williams[58]

SUNDAY: MARCH FOURTEENTH

LECTIONARY MESSAGE

Topic: Seeing the Light

TEXT: John 9:1–41

Other Readings: 1 Sam. 16:1–13; Ps. 23; Eph. 5:8 14

The lesson, 1 Samuel 16, tells a story of the one who does not see as human beings see, but who "looks upon the heart." The narrative connects with today's Gospel also in its theme of anointing: Samuel is enabled to see David as the one chosen to be king, and in the name of God anoints him. This anointing was itself a prayer that the new king would be given eyes to see clearly and to lead the people wisely. The Epistle, Ephesians 5:8–14, declares that those who are in Christ are light—no longer darkness—and are called to walk as children of the light. "Once I was blind, but now I can see."

Amos Wilder, writing on Mark's parallel to his story, calls this opening of the blind man's eyes a "mini-drama of the resurrection."[59] This story provides a picture of what it is like to enter into the death and Resurrection of Jesus: it is like having your eyes opened, just

as knowing Christ is like finding living water that sustains you forever.

I. *One thing I know.* In some regards, today's Gospel is quite a modern story, indeed a modern American story. When questioned by those in authority, the elders, the man born blind—now seeing—relies solely on his experience: "one thing I know, that though I was blind, now I see" (9:24). The heart of this Gospel story is a scene as clear as winter light, in the man's words: "The man called Jesus made clay and anointed my eyes and said to me, 'Go to Siloam and wash'; so I went and washed and received my sight." The elders have their agenda, to catch Jesus in a violation of Sabbath laws and to buttress their position of religious authority. All of this, however, is wasted on the man: "I can see."

Wouldn't you call this a text for our time? Of course it was not written to be so. These stories circulated in the early church as dramatic representations of the triumphant life of the crucified and risen Jesus, and of the new life that these witnesses had found in him. In the fourth Gospel there are "signs," whether we see Jesus providing wine at a

---

[56] *Selected Sermons, Vol. 1*
[59] *Early Christian Rhetoric*

[57] *Our Faith*
[58] *God's Grace and Man's Hope*

wedding or opening blind eyes, that manifest his glory, the triumph we will celebrate at Easter.

It would be a mistake to reduce this story to a merely psychological portrayal of the modern American tendency to refer everything to personal, indeed private, experience. But it is tempting to do so. The man turns aside the disbelief of his neighbors and of the authorities with "I can see." Vivid, firsthand experience is what matters. Hard to gainsay, easy for us moderns to recognize: he knows what has happened to him. The elders cast him out, his parents show little interest, and his neighbors do not even recognize him. All of this fades into insignificance before the one reality: he sees.

II. *The children of the light.* From the earliest days of the church, Lent has been the season of preparation for baptism on the eve of Easter. At the Great Vigil, those who had fasted and prayed and had been instructed in the faith were stripped of all their clothing—not even a hairpin could go into the baptistry—and plunged into water, just before dawn on Easter Day. In some of the early documents, the newly baptized are called "the illumined," those who have seen the light.

How we understand this—the nature of Christian experience and of the Church as shown forth in Holy Baptism—seems particularly crucial for us in the United States just now. What does it mean to have our eyes opened, to be the children of the light?

For example, David Koresh, whatever else we might say about him and the dozens of others who fall roughly into his camp, had "seen the light." As a consequence, he had no regard for church or state. This should not surprise us. One of the reasons for the success of fervent, evangelical religion must be its appeal to the idea that individuals can be illumined, can see the light. Hyperevangelical movements are amazing collections of individuals who have seen the same blazing light. In Jesus' anointing with the healing mud there is incipient evangelicalism: I have had an experience; I have heard the voice of God; I have seen the light; he touched me. Negotiation and compromise have little chance here.

The fourth evangelist writes as one who is himself so convinced of the truth that he stands apart from the traditions he knows so well—so much so that we have to be wary of the lectionary's gospel readings for this season. "The Jews, the Jews," John repeats, again and again. In today's Gospel, the man who has seen the light is finally alone with the one who has touched him. Such a story gives us the chance to ask whether we are content with the profile of the Christian life that it suggests and that is common among us: I have seen the light and I take my place among those who, like me, can be comfortable with "If you are saved and you know it, honk your horn."

III. *The light of Christ.* Those early Christians, catechized during Lent and baptized at Easter, were illumined not by superior knowledge but by entering more and more deeply into the mystery of Jesus' death and Resurrection. This is powerfully symbolized at the Easter Vigil when the new fire of Easter is kindled, the paschal candle is lighted and carried into the darkened church with the announcement, "The Light of Christ." In baptism, the individual not only acknowledges Christ as his or her Lord and Savior, but in this act he or she is also initiated into the community of faith. It is in this community that the light shines, that the Spirit moves, that the Word of God is rightly heard and the sacraments efficaciously received.

With the man whose eyes have been opened, we too confess that our eyes—our two eyes—have been opened by Jesus Christ. But it is all the more important in the modern, individualistic situation of life in America that we live in the light of Christ that shines forth among God's faithful people who day by day seek the light and truth of Christ present to the Church by the Holy Spirit.—Charles L. Rice

Illustrations

THE CRISIS.   The drama ends with the pronouncement of Jesus that his presence in the world is a judgment. Those who cannot see now have light and can see. Those who say they already see and have no need for light are blinded by the light. The reader is not allowed simply to enjoy a wonderful story about Jesus who gives sight to the blind. Christ's coming creates a crisis and two kinds of results follow: light comes to those who acknowledge life is darkness without him;

darkness comes to those who without him claim to see.—Fred B. Craddock[60]

THE OPENING OF THE EYES.   "Thou hast both seen me." How touching in this special story is the allusion to the light which the Lord had given only that day. Jesus reminds him of the lower mercy that He may assure him of the higher. "Thou has seen Him with the eyes that I have opened. Let that be a pledge and earnest to thee that I can and will open yet other eyes, and thou shalt see him more completely, more profoundly, in wonderful new ways." Still, you see, it is as the Saviour of the past life that He offers Himself for the future.

I love to think of this, that where men today are most unconscious of His presence, Christ is laying foundations for His future work. Here is a perfectly worldly man who cares nothing for Christ or Christianity, but yet Christ's touches are on him. He is surrounded with blessings; he is pressed upon with sorrows; he is led through apparently meaningless experiences; and all that some day, when he is really moved to cry out for a Son of God, Christ may be able to come to him, not new and strange, but with the strong claim of years of care and thought and unthanked mercy.—Phillips Brooks[61]

SERMON SUGGESTIONS

Topic: Holy—but Stained
TEXT: Exod. 28:38
The Aaronic priesthood had, as one of its functions, to intercede with God not only for the sins of the people, but also for the affectations in their holiness as well. Are we guilty of iniquity in holy things? (1) In our own penitence. (2) In our worship. (3) In our prayers. (4) In our service. (5) In our giving.—W. E. Sangster[62]

Topic: The Temptations of Maturity
TEXT: Luke 14:30
(1) Misused power. (2) Lost faith. (3) Foolish complacency.—Harry Emerson Fosdick[63]

[60] John
[61] The Light of the World and Other Sermons
[62] Can I Know God?
[63] What Is Vital in Religion

Hymn Suggestions

1. "Awake, My Soul, and with the Sun," Thomas Ken (c. 1670); TALLIS' CANON, Thomas Tallis (c. 1561)
An ancient morning prayer hymn reflecting the spirit of John 9:4, this is a natural selection for the beginning of morning worship.

2. "As Sons of the Day and Daughters of Light," Christopher Idle (1975); LAURATE DOMINUM, C. Hubert Parry (1894)
Recently written, this hymn spells out the implication of Ephesians 5:8 that we are to live as children of light.

3. "We Are Called to Be God's People," Thomas A. Jackson (1973); AUSTRIAN HYMN, Franz Joseph Haydn (1797)
In connection with the calling and anointing of David (1 Sam. 16:1–3), the singing of this hymn of commitment and mission would be appropriate.

4. "The Lord's My Shepherd, I'll Not Want," Scottish Psalter (1650); CRIMOND, Jessie Seymour Irvine (1872)
"The King of Love My Shepherd Is," Henry Williams Baker (1868); ST. COLUMBA, ancient Irish melody
"The Lord's My Shepherd, All I Need," Christopher L. Weber (1986); EVAN, William Henry Havergal (1846)
These are but three of numerous paraphrases of the great Shepherd Psalm (23), any one of which could appropriately be used in the place of the normal reading of it.—Hugh T. McElrath

Worship Aids

CALL TO WORSHIP.   "The Lord is my Shepherd; I shall not want" (Ps. 23:1).

INVOCATION.   Our Lord and our God, Shepherd of our souls, you provide for us in ways beyond our knowledge, certainly beyond our deserving, and we can trust in your love and care completely. Yet our faith is sometimes challenged. Our eyes, blinded by doubt and fear, must be opened so that we can see the truth. Help us today to view our lives and the world in which we live in the light of your love.

OFFERTORY SENTENCE.   "Like good stewards of the manifold grace of God, serve one another with whatever gift each of you has received" (1 Pet. 4:10 NRSV).

OFFERTORY PRAYER.   Lord, we would proclaim Jesus as Lord, so we give today and we ask that this gospel message be spread far and wide through our offering in Christ's name.—E. Lee Phillips

PRAYER.   Presence is what we seek as we gather, Father. Not just the presence of one another, but the presence of your Holy Spirit moving among us with power that transforms and renews.

We seek your presence that we may be forgiven for our sins. By ourselves we cannot resolve the sin issue, we only sink further into its grip where there is no light of redemption shining. Call our sinful natures to account, that we may enter the place of forgiveness and experience the power of restoration.

We seek your presence that we may be made aware of power beyond ourselves. So often we limit our expectations to what we can do in our own strength, forgetting that there is power available to your people that can do marvelous and wonderful things among us in our daily duties and responsibilities and needs. We seek your presence, Father, because we need a strong shield against temptation. On every hand we are tempted to take the short cut or compromise truth or engage in activity that is unacceptable for your children. We need someone to remind us again and again of the tragedies of yielding to temptation and becoming enmeshed in its tentacles. We need your presence to guide us, that we might not fall into the grips of temptation.

We need your presence that we may be given the ability and desire to be taught what is Godlike and right. We need you with us as we determine what is true and honest and just and pure. We need your presence so that we might understand what is holy and sacred and eternal. We need your presence so that we might have a love for your Word with all its power and insight and guidance. Without your presence as teacher, we remain ignorant and unable to follow the highest good possible.

We need your presence so that we may be sterling examples of Godlikeness as we walk in the community, as we show loyalty to your kingdom, as we serve in all humility among our fellow human beings, as we show care for your creation, and as we seek to enable others to be free, as we have found freedom in your presence.—Henry Fields

Sermon: Just Veggies and Water, Please
TEXT: Dan. 1

It was new student orientation weekend at the Royal Babylonian Palace Academy of Foreign and Civil Service, and the freshmen were getting adjusted. They all met the headmaster, who gave them the usual lecture about working hard, studying hard, and becoming future leaders. They all checked into their dorm rooms and unpacked their stuff and began to get used to their new roommates. They met with their academic advisers, who enrolled them in classes for the fall term: Fundamentals of Diplomacy 101, Babylonian Literature 101, Modern Political Thought 101, and History of the Babylonian People with Occasional References to the Rest of the World 101. Everything was going fine, until the first day in the cafeteria, when the four Jewish boys went through the line and said, "Just veggies and water for me, please."

To explain why they're on a diet, and to explain why they are there in the first place, we have to digress a little. Judah was part of the Babylonian Empire at this time, and one year the King of Judah decided that Babylon was too busy with its own problems to mess with Judah and opted not to pay the annual tax—as if Hawaii decided next year that, being an election year, nobody in D.C. would notice if they just never mailed in their federal taxes. But of course governments always notice delinquent tax accounts, and Babylon sent the troops out to punish Judah. The army sacked a bunch of cities, including Jerusalem; they took a bunch of captives back to Babylon, mostly the wealthy and the nobles, who could have led or financed another rebellion.

So Daniel, Hananiah, Mishael, and Azariah, sons of Judean nobles, wound up as unwilling guests of the Babylonian government. King Nebuchadnezzar decided that it would be good policy to take some of these Jewish youths and run them through his civil service academy. Why? Well, long term, these guys represented good insurance against any future rebellions. Think about it—Nebuchadnezzar was going to teach them to think like Babylonians. Take a look at verse 4: "They were to be taught the literature and language of the Babylonians." Now, that verse only spotlights the significant point of the story. We know something about the curriculum in these palace schools. Students learned how to act around royalty, how to avoid giving offense to people of different cultures, and so on. In those respects, Nebuchadnezzar's school would have been just like the one they would have attended in Jerusalem. But there was one significant difference: Nebuchadnezzar had them studying Babylonian literature and history. Daniel and his friends had to learn the Babylonian sacred stories, their version of how the gods had made them rightful masters of the world.

I. The aim was to teach them the Babylonian point of view, so that eventually these Jewish youths would think like Babylonians. In fact, they each got Babylonian names as part of their conversion process. Daniel, which means "God is my judge," was renamed "Belshazzar," which means "Bel is my protector." See the point? The school was to shape them into willing instruments of Babylonian policy. Maybe that was OK, so long as Babylonian policy was to punish thieves and murderers. But what if King Nebuchadnezzar decided that everybody in his kingdom had to worship a giant statue of his god? Would Daniel enforce the law? What if they passed a law saying that all prayers must be offered in the name of the king? Would Daniel punish offenders? What if the king told Daniel that he owed him, because he was fed at the king's table and educated at the king's school?

Nebuchadnezzar's policy works, doesn't it? The freshman congressman or congresswoman gets elected on a reform ticket—going to clean out all the special interest lobbies in Congress. Then the lobbyists line up to take the Congressman to dinner and to write checks for the Congresswoman's reelection fund. How long will the reform last? Not very long. We get upset about this because it is so blatant, but it happens to all of us. Things that seemed so clearly unfair when we were younger now seem more reasonable because we're more a part of the establishment. It isn't fair that your older brother can stay up

later than you, until you are the older brother, and then it makes perfect sense. It isn't fair for the administrators at the top to make two or three times what people on the bottom make, until it's your salary under discussion. It isn't fair for people of color to be excluded from places, until its your neighborhood or your club trying to keep them out—and on and on. I ask myself this question from time to time: how many principles do I really have that are absolutely not for sale? And the answer is, in all honesty, fewer than I used to have.

II. So what's the remedy? Nebuchadnezzar's stratagem gets us all in the end. We swap our true, inner names for the monikers stuck on us by the world. We start pretending to go along and say to ourselves, "I can do this and still stay the same person," but we end up becoming what we pretend to be. What's the remedy? We could withdraw completely, like the Amish or like monks in a monastery, but then we forfeit the chance to ever be of benefit to our own people. Think of the good Daniel could do in a top position if only he could avoid being co-opted by Nebuchadnezzar's gifts. So in the end Daniel and the three amigos matriculate in the Palace Academy, they study very hard, they graduate at the top of their class, and on graduation day they get appointments to top positions.

But they make a vow, while they're still in the orientation weekend, only to eat veggies and drink water. No meat, no wine—just veggies and water. Now there's the crucial thing to understand—this is not about kosher laws. This is not about obedience to the law. Sure, the meat could have been nonkosher and forbidden to Jews, but so could the veggies. And the wine would have been on their tables back in Jerusalem. This oath is not about obeying the Torah and not about moral scruples about wine. It is a decision to make a vow that would remind them every day that they belong to God and not to Nebuchadnezzar. It reminded these Jewish boys that their real names were Daniel, Hananiah, Mishael, and Asariah—God is my judge, God has been good to me, God is my protector, God is my helper.

III. I think we ought to do this, brothers and sisters. I'm talking about all of us, from school kids to college-bound to young adults to senior adults. It is not too early for any of us to start, and not too late for any of us to change. What we must do is to make a vow like Daniel's and stick with it. What kind of vow? Daniel's vow was to remind him of who provided for him. Refusing part of the kings' food was to remind him that he lived by God's help. We could vow to draw a line on our own expenses, to decide what we absolutely need, and then to give away a big chunk of the remainder—just as a way of reminding ourselves that money doesn't rule our lives, God does. We could vow to do without commercial TV—just as a way of reminding ourselves that we don't get our values and our sense of right and wrong from Roseanne and the beer ads but from God. We could vow to open our homes to needy children—just as a way of reminding ourselves that as God's people we have a higher mission than just making ourselves comfortable. Or maybe, like Daniel, we could make a vow about our dinners. Maybe we could decide to skip a meal or two or three each week, and give the savings to the poor.

The point is to do something that puts some distance between ourselves and Nebuchadnezzar's stratagem, something that helps us to remember our real names. Vow with your family to do something that helps you remember that you belong to God and not to your job or to your hobbies or to your house or to the values of the world around you. Just veggies and water for me, please, because God has made

me his own, and I want always to remember that—that's the gospel, brothers and sisters.—Richard B. Vinson

Illustrations

GOD AND OUR MOTIVES.   The Bible knows well that our motives are mixed. With all honor to Sigmund Freud, who discovered a continent even though his early maps may need revision, the Bible knew about "rationalizing" before the ancestors of Freud were weaned. Many a Bible story, beginning with Adam, shows man making "the worse appear the better reason." Adam said, "The woman gave me fruit of the tree," and she said the serpent was to blame. The Bible says, "The heart"—by which it means central motivation, the energizing will involving thought and feeling—"is deceitful above all things. . . . Who can know it?"—George Arthur Buttrick[64]

WORLD AND SOUL.   I remember a man who made a wise comment upon people of wealth and fashion who were pursuing the things of this world and forgetting the things of God. "They are trying," he said, "to get more out of this world than there is in it." How true that is. There is nothing in this world for the soul, and those who try to get out of the world lasting satisfactions for the soul are trying to get out of the world more than there is in it.—Clarence Edward Macartney[65]

SUNDAY: MARCH TWENTY-FIRST

LECTIONARY MESSAGE

Topic: Called to Life
    TEXT: John 11:1–45
    Other Readings: Ezek. 37:1–14; Ps. 130; Rom. 8:6–11

The connections to the other texts, Ezekiel 37:1–14 and Romans 8:6–11, are clear: the dry bones can live, and those in whom the Spirit of God dwells are delivered from death. In today's Gospel, the evangelist gives us one more way of setting forth on the new and triumphant life that comes through the life and death of Jesus. The preacher could make three forthright points based on this narrative.

    I. *Everyone dies.* Even Lazarus, who seems

at times to be the center of this story, will eventually die. The various ways in which death is described in Holy Scripture could lead us to forget that death is a part of what it is to be human: death is the result of the first transgression, death is the "last enemy," death is descent to some nether region away from God's presence. But in fact death would appear to be essential to creation, a necessary part of being a sentient creature of flesh and blood.

When does Lazarus die again? Will Mary and Martha face this situation again? What is

---

[64] *Sermons Preached in a University Church*
[65] *Macartney's Illustrations*

the purpose of bringing Lazarus back from the dead? Does his resuscitation imply his healing from what caused his death in the first place? How many of the departed that you and I know would we bring back from the dead if that were in our power?

All of these questions lead us to see that dying is part of living, and that this story is not finally about raising dead bodies from the grave. Jesus says that the raising of Lazarus is to lead us to see "the glory of God." Human beings confronting the universal experience of death have the opportunity, even there, to see the Glory of God. We know from our own experience that the truth does not lie in the assertion put forth by both Martha and Mary: "Lord, if you had been here, my brother would not have died." Everyone dies. Though we sometimes speak and act as if death were a surprise—and in the individual case it often is—it is in the face of this universal human experience that John the evangelist leads us to see the glory of God.

II. *Lazarus is dead.* The Gospel writer wants to be very clear about that. When Jesus commands the tomb to be opened, Martha—the fastidious one?—cautions: "Lord, by this time there will be an odor, for he has been dead four days." Lazarus, in other words, is good and dead. He is not just resting or sleeping, and without the cosmetics and refrigeration available to modern morticians the stark reality of death would have been apparent. The Gospel writer wants us to face the reality of death, in order to see, in the face of death, the glory of God.

The Moravians of Winston-Salem, North Carolina, celebrate the Resurrection in God's Acre, the large cemetery in Old Salem. On the day before, each flat white stone will have been scrubbed and decorated with a bouquet of fresh flowers. As the sun comes up on Easter morning the whole community is out among the gravestones and awakening birds and spring's fragrance celebrating, in the very teeth of death, the victory of Jesus Christ over sin and death.

That is where the Gospel writer puts us, when he shows us Lazarus decaying in the tomb. Even Jesus, faced with this, weeps. It is when we face up to the reality of death that we are in a good position to celebrate the Resurrection of Christ.

I remember well the first time I held in my hands, in the context of officiating at his funeral, the cremated remains of a person dear to me. As the small cardboard box was handed to me, I was surprised by the weight of it: Could ashes be so heavy? Here in my hands was all that remained in this world of a person I had known as a vivid, funny, loving Texan more than six feet tall. What had seemed at first so heavy now seemed so meager, and the stunning reality of death hit me. That, ironically, was a profound moment in which the power of the Resurrection became more palpable than ever.

III. *"Lazarus, come out!"* He comes forth with his grave clothes—at least as they are shown by artists—flying like banners, resembling the pennants of the triumphant Lamb often seen in liturgical art. Jesus' command is the one we have heard throughout his ministry, in one form or another: "Unbind him and let him go." The one who will soon himself suffer and die presides at the coming to life and freedom of a dead man.

From how many tombs has Christ called men and women to life? From how many bonds has he freed us? Hildegarde of Bingen once said that "by the sound of Christ's voice the entire creation was awakened and called to life."

Someone said that if we are to live well we must remember four things: "Life is hard. You are going to die. You are not the center of everything. You are not as important as you think you are. If you can remember this, you can have great joy." This goes against much of the avoidance and escapism of our culture, just as it carries some of the truth of the Christian Gospel, especially the reality of death, which we see in the story of Lazarus.

The Church of the Servant in Oklahoma City was celebrating Eastertide. In the narthex was an old garbage can, rusty and looking like it had been run over a few times, pretty badly beaten up. Someone had filled this can with an extravagant mixture of vivid flowers. That is what we see in today's Gospel. It is not so much "Lord, if you had been here he would not have died" as it is believing the Lord of life when he declares, "I am the resurrection and the life: he who believes in me, though he die, yet shall he live."

Does this mean that the more realistic we are about our situation, the more likely we are to hear the Gospel in all its power? Could be. I commented to my colleague that I was enjoying planting my garden, that I seemed to like digging in the earth more and more. "That, my dear Charles," he said, "is because with every passing year you are getting closer and closer to that dirt." There is something redeeming in that, is there not?

Jesus waits until Lazarus is good and dead and then calls him to life. It is relatively easy to avoid this in our culture, to use our affluence and cleverness to keep our vulnerability, that we are as "feeble as frail," out of sight. But it is there, where we are aware that all die, that Lazarus is really dead, that we can hear the one whose banner is love calling, "Come forth!"—Charles L. Rice

Illustrations

THE NEW LIFE.   Resurrection means the real conquest of death by God the Creator to whom the believer entrusts everything, even the ultimate, even the conquest of death. The end which is also a new beginning. Anyone who begins his creed with faith in "God the Almighty Creator" can be content to end it with faith in "eternal life." Since God is the Alpha, he is also the Omega. The almighty Creator who calls things from nothingness into being can also call men from death into life.—Hans Küng[66]

WHAT IT MEANS TO BELIEVE.   The most certain thing we know about our future is that we must die, and that therefore our life and everything that makes life worthwhile for us will be destroyed. No beautiful words can change that. Death is the end. The question is whether there is beyond this end still a hope greater than everything that this earth has to give us. This hope the gospel of Jesus Christ alone offers us, every one of us. But it offers us it at a price: the price is that we believe in him. To believe in him, however, means quite simply to be his disciple. If you will be his disciple, then take and receive what he promises you. If you really want to be his disciple, then there is no difficulty in receiving this. The difficulty lies only in whether you really want to be his disciple, whether you want to renounce your own

rights and will. If that happens, then henceforth you know: He is my resurrection and my life.—Emil Brunner[67]

SERMON SUGGESTIONS

Topic: Why a Nation Needs to Pray
TEXT: Dan 9:4–19
(1) We have sinned. (2) We have ignored those who have spoken God's message to us. (3) We have suffered in many ways for our sins. (4) God has been gracious to us in the past, and we can count on his mercies now.

Topic: Our Battle
TEXT: Eph. 6:10–17
(1) It requires the strength of the Lord. (2) It faces superhuman forces. (3) It utilizes the armor of God.

Hymn Suggestions

1. "Out of the Depths," Martin Luther (1524); tr. Richard Massie (1854); AUS TIEFER NOT, Martin Luther (1524)
One of the first chorales to be created by Martin Luther for congregational worship was this paraphrase of the penitential psalm (130). Its Phrygian melody aptly captures the psalm's poignant message and thus its singing could appropriately follow the Psalter reading.

2. "Sweet, Sweet Spirit," Doris Akers (1962); SWEET, SWEET SPIRIT, Akers
Following the reading of the passage in Romans that emphasizes the enlivening power of God's spirit, the singing of this newly written song would be appropriate, thus helping to evoke a sense of God's presence in the worshiping body.

3. "O for a Thousand Tongues to Sing," Charles Wesley (1739); AZMON, Carl G. Glaser; arr. Lowell Mason (1839)
Written on the anniversary of his conversion, Wesley pours out his praise for the power of God to cancel sin, heal, and raise the dead to new life. Its message makes its singing eminently appropriate to the theme of renewal of spiritual life, which runs throughout the readings for this day.

4. "I Want to Be Ready," African-American

---

[66] *On Being a Christian*

[67] *I Believe in the Living God*

Spiritual; arr. J. Jefferson Cleveland and Verolga Nix (1981); I WANT TO BE READY

Two stanzas of this popular spiritual have been added to the traditional text, both of which pertain to the story of Mary, Martha, and Lazarus as relayed in the Gospel reading. A leader could be used to sing the stanzas, with all choir and congregation members responding on the refrain.—Hugh T. McElrath

Worship Aids

CALL TO WORSHIP. "If thou, Lord, shouldest mark iniquities, O Lord, who shall stand? But there is forgiveness with thee, that thou mayest be feared" (Ps. 130:3–4).

INVOCATION. We come before you, O Lord, with confidence, though with confession that we have sinned in your sight. We dare to worship you, for you forgive our sins. Grant us now the blessing of your presence.

OFFERTORY SENTENCE. "Whatsoever ye do in word or deed, do all in the name of the Lord Jesus, giving thanks to God and the Father by him" (Col. 3:17).

OFFERTORY PRAYER. O Giver of every good and perfect gift, may we render unto you lovingly, faithfully, joyfully what belongs to you. We are not our own, we have been bought with a price, the precious blood of your only son. In his name let us bring these gifts that through the blessing of your love they may become the bread and the Bread of Life to many in this community and the world.—John Thompson

PRAYER. Father of all generations, dwelling place of humankind from the beginning of the ages, we come to this worship hour in an attitude of thanksgiving. We are thankful for your faithfulness, even when we have been unfaithful to you and the truth we find in your Word. We are grateful for your steadfast love, even when we are so often utterly unlovely and unlovable. We thankfully accept your mercy toward us, even though we many times show little or no mercy to others. We are grateful that you forgive us even while yet we are sinners and find it so hard to forgive one another as you have called upon us to do. Most of all we thank you for the sure knowledge that we are not orphans in this world, but are children of a Father of love who have been given the privilege of calling God Father.

To come before you with less than an attitude of confession would be to desecrate the time we spend in your presence. We confess that we often come to you out of habit more than from a sense of love. We come out of need more than out of a desire to know your will. We come filled with sins rather than seeking to cleanse our souls and lives from activities that generate sin. We come scarred with bitterness and drugged with hatred rather than with kindness and caring for others. We come with lying tongues and false promises rather than under the banner of truth and honesty. We come with loads of self-importance and self-worth rather than as humble seekers after righteousness and forgetfulness of self. Father, in confession for these and multitudes of other evils, wrongs, and sins, we come before you.

Yet we come also with a gladness and joy, Father. We are glad for Christ and for this special day when we remember his bravery, his challenge, his claim, and his commitment to our need. We are glad for the difference he made in human lives, not just in those days when he startled the world with his human presence, but throughout all the long years since. We rejoice in the Lord and give joyful thanks for all his benefits, which have so changed the world and those who follow him that nothing can ever be the same again. So we pray, come Lord Jesus, even now in this sacred hour.—Henry Fields

Sermon: The Only Way to See Jesus

TEXT: John 12:20–26

I. Several Greeks want to see Jesus. They do not belong to the religious crowd; they are not Jews.

"Philip went and told Andrew; Andrew went with Philip and they told Jesus." The Greeks have inquired of one of the disciples of Jesus, but he is confused and does not know for sure what to do with these people. They are complete outsiders, and he is not sure how serious their motives are. Sometimes such "Greeks" may come to church, and the church is often confused as to what it ought to do with them. Philip does the most sensible thing he can do under the circumstances. He speaks with another disciple about it. Then at last the issue comes to Jesus himself.

Now Jesus speaks. He speaks to his disciples and to these outsiders at the same time: "And Jesus answered them, 'The hour has come for the Son of Man to be glorified.'"

II. These Greeks wanted to see Jesus. But that is actually not so simple as it may seem. What sort of Jesus do they wish to see? We come with this image and really want to see only what corresponds to our image. When we stand before Jesus, we always see our image of him and never come to Jesus himself at all. For this reason, in this story the disciples are very good disciples, for they don't pretend to know anything themselves—everything depends on the fact that Jesus himself has something to say.

III. And now matters become serious for us, too. For Jesus says that he, the Son of man, will now be glorified by God. Only in this way does a man see Jesus aright, that is, with the glory of God upon him. If we do not understand that God's glory rests on Jesus, if his glory does not break through all of our mental images of him, then we have not seen Jesus. That is to say, as long as we continue to carry around with us *our* image of Jesus, we will keep on being the stronger ones. We have imprisoned Jesus within our views and are then his judges. If we really want to see him, we must be fully aware of what we are doing. Jesus is no longer just one of us. He is the one in whom God comes to us.

What is the glory of God? Once more Jesus says something very unusual and unexpected. "Truly, truly, I say to you, unless a grain of wheat falls into the earth and dies, it remains alone; but if it dies, it bears much fruit." The glory of God is manifested in the fact that Jesus dies very horribly and ignominiously—not even heroically—in the fact that he is executed.

Actually he can come to us only on this way that leads to his death. Just as the grain of wheat must die, must decompose, in order that the full ear of grains of wheat might come from it, so must the one Jesus die. He must die in order not to remain for himself alone but that a community might be born that really belongs with him, a community for which he remains not merely an image that a man gazes at, admiringly, but the one

with whom a man can live and die. So *that* is God's glory, Jesus says—not the glorious finishing off of all opposition with an unprecedented miracle. *This* is God's glory, that here on this earth one can be *completely* humble, can *completely* die, and can *completely* give himself up for the sake of these few disciples, these few Greeks, and for these few people here in the Fluntern Church.

IV. It all began so innocently. These Greeks fell in with these church people and just wanted to see Jesus one time. Why not, since they don't have anything against him. But Jesus turns to them and to us and tells us: "He who loves his life loses it, and he who hates his life in this world will keep it for eternal life." But in saying this he asks: "Do you wish to cling to yourself still? Do you still wish to keep unchanged your images of God and of Jesus, of that God and of that Jesus whom a man still has at his disposal?"

V. But what does that mean? Jesus puts it very simply: "If any one serves me, he must follow me; and where I am, there shall my servant be also; if any one serves me, the Father will honor him." To see him, actually to see him as he is, to see him in such a way that we see God's glory in him—that we can do only if we are where he is. Where is he?

He has always been present in both the joys of a wedding feast and the sorrows of the dying. He was never wrapped up in himself, but existed for other men. He always let his life go instead of clinging to it. When we begin to follow Jesus, we slowly learn this. Perhaps we learn to celebrate our festival a little bit differently.

Even those difficult hours when a man must seek God turn to sheer gift. But most of all the many living men whom one is permitted to meet are gifts. Take young men who are choosing their vocation. Some of them give up their career and a substantial salary to travel a road on which they are repeatedly showered with gifts, namely with people they serve. I know persons who care for the chronically ill. They are very simple people, no newspaper writes about them. Their work is very unromantic, but day after day they are richly blessed with the persons whose existence depends upon them. And even today some people literally follow Jesus into death, for the sake of those entrusted to them. Death is not easy, and it is not promised that the way will be easy. But it is indeed true that only the person who is where Jesus is sees the glory of God in Jesus.—Edward Schweizer[68]

Illustrations

GOD COMES TO US.   The message of the cross goes to the root of our ills, and it alone can cure them radically. Just for that reason it spells folly and scandal. How does it do so? In the Bible as a whole, and already in the Old Testament, the point always is that man does not find a way to God but that God comes to man. What is in question is not the recognition of higher worlds, not a vision which man might acquire by a special technique of mysticism. We do not hear in the Bible of any practice of mystical introspection, of otherworldliness, of cultivating the interior life, with a view to reaching ultimately the divine ground of the soul. It is not a question of man's own performances and exercises as a result of which he might hope

to become pious and well-pleasing to God. All that is man's way to God and in the last analysis self-praise. The central point is that God has mercy on man who is so stuck fast in the mire—if I may be pardoned the expression—that he cannot help himself. That is the meaning of the story which begins with Abraham and Moses and proceeds to the prophets, including that greatest of the prophets, who tells us of the servant of God who suffers for our sakes and burdens himself with our guilt.—Emil Brunner[69]

ON THE MOVE.   Life in Christ is a life which is growing, maturing, developing. It is on the move. It is energetic and vital, not content to stop at some point along the way and assume that everything has been accomplished. We are to "press on towards the goal of the mark of our high calling." We are to "grow up in every way into Christ . . . to the attaining of mature manhood, the measure of the stature of the fullness of Christ."—Norman Pittenger[70]

SUNDAY: MARCH TWENTY-EIGHTH

LECTIONARY MESSAGE

Topic: Our Hero
   TEXT: Matt. 21:1–11
   Other Readings: Isa. 50:4–9a; Ps. 31:4–16; Phil. 2:5–11
   The lesson from the Hebrew Scriptures is one of Deutero Isaiah's songs of the Servant, the one who comes in humility to teach and redeem. This is one more example of the liturgical function of scripture, that texts serve occasions. That is obviously the case on a day like Palm/Passion Sunday, as on those other Christological and sanctoral days when the occasion calls forth texts not so much for their exegetical pertinence as for their language and dramatic power.
   On this Sunday, two texts meet to start us on the ironic journey through Holy Week, the week in which a "triumphal" entry will lead to ignominious death, and in which Good Friday will issue in Easter. Putting these two texts together—the bright account of

Jesus' entering the city to cries of "Hosanna!" and the unfolding drama of his journey to the cross—is jarring, disorienting, and just what is needed as Holy Week begins.
   A tried and true homiletical rule is: the bigger the occasion, the smaller the sermon. Today is a very large occasion in the life of the Church. On this day we welcome, once more, Jesus to the city of his ancestors, David's royal city, the city in which the future of God's people resides. If a congregation is ever going to have a procession, it will be today. Today we voice our own Hosannas, calling out once more, "Save us, Blessed One who comes in the name of the Lord." And alongside this, we will read the story of the Passion, of betrayal, suffering, and death. What is the preacher's role today, and what shall we have to say?
   The preacher can consider saying a small but important word today. For example, if there is to be a procession, the entry narra-

---

[68] *God's Inescapable Nearness*

[69] *The Great Invitation*
[70] *Life in Christ*

tive (Matt. 21:1–11) can be read in the procession and the preacher can speak briefly about what day this is, what *Hosanna* means, Holy Week's beginning, and about the coming reading of the Passion. The remaining drama of the service will carry the day's meaning, as "all Glory Laud and Honor" recedes behind the account of Jesus' suffering and death. What could the preacher add to that? If, however, a sermon is called for, here are three points that would serve Matthew's witness well.

I. *The one who comes in the name of the Lord embodies the promise.* The colt, the branches of victory, the cries of "Hosanna!" the mere fact that Jesus enters the kingly city of Jerusalem—all suggest the coming of the Messiah. We would have to live under the oppression of occupation by a foreign power while remembering a glorious past to appreciate what the expectations of the Messiah were. He would set things right, restore the nation, even bring justice and peace. As governments go, Rome comes off quite well. But the Jewish hope was for the great, and greatly idealized, kingdom of David to be restored and for the land of promise to be theirs.

We still hope for that day of justice and peace, and we do not disconnect our very human hopes and dreams from our own expectations of the coming of the Lord. Nor should we. It should not be too difficult for us on a day in spring in America at the end of the twentieth century to cry out once more to the one who embodies the promise, on whom our hopes are pinned, to bring his salvation.

II. *He has no real power.* Homiletically, this is what Eugene Lowry, in *The Homiletical Plot*, calls the bottom of the loop. Somewhere in the first half of a sermon the preacher takes a dive, introduces something that does not fit, that disturbs the picture, that throws a shadow. Lowry compares this to playing jazz piano: unless the music somehow turns toward complication, it remains less than jazz moving toward satisfying resolution. So, the one who embodies the promise has no real power. The whole scene is highly ironic, even comic. A king rides into town on a borrowed donkey, welcomed with improvised wands of greenery and the coats of a ragtag crowd. That would be one way of seeing it, and it is probably closer to the truth than something that Cecil B. DeMille would do.

The Epistle for the day sees it that way: He "emptied himself, taking the form of a servant, being born in the likeness of men." Already, on Palm Sunday, we see him bowing his meek head, riding on in majesty, as the hymn has it, to die. The Palm Sunday procession is about as far as you could get from a military May Day parade in the Old Moscow, or something the Pentagon would stage. The Messiah comes in lowly pomp, riding toward ultimate humiliation in utter weakness.

A teacher of mine gave a window for the narthex of his congregation's new church, a depiction of a donkey. "Now," he said, "the congregation thinks that the window shows the donkey Jesus rode into Jerusalem, but actually that is Henry who lives on my farm." This little parade that brings Jesus to Jerusalem, far from being heroic, brings us to the unsettling realization that the one coming in the name of the Lord is riding very close to the earth on an animal something like Henry.

What we want, of course, is a hero to rescue us, a newly elected politician riding into town in a big car ready to set things right. A general to go over there and put those people in their place (and to ensure our place). And why not? There is plenty to be set right in this world. The AIDS Memorial Quilt came to the university in which I teach. The first prayer that was offered at a special service to open the weekend was given by a young man: "O God, what we could really use is a cure, now, today." Who cannot identify with the need of a hero? Hosanna is a cry for help, here and now.

But the one coming down the road on this Palm Sunday has no real power. That is about to become clear as we read the story of his suffering and death. Picture him on the colt, or standing outside the city, looking over Jerusalem, and lamenting: "If only you knew what it is that could give you peace."

III. But he is, this one who comes in the name of the Lord, both Messiah and Savior, our peculiar hero. He embodies the promise, and he brings it to fulfillment. In the early Church, Easter was celebrated as the great Three Days, what we now know as Good Friday, Holy Saturday, and Easter. Jesus, in John's Gospel, promises that in his being lifted up he will draw all to himself. The cross becomes his throne, and in his death he conquers. This is the great and saving irony of

Holy Week, that the powerless one does in fact embody and fulfill the promise. As he empties himself in obedience to his Father, he is raised in power and becomes the Savior of all who trust in him. That is the reason that, once more, we resolve on this Palm Sunday to walk with him, to take the way of the cross with him, and to find there our hopes fulfilled in God's salvation.

The collect, from *The Book of Common Prayer,* for Monday in Holy Week, captures much of this: "Almighty God, whose most dear Son went not to joy but first he suffered pain, and entered not into glory before he was crucified: Mercifully grant that we, walking in the way of the cross, may find it none other than the way of life and peace: through Jesus Christ your Son our Lord, who lives and reigns with you and the Holy Spirit, one God, for ever and ever. Amen."—Charles L. Rice

Illustrations

KNOWING AND DOING.   When the crowds cry "Hosanna to the Son of David!" and "This is the prophet," they use the right words, but they still miss the point. They have all of the notes and none of the music. They have the theology straight, but they will still end up rejecting Jesus and calling for his death (27:20–23). Matthew is striking a familiar note: Knowing the truth is not the same thing as doing the truth (7:21). What one social psychologist said of university students is also true of the Kingdom: "It is possible to make an A+ in the course on ethics and still flunk life."—*The New Interpreter's Bible,* vol. 8, p. 404

SUFFERING WITH CHRIST.   This is not simply solid theology; I have experienced it time and time again. I saw it most intimately in the living *Pietà* that was my mother cradling the lifeless body of my father and brother, dead within three weeks of each other. Until her memory deserted her, a quarter century later, she lived and relived the agony of a husband and a son wasting away on hospital beds. And still she lived for others—this seemingly frail woman who shoveled 25 tons of coal to heat the flats she janitored for several months after my father died, this sensitive woman who must have been unbearably lonely and yet was a ceaseless source of strength to the heavy-burdened. She simply lived, lived simply, in God's presence. The Christ of Calvary was real to her—the abiding experience of a God-man ever shaping her, roughly and rudely at times, in the image of his dying/rising.—Walter J. Burghardt, S.J.[71]

SERMON SUGGESTIONS

Topic: Between a Hard Place and the Rock of Ages
TEXT: 1 Kings 18:21–39
(1) *The story:* The Israelites apparently were at a stalemate in their religion. (2) *The meaning:* Life forces *the* ultimate decision on us. Historical examples—biblical and other. (3) *The application:* (a) Through God's providence, critical circumstances present us with vital choices. (b) Right choices are often painful. (c) God has ways of showing us what is right—sometimes dramatically, usually quietly and even subtly.

Topic: Facing Ourselves
TEXT: 1 John 1:8–9
(1) We cannot truthfully deny our sins. (2) We must not fail to receive the forgiveness freely offered us. (3) We will not be disappointed in our trust in a faithful God who makes all things right.

Hymn Suggestions

1. "Hosanna, Loud Hosanna," Jeanette Threlfall (1873); ELLACOMBE, *Gesangbuch der H. W. Hofkapelle* (1784); adapt. and harm. William H. Monk (1868)
One of the finest hymns depicting Jesus' triumphal entry into Jerusalem accompanied by the joyous songs of children, this hymn could serve well for a processional with palm branches at the beginning of worship on this particular Sunday.
2. "All Praise to Thee, for Thou, O King Divine," F. Bland Tucker (1938); SINE NOMINE, Ralph Vaughan Williams (1906)
Tucker's free paraphrase of Philippians 2:5–11 is an excellent version of this summons to possess the self-denying mind of Christ. It could well be substituted for the oral reading of this passage in worship.

[71] *Grace on Crutches*

3. "Behold the Savior of Mankind," Samuel Wesley (c. 1709); WINDSOR, William Damon's *Booke of Musicke* (1591)

This passiontide hymn by the father of the famous Wesley brothers depicts in awesome lines the details of the Crucifixion. However, the final stanza looks in hopeful anticipation at the victory over death in the Resurrection.

4. "'Tis Finished! The Messiah Dies," Charles Wesley (1762); OLIVE'S BROW, William B. Bradbury (1853)

Much in the same vein as his father's hymn (above), Charles Wesley's hymn waxes more personal, especially in its third stanza: "for me the Lamb is slain." Either hymn could serve as a response to the reading of the passion story.

5. "Eat This Bread," Robert Batastini and the Taizé Community (1982); BERTHIER, Jacques Berthier (1982)

This simple chantlike song repeatedly sung to varied accompaniments during the receiving of the elements in Holy Communion has been used with poignant effect in recent observances of the Lord's Supper.

6. "Fill My Cup, Lord," Richard Blanchard (1959); FILL MY CUP, Blanchard

Similarly, this modern chorus may be sung by the congregation as a prayer to be made whole or as a response in the communion service.

7. "To Mock Your Reign, O Dearest Lord," Fred Pratt Green (1972); KINGSFOLD, English melody, arr. R. V. Williams (1906)

Many are the hymns, ancient and modern, from which one could make selections for use in worship on this important Sunday in the Church year. Among the finest of the more recently written hymns for Passion Week is this one by one of England's greatest hymn-poets of the twentieth century. It effectively contrasts Jesus' crown of thorns with his crown of triumph, his purple cloak with a robe to cover our shame, and the reed thrust in his hand with his ruling scepter.—Hugh T. McElrath

Worship Aids

INVOCATION. "I trusted in thee, O Lord: I said, thou art my God. My times are in thy hand" (Ps. 31:14–15a).

INVOCATION. Gracious Lord, we know that we live by your providence, and now we pray that we may learn to be more than conquerors through Jesus Christ who loved us and gave himself for us. To that end help us to walk with deepening awareness with him as he faces the cross and as we face our own cross.

OFFERTORY SENTENCE. "And he said to them, 'Take care! Be on your guard against all kinds of greed; for one's life does not consist in the abundance of possessions'" (Luke 12:15 NRSV).

OFFERTORY PRAYER. Lord, as Jesus entered Jerusalem in triumph, help us to face every day triumphantly because of the life, teachings, Crucifixion, and Resurrection of our unvanquishable savior.—E. Lee Phillips

PRAYER. Our Father, we beseech of thee, let thy blessing follow the word spoken. If we are lights in the world, may our light shine. If we are the salt of the earth, let not the salt lose its savor. If we are thy soldiers and are put upon watch as sentinels, let us not leave the enemy to creep in upon our own friends to their destruction. May we be good soldiers, fearless, faithful unto the very end, doing battle for the right.

Give us, we beseech of thee, clearer views of thine own self. Every day, in prayer, take us into thine upper ocean, and cleanse us there. Wash us in those waters that shall return us to earth clean indeed. May we live in such communion with thee that nothing can dwell with us that is offensive to thee. Purify thy churches. Give tone, and courage, and perspicuity, and perspicacity to thy ministering servants. May they be the voice of God in this community. Brace up the loins of those who are members of our churches. May they come out of their sentimentality and look fearlessly upon the duties that are incumbent upon them in these days.

We beseech of thee that thy name may be glorified among the poor, and among the needy, and among the weak that are overborne in the struggle for life. Grant that power may not be tryannical. Grant that great capacities may not be given to avarice and corruption.

Lord God, we beseech of thee to look upon our nation with mercy and save us from our own infamous passions, and from the evil courses upon which we are bent. O Lord! Give ear, that all may see that our salvation is of thee.

And to thy name shall be the praise, Father, Son and Spirit.—Henry Ward Beecher

Sermon: By His Wounds You Have Been Healed

TEXT: Isa. 52:13–53:12

We cannot talk about the cross of Christ without talking about our own cross. The Crucifixion of our Lord was once for all, yet it was a prototype of every life. First Peter brings together the cross of Christ and our own cross: "He himself bore our sins in his body on the cross, so that, free from sins, we might live for righteousness, by his wounds you have been healed" (2:24 NRSV).

What a mistake Christ made! What a mistake we make when we follow in his footsteps! So some might suggest. They would free us from concern about other persons, from fretting over a selfish style of living, and from caring what other persons may think of our ideas, our speech, or what we do. For one person to suffer or die for another, for people to go very far out of their way for another person—that seems to be too high a price to pay. Yet that is what Christ did. In one way or another, to one degree or another, you and I cannot avoid it either. "Life is an altar."

So, it is a strange saying—"by his wounds you have been healed"—unthinkable to some, for if we had to enter into his suffering it would seem that "by his wounds we have been destroyed." But no! "We have been healed!"

We did not come by that healing easily. Some of us are too proud to acknowledge our brokenness, our need of forgiveness. Some of us are too formal, too squeamish to take up the cross—God could demean himself in this way, but we could not! Some of us are too determined to have our own way to let ourselves become the smitten agents of healing. And yet, even the proud, the disdainful, the self-willed—and don't we all deserve those labels?—even persons like that have to face the cross or something like it,

face it again and again, and consider what it means. It could make a difference in us—to think about the meaning of the words "with his stripes we are healed."

I. As I reflect on this suffering of our Lord, it tells me that God has taken into himself the pain and shame of our wrongdoing. The Servant Songs describe "the servant of Yahweh" and identify Israel—the suffering nation—as that servant. The prophet must have drawn his picture with some individual or individuals in mind, too—men like Jeremiah. But no one filled the outlines of that portrait so well as Jesus Christ. "With his stripes we are healed."

His stripes! Where did they come from, these stripes? He was wounded by the world into which he came. Herod was out to get him, then the Pharisees, then the Sanhedrin. Pilate condemned him, and Roman soldiers scourged him and drove nails into his hands and feet.

His stripes! Where did they come from, these stripes? He was wounded by his own people—but so much more subtly than by the world's powerful ones. "He came to his own home, and his own people did not receive him." What people in general did to him was bad enough. See what those closest to him did, and do! Our thoughts leap at once to Judas Iscariot, the disciple who betrayed him. And our preoccupation with what he did almost hides what the other disciples did. "The Christian Church," so Carlyle Marney charged, "has used Judas! We have our mileage out of Judas. He has been treaded and retreaded—how we have used him! . . . He is there to provide a contrast by which we look good." We must remember this: "Then the disciples all forsook him and fled." Not only Judas—the worst—but also the best added to his wounds.

His stripes! Where did they come from, these stripes? Don't forget—he had a choice in the matter too. He could have avoided the wounds. Of his life he said, "No one takes it from me, but I lay it down of my own accord." Christ willingly took the suffering upon himself. It was nothing new under the sun for the Righteous One, the innocent, to draw to himself and to claim as his very own those who were forever dishonoring him. God spoke to the children of Israel who, he said, "have been borne by me from your birth, carried from the womb; I have made, and I will bear; I will carry and will save" (Isa. 46:3–4 NRSV). And it was said concerning God, ". . . in his love and in his pity he redeemed them; he lifted them up and carried them all the days of old" (Isa. 63:9b NRSV).

It is because of love like that that we can be forgiven for our sins. With the stripes the world has given him, with the wounds we have made, he heals us. He has taken the venom of sin and guilt into himself and died the death that belongs to us. In this way, God has absorbed the pain and shame of our misdeeds.

II. As I reflect on the suffering of our Lord, it suggests further that *God brings us into a new relationship with himself in the cross.*

The cross of Christ becomes your cross and mine. It is not just a datum of history, nor a bright symbol to adorn a church, nor an amulet to hang about the neck. It is the very power of our life; the very wisdom of our life. When I know the cross in the forgiveness of my sins—truly know it—I also know that something has changed within me. I have a new relationship, a new standing, that gives a new outlook, new desires, new aims. Baptism is a sign of this. In baptism, I begin an open participation in the sufferings of Christ. He took the stripes that belonged to me. I now take stripes upon myself. And this is no mechanical transaction. What happens between me and God not only removes my guilt, it also touches my life at the depths of my motives.

This relationship to God in the cross of Christ indeed takes precedence over all other relationships, but it can and does transform or sanctify them.

III. A final meaning of our Lord's suffering is that *we receive a task of service in his cross.* The apostle Paul said, "I am completing what is lacking in Christ's afflictions for the sake of his body, that is, the church" (Col. 1:24b NRSV).

Only God knows the shape that this obedience will take. We would like to say that *we* know. We are superb when it comes to prescribing the obedience of our brothers and sisters. If we can get them to cut the contours of their life by our patterns, congratulations are in order—to them, of course, but mostly to ourselves. It makes us nervous or envious when the will of God for others does not con-

form to our notions. Simon Peter was sure of what was right for the unnamed disciple whom Jesus loved: "Lord, what about him?" Peter asked. Jesus answered, "If it is my will that he remain until I come, what is that to you? Follow me!" (John 21:21–22 NRSV).

This obedience does not always take a dramatic form. We honor Paul and Peter, Luther and Bunyan, Bonhoeffer and King. Rightly so! But is there not a place in God's scheme for a secret disciple—like Nicodemus, who simply because of his low profile at one point was able to do more for his Lord than might have been possible otherwise? I believe we do well to remember Tertullian's words: "The blood of the martyrs is the seed of the Church," but those who managed to stay alive also made a contribution.

In any case, service is costly. Some of us, of course, have a low threshold of pain, like the assistant minister who reputedly received the stigmata while carrying a tray of cocktails at a church fundraising social. But the one who says what he thinks and does what he feels pays a price for it. Rejection, persecution, prison, and even death could be his lot. He may have to suffer, in addition, the self-doubt produced by wondering if his prophetic stance is really for God or mostly to satisfy some ego need. The more cautious person pays a price, too. Inner turmoil, living with the knowledge that some think he is a coward and unworthy of his crucified Lord, the self-doubt that causes him to suspect that his critics may be right about him—this kind of suffering may be his lot. There is no discipleship that excludes the possibility that we shall feel the stripes that our Lord felt—wounds within or wounds without—although, strangely enough in both cases, wounds that potentially make people whole. Paul tells us that it has been granted to us that for the sake of Christ we should not only believe in him but also suffer for his sake.

Many of us could hardly claim to have suffered much for our Lord in any way. But to some of us here today, suffering for Christ is, or will be, a reality. These are the ones whom Dr. John Hutton called "Christians of the second degree." Their obedience, their service, and the worth of it are known to God, and because of their stripes, many will experience the healing of Christ.

Believing in Christ does make us available

for that second degree. Dr. Frank Gunsaulus of Chicago was preparing his sermon for Sunday. He was interrupted by a troubled young man for whom life seemed to have no meaning. Dr. Gunsaulus was to preach on the words of our Lord, "For this cause came I also into the world." He impressed those words on the young man, who went away reflecting on their meaning for his own life. The next day, the tragic Iroquois Theater fire occurred. That young man went into the flaming theater again and again until he had brought twenty-eight children to safety. The last time he went in he inhaled flames and gas. On Sunday afternoon Dr. Gunsaulus went to visit him in the hospital. He looked down at a face wrapped in bandages and heard the young man mutter, "Doctor, for this cause came I into the world." There is something doxological—something always singing the praise of God, something always glorifying God—in a cross-scarred life lived out in faith. The fourth Gospel tells us that Jesus called the Crucifixion that lay before him his glorification. How appropriate it is, then, as in the Eastern Orthodox churches, to place flowers on the altar even on Good Friday. Jesus, Hebrews tells us, "for the joy that was set before him endured the cross."

Anton Boisen was a patient in a state hospital for the insane. One night he lay on a cot in a screened-in porch, looking at the moon. The light filtering through made a cross on the screen. A world, a universe, with the cross—with utter tragedy—upon it was what Boisen saw and felt: his melancholy and depression told him that, and the vision on the screen symbolized and confirmed it. Then he shifted his position and saw the moon through a hole in the screen. The cross was gone, and Boisen was on his way to health.

The cross of Christ was no illusion—nor is ours—the cross—yet it is not a dead end. With his cross Christ was not destroyed; with our cross we are not destroyed. It is wounds that make us well.—James W. Cox

Illustrations

TALKING AND/OR DOING.   I recall sitting in an informal meeting with Karl Barth in 1962, when someone asked him why he did not speak out during the Hungarian Revolution. Barth, you will remember, had plenty to say in opposition to Hitler and the Nazis. Some criticized Barth, because he did not do the same in the Hungarian crisis. Professor Barth replied that there was no lack of persons speaking out on the issues—and speaking out was well taken care of. But there was something he could *do* by not speaking out. By his silence he was able to get some persons out of Hungary who were in mortal danger.—James W. Cox

THE CRUCIAL CHOICE.   Several years ago, I heard the Bishop of the Church of South India tell of a Hindu convert to Christianity. This convert, on the night before his baptism, sat in his room. On the table before him, he saw, as it were, two vessels—one containing the blood of Christ, who had died for him, and the other containing the tears of his mother, who had pleaded with him not to become a Christian. "And," said the convert, "I had to choose between the two."—James W. Cox

SUNDAY: APRIL FOURTH

LECTIONARY MESSAGE

Topic: Resurrection Faith
 TEXT: John 20:10–18
 Other Readings: Acts 10:34–43; Ps. 118:1–2, 1–24; Col. 3:1–4

Christianity's central claim concerns the return from the dead of one who was a close personal friend of many of those who proclaimed it. John 20:11–18 tells the story of

one such proclamation and one such friendship. This is Mary's story.

I. *Easter turns tears to joy* (vv. 10–13). The weight of a life can be measured by the extent of the loves it leaves behind. The love of Jesus had magnetized Mary. Mary had met Jesus, been drawn to him and changed by him. Now she had come to his tomb to do what little she could to honor and minister to the body of this man she loved. So it is not surprising to read that this Sunday morning, peering into the tomb of Jesus, Mary's eyes were filled with tears. She was crying because Jesus had been taken and tortured, mocked and killed. And now, just when she thought everything had been done that could be done, it seemed that someone had stolen his body.

We need to recognize that the good news of Easter comes to persons whose hearts are crushed by sorrow. Faith comes to fullest flower in lives that do not masquerade feelings. It may be tears that best make us eligible for Easter. Part of the power of Scripture is that it shows us human life before God that is full of rich, real, rugged emotions. A large part of the good news of Easter is that it comes to the hurt and the disappointed, the broken and the lonely.

II. *Easter announces the nearness of the Lord* (vv. 15–16). Mary is hardly prepared for what she finds. She encounters two souls (the text tells us they are angels) who announce that Jesus is not there. Bewildered and confused, Mary cannot take it in. Sometimes we can be so paralyzed by our pain that we stumble over angels unaware. Turning away, Mary almost bumps into a man she takes for a gardener. The text tells us it is Jesus. The story of John's Gospel drips with irony and never more so than here. Mary's mind is so focused on the dead Jesus she has come to remember that she does not recognize the Risen Jesus who is right before her. Easter means that the Lord is at hand. The Resurrection of Jesus means that there is no barrier or boundary, whether above or below, whether life or death, that can separate us from the love and presence of Christ. The Church Father Hippolytus, writing in the third century, described Easter as declaring: "No more bewailing your failings: forgiveness has come from the grave. No more fears of your dying: the death of our Saviour has freed us from fear. . . . Death . . . took earth and encountered heaven. It took what is seen and fell upon the unseen. Death played the master; but He has mastered death." Easter announces the truth that Christ is near.

III. *Easter opens ears and eyes to Jesus* (v. 16). At first Mary takes Jesus for a gardener. Though Mary is mistaken in this, a gardener is not entirely inappropriate as an image. When God created the first Adam and the first Eve, he placed them in a garden. On this first day of a whole new creation, the New Adam returns to stand in another garden, ready with his return to bring the world back to new bloom.

Significantly, what brings Mary to recognize Jesus is not her vision but her hearing. Jesus calls her by name. When Jesus took the first step back from death to life, what he came back with on his lips was a name: "Mary." It may have been less what he said than the way he said it. Nobody said her name just that way. Make no mistake about what Christianity offers. It is nothing less and nothing other than a personal relationship with the living God. It is Mary's hearing rather than her vision through which the identity of Jesus first became clear. This should not be surprising. The biblical witness regularly gives priority to the ear over the eye. It is not true that a picture is worth a thousand words. Pictures speak with power, but also with ambiguity. Biblical revelation is a revelation of and through the word. Words create worlds. It is of no small consequence that God spoke the world into being. It is of no small consequence that the Bible is called the Word of life, and Jesus is described as the Word made flesh. When John wants to write of the eternity of Christ's place in the Godhead and of his relation to the cosmos and to humanity, he finds it appropriate to use the term *Word*. By calling names, the Risen Jesus summons His people into fellowship with the God whose speech is the word of life.

IV. *At Easter, Christ's disciples are given a charge to mission* (vv. 17–18). Mary is sent by Jesus to carry the word of his presence into the world. The Risen Christ demands of those who meet him that they go back with him into the world he died to save. The heart of humanity is hungering for love. People looking at Jesus have come to know that God is love. At Easter they meet a loving God and a Risen Christ. As Joni Erickson Tada puts it: "Christianity isn't all that complicated . . . it's Jesus."

If, as Christians claim, Jesus Christ has risen from the dead and reigns as life's Lord, then he is available to be encountered and known by all who, in the power of the Spirit, would seek to look and see. Throughout the centuries, people from diverse races, continents, and nations have voiced their belief that Jesus is alive. Believers in Jesus have been united in their experience of the presence, power, and love of their Risen Lord. Faith in the Resurrection, however, is not to be confused with the fact of the Resurrection. They are related as effect and cause. The fact of the Resurrection declares that Jesus is the way to God. More than that, it establishes that he himself is the presence of God. It reveals what Hippolytus knew and proclaimed in his Easter homily: "Death swallowed a body, and met God face to face." In the Resurrection, death has not only been defeated, life has triumphed and love has prevailed. In the Resurrection, Jesus has been revealed as alive and as available to be known and loved by all who would trust him savingly.—John Shouse

Illustrations

SHARING HIS DIVINITY. When Jesus took our humanity, he made it possible for us to share his divinity. Eternal life is not poetic fancy. "Eternal life," Jesus said to his Father the night before he was to die, "consists in this, that they know you, the only true God, and the one whom you sent, Jesus Christ" (John. 17:3). This is not some abstract knowledge, some intellectual understanding a theologian might uncover, knowing *about* God from reason or revelation. Here, to "know" is to share by faith a living, intimate relationship with the Father and Jesus.

Your living oneness with a living trinity is so real and so mystery laden that the New Testament resorts to striking symbols, strong metaphors, to suggest how close it is. Jesus is the vine, you are the branches that live from that vine (John. 15:1 ff.). You are a dwelling place, and Father and Son make their home within you (John. 14:23). You are a temple, and God's Spirit dwells in you (1 Cor. 3:16–17).

So strong, so enduring, so eternal is this life that even death cannot destroy it. "Whoever feeds on this bread," Jesus declared, whoever feeds on his flesh given for the life of the world, "will live forever" (John 6:61).—Walter J. Burghardt, S.J.[72]

HE WAS THERE. When I was minister in residence of The Church for the Fellowship of All Peoples in San Francisco, I experienced this in a human relationship. For several weeks, every day, I visited a member of my church who was very ill. She had a disease for which there was no cure. For one-half hour every day, for several weeks, I read to her. Finally I stopped reading to her. I would simply go and sit. We would sit and "is" together. When I had to leave the city for several weeks, we entered into a very interesting little agreement. I worked out a timetable of the difference in the time between the Pacific coast and the various spots at which I would be stopping until I arrived in New York. At the same hour every morning, we met. For seven weeks every day with from two thousand to three thousand six hundred miles separating us, we touched each other outside of time.—Howard Thurman[73]

SERMON SUGGESTIONS

Topic: Conquered and Conquering

TEXT: Gen. 32:22–31

(1) *Then:* Jacob experienced pain and blessing in a crucial encounter with God. (2) *Always:* God can reveal himself most helpfully in the most parlous or dangerous personal events. (3) *Now:* (a) Life presents us each and all with true crisis, representing danger and opportunity. (b) Our decision making may involve prolonged struggle. (c) As a result of our struggle, we may in some ways be diminished, but stronger and better than ever in what matters most.

Topic: A Gospel of Our Own

TEXT: 2 Tim. 2:8

St. Paul was very fond of speaking of the gospel as "my gospel." (1) The gospel has not won us at all until we can say "my gospel"— an individual experience. (2) We cannot preach a gospel that is not our own. It has been said that every Christian life, in itself, is a fresh translation of the gospel. (3) But we must not confine the gospel to what we know of it ourselves.—James Reid[74]

---

[72] *We Would Like to See Jesus*

[73] *The Growing Edge*
[74] *The Temple in the Heart*

Hymn Suggestions

Group One

1. "This Is the Day the Lord Hath Made," Isaac Watts (1719); GRAFENBERG, Johann Crüger (1647)

Excellent for the beginning of worship, this hymn's first line is based directly on Psalm 118:24. The hymn, as usually found, is made up of the last four stanzas of Watts's twenty-stanza paraphrase of the psalm. As such, its singing could be substituted (in part, at least) for the Psalter reading.

2. "Good Christians All, Rejoice and Sing!" Cyril Alingtong (1931); GELOBT SEI GOTT, Melchoir Vulpius, (1609)

Next to "Christ, the Lord, Is Risen Today," this twentieth-century hymn is most often sung at Easter to express the Christian joy in the Resurrection of Christ. Like the older hymn, it can be sung antiphonally with each group—choir and congregation—answering the other phrase by phrase, and all joining on the final "Alleluia."

3. "Come, Let Us with Our Lord Arise," Chas. Wesley (1763); SUSSEX CAROL, Eng. trad. melody, R. V. Williams

Relating appropriately both Psalm 118 and the gospel lesson in John, this hymn was written originally for children. It is another Wesley Easter hymn that deserves more use.

4. "There's a Wideness in God's Mercy," Frederick Faber (1862); WELLESLEY, Lizzie S. Tourjée (1878)

This hymn reflects the spirit of the reading from Acts, in which Peter declares that there is no limit or partiality in God's love, which extends "like the wideness of the sea." It could appropriately follow the reading (Acts 10:34–43).

Group Two

1. "The Strife Is O'er," Latin hymn, trans. Francis Pott (1861); VICTORY, Giovanni P. Da Palestrina (1591); arr. William H. Monk (1861)

Celebrating the fulfillment of the Isaiah prophecy (25:6–9) that death will be swallowed up in victory, this old Latin hymn is particularly suitable for Easter worship. The choir could sing the triumphant words of each stanza, with the congregation responding on the "Alleluias."

2. "Come, Risen Lord," George Wallace Briggs (1931); SURSUM CORDA, Alfred Morton Smith (1941)

This contemporary hymn recalls the Emmaus Road experience of the two disciples, when they recognized Jesus in the breaking of bread. It is naturally a good selection for the celebration of Holy Communion.

3. "The Day of Resurrection," John of Damascus (eighth century); tr. John M. Neale (1862); LANCASHIRE, Henry T. Smart, (1836)

Recalling the teaching of the apostle Paul in the letter to the Corinthians (1 Cor. 5:7–8), this venerable hymn is obviously intended for Easter worship.

4. "Hope of the World," Georgia Harkness (1954); DONNE SECOURS, Louis Bourgeois (1551)

Especially in its third stanza, this profound hymn would appropriately accompany the reading of the gospel lesson having to do with the encounter of the disciples with the resurrected Jesus on the Emmaus road.— Hugh T. McElrath

Worship Aids

CALL TO WORSHIP. "The stone which the builders refused is become the head stone of the corner. This is the Lord's doing; it is marvelous in our eyes. This is the day which the Lord hath made; we will rejoice and be glad in it" (Ps. 118:22–24).

INVOCATION. In awe we come to this Easter morning, Father. We cannot comprehend the full meaning of the Resurrection. We do not understand everything concerning the return of the Lord from the grave. Give us in this hour the courage to accept what we cannot fully comprehend. Give us the ability to hear clearly the words of amazement uttered by those first visitors to the tomb that first Easter dawn. Let the light of newness shine on us, that our hearts may rejoice, our spirits soar, and our lips sing your praise, even as did those who first experienced the Resurrection of the Lord.—Henry Fields

OFFERTORY SENTENCE. "And I beheld, and heard the voice of many angels round about the throne and the beasts and the elders: and the number of them ten thousand times ten thousand, and thousands of thousands; saying with a loud voice, Worthy is the Lamb that was slain to receive power, and riches, and wisdom, and strength, and honor, and glory, and blessing" (Rev. 5:11–12).

OFFERTORY PRAYER. Today, Father, we have received the gifts of assurance that life is eternal. As with so many other gifts with which you have blessed us, our gratitude grows. Remind us that to receive is to give and that in giving we indeed do exemplify our Lord, who gave everything, even life for us. Receive these offerings, we pray, and use them for your glory in Christ Jesus.—Henry Fields

PRAYER. As a congregation, we come to you this morning, Father, to worship you in Spirit and in truth. Help us to be willing to be confronted by you and to be found by you. In truth we have misused our freedom and chosen to go far from you on many occasions. How grateful we are that you love us enough to seek us and find us and redeem us and save us.

You have given us a beautiful world in which to live and grow and serve. Yet too often we have chosen to build slums with our lives rather than plant gardens. We have chosen to waste limited resources for our own advantage rather than use them for your glory. We have chosen too often to use people rather than love them as fellow pilgrims and children of the heavenly Father. Too often we have created a climate of bitterness and mistrust and prejudice and hatred when we know that we should have been building your kingdom of love and grace among all people everywhere.

As we look upon the cross, help us to realize the pain and agony our waywardness has caused. Let us see it clearly in what our sinning has done to you, causing Christ's suffering.

But may we not miss the Resurrection. Let us be powerfully reminded by it as we ponder it, that all our sin, selfishness, prejudice, hatred, and willfulness cannot overcome your love for us and separate us from you. How thankful we are that the Resurrection reminds us of the mighty love of the Father that will not let us go.

Now, may we be ready to accept the responsibility that the Resurrection brings and with resounding alleluias celebrate the death of our self-centeredness, even as we accept the birth of our new lives in you.—Henry Fields

Sermon: Faith and the Resurrection
TEXT: 1 Cor. 15:1–28

What is Easter all about? It is a joyous time. Spring is bursting out all over. The gray days of winter are gone except for an occasional reminder. All nature leaps to the challenge to create.

What is Easter all about? It is a happy coincidence of the resourcefulness of earth and the resourcefulness of heaven. But it is especially about God and what he did about a tragic event two thousand years ago, and it is about what he continues to do in face of the tragedies of your personal history and mine. In a word, Easter is about the Resurrection of Jesus Christ and what that means to you and to me.

Easter came as a surprise to the early disciples. They were not expecting it, but it happened anyway. And they could never get through talking about it, telling the good news that their Crucified Lord had arisen from the dead; the church sprang to life like some young giant born full-grown. They did not give us a clear picture of how it all happened—what God did when he raised Jesus from the dead—but they left no room to doubt that it did happen, gloriously, victoriously.

I cannot explain the Resurrection. Yet I can believe it; I can experience its power; I can affirm and proclaim it. And so I do, with a thankful, hopeful, and joyful heart. I pray that God will make this a festival of renewal of faith by giving us eyes to see and hearts to believe the remarkable consequence of our Lord's Resurrection.

I. In the first place, because God raised Jesus Christ from the dead, we can believe that our sins are forgiven. I am taking it for granted that you and I still believe in the reality of sin—those things we have done that we ought not to have done, and those things that we have left undone that we ought to have done. I speak of whatever it is that separates us from God, that makes us feel at a distance from him and estranged from him, or that makes us feel guilty. We may not think about it all the time, but whenever we do think about it we know it is true. We know it especially and painfully when we have failed.

I suppose that no personality in the Bible presents our situation so well as Simon Peter. In our human weaknesses and failures, all of us can identify with him. We are so much like him. We love God and are committed to Jesus Christ; we have good intentions; we want to serve our Lord and we promise to serve him. In some euphoric moments, we even fancy we would die for him. But like Simon Peter, we get under pressure. Nothing is so real at the moment as the pressure. God, right, good intentions, vows, and conscience can hardly be heard. Only the steady, dinning torture of physical desire, of the need for social approval, of the demand for money or power gets through to us. And then what happens? We yield to the pressure, we sin, we deny our Lord. After we have realized what we have done, too late to reverse our decision, we are demoralized. We know that we have wronged our Lord. We can scarcely believe that we belong to him. Like Simon Peter, we may go out and weep bitterly.

But it is when we have sinned that he comes to us. Actually, he has been present all along, though we have not recognized his presence. But how obvious his presence when we have sinned! In that moment, we want both to run from him and to cry out to him. And he comes to us, for that's his business, for he is the Savior.

He says, "You have done wrong. You know it. No one has to tell you. And now you are saying to yourself, 'I really never knew him.' But you do belong to me. I knew what you were when I called you to follow me. I also knew what you could become. You have failed me, but you still belong to me. You will bear my name forever. You may deny me a thousand times, but because you belong to me, I will make you confess me a thousand times. I have carried the burden of your sin, and I will carry it again."

What pain such words of love can inflict! Like a father's look of disappointment or like a mother's tears, our Lord's persistent commitment to us makes us see what sin is and what it does. It makes us see that our cowardly silence and our indolent neglect, as well as our feverish acts of disobedience, are betrayal and crucifixion of him, new denials and new wounds compounded of the same evils

that did him to death two thousand years ago. And so comes the haunting question:

Once, oh, once I crucified him.
Shall I crucify my Lord again?

But that is not all. He does not come to avenge the wrongs we have done him. He comes not to avenge but to save. He forgives us freely and fully, saying, "Go, and sin no more," knowing full well that we will sin again and again. And still he is willing to take upon himself once more the burden of our guilt and the humiliation of our dishonor. For where sin abounds, grace abounds much more. He is determined that love shall at last win the victory over all our sins.

II. Not only can we believe that our sins are forgiven because God raised Jesus Christ from the dead, but we can also believe in a future life in Christ.

Those who walk with Jesus Christ, who enter into the struggles and triumphs of fellowship with him, realize that this new life and relationship is the beginning of something that has no end. The apostle Paul said, "Therefore, if any one is in Christ, he is a new creation; the old has passed away, behold, the new has come" (2 Cor. 5:17 RSV). Because of Christ, life has a new quality, a new dimension. The fourth Gospel calls it, "eternal life." It is something of the life of God himself brought into our existence. That is why we hear Jesus say, "And this is life eternal, that they might know thee, the only true God, and Jesus Christ, whom thou hast sent" (John 17:3). And that is why the apostle Paul said, "For me to live is Christ, and to die is gain" (Phil. 1:21). As Paul saw it, "To depart and be with Christ . . . is far better" (Phil 1:23).

Now let me ask: How could Paul have felt this way if Christ has not been raised? How could you and I have radiant certitude and hope about the future if Christ has not been raised? Our belief about the future life is based on the risen Christ. It is inextricably tied up with him. He is the first fruits, the first harvest, of those who have died. And he says to us as we shudder at the thought of our own death, "Because I live, you shall live also" (John 14:19).

We can be certain of this: God will handle your death and mine in a way best suited to his purposes and to our needs. I do not quarrel with my Creator about this life that he has given me, nor do I question his wisdom and love with respect to the next world. I was born into a world compatible with my physical needs; I received a Savior adequate to my spiritual needs. Surely I can trust God to meet whatever the next world requires.

But did it ever puzzle you that the Bible speaks a great deal about resurrection and very little about immortality? And when it speaks about immortality, it is either a quality that God alone possesses or it is something that we "put on," not something that we possess by nature. "For this perishable nature must put on the imperishable, and this mortal nature must put on immortality" (1 Cor. 15:53 RSV). The robust way in which the Bible speaks should comfort us. For the Bible talks in terms of the reconstitution of the redeemed personality. We shall be total persons, not just disembodied spirits floating aimlessly in space. So the term *resurrection,* rather than *immortality,* is the biblical term, the rich word that describes the future life of those who belong to Jesus Christ. And as Paul makes plain, our resurrection will be not a gathering together of our individual dust and ashes but a giving to each of us as individuals "a body as he has chosen" (1 Cor. 15:38 RSV). That is, as it has pleased God. "Beloved," wrote John, "we are God's children now; it does not yet appear what we shall be, but we know that when he appears we shall be like him, for we shall see him as he is" (1 John 3:2 RSV).

III. Now all of this is wonderfully comforting to believe, but it is not enough. One other conviction must complete the triad. Because God raised Jesus Christ from the dead, we can believe in the ultimate victory of God. The Resurrection of Christ is the decisive clue to the meaning of the universe and the final purpose of God. The truth of the Resurrection is of cosmic proportions.

The purpose of God to redeem includes not only the forgiveness of sins and the life everlasting. All creation shares in his redemption. Borrowing a figure from the process of natural birth, Paul described the whole creation as groaning and travailing in pain together, awaiting God's final act of redemption. The God revealed in Jesus Christ, who brought him again from the dead, this God is infinitely resourceful and redemptive. Nothing can stop him from achieving his purpose.

Sin is an obstacle—he conquered it in the cross. Death is an obstacle—he conquered it in the Resurrection. All the evil in an untamed universe is an obstacle—he will conquer it when, to use the words of the apostle Peter, we see "new heavens and a new earth in which righteousness dwells" (2 Pet. 3:13 RSV).

Again and again, the momentary victories of evil—crime, sickness, death, flood, and tornadoes—confront us with the cross and its tragedy. These victories of evil seem to be saying to us, "God is dead." And circumstances sometimes force us to live out many of our days in the noonday darkness of Good Friday. But Easter says to us, "God is alive. God has won the victory over sin and death. The power of the enemy is broken." It was this assurance that rescued the disciples from defeat, discouragement, and despair and made them the heralds of the good news to the ends of the earth. It is this assurance that can defeat the power of sin over us, that can give us something eternal to hope for, and that can make us bow ever more humbly before the loving Father who will make all things new, and who will be "all in all."—James W. Cox[75]

Illustrations

THE NEXT WORLD.   Perhaps you have asked yourself dozens of times, "What will the next world be like?" And it is only natural that you should. On Easter 1965 I preached in New York City. In my sermon I said, "Next Thursday I am scheduled to sail for Europe for my first visit. I have wondered over and over again what it will be like, I've read books, I've talked to people, I've used my imagination, and I've tried to prepare for the new experiences I will have. But I am sure there will be many surprises. As to heaven, I am convinced that none of the speculations of men, even the fabulous visions of apostles, prophets, and seers can do justice to what awaits us there. If we have walked with the living Christ, surely we have some idea of what it is like." My subsequent sojourn in Europe, with its gratifying fulfill-

[75] *Surprised by God*

ment and happy surprises, persuaded me that my analogy was reasonable and proper.—James W. Cox[76]

LIFE AFTER DEATH.   Dorothy Sayers, the great English detective-story writer, once put it this way. "The people who saw the risen Christ were at least convinced that life was worth living and that death is nothing—a very different attitude from that of the modern defeatists who are so convinced that life is a misfortune, and that death, somewhat illogically, is still a greater catastrophe." How could this decision between two basic possibilities so crucial in my life leave me cold or "not make any difference?"—Helmut Thielicke[77]

SUNDAY: APRIL ELEVENTH

LECTIONARY MESSAGE

Topic: The Power of the Resurrection
  TEXT: John 20: 19–31
  Other Readings: Acts 2:14a, 22–32; Ps. 16; 1 Pet. 1:3–9;
  In the nineteenth century, G. K. Chesterton wrote: "The Christian ideal has not been tried and found wanting. It has been found difficult; and left untried." A hundred years later, however, it would have to be said that the Christian ideal has not been found difficult, it has not even been entertained. We are living in an age that thinks it has moved beyond the Christian faith when, in fact, it has never considered it. We are living more in a pre-Christian era than in a post-Christian one. To the question, "What does it mean to be a Christian?" the Church's answer has always been: "Making Jesus Lord." Being a Christian means falling in love with Jesus, recognizing Jesus as eternally one with the Father, and committing one's life in obedience, service, and love to him. There is more, but everything else starts with and emerges from this beginning. All this, of course, presupposes that Jesus is available to be known. A fitting place to start thinking about Jesus, then, is with his Resurrection.

  I. *The blessing of the Risen Christ replaces fear with peace (v. 19).* John's Gospel says that when Jesus first appeared to his disciples away from the tomb, they were gathered behind closed doors "for fear of the Jews (v. 19)." Jesus threatens the status quo because he relativizes rival powers. Christianity makes ultimate claims. In the face of the Christian claim, all other claims, associations, and loves become secondary. As our culture moves increasingly back to pre-Christian assumptions, we can expect biblical people to represent more and more of a threat to the reigning powers. To be an ambassador for Christ is to be a refuge of hope, but also a lightning rod for resistance in a world that does not know Christ.

  The one response that Jesus explicitly refuses his people to luxuriate in is fear. The most frequently repeated command in all of scripture is "Fear not." Perfect love casts out fear. "The one who is in you is greater than the one who is in the world" (1 John 4:4). To his people in dire straits, Jesus brings peace. The Resurrection of Jesus trumpets the assurance that no matter what we see, or what life brings, God is Sovereign—he is in control, and his purposes will not be thwarted. The fact of the Resurrection means that no matter what situation we are in, or what the visible strength we see arrayed against us, we can face it with confidence rather than with fear.

  II. *Real joy springs from seeing the Risen Lord (v. 20).* Joy comes from having one's heart's desires met. Happiness is the world's virtue, but joy is the distinctively Christian one. Lives that practice the presence of Christ radiate exuberance and joy. Our hearts have each a God-shaped hole that he alone can fill. The key to joy is life that is open to the companionship and reality of the Risen Christ.

  III. *The Risen Christ sends his disciples on a mission (v. 21).* The common assumption in many minds is that there are a variety of roads up the mountain to God and it does not matter which one is taken. Different paths, however, usually lead to different destinations. Christianity has a story to share with the nations. It is the path that leads us

[76] *Surprised by God*   [77] *I Believe*

reliably and directly to entering a life-long and eternal love relationship with the living God. To be a Christian is to be sent.

IV. *The Risen Christ sends the Spirit to his disciples (v. 22).* Why does this life of joy and mission so often seem to elude Christian disciples? Surely it is due, in part, to our failure to avail ourselves of what God gives—his Spirit. We can either walk in the flesh—which will inevitably fail us—or we can rely on the Spirit. Too many Christians live weak and struggling spiritual lives, dying of spiritual thirst, when they are surrounded by an ocean of God's transforming power and presence. Because of the failure to live in the Spirit, there are reaches of human experience that are never traveled; there are depths of God's joy that are never plumbed; there are dimensions of God's love that are never touched. The Holy Spirit is the power to live a life in the company of the Almighty. Charles Spurgeon described the Christian walk as the taking of the faltering taper that is human life and the thrusting of it into the blazing fire that is the life of God. In the gift of the Spirit, God has given us the strength we need. He calls us to believe it, claim it, use it, and give him the glory. Christians are seldom better than when they are up against insuperable difficulties, because it is then they have to rely not on *their* strength but on the Lord's.

V. *The Resurrection is based in history but experienced through faith (vv. 24–25).* Some people attempt to hold the claims of Christ at bay by saying, "I choose not to live by faith." There are two problems with this: (1) the implied charge that Christianity has no credible, rational, objective support; and (2) the implication that there are some positions that are entirely "objective" and for which "faith" is irrelevant.

1. *The Resurrection of Jesus has strong evidentiary support.* The Christian faith loves cynics. Christianity is more for the hardheaded than for the credulous. The apostle Thomas reflects a pragmatic, empirical approach that many Americans could admire. He demands evidence. He wants to see, hold, and touch. The contemporary secular spirit has worked hard to spread the myth that to be a Christian is to check one's brains at the door. Although Christianity is experienced and known through faith, it is based on a historical claim that has withstood the most rigorous historical investigation.

a. *The evidence of the empty tomb.* Travel the globe and you will find shrines, mausoleums, and tombs commemorating the revered lives of those who have passed on. There is no memorial for Jesus. There is no tomb or monument made of stone. Could the critics of Jesus have produced his body, the church's claim to have contact with the Risen Christ could have been exposed. It has never been done. It never will be.

b. *The evidence of the appearances of Jesus to his disciples.* The record we have of the witness to the Resurrection of Jesus dates back almost to an exact contemporaneity with the event itself. We know that Paul's testimony in 1 Corinthians was written in about 55 A.D. It would be difficult to date Paul's conversion any later than 35 A.D. In 1 Corinthians 15, Paul uses the phrase "I delivered . . . what I received." This is technical language indicating that Paul is passing on not a tradition that he is creating but one that he was given— presumably in 35 A.D. or within five years of the events themselves. Paul's fourfold use of "that" indicates with precision four critical elements of this tradition: (1) that Christ died for our sins according to the Scriptures, (2) that he was buried, (3) that he was raised on the third day according to the Scriptures, and (4) that he appeared to many close friends and to five hundred others. We have reason to be confident, then, that we have a record of the claim of more than five hundred eyewitnesses to the Resurrection of Jesus that is almost exactly contemporaneous with the event itself.

c. *The evidence of the early church.* A historical fact beyond dispute is that shortly after Jesus was put to death on a Roman cross, a religious movement of enormous energy and vitality arose around his name. Judea was used to seeing messianic claimants come and go, their followers dispersing in disillusionment following their ministry's demise. The record of the Christian community is altogether different. The Roman historian Tacitus records about the Christians that "a most miraculous superstition, thus checked for the moment (presumably by the crucifixion of Jesus) again broke out." No one can deny the Church's own account of her origin. It is plain. The Church understood herself to be brought into being as a consequence of the fact that Jesus Christ had risen from the dead.

2. *Faith is not optional but essential.* There is another problem with the claim that it is possible to live without faith. The implication is that there is something more fundamental, scientific, or objective than faith. This is naive in the extreme. Faith is not an optional appendage to life. It is the inescapable situation in which all of us live. Recent decades have made us increasingly aware of how much "paradigms" affect what we see—even in such supposedly "objective" spheres as science. Often the paradigm that is chosen determines not only what one "sees" but what one "says" (that is, how the "objective" data is interpreted). Finally, life is lived out of the stories we adopt, embrace, and choose. There may be better or worse reasons for choosing a faith, but finally life is a choice. There is no escaping this. To live is to live by faith. The question is not whether to believe or not to believe. It is, Where will you decide to place your trust? To whom will you give your life? Although there are good reasons for believing in God, his existence will never be "proved" or "disproved." The reason is that the God of the Bible is not deduced; he is encountered. The only God the Bible knows is not some "Unmoved Mover" of philosophical discussion but the living God who made us, and cares for us, and comes to meet us in Jesus Christ.

It is a fitting irony that the most passionate articulation of faith in the Gospels comes not from Simon Peter, or from John, but from the one who is remembered as "Doubting Thomas." Seeing the wound in the side of the Risen Jesus, Thomas cries out: "My Lord, and My God." Christianity is a faith for the cynics who (like Frank Morrison in his book *Who Moved the Stone?*) are wise enough to look long and hard at the claims for and the truth of the Resurrection of Jesus.

The Resurrection reveals the truth and presence of a loving, personal God who has created all there is. It reveals that despite our cowardice, waywardness, and rebellion, this God has chosen to come and share our lives. Through his life, teaching, death, and Resurrection, Jesus has shown in human life the face and character of the living God. In Jesus, God has revealed himself to be personal, loving, merciful, and holy. Through the Resur-

rection of Jesus, God has declared that grace rather than law and goodness rather than evil will have the final word. The meaning of the Resurrection is that humanity can meet in actual history the very presence of the Risen Christ.—John Shouse

Illustrations

DOUBTING THOMAS. "Doubting Thomas" has long been a fixed part of our vocabulary. But it may be that mere doubt is not a good description of his role when we see him in the light of Johannine thought. In his statement in verse 25 he does not just doubt, he refuses to believe. In demanding physical contact with Jesus, he actually sets up the conditions for a faith based merely on signs. He becomes one of those whom Jesus had referred to when he said: "So you will not believe unless you see signs and portents!" (4:48). Yet when Jesus confronts him, it is not said that he wants any longer to fulfill his conditions, that is, he does not have to actually touch Jesus. Instead he sees him and responds to his Word with a very lofty confession of Christological faith, the most explicit attribution of divinity to Jesus in the Gospel. Thus Thomas is more than a doubter, and we should translate Jesus' command to him more strongly than the *Jerusalem Bible* does: "Do not be an unbeliever but a believer!" (v. 27).—George W. MacRae[78]

THOMAS'S MISTAKE.   Thomas made one mistake. He withdrew from the Christian fellowship. He sought loneliness rather than togetherness. And because he was not there with his fellow Christians he missed the first coming of Jesus. We miss a great deal when we separate ourselves from the Christian fellowship, and when we try to be alone. Things can happen to us within the fellowship of Christ's Church which will not happen to us when we are alone. When sorrow comes to us, and when sadness envelopes us, we often tend to shut ourselves up and to refuse to meet people. That is the very time when, in spite of our sorrow, we should seek the fellowship of Christ's people, for it is there that

[78] *Invitation to John*

we are likeliest of all to meet Him face to face.—William Barclay[79]

SERMON SUGGESTIONS

Topic: From Sacrifice to Song
TEXT: 2 Chron. 29:27
Sacrifice and joyous celebration belong together. (1) It was so in the reign of King Hezekiah, 2 Chron. 29:1–16. (2) It was so with Jesus Christ, Heb. 12:2. (3) It may be so with us today, Rom. 5:1–5.

Topic: On Loving Our Neighbor
TEXT: Mark 12:31
This requires that (1) we recognize the legitimacy of self-love, (2) we see our own good in the whole, and (3) we watch with wakefulness our awful bias to self.—W. E. Sangster[80]

Hymn Suggestions

1. "Jesus, Stand Among Us," William Pennefather (1873); BEMERTON, Friedrich Filitz (1847)
Recalling the appearance of the resurrected Jesus to the disciples when he breathed on them the Holy Spirit (John 20:19), this short hymn could well serve as a call to worship for this day's service.
2. "When in the Night I Meditate," The Psalter (1912); ST. FLAVIAN, Dayes Psalter (1562)
This full paraphrase of Psalm 16 could be sung responsorially by soloist and congregation in place of the oral reading of the Psalter lesson.
3. "Moment by Moment," Daniel W. Whittel (1893); WHITTLE, May Whittle Moody (1893)
This chorus from a gospel hymn reminds us of God's constant care of our lives and could thus logically follow the reading of the Epistle lesson (1 Pet. 1:5).
4. "Oh, How I Love Jesus," Frederick Whitfield (1855); OH, HOW I LOVE JESUS, American melody (nineteenth century)
The unutterable joy experienced by those who, though having not seen Jesus, love him

[79] The Gospel of John, Vol. 2
[80] The Craft of Sermon Construction

(1 Pet. 1:8) is given appropriate expression in this popular gospel song.—Hugh T. McElrath

Worship Aids

CALL TO WORSHIP. "Thou wilt shew me the path of life: in thy presence is fullness of joy; at thy right hand there are pleasures for evermore" (Ps. 16:11).

INVOCATION. Heighten our joy today, O Lord, as we think on the meaning of our Lord's Resurrection. Let the prayers we pray, the songs we sing, and the written and spoken word that comes to us open ever more widely before us that path of life that blesses us and that blesses others through us.

OFFERTORY SENTENCE. "And he commanded us to preach unto the people, and to testify that it is he which was ordained of God to be the Judge of quick and dead. To him give all the prophets witness, that through his name whosoever believeth in him shall receive remission of sins" (Acts 10:42–43).

OFFERTORY PRAYER. God of the Resurrection, we pray that the offerings that we bring will help to tell the glad message everywhere that Christ is risen and that because of him life for everyone can be new and different. Grant that we may find the joy of sharing that good news.

PRAYER. Almighty and everlasting God, who in the Paschal mystery established the new covenant of reconciliation: Grant that all who have been reborn into the fellowship of Christ's body may show forth in their lives what they profess by their faith; through Jesus Christ our Lord, who lives and reigns with you and the Holy Spirit, one God, for ever and ever.—The Book of Common Prayer

Sermon: Forgiving the Past
TEXT: Ps. 51:1–14
We were new in Oak Ridge. At Christmas we were invited into a home to meet some of the young adults of the church, and we became auditors of a conversation by three young professionals at the threshold of promising careers. The conversation was a friendly competition of compared achievements and aspirations, a few subtle fears and anxieties

about the jungle out there, but absolutely no nostalgia. Not once did I hear the lead sentence typical of folks in the middle of life, "Do you remember when. . . ?"

The longer we live, the more we experience. The more we experience, the more we have to remember. The more we have to remember, the more we have to forgive. Midlife is burdened by memory. In addition to the funny things and the landmark experiences that shape us, every last one of us carries an encyclopedia of legitimate claims against parents, siblings, friends, and colleagues to justify hurt feelings, injured pride, and crippled performance. The middle of life, which Gail Sheehy calls "the Deadline Decade," is a time for cleaning house. At some point in life you have to turn loose your grudges and accusations along with your excuses for failure. If you are honest, you will also need to find forgiveness. Credit Jesus for linking the two together, forgiving and being forgiven. The Lord's Prayer is the prayer for midlife, "forgive us our trespasses (or debts) as we forgive those who trespass against us."

I. *Honest confession is the beginning of redemption.* Walter Brueggemann wrote about David as a paradigm for our understanding of the meaning of truth in general and the truth about ourselves in particular.[81] Human failure is portrayed in "The Painful Truth of the Man." If we learn anything about David and from David, it is the necessity of facing the painful truth about one's past. David should not have been shocked to hear Nathan's charge, "You are the man!" Yet, on top of personal moral failure, David had woven such a tangled web of deception that he had lost sight of the facts of personal history. Nathan's hypothetical case of the rich man who stole the poor man's lamb adds to the drama of the story, and it reflects the difficulty all of us have in facing personal failure. In this therapeutic age of searching out the psychological causes behind personality, the trend is to conclude, "Everything that's wrong with me is someone else's fault." During the Exile, the people learned to blame their parents for their tragic circumstances. "The fathers have eaten sour grapes, and the children's teeth are set on edge" had become

something of a chant of the next generation. Then Jeremiah and Ezekiel declared the Word of God that the children are responsible for their own sins. It was time for honesty in the heart of the king.

I strongly doubt that David subscribed to *Psychology Today* or watched one of the afternoon TV talk shows, yet he demonstrated the current trend to blame everyone but ourselves for our failures in life. The king did not wake up one morning overcome by a perplexing guilt and decide to call in the royal therapists to "work his way through his guilt." David was confronted with the truth about himself that he had managed to bury with Uriah. Truth is the business of prophets. We can overcome the obstacles in our lives that we are willing to acknowledge.

David's hope turned on the discovery, "You desire truth in the inward being." Psalm 51 is located by the editors of the Psalter at the point where Nathan confronts David for his sin with Bathsheba against Uriah. We could offer the prayer in unison as a liturgical petition for forgiveness, with general implications of our individual acts of transgression; but the assigned setting makes it biographical, about a particular man and specific acts of adultery and murder.

I have always felt an invasion of privacy here, as if we had jerked back the curtain of the confessional to gape at a man stripped to his soul. It is like a spiritual autopsy performed on a living person. To offer a congregational confession, "All have sinned," is a different matter. Here we see the face of a man overwhelmed with his sense of shame. The man has given up all defense. "Have mercy on me, O God." He senses the need for a holy bath: "Wash me," "Blot out my iniquities," "Deliver me from bloodshed."

II. *Life begins with forgiveness.* This prayer is more about God than about us, more about grace than about guilt, more about salvation than about sin. Whitney Brown wrote that every human history is one long list of mistakes, "complete with names and dates. It's very embarrassing." We might add that most autobiographies are embellishments of the truth, in fear that the real story might be told. The biblical biography of David begins to be believable when we read the latest exposé on Franklin Roosevelt or John Kennedy. Who knows what else there is to learn about Nixon?

[81]*David's Truth in Imagination and Memory,* p. 16

Yet we easily dissociate ourselves from David's sin. After all, he was the immortal King of Israel, and we are mere mortals. We can look on this favorite child of God and say, "Hey, my sins don't look so bad." Some marriages recover from adultery, but how does one adjust the conscience to accept murder? Yet David makes the most miraculous recovery recorded in the story of Israel. The man who made a disaster of every opportunity that God had given him lived to experience a new life.

Here is our hope in the midlife passage. David's God is the God of redemption. Sin bears the fruit of our own destruction. Nothing we can do will erase the past, yet every sin that can be committed can be forgiven. That is the divine nature. Salvation comes in the midst of history. We are never lifted out of the context in which we destroy and plunder, but we can be empowered of God to become the very opposite of what we have been. Uriah the Hittite might argue with the assertion, "Against you, you alone, have I sinned," but we can find inner peace only as we find peace with God. John Killinger observed that the midlife search is basically spiritual and noted that Carl Jung found a universal quest among middle-aged men for religious meaning.

The end result of finding divine forgiveness is about us. If we are forgiven by God, we can forgive ourselves. If we are forgiven by God, we can begin to mend the relationships that we have destroyed.—Larry Dipboye

Illustrations

TRUE PENITENCE.   The first step to true penitence is a clear recognition of one's own sin. The worshiper's confession "I know my misdeed, and my sin is ever before me" expresses the sincerity of his consciousness of sinfulness, which never leaves him and the firm resolve to be truthful to himself and candid in his intercourse with God. This is not the fleeting mood of a depressed conscience, but the clear knowledge of a man who, shocked by that knowledge, has become conscious of his responsibility; it is a knowledge which excludes every kind of self-deception, however welcome it might be, and sees things as they really are.—Artur Weiser[82]

SINNERS AS WITNESSES.   Verse 13. *Then will I teach transgressors Thy ways.* Reclaimed poachers make the best gamekeepers. Huntingdon's degree of S.S., or Sinner Saved, is more needful for soul-winning evangelists than either M.A. or D.D. The pardoned sinner's matter will be good, for he has been taught in the school of experience, and his manner will be telling, for he will speak sympathetically, as one who has felt what he declares. The audience the psalmist would choose is memorable—he would instruct transgressors like himself; others might despise them, but "a fellow-feeling makes us wondrous kind." If unworthy to edify saints, he would creep in along with the sinners and humbly tell them of divine love.—C. H. Spurgeon[83]

SUNDAY: APRIL EIGHTEENTH

LECTIONARY MESSAGE

Topic: On the Road
  TEXT: Luke 24:13–35;
  Other Readings: Acts 2:14a, 36–41; Ps. 116 1–4, 12–19; 1 Pet. 1:17–23
  Christianity is not a set of principles waiting passively to be discovered. Christian faith is not a collection of proverbial wisdoms waiting to be adopted. Christianity means meeting Jesus. Christian life is an encounter with a person. Meeting Jesus may initially be disruptive, disorienting, and even unwelcome. It is not an encounter that can be anticipated or predicted. When it comes, it sets life in a whole new direction with a whole new purpose.

  I. *Jesus meets his disciples on the journey (vv. 13–24).* Our text finds two followers of Jesus on a road leading away from Jerusalem. Confused, disheartened, and bewildered, they are still involved and engaged in the events of the past few days. In life they had found Jesus riveting. He had become the focus of their fondest hopes for the "redemption" of Israel. The death of Jesus had seemed to crush this dream. But now rumors and reports abounded that not only was Jesus' tomb empty but he was alive. At this juncture Jesus

[82]*The Psalms*
[83]*Psalms*

arrives incognito as a companion on their journey. The text tells us "their eyes were prevented from recognizing him" (v. 16). Ever the consummate teacher, Jesus opens not with a lecture but with a question. The good news means, in part, that the Creator of the universe waits to hear our words. The world's author is interested in knowing what we have heard and what we have understood about his story.

At first glance, one may be struck by how much these two pilgrims seem to get right. They recognize Jesus as a man of God "mighty in word and deed." In Jesus, faith and action fuse. Jesus is understood as a man with a message reflected in actions. The two travelers also admirably summarize the Resurrection accounts. Yet Jesus still speaks harshly to them: "O foolish men and slow of heart to believe in all that the prophets have spoken!" (v. 25). Why? The text suggests an answer: although they had heard of the Resurrection appearances, these disciples still did not see Jesus. Apparently seeing Jesus is something for which our lives are accountable. Not to see Jesus is to be "foolish" and "slow of heart." We are reminded of the scriptural observation: "The fool says in his heart 'there is no God'" (Psalm 14:1). Our lives will finally be weighed by whether or not our eyes are open to life's Lord.

II. *Jesus meets his disciples in the Scriptures (vv. 25–27).* There on the Emmaus Road, Jesus takes his disciples to the Scriptures. The time in which we live has been termed by some "postmodern." It has been characterized as the refusal to accept the existence of objective truth. The historic faith of the Christian Church counters this attitude by anchoring its access to truth in an objective standard—the witness of Scripture. "Sola Scriptura" was a central tenet of the Reformation faith. Jesus Christ is the head of the Church, but access to his authority comes through the Holy Spirit speaking in and through the Scriptures. The Bible is not just a record of revelation. It is itself a part of that revelation.

The decline of confidence in the authority of Scripture has had a corrosive effect on the Christian Church. The question of Jeremiah can be heard as a commentary on our contemporary soul: "Since they have rejected the word of the Lord, what kind of wisdom do they have?" (Jer. 8:9). Throughout his ministry Jesus directed his followers to view the Bible with the confidence that what Scripture says, God says. Writing in the first part of the twentieth century, the British Congregationalist theologian P. T. Forsyth observed: "The Bible is the book, as Christ is the person, where the seeking God meets and saves the seeking man. . . . The Bible is not a quarry for the historian, it is a fountain for the soul. The Bible is the one Enchiridion of the [Christian] still, the one manual of eternal life, the one page that glows as all life grows dark, and the one book whose wealth rebukes us more the older we grow because we knew and loved it so late."

III. *Jesus meets his disciples in the breaking of the bread (vv. 29–32).* Then Jesus is met by his disciples in the breaking of the bread. The one who was "mighty" in both word and deed reveals himself not only through the words of Scripture but also in the acts of his church. Eating is one of life's great acts of intimacy and shared life. Jesus, who spoke in parables, also left a parable for his disciples to enact. The oldest portrait that the Church possesses of her Lord is the broken bread and poured cup of his communion table. Jesus not only is remembered in the broken bread—he also is the giver of it. Death did not overtake Jesus; Jesus took up death (see John 15). The broken bread declares the cross of Christ to be not an accident or misfortune but the climactic event in the history of human redemption.

The encounter of the Church with the Risen Lord over the breaking of the bread points to a truth beyond the cross. The supper of the Lord speaks not only of Jesus' sacrificial death but also of his continuing life. To break the "bread of life" in the fellowship of the Church is to give witness to a dual reality: victory as well as sacrifice, joy as well as suffering.

The Christian Church has two foundational rituals: baptism (the rite of Christian beginnings) and the Lord's Supper (the rite of Christian growth). Both are rooted in the historical fact of the Resurrection. At the Lord's Table not only is the death of Jesus reenacted, but also the presence of the Risen Jesus is appropriated and affirmed. The Lord's Table declares that Jesus is the one by whom Christians are nourished and sustained. To come to the table of the Lord as a believer is to celebrate not only the death but also the presence of the Risen Christ. The experience and confession of the Christian Church throughout the centuries give witness to the Church's continuing experience of and participation in the Resurrection.

Our text today tells the story of three places where the risen Jesus regularly meets his disciples: (1) on the real roads walked in the course of the journey of their lives, (2) in the opening of the Scriptures, and (3) in gathering around the tokens of Jesus' broken body, shed blood, and present reign. The good news of the Resurrection of Jesus is that the Risen Christ is closer to us and more ready to fill us with his love than the next breath we take.—John Shouse

Illustrations

IN TIMES OF TROUBLE. The same Jesus who stilled the storm on Galilee is present with us today. He is with us in the stormy times of life and the calm ones; He is present when the going is rough and when it is great—and in the ordinary times as well. The storm may continue to rage, or it may grow calm, but we are not alone.

William Barclay lost his grown daughter in an accident at sea. Years later he would cite this passage (Mark 4:35–41) and say to his students, "As he stilled the storm on Galilee, so he stills the storm in our hearts."—Alton H. McEachern[84]

IN OUR HEARTS. There is a sense of course in which God *can* be known in our hearts, but the God of the Bible, the God revealed in the living Christ, also stands over against us in our "hearts." We do not take him captive in our hearts. Indeed *he* may take *us* captive in our hearts, and then perhaps we can know the peace of God which passes all understanding. But it is precisely beyond our understanding because God, if Christ is the clue to his nature, is different. He is surprising, like appearing as a stranger along the dusty road to Emmaus.—Edmund A. Steimle[85]

SERMON SUGGESTIONS

Topic: "Where Is the Lord, the God of Elijah?"
TEXT: 2 Kings 2:1–2, 6–14
(1) *The ancient story:* Elisha succeeds Elijah as God's prophet. (2) *The contemporary relevance:* (a) Prayer truly succeeds when it is for the right thing (v. 9); (b) spiritual insight complements genuine prayer (vv. 10–12); (c) the Holy Spirit today sets God's people "afire" for God and his work, and they can go forth in the power and spirit of Elijah and Elisha and the disciples on the day of Pentecost (vv. 13–14; see also Acts 2:17–21).

Topic: Good News Must Be Shared
TEXT: Mark 5:19
Certain facts about our Christian duty of witness are driven home by these words of Jesus. (1) They drive home the compulsion of Christian witness. "Go . . . and tell." (2) They also drive home the strategy of Christian witness. "Go home to your friends and tell them . . ." (3) They drive home the theme of Christian witness. "Tell them how much the Lord has done for you, and how he has had mercy on you."—John N. Gladstone[86]

HYMN SUGGESTIONS

1. "Open My Eyes That I May See," Clara H. Scott (1895); SCOTT, Clara H. Scott (1895)

The disciples at the table with Jesus had their eyes opened (Luke 24:31) when Jesus took the bread, blessed, and broke it. So worshipers can pray in the words of this appealing song for spiritual eyes to be opened to perceive the truths of God. This could be sung just before the Gospel reading, or at the very beginning of worship.

2. "What Shall I Render to My God," Charles Wesley (1742); ARMENIA, Sylvanus B. Pond (1841)

A rare Wesley paraphrase of the Psalter, this hymn is based primarily on Psalm 116:12–18 and as such would naturally follow the psalm reading for this day.

3. "I'm New Born Again," African-American spiritual; NEW BORN AGAIN, John W. Work Jr. and Frederick Work (1907)

[84] *The Lord's Presence*
[85] *God the Stranger*

[86] *A Magnificent Faith*

In its recurring response focusing on the message of 1 Peter 1:23 ("You have been born anew"), this spiritual would be appropriately sung following the Epistle reading.

4. "O Thou Who This Mysterious Bread," Chas. Wesley (1745); LAND OF REST, American melody, arr. Annable Morris Buchanan (1938)

This little-known hymn by Charles Wesley is based directly on the Gospel reading describing the Emmaus road experience. It is eminently appropriate to be sung at the service of Holy Communion.—Hugh T. McElrath

Worship Aids

CALL TO WORSHIP.   "I love the Lord, because he hath heard my voice and my supplications. Because he hath inclined his ear unto me, therefore will I call upon him as long as I live" (Ps. 116:1–2).

INVOCATION.   Almighty God, in whose presence we long to linger, listen, and wait, bless our worship this day. Give strength to the faint, hope to the weary, and peace to all who name the name of God in prayer.—E. Lee Phillips

OFFERTORY SENTENCE.   "As ye abound in everything, in faith, and utterance, and knowledge, and in all diligence, and in your love to us, see that ye abound in this grace also" (2 Cor. 8:7).

OFFERTORY PRAYER.   Gracious Lord, our God, give us a vision of the soul needs of others, the difference Christ makes, the place Christ deserves, the hope Christ offers. Then let us give accordingly.—E. Lee Phillips

PRAYER.   We thank thee, O God, for life, with all its wonder and beauty and power, and especially for the life of Jesus as we see him revealed on a day like this, when the limitations of time and space are set aside and he goes forward to his life among us as love and power and wisdom. Help us, O God, so to order our lives that the weight of our interest may be on the side of eternal things, and when it comes time to gather us together unto our fathers, we shall know whither we are going.—Theodore Parker Ferris[87]

Sermon: In the Furnace

TEXT: Dan. 3

This is a kids' story, a bedtime story like Hansel and Gretel or the Three Little Pigs. It could have happened—we know that Babylonian kings made giant statues, had royal orchestras for state occasions, and punished evildoers by burning them alive. But all of that is really beside the point. Look at the ways the story is told: the repeating phrases, the funny names, the bad guys. It's a bedtime story for kids, and like most traditional bedtime stories it has a killer-diller theme, an absolutely heart-stopping, gutwrenching, cold-sweat-in-the-middle-of-the-night theme.

The essence of the story is a question we all ask, if we live long enough: Why do I have to go through this hell that I am in? And where is God while I'm here roasting in the furnace? This is the kind of question that transforms ordinary pain into a furnace of blazing fire, superheated and deadly even to bystanders. It was the question that haunted Elie Wiesel, Holocaust survivor, who wondered why God would not hear the cries of his people as they were marched into gas chambers and as their bodies became fuel for the furnaces of Auschwitz. Where was God in the Holocaust?

I. Tough question, but that's what many of us bring to this story, and that's what this little tale faces. It starts with a tyrant named Nebuchadnezzar, a Babylonian king who decides to dedicate a statue to one of his gods. He decides to make it really big and to place it in a flat spot so that everyone can see it for miles around. So the royal artists are commissioned, and they make it about ninety feet high, about nine feet wide, and goldplated. It must have looked like God's toothpick from a distance, until you got close enough to see that it was a statue, and then it must have looked like Manute Bol—really tall, really skinny.

On the day it was dedicated the herald told everybody to listen for the music and whenever they heard it to stop, drop, and worship, under penalty of instant incinera-

[87]*Prayers*

tion. A bizarre sort of version of musical chairs, if you will. You have to imagine the people of the province going about their work with one ear cocked for the melodious sounds of the trigon and bugle corps, and hearing them, flopping down and saying, "Onomatopoeia! Owatagoosiam!"

II. This is too easy, folks. Play the game or die? Hop when I say frog or face the music? Where have we heard that one before? Anybody out there have to play by unreasonable rules sometimes? And it doesn't matter how much you point out that the rules are stupid and that worshiping the golden statue doesn't help; the tyrants of this world never listen. "This is top priority," they say, "government regulations, standard policy, good business strategy." How many times, you adults, have you had to go along with what they say just because they said so?

But they've never asked me to compromise my faith, you say. Oh, really? Never expected you to put the company ahead of your family? Never expected you to set aside personal feelings for someone and do the tough thing for the sake of the business? Never asked you to keep something under your hat so that the business could profit by it at someone else's expense?

III. Here's where the kids' story takes our question from us and turns it around on us. See, there's a test for the three amigos before they get to the furnace. In the course of their regular lives, in the give and take of their jobs, in the interactions they had with people who didn't like them and wanted to tattle on them to the king, the three faced a test. Here it is: Can they see the statue for what it is—not just a useless, annoying rule but a trap for their faith? Can they spot the trap and walk away from it? We all face this sort of test regularly and consistently, and the only answer we should give is the one the three amigos gave: we serve God, and if God exists, then God can take care of us. And if God doesn't exist, we are still not going to worship your stupid, skinny statue.

IV. The second test is the furnace itself. Nebuchadnezzar goes ballistic, orders in the goon squad, and before you know it the three are tied up and chucked into the furnace. Some of you know precisely how they felt; you wake up one day in hell, the bottom having suddenly dropped out of your life; or

maybe you wake up one day at the bottom of a long slide into hell. These guys were alone—none of their coworkers stepped up to protest, the man who had supported them and had given them a job was now their enemy, their careers were over, their reputations were shot, their lives were going up in smoke.

The test for them and for us, the second test, is whether we can see the angel in the furnace. That's what the story promises. The story doesn't promise avoidance; these three guys were as good as gold, they were movers and shakers in the kingdom, they were clearly God's people, but they got bound hand and foot and thrown in. The story doesn't promise deliverance, even; notice that they didn't get out until Nebuchadnezzar let them out. Not avoidance or deliverance, but presence: God was with them in the furnace. And that's the test, the second test, to see if we can spot the angel in the furnace.

Even in Auschwitz? Yes, even there, in the worst hell that humans could create, and even as the vehicle for God's presence, the angel resisted. Elie Wiesel saw the lines forming, knew that one line meant life and the other death, and the Nazi commandant pointed with his stick to seal the fates of the sick and the old and the children. Elie Wiesel hated God at that moment for what was happening, and vowed never to pray again. But as the death line moved toward the gas chambers, he heard a voice saying Qaddish, the prayer for the dead, and realized that the voice was his own. He, unwillingly, became God's angel in that dark place for others, and for me, too, when I found his books in a very dark time in my life.

The story starts with our question—Where is God?—and then asks us a couple of questions. Can you tell that the skinny statues around you are not God? If you are having trouble finding God in your life, then it is at least worth asking yourself whether you are bowing down in the wrong direction and bobbing to the wrong tune. In response to the second question—Can you see the angel in the furnace?—if you can't, it doesn't mean that you're not spiritual enough, or that God has abandoned you. It may just mean that you need to look again. The prophet says, "When you pass through the rivers, they will not overwhelm you, and when you walk through the fire the flames will not devour you. Do not fear, for I am with you." That's the gospel, brothers and sisters.—Richard B. Vinson

Illustrations

A MATTER OF CONSCIENCE. In the second century after Christ, Polycarp, a venerable Christian, faced such a choice when he was commanded by an authority to renounce Jesus Christ. He replied, "Eighty-six years have I served him, and he has never done me wrong. How can I now deny my King who has saved me?" Your life may not be threatened, but your job or your popularity may be at stake when someone with power over you demands that you violate what represents obedience to God in your life. The matter is clear-cut, and you may have to answer in the

spirit of Martin Luther, "Here I stand. . . . I can do no other. . . . God help me! Amen."—James W. Cox[88]

A TAINT OF SIN. The love of God and the love of self are curiously intermingled in life. The worship of God and the worship of self confront us in a multitude of different compounds. There is a taint of sin in our highest endeavors. How shall we judge the great statesman who gives a nation its victorious courage by articulating its only partly conscious and implicit resources of fortitude; and who mixes the most obvious forms of personal and collective pride and arrogance with this heroic fortitude? If he had been a more timid man, a more cautious soul, he would not have sinned so greatly, but neither would he have wrought so nobly.—Reinhold Niebuhr[89]

SUNDAY: APRIL TWENTY-FIFTH

LECTIONARY MESSAGE

Topic: The Good Shepherd
TEXT: John 10:1–18
Other Readings: Acts 2:42–47; Ps. 2:3; 1 Pet. 2:19–25
Love has been defined as the determination to seek the best for the other regardless of the cost. With one bold stroke, Jesus paints a picture of this kind of determined love, and writes his name beneath it. The shepherd with his sheep was a familiar sight in Palestine. Jesus uses this well-known relationship to serve as a parable for the truth and promise of life.

I. *Our lives are under siege (vv. 1, 10).* A graduate student observed one day that when he went to college the "ante in life went up." There comes a time when the wise soul realizes that the stakes of life are immeasurably high. Verses 1 and 10 warn us that thieves and robbers are ever looking for openings in order to "steal, kill, and destroy." Evil is not passive. It has an active, initiatory presence. The world surrounds us with a sea of disinformation that assails our souls. Truth is labeled a lie, and packs of lies masquerade as the truth. From humanity's earliest breaths, idolatry has been our habitual sin. This text suggests that there are those who falsely seek to claim our allegiance. Consequently, the

Church is involved in a battle for the minds and souls of human life. Humanity's fundamental choice remains whether we will follow Jesus or submit to thieves and robbers contending for possession of our lives. Jesus bids us see the fallen world as it really is: "a people harassed and helpless, like sheep without a shepherd" (Matt. 9:35).

II. *Jesus is the Good Shepherd (vv. 3, 11).* Verse 3 describes a common scene. Raised for the value of their fleece, sheep were kept for long periods. The sheep knew and were known by their shepherd, who called them by individual names. In the city, sheep were kept in large common pens that men were hired to watch. When the sheep heard the familiar sound of their shepherd's voice, they would leap and jump for joy. Following the shepherd's voice, the sheep naturally separated themselves from the other herds.

Christ's lordship over life could scarcely be put in stronger relief. Jesus commands our wholehearted allegiance and our unreserved devotion. He comes not to destroy and diminish life but to fulfill it. He comes not to steal but to protect; not to mislead but to direct; not to take but to give; not to kill but to

[88] *Surprised by God*
[89] *Discerning the Signs of the Times*

enliven. As the original word order puts it, Jesus declares that he is nothing less and nothing other than "the Shepherd—the Good One." With this image, Jesus once again makes the audacious claim to stand in God's place before Israel. Centuries before, Ezekiel had recorded the Lord's promise: "I myself will search for my sheep and look after them. As a shepherd looks after his scattered flock when he is with them, so will I look after my sheep. I will rescue them from all the places where they were scattered on a day of clouds and darkness. . . . I myself will tend my sheep and have them lie down, declares the Sovereign Lord. I will search for the lost and bring back the strays. I will bind up the injured and strengthen the weak" (Ezek. 34:12, 15).

III. *Jesus is the door (v. 9).* When the shepherd could not get his flock back to the pen by nightfall, he would search out a spot, preferably a cave, in which to keep his sheep for the night. The shepherd would lie down before the opening and become a living door. Nothing could pass in or out of the cave without passing over or through the shepherd's body. The promise here is twofold. Jesus with his very life will protect his sheep. In the face of the most heinous evil, Christ's promise is never to forsake us or abandon us. *The Hiding Place* is a film that tells the story of a Dutch Christian woman, Corrie Ten Boom, and her family who hid Jewish citizens from the Nazis in the Amsterdam of World War II. Eventually their hiding place is discovered and Corrie is imprisoned. Corrie's radiant faith and resistant attitude infuriate the megalomaniacal commandant of the camp. In one scene the commandant takes Corrie into his office. He sits behind his imposing desk in a room filled with the trappings of worldly power, looks at Corrie wearing only the apparel of a prisoner, and sneers, "So, do you still think your God is watching over you?" Unflinching as a rock, with a confidence born of truth, Corrie returns his gaze and almost sings back, "Yes, and I also believe he is watching you."

The second promise of this picture is that Jesus is the door through which we must pass not only to receive protection but also to reach pasture. Jesus not only affords safety, he also assures sustenance. Scripture affirms that "by no other name will people be saved" (Acts 4:12). This has been termed the "offense of the Gospel" or the "scandal of particularity." In actuality, it is simply the truth. Ultimately all paths do not lead up the same mountain. Not all claims to truth can stand. It is the glad claim and promise of the Christian faith that in Jesus Christ God is available to be met and known. In Jesus, God has come to us not by proxy but in person. Jesus is the door through which all must eventually pass if they are fully and truly to know the God who is the great "I Am."

IV. *For Christians the road to life leads through death (vv. 11, 17, 18).* Jesus knew himself to be a man born to die. However, the text tells us that not only does the Good Shepherd lay down his life, he also takes it up again. This means that Jesus was not a victim of the cross but the victor on it. The cross did not overtake Jesus; he took it up. The Christian faith proclaims that although the road of discipleship leads to death, it also leads through death to life again.

Following the Shepherd will lead us to pasture, protection, and life, but also to a cross. To those the Master calls, he bids them come and die. While it is not his cross we are called to carry, it is a cross nonetheless. Some in their Christian walk bleed just enough to be incapacitated but not enough to die. The cross of Christ bids Christian disciples come and die to all that is killing them and draining them of life.

The love of the Shepherd leads him not only to lay down his life for His flock, but also to take it up again. Love loved the world enough to die for it. According to C. S. Lewis, in his book *Miracles,* "[Jesus] has forced open a door that had been locked since the death of the first man. He has met, fought and beaten the King of death. Everything is different because He has done so." Once we have been captured by that love, we are called to kneel before that grace. The death and Resurrection of the Good Shepherd declares that death could not silence Jesus. He is alive and He is here. He is available to be known, experienced, and loved by all those who are wise enough to take His hand, trust Him implicitly, and follow Him courageously.—John Shouse

Illustrations

THE TRUE SHEPHERD.   Readers of Plato will remember how Socrates, in the First

Book of the *Republic,* insists on the difference between the true artist (not only in the fine arts) who practices his art—e.g., medicine—for the sake of its true object (in the case of medicine, health), and one who practices it "as a money-maker." That the doctor should in fact earn his fee is right enough; but the earning of the fee must not be the directing motive of his practice (*Republic,* 341c–346d).

So the shepherd—the pastor—may rightly be paid for his service. He must be kept alive, or he cannot tend his flock. But his dominant motive must be care of the flock; and nothing must ever take precedence of that. —William Temple[90]

SACRIFICES.   When a friend once wrote to Dr. Livingstone about the sacrifices he was making in spending his days amongst the savages of Central Africa, he made the spirited reply: "Is that a sacrifice which brings its own best reward in healthful activity, in the consciousness of doing good, peace of mind and the hope of a glorious destiny hereafter? Away with such a thought. I never made a sacrifice."—W. MacIntosh Mackay[91]

SERMON SUGGESTIONS

Topic: What It Means to Be Blessed
TEXT: Ps. 1
(1) Taking delight in God's Word. (2) Enjoying the abundant life. (3) Experiencing God's providential care.

Topic: Why Do Bad Things Happen to People?
TEXT: John 9
I. The way it seems: (a) It is the fault of the victim. Sometimes it is, sometimes it isn't. (b) It is the fault of other people. Sometimes it is, sometimes it isn't. II. The way it is: (a) In any case, God is not malicious. (b) In every case, God, the God of the Cross, overcomes all evil—either now or in eternity.

Hymn Suggestions

1. "I Lay My Sins on Jesus," Horatius Bonar (1843); AURELIA, Samuel S. Wesley (1864)

[90] *Readings in St. John's Gospel*
[91] In *Treasury of the Christian World*

This hymn of penitence would appropriately follow the Epistle reading (1 Pet. 2:19–25), where the emphasis is on dying to sin and living to righteousness. It is suitable for a time of commitment, a season of confessional prayer, or the observance of the Lord's Supper.

2. "My Shepherd Will Supply My Need," Isaac Watts (1719); RESIGNATION, Walker's Southern Harmony (1835)
One of the oldest but still most appealing paraphrases of Psalm 23, this Watts hymn also attracts with its lovely folklike setting from the Southern shape-note tradition.

3. "Jesus, I Come," William T. Sleeper (1887); JESUS, I COME, George C. Stebbins (1887)
This gospel hymn spells out in effective detail the joys and fullness of the life abundant (promised in the Gospel reading—John 10:10) to which the repentant one comes.

4. "O Spirit of the Living God," Henry H. Tweedy (1935); FOREST GREEN, trad. Eng. melody, arr. R. V. Williams (1906)
This twentieth-century hymn based on the Acts 2 account of the coming of the Holy Spirit on the Church is one of many on this subject that could be selected. Among other excellent hymns celebrating the coming of the Spirit are:

"Filled with the Spirit's Power," John R. Peacey (1969); SHELDONIAN, Cyril V. Taylor (1943)
"O Breath of Life," Bessie Porter Head (1920); BISHOP POWELL, David Ashley White (1887)

Worship Aids

CALL TO WORSHIP.   "Surely goodness and mercy shall follow me all the days of my life: and I will dwell in the house of the Lord for ever" (Ps. 23:6).

INVOCATION.   Lord, allow us in worship to contemplate the Christ: his priorities, his prayers, his compassion, his courage, his sacrifice, his Resurrection. Then as we face the world, leave us not the same.—E. Lee Phillips

OFFERTORY SENTENCE.   "Moses said to the whole Israelite community: 'This is the command the Lord has given: Each of you is to set aside a contribution to the Lord. Let all who wish bring a contribution to the Lord'" (Exod. 35:4–5a REB).

OFFERTORY PRAYER.   Grant us now, Father, the imagination to see the needs of our fellow men, compassion to feel their pains and longings, and a gracious spirit that gives sufficiently to meet their hungerings and thirstings.—Henry Fields

PRAYER.   O thou art our Father, reveal thyself to us by the heart, by thy providences. Reveal thyself to us in our own hearts and out of our own experiences. For thou hast made us capable of understanding thee by making us like thee. And when we have known our own best paternal relations, we have shadowed in them thy nature, and thy feelings toward us. And in all the work to which we are called, with so much patience and sacrifice and pain of love, of rearing our children out of helplessness into experience and strength, and out of irregularity and inexperience into self-governing creatures, in all the waiting for them, thou art shadowed forth in thy dealings with us. It is thy nature to wait. It is thy nature to be patient and gentle. It is thy nature to bring out of inexperience, yes, and out of faults themselves, the virtues of life, and to establish the soul in righteousness. Blessed by thy name, that thou art brought home to us in a way so near, so touching, that our hearts are opened in loving our children, and being loved by them, to the very government of God in the universe. Grant, we pray thee, that the thought of God may make fatherhood more rich and more glorious among us. Grant that thy love, though we learn it from ours, may return to us, when learned, with such dignifying power that our own affections shall stand up grander than before we knew thee. God, grant, we beseech of thee, that we may know what faithfulness is, and learn to be faithful; that we may have a higher lesson of patience; that we may carry all the rights and duties and blessings of true loving into the household, not as our necessity, our yoke, and our law. May we, out of the necessity of full hearts, perform the duties of love. Grant that it may be spontaneous, overflowing, abounding evermore.

O Lord! We thank thee that thou hast made us like thyself, and that thou art drawing us to thyself by the bond of love. And we thank thee that so we are knitted one to another. And for its fruition, and all its elevation and joys in times past, we thank thee.—Henry Ward Beecher

Sermon: A Praying Church
TEXT: Acts 2:42

The contention of this sermon is that our greatest need, our number one priority, is spiritual renewal—a rediscovery of the place and power of prayer. A vital church is a praying church, a church that is at home in the secret place of the Most High.

Certainly prayer was an essential feature of the early Church. "They devoted themselves to . . . the prayers." The Jerusalem Christians continued to attend the Temple for corporate and private prayer. They met in homes for prayer meetings. They prayed at regular, set times, and often, we may be sure, at all times. The phrase "the prayers" rings like a refrain through the Book of Acts. All the great deliverances of the apostles, all the great decisions of the councils, all the great ventures of the first missionaries were carried out against a background of continuous prayer.

The atmosphere of the modern Church is startlingly different. The volume of private prayer cannot, of course, be assessed; but it would seem that there is very little corporate prayer. The prayer meeting has either disappeared altogether or, at best, is kept alive by a zealous few. Not surprisingly, one man is alleged to have prayed at such a meeting: "We thank thee, Lord, that when thou didst say, 'Where two or three are gathered together,' thou didst know how things were going to turn out." Modern Christianity is not devoted to "the prayers." Is this, then, the root cause of our ineffectiveness? Informed and sensitive Christians have long told us that this is our trouble. "The whole work of the Church is being crippled by this," claims one great authority. "The real malady is not theological stagnation or social apathy. It is prayer-paralysis." We must recapture the devotion of the first Christians to this maker of the vital church—"the prayers."

As we come to grips with our theme, two main considerations thrust themselves upon us.

I. Consider, in the first place, *the relation be-*

tween work and prayer. In this activist age, many of us are inclined to become restless and impatient about the whole question of prayer. Time given to prayer seems suspiciously like wasted time, a pietistic luxury we cannot afford in our busy, crowded days. The thing to grasp is that it is an entirely false dichotomy that separates work and prayer and gives one the priority over the other. They belong indissolubly together.

Prayer without work is a pious evasion of duty. A lazy, slipshod, inefficient approach to life is never justified by any amount of time a man spends on his knees. The student who plays the slacker before an important examination and then bombards heaven with frantic prayers for success will find, as Dean Inge caustically pointed out, that God is on the side of the examiners. Why should we ask God to endorse our indolence? William Barclay, in his helpful book *The Plain Man's Book of Prayers,* lays down an inevitable law of prayer that God will not do for us that which we can very well do for ourselves. Pasteur was in his laboratory one day, bending forward over his microscope. A student entered, and seeing the scientist in what he took to be the attitude of prayer, he began quietly to leave the room. Pasteur glanced up and the student said, "Oh, I thought you were praying." Returning to his microscope Pasteur said: "I was. God's heeded prayer is an active brain." This truth authenticates itself to the mind and heart of every serious Christian.

On the other hand, work without prayer is a practical denial of God. "Paganism begins where prayer ends." This is so, however apparently spiritual the work we are doing may be. We are workers together with God—and God is sovereign and supreme in his work. How can we remain sensitive to his will and receptive to his guidance if we do not pray? How can we keep our vision clear and our motive true if we do not examine and renew them frequently in his immediate presence? The best of men are men at the best. When they try to do by themselves alone what no man can do unless God is with him, the result is fairly predictable; they will either be puffed up with pride or cast down in despair.

A balanced attitude to work and prayer is superbly illustrated in the life of that engaging Bible character Nehemiah. The first five chapters of his book are in the nature of a diary. To read the record of Nehemiah's statesmanship, and rebuilding of the city of Jerusalem, is to see how prayer inspires work and work reinforces prayer. "We made our prayer unto our God," he writes, "and set a watch against them day and night." Again, there is this striking prayer: "O God, strengthen my hands." This same balanced religion is also illustrated in the life of that magnificent missionary doctor, Sir Henry Holland, whose services to Pakistan, the Commonwealth, and to suffering humanity, were so outstanding. When a visiting Viceroy asked him how his team of eye specialists achieved such astounding results under such adverse conditions, he replied: "Your Excellency, it's all done by prayer—and strong antiseptics." Work and prayer are one, and "What God has joined together, let not man put asunder."

II. Consider, in the second place, *the relation between individual prayer and corporate prayer.* There is a real sense in which prayer is a very personal and private activity. We have the authority of Jesus for this: "But when you pray, go into your room and shut the door and pray to your Father who is in secret, and your Father who sees in secret will reward you." If there is to be any substance to our prayer life, this is a practice we must cultivate assiduously. Somehow or other we must take the time and find the place where we can be alone with God, in worship, praise, confession, dedication, and intercession. It will not be easy. Prayer requires as much discipline and industry as painting, music, poetry, or learning to write effectively. The giants of the spiritual life all tell us of the years of stern, resolute, and unremitting effort it took them before they mastered the art of prayer. They literally "devoted" themselves: to prayer. Brother Lawrence spent ten years teaching himself to pray—ten years!

To the end of our days we may exercise this ministry of individual, secret prayer. Indeed, it keeps us in the forefront of the Christian warfare. It has special reference to those who because of age, infirmity, sickness, or altered circumstances imagine that their days of usefulness are over. "We are not needed or wanted now" such people are inclined to say. They are wrong. No one has ceased to serve who cares to pray. The range of such intercessions is as wide as the needs of men. It is said that anyone feeling useless should get to work in the ministry of intercession, and they will be doing as much as ever—if not more—for the Kingdom of God and the needs of humanity.

But what of corporate prayer, someone may reasonably interject? Where does that come in? Is there any value in praying together that is not covered by praying alone? Indeed there is. The greatest value is the realized presence of the living Christ, in fulfillment of his own promise: "Again I say unto you, if two of you agree on earth about anything they ask, it will be done for them by my Father in heaven. For where two or three are gathered together in my name, there am I in the midst of them." There are other values, too. Corporate prayer is a safeguard against spiritual egotism, liberating us from narrow prejudices, partial views, and self-opinionated ideas. It adds new dimensions to our praying; we learn how to pray as we converse with God in the company of some who have achieved a relationship with him that is richer and deeper than our own. There is a strengthened unity of purpose, an added vitality, a new joy and confidence in believing to be found in praying with others that we could never experience in isolation. John Trapp, an old puritan expositor, has a quaint comment on Acts 12, verse 12, where we read that "many were gathered together, and were praying." He says: "Great is the force of joint prayer when Christians set upon God. . . . They sacked and ransacked heaven by their prayers. . . . We beseech not God only, but we besiege Him, too; we beg not barely, but bounce at heaven-gates." Oh! for more of this prayerful bounce in the Church today!

I know the arguments against the traditional prayer meeting. The long-winded prayers, the embarrassing pauses, the fidgety silences, the sheer dullness of it all. No one who knows anything would deny that these difficulties exist, or attempt to defend them. But let us be honest. We offer these arguments as excuses for our nonparticipation in corporate prayer. In fact, they are clear examples of what Freud meant by rationalization. The real reasons that we do not pray corporately are in ourselves. We do not believe enough in the power of prayer. We do not care enough for God and his people. We are afraid to expose the poverty of our own inner life in public. The desire to pray with others is surely a natural, inevitable outcome of faithful individual prayer. It is curious, to say the least, if our sense of the "koinonia," the sharing Church, stops short of fellowship at its deepest level, which is prayer. Individual prayer and corporate prayer belong together. As one writer on this theme has pointed out, we "maintain the spiritual glow" in our private prayers by praying with others, and in our corporate prayers by praying privately.

Prayer is the way to a revived Church and a transformed world. The power of God is available to deal with this gone-wrong human situation in which we find ourselves. It comes in at the point of believing prayer. Listen to this promise of God: "If my people who are called by my name shall humble themselves and pray and seek my face and turn from their wicked ways, then will I hear from heaven and will forgive their sin and will heal their land." Prayer is the way. The prophet Isaiah has a dramatic passage in which he shares a vision that came to him at a time of national crisis and calamity. It was a vision of God watching the indifference and indulgence of his people. "And He saw that there was no man, and wondered that there was no intercessor . . ." Is he wondering today why his people are not devoted to "the prayers?"— John N. Gladstone[92]

Illustrations

PRAYING TO THE END.   Take the deeply moving example of Dr. W. E. Sangster. Already in the grip of the incurable illness that was to end his glorious ministry in its prime, he made his last public contribution as the Methodist Church Home Missions Leader. Characteristically, it was a passionate call to prayer: "Oh that God would give us a man who could call our people back to prayer, someone who could teach them how to pray. Perhaps that is our sorest need." Sangster's son, and biographer, comments: "In the passing of the few weeks he had become, though ill and incapable of active work, the man he had longed for, leading

[92]*All Saints and All Sorts*

the movement from his sick bed."—John N. Gladstone[93]

WHO NEEDS OUR PRAYER? Billy Sunday, the evangelist, preparing for a great city-wide mission, sent to the mayor of the city requesting a list of people who were in need of special prayer. The mayor—surely a man of imagination—sent him the city directory.— John N. Gladstone[94]

SUNDAY: MAY SECOND

LECTIONARY MESSAGE

Topic: The Disciplined Heart
TEXT: John 14:1–10
Other Readings: Acts 7: 55–60; Ps. 31:1–5, 15–16; 1 Pet. 2: 2–10

Troubled hearts left unattended lead to a troubled life. Distress left unresolved dismantles our ability to meet life's demands creatively and responsibly. Jesus does not criticize us for having troubled hearts; rather, he shows us how to discipline our hearts into God's peace. This context gives us the diagnostic cause of the disciples' depression. The sweet fellowship of the private Passover celebration had been disturbed. First, Jesus had declared that one of them was a betrayer. Then he refused to lie politely about Peter's pending failure of nerve. Jesus had ruined his own dinner by speaking family secrets! No disfunctionality is allowed in the Father's family! No secrets to make us sick as long as Jesus is Lord! Especially because this was his farewell dinner with those he loved. The comprehension of his pending departure cut like a cold scalpel.

But now that the truth had laid open the disciples' hearts, Jesus showed the disciples, and shows us, how to heal their hearts with hope. He dares us to face down our fears with faith in God and in him. "Believe in God, believe also in me" (14:1). This passage could alternately be translated, "You believe God, so now also believe in me." With this injunction Jesus gave instruction. He instructed the disciples in how to out-faith their fears. Within this instruction we can discover six truths by which trust disciplines the heart. We can trust that:

I. *The Father has a big house.* Jesus said, "In my Father's house are many rooms." The Greek word often translated *mansion* in Eng-

lish translations actually means *abodes, resting places,* or *bedrooms.* The disciples were used to Jesus referring to the Temple as the Father's house (John. 2:16). His explanation for cleansing the Temple came with a sense of a son's right to carry out the will of his father in his father's house. So the disciples were aware of the intent of Jesus to arrange God's house according to the Father's will. They also were used to the striking manner of divine address used by Jesus. He characteristically addressed God as *abba,* which was the Aramaic household name that little children used to address their own biological fathers. Could not the Son invite his friends for a sleepover in the Father's big house? We can trust that:

II. *Disciples have a place in the Father's house.* In the book of Revelation, John paints the conclusion of history as a wedding feast. Redeemed humanity is the bride-to-be at last united with Christ as the groom. Could the comforting words of Jesus, "I go to prepare a place for you, and when I am finished, I will return for you that you may be where I am also," have been the customary words spoken following an engagement dinner by the groom to his future bride? Words like these would be spoken to comfort a fearful bride as to the pending separation and its joyful ending. There are only two methods to managing distress: the world's way and God's way. The world's way is to seek elimination of the external causes of stress. God's way is to discipline the distress by meditating on our future with God. Hope heals the heart and restores our ability to control our lives. Hope counts on the faithfulness of Jesus. So we can trust that:

III. *Jesus goes ahead to prepare a place for us in the Father's house and will return for us when it is ready.* All separation is painful, but meaningful separation is bearable and even strengthen-

---

[93]*All Saints and All Sorts*

[94]*All Saints and All Sorts*

ing. The pending departure of Jesus was to prepare a place in which there would never again be separation. Troubled hearts are manageable when we believe in Christ's heavenly provision for us. He goes ahead to prepare a place for us.

a. *We manage our troubled hearts by trusting in the motivation of Jesus.* He is motivated to prepare a place for us so that we might be with him forever. We always prepare for the coming of the ones we love. Our separation anxiety becomes meaningful as we know we are loved and prepared for by the Lord.

b. *Hope is the capacity to manage troubling of the heart.* Hope enables the self to steer by God's chart through life's storms. The men who heard these words were in need of hope. They had given up their places of comfort and career to be with him. They had no place but with him. His promise gave hope. If we believe the provision and motivation of Jesus, then we must go on to believe also his instruction. We must trust that:

IV. *Jesus is the way to the Father's house.* John 14:6 is a pivotal New Testament text for understanding Christianity. When interrupted for clarification about the way to the Father's house, Jesus makes the following self-declaration, "I am the way, the truth, and the life." Some commentators suggest fusing the three predicates into "I am the way to true life." With this statement, however it is translated, Jesus moves beyond being merely a good teacher or a great man. With this declaration, Jesus must be understood as C. S. Lewis insisted, as either a megalomaniac, a liar, or the unique Son of God. His words make an exclusive religious claim upon our ears, which are so used to inclusive and pluralistic religious claims.

We are told by others that there are many ways to the Father's house. However politically correct it may be to say otherwise, it is Christologically correct to affirm Jesus as the only way to the Father's house. "No one comes to the Father's house except through me" (John. 14:6). If you will not have the Son, then you will not have the Father. Such is the will of the Father. To know the Son is to know the Father. What human father would ever think well of anyone who gave poor treatment to his son or daughter? To love the Son is to love the Father. To know the Son is to know the Father. We must believe that:

V. *The words and works of Jesus are the very words and works of God.* Jesus reveals God. To know Jesus is to know God as God wants to be known. God was in Christ revealing himself to humanity in a definitive, transforming way. Jesus said, "Anyone who has seen me has seen the Father" (v. 9). This revelation demands our response of faith. The miraculous works and actions of Jesus are meant to validate that the words of Jesus are the Father's own words. "It is the Father, living in me, who is doing his work." The words of Jesus are the reliable instruction to the Father's house. Jesus is the way to the Father's house. The unity of the Father and the Son means that the Son comes to bring us to the Father's house. Jesus is heaven's open house. However, God has even greater plans still, because Jesus is returning to the Father. So we can also trust that:

VI. *The words and works of Jesus will continue in the words and works of the disciples.* Men and women will ever find the way to the Father's house because God and Son will be known through the ministry of the disciples. Prayer in Jesus' name will give the disciples access to the very words and works of God. "I will do whatever you ask in my name, so that the Son may bring glory to the Father." The glory the Father seeks is the restoration to himself of those who were lost through sin and rebellion. The glory the Father seeks is that found in the repentant human heart. We experience God's pleasure through forgiveness of our sins. We experience God's pleasure as assurance of reception into the Father's house through trust in his Son.

The mission of the Church is to bring the words and works of God to a lost world, that they might know that Jesus is the way to the Father's house. Jesus is the way to the big house of heaven.—Rick K. Durst

Illustrations

A NEW HEART. After an extensive recovery following heart transplant surgery, a beloved Santa Barbara pastor at last returned to the pulpit and congregation. During the service a mother quietly explained to her young daughter what had happened to the pastor and that he now had a new heart. This explanation caused some theological distress within the mind of the six-year-old.

She resolved it by asking the pastor the following question at the end of the service: "Pastor, now that you have a new heart, do you have to ask Jesus to come into your heart again?"—Rick K. Durst

CHANGES AND CHANCES.   Do not look forward to the changes and chances of this life in fear; rather look to them with full hope that, as they arise, God, whose you are, will deliver you out of them. He has kept you hitherto—do you but hold fast to His dear hand, and He will lead you safely through all things; and, when you cannot stand, He will bear you in His arms. Do not look forward to what may happen tomorrow; the same everlasting Father who cares for you today will take care of you tomorrow, and every day. Either He will shield you from suffering, or He will give you unfailing strength to bear it. Be at peace, then, and put aside all anxious thoughts and imaginations.—Francis de Sales

SERMON SUGGESTIONS

Topic: Healthful Living
TEXT: Dan. 1:1–21
(1) *Then:* Daniel and his colleagues showed that disciplined living is superior. (2) *Always:* A life of prudent habits will lead to personal and social fulfillment. (3) *Now:* (a) Temptations to weakening or destructive lifestyles are all about us. (b) God helps and prospers those who resist such temptations.

Topic: New Life in Christ
TEXT: Rom. 12:1–2
(1) Its source. (2) Its purpose. (3) Its requirements. (4) Its means of attainment.

Hymn Suggestions

1. "God of Our Life," Hugh T. Kerr (1996); SANDON, Charles H. Purday (1860)
The psalmist reminds us that our times are in God's hand. This twentieth-century hymn acknowledges God to be the God of all times, past, present, and future. Its regular periodic structure makes it suitable for antiphonal singing.
2. "We Are God's People," Bryan Jeffery Leech (1976); SYMPHONY, Johannes Brahms (1877); arr. Fred Bock (1976)

Based in part on the passage in 1 Peter 2:2–10, this hymn could logically follow the Epistle reading.
3. "When I Can Read My Title Clear," Isaac Watts (1797); PISGAH, trad. Amer. melody, Kentucky Harmony (1816)
One of Watts's finest hymns contemplating heaven, it can be sung in connection with the Gospel reading (John 14:1–14) with its assurance of not only the life hereafter, but also of the only way to secure it, through Jesus, the way, the truth, and the life.
4. "Christ Is the World's Light," Fred Pratt Green (1968); CHRISTIE SANCTORUM, Paris Antiphoner (1681)
This contemporary hymn of praise asserts in its first stanza, if we have seen Christ, we have seen the Father. The hymn bathes this and other thoughts about Christ in an outpouring of "Glory to God on High."—Hugh T. McElrath

Worship Aids

CALL TO WORSHIP.   "Thou art my rock and my fortress; therefore for thy name's sake lead me, and guide me" (Ps. 31:3).

INVOCATION.   O God, you are our advocate and friend, give us sensitive souls today in the presence of your Word and may its precepts and saving power find a lasting place in our lives.—Donald Macleod[95]

OFFERTORY SENTENCE.   "God was making all mankind his friends through Christ. God did not keep an account of their sins, and he has given us the message which tells how he makes them his friends" (2 Cor. 5:19 TEV).

OFFERTORY PRAYER.   Father, you have given us all that we possess. Grant us the grace to honor your gift with one of our own as we return a portion of our bounty for the glory of your kingdom in all the world.—Henry Fields

PRAYER.   O Savior of the world, in whom we find love to live and faith to die, we have

[95] *Princeton Pulpit Prayers*

your word that if you would be lifted up from the earth, you would draw all of us to yourself. Unveil for us afresh the "wondrous Cross on which the young Prince of glory died" so we shall see and feel how love was given to the loveless and in dying, desolate and forsaken, you yielded your soul to God. Help us in our time to die more and more to self and to live daily unto righteousness. Give us to trust more earnestly in your work of grace and through it, as in ages past, may all loyal hearts be heirs of your fullness and once and for all set free. Keep us and possess us as your own forever and may we live to the end in the solemn thought that they who die believing die safely through your love. These things we say in the name of the Father and of the Son.—Donald Macleod[96]

Sermon: So Far, So Good

TEXT: 1 Sam. 7:12–17

"Historical landmarks," we call them— brass plates posted at significant stopping places all over the land, with a synopsis of some historical event or person connected to the place. While you are stretching your legs or taking in the view, you can expand your knowledge of history and add a bit of trivia to your memory for future reference. Who knows when you might need information about what happened here in 1798? More important is the sense of history that comes from being in the very place where a noteworthy event has occurred. Words on the page of a history book cannot quite compare with seeing the lay of the land, a building, or a tree where an event in history took place.

I. *Spiritual landmarks direct your paths.* The practice is not new. The Jews worshiped the God who acts in history. Because historical knowledge was basic to faith, the landmarks of national memory had not only educational but also ritual importance. Samuel named the place Ebenezer, "stone of help." If for no better reason, we now have a textual landmark for the strange phrase, "Here I raise mine Ebenezer; hither by thy help I'm come," in the hymn. The story stands in the early records of Jewish history as an explanation of a landmark on the road between Mizpah and Jeshanah. Long after the smoke and dust of

[96] *Princeton Pulpit Prayers*

battle had settled on the landscape and all of the principals in the conflict had become one with the ancestors, Samuel wanted the children who passed by this place to be reminded of their debt to their spiritual heritage. Yet Samuel's concern was not for historical trivia. The landmark stood as a reminder of the faithfulness of God. More than a memory of the national heritage, this place was marked as a sacred altar. Here the people remembered their dependence on God.

Samuel is no longer a child. He has assumed the role to which he was called by God, and he is responsible for the spiritual welfare of the nation. Perhaps this is also a reminder of life before kings, when the land had to be claimed inch by inch. Ebenezer is about the national heritage, but I cannot help but believe that Samuel's personal pilgrimage is represented here. Samuel did not initiate his own existence. His life was the issue of the marriage of Elkanah and Hannah, but something more basic than biology contributed to Samuel's existence. His life began in the fervent prayer of his mother. His life developed in the house of worship, attending to the spiritual needs of the people. In spite of personal failures, Eli must have contributed significantly to the person Samuel became. This stone on the landscape of Israel was not just about a war with the Philistines. It was a pause to look back over a life lived to fulfillment, to say, "Thus far the Lord has helped us."

II. *Spiritual landmarks are humbling.* Where are your Ebenezers? What are the spiritual landmarks on which your life has turned? Do you have a sense of having been brought to this place by a power greater than yourself? The recognition of the Ebenezers in life is a sure sign of growing up. All of us begin as children with a sense that everything of importance in this world began with "my" birth, but maturity opens up a larger world of friends and family to whom we owe both our existence and our development. Dale Moody recalled his childhood fear at discovering that this existence depended on events in history. If his mother and father had never met, he would not have come to be. To discover that your existence is totally dependent on the decisions of people who were here before you were born is humiliating. We are totally powerless before the acts and decisions of our ancestors, yet we are beneficiaries and victims of those decisions.

One of my favorite passages out of the Old Testament is the posting of the law in Deuteronomy and the warning, "Take care that you do not forget the Lord your God." The danger is clearly registered in conversations people have with the mirror. The writer suggests that the people might be prone to talk with themselves and to have the audacity to suggest, "My power and the might of my own hand have gotten me this wealth." That is the child's view of life. Only with spiritual maturity does one come to the conclusion, "thus far the Lord has helped us."

Steven Covey's formula for success majors on the choice of our paradigms. A paradigm is a vision of the shape of our future, a mental image of where we want to be and how we want to live. Our models of the future are never born in a vacuum. All of us are imitations of people who have gone before us. If I did not believe in our spiritual power to overcome the past, I could not possibly believe in the transforming grace of God. Yet we are the product of the past—biologically, emotionally, spiritually. Our paradigms are either the direct inheritance of models who have gone before us or a combination of people who have set in motion the events that have led us to this moment. In every case we have to come to the humbling conclusion of the psalmist: "It is he that has made us, and we are his." The inaccurate statement of the King James translation is also true, "and not we ourselves." The people who have touched our lives are the hands of God shaping and directing our future.

III. *We are heirs according to the promise of God.* In *Roots* Alex Haley contributed more than another historical novel about the terrors of slavery. He posted a landmark in his own debt to history, and he registered the importance of heritage to personal identity and dignity. The insult of treating a person as property, something to be bought and sold, to be bred, beaten, and slaughtered like cattle has always been viewed as the ultimate offense of slavery, but Haley saw something more. To cut off family, to steal a people's sense of inheritance, is an even greater insult.

Paul brought his Jewish sense of history to the Gentile situation of Galatian Christians in his declaration that we are "heirs according to the promise." Gentile Christians received their inheritance through faith in Christ. Lacking a sense of history, they lacked a sense of themselves. Paul's mission to the Gentiles began with heritage. If our children are to know who they are, we must set the landmarks of faith before them. Our task is never final, complete within itself. We are always laying the foundation on which our children will live and build toward the Kingdom of God.—Larry Dipboye

Illustrations

THE TRIUMPH OF MATURITY.   The best insurance against melancholia, depression, and a sense of futility in old age is the development of wide horizons and the cultivation of mental elasticity and interest in the world. Unlike the flesh, the spirit does not decay with the years. Many of the happiest individuals in the world are men and women in their sixties, seventies, or eighties, who have contributed richly to the world's work during their maturity, and at the same time have cultivated sufficient awareness and interest in the undying cultural activities to make their leisure a delight.—W. Béran Wolfe[97]

THE BEST.
Grow old along with me!
The best is yet to be,
The last of life for which the first was made.
Our times are in His hand
Who saith: "A whole I planned,
Youth shows but half; trust God:
see all nor be afraid."
            —Robert Browning (1812–1889)[98]

[97] *How to Be Happy Though Human*
[98] "Rabbi Ben Ezra," in *Poems*

SUNDAY: MAY NINTH

LECTIONARY MESSAGE

Topic: The Way of Obedience
TEXT: John 14:15–21
Other Readings: Acts 17:22–31; Ps. 66:8–20; 1 Pet. 3:13–22

If Jesus is the way to true life, and he is, then that way is the way of obedience to the will of the Father. Jesus teaches this way of obedience in the second half of John, chapter 14.

I. *Love expresses itself through obedience.* "If you love me you will obey my commands." Love for Christ demonstrates itself as obedience to the commands of Christ (v. 15). The obedient authenticate their love for Christ through acts of obedience. Obedience is our opportunity to love the Lord in a way that he appreciates.

a. *Relationship engenders influence.* New affections have power to change behavior. First loves transform personality. Jesus had expectations for the devotion he had developed in the disciples. He expected their devotion to enable his commands to influence their choices. Leaders do well to learn this principle from Jesus. Love is the path to influence. Jesus loved the disciples into loving and obeying. Real leadership is the accumulation of relational influence. The resulting obedience has an additional effect.

b. *Obedience overcomes doubts.* Only of the disobedient does Christ ask, "Do you love me?" If doubt is your experience today, obedience may be your solution. Is there some act of obedience you know Christ is now expecting of you, yet you have been reluctant to carry through? Obey that command immediately and you may well experience a new sense of Christ's nearness. The disciples in this text were riddled with questions and doubts. Jesus points them to obedience as the antidote to doubts. But such obedience will require help.

II. *Consistent obedience requires counsel and company.* Jesus was the obedient son. He learned obedience even though he was a son (Heb. 5:8). Out of his own experience of obedience, Jesus learned that consistent obedience in living and serving requires divine company and counsel. All the Gospel accounts of Jesus' baptism describe the descent of the Spirit upon Jesus. The Spirit counseled and accompanied Jesus into the wilderness and into his ensuing ministry. The Holy Spirit was Jesus' counselor and companion from the beginning. Now Jesus promises that the Spirit will be sent to the obedient. The Spirit of truth will be sent by the Father at the request of the obedient Son. "I will ask the Father and he will give you another Counselor" (v. 16). The enduring and enabling Spirit of God guides the obedient in the true way.

a. *The obedient experience counsel and company.* The obedient will not be forsaken. They will be accompanied. They will not lack for divine fellowship. The word translated *counselor* literally means "one who comes alongside of." The obedient will not lack for counsel, for the one who accompanies counsels us in truth. He can do this because he is the Spirit of truth. The need created by Christ's absence will be met by the Spirit's presence. His presence will be reliable. He will forever be our mentor in the truth.

b. *The obedient are counseled in the truth.* We must remember that to follow Christ is to admit to and side with the truth in so far as we know it. The disciples of Christ are ever to be marked as truth speakers and truth affirmers, no matter the cost to their personal concerns. Christian lives speak the whole truth and nothing but the truth because God the Spirit helps them to do so. The obedient know where to stand because they have the Spirit of truth to guide them. The obedient find the courage to stand for truth because they have the Spirit of Christ for their constant companion. We need not even worry about the words we will speak in public witness, for the Spirit will make us articulate in defense of the truth about Christ (Matt. 10:19–20).

III. *Consistent obedience requires discernment.* "Before long, the world will not see me anymore, but you will see me." Christian obedience is not blind faith; rather, it is discerning faith. There are eleven Greek verbs for *seeing*. This seeing is the careful perusal of the details revealed. The obedient are able to observe God's presence and activity in the world. The believers will see the resurrected Jesus (v. 19). They will see and know the Spirit of truth. The Father and the Son will manifest themselves to the obedient (v. 21).

a. *The world, on the other hand, is blind to the things of God.* It is the obedient ones who testify that "once I was blind but now I can see" (John 9:15). Jesus asserted that the world would not accept the Spirit of truth because it could not see, discern, or even realize the truth. It is the world that operates in blind obedience to the ways that seem right but the end of which is death (Prov. 14:12).

b. *Obedience is encouraged by seeing what God is doing.* Revelation is God disclosing himself to the ones he trusts and loves. "Whoever has my commands and obeys them, he is the one who loves me. He who loves me will be loved by my Father, and I too will love him and show myself to him" (v. 21). The world has no capacity for spiritual discernment. Spiritual discernment is the result of divine indwelling. "On that day you will realize that I am in the Father, and you are in me and I am in you" (v. 20).

c. *The obedient discern what the world cannot.* The obedient are the habitat of the triune God. God the Father, Son, and Spirit tabernacle with the obedient. The obedient know God because God lives with them, loves them, and shows them what he is doing.

Through obedience we come to know God intimately. Remember the mobilizing words of Daniel 11:32 (KJV): "They that know the Lord their God shall do exploits." Are you ready to do exploits? Commit yourself to Jesus and follow him in the way of obedience.—Roderick K. Durst

Illustrations

THE TRIAL.   The Catholic layman G. K. Chesterton once declared, "It's not that Christianity has been tried and found wanting, but that Christianity has been tried and found difficult."—Roderick K. Durst

THE HOLY SPIRIT AND OBEDIENCE.   Recently, someone speaking of the value of religious belief for physical health and healing said that we humans are "wired for God." This is certainly true for the experience of salvation in its various dimensions and dramatically so in the experience of regenera-

tion. Two important factors are at work, therefore, when we proclaim the gospel: human need and the precise remedy for that need. If this is true, then our sometimes frantic anxiety about communicating effectively with those to whom we witness should be eased and our cheap efforts to "make" the gospel relevant must be brought into question. While every laudable effort should be made to honor the Christ of the gospel by our care in presenting the message, we can take comfort in the fact that in the end it is the work of the Holy Spirit, the Advocate, who proves the world "wrong about sin and righteousness and judgment" (John 16:8 NRSV).—James W. Cox[99]

SERMON SUGGESTIONS

Topic: Essentials of Spiritual Leadership
TEXT: Joshua 10:1–9
(1) Confidence in the power of God (vv. 1–2). (2) Appreciation of the promise of God (vv. 3–4). (3) Dependence on the presence of God (vv. 5, 6, 9). (4) Obedience to the Word of God (vv. 7–8).—James Brage[100]

Topic: A Sermon in a Hymn
TEXT: "O Jesus, I Have Promised," by John Ernest Bode
(1) Stanza 1: commitment. (2) Stanza 2: comfort of the Divine Presence. (3) Stanza 3: lordly guidance. (4) Stanza 4: grace to obey.—Suggested by Donald Soper[101]

Hymn Suggestions

1. "To God Be the Glory," Fanny J. Crosby (1875); TO GOD BE THE GLORY, William H. Doane (1875)
Reflecting the spirit of the Psalter reading (66:8–20), this popular song is one of the few of its genre that voices objective praise for God's mighty acts.
2. "Because He Lives," Gloria and William J. Gaither (1971); RESURRECTION, William Gaither (1971)
"Because I live, you will live also" (John 14:19) is the basic theme of this popular

[99]In *Review and Expositor*
[100]*How to Prepare Bible Messages*
[101]*Aflame with Truth*

gospel song that would be effective when sung after the Gospel reading.

3. "All Authority and Power," Christopher Idle (1971); UNSER HERRSCHER, Joachim Neander (1680)

This modern hymn magnifies the thought in 1 Peter 3:22 that Christ has gone into heaven, where he has all authority over angels and all other powers.

4. "God Our Author and Creator," Carl P. Daw Jr. (1985); JEFFERSON, Southern Harmony (1835); harm. John Ferguson (1973)

Appropriate for many of the ideas in Paul's sermon in Athens (Acts 17:22–31), this contemporary hymn lends itself to antiphonal singing between two parts of the worshiping group or between choir and congregation.—Hugh T. McElrath

Worship Aids

CALL TO WORSHIP. "Blessed be God who has not turned away my prayer, nor his own faithful love from me" (Ps. 66:20 NJB).

INVOCATION. "As a mother stills her child," so you have often calmed the wild waves of our lives, O God. You have faithfully heard our cries. Now hear us as we pray in this quiet time, and let the remembrance of past mercies make your love real, healing, and challenging in this time of worship.

OFFERTORY SENTENCE. "Offer the right sacrifices to the Lord, and put your trust in him" (Ps. 4:5 TEV).

OFFERTORY PRAYER. Teach us, good Lord, to serve thee as thou deservest: to give and not to count the cost; to fight and not to heed the wounds; to toil and not to seek for rest; to labor and not to ask for any reward, save that of knowing that we do thy will.—St. Ignatius of Loyola

PRAYER. Eternal God, on this Mother's day we pause to thank you for the gift of the home. We thank you for the oasis it often provides. We thank you for the nurture of good parents, the openness of children to new adventures. Give us the courage to respond to life and commit ourselves to causes that give us meaning and purpose.

Give us this day the willingness to listen openly, as parents to our children, and to each other, when we and they have failed. Forgive us for wallowing in self-pity and being quick to condemn or blame instead of seeking to forgive and understand. We thank you for the joys that we have shared together. Teach us how to celebrate these joys more fully. We thank you also for the assurance of your presence with us even during the times of sorrow. Teach us how to learn from them. Give to us the grace to know how to embrace those we love. And in that embrace may we feel the nearness of your presence with us in both good times and difficult times. We thank you for the assurance that your spirit is ever present to sustain us and direct us.

Grant to those who are here today, parents or children, or those who are single, that we might be open to your love as we come waiting before your Spirit. We seek this day to know your direction and guidance in how to love better, as we look to Jesus Christ who loves us so much that he gave his all for us.—William Powell Tuck

Sermon: A Family Inventory

TEXT: 1 Sam. 2:12, 22–26; 1 Tim. 5:1–8

The apostle Paul, writing to young Timothy, touched on a problem they were evidently having in one of the early churches. Part of the problem centered on what to do with the widows who have no family to care for them. Some widows were obviously taking advantage of the situation, and some were not getting the proper support from the Christian community. One of the most interesting lines in that discussion is the last one, which I read in our text today. Paul puts the burden back on the children of the parents. He says: "If any one does not provide for his relatives, and especially for his own family, he has disowned the faith and is worse than an unbeliever." Paul tied the Christian faith together here with an awareness that how one treats family, parents, children, husband, and wife is evidence to the wider community of whether or not he or she has really understood the essence of what constitutes the Christian faith.

What I would like for us to attempt today is to see whether we can put some things on a checklist for a family inventory of our own.

I. *We need to make our homes a place where everyone feels accepted.* Each one wants to be accepted as an authentic person and appreciated for who they are and for what they do. In our society today there are so many places where we are not really accepted for who we are. Many seem to demand of us that we become somebody else or put on a kind of mask for them. We all hunger for a sense of feeling accepted.

II. *We need also on our list a sense of expectancy.* So much of life is lived as though it was all plain vanilla. For many of us there are no varieties of color in our life, and no sense of excitement or adventure, no awareness of something other than what has already been. Everything is so routine, so humdrum, and so daily. Parents need to create a sense of excitement in the lives of their children. And so do husbands and wives. Expectancy pulls us joyfully toward the future while routineness often leads to dullness and disinterest. What we have had, we remind ourselves, is not as good as it may be, because there is still an expectancy and excitement about the life that lies ahead of us.

III. *Third, we need to learn to listen to each other.* I do not mean that we are to talk more. I think we need to listen to one another and really hear what the other person is saying to us. Let us listen so that we do not let the other's conversation go in one ear and out the other. We must really genuinely listen to our children when they come to discuss a problem, need, hurt, or pain with us. When our wife or husband talks with us, we will learn to hear them when we really listen.

IV. *We also want to learn to understand one another.* We all long to have someone who understands our goals, ambitions, dreams, feelings, hurts, excitements, frustrations, and failures. All kinds of emotions bubble up within young people, children, parents, husbands, and wives. We can learn to get inside another's feelings and show we care. Understanding opens doors and removes barriers.

V. *There is also a drive to have a sense of security in our home.* That was a part of the issue that Paul was addressing in his letter to Timothy. In the early Church many of the widows felt insecure because they had no one to make provision for them in their old age. Of all places, our homes should be the place where security is realized. Small children want night lights, and some of them want

security blankets. We all want some kind of security blanket in one form or another.

VI. *We all also want and need recognition.* Every child, parent, husband, and wife needs some recognition for what they have done. Recognition says to a person, "I see you as a person of worth and importance." Who and what you are is significant to that person and that makes you feel good inside. You have been affirmed.

VII. *One of the most important things we need to do in our homes, though, is to give our children religious teachings, affirmations, and directions.* The home should be the central place where religious convictions are taught. It is the place where we have opportunity to teach our children through word and example that religion is important to us. We affirm that the worship of God and the ministry of his Church are important and essential to us and to them. Our children need to learn from us that following Christ is the central thing in our life.

One of the saddest things is for parents to telegraph to their children, either by not coming to church or by constant criticism or indifference, that religion is just for children. Religion is more caught than it is taught in a family. Children will learn very early whether or not the church, religion, God, and Christ are important to their parents. I hope they will learn that it is very important to you.

VIII. *I hope also that you and I can learn to admit that we are wrong* and say, I'm sorry. We expect our children to do this sometimes, and we often demand it of them. But sometimes as parents we need to say to our children, "I'm sorry." "I'm sorry, son, or daughter, but I really misunderstood that and I goofed. It was my mistake." Maybe we need to say to our husband or wife, "I was wrong, you were right. I really blew it. I didn't see it." It is difficult, but I think it is authentically Christian to be able to admit that one is wrong and attempt to start anew.

I hope that we can learn to make our homes Christian. We have gathered together in this church today, on this Mother's Day, to say that we want our home to be Christian. Let us begin to make a family inventory and put on it a checklist of things that we want to incorporate into our homes to make them more Christian. My prayer is that our home life may indeed reflect that we walk with Jesus Christ as Lord.—William Powell Tuck

Illustrations

DIFFERENCES.   A boy and a girl were walking down the street one day and the little girl said: "Don't you wish you could be a bird and flap your wings and fly up into the sky way off yonder someplace?" He said, "No. What I wish I could be is an elephant and squirt water through my trunk at you." Children have many goals, some known and some unknown verbally at a young age. We all have different kinds of wants and desires in what makes us who we are. We want to understand what constitutes another person and try to be more understanding and caring.—William Powell Tuck

IN LOCO PARENTIS.   I know that sometimes people who are good parents are not physical parents at all. I can think of a particular couple, Frank and Mary Marney. Frank was the executive director of the YMCA in the community where I lived. He served in that capacity for about forty years. He and his wife never had any children of their own, but Frank and Mary were parents to literally hundreds of children through their work in the YMCA and community programs. Many adults spoke about the "parental" guidance the Marneys gave to them when they were young.—William Powell Tuck

SUNDAY: MAY SIXTEENTH

LECTIONARY MESSAGE

Topic: Preparing for a Pentecost
TEXT: Acts 1:6–14
Other Readings: Ps. 68:1–10; 1 Pet. 4:12–14, 5:6–11; John. 17:1–11

Living happily ever after depends on what you are after. The book of Acts is an "after" book. It comes after the Gospels. It comes after Jesus rises from the dead. It tells what happens to the disciples and the Church after Jesus ascends back to heaven. However, chapter 1 is critical if the Church wants to live happily ever after, for the Church is apt to be after the wrong thing. In Acts 1:6–14, Jesus tells the first church what to be and what not to be after in order to live happily ever after.

I. *Avoid the desire to calendarize.* Do not be after the date for the Kingdom's coming. For the forty days following the Resurrection, Jesus had been appearing to the disciples. He had been teaching them about the Kingdom (v. 3). It was at his concluding appearance that the disciples asked, "Lord, are you at this time going to restore the Kingdom?" (v. 6) to which Jesus answered, "It is not for you to know the times or the dates the Father has set by his own authority" (v. 7).

a. *The Kingdom's coming is marked only on the Father's private calendar.* It is not for us to know the times or dates of Christ's return. We are not to allow ourselves to focus on the calendar. The timing of Christ's return is the Father's sovereign secret. Even as we draw near the year 2000, we must trust the Father's tim-

ing. He is never in a hurry and he is never late. He acts in the fullness of time (Heb. 1:1). He makes all things beautiful in his time (Eccl. 3:11). We must anticipate Christ's return without requiring a date.

b. *A genuine eschatology energizes Christian ethics and not Christian antics.* If we declare a date, then we will have forgotten the lessons of Church history that tie disillusionment, division, doctrinal heresy, and death to all who have set such dates. We must long and live for Christ's return without pressing him for a time frame. People who want the date only really want to know how long they have before they have to repent, or they want insider information to enable them to have first opportunity in a kingdom power grab.

II. *Avoid the desire to politicize.* If you want to live happily ever after, do not be after a crown or kingdom. "Lord, are you at this time going to restore the kingdom of Israel?" The disciples hungered for kingdom restoration in their time. They longed to see political authority exercised against their enemies and God's. They wanted the kingdom of this world when Jesus had told them that the Kingdom of God was not of this world (John 18:36). In their search for significance, the disciples sought for control through calendars and kingdoms.

We must anticipate Christ's return without desiring or requiring a political agenda. A genuine eschatology emphasizes the spiritual and not the political. The power God would have us be after is power to witness in the world to new life in Christ. Do you want to live happily ever after? Then don't be after an earthly restoration of the Kingdom. To be happy we must seek the Spirit.

III. *Anticipate the Spirit's empowerment to witness.* In verse 4, Jesus warned the disciples not to leave Jerusalem until they had received the gift of the Spirit. Now, in verse 8, which most scholars agree is the key verse to the book of Acts, Jesus promises, "But you will receive power when the Holy Spirit comes on you, and you will be my witnesses." The point of Christ's Ascension was the Father's sending the Spirit at the request of the Son (John 14:16, 28). The atoning work of the cross was to be proclaimed to the world by the Church with power from on high. This power was to mark and seal the disciples as belonging to Christ (Eph. 1:7).

a. *Never proceed without God's power.* Seek to achieve what requires God's power. God supplies according to his purpose. God's supply neither is outrun nor does it run out as long as we are proceeding according to his purpose. God feels no obligation to empower outside his purpose for the Church. We must stay on task if we wish his power. The primary task of the Church is to bear witness to Jesus Christ. His power is for witnessing to our world.

b. *God's power is sufficient to witness to our neighbors, to our nation, and to the Nepal.* Note that this power has a centrifugal force. Its coming enables concentric waves of influential witness for Christ. Its power enables cross-cultural ministry. Do you want to live happily ever after? Then seek after the power of God to witness at home, at work, and in the world.

IV. *Accept Christ's Ascension.* Having promised the disciples to send the Spirit down, Jesus went up to fulfill that promise. Verse 9 records that while they were watching, Jesus ascended up until clouds blocked him from their sight. Verse 11 records the angelic interpretation of this event: "This same Jesus, who has been taken from you into heaven, will come back in the same way you have seen him go into heaven." If we disciples are to live happily ever after and to be prepared for the coming baptism of the Spirit at Pentecost, we must make three observations about Christ's ascension into heaven.

a. *Ascent follows descent.* The ascent of Christ into heaven answers Christ's descent into hu-manity, humility, and crucifixion. The crown follows the cross. Triumph follows suffering. Reward follows service. Up follows down. This pattern characterizes Christ and it must characterize the Christian and the Church. This is the mind of Christ, which must be in us (Phil. 2:5). The prepositional phrase "into heaven" is repeated twice to emphasize that the measure of the ascent is more than equal to the measure of the descent into suffering and service. Present suffering for gospel service is nothing compared to the glorious future in God's presence. Jesus will initiate this reward at his return.

b. *The same Jesus who ascended will return for his disciples.* There is continuity of identity in eternity. Present recognition of and relationship with Jesus will be renewed at Christ's return. The dissolution of personal identity in eternity is not true. Relationships are lasting. Nothing can separate us from the love of God in Christ (Rom. 8:39).

c. *Accepting Christ's ascent results in expectation, obedience, and evangelism.* The angel asserted that "this same Jesus . . . will come back." There is no need to stand watching and waiting. Our best waiting for Christ's return is done in waiting for his Spirit to give us the power to be his witnesses to the world.

V. *Unite in prayer to prepare for Pentecost.* The disciples demonstrated assent to Christ's ascent and return by obedience to Christ's instruction. Jesus had instructed them to return to Jerusalem and await the advent of the Spirit. Luke records their obedience in detail. He even gives the attendance record of those involved in what became a ten-day prayer meeting. What a privilege to be named among those who prepare for a Pentecost through prayer. Luke emphasizes three essentials to this pivotal prayer meeting.

a. *Maximize attendance at prayer times to adequately prepare for Pentecost.* Luke states that "they all joined" in the prayer meetings. Is there some relation between the measure of participation and the measure of the power that God sends? Ten days of total attendance seems a small price to pay that three thousand might find salvation in Christ. Pentecost demands serious preparation. We undervalue uniting in prayer because we overvalue personal schedules. Prayerfulness for these disciples was faithfulness. Could our prayerlessness be our faithlessness and the cause of our powerlessness? Luke records two qualities of their prayerfulness worthy of our emulation.

b. *Match prayer meeting attendance with steadfast focus.* The original language of the passage indicates that their hundreds of prayers consistently focused in the same direction. They experienced consensus that the Father would keep his promise to send the Spirit. The Ascension of Christ would be successful.

c. *Match petition with praise.* The word Luke uses for *prayer* in this passage is the general word for *worship.* It suggests that proper honor is to be given before any asking is done. This *worship* word demands that we measure God's majesty before we ask of his treasury. The word also demands that gratitude be the abiding attitude of all the petitions. "Praise ye's" and "Thank ye's" should exceed all "Give me's."

Pentecost has a price. The price is paid in preparation. Prayer is the preparation. Any church may have a Pentecost of power for worship and witness. Personal calendars and kingdoms distract us from paying the price. To proceed without Pentecost is to minister without effect. God's work can be done only with God's power. United prayer is the preparation for God's power. Little prayer, little power. Much prayer, much power.—Roderick K. Durst

Illustrations

PENTECOST AND POLITICS.   In 324 A.D. Constantine established Christianity as the state church of the Roman empire. The state of the church then became one of political compulsion rather than spiritual conviction. Inspiration gave way to inquisition. Constantine enabled the persecuted church to become the persecuting church. Restoration to fellowship was replaced with retribution for rebellion. No longer could the Kingdom of God be distinguished from the kingdom of humankind. Pentecost had been politicized. —Roderick K. Durst

AN EMPOWERER.   To the disciples, the living Christ said, "You will receive power when the Holy Spirit has come upon you, and you will be my witnesses" (Acts 1:8a NRSV). The apostle Paul spoke of what Christ had accomplished through him "to win obedience from the Gentiles, by word and deed, by the power

of signs and wonders, by the power of the Spirit of God" (Rom. 15:18–19 NRSV). To the Corinthians he declared, "My speech and my proclamation were not with plausible words of wisdom, but with a demonstration of the Spirit and of power, so that your faith might rest not on human wisdom but on the power of God" (1 Cor. 2:4–5 NRSV). Again and again, it has been demonstrated in the history of the Church that at the growing edge of the Church's outreach, extraordinary demonstrations of the power of the Spirit have emboldened Christ's witnesses and enabled them to achieve remarkable results.—James W. Cox[102]

SERMON SUGGESTIONS

Topic: Prayer, Praise, and Proclamation
TEXT: Ps. 68:1–10, 34–35
(1) Prayer for justice. (2) Praise for providence. (3) Proclamation of God's power.

Topic: God's Wisdom for the Asking
TEXT: Jas. 1:5–8
By meeting three conditions, believers can obtain wisdom: (1) By recognizing that you lack it (v. 5). (2) By asking God for it (v. 6). (3) By believing that you will receive it (vv. 6–8).—Lloyd M. Perry and Faris D. Whitesell[103]

Hymn Suggestions

1. "Rejoice, Ye Pure in Heart," Edward H. Plumptre (1865); MARION, Arthur H. Messiter (1883)

Appropriate for a processional (for which it was originally written), this hymn, expressing the invitation to sing joyfully (in today's Psalter reading: Ps. 68:1–10, 32–35), could also serve as a call to worship (stanza 1), after which the congregation could make joyful response by singing the remaining stanzas.

2. "Alleluia, Sing to Jesus," William C. Dix (1866); HYFRYDOL, Rowland H. Prichard (c. 1830)

This Ascension hymn is effective when sung antiphonally. It could appropriately follow the reading of the lesson from Acts (1:6–14).

[102] *Review and Expositor*
[103] *Variety in Your Preaching*

3. "Give to the Winds Your Fears," Paul Gerhardt (1653); tr. John Wesley (1739); DIADEMATA, George J. Elvey (1868)

Reflecting the empowering words of 1 Peter 5:6–11, this important Wesley translation of Gerhardt's strong hymn could be sung prayerfully following the reading of the Epistle lesson.

4. "This Bond of Love," Otis Skillings (1971); BOND OF LOVE, Skillings (1971)

This simple chorus would be appropriately sung after the Gospel lesson (John 17:1–11: Christ's earnest prayer for unity among his followers).—Hugh T. McElrath

Worship Aids

CALL TO WORSHIP.   "Sing to God, celebrate his name, extol him who rides on the clouds, bless him, exult before him" (Ps. 68:4–5a Moffatt).

INVOCATION.   Let there be song in our hearts as we come before the Lord our God. Let there be praise on our lips as we enter into his everlasting presence. For the Lord our God is good, his mercy is everlasting and his truth endures unto all generations. Lord, if our hearts are heavy, may the praise of this people lift our burdens. If our lives are weary and worn with the cares of the day, may we find renewed strength in your presence as we come before you with expectation. If the future seems dark because of the many shadows that hide the sunshine of your grace, may the light of truth scatter the clouds and illuminate our hopes. In our worship let us experience the power and wonder known by those first followers of Jesus.—Henry Fields

OFFERTORY SENTENCE.   "If you offer food to the hungry and satisfy the needs of the afflicted, then your light shall rise in the darkness and your gloom be like the noonday" (Isa. 58:10 NRSV).

OFFERTORY PRAYER.   O God our Creator, our Judge, our Father, may love constrain us to do all that we ought to do in our stewardship, that joy may be in our hearts when we give and that your name may be glorified.

PRAYER.   Sometimes, Lord, we want to cry out in the silence. Sometimes it feels to us as though you have been silent too long—our ears strain for a healing word; our hearts long for a soothing touch. We want nothing so much as to be wrapped in your embracing arms. But our faith is small, and so we look where you can't be found. We listen to the nonsense and the static that passes for wisdom in our world. Forgive us our little faith. Forgive us our foolish attempts to satisfy our needs with lesser answers than you give. Teach us, loving Father, to trust your love. Remind us again to wait and to listen and to rest content in the assurance of your steadfast, eternal loving care. Help us, we pray, to reassure one another. Help us to reach out to one another. To be for one another your hands to soothe, your voice to comfort, your arms to embrace.

We pray for the families of this community, for the children among us who need to know a mother's love and a father's steadfast caring. We pray for the outcast of our community, those who need to understand the depth and breadth and height of your care. Make of us a church ever more sure of our mission, ever more eager to share ourselves, ever more willing to draw wide the circle of your love.—Ronald D. Sisk

Sermon: God Can Help You Hang In There

TEXT: Mark 4:31–32

The world is literally filled with people who are ready to give up. "I can't take this pressure much longer. I have just about reached the limits of my endurance." People who hurt and see no end to their pain often have difficulty wanting to live.

Early in the new movement, many people followed Christ. Who were they? The kids on the streets, sick people looking for a cure, desperate people looking for a friend, and poor people looking for anything or anyone. But to be really honest about it, the city fathers hardly gave Jesus the time of day, and Jesus' disciples would never qualify for Palestine's *Who's Who*. But Christ had a way of getting people attached to him. There was a winsomeness about him, a magnetism that drew people to him. He wasn't easy to leave. That doesn't mean that people didn't want to leave or give up. No doubt they did.

But if you're the leader, what do you say to someone who has doubts about the future? How do you encourage the discouraged?

How shall we picture the Kingdom of God, or by what parable shall we present it?

Those were the questions Christ asked, as if he were talking to himself. He said, in effect, "Fellows, I want to tell you about a kingdom and the way it is going to develop."

If you and I can understand the depth of meaning that is contained in that parable, perhaps we can gain the wisdom and strength that will enable us to hang in there when quitting might be easier.

I. *The dynamic power of life.* Jesus likened his Kingdom to a seed. It doesn't take a genius to know that there is an awesome power latent within any kind of seed. So long as the dynamic quality of life exists in an organism, the possibility for change and development exists.

Think of the things you'd like to see altered, the people you love and the changes you'd like to see made in their lives. That possibility for change exists as long as there is life.

When we think about a seed, we are looking at something with the ability to become more than what it is in its present form. What you see is not what you get. What you get can be far greater than anything you can see. The Kingdom dream is latent with power, just as the seed contains the power of life. Don't give up until God does.

II. *Don't misjudge the future by the present.* Maybe what we see at times isn't much. But let us not forget that the greatest life ever lived was once a babe "wrapped in swaddling clothes, lying in a manger" (Luke 1:12 KJV).

Jesus said to his friends, "Day after day, night after night, week after week, and month after month, the seed will grow and produce a plant large enough for birds to nest in its branches" (Mark 4:32, author's paraphrase).

Maybe the present doesn't look like much. It may be rather glum. You don't like what you presently have. Maybe you can see no future for yourself because of the circumstances. Don't misjudge potential.

Alcoholics have been rehabilitated. Those who have been drug dependent have gotten well again. Prodigal sons and daughters have repented and returned home. Saul, the persecutor of Christians, became Paul, the prisoner of the Lord Jesus Christ.

III. *An analogy to faith.* Faith means to hang on when there seems to be nothing on which to hang. The writer of Hebrews said, "Faith is the assurance of things hoped for, the conviction of things not seen" (11:1). But how can one be sure? Faith. How can one be certain? Faith. What keeps a person looking for something he cannot see? Faith. Our faith is a response to God's acts on our behalf. Signs of God's presence and greatness were given to Moses before he was commissioned to lead the people out of Egypt. Jesus came doing signs and wonders, and many responded to him. Faith is our response to the outward acts of God.

We plant seeds in faith, don't we? How do we know they will grow? Of course, we have the record of the past. Other seeds have grown. Our faith is based on reason, isn't it? We have confidence in the power of nature that is at work. There is something in the soil that will affect the seed and enable it to grow. Sunshine and rain do their part. Even the moon has an effect on the seed. All of these things are beyond our control, but they are necessary to a good harvest. Likewise in the spiritual realm, we can do everything possible to provide a climate for something to happen, but then we must surrender it to the hands of God.

People who are hanging in there have accepted that reality. When we have done all we can do, then we must leave the rest to God.

IV. *What about the darkness?* What about the dark times? Are there not times when you think perhaps God has forgotten you and your difficult situation?

Remember, when we plant the seed it spends a considerable amount of time underground, out of view of the naked eye, in the dark. Do we need to be reminded that just because it is out of sight does not mean it is doing nothing? Quietly but effectively, something is happening to the seed, something very important. Changes are taking place that you and I cannot see.

Maybe Jesus told his friends the story of the mustard seed because they could not see anything happening to indicate that a great kingdom was budding and developing. Maybe he was saying to them that God works just as well in the darkness as he does in the light.

Hanging in there can be done when we hang onto the promises of God. God can be trusted. God's word is his bond. As we study those words of his, spend time in prayer and contemplation, and exercise our faith in worship and service, strength comes to us. Learning to hang in there means learning to hang on to God.

Don't give up. Keep on believing in the one who has put life in the seed. He can make the mustard seed grow, and he can make your dreams come true.—Jerry Hayner[104]

Illustrations

A WORLD OF DIFFERENCE. Halford Luccock once told of an error that was made in the printed program of a performance of Handel's *Messiah*. In the "Hallelujah Chorus" the print read: "The Lord God Omnipotent Resigneth." *Resigneth* or *reigneth*? There is a world of difference between the two words. It's the difference between quitting and winning, failing and succeeding.—Jerry Hayner[105]

FAITH.   Starting in 1881, the College of William and Mary closed its doors for nearly seven years. Battles of the Civil War had been fought up and down the peninsula and had left the college physically in ruins. Although it struggled to keep going during the better time of reconstruction, financial catastrophe finally swamped it. But every morning during those seven barren years the school's president, Benjamin Stoddert Ewell, rang the chapel bell. There were no students. The faculty had disappeared. Rain seeped through the roofs of the desolate buildings. But President Ewell still rang the bell. It was a gesture of defiance. It was an act of faith! And there came a day when William and Mary opened its doors once more and grew into one of the outstanding educational institutions of the nation.—Cecil Taylor[106]

SUNDAY: MAY TWENTY-THIRD

LECTIONARY MESSAGE

Topic: Pentecost Is the Norm
TEXT: Acts 2:1–21

Other Readings: Num. 11:24–30; Ps. 104:24–34, 35b; 1 Cor. 12:3b–13; John 7:37–39, 20:19–23

Pentecost hounds us. Pentecost will not let us go. Is the Pentecost of Acts, chapter 2, the Big Bang used by God to start the Church of Christ after the first Easter? If so, we can hardly be expected to repeat the effectiveness of the initial explosion, can we? But what if Pentecost 30 A.D. was meant as the norm for the Church and not the initiation? Is there a possibility that God meant Pentecost as the norm for Christian worship? Let's take a fresh look at Acts, chapter 2, and restate its narrative in terms of the conditions required to make Pentecost the norm of Christian worship. Pentecost becomes the norm when we:

I. *Plan spontaneity.* Pentecost gives the appearance of spontaneity, but Pentecost is no more spontaneous than is incandescent light. When electrical energy is channeled through carefully laid wire and superbly manufac-

tured metal alloys, the result is an incandescent light that is remarkably brilliant, illuminating, and constant.

a. *Pentecost was planned.* Pentecost was planned by God the Father from before the beginning, enabled by the Atonement of the Son, and achieved by the operation of the Spirit. God previewed the Pentecostal prototype in the wilderness in about 1300 B.C. (Num. 11:24–30). There the Spirit that was upon Moses was distributed among seventy other leaders. This distribution of the Spirit empowered these consecrated leaders to speak God's word with prophetic accuracy and conviction. When Moses was asked whether he was threatened by this egalitarian distribution of the empowering Spirit, he made a majestic response: "Would that all of God's people were prophets and that God would put his Spirit on them" (Num. 11:29). Moses discerned intuitively that God planned to make Pentecost the norm for the people of God. The future Kingdom would be marked by distribution of the Holy Spirit.

b. *Pentecost was promised.* Pentecost was the Father delivering on his promise. Jesus told the disciples to "wait for the gift my Father promised" (Acts 1:4). He had also announced

---

[104] *Yes, God Can*
[105] *Yes, God Can*

[106] *Proclaim*

his intention to ask the Father to send the Spirit as the second counselor so that the disciples might walk in the truth (John. 14:16).

c. *Pentecost was prayed.* For ten days the committed company gathered, prayed, and worshiped. They developed a liturgy of anticipation of the Spirit's leadership. We too must plan and pray the liturgy to let the Spirit assert leadership. Liturgical planning does not mean you know what is going to happen on Pentecost. If you know everything that is going to happen, there is no room for expectation or anticipation. Worship planning and prayer anticipate an ardor of God that sets a new order for the Church. Pentecost becomes the norm when we:

II. *Order ardor and put ardor in order.* Many churches so fear wildfire that they put out any fire of enthusiasm and spontaneity. For such, the serendipity of the Spirit has been shortened to "pity" at best and "dip" at worst. Without ardor, worship is dead. Without order, worship is divisive. Pentecost is about living the healthy tension between order and ardor.

a. *Peter explained the fire of their ardor in terms of God's prophetic order.* When Pentecost becomes the norm, ardor is ordered by the Spirit through all generations and genders. Everyone experiences the zeal and thrill of leadership and ministry. Old men put aside reminiscences because they now dream God's future. Young men see the long-term vision. Sons and daughters speak God's truth with the accuracy and currency that all ears know as divine prophecy. Peter interpreted the multilingual manifestations on 30 A.D. as the promised fulfillment of Joel. "In the last days, God says, I will pour out my Spirit on all people" (Acts 2:17; Joel 2:28).

b. *Order ardor by ordaining the laity.* God was planning to pour out his Spirit on all his people. He was planning to ordain all members to be ministers of his Word. Pentecost is God the Spirit ordaining members into the ministry. People today want to participate. Participation magnifies meaning for the participant. Unleashing the laity will maximize participation and meaning in worship. Pentecost becomes the norm when we:

III. *Maximize participation.* Every believer present had a part to play on Pentecost. Every believer had the power to play their part. "All of them were filled with the Holy

Spirit and began to speak." Participation enables satisfaction and meaning in worship. Pentecost becomes the norm when every believer has a meaningful ministry to fulfill.

a. *We all fear what and whom we cannot control.* We would rather skip Pentecost because it holds no guarantees about with whom we will sit, what we will experience, and what ministry we will be doing. When Pentecost is dismissed by focusing on the wildness of unknown tongues, we miss the point of Pentecost.

b. *When every believer present was Spirit-filled, then every unbeliever present was able to hear the saving work of Christ praised in their own tongue (Acts 2: 6–12).* Far from chaos, Pentecost was a Spirit-administered event of worship evangelism. There is a direct connection between the fact that every believer present was Spirit-filled and spoke and the fact that three thousand were added to the church that day (Acts 2:4, 41). Little wonder that the apostle Paul commanded all believers to put themselves in the way of continuously being filled and directed by the Spirit (Eph. 5:18).

c. *This administration of the Spirit means all members are united in the Spirit-filling joy of the Risen Christ.* The administration of the Spirit also means that all believers are diversified in the specific ministries and manifestations that the Spirit gives and directs (1 Cor. 12:3b–13). Each speaks in a specific tongue different from that of their fellow believers. The Church is adequately organized only when its membership is ardorized into gifted ministry for the common good.

Pentecost becomes the norm when we:

IV. *Seek God's order through his ardor.* People who heard the Easter message proclaimed in a way they could understand asked for explanation. "What does this all mean?" (Acts 2:12b). Peter answered with the prophecy in Joel 2:28. This Pentecost was an eschatological event that God himself had planned and now was implementing. Peter used Joel's text to teach the hearers that Jesus was the Lord on whom they must call for salvation (Acts 2:21, 4:12). The time to call was the present because they had seen the Spirit poured out of those committed to Christ.

a. *Depend on whom he pours.* Wait for heaven's wind. "Not by will nor by strength, but by my Spirit says the Lord God" (Zech. 4:6). Effective Christian community comes only through Pentecostal power. The outer fruit of praise, witness, and ministry and the inner fruit of spiritual character are the magnetic evidences of Spirit-filled ardor. Such fruit enthrones the evangelizing presence of God so forcefully upon the visitors' hearts that they cry out for the Savior and salvation (1 Cor. 14:25).

b. *When Pentecost becomes the norm all members feel equally responsible to be aflame for Christ by daily surrender to his leadership.* Such members refuse to be antiworship agents. They will not participate as fleshly, carnal Christians. Pentecost becomes the norm because all members consider themselves as worship agents. They know that believer-inflamed worship is the engine of evangelism, ministry, and missions. Such people gladly hurl themselves as fire brands into holy surrender at the altar. When all believers present in a service are Spirit-filled, Pentecost becomes the norm of that congregation. When all members are Spirit-directed ministers, then outsiders visiting are apt to cry out for salvation.

The tragedy of Christendom is not its sins of passion. Nor is the tragedy of Christendom the contradiction created by its obvious attitudes. The tragedy of Christendom is that in the face of so much need, so little effectiveness is tolerated when so much power is available. Let us so surrender to Christ that he might make Pentecost our personal and congregational norm.—Roderick K. Durst

Illustrations

HANDS-OFF.   I recently heard a church growth lecturer say that in order to stimulate church growth, a pastor had to be willing to surrender the one thing that pastors want more, namely, control. God's utter involvement always demands a hands-off posture. This means that the greatest accomplishments of the church will not be our achievements. Neither will all our excellent sermons be fodder for career boasting. The sermons themselves will have a hands-off quality that enables the pastor to challenge and confront so that God may get on with his specific agenda for his world.—Calvin Miller[107]

GOD'S HANDS AND OURS.   The best weather for crops can be so carefully calculated that the vintners in California's San Joaquin Valley can know exactly how many very hot nights in a summer are necessary to the proper sugar content in the raisins. It is not thus with the harvest of souls. Even given a certain atmospheric condition, the yield itself is still in the hands of God. If one were to change the figure to a more crude parallel in baseball, this truth would be lifted up more accurately. Although players practice hitting for hours, and although the managers know well that a .350–average hitter is always a better basis for hope of a score, no given hitter can be *sure* of hitting at any given turn at bat. Whether or not there will be a hit and for how many bases is never within the power of human beings accurately to predict. There is no exact cause-and-effect relation between the hitter's effort and the result of any given stand at the plate. Success follows a plan beyond any human's precise wisdom.

Nevertheless, every batting coach knows that for certain hitters, certain stances, grips, and swings are more productive than others. The percentages over time reflect the value of good coaching, as well as the genius of the hitter.—Henry H. Mitchell[108]

SERMON SUGGESTIONS

Topic: The Rewards of Patience
TEXT: Ps. 40:1–3
(1) Assurance of God's concern. (2) Experience of God's faithfulness. (3) Joy in witness to God's goodness.

Topic: Perpetuating Pentecost
TEXT: Acts 1:14, 2:14a, 36–42
(1) Through fervent prayer. (2) Through faithful preaching. (3) Through an urgent call to decision and commitment. (4) Through guidance in Christian growth and service.

HYMN SUGGESTIONS

1. "O Worship the King," Sir Robert Grant (1833); LYONS, attr. to Johann M. Haydn (eighteenth century)

---

[107] *Spirit, Word, and Story*

[108] *Celebration and Experience in Preaching*

Based on portions of Psalm 104—an impassioned description of God the Creator and God's works—this fine hymn by an outstanding layman high in British government circles in the eighteenth century is a natural selection for the beginning of worship on this signal day.

2. "Come, Holy Spirit, Our Souls Inspire," attr. to Rabanus Maurus, (ninth century); VENI CREATOR SPIRITUS, plainsong; Vesperale Romanum, Mechlin (1848)

For ten centuries, this ancient hymn has been used to express the Christian longing to know the presence and power of the Holy Spirit as it was known originally on the day of Pentecost. In those churches not familiar with plainsong, this hymn could be sung by a choir as a call to worship or invitation to prayer.

3. "Every Time I Feel the Spirit," African-American spiritual; adapt. Melva Costen (1989); arr. J. T. Jones (c. 1989)

Gathering up the spirit of Pentecost, this spiritual could be used as a response to any one of the readings for this day.

4. "I Heard the Voice of Jesus Say," Horatius Bonar (1846); VOX DILECTI, John B. Dykes (1868)

In its second stanza, echoing the invitation of Jesus to come quench spiritual thirst with the water of life (John 7:37), this hymn would be effective if sung antiphonally—one group singing the first half of each stanza (minor key) and another group the second half (major key).—Hugh T. McElrath

Worship Aids

CALL TO WORSHIP.   "I will sing unto the Lord as long as I live: I will sing to my God while I have my being" (Ps. 104:33).

INVOCATION.   In your mercies, O Lord, you have given us this day and this hour to praise you. Help us to seize each moment to lift our hearts to you—in gratitude, in hope, and in renewed dedication.

OFFERTORY SENTENCE.   "Thine, O Lord, is the greatness, and the power, and the glory, and the victory, and the majesty: for all that is in the heaven and in the earth is thine; thine is the kingdom, O Lord, and thou art exalted as head above all" (1 Chron. 29:11).

OFFERTORY PRAYER.   Father of our Lord Jesus Christ, we thank you for the gift of your Son and for his willing obedience to you, which brought him to the cross. We thank you for the love for you and for us in it all. Now we bring our offerings to you as tokens of our gratitude.

PRAYER.   O Lord of all truth and love, the source and end of our believing and loving, we gather in your presence this hour as a community of faith and rejoice as we lift our voices in hymns and songs of praise. You alone are worthy of the homage of the whole human creation, and within the courts of this house we unite with those who love your name to sing blessing, honor, glory, and power unto your great Spirit forever and ever.

We thank you, our God, for this opportunity of separating ourselves from the clamor and clangor of the world, and for the privilege to take time and rest as we await the entrance of your living Spirit. We are your Church on earth, but our drooping faith tells us we need the baptism of your heavenly fire. We thank you for the gift of your dynamic presence, which can turn this time of worship into an hour of power, especially when souls are moved to aspire to holiness and to union with one another, to become forces of righteousness across the earth. We remember with gratitude that first Pentecost day when your Spirit breathed upon desolate and discouraged hearts and launched a movement that has changed the world. We bless you for that little company of disciples and fellow travelers who were of one mind in one place, and for their readiness to receive a living flame from the altar of heaven and to declare to all who would hope that salvation was near through Christ's death and risen power.

And now we ask from your gracious hand those special gifts that we need to extend your Kingdom and to keep our Christian mission strong and great. Purge us from evil and every wrongdoing and anoint us with a sure sense of duty and service. Pour fresh life into every part of our being so that our disordered conduct may give way to the harmony and beauty of your peace. Set our ideals and desires aflame with your undying love so that the reign of Christ may become a reality in every temple, home, and sanctuary, and especially in all the needy places of the earth. Revive, we pray, your Church in the midst of the years to become the means to righteousness and justice among all people everywhere, and bless with abundance the fruits of Christian service now and forever.— Donald Macleod[109]

Sermon: Under the Influence

TEXT: Eph. 5:18

Since the days when I first became a pastor, I have listened to many people weeping over marriages that dissolved because of drinking or drugs. You could tell stories of your own about people who died, or got in trouble with the law, or ruined their families, or just plain messed up their lives while "under the influence."

The best and happiest life is when your thoughts, emotions, and actions are affected by some other power, when you're under an influence that makes you someone you wouldn't otherwise be. The influence I'm talking about, though, isn't the power of alcohol or drugs; it's the power of the Spirit of God.

In Ephesians 5:18 the Bible says, "Do not get drunk on wine, which leads to debauchery. Instead, be filled with the Spirit." Scripture is making a shocking comparison here. Getting drunk and being Spirit-filled are different, of course, but by putting the two side by side, the Bible is saying that they are also comparable in some ways. When you get drunk, you do some things you wouldn't otherwise do; and when you're filled with the Holy Spirit, you also do some things you wouldn't otherwise do. In both cases, you're under the influence of another power.

On Pentecost the Christian church marks the day when the Holy Spirit came upon Jesus' disciples. When they were filled with the Spirit, they began to praise God and to speak of him in such a way that all who heard them reacted in one of two ways. They were either amazed at what they heard about the mighty wonder of God, or they made fun of the disciples and said, "They have had too much wine" (Acts 2:13).

So being under the influence is either a terrible and deadly thing or it's a life-giving

and joyful thing. It all depends what influence you're under. The Bible says, "Do not get drunk on wine, which leads to debauchery. Instead, be filled with the Holy Spirit."

Now, if you're like me, *debauchery* isn't exactly a word you use everyday. It means "to squander, to overdo, to go to excess, to waste, to throw away." Debauchery means throwing away money, throwing away time, throwing away energy, health, family, dignity, purity, intellect, oneself, even one's life. Living under the influence of alcohol leads to debauchery—trashing everything that matters. There's a sharp contrast between that kind of life and the Spirit-filled life.

Genuine Christianity isn't just a matter of words, it's a matter of power. Jesus didn't come into the world just to give us a new set of ideas. He came to give us new life, and to bring a new power to bear in our lives: the power of his Holy Spirit living within us.

Real Christianity is a matter of being under the influence of a person and a power, not just looking at words on a page and reciting doctrinal formulas. The Bible's words are marvelous, and doctrinal formulas can be very helpful, but Christianity is more than just words. It's new life and power as you are filled with the Spirit and come under the influence of Jesus. We could almost say that getting drunk is the evil twin of being filled with the Holy Spirit.

Just before the Bible speaks in Ephesians 5 of being filled with the Spirit, it says, "Be very careful, then, how you live—not as unwise but as wise, making the most of every opportunity, because the days are evil. Therefore do not be foolish, but understand what the Lord's will is" (5:15–17). Wise, clear thinking that sees God's will—that's what happens when you're under the influence of the Holy Spirit.

The Spirit opens your mind to the deep things of God, things that have always been there but that you never saw until you came under the influence of the Spirit. In fact, if we are filled with the Spirit, the effect on our thinking is so great that it can be said that "we have the mind of Christ" (12:16).

When you're under the influence of the Spirit, you don't try to run from sorrows or look for a way to pretend they're not there. Instead, the Spirit helps you to face your sorrows and moves you to rejoice anyway, be-

[109]*Princeton Pulpit Prayers*

cause you belong to the Lord Jesus Christ. The Bible says, "We rejoice in the hope of the glory of God. Not only so, but we also rejoice in our sufferings. . . . And hope does not disappoint us, because God has poured out his love into our hearts by the Holy Spirit, whom he has given us" (Rom. 5:2–5). —David Feddes

Illustrations

THE FEAST.   Pentecost has Easter as its premise. The experience of the creative and therefore immortal spirit of life in us is nothing other than the new experience of the whole of life in the light of the resurrection. For this experience of the Spirit is the feast of a life that conquers death. It is the feast of a life that no longer knows any want. It is the

feast of the rapturous, overflowing divine joy of living.—Jürgen Moltmann[110]

THE CONTRAST.   Draw a contrast between two kinds of gatherings—a pagan gathering and a Christian gathering. The pagan gathering is apt to be a debauch. It is a significant thing that we still use the word *symposium* for a discussion of a subject by a number of people. The Greek word *sumposion* literally means a drinking party. Once A. C. Welch was preaching on this text: "Be filled with the Spirit." He began with one sudden sentence: "You've got to fill a man with something." The heathen found his happiness in filling himself with wine and with all the pleasures which are worldly pleasures; the Christian found his happiness in the fact that he was filled with the Spirit.—William Barclay[111]

SUNDAY: MAY THIRTIETH

LECTIONARY MESSAGE

Topic: The Mission of the Trinity

TEXT: Matt. 28:16–20

Other Readings: Gen. 1:1–2:4a; Ps. 8; 2 Cor. 13:11–13

The triune God is on a mission. Redemption is that mission. God has set himself the work of reaching and redeeming the creation lost to him through human rebellion and self-centeredness. The Bible is the inspired record of the minutes and motions of God's mission activity. Any analysis of those mission minutes must conclude that God never works alone. God develops mission teams and partners. God's decision to redeem includes his decision to recruit the redeemed onto his mission team. The redeemed are commissioned to team with God to move his redemptive mission forward and outward. Matthew 28:16–20 concisely words that *co-mission*. This great commission statement requires five responses of any who would become a missionary with the Triune God.

I. *Mobilize under the authority of Christ.* "All authority in heaven and on earth has been given to me" (v. 18). These words are the last words in the Gospel of Matthew. They record the scope of the authority of the Risen Christ. Jesus identified his rank before he directed

his disciples for mission. What Christ had surrendered in order to make atonement for sin had now been restored. His obedience had been answered with exaltation from God the Father. This Jesus whom the disciples had come to know now had authority more than sufficient to support his disciples on the mission he was about to commission.

These words about Christ's authority call us to worship before we evangelize. Worship energizes evangelism. Worship encourages evangelism. Commission is given to disciples who have witnessed the reality of Christ's death and Resurrection and have responded with worship. The commission is to those who have responded to the Risen Jesus by confessing, "My Lord and my God" (John 20:28). Affirmation of such authority enables us to evangelize.

2. *Evangelize all with the gospel of Christ.* Verse 19 is traditionally translated, "Go and make disciples of all nations." However, it could also be translated "as you are going" or even "in your going, make disciples of all nations." We must not make the mistake of missing the main verb of the commission, "to

---

[110] *The Power of the Powerless*
[111] *The Letters to the Galatians and Ephesians*

make disciples." If the main thing is to remain the main thing, then the Church must evaluate itself on whether or not it can point to people who are following Christ today, not followers of Christ yesterday. To disciple involves informing and infecting persons with the story and meaning of Jesus' life. All members are responsible to fulfill this command of Christ. If we aim to please the Master, we must aim to reach the unreached.

a. *Evangelize by targeting the unreached.* Contemporary missiologists have identified the unreached but reachable. Their studies show that about 1.6 billion people living between the fortieth and the tenth parallels north of the equator had little or no access to the gospel. Living within this global corridor are 2,161 unreached language groups, each having at least 100,000 speakers. O, for these two thousand tongues to sing our great redeemers praise! There is only one source of missionaries sufficient in our generation to complete the unfinished task of making disciples of these peoples. Our church members must become missionaries. Members must personalize and mobilize the great commission.

b. *Evangelize by mobilizing members as missionaries.* A new reformation is needed in which the priesthood and the missionhood of the believer is a given. Members of our churches must hear Christ's calling and affirm their gifts for ministry. They must realize the mobility afforded them by their international corporate deployments or by their retirement resources. Like Priscilla and Aquila, they must become the modern tent-making partners of Paul (Acts 18). There are not enough Pauls and Paulettes to finish the task. If the unreached are to become the reached in our generation, all disciples must agree to become personally responsive to the great commission.

c. *Members and vocational ministers must awaken to God's sending us to the world and to God's sending the world to us.* Many unreached or less reached language groups now live near our homes and churches. Ministry to and evangelization of these people presents the opportunity of their returning to their own people as did the Ethiopian eunuch in Acts 8.

d. *The Triune God is the prime mover in this new volunteer missions movement.* God is stirring members to become missionaries. The Fath-

er's passion to complete the commission is undiminished. He longs to see human response to the saving work of the Son at the direction of the Spirit. He longs to see churches place the watermark of baptism upon these unreached peoples.

III. *Baptize all believers in the name of the Trinity.* Baptism is an initiating mark of commitment to discipleship. Christian baptism is in the name of the Trinity: the Father, Son, and Holy Spirit. After all, we are to respond to God as he has revealed himself, and God has revealed himself as Father, Son, and Spirit. As the watermark of Christian obedience, baptism is to be distinctively Trinitarian.

a. *Baptism praises the Father for his call to salvation.* Jesus taught his disciples to pray to "our Father who is in heaven." He called God "Father" and taught his disciples that to obey the Son is to know and obey the Father (John 14:7). It was the voice of God the Father who declared at the baptism of Jesus, "This is my own Son in whom I am well pleased" (Matt. 3:17). The atoning work of the Son on the cross also pleased the Father.

b. *Baptism remembers the saving work of the Son on the cross.* Baptism in the name of the Son becomes a remembrance through reenactment of his death and Resurrection in our own baptism (Rom. 6:4). None ought to be baptized in Christ's name who do not affirm the power of the cross to forgive sins. Whom we baptize with water in Christ's name, Christ would baptize with his Spirit. Therefore we also baptize in the name of the Spirit.

c. *Baptism in the name of the Spirit acknowledges the presence and power of the Spirit.* John baptized with water but longed for more (Matt. 3:11). He knew that a baptism of the Spirit would mark the Kingdom's coming. He knew that a baptism of the Spirit alone was sufficient to transform a life. When John saw Jesus, John proclaimed him the Messiah, the one who baptized with the Spirit. Baptism in the name of the Spirit is a messianic baptism, which marks us as followers of Jesus as God's promised Savior and Christ. Baptism in the name of the Spirit reminds us to depend on the Spirit for guidance and giftedness in ministry and mission (John 14:26; 1Cor. 12:7).

d. *Baptism is the beginning of discipleship and not its completion.* If new members are to be effective followers of Christ and contributing members of the mission, they must be educated and equipped for missionary employment.

IV. *Catechize into observance of the commands of Christ.* The goal of catechism is to see the Christian life reproduced in the life of new disciples. The commission says that we are "to teach to observe all that I have commanded you." Authentic Christian education programs must produce transformed persons. The goal of a great commission church is intellectual understanding demonstrated in consistent obedience to the commands of Christ. We know a church has institutional effectiveness when its members have a vision and passion for the life of Christ. We know a church has effectiveness when its members practice the presence of the living Christ.

V. *Realize at all times the presence of Christ.* Commission suggests accompaniment. Jesus promised that he would not leave his disciples orphaned (John 14:18). Now he repeats that promise: "Behold, I am with you always, even to the end of the age" (v. 20). Practicing Christ's presence is essential to fulfillment of the Church's mission. Practice makes perfect and it makes permanent. Christ's presence supplies the power for effective mission and ministry. His presence comforts and counsels us as we penetrate and have an impact on cultures and communities for Christ, to the uttermost parts of the world.

Practicing the presence of Christ is made possible because Christ will allow nothing to separate us from the love of God. The Spirit of Christ dwells in us to guide and gift us for effective service in Kingdom work to the fallen world. If you sense his presence today, hear his call to join his mission, hear his command to unite with his cross-bought people and obey his commission.—Roderick K. Durst

Illustration

A GOSPEL FOR ALL. Francis of Assisi was an urban evangelist in the twelfth century. He used the Christmas Carol to share the good news of the shepherds with the desperately poor citizens of Italian cities and farms. He invited all to submit to Christ's rule and to preach the gospel to the living. His simple love for Christ gave birth to enduring movements of faithfulness among men (the Franciscans), among women (the Poor Clares),

and even among laymen. He kept as his personal mission statement a paraphrase of Matthew 28:19–20. He said, "If I do not preach the gospel everywhere I go, then I should go nowhere to preach the gospel."—Roderick K. Durst

DOCTRINE OF THE TRINITY. The story is told of a pastor who faced the task of preaching on Trinity Sunday with much misgiving. He solved his problem by informing his congregation that the Trinity was such a great mystery that in honor of it there would be no sermon that morning!

Despite these widespread feelings, the doctrine of the Trinity represents the distinctively Christian understanding of God. The Trinitarian understanding of God pervades Christian prayer and worship. We baptize in the name of the Triune God (Matt. 28:19). We bless in the name of the Triune God (2 Cor. 13:14). We sing praises to the Triune God:

Holy, holy, holy,
Merciful and mighty,
God in three Persons
Blessed Trinity.

The doctrine of the Trinity is indelibly stamped on Christian creeds, liturgy, hymns, and prayers. And it is, after all, in our worship and prayer that we express our deepest convictions about God.—Daniel L. Migliore[112]

SERMON SUGGESTIONS

Topic: A Lover's Quarrel with the World

TEXT: The Wisdom of Solomon (Apoc. 11:24, 12:1)

Engraved on Robert Frost's tombstone is "I had a lover's quarrel with the world." This is the key to a creative and fulfilled life. Five instances: (1) Make sure that your quarrels with other people are lover's quarrels. (2) Make sure that your quarrel with the church is a lover's quarrel. (3) If you have a quarrel with the Christian faith, make sure it is a lover's quarrel. (4) Have a lover's quarrel with God. (5) We ought to have a lover's quarrel with the world. God has a lover's quarrel with the world, but at the last what

[112] *The Power of God*

remains is not the quarrel, but the love.—R. Maurice Boyd[113]

Topic: Our Faith in the Kingdom of Heaven
TEXT: Matt. 13:31–35
(1) A divine Kingdom. (2) An unending Kingdom. (3) A world-embracing Kingdom. (4) A soul- and life-renewing Kingdom. (5) A triumphant Kingdom.—R.C.H. Lenski[114]

Hymn Suggestions

1. "Lord, Our God, Thy Glorious Praise," The Psalter (1912); GOTT SEI DANK DURCH ALLE WELT, Feylingshausen's Geistreiches Gesangbuch (1704)
This paraphrase of Psalm 8 would make a good opening hymn for worship. Two groups of the congregation could alternate the singing of the stanzas.
2. "God, Who Stretched the Spangled Heavens," Catherine A. Cameron (1967); HOLY MANNA, attr. to William Moore (nineteenth century)
Praising the creating God of Genesis 1, this modern hymn voices for the worshiping congregation their obligation to share in God's creative powers and thus conform to God's intention for them in time and space.
3. "Lord, You Give the Great Commission," Jeffery Rowthorn (1978); ABBOT'S LEIGH, Cyril Taylor (1941)
Should the homily and theme of worship focus on the Gospel reading concerning the great commission (Matt. 28:16–20), this contemporary hymn would be quite appropriate to climax the service of worship.
4. "Creating God, Your Fingers Trace," Jeffery Rowthorn (1979); HANCOCK, Eugene Hancock (1989); KEDRON, attr. to Elkanah K. Dare (1799)
Of the numerous Trinitarian hymns available for use on Trinity Sunday, this modern one, set to either tune, is unique in its prayer that God's nature will meaningfully influence human behavior.
5. "We All Believe in One True God," Tobias Clausnitzer (1668); tr. Catherine Winkworth (1863); RATISBON, J. G. Werner's

Choralbuch (1815); arr. William H. Monk (1861)
For those congregations that recite the Apostle's Creed in public worship, this metrical version of the Trinitarian articles of that creed could well be sung in its place, thus highlighting the principal theme of Trinity Sunday.—Hugh T. McElrath

Worship Aids

CALL TO WORSHIP.   "I will praise thee, O Lord, with my whole heart; I will show forth all thy marvelous works" (Ps. 8:1).

INVOCATION.   Holy, holy, holy, Lord God of Hosts. Great is your name and greatly to be praised. The whole earth is full of your glory. Lead us today to a righteous and fitting worship that shapes us for our daily living and binds us ever closer to the heart of God.—E. Lee Phillips

OFFERTORY SENTENCE.   "If you put an end to oppression, to every gesture of contempt, and to every evil word; if you give food to the hungry and satisfy those who are in need, then the darkness around you will turn to the brightness of noon. And I will always guide you and satisfy you with good things" (Isa. 58:9b–11a TEV).

OFFERTORY PRAYER.   Lord, these gifts are but the outward manifestation of the inner person. Let what is revealed match what is hidden, that in every generous act of gratitude the Lord Jesus Christ may be glorified.—E. Lee Phillips

PRAYER.   Our Father, we need forgiveness; we need divine forbearance; we need a new creation; we need to be inspired by the energy of thy mind, which never faints and never is weary. Blessed be thy name that thou art our watch, our guide; thou art our Captain in the hour of conflict. Thou who art in the night the bright and morning star and in the day the sun of righteousness, thou art to us the shadow of a rock in a weary land—our tower, into which we run when pursued; our Savior, our pavilion, where we can hide until the storm be overpast. What is there that we know of grace or purity or comfort or strength in things of earth, that thou hast not selected

---

[113]*A Lover's Quarrel with the World*
[114]*Eisenach Gospel Selections*

them and called them by their name, so that we can neither by day nor by night touch any thing that is made of thee, that it hath not some message impressed upon it from thee to us. All things are speaking to us of God, if we were not deaf and would hear. We pray, O Lord, that thou wilt grant that the experience, little though it be, of our love and joy in thee in time past may not fade out but rather augment; grant, we beseech of thee, that the things that aforetime have held us away from thee may now lead us more closely to thee.—Henry Ward Beecher

Sermon: Jacob's Ladder

TEXT: Genesis 32:22–32

What a strange story this is, Jacob's all-night wrestling match with a man who comes out of nowhere, jumps him, cripples him for life, gives him a new name but stays incognito under questioning, and then apparently vanishes. What a strange story, but then how life-like; I think when we see Jacob a little clearer, we'll see that his is really our story, too.

I. We start with a little distance, backing up a little to see what led to the nocturnal altercation. In fact, back up all the way to Jacob's birth, when he came out of the womb holding onto the heel of his twin brother, Esau. Like most of the birth stories in the Bible, this one is a destiny-setting, character-revealing moment. Destiny-setting, because for the rest of Jacob's life he'll be the second-born. Just a few minutes later than Esau, but those few moments made all the difference. Esau, firstborn, would inherit the majority of the family estate. Esau, firstborn, would take first place in his father's affection. Esau, firstborn, would be the dominant brother, according to the standards of his time: he was the one with the muscles, the hunting skill, the hairy body. Esau was a manly man, a Tim Allen kind of guy who grunted and ate a lot and was not too clever.

Jacob, on the other hand, was second son, second place, second rank; Esau was his father's favorite, so Jacob had to be his mother's favorite. Esau was the one with the muscles and the hair, so Jacob had to be the clever one. If Esau is the poster boy for the establishment—traditional values and all that—then Jacob is the icon for all those who never quite measure up. Esau is the football team; Jacob is the chess club. Esau is the board of trustees; Jacob is the employee grievance committee. Esau is the good old boys network; Jacob is a brand-new female storefront lawyer looking for a way to sue the pants off of them. Jacob's hand on Esau's heel—that's his destiny, which he plays out by cheating dumb old Esau out of his place in his father's estate, by cheating blind old Isaac, his father, into giving him Esau's blessing, by cheating wily old Laban, his uncle, out of a whole portfolio of movable assets. His destiny is to play catch-up to the system, to attack the system, to try to cheat the system.

And that becomes his character as well. When they saw his hand on his brother's heel, they named him Jacob, "Cheater." I suppose there are worse names to be saddled with. But talk about a self-fulfilling prophecy! Name a kid "Cheater" and then wonder what kind of person he'll be? Jacob was one to exploit the weakness of others—he used his brother's love for food to gain the inheritance, and his father's dim eyesight to gain the blessing. And when confronted by strength, he ran away. He first fled from Esau, who wanted to kill him, and then from his uncle Laban, who wanted to kill him, until there was really nowhere else he could go—no place to flee to, no more relatives to cheat—so he retreated behind a river to wait.

II. Now, is that life, or what? Some folks are born into power or come into it without much effort, and I'm not talking to folks like those today. I'm talking to the rest of us, who have never occupied the top rungs of the ladder. Most of us find that the world conspires to hold us back for some reason: because of the way we talk or the way we look, or because we don't know the right people or haven't been to the right schools or don't live in the right neighborhood. Or maybe it was just the way things worked out; had things been a little different, my life would have been so much better or so much easier. It's my experience that most people feel that way to some degree or another—my life has not turned out the way I would have hoped—and so most of us become like Jacob, some more, some less, feeling that life is unfair, so we might as well grab it by the heel.

My life didn't turn out the way I want, so I deserve to find some happiness somewhere. My life didn't turn out the way I want, so it's OK for me to cheat on my spouse. They make all the rules and hold all the power, so it's OK for me to misrepresent the truth just enough to make the sale or get the promotion. I deserve a few good things in life, so it's OK for me to ignore the poor in order to provide for myself. We climb Jacob's ladder by climbing over or around others, and we blame our lack of character on the way the world is set up; like my students say sometimes, "If you wouldn't make the test so hard, we wouldn't have to cheat."

III. Our real opponent in all of this, although it goes unsaid, is God. We may say we're angry at the boss or the government or society, but the one we're really mad at is God. God made the world, right? God made the rules, right? Didn't God say that the eldest should inherit and that men would rule over women? All along, Jacob's real argument, and ours too, has been with God for creating a world like this that stacks the deck against us.

God knows this, and in this story God obliges by giving Jacob a chance to face his real opponent. God pounces on Jacob when he's in a corner with no place else to go. And for the first time in his life, Jacob does not run away. Jacob faces his challenger and by simply hanging on he prevails. He survives the dislocated leg and hangs on until God transforms him, changing him from "Cheater" into "God-fighter." In theological terms, when Jacob finally faces God with his problems, he finds faith and grace and salvation. Not easy faith—he has to hang on all night long. Not cheap grace—he must endure his pain, he has to live with his injury. Not a pie-in-the-sky salvation, either; Jacob has to leave the wrestling ring and go to face his brother. But after facing God, who is there left to fear? "I have seen God face to face, and I'm still alive"; that's the motto of a man who never needs to run away or cheat again.

IV. Brothers and sisters, if life has been unfair to you, you are not alone. I do not mean to minimize the hurt or the damage that I know some of you have felt. But you are not alone. And if life's hurts and the world's unfairness have left you feeling that your only choices are either to run away or to fight, then you're facing the wrong adversary. Your fight is not with the world, though you may think it is. Your fight is not with this world, and the longer you fight the world, the more like the world you will become. Turn and embrace God, even if at first it feels like a wrestling match. Take your complaints to God and fight it out. What you'll find is that God loves the second sons as much as the first, God loves the cheaters as much as the dominators, God loves the folks on the bottom as much as those on the top. Turn and embrace God, and you'll find that the rules that held you down are not God's rules after all. Turn and embrace God, and even if you have to hold on all night long, you will find faith and face and salvation. That's the gospel, brothers and sisters.—Richard B. Vinson

Illustrations

PLAYING SECOND FIDDLE. So many of these domestic difficulties have grown out of an unwillingness on the part of certain members of the family to play second fiddle! I remember when our second baby was born, our first was delighted. He looked at his younger brother with eyes wide with joy and wonder. He regarded him as a new and thrilling toy. But before many days this first-born began to discover that the newcomer was to make a difference in his own life. He realized that he was not quite the center of the stage as he had once been. He began to get indignant over it. One day he boldly spoke his mind. "I am going to send that little old baby back to God," he declared. There you have it. We do not always propose to send those that get in our way back to God. Sometimes it is in the opposite direction. But we feel that we must get rid of them by sending them somewhere, for we simply must have first place!—Clovis G. Chappell[115]

EXPERIENCING GOD'S MERCY AND LOVE. Our relationship with God and our relationship with our neighbors are never two different things, but are one and the same. We cannot sin against God except by doing wrong to one of our brothers. The opposite is true, too. If our relationship with God is made new, our relationship with our fellowmen is made new by the same token. In other words, we cannot receive mercy and

[115] *Values That Last*

love from God unless we are in turn full of love and mercy toward our brothers. The one is not possible without the other. He who basks in the sun becomes himself a light, radiating warmth. He who lives in God's love cannot but reflect it upon his fellowmen. He who has found Christ must, as Luther boldly affirms, become a Christ to other people. He who is not himself a forgiving, merciful, and loving person only demonstrates that he has not truly experienced God's mercy and love. He who does not help to carry the guilt of others has not yet made the cross of Christ his own.—Emil Brunner[116]

SUNDAY: JUNE SIXTH

LECTIONARY MESSAGE

Topic: The Long Journey

TEXT: Gen. 12:1–9

Other Readings: Rom. 4:13–25; Matt. 9:9–13, 18–26

At some point in any sensitive life there comes a sense of strangeness, of isolation, of longing for something else. It may be a desire for better health, or different family circumstances, or to have chosen a different path of life. The heart may revolt at senseless cruelty and long for more fairness, or beauty, or love. The restlessness may be nameless, but the critical moment comes when it dawns on the longing heart that it is not to be satisfied. No diversion, no excess, no dedication, no good works, good thoughts, or good prayers fill the hole. We are truly "strangers in a strange land." We have, unknowingly, set out on the biblical journey of faith.

I. *The story of God's people really begins with Abraham, "the father of all of us" (Rom. 4:16).*

a. *It's a story that begins with the command to "go" (v. 1).* It's the story of our exile. It begins with birth, with the entrance of the spirit into this world, with the loss of the immediate presence of Love. No matter how we care for each tiny new life, its eyes wander off searching for a lost paradise. It wakes from dreams weeping with the loss, even when it wakes in loving arms. We come "trailing clouds of glory," as the poet Wordsworth said, and as they dissipate we are bereft.

b. *Oh, we adapt.* We realize fairness is not to be had here. We despair of perfect love. We tell one another, "Grow up!" when there is too much longing for bliss or beauty or bounty. We abandon idealism and sell our souls for the trinkets and glass beads of the world. Sex replaces love, pleasure replaces joy, self replaces service, money replaces hope, and we shrink to the measure of our self-made gods.

c. *But the Spirit that brooded over chaos is still abroad in the world,* whispering its still, small message to our spirits. Over and over we become discontent with the choices we've made, the hopes we've abandoned, the love we've betrayed. Perhaps even today a voice is whispering, calling, saying to you, "Look around; look again."

II. *This life is a journey, not a goal.* "Abram passed through the land" (v. 6).

a. *Even when Abraham came to the land of promise itself, it was not yet his resting place.* The fairest experiences, highest dreams, and deepest blessings we find along the road of this life are not places we can stop and say, "I have arrived." They are stages on the way to the place of which they are foretastes. A loving home, a profound love, a rewarding job, a joyous and blessed family life, of none of these can we say, "This is the place."

b. *This is not to say we are to ignore the present.* This world is not our home, but it is the land through which we pass. If we are not to settle in it, we are called to leave it better than we found it. Like campers or scouts, we try to leave our campsites in good shape for those who will follow. We often hear that we must choose between this world and the world to come, between care for the soul and care for the environment, between prayer and political action. If this is true, we are stuck.

c. *But it's a false distinction.* Only those who have a dream of a better world can act to transform this one. Dr. Martin Luther King Jr. left us that as an enduring legacy with his "I have a dream" speech. He came from a people denied this world by slavery and oppression; yet their focus on the world to come transformed the world they were passing through.

[116] *Sowing and Reaping*

III. *"The journey is our home."*

a. "Then the Lord appeared to Abram" (v. 7). Our uneasiness, our discontent, our longing for a better world, these are the first signs of God appearing to us. This is the voice of God calling to us, telling us that "here we have no lasting city, but we are looking for the city that is to come" (Heb. 13:14). And when we confront our Teacher, the homeless one, the one who was driven into the wilderness by the Spirit (Mark 1:12), the one who said, "Foxes have holes, and birds of the air have nests; but the Son of man has nowhere to lay his head" (Matt. 8:20), then we know that the Lord has appeared to us and for us, showing us our own situation and giving us hope.

b. *"So he built there an altar to the Lord, who had appeared to him" (v. 7).* By ourselves we cannot sustain the illuminating, hopeful realizations that we are aliens and exiles in this world, that we are citizens of another realm who "desire a better country, that is, a heavenly one" (Heb. 11:16). So we say, "I will go to the altar of God" (Ps. 43:4). We go to church, we sing the songs of Zion, we look into the Word, we pray at table and bedside. We build an altar where we can come often to the one who says to us, "You are right; heaven is your home."

c. *"From there he moved on to the hill country" (v. 8).* So with Abraham, we move on toward the distant hills, the shining heights we left so long ago and miss so deeply. As we go, our very longing transforms the land through which we pass; "As they go through the valley of Baca they make it a place of springs; the early rain also covers it with pools" (Ps. 84:6). But still, here we find no abiding place. Like Abraham, we journey always toward the everlasting hills, toward the mountain of God, the source and goal of our life. "Therefore God is not ashamed to be called their God; indeed, he has prepared a city for them" (Heb. 11:16).—Donald F. Chatfield

Illustrations

OUR BIRTH IS BUT A SLEEP AND A FORGETTING.

The Soul that rises with us, our life's Star,
Hath had elsewhere its setting,
And cometh from afar:
Not in entire forgetfulness,
And not in utter nakedness,

But trailing clouds of glory do we come
From God, who is our home:
Heaven lies about us in our infancy!
Shades of the prison-house begin to close
Upon the growing Boy,
But he beholds the light, and whence it
   flows,
He sees it in his joy;
The Youth, who daily farther from the east
Must travel, still is Nature's Priest,
And by the vision splendid
Is on his way attended;
At length the Man perceives it die away,
And fade into the light of common day.
                    —William Wordsworth[117]

LIVING IN DIFFICULT TIMES.   "A great door and effectual is opened unto me, and there are many adversaries" (1 Cor. 16:9). There are open doors enough and necessary work to be done if only we will look beyond, and thus overlook, the intervening difficulties. Let me quote . . . , as a footnote to our text, an inscription on the walls of the Chapel of Staunton Harold in Leicestershire:

In the year 1653
when all things sacred were
either demolished or profaned
Sir Robert Shirley, Baronet,
Founded this church:
Whose singular praise it is
to have done the best things in the
worst time and
hoped them in the most calamitous.
                    —Willard L. Sperry[118]

SERMON SUGGESTIONS

Topic: Learning to Do Good
    TEXT: Isa. 1:18–20
    (1) A gracious invitation. (2) A generous proposal. (3) A radical promise. (4) A critical choice.

Topic: *STOP!*
    TEXT: Various in RSV
    (1) "Seek the Lord while he may be found" (Isa. 55:6). (2) "Take my yoke upon

[117]From "Ode on Intimations of Immortality from Recollections of Early Childhood"
[118]*Sermons Preached at Harvard*

you, and learn from me" (Matt. 11:29). (3) "Obey my voice, and I will be your God, and you shall be my people" (Jer. 7:23). (4) "Pray constantly" (1 Thess. 5:16b).

Hymn Suggestions

1. "Jesus! What a Friend for Sinners," J. Wilbur Chapman (1910); HYFRYDOL, Rowland H. Prichard (1830)

The Gospel lesson about Jesus' eating with tax collectors and sinners could appropriately be followed by the confessional singing of this hymn exalting the friendship of Jesus in all human circumstances.

2. "Faith While Trees Are Still in Blossom," A. Frostenson (1960); tr. Fred Kaan (1972); FOR THE BREAD, V. Earle Copes (1960)

This contemporary hymn celebrates the spirit of faith that Abraham manifested as set forth in the Genesis passage and the apostle Paul's teachings in Romans (4:13–25).

3. "Thanks to God Whose Word Was Spoken," R. T. Brooks (1954); WILDE GREEN, Peter Cutts (1955)

Gathering the thoughts of Psalm 33:6 and 9—and the call of Abraham (Gen. 12:1–9 and Rom. 4:13–25)—that God spoke the earth as well as a nation into being, this contemporary hymn is appropriate when sung in connection with any of the readings appointed for this day.

4. "Immortal Love, Forever Full," John G. Whittier (1866); SERENITY, William V. Wallace (1856)

This hymn by the great Quaker Whittier, encompasses the assertion of Psalm 33:5 that the earth is full of God's steadfast love and—in its stanza 5—the truth that, like the woman in the gospel lesson (Matt. 9:20–22a), "we touch him in life's throng and press, and we are whole again."—Hugh T. McElrath

Worship Aids

CALL TO WORSHIP. "For the word of the Lord is right; and all his works are done in truth. He loveth righteousness and judgment: the earth is full of the goodness of the Lord" (Ps. 33:4–5).

INVOCATION. Still us, Lord. Quiet us. Calm us in the presence of a community of faith held together in bonds of love. Seal the Word in our hearts that we might not sin against you and by the power of the Word fit us for service in Jesus' holy name.—E. Lee Phillips

OFFERTORY SENTENCE. "For God is not unrighteous to forget your work and labour of love, which ye have shewed toward his name, in that ye have ministered to the saints, and do minister" (Heb. 6:10).

OFFERTORY PRAYER. God of grace from whom all blessings flow, accept these offerings we bring in stewardship and use them to further the Kingdom into which all who will may enter through our Lord Jesus Christ.—E. Lee Phillips

PRAYER. O Father, who has set us amid the bonds of time; this hurrying pace of life frightens and amazes us. We cannot crowd our purposes into such a narrow space. Ere ever the day has worn to noon, or we have even planned the work we meant to do, the night comes down upon us and we can work no more. The swift years pass and find us little farther on. We wake to mourn what we have missed, to value most what comes no more.

Forgive our waste of precious moments, our loitering feet, our procrastinating will. O teach us to number our days, that we may apply our hearts to wisdom; to lengthen our brief life by intensity of living; to fill swift hours with mighty deeds; to lay up treasure where neither moth nor rust doth corrupt.

Seeing we spend our days as a tale that is told, let us haste to speak that which is within us, lest we be called away before the story is begun. If there is anything Thou hast meant us to do in life, O spare us till we have accomplished it. If there is any kindness we can shew, may we not neglect or defer it, seeing that we pass this way but once.

So may the very stress of earthly life educate us for the life eternal.—W. E. Orchard[119]

Sermon: Doing God's Will

TEXT: John 7:17

If there is one question that Christian people—especially Christian young people—like

[119] *The Temple*

124THE MINISTERS MANUAL FOR 1999

to have answered, it is, How can I *know* God's will for my life?

With all due respect for the importance of our knowing God's will for our lives, there is another more basic question that we ought to consider—namely, do I have a disposition to *do* God's will?

Jesus emphasized the importance of this disposition to do God's will when he said, "If any man will do his will, he shall know of the doctrine, whether it be of God, or whether I speak of myself" (John 7:17).

The enemies of Jesus had seen his miracles, such as the healing of the impotent man and the feeding of the five thousand, but they had rejected his power. They had heard his claims, which were exalted beyond the claims of any mere man, but had resisted his overtures. They had examined his witnesses, including Jesus himself, John the Baptist, the Father, his works, and the Scriptures, but had repudiated his teaching or doctrine. To these knowledgeable but incorrigible recalcitrants the Savior said, "If any man will do his will, he shall know . . ." (John 7:17).

The Old Testament provides some interesting illustrations of the spiritual principle that we have enunciated. From the experiences of the Israelites during their wilderness wanderings come three stories that are noteworthy.

I. *Doing God's will promptly.* The first of these stories is taken from Numbers 14. The Israelites were encamped at Kadesh. Under God's direction, Moses sent twelve men, a representative from each of the twelve tribes, to spy out the land of Canaan. Ten of them brought back a majority report that said that the land's inhabitants were so strong they could not be conquered. Joshua and Caleb brought back a minority report that said that, with God's help, the land could be conquered. The masses sided with the viewpoint of the ten, talked about returning to Egypt, and even contemplated stoning Joshua and Caleb.

The sequel to this story is well known. For forty years the Israelites wandered in the wilderness. The writer of the Epistle to the Hebrews succinctly explains this by saying, "They could not enter in because of unbelief" (3:19).

One aspect of the episode deserves careful consideration. In the closing verses of Numbers 14 we are told that early the next morning the Israelites decided to do what they had refused to do the day before. Surely Moses and the Lord would be happy about this change of heart!

All of the details of this story may not be understandable. One thing, however, seems clear: that which had been God's will the day before was no longer his will. This shows the necessity of doing God's will promptly. Tomorrow may be too late.

II. *Doing God's will exactly.* The second story is found in Numbers 20. Forty years had elapsed since the time of the first episode. The Israelites were desperately in need of water. Moses, for the second time, smote a rock; and a life-giving stream was provided for the people.

But what a sequel there was to this event! Moses and Aaron were rebuked by God and informed that they would not be permitted to bring the congregation of Israel into the land that God had promised to give to them. What had gone wrong?

A study of the context shows that God had told Moses to *speak* to the rock, not *smite* it. Because Moses did not do God's will exactly as he was instructed, he surrendered the opportunity to do what he wanted most: to lead his people into Canaan.

Have we accepted the whole counsel of God, or do we, as C. S. Lewis charged, tend to pick out certain parts of Christianity to follow and forget about the rest? God expects us to obey him completely. This is the way of spiritual victory, and this is a prerequisite for effective service.

III. *Doing God's will honestly.* By this time the Israelites were encamped on the borders of Canaan, in Moab, east of the Dead Sea. In Numbers 22 to 25 we are introduced to one of the most enigmatic characters in all of the Old Testament: a prophet by the name of Balaam who was hired by Balak, the king of Moab, to curse the Israelites.

Three times over Balaam tried to curse the Israelites, but each time the Spirit of God came upon him and turned his curse into a blessing. Failing in this venture, Balaam, according to Revelation 2:14, "taught Balak to cast a stumbling block before the children of Israel, to eat things sacrificed unto idols, and to commit fornication."

What was Balaam's basic problem? There

seemed to be indications that he wanted to do God's will. Did anyone ever make a more noble declaration of allegiance to God than Balaam? He declared, "If Balak would give me his house full of silver and gold, I cannot go beyond the word of the Lord my God" (Num. 22:18). When a better offer came from Balak, he questioned his first decision.

In 2 Peter 2:15 we are told that "Balaam . . . loved the *wages* of unrighteousness." This same charge is also found in Jude 11, where the "error of Balaam" is identified as the "reward" for which he longed. Balaam's true god was money.

The lesson for our day and age is obvious. We must be careful that we do not have mixed motives. To paraphrase the words of our Savior, we must watch to see that our eye is single (Matt. 6:22). We too must do God's will honestly.—William R. Shunk[120]

Illustrations

GOD'S PRESENCE.   As sure as God ever puts his children in the furnace, he will be in the furnace with them.—C. H. Spurgeon[121]

THE LORD'S PRAYER CONTINUED.   The prayer also means in great joy "Thy will be done" *for me and for all mankind.* For the will of God is not a dark line in God's face. It seems so only to our dim and shortened sight. Jesus said, "My meat is to do the will of him that sent me," for the will of God is food and drink to our famished life. Sunrise is His will, and friends, and pardon for our sins, and the sure hope of life eternal.—George A. Buttrick[122]

SUNDAY: JUNE THIRTEENTH

LECTIONARY MESSAGE

Topic: Laughter Is God's Middle Name
TEXT: Gen. 18:1–15 (21:1–7)
Other Readings: Rom. 5:1–8; Matt. 9:35–10:8

We have heard that laughter is good for the soul; doctors tell us it is good for the body as well. Sometimes, though, Christians forget not only that it is a good gift of God to laugh but also that laughter is central to our heritage. In fact, we could even say that laughter is God's middle name. As God initiates the history of salvation, the voice from the bush says to Moses, "I am the God of your father, the God of Abraham, the God of Isaac, and the God of Jacob" (Exod. 3:6). It is by these three names that the covenant of God is often recalled in Hebrew Scripture, and Jesus refers to God in these same words more than once (Matt. 22:32; Mark 12:26). Each of these great names has a meaning, and the middle one means "laughter."

I. *We laugh because it's impossible.* God comes to Abraham with news so impossible it's silly: Sarah—old, dried-up, wizened Sarah—will bear a child. Abraham may be so impressed with his heavenly visitors that all he can do is nod at the nonsensical news, mouth agape. But Sarah, hidden in the tent, runs her knobby, rope-veined hands over the barren husk of her old body and laughs, quietly, hand to mouth, shoulders shaking (18:12). This is the releasing laughter of incredulity. We clench our hopes and longings to us so tightly for so long, believing that all we need to do is believe, that we become locked around them and cannot let go. What a release to laugh at ourselves, to recognize that we will never be president, or CEO, or married, or parents, or handsome, or pretty, or famous, or perfect. What a relief, to accept ourselves as we are. (We'd better; it's the only "we" there is!) What a tonic, to abandon pointless dreams, foolish hopes, and proud ambitions, to laugh at ourselves, to see and accept ourselves and our situations honestly. Are there even times when it is good for the soul to laugh at the outrageous promises of God: a child who brings peace, plenty for the nations, life that will never end, the final defeat of evil? Impossible! Perhaps when Sarah heard the strangers' promise to Abraham—that she, wrinkled and old as she was, would have a child—perhaps she heard finally how foolish that ancient dream of hers had become. Perhaps in hearing another say it she found release in the laughter of the impossible.

[120]In *Award Winning Sermons,* Vol. 4
[121]*Privileges of Trial*
[122]*So We Believe, So We Pray*

II. *God laughs at our foolishness.* We are like children to God; and sometimes we laugh at our little children, even as we comfort them. They burst out crying because Mama is gone, when we know she will be back. "The Lord said to Abraham, 'Why did Sarah laugh, and say, "Shall I indeed bear a child, now that I am old?" Is anything too wonderful for the Lord?'" (18:13–14). God has great plans for us, plans already in motion in our gifts, situations, work, friends, families, and talents. It must be amusing to God, at times, how we cling to our own notions. Have you never looked at another's life and shaken your head in amused wonder at their foolishness? There are those who struggle for achievement in order to win love, when those who love them already are not the least impressed. There are parents who urge on their children a path not suited for them. There are those who have plenty yet are restless because they think it's never enough. Sometimes we struggle to get what we already have; sometimes we despair of getting what lies just around the corner; sometimes we think, "If only I had *this*," when *that* (which we have already) will do the job quite nicely. God hears Sarah's nearly derisive laughter and says, "Why did Sarah laugh? . . . Is anything too wonderful for the Lord?" Can you hear the gentle humor in God's voice? No? "Sarah denied, saying, 'I did not laugh'; for she was afraid. He said, 'Oh yes, you did laugh'" (18:15). Sarah fears God will be angry, but no punishment or even rebuke follows; just the gentle, smiling response of understanding and empathy: "Oh yes, you did laugh." When we insist on our plans to the point of obsession, when we despair of our lives to the point of tears, when we fear that God will not give what we long for but will punish instead, we can remember: "He who sits in the heavens laughs" (Psalms 2:4), so we can laugh too.

III. *We laugh at God's mercy and love.* One of the loveliest moments in the Psalter is this: "When the Lord restored the fortunes of Zion, we were like those who dream. Then our mouth was filled with laughter, and our tongue with shouts of joy" (Ps. 126:1–2). How Sarah must have laughed when she began to show; how she must have shouted with glee, even between the gasps of the birthing; how she must have chortled as her bony old arms clutched the newborn boy to her heart. She must have, for she named him "Laughter," Isaac. The unrestrained glee of a winning team at tug-o-war, or a child who gets just what she wanted for Christmas, or a people delivered from slavery—and what shall we say who have been snatched from the jaws of death eternal, freed from the pain and penalty of sin, called to the fellowship of undeserving blessing, made sisters and brothers of Christ, adopted children of the great God Almighty? Laugh, Christian! Laugh for joy and unbelief. Laugh with all the saints, and sing to heaven, "Thanks be to God, who gives us the victory through our Lord Jesus Christ" (1 Cor. 15:57).—Donald F. Chatfield

Illustrations

LAUGHING IN CHURCH.   When I was doing graduate work in Scotland, back in the 1960s, I often preached in one particular parish church. These Scottish Christians were a wonderful lot, but for them worship was a serious, even a dour, business. I decided to loosen them up, and one Sunday I preached on "The Humor of Jesus." I showed the Savior portraying the impeccable Pharisee swallowing a camel, the man with a railroad tie jutting from his eye trying to see to remove a speck from another's eye, and so on. But there was not even a smile out among the kirk. Afterward, I despaired, both of my message and of those irrecoverably serious Scots Christians. But at the door, all were smiles and praise. One woman summed up the paradox beautifully: "Och, that was a wonderful message," she chortled, "it was all I could do not to laugh."—Donald F. Chatfield

THE LITTLE THINGS.   A man once said to me, "When I was ten years old, I was walking across a field not ten miles from this spot, and I saw God. He was immense, head and shoulders rising up just beyond the tree line against the sky. And God said to me, 'You and I will do great things together.' And what I keep wondering is, when is it going to start?" This man could be forgiven his bafflement; he was in his late fifties, out of work after a lifetime of low-end jobs, long divorced, and isolated from his children. I chewed on his words for a long time. I believed he had heard God rightly, and like him I wondered how God could make such a promise and not follow through. But then I thought, What if it *did* come true? What if this man's life has been full of small acts of kindness—like the hot coffee he invited me to share in his tent at a cold, rainy campground that day? Perhaps God was laughing gently at the man's nearsightedness; perhaps they will both laugh together, on that day when his eyes are opened to all the great little things God *did* do with him in his lifetime.—Donald F. Chatfield

SERMON SUGGESTIONS

Topic: Going into Business with God
TEXT: Exod. 3
(1) Encounter (vv. 1–6). (2) Call (vv. 7–10). (3) Promise (vv. 11–17).

Topic: Getting Life in Proper Order
TEXT: Rom. 12 NRSV
(1) An urgent challenge: "Present your bodies as a living sacrifice" (v. 1). (2) An adequate resource: "by the mercies of God" (v. 1). (3) A practical procedure: "Be transformed by the renewing of your minds" (v. 2). (4) An appropriate outcome: "that you may discern what is the will of God" (v. 2).

Hymn Suggestions

1. "Come, Holy Spirit, Heavenly Dove," Isaac Watts (1707); ST. AGNES, John B. Dykes (1866)
In response to the truth expounded by the apostle Paul (Rom. 5:5), that God's love has been poured into our hearts through the Holy Spirit, this classic hymn could be used as an invocation near the beginning of worship.
2. "O Thou, My Soul, Return in Peace," Murrayfield Psalms (1950); The Psalter (1912); MARTYRDOM, Hugh Wilson; arr. R. A. Smith (1825)
This metrical version of verses from Psalm 116 could appropriately be sung following the Psalter reading. In keeping with ancient practice, it could be sung line by line antiphonally throughout.
3. "Pass It On," Kurt Kaiser (1969); PASS IT ON, Kaiser (1969)
"Freely you have received, freely give" (Matt. 10:8b). This scripture at the end of the Gospel reading could find suitable response

by the worshiping group's singing of this contemporary song.
4. "Freely, Freely," Carol Owens (1972); FREELY, FREELY, Owens (1972)
Similarly, this mini-hymn could be used as suggested for the previous hymn. It pertains even more closely to the sending of the twelve disciples as recorded in Matthew 10:1–8.—Hugh T. McElrath

Worship Aids

CALL TO WORSHIP. "What shall I render unto the Lord for all his benefits toward me? I will take the cup of salvation, and call upon the name of the Lord. I will pay my vows unto the Lord now in the presence of all his people" (Ps. 116:12–14).

INVOCATION. Lord, your blessings have amazed us again and again, so unbelieving we often are. Yet you continue to teach us in the midst of weakness, struggle, suffering, and temptation. Grant that we may now in sheer faith show our gratitude by a renewal of our intentions to serve you faithfully.

OFFERTORY SENTENCE. "The earth is the Lord's and the fullness thereof; the world, and they that dwell therein" (Ps. 24:1).

OFFERTORY PRAYER. Help us, O Lord, to discern the meaning of your ownership of the world and of us, and help us to give a faithful account of our stewardship.

PRAYER. Thou Savior of the world, thou hast occasion to bear even with our knowledge. Our best things are so imperfect that thou has to bear with them. Our very love is frigid, if it be measured by the golden tropic of heaven. The ripest fruit that hangs upon our bough, spirit-ripened on earth, is yet acerbic, and unfit for the heavenly garden. Thou hast occasions, O gentle and loving and ever-blessed God, to carry us all as little children are carried. We are ignorant, we are weak, we are stumbling all the time; and yet we arrogate to ourselves such knowledge that we take one another by the throat, and cast out men that differ from us. We are perpetually proving one another and judging one another, and yet, all the time, we are depending upon the infinite forbearance and love of

God. Teach us, we beseech of thee, the whole lore of love—of its forbearance and gentleness, of its kindness and patience, of its charitableness and richness; and make us to be thy dear children; and work out in us thine attributes; and finally draw us, by that in us which is like thee, to the open arms of Jesus, and to the bosom of our heavenly home where we will praise thee, Father, Son and Spirit.—Henry Ward Beecher

Sermon: Who's to Blame?

TEXT: Gen. 2:15–17, 3:1–7; Rom. 5:12–19; Ps. 32

"All you preachers ever do is talk about sin. I don't go to church to feel bad. Why don't you talk about something good for a change?" Have you ever heard those words expressed? Have you ever thought them? Sure you have—and I have as well. Why do we preachers talk about sin? Have you looked at a newspaper recently? The picture is too clear.

I. Adam and Eve are in the Garden of Eden and God has given them explicit instructions not to eat from the tree of the knowledge of good and evil. However, Satan arrives in the form of a serpent—traditional interpretation has seen the serpent in this understanding—and before you know it the deed has been done, the sin committed, and quite literally all hell is getting ready to break loose. When God comes looking for Adam and Eve they hide, incredibly naive concerning the ability of God to know where they are and what they are doing, but also not so naive in that they know that no longer can they remain in the presence of the Creator.

When God asks Adam concerning the deed, Adam replies: "The woman you gave me, she deceived me and I ate." God then turns to Eve and she replies, "The serpent deceived me and I ate." In other words, each was trying to blame someone else for their sin. Adam blamed Eve—and also God for giving Eve to him—and Eve blamed the serpent, the deceiver, that is, Satan. The blame game was on—and continues to this day. Nowhere in all of Scripture is the responsibility for human actions removed from the people involved and placed at the feet of Satan.

Could not God have created us without the ability to sin? The traditional answer of Judaism—and it was their text before it became ours—is that God created us as moral creatures who are able to make decisions of our own free will.

II. Some people blame nature, that is, genetics. Geneticists examine DNA and tell us that there may be a "criminal gene" that causes the antisocial behavior that results in crime. I do not know about this, but though I believe in the power of genetics far more than I did in the past, I cannot believe that moral responsibility would lie in this realm.

Others desire to place the blame on nurture, that is, on family environment. These look at the structure of the home in which persons are raised and note that most criminals come from homes of broken marriages and absent fathers that are mainly of the lower economical strata. Still, today most children raised in poverty do not become criminals, even though most of the criminals come from that particular stratum of society.

III. What are we to do? Play the blame game? Or deal with the reality of our sin? God would not allow Adam and Eve to get away with their shifting of personal responsibility, and neither will Holy Scripture allow us to do the same. If we would grow as persons and as followers of Jesus, then we must deal with our shadow side, with the presence of Adam in each and every one of us.

What do we see when we look at the dark side? Quite simply, that even in the best of us—and that's a contest no one wants to play—there is more than enough evil and sin to go around.

There's a huge problem with using people—and the problem is not just what it does to others but what it does to ourselves. If we use others, then we must harden our heart to their plight in order to do that—and every time we harden our heart we move one more step away from the one who is love.

IV. What, then, are we to do? How do we deal with the sin of our lives? Confession is the beginning point, but confession that does some good. Too often our confession runs generic, simplistic, and half-hearted: "Lord, forgive me for my sin, Amen." That confession does no one any good—God or the sinner. Confession means to look at our lives and through the power of the Spirit speak the truth about them. Without the incredible love of God permeating our lives we will never have the strength to look inside and see the nature of the zoo that resides within.

Repentance follows confession, but there is much confusion about repentance today. Repentance involves definitive actions that are taken to correct the sin and restore any broken relationships that may have resulted from it.

What does it take for us to do all this? We must accept the power of God as necessary and able to break the hold of sin upon our lives. When we come face to face with the greatness of what Christ Jesus has done for us and will do in us and through us, then we will accept amazing grace and place ourselves on the path of transformation.—Robert U. Ferguson Jr.

Illustrations

PERSONAL GRATIFICATION. A university chaplain tells the story of preaching against premarital sex at a major university. After the sermon a student asked this question: "Why do you want us to say no to sex before marriage?" The chaplain replied, "Because if we can get you to say no to anything in a society that teaches you to say yes to everything, why, there's no telling what we might make of you."

We live in a world that says yes rather than no to any and all opportunities for self-gratification. When everything becomes an instrument for my personal satisfaction, including the church and worship, then the almighty "I" has replaced the Almighty God and we are not aware of it. We are all sinners and the sooner we admit that the sooner we will be on our way to spiritual and emotional health. The shadow side is real.—Robert U. Ferguson Jr.

WHO'S TO BLAME? In *Death of a Salesman* by Arthur Miller, Biff slowly learns the truth about his father, Willy. He learns that his father is no hero but rather is a failed salesman, a has-been who is really a never-was. Biff says to his father, "You are a phony. . . . We never told the truth for ten minutes in this house." However, Biff eventually comes to realize that he is no better than his father, that he is a liar and thief just like his Dad. "I stole myself out of every good job since high school," Biff confesses. But then he blames it on his father: "I never got anywhere because you blew me so full of hot air I could never stand taking orders from anybody. That's whose fault it is!"—Robert U. Ferguson Jr.

SUNDAY: JUNE TWENTIETH

LECTIONARY MESSAGE

Topic: God of the Outcast
TEXT: Gen. 21:8–21
Other Readings: Rom. 6:1b–11; Matt. 9:35–10:8

For generations Americans have heard the biblical story in a striking way. We in this land have applied to ourselves the images of a chosen people that recur again and again, in the Hebrew Scriptures especially. We have fed our spirits with tales of our hardy ancestors who came to this land like the Hebrew people, crossing the sea to freedom, turning exile into conquest, founding in this hemisphere "a new nation under God, conceived in liberty." We have followed only the main line of the story of God's people, ignoring the Bible's tales of repeated faithlessness, destruction, and exile. This identification has given us courage and pride, but its day is fading before a new global awareness and a hard

historical honesty. Our certainty that this land comprised a new people of God, a new elect, nurtured destruction of old native cultures and peoples, sanctioned slavery and oppression, led to wars of economic conquest and political dominance, and left us ill-prepared for a day when waning American hegemony stands facing the economic might of the European Union, the awakening power of a massive China, and the export of jobs, technology, and wealth across the seas. As our national story changes, our personal stories lose their roots; as many among us already know, we are not the triumphant chosen race. Many among us are ill-educated, handicapped, downsized, aged, alone, or fearful. Perhaps it is time to open our eyes to another part of the biblical story: the story of the God of the outcast.

I. *"Cast out this slave woman with her son; for the son of this slave woman shall not inherit along with my son Isaac" (v. 10).* Hagar was Sarah's

Egyptian slave girl, abused by being given to Abraham like a brood mare to provide barren Sarah with a child by proxy. But now Isaac has been born, and Sarah, ungrateful, jealous, and not content with God's fulfillment, tells Abraham to cast out Hagar and her little boy Ishmael. Abraham passively complies, and sends the woman and the son she had borne him out into the inhospitable desert. The two chosen people behave in a less-than-choice way. Nations, churches, and individuals who think that God has something special for them to do have often behaved in an ungodly way, covering the full spectrum of shamefulness, from pride to genocide. What is racism but a fruit of the improbable contention that God has chosen one race over all others? What is sexism but the contention that males are more the image of God than females? What was emblazoned on German Nazi emblems as whole peoples were exterminated by them but "Gott mit uns"—"God with *us?*" As we watch Sarah and Abraham, God's chosen, behaving so abominably toward the slave woman and her child, perhaps we will make a silent vow, that inasmuch as God has chosen and blessed us, we will behave in Godly ways: "and what does the Lord require of you but to do justice, and to love kindness, and to walk humbly with your God?" (Mic. 6:8). For our God is not only the God of the chosen, but also the God of the outcast.

II. *"When the water in the skin was gone, she cast the child under one of the bushes. Then she went and sat down opposite him a good way off, about the distance of a bowshot; for she said, 'Do not let me look on the death of the child.' And as she sat opposite him, she lifted up her voice and wept" (vv. 15–16).* Is someone here saying, "I don't feel chosen; I feel rejected, lost, bereft; I identify with this poor forsaken woman and her tears and her dying child"? Isn't this why the text of Scripture suddenly takes this detour, leaving the history of the chosen and choosing to follow the lost? Isn't it to let us know that the God who chose the descendants of Abraham, Isaac, and Jacob is still the God of all Earth's tribes and peoples? The mission of Israel was the same as what Jesus told his followers theirs was to be: "You are the light *of the world.* A city built on a hill cannot be hid" (Matt. 5:14; compare Isa. 2:2, 42:6, 49:6, 60:3; Mic. 4:2). Israel was not cho-

sen to have salvation for itself, but to give "light to all." The story is told this way lest the chosen people forget that the God who chose them is truly the God of all.

III. *"And God heard the voice of the boy; and the angel of God called to Hagar from heaven, and said to her, 'What troubles you, Hagar? Do not be afraid; for God has heard the voice of the boy where he is'" (v. 17).* The God who saw the burdens and heard the cries of the Hebrew slaves in Egypt and came down to save them with a mighty hand and an outstretched arm sees the outcast child under the bush in the desert, hears his mother's weeping, and tenderly brings them to water and promises that they too are regarded by God. For the message is not just about nations and tribes; it's about people, about individuals. It's about us, when all have forsaken and forgotten us, when life has passed us by and all around us is a desert, and our dreams are dying under yonder bush. What a comfort to remember this old story, then, to know that God sees the tears of an outcast woman and an abandoned child, to realize that God hears us in our godforsakenness. What a comfort to know, then, as the old hymn says, that "God hears thy sighs and counts thy tears, God shall lift up thy head." It is this that makes us the chosen people of God, for it is the experience of God's mercy that makes us merciful.—Donald F. Chatfield

Illustrations

AN OUTCAST.   A woman came to her pastor to ask his prayers. Her only son—a man in his early thirties—was dying, and she was going out of town to be with him at the end. With great reluctance she agreed to let the pastor ask their little congregation to pray for her and her son. But she didn't want the people to know what he was dying of. With great reluctance she confided in the pastor that he was dying of complications brought on by AIDS; but she begged him not to tell the people. They might suspect from that, she said, that her son was gay. The pastor complied with her wishes. The people did pray for her while she was gone, of course, and gathered around to comfort her when she returned. But a strange distance was created between her and her church by her vagueness about what had killed him. In effect, she became outcast in her time of need because she suspected (with justification) that some church members—some of God's chosen people—would shun her if they thought her son might possibly be gay.—Donald F. Chatfield

GOD'S STRONG HAND.
Give to the winds thy fears;
Hope and be undismayed;
God hears thy sighs and counts thy tears,
God shall lift up thy head.

Through waves, and clouds, and storms,
He gently clears thy way;
Wait thou His time; so shall this night
Soon end in joyous day.

Leave to His sovereign sway
To choose and to command;
So shalt thou, wondering, own His way,
How wise, how strong His hand.

Far, far above thy thought
His counsel shall appear,
When fully He the work hath wrought
That caused thy needless fear.
—Paul Gerhardt, 1656[123]

SERMON SUGGESTIONS

Topic: Power Belongs to God
TEXT: Ps. 62
Because power belongs to God: (1) I can confidently and quietly await God to come through for me (v. 1); (2) I can freely and honestly pour out my heart to God in all circumstances (v. 8); (3) I can resist temptations to take unethical shortcuts (v. 10); (4) I can expect God to reward my faithfulness (v. 12).

Topic: Called to Freedom
TEXT: Gal. 5:13–26
(1) Not for self-indulgence. (2) Rather, for the experience of love for others. (3) By the leadership of the Spirit.

Hymn Suggestions

1. "We Know That Christ Is Raised," John B. Geyer, (1969); ENGELBERG, Chas. V. Stanford (1904)

[123]Tr. John Wesley, 1739

This contemporary hymn is an admirable paraphrase of the Romans 6:1b–11 passage in today's lectionary. As such, its singing could logically follow the reading from the Epistle.
2. "To My Humble Supplication," J. Bryan (c. 1620); GENEVAN 86, Genevan Psalter (1551)
Rather than the Psalter lesson (Ps. 80), this metrical version could be sung by the worshiping group.
3. "Mighty God, While Angels Bless Thee," Robert Robinson (1774); RUSTINGTON, C.H.H. Parry (1897)
A good general praise hymn that in its second stanza reflects God's care and guidance of the sparrows (Matt. 10:29), this would be a worthy and effective item for the beginning of worship.
4. "Make Me a Captive, Lord," George Mattheson (1890); DIADEMATA, George J. Elvey (1868)
As a reflection of the paradoxes of the Christian walk (found in Matt. 10:29), this hymn is a prayer expressing obedience and commitment. Appropriately, it could either precede or follow the Gospel reading.—Hugh T. McElrath

Worship Aids

CALL TO WORSHIP. "Rejoice the soul of the servant: for unto thee, O Lord, do I lift up my soul. For thou, Lord, art good, and ready to forgive; and plenteous in mercy unto all them that call upon thee" (Ps. 86:4–5).

INVOCATION. Lord, hold on to us today. Some of us are wandering and want to walk away from it all. Others of us are hurting and do not want to be embittered. Some of us are grief-stricken and cannot see the way. Others of us face a door of opportunity and come rejoicing. Grant to us all the faith that steadies in sunlight or storm because we paused to pray and worship the Lord our God.—E. Lee Phillips

OFFERTORY SENTENCE. "Walk in love, as Christ also hath loved us, and hath given himself for us an offering and a sacrifice to God for a sweet-smelling savour" (Eph. 5:2).

OFFERTORY PRAYER.   Now with this offering, dear Lord, accept our commitment of time and prayer, that how we live will match what we believe and the light of Christ's love will shine even more brightly in the dark corners of this world.—E. Lee Phillips

PRAYER.   Eternal Father, we come today as your children seeking to be reminded of who we are and who you are. We confess that our memories are often so short and that we quickly turn away from your way to self-made paths and trails of self-interest. Teach us that the abundant, meaningful life is found only within your will and your way. Help us to remember how to walk in that way if we have found it, and how to find it if we have missed it altogether.

We pause this day to express thanksgiving for all of your blessings. If we will, we can fill our minds with the greatness of these blessings. We thank you first of all for the gift of life, health, friends, good food, music, and books. We pause to remember the impact that parents, family, schools, and churches have had upon us for goodness, honesty, integrity, and faith. We remember the new worlds that have been opened for us by so many through their conversations, teachings, and writings.

We remember this day those who have stuck by us even when others thought we were hopeless. We remember the dry days and thank you for the rain. We remember those who cheered us up when we were low. We remember those who gave us hope when life tumbled in. We remember those who believed in us when we were weak or when we failed. We remember especially today our fathers or those who have been father models for us. Help those of us who are fathers or father models to express your love through our own words and behavior.

Teach us how to remember. Teach us the proper use of the past that we might serve you better in the present. Help us, O Lord, that we might know how to live as individuals and as a church. Through Jesus Christ our living Lord, we pray.—William Powell Tuck

Sermon: No Fear

TEXT: 1 John 4:7–21; John 15:1–8

The author of 1 John is addressing a church that has lost its vision. John writes to them to say that it is really very simple. We are here to make real the love that God has for the world. We are the recipients of God's love, those of us who call ourselves Christians, that is given to us, unexpectedly, undeservedly, unconditionally. John says, "In this is love, not that we loved God but that he loved us and sent his Son to be the atoning sacrifice for our sins," which is the whole point of the gospel. God took the initiative. God loves us even if we are unlovable. God still loves us.

That is the good news, and it is still new for many people who still think that love is to be a reward for good behavior. If you shape up, then I will love you. If you love me, then I will love you. If you do what I want, become the person I want you to become, then I will love you.

We ordered our relationships with one another conditionally, so we expected God to do the same, to love us when we shaped up. And that was the surprise: God didn't treat us that way.

In this is love, not that we loved God but that he loved us.

Then John makes it personal. Some might feel that he makes it too personal, because if you have received this amazing love of God in your life, as you claim, then it will show. John says, "No one has ever seen God; if we love one another, God lives in us, and his love is perfected in us."

And according to John, there are two places especially where you can see that. You can see it when you approach death, and you can see it when you approach your neighbor.

Look first at what the end of life would look like if, in fact, God dwells in us. If God's love dwells in us, then "we will have boldness on the day of judgment." That is the way John puts it. We will have boldness on the day of judgment because "there is no fear in love, perfect love casts out fear."

The fear he is talking about is the fear of what is going to happen to us at the end of our life. It is expected in our time that we will not talk about such things, or at least when we do we will use euphemisms; or we will rationalize it, which is what we generally do—we rationalize it. We say death is "only natural." We have analyzed the process of dying, the way science does. We have objectified it. We have laid it out in its various stages. This is what you can expect. So it looks like it's natural. That is the assumption of science—if a phenomenon is repeated enough times, it becomes natural.

Well, it may be natural for you to die, but not for me. For me, it is the most unnatural thing that I can think of. The natural thing for me is to keep on living.

A woman's mother dies. Somebody hears about it and says to that person, "I am sorry. You have our sympathy." Then she asks, "How old was your mother?" Well, she was ninety years old. "Oh, well, then it is all right." As if it matters how old the person is. As if it is less painful. As if it is less a sorrow when we lose a parent, or a friend, or a spouse.

The problem is, we are the only animals that know that we are going to die. That knowledge creates anxiety in us. We cover up the anxiety with euphemisms, objectify it with science, and soften it with cosmetics.

I prefer the biblical way. In the Bible, death is the enemy, "the last enemy." God has sent his Son to conquer it, which he did in his Resurrection on Easter. Now because he lives, we too shall live. So John says you have "boldness" in approaching this enemy.

I say, no more of this natural business. I don't want to die a natural death, like a plant. Just fade, wither, and flop over. I don't want that. I want to face death with courage, boldness, and hope, because I know that though I die I will live, because of the victory given to me through my Lord Jesus Christ.

No one has seen God. But you can see God's love in the way Christians approach death with boldness, hope, courage, and no fear, "for perfect love casts out fear."

You can also see God's love in the way Christians approach their neighbor. There are no more unequivocal words in all of scripture than these: "Those who say, 'I love God,' and hate their neighbor, are liars; for those who do not love their neighbor whom they can see, cannot love God whom they have not seen."

John was writing to a congregation that had lost its vision and had turned inward. The Church's vision is outward. They had turned inward, as churches so often do, arguing with one another about all kinds of things. In this case, they were arguing with one another about theology, some saying,

"We have all the truth and therefore the rest of you are benighted." The results were predictable. There were hurt feelings, divisions, things said that shouldn't have been said, recriminations. You know the way it happens.

John writes to them: If you say that you are a Christian, then give the evidence, not only in the way you face death with boldness, but in the way you face your neighbor in love. "For if you say you love God, and you hate your neighbor, then you are a liar."

If the only way anybody is going to be able to see God is to see God's love at work in the lives of people, then make that love visible. St. Francis said, "Preach the gospel at all times and if necessary, use words."

What young people need at the minimum are two things: they need a loving community, and they need an adult who cares for them. For all of these years the Church has been the one enduring institution that has provided that safe environment, that loving environment, and adults to model for young people what the Christian life is all about.

Jim Wallis is the founder of the Sojourner's Community in Washington, D.C. He tells the story of a friend of his who happened to be in Sarajevo when that city was under siege. His friend saw a young girl shot by a sniper fall to the street. A man came over and picked her up. Wallis's friend had a rented car. He drove the car over and said, "Get in. I will take you to the hospital."

They started heading for the hospital. On the way the man holding the girl in the back seat on his lap said, "Hurry, mister, she is still alive." A little while later he said, "Hurry, mister, she is still breathing." A few moments later he said, "Hurry, she is still warm." They got to the emergency room of the hospital and turned the child over to the doctors. The man said, "Hurry, please. She is getting cold."

She died. The two men were washing the blood from their hands. The man who had picked her up said, with tears in his eyes, "I don't know how I am going to tell her father that she is dead." Wallis's friend was astonished. He said, "I thought she was your child." He said, "Aren't they all?" That is the way God looks upon it. They are all God's children.

No one has ever seen God; if we love one another, God lives in us, and his love is perfected in us.—Mark Trotter

Illustrations

A REAL GLIMPSE OF GOD.   Carlyle Marney told about an old man who was asked once,

"Have you ever seen God?" He said, "No, but I have known a couple of Jesuses in my lifetime."—Mark Trotter

CHILDREN AND THE COMMUNITY.   What the best and wisest parent wants for his own child, that must be what the community wants for all its children.—John Dewey

SUNDAY: JUNE TWENTY-SEVENTH

LECTIONARY MESSAGE

Topic: The Waiting Altar
    TEXT: Gen. 22:1–14
    Other Readings: Rom. 6:12–23; Matt. 10:40–42

Do you seriously believe that the God and Father of our Lord Jesus Christ ever told anybody, even to test him, to sacrifice his only son? Or her only daughter? Or anybody else? That Abraham heard—or thought he heard—the voice of God saying that is certain. Just as we know that somewhere in this story the voice of God is speaking to us. But *how* the voice of God speaks to us in this story is not so certain!

I. When astronomers pointed radio telescopes at the heavens, they discovered out there a noise, a background noise, that's all over the universe. It sounds a little like a kind of a hiss. It's like the faint hiss you hear sometimes on a long distance telephone call. And finally somebody came up with a theory that a lot of scientists agree must be the answer to what it is, this thing that we hear as a distant hiss that echoes all around the universe, no matter where you listen for it and look for it. And what they say is wonderful: they believe that it's the echo of the big bang of creation, itself an event so vast that billions of years later the echo of it is still bouncing around, inside the skull of this universe, and we can hear it—a faint hissing noise—if we're quiet enough and listen hard enough with the right instruments. And so I wonder if what Abraham heard wasn't a vast and cosmic sound, deeper and older than the echoes of that primal explosion they call the "big bang."

The author of the book of Revelation heard it, rumbling like the bass organ note that shakes a cathedral, so deep it can scarcely be

heard. And when he came to speak of the deepest thing he saw, he called it "the Lamb slain from the foundation of the world" (Rev. 13:8 KJV). Maybe that ancient visionary figured out what it was that Abraham had overheard and misunderstood. Maybe the truth is that the sacrifice Abraham heard God cry out about was not the sacrifice of a nomad's smiling, dark-skinned boy; maybe the cry of sacrifice that Abraham heard really came from before the foundations of the universe.

II. I picture in my mind's eye the Father and the Son (the Parent and the Child, the Lover and the Loved One, who have been with each other since before there was anything) pacing out where the foundations of the universe are going to be dug. With the joy and the love they share they are planning a place where there can be a family with whom to share it. They're pacing out where the foundations are to be laid for this home, for us, and it comes over them both at once, long before the foundations were laid, long before there was anything. In their wisdom, God the Parent-Child can see that from the crown of the house down through the foundation there will be the most awful chasm of a crack. Why? Because some of us will take our freedom not to love but to destroy; to be hateful, to choose evil rather than good, and self rather than God. God saw before it was made that the thing they were planning would break. And at the same instant they saw that someone must heal that break. And the Son said to the Father (the Child to the Parent, the Loved one to the Lover), "Let it be me." So before the universe was, the death of Christ was. And from that moment on, the joy that the Father shares with the Son was mingled with the knowledge of, with the presence of, death. And did not God cry out then? That's what it means to say that the

Lamb was slain before the foundation of the world.

III. Well, at last it was all created. And the Son left the Father's side and was born. They were separated by long distance. Oh, they talked to each other. But always it was over the long-distance wire, with the lonely hiss that you hear sometimes like the cosmic background noise. And then came the final call. "O Father, if it's possible, let this cup pass from me." And then, over the wires, the Parent hears it all: the shouts and the sound of blows, and the ring of a hammer against cold iron. Until finally, the Son of Man could no longer hear the voice of God. But God could still hear across the distance that chilling cry, "My God, my God, why have you forsaken me?" Then silence. And then the cry of the Parent, the cry that made the heavens shudder: "My son, my only son, sacrificed on *this mountain!*" But then (in my imagination) God hears someone else, on a crossed wire, muttering, "Take your son, your only son, Isaac, and sacrifice him upon this mountain." Somehow Abraham overheard God's cry— "My only son, sacrificed!"—the way scientists can overhear the cosmic noise, and he misunderstood it. He thought it meant sacrifice your joy (Isaac means "laughter"). Haven't you said something like that to yourself? "To be a Christian I must give up what I love"? But in a moment, even in the depths of grief, God dispatches an angel, shouting, "Abraham, Abraham, stay your hand!" And Abraham looks around and there is a ram, caught by his horns in a woody thicket—as Christ was caught and held fast for us by the wood of the cross.

So take back, as God's gift to you, your joy, your laughter; take as God's gift to you today the sacrifice of Jesus Christ. "On the mount of the Lord it shall be provided" (Gen. 22:14). God will provide for you the Lamb, slain (on Mount Zion) from before the foundations of the world.—Donald F. Chatfield

Illustrations

FOLLOW YOUR BLISS.   Career counseling services charge fees, sometimes substantial ones, to help people find out what sort of work would be best for them. But the basic secret underlying all they do was discovered generations ago: if, in your work, you can spend at least half of your time doing something you love, you will be happy. On the other hand, if over 50 percent of your time is spent performing functions you dislike, you will begin to become maladjusted, even to develop illnesses and psychological problems. Mythologist Joseph Campbell was on target when he advised us to "follow your bliss." It seems that God made us with different gifts, that using those gifts will bring us joy, and that being unable to use them will weaken us. Perhaps when Jesus says, "My yoke is easy, and my burden is light" (Matt. 11:30), he means in part that giving up our legitimate joys for God is not a sacrifice with which God is well pleased.—Donald F. Chatfield

OUT OF THE DEPTHS.   Because he cried out his godforsakenness, he was utterly human; he was man visited by the most terrible suffering and death.

Nevertheless, he is the Son of God, who as the darkness clutched at him from below reached out for the hand of the Father by calling out to him. And so, even as he was horribly abandoned and deserted, he was nevertheless secure in those hands and lifted above all woe. He was held suspended above the abyss of nothingness, but he was held by the majesty of God himself. As he was cast down to death, so he was secretly lifted up to an invisible throne. As he cried out like a tormented creature, so he lived in eternal communion with the Father. He is man and he is God; he is cast down into death and lifted up into life.—Helmut Thielicke[124]

SERMON SUGGESTIONS

Topic: Perfect Peace
TEXT: Isa. 26:3
(1) God's gift of peace is special: it is *Shalom*—protection and prosperity—and it is available to God's people. (2) It is peace that prevails in the most difficult circumstances (John 14:27). (3) The key is firm trust in God.

Topic: Listen to the Spirit
TEXT: Rev. 3:14–22
(1) Because you may be self-satisfied (vv. 15–17). (2) Because the Lord may be dealing

[124]*Christ and the Meaning of Life*

with you through disciplines you are experiencing (v. 19). (3) Because you can have an intimate and rewarding fellowship with the living Lord (vv. 20–21).

Hymn Suggestions

1. "God Is Love, Let Heavens Adore Him," Timothy Rees (1922); ABBOTT'S LEIGH, Cyril Taylor (1941)

This twentieth-century hymn expands on the assurance of Romans 6:14 that sin will have no dominion over those who are the recipients of God's grace and love. Its singing could set the tone for the hearing of the Epistle lesson to be read.

2. "How Long, O Lord?" Barbara Wollett (c. 1983); BINNEY'S, Eric H. Thiman (1951)

Because this modern paraphrase so closely follows the original Psalm 13, it could be sung in place of the Psalter reading. Its plaintive minor tune is a suitable musical vehicle for this psalm of lament.

3. "Where Cross the Crowded Ways of Life," Frank M. North (1903); GERMANY, Gardiner's Sacred Melodies (1815)

As a response to the reading from the Gospel—Matthew 10:40–42, with its assurance of reward to those who serve the needy—this fine hymn could be prayerfully sung.

4. "I Gave My Life for Thee," Frances R. Havergal (1884); KENOSIS, Philip P. Bliss (1873)

The Old Testament reading depicting Abraham's willingness to sacrifice his son could be followed by the thoughtful singing of the poignant questions of this gospel hymn.—Hugh T. McElrath

Worship Aids

CALL TO WORSHIP.   "I have trusted in thy mercy; my heart shall rejoice in thy salvation! I will sing unto the Lord, because he hath dealt bountifully with me" (Ps. 13:5–6).

INVOCATION.   Come, Holy Spirit, come and indite our petitions with love and faith and hope. May we know that someone else is helping us to pray, for we know so little. Our horizons are small and fade in the mist. Let this hour be an hour of prayer. All the way through this service may we be looking unto Thee, O God, and wilt Thou teach us how to pray. We ask in the name of our Lord and Savior, Jesus Christ.—Frank W. Gunsaulus

OFFERTORY SENTENCE.   "Thanks be unto God for his unspeakable gift" (2 Cor. 9:15).

OFFERTORY PRAYER.   Father, you have filled our lives with good things beyond measure. Now open our hands to others that we may give generously, that their hopes and prayers sounded out of deep need may be answered as our offerings are laid before you today in Jesus' name.—Henry Fields

PRAYER.   Almighty God, whom we do praise on high because the highest hast come to us through the highest, even our Lord, to us and to the highest within us, making appeal to that which is loftiest, so that we cry out in prayer and sing rejoicing, "Holy, Holy, Holy, Lord God Almighty," to thee we bring from all the lower experiences of our lives the prayers expressed and unexpressed of our very souls, knowing that thou on high hast proven to us the highness and loftiness of thy divine nature by reaching down to us. Now the weakest of us comes and the weariest and the saddest, the most mistaken, and the most sinful, crying—the lowliest and the highest—"O God of Jesus Christ forgive us our sins in the Name of our Lord and Savior, Jesus Christ."—Frank W. Gunsaulus

Sermon: The Integrity of Job and the Mystery of God

TEXT: Job 1 and chapters following

The book of Job begins with an artful retelling of an old legend familiar throughout the Near East. In this legend, Job is immensely wealthy, immensely pious, and immensely respected. He loses everything that makes life worth living, yet he refuses to blame God. Instead, he patiently resigns himself to his fate with the consolation that God gives or takes away as God pleases. God, who has wagered with Satan over Job's fidelity, wins the bet and rewards Job with a twofold increase in material assets and another set of seven sons and three daughters. Job also regains his lost status in the community and lives to "a very great age." Job is the wise one, who deals wisely with adversity—patient acceptance, faithfulness to God—assured that in the end everything will be right. The prologue and epilogue put Job on trial, and he is found innocent.

In the poetry, however, which constitutes the bulk of the book, we discover a second, very different Job. In this second version, Job is still a good man who loses everything that makes living worthwhile. But in this version, Job almost loses his religion as well. His whole world has crumbled, and instead of being patient and submissive, he demands an explanation. He believes he has a right to an explanation because it is *his* life that has been ruined. If God will not give him the explanation he desires, then he will be forced to conclude that God is not really just after all. In the poetry, Job puts *God* on trial. His friends, who have heard about his distress and have come to console him, are horrified at his disfigured countenance *and* his unorthodox, shocking, dangerous questions. Job is flirting with blasphemy, and the friends see it as their duty to discourage this romance. The only way they know to do this is to assume that Job is guilty of something and to make him admit his guilt, because if Job has not sinned, then God *does* seem to be unjust as Job has charged. Implicitly at first, then explicitly, with growing anger toward Job, they argue that he deserves the suffering visited upon him. Job responds by defending his integrity and accusing his friends of faithlessness. He rejects in no uncertain terms their explanation that suffering always results from sin, but he is unable to discover a better one. Instead, Job explores the ways he might get satisfaction—either a third party could arbitrate, or God could appear and Job could question God. Job finally silences his friends with a summary of his defense, ending with a mighty oath of clearance. He too falls silent and awaits God's response.

This response is delayed, however, by the longest continuous series of speeches, those of the pompous, bombastic, and earnest youth Elihu, who repeats many of the friends' arguments but who also contributes two new elements. The first is the idea of suffering being a signal from a gracious God to turn the sinner from sin, instead of being merely punishment. The second is a magnificent, thrilling description of the thunderstorm, which introduces, finally, the speeches of God. The divine speeches out of the thunderstorm consist of overwhelming rhetorical questions that have the effect of silencing Job. Job had demanded God's appearance so he could question God. But when God does appear, God does the questioning, not Job. Job the rebel "melts away" and his questions no longer seem relevant in the light of his encounter with the living God. Curiously, though, God vindicates Job because, when the speeches are ended, God says to Eliphaz: "My anger is aroused against you and your two friends, because unlike my servant Job you have not spoken as you ought about me" (42:7).

The purpose of the book of Job (that is, of the poetic dialogue) is to confront human suffering in a world created by God. Job insists throughout that there must be some satisfactory answer to this question, but he never finds it. The book of Job never offers us an intellectual, philosophical answer to the question of human suffering. Instead, it does something else. Job has dared to say things that are scandalous and that border on blasphemy. He has accused God of being his enemy and of being unjust. Such charges cannot go unanswered. Thus God finally appears to correct Job's error and be vindicated, though at the same time God acknowledges Job's righteousness. Job's questioning, petulance, and anger melt away in the heat of God's overwhelming rhetorical questions. Job, who has known of God only by "the hearing of the ears," now confronts God face to face in personal encounter. God is now no longer simply the object of formal piety but is also a living, inescapable presence. The poet's purpose, therefore, is to call into question the friends' traditional explanation of suffering and show that it is inadequate. Yet the poet does not propose a new solution and so is not engaging in theodicy. The existence of both God and suffering remains a mystery.

But this intellectual mystery is transformed by an even greater mystery—that of the divine-human encounter. God's appearing to Job affirms Job's self-worth. Job maintains his integrity in the face of powerful pressures to conform and compromise. Job therefore exemplifies the "courage to be." God's address to Job affirms Job's self-valuation and invests Job with new dignity and honor. Job is no longer the wealthy, pious, wise man. He is now the one-addressed-by-God, the one who because of his integrity and refusal to conform is worthy now to stand in the presence of God.—Bill Thomason[125]

Illustrations

SUFFERING.   Bacon thought of God sitting serenely remote from suffering. "In this world God only and the angels may be spectators." Bacon had forgotten his Bible. "When thou passest through the waters I will be with thee and through the rivers, they shall not overflow thee. . . . Fear not, for I am with thee." No one who has grasped the meaning of the Cross of Christ's deathless

words, "He that hath seen Me hath seen the Father," thinks of a remote God. He is in your tragedy with you, sharing with you His spiritual power and leading you on to victory.—J. Leonard Clough[126]

WHEN GOD HAS DISAPPEARED.   The courage to take the anxiety of meaninglessness upon oneself is the boundary line up to which the courage to be can go. Beyond it is mere nonbeing. Within it all forms of courage are reestablished in the power of God above the God of theism. *The courage to be is rooted in the God who appears when God has disappeared in the anxiety of doubt.*—Paul Tillich[127]

SUNDAY: JULY FOURTH

LECTIONARY MESSAGE

Topic: Behold, the Camels Come

TEXT: Gen. 24:34–38, 42–29, 58–67

Other Readings: Rom. 7:15–25a; Matt. 11:16–19, 25–30

In the fortunes of Isaac, we see expectation, loneliness, meditation, promise, and finally, fulfillment. In this way God directed the life of Abraham's son, Isaac, the son given by God to keep his promise to Abraham.

In the person of Rebekah are kindness, caring, helpfulness, and the willingness to serve God. So life under God brought Rebekah into the path of God's eternal purpose.

I. *From expectation to fulfillment.* The details of life pile up moment by moment. Years and decades are full of the details, leading to some strange experiences, composing series of events, resulting in lives. Here was Isaac, coming from the well Lahairoi in the south country, and he went out to the field to meditate at about sundown. He experienced the moment of fulfillment that proved that his life belonged to the Lord of the universe—*the camels were coming!*

Isaac had once been taken by his father, Abraham, to a hilltop altar, carrying the sticks for the fire by which he was to become the proof of his father's obedience and faithfulness to God.

II. *Faith, the basis of expectation.* Imagine Abraham's faith! A promise was fulfilled in Isaac's birth to Abraham and Sarah, when Abraham was one hundred years old and Sarah was well past the normal age of motherhood. Isaac was the sole heir of the promise of God, because Ishmael was the son not in the purpose of God. God commanded Abraham to sacrifice Isaac! Let's look at the human side a moment. *Be real!* You are Abraham, and your miracle of a son is now required to be sacrificed. Do you not stop and at least think to yourself, "Come on, Lord—surely you don't mean it!" But still, Abraham had perfect faith—God had given, he could require. Abraham saw no way but to obey.

God renewed his covenant—a sacrifice was provided—and Isaac was reprieved by God. Especially for this day, when Isaac saw the camels coming, carrying his promised bride, had he been renewed in God's promise, redeemed by a ram. Now God had brought the grace not only of human contentment and satisfaction but also of continued provision for racial as well as individual redemption, by bringing to his chosen man his chosen bride.

The series of events leading up to this momentous meeting proves once again how valuable the book of Genesis is to the Christian. All the great issues of time and eternity are faithfully dealt with, and God's loving

---

[125] *God on Trial: The Book of Job and Human Suffering* (Collegeville, MN: The Liturgical Press, 1997), 8–10.

[126] In *Treasury of the Christian World*

[127] *The Courage to Be*

grace and his power to redeem and sanctify his wayward creatures are fully demonstrated. Because we believe the Scriptures to be the Word of God, we must assign as prominent a position to the events of this family compact, to the account of the servant successfully guided each step of the way to the fulfillment of his master's instructions, as the lengthy account occupies in this Book of Divine Beginnings. This story is to be constructively viewed as showing the pattern of God's infinite provision for the lighting of the flame of faith and salvation, for the sanctification of every dedicated life in the ages of God's relation to humankind. Our account reveals (in verse 37) that the servant refers to Abraham's requirement of the oath that the line of the chosen people would not be mixed with any line but that of the people of God.

III. *The fulfillment of the faithful servant's oath.* Thus the oath between Abraham and the servant had as its object the provision of a lifelong partner for his son. It is a fitting forecast of all the subsequent elements of God's provision of a partner—the Church—for *his* son, Jesus Christ. Jesus speaks in a parable (Matt. 22:2) of the king who provided a marriage for his son—a mission call to believers as servants of God to form the all-time partnership with him.

This servant of Abraham was faithful to his master's trust. He described Isaac as the son of old age, unto whom his very wealthy father—with great blessing, and possessing "flocks, and herds, and silver, and gold, and menservants, and maidservants, and camels, and asses" (v. 35)—"hath given all that he hath."

The renewed emphasis in the church on spirituality seems to be preoccupied with looking inward to see the depth of devotion in each heart; but that is not the proof of spirituality. The proof of spirituality is not in the extent of the Holy Spirit's work within a believer, but rather in that the servant speaks not of himself but of the magnificent greatness of him for whom he seeks the companion and partner. Just as the servant won Rebekah by holding up Isaac, the Spirit draws the souls of humans to Christ by holding up his perfection.

Such winsome testimony and selfless service will always be successful. When one preaches, teaches, and upholds in conversa-

tion the glory of Jesus Christ as the one in whom "dwelleth all the fullness of the Godhead bodily" (Col. 2:9), the hearts of the lost, the weary, the hopeless, the overborne, the bruised, and the lonely will find in him their renewal and their eternal inheritance, just as Rebekah saw her future fulfilled in her partnership with Isaac.

The result on which we focus—that moment when Isaac roused out of his sole meditation and saw that, behold, the camels were coming—is the effect of trust in God, the realization that when we trust, he brings to pass, puts into effect, makes happen just what it takes to make life and eternity complete.—John R. Rodman

Illustrations

THE YET UNKNOWN.   The definite and the tangible have their value, and so have the indefinite and the intangible. The man who knows exactly where he is going may not go very far. He may merely go across the street or into the next town to buy and sell and get gain. The man who goes out on some moral quest "not knowing whither he goeth" often goes a long way and he arrives at some glorious destination. "Alas for him who never sees the stars shine through the cypress trees!" Trees are all very well—they furnish us lumber to build houses, material to make furniture, fuel to bake our bread. But the stars!—Charles R. Brown[128]

HOW WE FIND OUT.   "Obedience is the organ of spiritual knowledge," Robertson of Brighton said. "If any man has the will to do His will, he shall know." It sounds dogmatic—it is dogmatic. The promise made to those who strive to do His will is not that they will be able to make a shrewd guess at the truth—"Ye shall know." The promise is not for a few gifted minds alone—it is universal. "Any man"—that takes us all in. The offer was not restricted to college professors or to doctors of philosophy.—Charles R. Brown[129]

---

[128]*Dreams Come True* (Old Tappan, NJ: Macmillan, 1945), 5.

[129]*Dreams Come True*, p. 112.

SERMON SUGGESTIONS

Topic: Your Everlasting Light
TEXT: Isa. 60:19–20
(1) Potential for Israel (v. 60:1). (2) Fulfillment in Jesus Christ (John 8:12). (3) Extension through believers (Matt. 5:14).

Topic: Losers and Gainers
TEXT: Phil. 3:7–21
(1) A goal to die for (vv. 7–11). (2) A past to overcome (vv. 12–16). (3) An identity to cherish (v. 20).

Hymn Suggestions

1. "The God of Abraham Praise," Yigdal of Daniel ben Judah (1400), para. Thomas Olivers; LEONI, Hebrew Melody (1780)
This great hymn of praise stemming from the Jewish tradition is quite suitable for any Sunday's worship, but it is especially so when the focus is on the God of Abraham and Isaac, of Sarah and Rebekah (Gen. 24).
2. "O Crucified Redeemer," Timothy Rees (1946); LLANGLOFFAN, Welsh melody, harm. David Evans (1927)
The penitent confessional spirit of this twentieth-century hymn would be appropriate when sung in connection with the apostle Paul's confession of his inward struggle with sin (Rom. 7:15–25a).
3. "I Praise the King with All My Verses," vers. Marie J. Post and Bert Polman (1986); O DASS ICH TAUSEND, Johann B. König (1738)
This chorale could be sung by the choir, alternating with readings from Psalm 45, on which it is based, for the first three stanzas. The congregation may then join in singing the final two stanzas. This is a beautiful example of a modern paraphrase of a rather unique psalm.
4. "I Heard the Voice of Jesus Say," Horatius Bonar (1946); VOX DILECTI, John Bacchus Dykes (1868)
This hymn, based on three gracious sayings of our Lord, could be sung stanza by stanza in response to the following readings: Matt. 11:28, John 6:35, and John 8:12. Antiphonal treatment of each stanza, with the choir singing on the three invitations of Jesus (in minor key) and the congregation responding with the joyful result that answer-

ing Jesus brings (in major key), would be effective.—Hugh T. McElrath

Worship Aids

CALL TO WORSHIP. "What a miserable person I am. Who will rescue me from this body that is doomed to die? Thank God! Jesus Christ will rescue me" (Rom. 7:24–25 CEV).

INVOCATION. We look to you, O God, for life, true life, here and hereafter. To that end, bless and empower us as we worship you in praise and prayer, in sermon and song, and in quiet waiting in your gracious presence.

OFFERTORY SENTENCE. "What you are doing is much more than a service that supplies God's people with what they need. It is something that will make many others thank God" (2 Cor. 9:12 CEV).

OFFERTORY PRAYER. Whether we bring to you much or little, our Father, we know that you are able to do with it exceedingly abundantly above all that we ask or thank. So receive and multiply our tithes and offerings, we pray (Eph. 3:20 KJV).

PRAYER. O Lord, we take into our prayer this morning all conditions, all achievements, all frustrations of hope, all blighted buds that shall never fully bloom, all the grief and all the tears, that we may take them into the little cup which we offer to thee; and we recognize that on the outside there are millions untouched by our comprehension. Thou knowest all; thou knowest everybody's need. We commend unto thee the child Humanity, the blundering, faithless, mistaken, rising, hoping, believing child Humanity—in the Name of our Lord and Savior, Jesus Christ.—Frank W. Gunsaulus[130]

Sermon: Public Tears

TEXT: 2 Sam. 1:17–27
Saul and David have been political enemies for years. We were present when Samuel anointed David and declared that David was

---

[130]*Prayers*, p. 23.

God's new servant and that the kingdom had been taken away from Saul. The story has rushed along as Saul has attempted to capture and eliminate David. But David has refused to fight back. He would do nothing to help advance his claim to the throne. He would not put forth his hand to harm the Lord's anointed. If David were to become king, it would be because God pushed him into that position. David would not be Macbeth. He would forever be a loyal servant of Saul.

I. Now the news comes that Saul and Jonathan have died. Like the beat reporter who wants to be first with the story, the messenger thought there would be a reward from David to the first one who brought him the news of Saul's death. The king and the heir apparent are both dead. The door has opened wide for David to move in. David should be delighted with the news. But David does not rejoice. He knows a great tragedy when he sees it. There is no joy where there is a great divide. The punishment of the youths who removed a stop sign brings no joy and celebration to those who have lost a child.

II. David, the psalmist, gathers up his pain, gathers up the broken plans and hopes of the people, gathers up the vision and providence of God, which were not able to accomplish in Saul all that God had intended, and brings them to song. This is a song of public tears. This is David acting in front of and on behalf of the people. This is David in the leadership role of being able to express the power and emotions of his nation.

It has been suggested by many recently that it is always part of the government propaganda effort to discourage events of public grief and national tears. "The prospect of public grief is a scarce practice in our society, where we are so engaged in self-deception, pretending that everything is 'all right.'"[131] There are those who suggest that it is part of the permanent mind-set of political consultants that you never acknowledge that things are not going well. Never admit a mistake. Never acknowledge a sorrow. Never confess a failure.

But these words of David are public tears

expressing public pain and grief. David's public tears suggest that there is no healing where there is no acknowledgment of pain. If you refuse to admit your pain, then you never get help. But Freud was right: if you repress and deny your tears, your pain, and your sorrow, it will find a way out. Others will have to debate whether or not we as a society have been repressive in our public pain, but in my lifetime we have certainly seen some changes in the expression and processing of our public tears.

III. We have a traditional and formal laying of a wreath at the tomb of the Unknown Soldier, but we have an ever-expanding informal tradition of thousands of people coming and placing flowers and gifts at the Vietnam Memorial. Where there could have been more organized expressions of public sorrow, we now have spontaneous and massive displays of emotions: people coming to the government building and putting flowers around the old tree; strangers bonding and crying together at the site; a couple of bright happy teenagers go off the road and hit a tree, and immediately a long, steady stream of people come and leave notes, flowers, signs, and memorabilia. These are public tears coming to expression in new ways.

Public tears and public sorrows are finding new and different ways to come out. No one came to my high school when a drunken driver crossed the center line and hit a bright, happy young girl head-on and killed her. There was no army of mental health counselors, no calling in of all the clergy to be present at the school for the next three days. We gathered at the funeral home. We went to the funeral service. These venues gave us channels to express our public sorrows. These days, public sorrows and public grief come out and find expression in different ways.

But David was right: they must come out. In the end we must face our pain and acknowledge our hurt. We have to confess what hurts. The death of JFK shattered a lot of hopes and expectations. We have to acknowledge that a denial of our public pain and sorrow means a barrier to our recovery. There are those who suggest that because we have never acknowledged our public pain and sorrow about slavery, we have never been able to move closer in our race relations. There are those who suggest that because

[131]Walter Brueggemann, *First and Second Samuel: Interpretation* (Louisville: John Knox, 1990), 218.

there is that public pain and sorrow that has not been openly acknowledged and that keeps oozing out at the Vietnam Memorial, we have not been able to recover well.

IV. The news of Saul and Jonathan's death was a moment of deep personal and public pain for David, and David spoke these words of pain. Notice that there is not a hopeful word within the song. David does not rush to try to make us feel better. In the speaking of our public pain, we are so often too eager to try to make people feel better. "How the mighty have fallen." What a blow to our hopes. It is not just that Saul and Jonathan are dead; that grief comes later. But our very best military heroes have been beaten.

The public song of the public tears confesses that our best is not good enough. Perhaps that is why it is not easy for politicians to say. The public song of the public tears begins by acknowledging that our best warriors were not able. They are dead. Those who come back in body bags were the mighty, the fit, the able. The public song of the public sorrow starts with our confession that even the best of our species is vulnerable. Saul and Jonathan are dead. The mighty have fallen and the dreams and the hopes for the Kingdom of God have not been accomplished. In our western civilization—with its continued confidence in the perfectibility of humanity, with its self-confidence that if the mind can conceive it, the hand can achieve it—the recognition that the mighty have fallen without success is a direct admission of misguided confidence.

V. David just looks at the reality that the heroes of Israel are dead. We had thought he was the one to redeem Israel. There is an awesome need for us to look long and hard at all of our pretending that we are able, at our belief that all our young people need is a dose of self-confidence. We have to believe in ourselves. To acknowledge our public tears, to give voice to our pain, to express our grief in times of tragedy, is to acknowledge that there is in a Timothy McVeigh some power of evil that we will never be able to get rid of by our own efforts. That even our brightest and best cannot and do not often take us very far from where we already are, and if we are ever to come to the Kingdom of God, it will be by the grace of God to give us the Kingdom, because in our moments of public tears we have

realized that we will never be able to make the Kingdom come by our own efforts.

David does not talk about God in this song. But that is what David lived by. If God wanted David to be king, God would give him the kingdom, because David could not, would not, make it happen. If God wants to bring us into the Kingdom, God has to make the Kingdom available to us as a gift, because "How the mighty have fallen!" That is the good news we hear in the story of Jesus Christ, that God in his love and mercy has come to give us the Kingdom because not even the best of us is able to win all the battles by ourselves all of the time.

Jesus says to his disciples, "Fear not, little flock; it is the Father's pleasure to give you the kingdom."—Rick Brand

Illustrations

GOD'S CHOICE. Man can certainly keep on lying . . . but he cannot make truth falsehood. He can certainly rebel . . . but he can accomplish nothing which abolishes the choice of God.—Karl Barth

RIGHT LIVING.
From the cowardice that dare not face new truth,
From the laziness that is contented with half truth,
From the arrogance that thinks it knows all truth,
Good Lord, deliver me.
—Prayer from Kenya[132]

A PASTOR'S CONFESSION. I was lamenting this morning my unfitness for work, and especially for the warfare to which I am called. A sense of heaviness came over me, but relief came very speedily, for which I thank the Lord. Indeed, I was greatly burdened, but the Lord succored me. The first verse read at the Sabbath morning service exactly met my case. It is in Isaiah 43:1: "But now thus saith the Lord that created thee, O Jacob, and he that formed thee, O Israel, fear not." I said to myself, "I am what God created me, and I am what he formed me, and there-

[132]George Appletone, ed., *The Oxford Book of Prayers* (Oxford: Oxford University Press, 1986), 115.

fore I must, after all, be the right man for the place wherein he has put me." We may not blame our Creator, nor suspect that he has missed his mark in forming an instrument for his work. Thus new comfort comes to us. Not only do the operations of grace in the spiritual world yield us consolation, but we are even comforted by what the Lord has done in creation. We are told to cease from our fears; and we do so, because we perceive that it is the Lord who made us, and not we ourselves, and he will justify his own creating skill by accomplishing through us the purposes of his love.—Charles H. Spurgeon[133]

SUNDAY: JULY ELEVENTH

LECTIONARY MESSAGE

Topic: God's Continuing History
TEXT: Gen. 25:19–34
Other Readings: Rom. 8:1–11; Matt. 13:1–9, 18–23

Many distinguished authors and editors have researched, compiled, and published books telling the history of the Christian Church. The story is fascinating, at times heroic, and always intriguing. As a person reads of the continuing evolution of the Church from a small group of tried and devoted disciples into the great present-day body of Christian believers, in every country and among every race of people, he or she is newly equipped to appreciate how God leads his people through trials, difficulties, and challenges to become his body of witness for his own glory.

Our great "Book of Divine Beginnings," Genesis, develops important principles of God's dealings with, and provisions for, some highly unlikely persons—people somewhat like us.

I. *Taking another's place.* What caused the second-born son of Isaac and Rebekah to become the man of God, the eventual father of a great nation, the eponym of that nation, and the avenue of God's blessing on all future generations of humanity? Why would God bless in every way a man who supplanted his firstborn brother? There may be a sensible explanation.

Que sera, sera—whatever will be, will be—is not quite the true viewpoint on life, not quite the enlightened outlook, for any individual or nation. It is, for one thing, atheistic—it reckons without the plan, purpose, predestination, or provision of God, who rules in the universe and in people's hearts and lives. It is also fatalistic, endorsing the philosophical idea that events occur because of the laws of the universe, and denying the force of personal variations and the influence of faith and prayer in individual lives.

Contrary to this viewpoint is the truth that personal outcomes are the results of personal acts, whether those acts are based on impulse or caused by long and thoughtful research and consideration.

II. *Taking over God's plan.* One possible reason for Jacob's replacing Esau is that his desire drove him. The name *Jacob* is attributed to the event of his birth, in which he "took hold of the heel of Esau," and it means, as nearly as we can tell, that he thereby supplanted Esau. We can attribute his grasping the heel of his brother only to an innate, congenital urge to be first instead of second, and later, to the desire to replace Esau in his father's affection and in his blessing.

Another reason might be the coarse and carnal nature of Esau, which may have led to his disdain for his birthright and caused him to prefer instead a bowl of Jacob's stew. The Spirit of God had indwelt Jacob and had found Esau rejecting spiritual things. The present time was most important to Esau; his bodily comfort influenced his choices, and he could not delay the desire of the moment for the sake of realizing a greater good in a later time. Esau was the personification of those who seek instant gratification at the expense of future health, safety, or reward.

III. *Making fateful decisions.* Esau said to Jacob, "I am at the point to die," so Esau gave up his claim to his future life. Many people—young and old—believe that present conditions are all that is important; they adopt the philosophy *carpe diem*—seize the day—and fail, or refuse, to consider the fruit of today's

[133]*Great Pulpit Masters* (Grand Rapids: Baker Book House, 1972), 175.

impulsive expenditures of physical or spiritual capital in the harvest of the future. One is reminded of the sick old person who said, "If I had known I was going to live this long, I'd have taken better care of myself."

So much is involved in the early choices and patterns of a human life. It is almost as if, as someone once remarked, "youth is too good a thing to be wasted on the young." It is extremely difficult for a child to see the possible long-term effects of his or her own impulsive actions; it is therefore essential that a child be guided and protected from dangerous behavior. Great life-making decisions are required of youth—choice of education, choice of career, choice of a mate, and most serious of all, choice of religious faith or a secular life. It seems as though the most serious decisions must be made when one is least equipped to make them. That is all the more reason to determine in one's youth, on the basis of what one wants the future to be like, to follow God, who is the author and the finisher of life; to learn his ways of grace and love; and to care for the welfare of others.— John R. Rodman

Illustrations

THE FOOL.   Down the street, from His old home, just outside Nazareth, there was a farmer so prosperous that he had to enlarge his barns, and while still young he retired, the lucky fellow, as we all would like to do. And then he died: and people went about saying how well he had done, and how much he had left, more even than they had imagined it could be. But into Jesus' eyes for once there came contempt. To Him it seemed so monstrous that a life, a whole rich human life, should have been thrown away only for that! And He stooped down and wrote with His own hand across the tomb that stinging epitaph, "Thou fool!" And that is why He looks so anxiously at you. For He knows He can offer you something infinitely bigger than these cheap nothings you keep handling wistfully; knows that what He has to give is not just something additional that can be joined on to the rest, but something so central, so foundational, so essential, so splendid, that without it no one can have anything worth reckoning at all. "I am come," He said, "to give you life."—Arthur John Gossip[134]

WHO LIVES BEST?   "He lives the best," Luther once said, "who does not live to himself; and he lives the worst who lives to himself." Only the self-forgetful person finds the peace of God and thus becomes secure within the consciousness of those higher thoughts. The only place I can reach God is where he chooses to be present: in my fellow man, whom I help without thinking of myself, the fellow man for whom I am available and whom I love. That is exactly what Nebel meant by saying, "Self-sacrifice is the only remedy for neuroses and depressions." The prescription appears to be that simple when the issue is the ultimate questions of life.— Helmut Thielicke[135]

SERMON SUGGESTIONS

Topic: Keep God in Mind
TEXT: Prov. 3:5–6 REB
(1) Some practical, even good ways of setting our course: (a) thinking matters through for ourselves; (b) getting the opinions and advice of others; (c) patiently waiting for circumstances to change. Each of these ways has its limitations. (2) The ways of wisdom: (a) trust God completely; (b) pray about every significant decision you make; (c) listen to the sound counsel of devout, caring people (Prov. 4:1–4), (d) then go forward with confidence.

Topic: The Invitation
TEXT: Matt. 11:27–30 NIV
(1) A gracious, universal invitation: "Come." (2) A specifically focused invitation: "Come to me." (3) A caring, compassionate invitation: "Come to me, all you who are weary and burdened." (4) An invitation with a promise: "Come to me, all you who are weary and burdened, and I will give you rest." (5) An invitation with an imperative: "Come to me, all you who are weary and burdened, and I will give you rest. Take my yoke upon you."

[134]*From the Edge of the Crowd*
[135]*How to Believe Again*

Hymn Suggestions

1. "Praise the Lord, Ye (O) Heavens, Adore Him," Anon. (1797); HYFRYDOL, Rowland Hugh Prichard (1831)

Originally a children's hymn found in *Foundling Hospital Psalms and Hymns* (1798), this is a great hymn for beginning worship. Its first stanza ends with reference to God's laws—the theme of the Psalter reading for today.

2. "O Word of God Incarnate," William W. How (1867); MUNICH, Meiningen Gesangbuch (1693)

This stately chorale is an elaboration of Psalm 119:105 and thus a good response to the Psalter reading.

3. "Open My Eyes, That I May See," Clara H. Scott (1895); OPEN MY EYES, Clara H. Scott (1895)

The second stanza of this devotional hymn is particularly suitable as a response to the Gospel reading. The hymn could also be sung as a prayer in preparation for the Scripture reading in Matthew.

4. "And Can It Be," Charles Wesley (1738); SAGINA, Thomas Campbell (1825)

This popular Wesleyan hymn on confession, forgiveness, and the amazing love of God is perfect for use with the reading from Romans. Indeed, its fourth stanza paraphrases Romans 8:1.—Hugh T. McElrath

Worship Aids

CALL TO WORSHIP. "Thy word is a lamp unto my feet, and a light unto my path" (Ps. 119:105).

INVOCATION. O Lord, most righteous, we pause to pray, for prayer is the breath of the soul. We come to sing, for rejoicing is the joy of the soul put to music. We come to worship, for worship is the heartbeat of the soul. Bless what we do here that God may be glorified in this place and in our lives all through the week ahead.—E. Lee Phillips

OFFERTORY SENTENCE. "God has chosen the weak things of the world to confound the things which are mighty" (1 Cor. 1:27b).

OFFERTORY PRAYER. Because of your amazing resourcefulness, O Lord, we believe that even the smallest of our gifts can do astonishing things. So we give boldly, trusting in your providence and power.

PRAYER. Our Heavenly Father, why should we lift our praise unto thee this morning when we cannot add a single ray of glory to the throne nor pour into the great chord of the universe and joy? We ask ourselves this question as we come into the very presence of the Omnipotence and Omniscience ruling the universe. Then there steals over us the sweet and encouraging thought that thou desirest communion. Thou hast come all the way to us, through our Lord; thou hast come, by way of the Holy Spirit; thou hast come, so many, many times, thou hast come to us in familiar ways; by providence thou hast come; through sorrows and joys thou hast come. Thou are so rich and yet thou wouldst have thy children around thy throne in communion, as a father would have his children. We thank thee for the fellowship of this service. May it be ours through all our lifetime. We ask through our Lord and Savior, Jesus Christ.—Frank W. Gunsaulus

Sermon: Old Men, Dreams, and the Spirit

TEXT: Acts 2:14–21

How can we ensure that when we reach retirement age or beyond that we will be better, not bitter; that we will find ourselves to be compassionate, not cranky, jubilant rather than judgmental as senior adults?

I. *First, some scriptural background.* Simon Peter is preaching to the Jews gathered from all over Asia and the Mediterranean. Filled with the Spirit of Christ, he explains to them how they are able to hear the gospel in their own native language, and then he ties this phenomenon into the prophecy of Joel as to what would happen in the final days, when the Spirit of God descended upon his people.

Joel was an interesting choice, primarily because we know little or nothing about him and even less about when he spoke and wrote. To the best of our ability to date him, we can determine that Joel came after the exile, after the Jews had returned to Israel and rebuilt the walls and the Temple, somewhere around 400 to 350 B.C. Israel had pulled back into herself and was waiting on God to come with the "Day of the Lord," that day when God would restore Israel to her rightful place. Joel watched as a plague of locusts came and literally destroyed the vegetation of the land. After seeing this, Joel was struck by an analogy to the "Day of the Lord." He saw that Israel was not fulfilling her function under God and that she too would be destroyed. After that destruction, however, Joel offered hope. After Israel was brought low, he said, she would be restored as the Spirit of God came upon His people. The Spirit had been thought to be silent for several hundred years—and would be silent until the coming of Jesus. With this coming of the Spirit, there would be a new vision and new dreams for God's people, even the old men. For some reason it was hard for old men to dream anymore; but Joel knew that through the presence of the Spirit they would.

Simon Peter understood what was happening that day in Jerusalem. He knew what it was like to be a part of a temple, a faith, a people who had lost their vision, who had no dreams. Simon Peter knew that the Spirit could and would cause even old men, even those who had surrendered their dreams to the press of reality, to dream again. Both Joel and Simon Peter saw that even in one's last days, even in the twilight years, even in the agony of physical and intellectual deterioration, one could dream again as the heart was opened up to the Spirit of Christ.

Here is the answer for growing old gracefully! Here is the answer for living life to the fullest, no matter what the circumstances may be. Every person, both young and old, needs the Spirit of Christ. How does the Spirit of Christ work in and through us as we move toward the end of our years upon this earth? I want you to think with me about four words that are keys to unlocking the secret as to how we can thrive in our later years: *pondering, prayer, passion,* and *perseverance.*

II. *The Spirit works to help us gain a greater knowledge of ourselves and God, and of ourselves in relation to God.*

a. *Pondering* is the beginning step of hearing the Spirit of God. Pondering means looking deep within ourselves to see who we are and what we have been about in our lives—and what we should be about at this stage of our lives. Many people shy away from pondering because they are afraid of what they will find hidden deep within. A minister was

visiting a nursing home when he saw a member of his church who was old and suffering from dementia. He walked over to her and said: "Do you know who I am?" She replied, "No, but I get that way sometimes and if you'll ask that nurse over there she will tell you who you are."

As we reflect, we will find ourselves reviewing the story of our lives and in so doing we will involved ourselves in recollection and remembrance. The first word in such an action is always *grace,* both God's and ours. Too often we are hard on ourselves when we do not need to be. There will be those things about which we need to ask forgiveness and there will be those things about which we need to forgive ourselves. Most of the time we just need to remember and be grateful to God for the blessed lives that we have lived. We are the children of a loving Father who leads, guides, nudges, and rescues, all to get us safely to the Kingdom. Spend time in pondering.

b. We also need to spend time in *prayer.* One of the fallacies of life is that as we grow older we become necessarily more holy. Wrong! Senior adults are just as likely to move away from God as middle adults—if not more so. There are several forms of prayer that are helpful:

Sharing prayer: When we share with God our deepest needs and concerns

Listening prayer: When we do just what this says—listen to the Spirit

Praying the Scriptures: When we use God's word to illumine our prayer life

Communal prayer: When we just bask in the presence of our loving God

Prayer stirs our holiness so that we are nourished in the depths of our soul. If we do not nourish our soul, we will discover that either it is starving or it is being nourished by the food of the world: addictions, old habits, worrying, and the quick fix of the thrill. Prayer nurtures our soul as we develop a sense of awe and wonder at who God is and what God has done and is doing. Awe and wonder give birth to gratitude, and gratitude brings forth a life that is pleasing to God. The truth is that it is in the living of our lives that our experience of God—and our response to that experience—is seen.

c. *Passion* is a word that we usually hear only on soap operas or in the movies, yet passion is crucial to a well-lived life. Most of us are passionate about some things: athletics, gardening, reading, boating, ecology, music, mission trips, and so on. The problem is that so many of us have seen misguided passion in religion, so we have dropped our passion in favor of a cool aloofness. Yes, we believe, and yes, we want our children to grow up in the Church, but for goodness' sake, do not expect me to get too excited or too involved. Only kooks, weirdos, and people who have no other interests do that. Especially as we grow older, as we have "been there, done that," we lose our passion.

How do we regain our passion? Through the power of the Spirit. Simon Peter had lost his passion because of his failure. But he waited on the Spirit of Christ and on Pentecost we find him preaching the gospel at great danger to his physical well-being. From this point on Simon Peter is passionate about the good news of Jesus and proclaims it until his death upside down on a cross.

d. *Perseverance* is an expression of both our search for God and our gratitude to God. When the breath of the Spirit blows through our lives, when the fire of the Holy One burns on the altar of our heart, then we will be stirred to a commitment and perseverance that is life changing. There is probably no quality that I appreciate more deeply than perseverance. Once I was impressed with ability, with those preachers who could sway crowds or those musicians who could stir one

to tears. Now I am much more impressed with perseverance, because it is through faithful service that God's Church is built. Dreams and visions come to many, but only the faithful see them through to the finish.—Robert U. Ferguson

Illustrations

COMMUNICATION AS A PROBLEM. Prayer gives us a new perspective on life and helps us to understand what God wants us to do. Communication is not always easy. I heard about a blacksmith who hired a young man to work as his apprentice. This young man was not extremely bright but was enthusiastic. The blacksmith took a shoe out of the fire with his tongs, put it on the anvil, and said to his apprentice: "When I nod my head, you hit it with the sledgehammer." The next day the town had a new blacksmith. There was definitely a communication problem.—Robert J. Wicks[136]

TEACHING AND LEARNING. Howard Hendricks told the story of going to a Sunday school convention in Chicago and, while there, sharing a cab ride with an eighty-three-year-old lady. She was at the convention to learn more about teaching young people—she had been doing it for sixty years. At last count eighty-four persons in vocational ministry were there because this lady had a passion to teach and share with young people—and they continually connected with that passion, even across generational lines.—Robert J. Wicks[137]

SUNDAY: JULY EIGHTEENTH

LECTIONARY MESSAGE

Topic: Visions of Grace from a Stone Pillow
TEXT: Gen. 28:10–19a
Other Readings: Rom. 8:12–25; Matt. 13:24–30, 36–43

When a person hits bottom, it is said, he or she should rejoice—the only way left to go is up. But there is another possibility: without help, he or she could stay right on the bottom.

I. *Emptiness and loneliness.* Jacob's nature

and behavior had put him in the middle of nowhere—"a certain place"—with a stone under his head for a pillow and the stars above him for a blanket. What hope did he have? Certainly none, if left to himself. He was helpless, and would have failed completely if he had been forced to face responsibility before God.

[136]*After Fifty*
[137]*After Fifty*

His condition parallels that of many other people. He was alone, entirely on his own. He was on a journey to seek a lifelong companion in the land of his grandfather's people. A refugee, in fear for his life, he was under a threat of death from his brother, from whom he had stolen their father's blessing. His mother had sent him away for a "cooling-off period," until his brother's anger should fade away. He had no road map to his destination, except the general direction to the early homeland from which he was to bring a wife suitable to his family.

I am reminded of a student of Japanese ancestry named Masao, who was a good friend of mine at Antelope Valley Junior College in California. He left the United States in 1938 to return to Japan to seek a wife suitable to his family heritage. I learned later that he had found her, and that he had remained in Japan to serve in the military force. His last letter, in 1939, contained a mystifying remark about a "hope that relations between Japan and the United States can be settled peaceably and without conflict." This remark was a mystery to me and other friends because we had no inkling then that any threat was arising to Japanese–U.S. relations. Just as the destinies of Jacob and Esau were formed by the forces of Esau's desperate, smoldering hatred and resentment of Jacob, there were forces of desperate ambition, greed, and hatred that shaped Masao's destiny and ours in years to come. As did Jacob, many people have found themselves in the empty place of loneliness and need.

II. *Receiving a vision and hearing a voice.* If anyone needs confirmation of the adage "Man's extremity is God's opportunity," then this event in Jacob's life is it.

"And he dreamed" a dream that presented him with hope for his life and a promise for eternity. Jacob's dream seems to be like the "American Dream," in a way, except that Jacob's was purely based on God's freely given grace and power, whereas the American Dream requires hard work and intelligent planning.

Jacob's vision was of a ladder "set up on the earth" with its top reaching to heaven. It started where he was. Any attempt of a person to improve his or her fame and fortune, to engage in meaningful, successful work leading to achievement of individual or family welfare, must begin as Jacob's vision did—on the ground, from where that person is to start. Each person needs to make a careful assessment of present conditions; to examine assets of character, intellect, personality, strength, and faith; and to recognize handicaps and deficiencies, if any, in order to appreciate what God may do for him or her in return for faith and trust in Jesus Christ—and what God would have one do for oneself with his help.

Jacob's vision brought angels delivering God's message. It is strange to note that the text describes the angels as "ascending and descending" the ladder. Is it an accident that *ascending* is mentioned first? They were actually starting from the bottom, from where Jacob was! They were obviously with him all the time, arising on the ladder only to receive fresh messages from God, who was revealed at the top speaking to Jacob. The voice brought Jacob God's assurance of a permanent place for life and a plentiful population to fill it.

III. *A recognition and a memorial.* Jacob belatedly realized that he was in the presence of God, and it made him fearful. He was not yet a trusting, faithful follower, but he was awake to the presence of his everlasting companion. God's first man, Adam, heard the voice of God in the garden of Eden after he ate the forbidden fruit, and he said, "I was afraid, because I was naked; and I hid myself." So Jacob, running from the dire consequences of his sibling rivalry, hears the voice of God and is afraid, no doubt, because for everyone who awakes to the voice of God in his inner being and utter loneliness, fear is the first emotion.

Not everyone has a stone pillow to erect into a memorial pillar, but everyone marks permanently in his or her memory the time and place of his or her first recognition that God would always be with him or her, to claim ownership and promise enabling companionship. The lives of all great people and the great events of human history are honored with memorials as permanent as it is possible to make them, with stone walls and marble or granite statuary. It is fitting that each person strike a permanent mark at the place in his or her life where God was met. The realization that "God is in this place—it is none other than the gate of heaven" cannot help being of permanent significance for every life.

Beth Elohim—Bethel, the House of God, the Gate of Heaven—is wherever the lost and lonely find themselves and God.—John R. Rodman

Illustrations

THIRSTING FOR GOD. Now it was this loneliness and this repentance that made it possible for God to reveal Himself to him. They made it possible for God to make real to him the eternal and the unseen. When he had come to the end of himself, when he had got to the place where his soul was thirsting for God, when his sense of sin had made him sorrowful and ashamed, then it was that God spoke to him and enabled him to say, "This is the gate of heaven."

And it is to such that God is able to grant this thrilling discovery still. If you have no need, you will never make it. But if there is a need, if you are thirsting for God; if your losses, your broken hopes, your broken vows, drive you to bow at His feet, then this discovery is ahead of you. We do not all come to it by the same road. Sometimes we find it at the door of disappointment. Sometimes the sick room becomes transformed by the grace of God into the gate of heaven. Even sometimes the door behind which a loved one lies dead leads us to the discovery of the gateway to the Father's house.—Clovis G. Chappell[138]

GOD ENTERS. "God," says Emerson, "enters into every life by a private door." And the wicket through which he slipped into Jacob's was no tremendous spiritual experience (that came later), but just a wondering recognition of God's faithful kindness day by day. For Jacob, once he saw, never forgot. That moment made a lasting mark upon his heart and mind. From that day on, the thought of God was never far away from him. He was no saint, was never proficient in these holy things, was to the end a plain man leading a plain life, like most of us. But that blank in his soul was gone. For God was there, the background of his being all his latter years.—Arthur John Gossip[139]

[138] Old Testament Characters
[139] The Hero in Thy Soul

SERMON SUGGESTIONS

Topic: Sour Grapes
TEXT: Ezek. 18:1–4, 30–32
(1) There is often a direct relationship between the destructive behavior of a parent and a similar behavior of a child. (2) However, the parent's behavior does not have to determine what the child becomes (vv. 2–3). (3) God desires the well-being and salvation of all (v. 32). (4) The key to the new life is repentance (v. 30).

Topic: Our Way of Life
TEXT: Eph. 2:8–10 NRSV
(1) Becoming and being Christian is not our own doing, though we may try to win God's favor by our good works. (2) God, by his totally undeserved grace, does for us and in us what we cannot accomplish ourselves. (3) God's ultimate purpose for us is to be good and do good, in ways that only God can bring about.

Hymn Suggestions

1. "Nearer, My God, to Thee," Sarah F. Adams (1841); BETHANY, Lowell Mason (1856)
This once quite popular hymn is based on the experience of Jacob dreaming of the ladder from earth to heaven at the place he named Bethel. It would therefore be appropriately sung in connection with the reading in Genesis.

2. "Lord, You Have Searched Me," Marie J. Post (1986); FEDERAL STREET, Henry K. Oliver (1832)
This song freely paraphrases parts of Psalm 139. Thus it could be used either in place of the Psalter reading or as a response to it.

3. "Every Time I Feel the Spirit," African American spiritual (nineteenth century); PENTECOST, spiritual arranged by William F. Smith (1986)
A song such as this one that magnifies the action of God's Spirit in the heart would be a suitable response to the reading in Romans (8:12–25), in which the apostle discusses life in the Spirit.

4. "Come, Ye Thankful People, Come," Henry Alford (1858); ST. GEORGE'S WINDSOR, George J. Elvey (1858)
Too often confined to the season of Thanks-

giving, this hymn is in reality based on Jesus' parable of the good wheat and the weeds recorded in the Gospel lesson for this day (Matt. 13:36–43).—Hugh T. McElrath

Worship Aids

CALL TO WORSHIP.   "Search me, O God, and know my heart: try me, and know my thoughts: and see if there be any wicked way in me, and lead me in the way everlasting" (Ps. 139:23–24).

INVOCATION.   Lord, surprise us today with new insights of grace and new epiphanies of joy that grant glimpses of the holy. Then let our week be different because we have met with God and walk with the living Christ.—E. Lee Phillips

OFFERTORY SENTENCE.   "We have access by faith into this grace wherein we stand, and rejoice in hope of the glory of God" (Rom. 5:2).

OFFERTORY PRAYER.   Help us to know, O God, that we can right here and now share your glory as we bring our tithes and offerings to further your cause on this earth, even as we are confident that we shall share that glory in the world to come.

PRAYER.   O God, in this place, the House of the Interpreter, we have heard your word calling us out from the comfort of some Ur of the Chaldees, inviting us to pilgrimage, to go out not knowing where we are going, to live by faith. You do call us to the road less traveled, for "straight is the way and narrow is the gate which leads to life, and few there are who find it."

Some of us here this morning find ourselves confronted with new realities that we did not invite or desire, but here they are, like some bolt out of the blue, disturbing our complacency, even threatening our life. Whatever these eventualities, may we discover the faith, the courage, and the grace to accept them as the facts of our life, that our healing may begin.

From any brokenness in body, in mind, in spirit, in relationships, heal us, and we shall be whole. We pray, too, for the healing of the nations. For all of those who persevere in ways of compassion, justice, and peace, we pray for the courage born of faith in your purposes and the hope assured through your steadfast love.

Through him who as your eternal Word is here leading us to pray together: "Our Father. . . ."—John Thompson

Sermon: And Sarah Laughed

TEXT: Gen. 17:15–19, 18:9–15, 21:1–7

God said to Abraham, "Sarah shall be her name. I will bless her, and moreover I will give you a son by her. Kings of peoples shall come from her." And Abraham fell on his face and laughed. This whole section of Genesis is the story of God's covenant with Abraham and Sarah, of the promise that Abraham would be the father of a great nation and Sarah would be its mother. If Abraham was hurt because he and Sarah had no children, Sarah's pain has to have been far greater. All a woman had in those days was her children. A wife was the property of her husband, and if she bore him no children, he could divorce her and find a more fertile woman. Barrenness was held to be a curse from God. It was thought to be always the woman's fault. Thirteen years before we pick up our story, Sarah had been so deeply embarrassed by her barrenness that she had given her own maid to Abraham to bear him a child. And now, at ninety, not even Abraham, who loved her, believed Sarah would ever be a mother. He laughed at the very idea. So it is for some of us.

Abraham fell on his face and laughed. It wasn't a very polite response to the promise of God. It was putting Sarah in the category of hopeless. But it was just like the laughter Sarah had been hearing from those around her all her life. I never understood that curious little verse in Matthew 18 until I saw it happen to somebody. But it's true: whatever you or I bind on earth will be bound in heaven. You and I can script someone and make it almost impossible for them to find hope. We can decide that Johnny is stupid or that Susie will never make anything of herself. And we can make them begin to believe it. I've seen it again and again in families. By deciding that nothing can happen for the good, you and I make certain that nothing does. Abraham stopped believing that even God could make a difference in Sarah's life. So he laughed at the very idea.

And Sarah laughed, too. She laughed bitter tears and her laughter hid a lifetime of pain. Barrenness was the central fact of Sarah's life. From the time we meet her in chapter 11, the most important thing that's said about her is that Sarah had no child. Childlessness is not quite the same thing today. Many people choose to have no children, or find that they cannot, and still live quite happy, meaningful lives. But if you've ever wanted a child and been unable to have one, if you've ever wanted a mate and been unable to find one, or a career and been unable to make it happen, if you've ever had a personal goal and been unable to reach it, you know exactly how Sarah's laugh felt. In a day when wealth was counted in sons and daughters, Sarah was the poorest of women. Even at fifty, the promise of a child might have caused a hope to start up within her, her heart to skip a beat for joy. But Sarah was long past it now. Her childbearing years were over.

Sarah heard the promise to Abraham, but she laughed because she just didn't believe it anymore. That's why she had given Abraham the maid Hagar and had let Hagar bear Abraham a son named Ishmael. One of the greatest temptations for any of us is the temptation to live by our wits instead of by our faith, to try to create our own solutions instead of waiting on the Lord. Of course the Lord expects us to use our heads in this life, but when we spend all our energy figuring the angles, when you and I fall into anguish of spirit because we don't have everything we want right now, we lose the ability to enjoy life today. We forget that God promises to care for you and me if we put our trust in the Lord. We put ourselves in the category of practical atheists.

It isn't all that hard to understand how Sarah felt when she heard the promise. "Shall I have pleasure?" she laughed. What, who me? My life can't get any better now. It's gone on too long the way it is. Wouldn't I look silly in a maternity ward at my age? Laughter, you see, can be an evil thing. The wrong kind of laughter can make fun of hope. One of the most interesting statistics about American Christianity is that very few people in the United States become Chris-

tians after age twenty-five. Grown-ups get too cynical, too sophisticated. You've got to come to the Kingdom like a child. You've got to be willing to trust that what seems impossible really can happen, to believe in what Niebuhr called the impossible possibility. For that is what happened in Jesus Christ. That's what the Lord does as a matter of course. Sarah was too old to believe the impossible, so she laughed. But the Lord heard that laugh, and God challenged her disbelief just the way God challenges yours and mine.

Maybe that's what you think about your dream, too. You have heard the promise of God that you can have a meaningful life in Christ, that God will give you the strength you need, that God will help you to make that change you need to make. But you just don't believe it can happen to you. Well, my friend, neither did Sarah, but skeptical as she was of the prospects for a geriatric baby boom, she gave herself to the purposes of God.

And Sarah conceived and bore Abraham a son. And the two of them became among the first in that long list of sisters and brothers you and I know as believers, and the world knows as the clowns of God. Goodness knows they must have felt a little silly at Lamaze classes. But there they were, shoo-ins for the title of oldest couple at the PTA. And there was the child. God kept God's promise in God's time. God's call to you this morning may seem to be similarly ridiculous. It may be to believe the impossible. It may even be to believe in yourself. But the promise is that if you and I say yes, as Sarah did, God will see us through. With Sarah we will say, God has made laughter for me.

God named the boy Isaac, which means "he laughs." Maybe the Lord figured that any kid with parents that old would need a sense of humor. Certainly for Sarah, Isaac was sheer unadulterated joy. She learned what each person who has chosen to trust God has learned for himself or herself from Sarah's day to the present: to give yourself to God is to find joy in the midst of suffering, comfort in the midst of pain, confidence in the midst of doubt. It is to discover the deep-down, incredible relief of being accepted by God and used by God just the way you are. It is to learn what it means to laugh for joy. The writer Frederick Buechner was converted under the preaching of

George Buttrick at the Madison Avenue Presbyterian Church in New York City. Buechner says he gave himself to Jesus when Buttrick said that a Christian is someone who has the right to fall down before the throne of Christ "with tears and great laughter." When he heard that, Buechner understood for the first time in his life, just as Sarah did when she laughed after the birth of Isaac, what it means to be loved by God. It's to realize that the impossible can come true.

It is to know that God has made laughter for me. Much of the time this doesn't seem like a very funny world. This week alone we have grieved with the families of the airliner disaster and have learned with horror of the rape of a six-year-old here in our own city. In our own fellowship there are illness and economic difficulty to be faced, and life to be lived the best we can from day to day. All these things are very important and very serious indeed.

Still, for those of us who follow Jesus, it's good to stop from time to time and remember that, as impossible as it sounds, in Christ you and I have already won, just as Sarah won against all odds that year so long ago. I tell you this story in part, you see, because its modern version happened to me. If you went by our ages, which were too high, or our income, which was too low, or our influence, which was nonexistent, the Edna Gladney home should never have given us a child. We will always believe that God intervened. In the years since God gave us Douglas, Sheryl and I have laughed more than we ever thought

possible for us. In the Disney classic *Mary Poppins,* Ed Wynn played a magical old gentleman for whom laughter was the stuff of life. "I love to laugh," he sang, "loud and strong and clear. I love to laugh. It's getting worse every year. The more I laugh, the more I fill with glee. The more the glee, the more I'm a merrier me." It sounds almost sacrilegious to put it this way. But the great thing about trusting Christ to take care of us is that for the first time in your life and mine, we've really got something to laugh about. The laughs are on God. I don't know about you, but I love to laugh. And this morning I've got something to laugh about. Hopeless sinner that I am, God has loved me and made me God's own through Jesus Christ, and God is giving me the life and the laughter I was meant to have. Tell me, my friend, when's the last time you had a really good laugh?—Ronald D. Sisk

Illustrations

TEARS AND LAUGHTER.   "Blessed are they that weep, for they shall laugh!" Only he that has wept can laugh! The laughter of Heaven sows earth with a rain of tears, and out of Earth's transfigured birth-pain the laughter of Man returns to bless and play again in innumerable dancing gales of flame upon the knees of God!—Eugene O'Neill[140]

MAY WE LAUGH?   It is the heart that is not yet sure of its God that is afraid to laugh in His presence.—George Macdonald[141]

SUNDAY: JULY TWENTY-FIFTH

LECTIONARY MESSAGE

Topic: A Taste of His Own Medicine
TEXT: Gen. 29:15–28
Other Readings: Rom. 8:26–39; Matt. 13:31–33, 44–52
I. *Jacob's responsibility.*
a. We can hardly hold Jacob responsible for the manner in which he earned his name, "Heeler." After all, he was barely even born when he caught hold of his brother Esau's heel. But we must hold him accountable for the series of events described in Genesis 27, even though his mother, Rebekah,

plotted it and put him up to it. He was then also of an accountable age, when he fed Esau from his mess of pottage, taking advantage of Esau's fatigue and faintness to barter the savory meal for the firstborn's privileged birthright.

b. When Isaac was about to die and called for Esau to give him some venison so he could happily satisfy his hunger and give Esau his blessing before the Lord, and while

---

[140] *The Great God Brown* (Act IV)
[141] *Sir Gibbie*

Esau was out with bow and arrows hunting the deer, Rebekah persuaded Jacob to cook up some tender mutton from two kids in the flock, then covered Jacob's smooth skin with the kids' hairy skin and sent Jacob to supplant Esau in his father's blessing.

c. Jacob had heard the voice of God at Bethel promising him that the land where he had slept would belong to his descendants, who would bless all the families of the earth, and that wherever Jacob went, God would be with him, not leaving him until the promise was complete. Jacob was thereafter still not a child of faith, and the best he could say was, "This is an awesome place, the house of God, the gate of heaven," and he vowed, "*If* God will be with me . . . then the Lord will be my God." Jacob was responsible for doubting the promise of God, which had been unconditionally given. He was a difficult person for God to teach. The faithfulness of God was already assured; Jacob still had much to learn.

II. *Jacob met his match.*

a. Thomas Carlyle, in his book *Sartor Resartus* ("The Tailor Reclothed"), expounds the theory of accomplishing changes in personality by putting on and taking off articles of clothing, thus illustrating the theory of the spiritual nature of individual life in relation to the universe. Carlyle's theory was based on his own experience of loneliness and isolation. The book delves sternly into the mistaken assumption, held by many people, that one can "grind me out Virtue from the husks of Pleasure"—that is, indulge in selfish satisfactions, as Jacob did, hoping to emerge as a spiritual being. Carlyle proves that it is not to be that way—that such a life leads to "shouting question after question into the Sibyl cave of Destiny, and receive no Answer but an Echo."

b. Jacob evidently considered himself the only one who could successfully deceive another person. He accepted his uncle's promise at face value—that after seven years of labor for Laban, he would be given the beautiful and well-favored Rachel as his wife. Jacob served what to him seemed but a few days because of his love for Rachel. Then, when the time came for his marriage, he awoke to find himself married to Rachel's older sister, Leah. With the explanation that the younger daughter was not permitted to precede the older (a lesson Jacob needed to learn), Laban then offered Rachel to Jacob for seven more years of work.

c. There is a satisfaction in finding that Jacob learned certain of life's truths. That God was guiding him is evident in his commitment to serve the seven more years for Rachel. But he had other lessons to learn as well.

III. *Jacob's spiritual awakening.*

a. Jacob learned that evil actions bear bitter fruit. Whenever a person plans to deceive another and profit from another's weakness, he or she casts himself or herself on the scales of a just and righteous God, and will be weighed in the balance and found wanting. Jacob had taken matters into his own hands. God's timing would have blessed him, but impatience and unbelief urged him into dark paths, and he had to go to Haran to escape his wronged brother's vengeance. There he fell in love with his cousin Rachel. Psalm 46:7 declares, "The God of Jacob is our refuge," and commands, "Be still, and know that I am God"—something Jacob learned with great difficulty.

b. One who cheats another lives in a world of deception and false promises. What he makes of his opportunities and desires leads him to finds others who are ready to practice in the same way. When Jacob awoke with Leah, he realized that Laban had kept his principle of priority of daughters a secret at the time they had set the terms of Jacob's employment. God was showing him that his plan was of his own doing, and that God had plans that superseded Jacob's.

c. Still, it is God who makes his own followers and agents. Jacob's children with Leah; with Zilpah, Leah's handmaiden; and with Rachel and her handmaiden, Bilhah, are all the heads of tribes of Israel, by God's blessing. God fulfilled his own plan in his own time, as he does with each of his believers who follow in his promises.—John R. Rodman

Illustrations

DOES ROGUERY PAY? Eugene Aram committed a murder and lived for thirteen years undetected; it was thirteen years of hell. He was a schoolmaster, and he said that he used to watch the boys at their play and be sick with envy for their carefree hearts. The first moment of peace he had in all the years since he had committed the crime was the moment when the handcuffs were slipped around his wrists. Be warned! You have read a novel perhaps or seen a film, in which the rogue is made into a hero and makes his roguery pay. But that isn't real life; that is only a story. Don't be deceived. It is the height of folly to think that it pays to be a rogue.—W. E. Sangster[142]

WINNING IS POSSIBLE. In *Pilgrim's Progress* two men fell into the Slough of Despond. They both wallowed around in the mud and for a time it seemed that both men would lose their lives. But strength and persistence triumphed and both men stood once more on solid ground. One of them was a man with a purpose, and he climbed out on the side toward the Celestial City and went on. The other man lived by whim and chance. He finally crawled out on the same side where he fell in and was no further along. Mud, obstacles, disappointment, adversity—there is nothing final about them. They all come in the day's work. It all depends upon how one faces them. If he accepts them as a challenge to his best powers, he too can win out.—Charles R. Brown[143]

SERMON SUGGESTIONS

Topic: How to Know God
TEXT: Jer. 31:31–34
(1) Knowledge of God does not come by merely knowing the words of Scripture and their meaning. (2) Nor does it come through the well-intentioned efforts of good people. (3) Knowledge of God comes when God takes the witness of those who love him and the good news contained in Scripture and makes his truth a living, transforming reality in the hearts of those who trust his forgiving love.

Topic: Keep the Faith
TEXT: Jude
(1) What is the faith? It is the truth of God as manifested in and taught by the Lord Jesus Christ. (2) How can this faith be perverted?

[142] *Why Jesus Never Wrote a Book*
[143] *Being Made Over*

(a) By lack of understanding (v. 10a); (b) by immoral living (v. 10b). (3) How can this faith be preserved? (a) By depending on God's keeping of you (v. 24); (b) by doing your part in what God is doing in you (vv. 20–21); (c) by helping those about to fail (vv. 22–23).

Hymn Suggestions

1. "O Day of God, Draw Nigh," Robert B. Y. Scott (1737); ST. MICHAEL, *Genevan Psalter* (1551)
Particularly in keeping with verse 7 of Psalm 105, which asserts that God's judgments are present in all the earth, this apostrophe to "the Day of God" and to the prayer that it will come with "timeless judgment" is apropos.
2. "Spirit Divine, Attend (Inspire) Our Prayer," Andrew Reed (1829); GRÄFENBERG, Johann Crüger (1647)
This prayer-hymn echoes Romans 8:26 in the truth that the Holy Spirit helps us in our weakness to pray as we ought. It could suitably follow the reading of the Epistle lesson for this day.
3. "Jesus, Priceless Treasure," Johann Franck (1653); JESU, MEINE FREUDE, Johann Crüger (1647)
A venerable chorale voicing the inestimable value that Christ has for the faithful believer, "Jesus, Priceless Treasure" could appropriately follow the Gospel reading concerning the parable of the kingdom—especially Matthew 13:44–46.
4. "God Moves in a Mysterious Way," William Cowper (1774); DUNDEE, *Scottish Psalter* (1615)
The frustrations of Jacob in claiming Rachel for his wife (Gen. 29:15–28) reminds us that God works in inscrutable ways to accomplish his purposes. Cowper's great hymn on divine providence gives expression to such comforting thoughts.—Hugh T. McElrath

Worship Aids

CALL TO WORSHIP. "O give thanks unto the Lord; call upon his name: make known his deeds among the people" (Ps. 105:1).

INVOCATION. O God, our days should begin and end with thanksgiving. Make our lives so responsive to your goodness that no one can mistake that we live by your grace. To that end, strengthen us during this time of prayer and praise.

OFFERTORY SENTENCE. "And whatsoever ye do, do it heartily, as to the Lord, and not unto men; knowing that of the Lord ye shall receive the reward of the inheritance: for ye serve the Lord Christ" (Col. 3:23–24).

OFFERTORY PRAYER. This is all for you, O God, whether our hearts can fully embrace your claim or not. Teach us more and more through each offering we bring the joy of partnership with you in your redeeming work in the world.

PRAYER. Father, in this world so rife with bitterness, selfishness, and indifference—a world stumbling from blunder to blunder, hollow with graves resulting from war, hard with hate—fill us with the power of your grace and forgiveness and hope and make us bold enough to share your salvation with people everywhere.

Give us a broad vision of our responsibility to one another, both friend and stranger, so that we will have compassion enough to meet one another's needs. Lead us to plant the seeds of concern in the hearts of others and to tap the wells of generosity, so that hands and hearts may be opened to do your will.

Help us to live as people who have been forgiven a great debt. Help us to be gentle with those who are weak and to walk softly with those in pain. Help us to speak encouragingly to those who are lost and kindly to those who are troubled. Let your truth be shared through our lips and lives, so that the world may be changed for some struggling soul in the midst of life's demands and pressures. Deliver us from causing one useless tear to fall because of our callous and unthoughtful words or actions. Give us the ability to see all persons as your children and as our brothers and sisters, no matter their origin or circumstance in life.

Father, help us to be ministers of mercy and ambassadors of truth as we bring good news to our world in Jesus' name.—Henry Fields

Sermon: A Word for All Seasons

TEXT: Rom. 8:26–39

This text is one of my favorite passage in all of Holy Scripture.

I can hardly think of any condition of our existence that is bypassed in these words. On the underside of this text we can find a laundry list of the grimmest words imaginable. Listen to some of them stated or implied here: *anxiety, despair, fear, meaninglessness, help-lessness, weakness, defeat, opposition, accusation, condemnation, death, life itself, unseen negative forces.* Over against all of these chilling words stands one word. It is not used anywhere in the text, yet it is everywhere in the text. The word is *hope.* The psychiatrist Karl Menninger called hope "an adventure, a going forward—a confident search for a rewarding life."

Hope, as taught in the New Testament, is nothing like the nervous belief that you may win the lottery. What the New Testament calls hope is an assurance that reaches two ways. It reaches back in faith to what Jesus Christ did in his cross and resurrection, and it reaches forward in trust to the promise of the Christ event and its fulfillment in the future, as God brings all things to a glorious consummation in Christ. Hope is the work of God from first to last. Although we may be predisposed to it, it is nevertheless what God intervenes to bring about.

George Buttrick told about a man who was converted when he considered the miracle of gravity—that we are able to live on this planet and not be flung off into space. This man came to realize that there is something solid, reliable, and predictable that we can depend on, that there is *someone* out there, in there, down there, up there, everywhere, on whom we can depend. What he saw in nature was a sign pointing beyond nature itself to God. And that is precisely what John indicated was the purpose of the miracles of Jesus: they were signs.

Many thinkers have observed that in every culture there are expressions of either a wish for or an expectation of a future life in which the present life is completed, expanded, or glorified. In recent years we have read of near-death experiences in which people have come back to tell of celestial sights that they have seen, sights so real that they have come back to live lives transformed by what they experienced at the frontier.

One of the most triumphant biblical statements on hope is found in the First Letter of Peter (1:3–5, RSV). Such a statement is what really defines hope for us. Other faiths and philosophies point somewhat in this direction, but the biblical declarations surpass them all.

When genuine hope is at work in our lives, things happen. Positive and creative forces are released within us.

For one thing, we feel accepted, we feel that we belong to God, we feel that we have a place in God's kingdom. A famous sermon of the theologian Paul Tillich bears the title "You Are Accepted." Tillich said—and how right it feels!—"We experience moments in which we accept ourselves, because we feel that we have been accepted by that which is greater than we. . . . For it is such moments that make us love our life, that make us accept ourselves not in our goodness and self-complacency, but in our certainty of the eternal meaning of our life."

Can you imagine how it would be possible for someone like Saul of Tarsus, later known as Paul the apostle, to come to the place of self-acceptance without the assurance within his heart that the Christ whom he had persecuted had accepted him? He could he in one breath call himself "the chief of sinners" and in the next speak of having been made an example to those who would come to believe in Jesus Christ for eternal life? The fact that you and I are accepted by God makes it possible for us to accept ourselves.

This is not "cheap grace," however. Anything so costly to God—namely, his gift of his only Son, who suffered the cross and all the rest for us—ought to and will produce in us a type of life and character that corresponds to what God has done for us in Christ. John, in his first letter, tells us that "we are God's children now; what we will be has not yet been revealed. What we do know is this: when he is revealed, we will be like him, for we will see him as he is. And all who have this hope in him purify themselves, just as he is pure."

Embedded in that hope and our proper response to it is the answer to the question, What does it all add up to? Many people today are saying about life, with Shakespeare's Macbeth, "It is a tale told by an idiot,

full of sound and fury, signifying nothing." It is an unavoidable issue, and sooner or later every intelligent person will likely ask, What does it all mean? We reach for ultimate meaning, that which enabled the apostle to say, "I consider that the sufferings of this present time are not worth comparing with the glory about to be revealed to us." No wonder Robert Louis Stevenson could say, "I believe in an ultimate decency of things; ay, if I woke in hell, I should still believe it."

In all of this—acceptance, character, and meaning—comes empowerment: "We are more than conquerors through him who loved us." Does it puzzle you a bit that Paul speaks of predestination? What is it all about? Why is God doing this and that for us? His eternal purpose for us is summed up in the words *to be conformed to the image of his Son*— and that image is cruciform. He calls us to take up our cross and follow him, not in this life only but also in the life to come.

The apostle Paul stated his hope in these words: "I am convinced that neither death, nor life, nor angels, nor rulers, nor things present, nor things to come, nor powers, nor height, nor depth, nor anything else in all creation, will be able to separate us from the love of God in Christ Jesus our Lord."— James W. Cox[144]

Illustrations

FOR HER.   Viktor Frankl of Vienna [in his book *Man's Search for Meaning*] told of a grieving general practitioner whose wife had died two years before. He had loved her more than anything or anyone. Apparently no one had been able to help him out of his severe depression. Frankl wondered how he could help him. What should he tell him? Frankl refrained from telling him anything, but instead confronted him with the question, "What would have happened, Doctor, if you had died first, and your wife would have had to survive you?" "Oh," he replied, "for her this would have been terrible; how she would have suffered!" Then Frankl said, "You see, Doctor, such a suffering has been spared her, and it was you who have spared her this suffering; but now, you have to pay for it by sur-

[144]*Best Sermons*, vol. 7

viving and mourning her." The man said nothing but shook Frankl's hand and left.— James W. Cox[145]

A REAL FIGHT.   If this life be not a real fight, in which something is eternally gained for the universe by success, it is not better than a game of private theatrics from which one may withdraw at will. But it feels like a real fight—as if there were something really wild in the universe which we, with all our idealitites and faithfulness, are needed to redeem; and first of all to redeem our own hearts from atheisms and fears.—William James[146]

SUNDAY: AUGUST FIRST

LECTIONARY MESSAGE

Topic: Keep the Change
 TEXT: Gen. 32:22–31
 Other Readings: Ps. 17:1–7, 15; Rom. 9:1–5; Matt. 14:13–21

It will be helpful if the preacher has been following the lectionary readings for the previous few Sundays, so that both preacher and congregation will have formed a mental picture from the Old Testament lessons. This is necessary to make sense of the episode recorded in this pericope. Through reading the larger Jacob saga we will become conversant with Jacob's family history, checkered as it is: Isaac, his blind, aged father who could be deceived; Jacob's mother Rebekah, who consistently favored her younger son; and Esau, who had good reason to be angry with Jacob. We will learn about Jacob's dealings with his crafty father-in-law, Laban, and about Jacob's devotion to his wife, Rachel. We may conclude that Jacob is the sort of character we find interesting, but not the kind of person we would want living next door to us. It is difficult to see him as a heroic figure, or as a model for modern men and women. Nevertheless, he may be a prototype, reflecting "our own lives, writ large."

I. *What it means to be like Jacob.* By and large, Jacob had a good life. He was upwardly mobile and had plans for the future. We may conclude that he was shrewd, for no one got the best of him for long, and he was perhaps smarter than the rest of his family. He had to have been in good physical health to wrestle all night and prevail. We may infer that he was handsome and sexy, for his wives and their maids fought for his attentions. He was rich enough to be able to afford expensive presents for others. And he knew that he had been blessed by God.

Although we may not claim to have Jacob's advantages to the same degree, everyone has hopes and dreams for the days to come. We may not claim to be geniuses, but each of us occasionally marvels at the stupidity of those around us. Everyone present is in good enough health to have made it to church today. We're better looking than some we could name. Jacob's wealth may be foreign to us, but the blessings of a merciful God have sustained us to this point, and the Lord has made us stewards of however little or much we have. Jacob's values and attitudes may be ours, too. One popular motto found on bumper stickers and T-shirts is "He who dies with the most toys wins." Jacob could be competitive and ruthless when he thought the situation required it. Estrangement and alienation were part of his experience, as they are of our own. His prayers, too, may resemble ours. Earlier in the thirty-second chapter he called on God to aid him in his upcoming confrontation with Esau. After reminding God of his divine promises and mouthing a few phrases about unworthiness, Jacob figuratively handed God an agenda, asking for further blessing and deliverance. Contemporary extemporaneous prayers tend to be weighted on the side of supplication and intercession, at the expense of praise and confession.

II. *How God dealt with Jacob.* God heard the cry of Jacob's prayer and responded—but not as Jacob had expected. As Jacob waited alone that night, he was approached by an angel or a man (depending on which translation you use). He recognized this being as divinely sent, in any case. Instead of "fixing" Jacob's circumstances, the angel wrestled with him, dislocating his thigh and demanding to know his name. The dislocation was a painful symbol of Jacob's whole world being "out of joint"; this is confirmed by his confession of his name, which means "supplanter" or "cheater." Once Jacob acknowledged the truth about himself, the divine being changed his name to Israel, which means "God rules." This renaming was a transformation of Jacob rather than a magical solution to his problems. Esau would not have been bought off by the substantial gifts offered by his brother, but he was reconciled by the change he could see in Jacob, who bowed to him seven times. And Jacob recognized the transformation in himself when, in 33:10, he said to Esau, "Truly to see your face is like seeing the face of God."

III. *How God deals with us.* When we pray, God responds to our needs, not to our wishes. Like Jacob, we may become defensive and resist with all our might the transformation the Lord wants to work in us. We're prone to ask God to hand over the blessings but keep the change. When we struggle against God's good purpose, we not only feel the alienation and brokenness that Jacob did, but we also cause ourselves and God pain. Instead of a wrestling angel, God comes to us in his son, Jesus Christ, who grappled with sin and death and emerged the victor, so that you and I may be changed and blessed. The God of Jacob can give us new names, too: Redeemed and Sanctified. He can change our world—beginning with us.—Carol M. Noren

Illustrations

CREATIVE DISCIPLINE.   The Lord disciplines him whom he loves, and chastises every son whom he receives (Heb. 12:6).

"Wrestling Jacob" has been regarded as one of Charles Wesley's greatest poems. Written in 1742, the first two stanzas are as follows:

Come, O thou traveler unknown, who still
    I hold, but cannot see!
My company before is gone, and I am left
    alone with thee;
with thee all night I mean to stay and wrestle till the break of day.
I need not tell thee who I am, my misery
    and sin declare;

thyself has called me by my name, look on
    thy hands and read it there.
But who, I ask thee, who art thou? Tell me
    thy name, and tell me now.
                                    —Carol M. Noren

CHANGES REQUIRED.   A woman who had been unsuccessful in keeping off excess pounds heard a friend talking about the "cabbage soup" diet and its effectiveness. The friend gave her the recipe and a sample portion of the soup, suggested ways to keep the diet from becoming too boring, and advised her how long it would be before she began to see positive results. The woman listened with interest and said, "That sounds pretty easy. Just one thing, though; chocolate chip cookies are my favorite thing to eat, and I'm not going to give them up. I'll just have them along with the diet." Of course she didn't lose any weight. She was unwilling to make the necessary changes in her life to achieve her goal.—Carol M. Noren

SERMON SUGGESTIONS

Topic: Canceling Complaint
TEXT: Isa. 40:27–31
We can be reassured: (1) because God is always at work for us, though we cannot fathom his ways (v. 28b); (2) because our very expectations of God's blessing prepares the way for the seemingly impossible to happen to, in, and for us (vv. 28–31).

Topic: When Tempted
TEXT: James 1:12–15
(1) Don't blame God. (2) Ferret out the true reasons for temptation. (3) Consider the consequences of yielding. (4) Anticipate the blessings of perseverance (v. 12).

Hymn Suggestions

1. "O Worship the King," Robert Grant (1833); LYONS, Johann M. Haydn; harm. William Gardiner (1815)
Though this great hymn of praise is based on another psalm (104), it gathers up some of the thought and mood of today's Psalter selection.

2. "Your Hands, O Lord, in Days of Old," Edward Plumptre (1866); ST. MICHAEL'S, W. Gawler's *Hymns and Psalms* (1789)

This durable hymn recalls the healing ministry of Jesus, with which the Gospel reading for this day is concerned.

3. "Lord, Listen to My Righteous Plea," vers. Helen Ott (1982); BERNARD, Jack Grotenhuis (1983)

Closely paraphrasing the entire Psalm 17, this metrical version could well replace the Psalter reading.

4. "Come, O Thou Traveler Unknown," Charles Wesley (1742); CANDLER, Scottish melody, harm. Carlton Young (1963)

Considered by Isaac Watts as worth all the verses he himself had written, this memorable hymn is Charles Wesley's meditation on Jacob's wrestling with the angel (presented in today's Old Testament lesson, Gen. 32:22–31).
—Hugh T. McElrath

Worship Aids

CALL TO WORSHIP. "God, I call upon you, for you will answer me. Bend down your ear to me, listen to my words. Show me how marvelous is your unfailing love" (Ps. 17:6–7a REB).

INVOCATION. As we call upon you, God, we are assured that you hear us, that you care for us, that you will act on our behalf. Strengthen us against the times of doubt, when we find it hard to deal with disappointment and pain.

OFFERTORY SENTENCE. "And it is in God's power to provide you with all good gifts in abundance, so that, with every need always met to the full, you may have something to spare for every good cause" (2 Cor. 9:8 REB).

OFFERTORY PRAYER. We thank you, O God, that we can use your good gifts to us for the blessing of others and to witness to your love and grace. Open our eyes and hearts to ever new possibilities to share in this ministry of stewardship.

PRAYER. In this sacred moment, Father, help us to clear the way for a powerful encounter with you. Help us today to see the revelation of your glory on the face of Jesus who, being rich, for our sakes became poor and laid down his life that we might have life and have it more abundantly.

Develop within us his vision, that we might see and follow the things that lead to our personal peace, and to peace for all mankind.

Develop within us his understanding and compassion, that we may help one another and live with one another in love and good will.

Develop in us his devotion to your Kingdom, that we may discover the meaning and true glory of life as we live by the eternal precepts that govern your Kingdom.

Develop within us Christ's faith in you. Then we will not be overwhelmed by any circumstance that occurs, by any disaster that comes, or by any struggle that may arise. With Christlike faith in you, Father, we, like him, will face each life event bravely and creatively.

Here in your presence, we ask that out of your mercy you forgive us for past failures and sins and lead us to be true followers of Christ, enhancing the growth and welfare of all mankind.

Call us now unto you—the bereaved, the wounded, the struggling, the lonely, the sad, the weak, the strong, the wealthy, the poor, and all who need a father's strength and love.—Henry Fields

Sermon: The Revolution of a Revolutionary
TEXT: Gal. 1:13–24 (RSV)

The apostle Paul was a revolutionary both before and after he met Christ. Paul worked in Galatia, where he started a church. After leaving the area, he heard that they were straying away from the truth that he had taught them, that they were even doubting his credibility as a teacher. Therefore, to reaffirm the truths of the faith and to renew his own credibility, he wrote them a letter. In the letter he reminded them of the source of his authority: a personal encounter with Christ that had turned his life around. The text illustrates a life both without Christ and with Christ.

I. *Life is meaningless without Christ* (vv. 13–14). How would you like to achieve a high level in your occupation or in your social strata but still feel very empty? Evidently Paul felt that way.

Paul was the kind of man who often overdid whatever he did. For instance, if he persecuted the church, he did so "beyond measure." He attempted to be true to what he had been taught. He deliberately planned to climb a ladder of recognition, and succeeded in climbing above his social and religious peer group.

It is evident in these verses, however, that even in the face of success he felt failure. To vent his personal frustrations and to stamp out the group called Christians, Paul the pious became Paul the persecutor.

I can think of two men who were a lot like Paul; one was a contemporary of Paul, one is our contemporary. Both had achieved a great deal in their separate careers, but neither had achieved any inner peace. Paul's contemporary was a man named Nicodemus. This high-ranking, ethically unimpeachable Jewish official approached Jesus Christ at night. To paraphrase his statement and thoughts: "I know that you, Jesus, are a great man. Evidently you have something that I don't, and I want to find out about it." It was perhaps that night that Nicodemus not only found the answers to his questions, but found the answer to an empty life (see John 3:1–21).

In our day, Dean Jones had achieved a great deal in his own career. As he recently stated, "I had everything I thought I wanted—a growing career as a movie actor, a good family; but there was something missing." Dean Jones stated that Jesus Christ had filled that vacuum and changed his life, and that he was living proof of it.

Where do you stand in life? Stop and consider: "What will I have after I reach the top?"

According to Paul's testimony and the Bible's teaching, no success in life is adequate to provide for the lasting fullness that each individual longs to possess. There is a built-in mechanism that inevitably leads us in search of fulfillment. Paul declared that fulfillment to be Christ. Christ can enter an individual's life and give meaning—but how and where do we find him?

II. *Christ reveals himself in human experience* (vv. 15–16). Paul called on his personal experience to validate his relationship to Christ. It was clearly seen that Christ came to Paul, rather than that Paul directly sought Christ.

Paul wrote that Christ had revealed himself in Paul's life. This illustrates that God did something in Paul's life for a purpose. Paul declared that God had it all in mind even before Paul was born. Evidently Paul was important to God; and that which God had been planning all along climaxed at a place that was not necessarily holy but that was necessarily appointed. It was on a road to Damascus. I imagine that Paul began a conversation with many persons with the words, "Have you ever heard of what happened on the road that leads from Jerusalem to Damascus?"

Christ came to Paul right where Paul was: physically, on a dusty road; spiritually, in an empty shell. It may have been a long time before Paul understood all that took place that day. But one thing he never forgot or doubted was that he had encountered the living Christ and that Christ had changed his life. The emptiness had been invaded and filled to overflowing. The revolutionary had been revolutionized by Christ.

Today we can find him where we are. Whether you are in a church building or at work, Jesus Christ is where you are, and he is continually revealing himself. Whether you have sensed his activity in your life before or you sense it now for the first time, he is offering meaning and purpose and forgiveness to you.

God plans no accidents. Just as God wanted Paul to respond on that Damascus road, he wants you to respond.

You may ask, If God is revealing himself to me and I acknowledge that fact, what will happen if I respond?

III. *Christ transforms the lives of willing persons* (vv. 23–24). The Damascus road was not the end; it was the beginning of new life. Paul the persecutor became Paul the peacemaker. The one driven by hate became the one motivated by love. Emptiness was displaced by a fullness that poured into the lives of other empty people.

You can imagine the skepticism with which Paul was received by Christian groups. After all, would you want someone who was notorious for jailing Christians to be next week's honored guest? Paul's bad reputation had even spread to those who had never met him. A new rumor began to spread, however: "He who once persecuted us is now preaching the faith he once tried to destroy" (v. 23 RSV). Christ had transformed Paul's life.

Paul had hidden potential within him before he met Christ. Who knows what great things God has in store for you when you give your life to him.—James E. Lamkin[147]

---

[147]*Award Winning Sermons,* vol. 2

Illustrations

OUT OF THE DARKNESS. It is not always easy to be willing. It wasn't easy for Horace Bushnell. Bushnell was an agnostic professor at Yale University. During a week of revival services on campus, the preacher asked Bushnell, in private, if he did not think he should give heed to the truth of which he was preaching. Mr. Bushnell replied: "Sir, if the things you are preaching are true, I am utterly missing it, missing it personally because my life is falsely and wrongly positioned, but I have no way to find the truth." The preacher replied saying that he should call out to God on the hypothesis that he exists, then promise him to follow the light which he gives. Bushnell, being a man that never refused a challenge, said that he would. Three days later Bushnell came back and stood on the rostrum of the Yale chapter and said to the men: "Men, I have been in utter darkness, I have come through it to the light. Jesus is my personal Savior"—James E. Lamkin, citing George W. Truett[148]

THE COMING OF DAWN. One is reminded of a story told by Hilaire Belloc. With a friend he set out one evening to climb in the Pyrenees. They were caught in a terrible storm and the night came on. Thunder roared and lightning flashed. Rain drenched them and tempest all but dragged them from their hold on the rocks among which they sought to shelter through the long and terrifying night. Belloc's friend was new to the experience. "Isn't this terrible," he shouted to his friend. "It seems like the end of the world." Back came the reassurance of the more experienced traveler: "This is how the dawn comes in the Pyrenees," he said.

And again and again in Christian history, both widespread and personal, the dawn has seemed born of storm and tempest, danger and horror, tears and death, but it has come, and its light has spread across the world.—Leslie D. Weatherhead[149]

SUNDAY: AUGUST EIGHTH

LECTIONARY MESSAGE

Topic: Show Boat

TEXT: Matt. 14: 22–33

Other Readings: Gen. 37:1–4, 12–28; Ps. 105:1–6, 16–22, 45b; Rom. 10:5–15

The stories of Jesus and Peter walking on the water (see also Mark 6:45–52, and John 6:15–21), along with the accounts of Jesus stilling the storm (Mark 4:35–41), have stimulated the creativity of artists and musicians through the years. The boat, the tempest, and a cross signifying the presence of Christ appear frequently as liturgical symbols. Christians identify themselves with Jesus' disciples in these stories with songs like "Love Lifted Me," "Throw out the Lifeline," and "Rescue the Perishing." We sing them as testimony to what miracles can happen—such as walking on water—if we only have faith. When the storm surrounding the boat is the focus of a sermon, more often than not the preacher proclaims that Jesus will still the storms in our lives and lift us up when we would otherwise perish. These are positive, upbeat messages; they reflect, however, neither the action of the story nor the intention of the author.

I. The account of Peter's walk on the water is about not faith but the lack of it. What is worse, it appears that the other disciples were equally faithless; they cried out with fear and supposed that Jesus was a ghost. Peter demanded that the Lord prove his identity by performing a miracle—one for Peter's own gratification, and of no lasting benefit. The disciples' misunderstanding of Jesus and their absence of faith are underlined by the setting of the passage. Just prior to this, Jesus had fed five thousand with five loaves and two fishes. He had already cast out demons and healed a paralytic. The disciples spent more time with the Messiah than other people did. You would think they would recognize him, and have confidence in his authority over wind and wave. Matthew paints an unflattering portrait of Peter and the others, carefully recording Jesus' rebuke along with their confession of faith in verse 33. It is appropriate to ask why the story is presented in this manner.

[148] *The Prophet's Mantle* (Grand Rapids: Baker Book House, 1948), 22.
[149] *Best Sermons* (1959–1960)

II. The early Christians hearing (and later reading) this story would see in it a reminder: that the worst fear is caused not by storms or the possibility of drowning but by forgetting what God has done and promises to do. The men in the boat that night had grown up hearing about the wondrous works of God in preserving Noah through the flood, delivering Moses through the Red Sea, and bringing Jonah out of the depths in order to proclaim the Word of the Lord. But they temporarily forgot divine power and purpose. The Church in the Apostolic Age heard about Jesus walking on water in the midst of the storm and remembered—and a church that recalls and retells the mighty acts of God has a future. Even as some of them faced martyrdom, they sang praise to the Redeemer, looking forward to a new heaven and new earth where "the sea is no more" (Rev. 21:1). Their faith lives on. The places where the church of Jesus Christ is growing larger and stronger today are paradoxically those places where it is unsafe and uncertain—those places where the people of God *must* remember.

III. There is good news in this text for fainthearted followers, too. The story of Peter's fall and rise tells us that even our failures in faith can be used by an all-powerful God to proclaim the gospel. Peter's confession of faith, recorded in Matthew 16, has that much more impact because we know how far he had come. The bold postresurrection witness of the other apostles stands out in sharper relief because we know they once fearfully mistook Jesus for a ghost. Matthew's record of this event is a gift to every imperfect disciple, if we read it as a promise that the truth of Christ can be proclaimed even through the likes of us.

IV. Finally, this episode on the Sea of Galilee shows us something of the nature of Jesus Christ. He is Lord of wind and wave, sovereign over gravity and all the forces of nature. His power and love are infinite. The Savior did not abandon Peter in his unbelief, or let the waves of death encompass him alone. God's love made visible does not give up on people. Whether we ascend to heaven, make our bed in Sheol, take the wings of the morning or dwell in the uttermost parts of the sea, his hand shall lead us, and his right hand shall hold us. Thanks be to God for such steadfast love and power.—Carol M. Noren

Illustrations

SOMEONE KNOWS BETTER.   A few years ago I went to have two teeth pulled by a highly respected dentist. From previous dental work elsewhere, I had some idea of how long it would take for a local anesthetic to work. I was surprised, therefore, when the dentist picked up the tools to pull the teeth as soon as he had set down the hypodermic syringe. "I don't think it's taken effect," I told him. He replied that he was sure the area was numb. I protested that I was sure it wasn't ready but agreed to let him check it. In a moment, to my astonishment, the two teeth had been extracted. The dentist knew better than I did the strength and speed of the anesthesia. I felt mildly embarrassed and ashamed for not trusting his skill and wisdom.—Carol M. Noren

FOOLS FOR CHRIST.   When Katherine Anne Porter published her long-awaited novel *Ship of Fools,* she explained why she had borrowed the title from a fifteenth-century moral allegory: "I took for my own this simple, almost universal image of the ship of this world on its voyage to eternity. . . . I am a passenger on that ship." We too are passengers on a ship. Shall we call it a ship of fools? Let us hope that we are, as Paul phrased it, "fools for Christ's sake" (1 Cor. 4:10). When he twice used the word *moros* (fool), he had discipleship in mind, like Matthew when he told the story of the stilling of the tempest.—James W. Cox[150]

SERMON SUGGESTIONS

Topic: Who Is Like the Lord?
    TEXT: Mic. 7:14–20
    (1) He cares for his people like a shepherd (vv. 14–15). (2) The work of his wrath often leads to repentance (vv. 16–17). (3) He has compassion and forgives sin (vv. 18–19).

Topic: Model of Humility
    TEXT: John 13:3–5
    (1) *Our problem:* (a) we may be too insecure to render humble service, (b) or too

---

[150] *Surprised by God*

proud. (2) *Jesus' solution:* (a) his standing came from God, not from human opinion; (b) he did what was needed under the circumstances; (c) he left an example of self-forgetfulness.

Hymn Suggestions

1. "Eternal Father, Strong to Save," William Whiting (1860); MELITA, John Bacchus Dykes (1861)
This hymn that prays for those at sea may appropriately be sung as a response to the Gospel reading depicting Christ walking on the sea and saving Peter who dared to try to do the same.
2. "We Have Heard the Joyful Sound," Priscilla Owens (1887); JESUS SAVES, William J. Kirkpatrick (1882); LIMPSFIELD, Josiah Booth (1889)
Reflecting the central message of the Epistle reading for this day, this gospel hymn—enthusiastically sung to either tune—could be used as a response to the Romans 10:5–15 passage.
3. "To God Be the Glory," Fanny J. Crosby (1875); TO GOD BE THE GLORY, William H. Doane (1875)
Psalm 105 and "To God Be the Glory" in quite different ways give praise to God for "his wonderful works." One of the few songs of Fanny Crosby to voice objective praise of God, this one is quite suitable to accompany the Psalter reading, for "great things he hath done!"
4. "I Sought the Lord, and Afterward I Knew," anon. (1878); FINLANDIA, Jean Sibelius (1899)
This anonymous hymn beautifully expresses the truth, exemplified by Jesus reaching out to save Peter in the stormy sea (Matt. 14:22–33), that God is the prime mover. Peter not so much took hold of Jesus' hand as Jesus took Peter's hand to rescue him from drowning.—Hugh T. McElrath

Worship Aids

CALL TO WORSHIP. "Seek the Lord, and his strength: seek his face evermore" (Ps. 105:4).

INVOCATION. Grant, our heavenly Father, thy blessing to rest upon us. Bless to our use and profit the lesson of the hour. May we bear with us a thought of the fruitfulness of thy sacred scripture. It hangs as clusters hang on the vine, covered with fruit for our need. May we learn how to search. May we learn how to find. May we learn how to feed upon thy word. Prepare us for the duties of life. Make us joyful in them by the consciousness of thy presence. Make us royal ourselves by sympathy with our royal Head. And at last bring us, through much tribulation, to reign with thee in the unclouded glory of the upper sphere, where we will praise the Father, the Son, and the Spirit evermore.—Henry Ward Beecher[151]

OFFERTORY SENTENCE. "Let your light shine before others, so that they may see your good works and give glory to your Father in heaven" (Matt. 5:16 NRSV).

OFFERTORY PRAYER. Bless the mission enterprise of the church, O Lord, through our gifts this day, and may Jesus Christ be magnified because we pause to give and pray and believe.—E. Lee Phillips

PRAYER. We thank thee for thine exceeding bounty and love, O Lord Jesus, our Redeemer. We thank thee for our souls' own experience. What to us is the heaven around us, and the earth filled with tokens of thy love and kindness; what are food and raiment; and what are all the blessings of the household compared with the glory which thou dost bring to the soul in the assurance of thy love today. For the earth fades and passes away. At longest, we are here but a little time. In our Father's house eternity dwells. But when thou dost disclose thyself to us, and call us thine, speaking our sins forgiven, and giving us the promise of thy life as the assurance of ours, saying, "Because I live, ye shall live also," then, O blessed Savior, with what transport do we hail the gift of immortality, and all its blessedness, with thee, with thine, with ours. Cleansed from every sin, redeemed from every weakness, knowing as we are known, we shall forever and forever, in thy presence, in thine own immediate love and care, hold on our exalted being through endless ages of blessedness. Eye hath not seen, nor ear heard, nor hath it entered into

151 *The Plymouth Pulpit*

the heart of man to conceive, what thou hast laid up for those that love thee, and whom thou dost love.—Henry Ward Beecher[152]

Sermon: How to Cope? Trust the Uplook, Not the Outlook

TEXT: Ps. 119:50

In every problem, God has wrapped up a promise. Obstacles can be opportunities and burdens can be blessings. Attitudes are more important than facts. Not what happens *to* us but what happens *in* us is the important matter. In our problems there is a golden heart of meaning. The psalmist calls us to new life in the midst of trouble through the promises of God. We are meant to live *above* our problems, not *in* them, to lift up our hearts to God. When the outlook is bad, the upward look gives us power to cope!

I. *The upward look of faith gives us perspective.* St. Paul gave powerful witness out of his life of suffering: "I consider that the sufferings of this present time are not worth comparing with the glory that is to be revealed to us" (Rom. 8:18). We often describe life in negative terms—as a "rat race," a "tedium," a "vale of tears"; but Paul describes life in positive terms: "this grace wherein we stand." (Rom. 8:28). In the school of Christ, Paul had learned the practical power of perspective! Here is his courageous testimony: "We are afflicted in every way, but not crushed; perplexed, but not driven to despair; persecuted, but not forsaken; struck down, but not destroyed . . . so we do not lose heart" (2 Cor. 4:8–9, 16). In every trouble, Paul found that God was there with him, and the perspective of faith gave him the power of the going on.

II. *When we look to Jesus, we find the secret of confidence in the gospel story—both what he did and what he said.* In his ministry of compassion, he brought help and hope to multitudes. Not only specific instances but also the summary statements are impressive.

Multitudes have found their confidence in Jesus' words. Not only what he did but also what he said gives us new life and spirit. "Come to me, all who labor and are heavyladen, and I will give you rest. Take my yoke upon you, and learn from me, for I am gentle and lowly in heart, and you will find rest

for your souls. For my yoke is easy, and my burden is light" (Matt. 11:28–30). Jesus lights up our lives with his love.

Not only does God promise us power to cope, he also promises us victory in life's struggles. St. Paul sounds the victory note, despite his hardships and sufferings: "Who shall separate us from the love of Christ? Shall tribulation, or distress, or persecution, or famine, or nakedness, or sword? . . . No, in all these things we are more than conquerors through him who loved us" (Rom. 8:35, 37).

The love of Christ puts us on victory ground. Love is the gospel magic. Our hopes will not disappoint us, because God loves us, and God is with us and for us. Nothing can "separate us from the love of God in Christ Jesus our Lord" (Rom. 8:39). When we live in the light of his love, life becomes a thing of beauty, not just a round of duty.

III. *But there is something we must do.* We must look up to God. His saving help is at hand, but we must look to him to see it. His miracles are waiting for us, but we must look to him to receive them. When we stop staring at our problems and look to God, wonderful things will happen. The psalmist gives happy witness: "He put a new song in my mouth, a song of praise to our God" (Ps. 40:3). The promise is for all who turn to God. "He will speak peace to his people, to his saints, to those who turn to him in their hearts" (Ps. 85:8).—Lowell M. Atkinson[153]

Illustrations

LOOK UP!   John Wesley wrote to one of his preachers, "You look inward too much, and upward too little." That was the letter, and it says it all. Never doubt the power of the upward look. When troubles come, we are made strong by the promises of God that give us new life. We learn the secret of successful living—get on the God-lighted side of our troubles!—Lowell M. Atkinson[154]

THE BIG PICTURE.   Perspective helps us see the big picture. On one of our trips to Europe, my wife and I were flying over the Alps,

---

[152]*Prayers from the Pulpit*

[153]*Apples of Gold,* (Lima, OH: Fairway Press, 1986), 155–158.
[154]*Apples of Gold,* p. 156.

reveling in the beauty of the bright blue sky above and the magnificent panorama of the sun-drenched mountains below. Then we began a long descent to Schiphol Airport in Amsterdam. Suddenly a gray blanket of cloud appeared beneath us. Then rain spattered against the window. Looking out, we could see only rain and cloud. The bright view was gone; we were in the storm, and all was gray. On the airfield beneath us we could see figures in rain gear scurrying about. I turned to my wife and said, "And to think, a few moments ago the sun was shining." To which she replied, "It still is." Of course! Her reply restored my perspective. Above the storm, the sun still shone!—Lowell M. Atkinson[155]

SUNDAY: AUGUST FIFTEENTH

LECTIONARY MESSAGE

Topic: Going to the Dogs
TEXT: Matt. 15: 21–28
Other Readings: Gen. 45:1–15; Ps. 133; Rom. 11:1–2a, 29–32

The Gospel writers are assumed to bear witness to the good news about Jesus Christ, but today's reading from Matthew makes one wonder if the author was having an "off" day. Although a healing miracle occurred, the story lacks the sympathetic characters and appreciative bystanders of, for example, the healing of the daughter of Jairus (Mark 5:22ff). A modern publicist would quietly excise the first twenty-eight verses of chapter 15, because none of the persons depicted is presented in a particularly flattering light.

If we considered them in the order in which they speak, we would conclude that the Syrophoenician woman was a nag who wouldn't take no for an answer. In Mark's version of the story, the woman gate-crashed a private party at someone's home. She approached Jesus three separate times, and at least once she made her case to the disciples. Her quick retort to the Messiah (v. 26) strikes us as impertinence, if not outright irreverence. The author makes her look bad by noting that she was from the region of Sidon and Tyre. For Jews of that time, the Canaanites symbolized all that was wicked and godless.

The disciples don't come off much better in this section of the Gospel. In the previous chapter, they suggested that Jesus send the crowds away to fend for themselves, rather than feeding the five thousand. When the next person in need came along, they said, "Send her away, for she is crying after us." They weren't interested in helping her. They lacked faith that Jesus could and would do anything *but* send her away.

The portrait of Jesus painted is most troubling of all. Is this a harsh, indifferent Messiah who is unmoved by the plea of a mother? His words sound insulting: "It is not fair to take the children's bread and throw it to the dogs." It's so unlike other healing miracles in the Scriptures. When a centurion asked Jesus to restore his servant to health, the Master didn't disqualify him for being a Gentile (Matt. 8:5). We wonder why he made this seemingly narrow-minded response in verse 24: "I was sent only to the lost sheep of the house of Israel."

It is hard for us to understand why Matthew repeated this story, even if it is true. But Matthew's intended audience would have heard it quite differently than we do. For first-century Jewish Christians, the Lord's encounter with the Canaanite woman answered questions rather than created problems.

The first listeners and readers came from a tradition that had waited many generations for the Messiah promised to Israel. Matthew took special care to preserve those sayings that showed Jesus of Nazareth to be the fulfillment of Old Testament prophecy. If we reread the woman's lines in this episode, we note that she addressed Jesus as "Lord, Son of David," and Jesus identifies himself as the Savior of Israel. These words would underline Jesus' messianic identity. At the same time, the woman's confession of faith stands in contrast to Jesus' own people rejecting him. Unlike his fellow Jews, the woman claimed no right to the Messiah's compassion, no privileged relationship. Her only hope was in his mercy without bounds. This was the first time Jesus ministered outside Jewish territory. Read in context, it would suggest to the Apos-

155*Apples of Gold*, p. 156f.

tolic Church that their mission was now to the very people they considered dogs—or worse: to outsiders and enemies and those they'd rather send away.

Even the Savior's words and actions appear in a new light when we imagine their reception by Matthew's audience. The early Christians, shunned and persecuted, would cry out to God in times of pain and trial just as the Syrophoenician woman did, saying, "Lord, help me." Remembering this story would have encouraged them to be constant in prayer, trusting that the God of mercy could deliver them or use their suffering for a purpose greater than they understood. And what about Jesus' reference to the woman as a dog? Speaking to her at all broke with convention. Jesus took her words seriously, and the term of derision set up the disciples for the surprise ending: someone they disqualified because of her sex and background was included because of her faith in Christ. Jesus contrasted the unbelieving Jews of the time with a believing Gentile, and showed that the Kingdom of God is going to such dogs.

This makes the story good news for us, too; none of us can claim a birthright to God's favor. We bring nothing to the Son of David but our own neediness and the hope that he will have mercy on us. And he awaits us still today, at the sacred table where he is both host and feast. We are not worthy to so much as gather up the crumbs under God's table, but by faith we may receive the Bread of Life and be made whole. The Kingdom of God is going to the "dogs," to all who place their trust in Jesus Christ.—Carol M. Noren

Illustrations

AS WE ARE.
Just as I am, without one plea,
but that thy blood was shed for me,
and that thou bidst me come to thee,
O Lamb of God, I come, I come.
Just as I am, thy love unknown
hath broken every barrier down;
now, to be thine, yea thine alone,
O Lamb of God, I come, I come.
—Charlotte Elliott, 1835

THE WAY GOD WORKS. The righteousness of God is his forgiveness, the radical alteration of the relationship between God and man which explains why, though human unrighteousness and ungodliness have brought the world to its present condition and are intolerable to Him, He nevertheless continues to name us His people in order that we may *be* his people. Unlike any other verdict His verdict is creative: He pronounces us, His enemies, to be His friends.—Karl Barth[156]

SERMON SUGGESTIONS

Topic: Sound the Alarm!
TEXT: Hos. 8:1–14
(1) When God's people rebel against him (v. 1); (2) when obedience to God is selective (vv. 2–4); (3) when idolatry takes over (vv. 5–6); (4) when God's purposes for his people are forgotten (vv. 11–14).

Topic: Why Christ Deserves to Be Lord
TEXT: Rev. 1:5–6
(1) He was faithful unto death. (2) He brought us salvation. (3) He gave us a redemptive role in the world.

Hymn Suggestions

1. "Behold the Goodness of Our Lord," Fred Anderson (1872); CRIMOND, Jessie Seymour Irvine (1872)
This free paraphrase of Psalm 133 could well replace the Psalter reading in this day's worship.
2. "How Good and Pleasant Is the Sight," The Psalter (1912); PRESSLY, Charles H. Gabriel (1912)
Set to a more lively tune by the prolific Charles H. Gabriel, this paraphrase of Psalm 133 could also be used in connection with the Psalter reading.
3. "God Moves in a Mysterious Way," William Cowper (1774); DUNDEE, Scottish Psalter (1615)
4. "There's a Wideness in God's Mercy," Frederick W. Faber (1854); WELLESLEY, Lizzie S. Tourjee (1877)
Jesus responded to the Canaanite woman's plea for mercy (Matt. 15:21–28) because of her great faith. This hymn suitably celebrates the universality of that divine mercy.—Hugh T. McElrath

[156] *The Epistle to the Romans*

Worship Aids

CALL TO WORSHIP. "How very good and pleasant it is when kindred live together in unity! . . . It is like the dew of Hermon, which falls on the mountains of Zion. For there the Lord ordained his blessing: life forevermore" (Ps. 133:1, 3 NRSV).

INVOCATION. Our Father in heaven, help us through your Word, through your Holy Spirit, and through our fellowship with our brothers and sisters in worship, to know the blessings of belonging to one another through Christ Jesus, the Savior and Lord of us all.

OFFERTORY SENTENCE. "We then that are strong ought to bear the infirmities of the weak, and not to please ourselves" (Rom. 15:1).

OFFERTORY PRAYER. We would not come in pride and arrogant superiority, but in loving and caring humility, our Father. Accept these tithes and offerings, that the weak may be strengthened and encouraged and the able challenged.

PRAYER. Our Father, we come this morning, seeking your presence more fully in our lives. Teach us your ways, impart to us your thoughts, lead us into your purposes, we pray. We have heard of you with the hearing of the ear. We have glimpsed you in the majesty of life and the grandeur of creation. We have felt your presence in rare moments when life was receptive to your spirit. Yet we have not allowed you to be Lord of all of life, nor master of our destiny. Large compartments of our daily habits we have closed to your presence. Big segments of our thinking we have neglected to align with your truth. As only you can, create the circumstances in which you can have our undivided attention and enable us to amend our straying ways, that we might follow you in all things. Bless us, Father, as we come before you repentant and seeking renewal, which comes through the realization that we have been forgiven and loved even when we were unlovely sinners. Then will our hearts be glad. Then will our thanksgiving be unending. Then will our lives be worthwhile in the building of your Kingdom among our fellow human beings.—Henry Fields

Sermon: Stick-to-itiveness

TEXT: Rom. 12:11

Does your faith shine as brightly today as it once did? Have you the kind of spiritual life that has staying power, constantly deepening in devotion, always growing in love, ever better in behavior, openly continuing in zeal, and overflowing with strength?

This faith is the kind of which Paul speaks in Romans 12:11. This chapter begins with a call to practical surrender, personal transformation, and service in the will of God (vv. 1–2). Counsel on right relations with God, others, and oneself (vv. 3–10) culminates in a call to continuity in the quality of personal spiritual life.

Verse 11 in the Revised Standard Version reads, "Never flag in zeal, be aglow with the Spirit, serve the Lord." In these imperatives we see some clear aids for spiritual continuity.

I. *Our outward activity—the need for a disciplined life.* The apostle knew how easy it could be to withdraw from active spiritual service, to stop being busy for the Lord, to allow one's zeal to flag and the spiritual barometer to fall. Hence his warning against carelessness and sloth.

Every man suffers from the desire to avoid hard work when possible. We can rationalize our actions in many ways: "I've done my share—let the young folks take their turn in carrying the burdens of the church and its leadership now." "Most of my get-up-and-go has gotten up and gone; I think I'll be a spectator rather than a participant for now!" "I believe I need and deserve a rest!"

Against this attitude, Paul butted his solid counsel: "Never flag in zeal!" To do so is to court danger. To sit back invites disaster. The Christian who steps down and by choice refuses to be busy for the Lord, who turns away from a disciplined life of spiritual action, opens a clear path for the forces of evil to attack.

Second Samuel 11:1 says of David that "in the spring of the year, the time when kings go forth to battle, David sent Joab, and his servants with him, and all Israel; and they ravaged the Ammonites, and besieged Rabbah" (RSV). David was the king, but he stayed at home in the time when kings go forth to battle. Instead, he sent a substitute to do the service that was his responsibility. He fell into temptation and deep sin because he was not in the front line of the battle, where he ought to have been.

The devil is a specialist in strategy. He knows exactly how to work out the situations and circumstances of our lives to help him get his hands on us, and he did just this with David. The safest place for the king was in the front line of the battle, serving God with unflagging zeal. Instead he fell into a wrong experience because he slackened off in that discipline that would have kept him active in the right place and in the right way. The zealous approach to Christian service is a primary aid to safety, success, and satisfaction.

"Beware of the natural human desire just to hang there limp and lifeless, to allow your zeal to flag," cried the apostle. We must adopt drive, method, application, system, and commitment as essentials in our outward activities for God, or else we shall fail to keep on keeping on.

That is the way in which God himself works. Several times the Scriptures mention a seemingly impossible objective and then add, "The zeal of the Lord will perform this." God does not abandon his projects and programs because they are tough. He also sent his only Son as a final word to reach us, despite the cost. His purposeful, disciplined activity for us can be seen in Jesus' words: "I have a baptism to be baptized with; and how am I straightened till it be accomplished" (Luke 12:50)! "He steadfastly set his face to go to Jerusalem" (Luke 9:51). God's zeal would not allow him to give up his purpose— to redeem; and as Paul also said, "He which hath begun a good work in you will perform it" (Phil. 1:6).

Jesus worked a full three years with Peter and saw little change, but still sought him after the resurrection, to be forgiven and restored again. And in later days we find that same apostle actually becoming the rockman that Jesus had him in mind to be. And God made him grow like that because he refused to give up on him.

II. *Our inward motivation—the need for a burning heart.* The King James Version of the Bible reads, "fervent in spirit"; the RSV says, "aglow with the Spirit"; Moffatt's translation reads, "maintain the spiritual glow" (Rom. 12:11). All these translations speak of the inner life of spiritual power, enthusiasm, love, and devotion that fans the flame of the Holy Spirit's guidance within, which in turn affects our outward behavior.

The wisest man who ever lived advised, "Whatsoever thy hand findeth to do, do it with thy might" (Eccl. 9:10)! Paul himself knew the power of commitment needed in order to achieve. He told the Philippians, "This one thing I do. . . . I press toward the mark" (Phil. 3:13–14).

Paul's call here is to turn away from half-hearted commitment, to feed the inner glow of the spirit, to stoke up the fire within; then outward zeal will not flag.

III. *The upward vision of an eternal perspective.* "Don't be limited by the immediately visible results," Paul said. "If you want to keep on keeping on, you need to look at the future, not the present. You are not serving the current situation. You do not work only for immediate results. Look upon what you are doing in the light of eternity. Serve the Lord!"

Too often we grow cold because we get so tangled with the present. We consider present results. We respond to present pressures. Others misunderstand and misjudge us, and we stop too long to consider how things are right now. We need to remember that the spiritual life has its anchor in eternity and can never be fully evaluated until we finally view it from that perspective. It is only those whose eyes are fixed on the eternal dimensions of service to the Lord who can continue (2 Tim. 4:7–8; 2 Cor. 4:8, 16–18).

Too many people are eliminated from fulfilling their spiritual best in the runoffs! Too many never last the distance, but drop out before the finish. To keep on keeping on takes stick-to-itiveness. As Paul told the believers in Galatia, "Let us not be weary in well-doing: for in due season we shall reap if we faint not" (Gal. 6:9).—Craig Skinner[157]

Illustrations

EVERLASTINGLY AT IT.   Sometimes in a museum you see one of the old prairie schooners on which the pioneers crossed the continent. If they had stopped to contrast

---

[157]*Back Where You Belong* (Nashville: Broadman Press, 1980), 89–99.

each day the distance they had traveled with the vast stretches of the continent before them, they would never have reached their goal. But day by day the oxen plodded on; night by night the wagons were halted, the cattle watered, and the fires lighted. Thus, by going on, day by day, they crossed plains and mountains and reached the lands on the Pacific. It is not doing something brilliant or striking that wins you the victory and brings you to the journey's end, but keeping ever-lastingly at it, sailing on from port to port, island to island, this day and then the next day. The ministers of the old time used to ask in their prayers that we might be granted an "honorable through-bearing." A fine phrase that, signifying perseverance up to the very end.—Clarence Edward Macartney[158]

PERSEVERANCE. By perseverance the snail reached the Ark.—Charles Haddon Spurgeon

SUNDAY: AUGUST TWENTY-SECOND

LECTIONARY MESSAGE

Topic: The Weak Confounding the Strong
TEXT: Exod. 1:8–2:10
Other Readings: Ps. 124; Rom. 12:1–8; Matt. 16:13–20

The saga of Moses, so crucial to the identity of Israel as God's covenant people, is familiar to any child in Sunday school. The story of hiding a baby in the bulrushes charms the imagination and captures a listener's attention. In focusing on the infant, however, we are apt to miss the interaction of other characters in the tale. And at this stage of the story, God's ultimate purpose is manifested as much in these characters as in young Moses.

I. Today's passage begins with the pronouncement, "Now there arose a new king over Egypt, who did not know Joseph." Reading the narrative that follows creates the impression that this new king had qualities we look for today in national leaders. He was shrewd in formulating policy to serve his country's best interests (v. 10). He looked out for national security (v. 10). He had a long-range economic plan, a circle of advisers who reported to him, and a public works program to cut down on unemployment (v. 11). He shared his people's concern about the problem of resident aliens. Like many new leaders, he tried to distance himself from his predecessor's policies—even to the point of saying he didn't know Joseph, the famous deputy who had saved Egypt from famine. All of this sounds admirable, on the face of it. But as we read on in chapter 1, it becomes clear that this leader was unprincipled. He did whatever seemed expedient at the time, whatever served his own ends. Feeling secure in his own power, he did not fear God or show any reverence to the Lord. And so he had no qualms about oppressing God's people. It is paradoxical, then, that some of the least powerful and influential in his kingdom, who feared and served God, were his undoing, though they never took up arms against him.

II. The midwives, Shiphrah and Puah, through their passive resistance, foiled the king's plan to reduce the Hebrew population. Scholars vary in their opinions as to whether the midwives were actually Hebrews or in fact Egyptians. It seems unlikely that the Pharaoh would communicate directly with two low-status Hebrew women—but it is also unlikely that the Hebrew people would willingly use outsiders as midwives. In any case, they are described as "fearing God"—a term usually applied to someone outside the covenant community who nevertheless revered the God of Israel. Shiphrah and Puah played on Pharaoh's ethnic or racial prejudice when they explained that they could not keep up with the speed with which those vigorous (read: primitive) people delivered babies.

III. Moses' mother and sister, too, had the last laugh on Pharaoh. His mother followed the letter but not the spirit of the law when she obeyed the king's decree to cast all male babies into the Nile; she did, after all, set her son in the water. It may or may not be deliberate irony that the vessel in which she placed the child was like those used for housing images of Egyptian gods. This helpless child would be more powerful than the

[158] *Macartney's Illustrations*

Pharaoh or the Pharaoh's gods. The sister, too, was in collusion to confound the king's purpose. She had the last laugh when she was able to restore the baby to its mother—under the protection of the royal family.

IV. Even the princess, though she could not know what this infant would grow up to be, undermined the power of the king. Instead of complying with Pharaoh's decree to kill the male Hebrew babies, she adopted his enemies' child as her own son. She raised him up to privilege and power, so that years later he was not on unfamiliar ground when he returned to demand liberation for God's chosen people.

V. Moses, whose name in Hebrew means "to draw forth," would himself draw forth his people in defiance of Pharaoh's will. In the same way, Jesus Christ, poor and weak in the eyes of the Roman government, was born with a price on his head. Our Savior, who was delivered by angelic guidance to the relative safety of Egypt, became the Great Deliverer for all who follow him. As 1 Corinthians 1:27 and 30 say, "God chose what is foolish in the world to confound the wise; God chose what is weak in the world to confound the strong. . . . He is the source of your life in Christ Jesus, whom God made our wisdom, our righteousness and sanctification and redemption."

Whoever we are, kings' daughters or enslaved people, God can use us to accomplish his good purpose and to confound the powers and principalities of the world. The world may forget our names, as it did in noting the roles of the princess, the mother, and the sister. But God remembers, and having a part in his saving work is reward enough.—Carol M. Noren

Illustrations

ON OUR SIDE.
Did we in our own strength confide,
  our striving would be losing;
Were not the right man on our side,
  the man of God's own choosing.
Dost ask who that may be?
Christ Jesus, it is he;
Lord Sabbaoth, his name,
  from age to age the same,
  and he must win the battle.
And though this world,
  with devils filled,

should threaten to undo us,
We will not fear,
for God hath willed
his truth to triumph through us.
The Prince of Darkness grim,
we tremble not for him;
his rage we can endure,
for lo, his doom is sure;
one little word shall fell him.
          —Martin Luther, "Ein Feste Burg"

BIGNESS AND GREATNESS.   I am against bigness and greatness in all their forms, and with the invisible molecular moral forces that work from individual to individual, stealing in through the crannies of the world like so many soft rootlets, or like the capillary oozing of water, and yet rending the hardest monuments of man's pride, if you give them time.—William James

SERMON SUGGESTIONS

Topic: God's Muted Voice
TEXT: Exod. 20:18–21; John 1:16–17
(1) Our human weakness and our sins may cause us to dread or feel threatened by God. (2) We may wish for a human voice to speak for God to us—someone like us who understands us. (3) Moses did what God willed in his day, but Jesus Christ brought to us God's love and grace in its fullness.

Topic: Why We Don't Lose Heart
TEXT: 2 Cor. 4:16–18
(1) God is making us stronger on the inside. (2) Our little troubles are preparing us for a wonderful celebration in eternity.

Hymn Suggestions

1. "If God the Lord Were Not Our Constant Help," vers. Calvin Seerveld (1981); OLD 124TH, *Genevan Psalter* (1551).
Using this contemporary paraphrase set to the ancient tune for Psalm 124, the reading of Psalm 124:1–5 could be followed by the singing of the first stanza of the paraphrase. The reading of Psalm 124:6–8 could then be followed by the second stanza of the paraphrase.
2. "Built on the Rock," Nicolai F. S. Grundtvig (1854); KIRKEN, Ludwig M. Lindemann (1840)

Peter's confession—the rock on which Christ built his church—is the burden of this great Scandinavian chorale. It would naturally accompany the New Testament reading (Matt. 16:13–20).

3. "Come, All Christians, Be Committed," Eva B. Lloyd (1912); BEACH SPRING, *The Sacred Harp* (1844)

This twentieth-century hymn issues a call to sacrificial worship—the theme of the Epistle lesson for this day.

4. "You Are the Christ, O Lord," William W. How (1871); WYNGATE CANON, Richard Wayne Dirksen (1974)

This little-known nineteenth-century hymn is based directly on the Epistle reading and thus could be appropriately sung either before or after its reading.—Hugh T. McElrath

Worship Aids

CALL TO WORSHIP. "Our help is in the name of the Lord who made heaven and earth" (Ps. 124:8).

INVOCATION. Gracious Lord, we look to you for help, in the ordinary challenges and demands of life and in our day-to-day effort to find and do your will. And we look now to you for your special help in this service of worship, that we may be strengthened to do what life in general requires and what you show us to be the special tasks to which we should put our hearts and hands.

OFFERTORY SENTENCE. "Every good gift and every perfect gift is from above, and cometh down from the Father of lights, with whom is no variableness, neither shadow of turning" (James 1:17).

OFFERTORY PRAYER. Your love, O God, is unchanging, however much we change. You have blessed us far more than we could ever deserve. Let that love make us more consistent in what we are, in our concern for those causes and for all people who are near and dear to you.

PRAYER. Look upon us, O Lord, and let all the darkness of our souls vanish before the beams of Thy brightness. Fill us with holy love, and open to us the treasures of Thy wisdom. All our desire is known unto Thee; therefore perfect what Thou hast begun, and what Thy Spirit has awakened us to ask in prayer. We seek Thy face; turn Thy face unto us and show us Thy glory. Then shall our longing be satisfied, and our peace shall be perfect. Amen.—St. Augustine[159]

Sermon: Death Be Not Proud

TEXT: Rev. 1:17–20

In the following poem, John Donne pictures death conquered and humbled by Jesus Christ:

Death, be not proud, though some have called thee
Mighty and dreadful; for thou art not so.

In Revelation, John gives three reasons why death can no longer be proud and arrogant toward those who are trusting in Jesus.

I. *Death can no longer be proud toward us because Jesus has fully experienced it.* "Fear not, I am the first and the last: I am he that liveth and was dead" (Rev. 1:17–18), John wrote to the suffering believers in Asia Minor. Domitian, the Roman Emperor, had already put some of them to death because they refused to bow down and worship him as a god. The surviving Christians were terribly afraid. Death stood knocking at their door. It rattled its terrifying chains at them. But to those frightened Christians, the Savior had something to say about death, and what he said brought great comfort to them.

The original language in verse 17 is very graphic: "Stop being afraid; I became dead," Jesus said. He told them that he had experienced all that death can do to them and more, and that there is no reason for them to keep on fearing it. Having experienced it all, he tells us to stop being afraid of it. Many things frighten us, but we fear the unknown most of all.

Jesus has returned from that unknown realm, courageously saying to all of us: "Stop being afraid of death; I have experienced it all!"

London must be a wonderful place to visit. Friends have gone there and returned telling me about the old city and its marvelous sites. I would not be afraid to visit

---

[159] St. Augustine (354–430 A.D.)

London, because my friends have been there and have told me what it's like.

I have a dear friend who died and was raised from the dead. In quiet moments of worship and meditation he has said to me: "Stop being afraid, I have experienced it all! I know what it's like! There is no reason for you to continue being afraid!"

So death can no longer be proud and arrogant in its attitude toward believers because all of its mysteries have been explored and revealed by Jesus. He has experienced it all!

II. *Death can no longer be proud toward us because Jesus has completely conquered it.* "I am he that liveth, and was dead; and behold, I am alive and for evermore. Amen" (v. 18). Jesus identifies himself: "I am the Living One," "I am the one who is alive forevermore." He will never die again. In his resurrection he conquered death. Its power and sting have been removed. Death be not proud, for Jesus has conquered you!

For centuries death held its victims in its proud and greedy hands. Death gloated in arrogant pride as it pointed its scepter at men and rattled its chains in their faces.

III. *Death can no longer be proud toward us because Jesus has total control of it.* "I am he that liveth, and was dead; and behold, I am alive for evermore, Amen, and have the keys of hell and of death" (v. 18).

Death is the cessation of physical life; Hades is the grave, the world of the dead. Jesus tells us to stop being afraid, either of the cessation of physical life or the grave, because he has total control of both! So far as the Christian is concerned, Jesus has conquered both, and he has total control of them! Therefore, "stop being afraid of death and the grave," he says!

We Christians ought to approach our death simply and in faith. We are wrong to think of death as separating us from our Christian loved ones. Those who know Jesus never say good-bye. We only say, "Until then!" Those who love Christ never meet for the last time.

I think I would like to put my name to that, as well. When I die, I should like to slip out of the room without fuss—for what matters most is not what I am leaving but where I am going! I would like to do that because death is no longer a proud enemy but a van-

quished and chained foe; Jesus has control of it!

When life's day is over and our name is called, all of us who are Christians ought to answer our call without fear. With joy and expectation let us answer, "Adsum"—"Present." We will be able to do it because Jesus has total control of death and the grave. Its power has been removed!

"Death be not proud! Do not rattle your noisy chains in my face as though you can frighten me! Do not try to tyrannize me with your fearful scepter, for my savior has vanquished your terrible power!"—J. B. Fowler Jr.[160]

Illustration

FEAR OF THE UNKNOWN.   When Columbus sailed across the Atlantic, the sailors on his three ships were fearful of what lay ahead. They were sailing into unknown waters. When Magellan sailed around the world, his crew was fearful. They were sailing into the unknown. When Lindberg flew *The Spirit of Saint Louis* across the Atlantic to Paris, there was some fear in his heart. He was doing something that had never before been done.—J. B. Fowler Jr.[161]

CONFIDENCE IN THE FACE OF DEATH.   In 1756 John Wesley, the founder of Methodism, received a letter from a father whose son had been converted in a revival meeting that had swept York, England. When the father wrote, his prodigal son was in prison, awaiting execution. Writing to Wesley, the old father said: "It pleased God not to cut him off in his sins. He gave him time to repent; and not only so, but a heart to repent." The father's letter to Wesley continued as he described his son's execution: "His peace increased daily, till on Saturday, the day he was to die, he came out of the condemned-room, clothed in his shroud, and went into the cart. As he went on, the cheerfulness and composure of his countenance were amazing to all the spectators."—J. B. Fowler Jr.[162]

---

[160]*Award Winning Sermons,* Vol. 2
[161]*Award Winning Sermons,* Vol. 2
[162]*Award Winning Sermons,* Vol. 2

SUNDAY: AUGUST TWENTY-NINTH

LECTIONARY MESSAGE

Topic: Wonders—Why?
TEXT: Exod. 3:1–15
Other Readings: Ps. 105:1–6, 23–26, 45; Rom. 12:9–21; Matt. 16:21–28

We live in a culture of disbelief, but one that is nevertheless hungry for signs and wonders. Within the space of one week, the national news carried stories of two "miraculous" appearances of the Virgin Mary. A suburban Chicago homeowner told reporters that he was washing windows when he noticed that one of the sliding glass doors to the patio looked different. Dew had formed between the double panes, and it appeared to be an outline of the Virgin Mary. He called a reporter, told a few friends, and marveled that Mary would visit his humble abode. In no time, "pilgrims" were coming to the door, asking to see the Blessed Virgin, leaving flowers by the pane of glass, and lighting candles. In Clearwater, Florida, a rainbow-colored hue on the windows of an office building attracted hundreds of thousands of visitors, who believed it was an image of the Mother of Christ. In other parts of the world, Christians and skeptics alike are curious about weeping icons and miracle-working relics. The popularity of "trance-channelers," psychics, crystals, and tabloid newspapers also suggest that there is something in every person that is hungry for visions and eager to hear voices or read about others' holy thrills.

There's a reason for our simultaneous fascination with and skepticism about modern accounts of God's wondrous intrusion into human history. Both the longing and the critical attitude may be signs that the Holy Spirit is already at work within us. In addition, there is the sense that these signs and wonders, however exciting, aren't enough. Taken by themselves, they're not good for much. They don't make much difference in our lives.

Today's Old Testament reading supports such a viewpoint. The third chapter of Exodus presents a well-known theophany, and just as important, it offers implicit guidelines for understanding other encounters with the holy, in any time or place.

I. *Visions are not an end in themselves, but connect us to others.* Moses was not tending sheep in the fields of Midian in hopes of finding a burning bush. He was not seeking a sign; it happened at God's initiative. The Lord's words to Moses connected Moses with divine-human history: "I am the God of your father, the God of Abraham, the God of Isaac, and the God of Jacob." Moses knew the stories of his ancestors, and God's statement invited Moses to test his current experience with the faith stories of trusted leaders. In the same way, when we have inexplicable, wondrous experiences, a sign of their authenticity is that they conform to God's nature and work as revealed in Scripture. They connect us to other people, rather than separating us. The Holy Spirit, at work in the Word, the individual, and the community, helps us to discern the truth of our experience.

II. *Authentic spiritual experiences put us to doing the work of God.* If God's self-disclosure demanded nothing of people, Moses might never have left the wilderness of Midian. It is tempting, when we are overwhelmed and awestruck by the presence of God, to want to stay on the Mount of Transfiguration and savor the moment, to cling to this audience with the Almighty. But Moses' vision made him a servant, not a member of some spiritual elite. It must be the same with us. We should also notice that the episode of the burning bush did not give Moses the green light to start a project he'd been itching to begin for ages. He had fled Egypt years before; now God told him to return to deliver the chosen people. It was with reluctance and hesitation that he undertook what was ultimately God's vision, not his own. An indicator that modern religious experiences are of God is that we are led where we did not expect to go. We are used by our Lord to benefit others. The saints of history have been obedient souls, faithful to God's vision for his people even at great personal risk.

III. *Genuine "wonders" inevitably result in the worship and praise of God.* Verse 12 of this passage reads, "This shall be the sign for you, that I have sent you; when you have brought forth the people out of Egypt, you shall serve God on this mountain." Signs and miracles of any age must lead to the greater glory of God: the God to whom we and Israel and all humanity belong, the one who is worthy of our loyalty and adoration. It is good, but not enough, when a religious experience gives us insight, healing, or a "warm glow." A vision that fosters community or inspires us to acts of justice and mercy may be quite noble; but unless it moves us to adoration, we have turned away from the burning bush too quickly and not listened to all God has to say. The God of Moses does indeed speak and act in our time. It is as the result of such encounters in us that others may see the flame of divine mercy, and give glory to God.—Carol M. Noren

Illustrations

SEEING GOD.
Earth's crammed with heaven,
And every common bush afire with God;
But only he who sees takes off his shoes;
The rest sit round it and pluck black-
berries.
—Robert Browning[163]

DISCERNMENT NEEDED.   Early in 1997, a coffee shop in Nashville, Tennessee, gained national attention when one of the cinnamon buns it sells reportedly looked like Mother Teresa. The popular press hailed it as a wonder. The coffee shop owner put the bun on display in a glass case and sold picture postcards of the "miracle bun." Business improved as tourists came to see and pay homage to this marvel. It suggests that our hunger for a sense of God's presence is greater than the hunger for food—and that we lack the discernment to discriminate between the real Bread of Life and cheap junk food.—Carol M. Noren

SERMON SUGGESTIONS

Topic: Dealing with the World in Which We Live
TEXT: 2 Kings 5:12 (NRSV)
(1) *Then:* The story of Naaman (vv. 1–14). (2) *Always:* People are strongly drawn to worthless remedies for their needs, such as . . . (v. 12). Others: Adam and Eve, Moses, David, even Jesus? (Matt. 4:1–11). (3) *Now:*

(a) The problems: "wanting your own way, wanting everything for yourself, wanting to appear important" (1 John 2:16).[164] (b) The remedy: doing the will of God (1 John 2:17). (c) The rewards: living forever.

Topic: Sober Judgment
TEXT: Rom. 12:3–8
(1) Being grateful for God's good gifts to you without looking down on others who are less gifted. (2) Considering our kinship with one another in Jesus Christ. (3) Working faithfully and individually in the one great cause.

Hymn Suggestions

1. "Take up Your Cross," Charles W. Everest (1833); QUEBEC, Henry Baker (1854)
This hymn of consecration and commitment is based on Jesus' summons to deny oneself and take up the cross to follow him (Matt. 16:24). Its singing would logically follow the Gospel reading as a response of dedication to Christ's call.

2. "We Are Standing on Holy Ground," Geron Davis (1979); HOLY GROUND, Geron Davis (1979)
This simple chorus could effectively accompany the Old Testament reading concerning Moses, who found himself on holy ground in the burning bush worship experience.

3. "Trumpet the Name! Praise Be to Our Lord!" vers. Calvin Seerveld (1983); GENEVAN 105, *Genevan Psalter* (1562)
A modern paraphrase of Psalm 105, this hymn is sung to its original tune in the Geneva Psalter. The parts of the nine-stanza version appropriate for the selected Psalter reading would be stanzas 1, 2, 5, 6, and 9.

4. "Lord, Make Us Servants of Your Peace," James Quinn (1979), based on the prayer attributed to Francis of Assisi (c. 1200); DICKINSON COLLEGE, Lee Hastings Bristol Jr. (1960)
The apostle Paul's exhortations to Christian living in the Epistle lesson (Rom. 12:9–12) could have no more meaningful response than the famous prayer attributed to the medieval monk Francis of Assisi. This metrical

---

[163]*Aurora Leigh,* Book VII, 1.820

[164]Translation by Eugene Peterson, *The Message* (Colorado Springs: Navpress, 1993).

version set to a contemporary hymn tune should be sung simply and prayerfully.—Hugh T. McElrath

Worship Aids

CALL TO WORSHIP.   "Oh, give thanks to the Lord! Call upon his name; make known his deeds among the peoples" (Ps. 105:1–2 NKJV).

INVOCATION.   Open us, Lord, to all that we need to see and hear and feel so we may return from worship to affect our world with the Spirit of the living God, through Christ our Lord.—E. Lee Phillips

OFFERTORY SENTENCE.   "He who has a bountiful eye will be blessed, for he gives of his bread to the poor" (Prov. 22:9 NKJV).

OFFERTORY PRAYER.   Lord, God, the same yesterday, today, and forever; make us faithful stewards in plenty or want, ever aware that we are held accountable for whatever we have through him who brings salvation to all who believe.—E. Lee Phillips

PRAYER.   Eternal Father, because we do not make ourselves, because we cannot keep ourselves and we cannot forgive ourselves, we reach out to you. We thank you for our creation, our preservation, and our redemption. We thank you for the challenge of living and for the opportunity to become your children, to grow and be nurtured by you.

We thank you for this church, for its commitment to service and love as your witness in this community. Strengthen us to be able to share the good news of Jesus Christ more effectively with all those in our community. We come this day acknowledging those in our fellowship who have illness, who have experienced accidents, hardship, grief, or pain. We ask you to sustain them.

Open our eyes that we might sense this day your presence. Open our ears that we might hear the sound of your presence. May our worship today give to us a real sense of the power of your eternal presence. Open our mouths that we might proclaim the good news of Christ to all persons, so that they might know of the redeeming grace that we have experienced in Christ. We come praying in the name of Jesus Christ, our Living Lord. Amen.—William Powell Tuck

Sermon: Somebody Must Stop the Cycle
TEXT: Rom. 12:14–21

During a trial in West Memphis, Arkansas, in which three young men were charged with murder, the father of one of the victims suddenly rushed at the men screaming, "I'll chase you all the way to hell." One writer observed, "I understand the father's fierce anger, but there is something almost prophetic about his words. If we allow our hatred for those who have wronged us to go unchecked, it will eventually destroy us. We will follow our bitterness 'all the way to hell.'"[165] Somebody must stop the cycle of hurt repaid by hurt, wrong repaid by wrong, hatred repaid by hatred, and injury repaid by injury. Paul tells us that as citizens of the Kingdom and disciples of Jesus Christ, that is what we are here for. And he tells us how to do it.

I. The first thing Paul tells us is that we're not here to even the score: *"Beloved, never avenge yourselves, but leave room for the wrath of God; for it is written, 'Vengeance is mine, I will repay says the Lord.'"*

The immediate temptation when someone does us wrong is to retaliate, to get revenge. Andrew Greeley states the problem succinctly with this tactic: "Revenge is a process that never ends, as Palestine and Northern Ireland are ample evidence. It only stops when one side says, 'Enough.'"[166] It takes real courage to say, "Enough!" It takes real spirit to say, "Enough!" It takes making one of the most difficult decisions you will ever make: the decision to live with an uneven score.

We must be willing to leave the future to God. We must be willing to leave judgment to God, whose prerogative it is and who is the only one qualified to do it. But the text from Deuteronomy 32:35, which Paul quotes, does not necessarily mean that God will take vengeance on our enemies. It means that *if*

---

[165] J. Ellsworth Kalus, *If Experience Is Such a Good Teacher, Why Do I Keep Repeating the Course?* (Nashville: Dimensions for Living, 1994), 113.
[166] *A Piece of My Mind* (Garden City: Image Books, 1985), 51.

there is any vengeance to be taken, God will do it. We're not here to even the score.

II. The second thing Paul tells us is that we're not in the cursing business; we're in the blessing business. *"Bless those who persecute you; bless and do not curse them."*

Genesis 4:15 tells us that God put a mark of some kind on Cain after he killed his brother, Abel. Usually when people talk about the mark of Cain they understand it as some kind of a curse; here is God taking vengeance and being a cursing God. A careful reading of the text reveals, however, that the mark God placed on Cain was to protect him from being killed by anyone who would attempt to take vengeance into his own hands. The mark God put on Cain was not a curse; it was a blessing.

From the beginning God is a blessing God and not a cursing God. And that is what he expects of us. Discovering the verb tense in what Paul tells us to do is even more jolting: *"Be constantly blessing those who are constantly persecuting you; be blessing and stop cursing."* Many feel that verse 15 of Romans 12 is out of place and belongs with the material that tells us how to live with other Christians. I am not so certain. The verse reads: *"Rejoice with those who rejoice, weep with those who weep."* Perhaps one of the ways to bless and not curse is to be sensitive even to the ups and downs of our enemies. Have you ever complimented an enemy for a valid achievement in some endeavor? Have you ever expressed sympathy to an enemy for some sorrow or loss in his life? If you have, I think you were a channel of blessing for that person. After all, the *only* business we are to be in is the blessing business; we are not in the cursing business.

III. The third thing Paul tells us is that we are to overcome evil with good. Abigail Van Buren has wisely said, "People who fight fire with fire usually end up with ashes." This is another way of saying that you never overcome evil with evil. In the attempt, everybody loses. Paul points out the real danger for all of us when he writes: *"Do not be overcome by evil, but overcome evil with good."*

The real tragedy in attempting to get even, to give back evil for evil, is that we become double victims—victims of the other's evil and victims of our own evil. It's just like the story with which this sermon began: We can follow our bitterness all the way to hell. For our enemies to hurt us once is their fault and bad enough, but to allow them to continue to hurt is often our fault.

A former inmate of a Nazi concentration camp was visiting a friend who had shared the ordeal with him. "Have you forgiven the Nazis?" he asked his friend. "Yes," his friend said. "Well, I haven't. I'm still consumed with hatred for them." "In that case," said his friend gently, "they still have you in prison."[167]

It came as a shock to me when I realized that the only solution God could come up with for the problem of sin is forgiveness—and that the price of that forgiveness was the death of his son. It was equally shocking when I realized that ultimately the only solution for the wrong my enemy has done to me is forgiveness—and that, too, is a very costly matter.

Three days before he died, Senator Hubert Humphrey called Richard Nixon. They had been long-time and frequently bitter opponents. When asked why he had made such a call Humphrey answered, "From this vantage point, with the sun setting in my life, all of the speeches, the political conventions, the crowds and the great fights are behind me now. At a time like this you are forced to deal with your irreducible essence, forced to grapple with that which is really important to you. And what I have concluded about life—when all is said and done, we must forgive each other, and redeem each other, and move on."[168]

If the only evil we overcome is the evil in our own hearts, that is a big victory—and it is a battle we cannot afford to lose. Maybe that is the first overcoming that Paul has in mind. Feeding our enemies when they are hungry and giving them water when they are thirsty may never make them into our friends or overcome their evil intentions toward us; but it will certainly have a great effect on us. Somewhere I picked up this anonymous quote: "Who is stronger: he who says, 'If you do not love me, I will hate you,' or he who says, 'If you hate me, I will still continue to love you?'"

[167]Ernest Kurtz and Katherine Ketcham, *The Spirituality of Imperfection* (New York: Bantam Books, 1994), 213.

[168]Kalus, *If Experience Is Such a Good Teacher,* p. 113.

Somebody must stop the cycle of hate and revenge, and Paul says that we are elected to do it. A modern paraphrase of Paul's words says it plainly: *"Don't insist on getting even; that's not for you to do. 'I'll do the judging,' says God. 'I'll take care of it.' Don't let evil get the best of you; get the best of evil by doing good. "*[69]—Ronald Higdon

Illustrations

RESENTMENT. There is a way to get over it. This is the redirection of life which comes from a sense of being forgiven by God and empowered by him to love even one's enemies. When the love of God takes possession of a life, good will crowds out the sense of injury. One begins praying in love for the person who has injured him. Then one day he realizes—perhaps to his own surprise—that he does not need to pray for his enemy any more, for the enemy has become a friend.—Georgia Harkness[170]

PEACEMAKING. For years two monks lived together in harmony. The monotony of their lives prompted one of them to say, "Let us get out of the rut of our humdrum round of daily tasks and do something different—let us do as the world does." Having lived such a secluded life, the second monk inquired, "What does the outside world do?"

"Well, for one thing, the world quarrels."

Having lived in an atmosphere of Christian love, the second monk had forgotten how to quarrel. So he asked, "How does the world quarrel?" The first monk replied, "See that stone? Put it between us and say, 'The stone is mine.'" His friend, willing to accommodate, moved the stone and said, "The stone is mine."

Pausing for reflection and feeling the compulsion of their years of friendship, the monk who had suggested the quarrel concluded, "Well, brother, *if the stone is thine, keep it.* "[71] And thus the quarrel ended.—Bessie Kennedy[172]

SUNDAY: SEPTEMBER FIFTH

LECTIONARY MESSAGE

Topic: Love Is the Answer
  TEXT: Rom. 13:8–14
  Other Readings: Exod. 12:1–14; Ps. 149; Matt. 18:15–20

The apostle Paul was driven with an insatiable desire to tell the good news of a new life in God through Jesus Christ. He who had resented the "Followers of the Way" had become a follower himself. Now he preached, taught, established local congregations, checked up on their spiritual growth, and instructed them through letters. No church received lengthier practical instructions than the believers in the world city of Rome.

Paul's letters to all the churches were filled with strong admonitions to lead an honorable, God-fearing life in the midst of a corrupt society.

I. *Let love guide you* (vv. 8–10)! Some people have a hard time forgiving and forgetting. Were there Christians in Rome who remembered Paul as the raging Saul, untir-

ingly prosecuting and persecuting the Church? The apostle tried to get through to all of the readers of his Epistle; thus he assured them: "I am telling the truth in Christ, I am not lying, my conscience bearing me witness in the Holy Spirit" (Rom. 9:1). Then, after having given them a detailed lesson on how to be subject to government, Paul offered them the key to a successful life regardless of governments, families, or other relationships: "Owe nothing to anyone except to love one another."

During tax return time, we look forward to the final calculation that will reveal whether we owe the government money or receive money back. The apostle gives the practical advice: "Owe nothing to anyone except to love one another." Now in September we usually don't think of government taxes, but there are many uncounted obligations in our daily lives that often tax us to the limit. Again,

[169]Peterson, *The Message*, p. 329.
[170]*Prayer and the Common Life*

[171]Walter B. Knight, *Knight's Master Book of New Illustrations* (Grand Rapids: Eerdmans, 1956), 466.
[172]*Open Windows* (The Sunday School Board of the Southern Baptist Convention, Winter 1994), page for January 25, 1993.

it is love, especially of our neighbor, that is more effective than our fulfilling the law.

Love will make us respect even the most enticing people and prevent us from committing adultery (not to speak of honoring our own marriage vows)! Murder, stealing, coveting, and breaking any other of the Ten Commandments will be out of the question if we "love our neighbor as ourselves" (v. 9), because in genuine love we will do no wrong to people who live close to us (v. 10).

II. *Love will keep you awake* (vv. 11–13). Do you remember the sleepless nights when you had just fallen in love with somebody? Or the days before your wedding? Each day, each hour, brought you closer to the big event, and with that anticipation, sleep suddenly was not at all important. You lived on air and love, as a German proverb describes the nature of love.

This is the attitude Paul wishes that all of the followers of Christ would have, especially because "the night is far gone and the day is near" (v. 12).

There comes a time when we must make up our minds "to lay aside the works of darkness . . . and live honorably as in the day" (v. 12). Yes, love loves light and hates darkness! The more we love, the more we will long for an all-encompassing and guiding light. People who prefer to live under the cover of darkness often are the ones in pursuit of reveling, drunkenness, sexual promiscuity, licentiousness, quarreling, and jealousy (v. 13).

III. *Live in the light* (v. 14). People who live in the light, on the other hand, know something of the joy of identifying with Jesus ("put on the Lord Jesus Christ," v. 14). Instead of using the obscuring darkness to "gratify their desires," they prefer to live a life out in the open, just as their Lord Jesus did during his earthly years. They don't look down on the predators who hunt in the dark, neither do they envy them. They have been there themselves, but the love of God has brought them into the light of Jesus Christ, who now expects them to "live as children of the Light" (Eph. 5:8). As such they are determined to make love their rule of life, and love thrives best in a transparent light that is not obscured by selfish desires. Love can even conquer hatred toward an enemy and turn him or her into a friend.

If we need a measuring device to discover how much we love God and others, let us look into ourselves to see whether we live in the light or in darkness. If there is more darkness than light, then we have not granted priority seating in our heart to the Prince of Light. However, where there is more light than darkness, there Jesus Christ has eminence, and we reap the benefits of his presence.

There are a measureless number of songs dealing with love. Most of them proclaim, "Love makes the world go round!" But love is not necessarily something to sing about; rather, it is to be lived daily.

If we want to please Jesus Christ, let's remember that he gave us a simple formula for how to achieve this goal: "If you love me, you will keep my commandments" (John 14:15). Let's do it!—Reinhold J. Kerstan

Illustrations

LOVE NOT AN EXCUSE.   It is disastrous to suppose that, in the name of "love," the intensity of our emotions can be used as an excuse to justify the waywardness of our passions. Perhaps, if we were honest, we would have to confess that few of us are capable of loving in the biblical sense. A more fruitful approach to our problem, because it is more humble, would be to accept the fact that we need help.—Maurice Nesbitt[173]

SEEKING AND FINDING.   If we really want to know God, so far as our little minds can know him; if we want to have a right understanding of life and how to live it, it is worth time, courage, and the extra effort to win it. How can we begin to seek to know God and his way and will for us? Let us begin by forming the habit of reading a Gospel through, one each month. Read slowly, with imagination, reproducing its scenes in our hearts, just listening to its music, and soon we shall find that we have a vivid, glad, glowing sense of God as near, real, closer than our own souls.—Joseph Fort Newton[174]

---

[173] *Where No Fear Was*
[174] *Everyday Religion*

SERMON SUGGESTIONS

Topic: Choosing Your God
TEXT: Ps. 121

There are alternatives to God that we might consider for ourselves, just as the psalmist asked the rhetorical question when he in imagination scanned the hills on which altars were raised to false deities. He immediately chose the only viable alternative. For what reasons? (1) God's commitment to us; (2) God's protection of us; (3) God's guidance of us.

Topic: The Anatomy of Love
TEXT: 1 John 4:8–12

(1) The essence of love (v. 8); (2) the revelation of love (v. 9); (3) the cost of love (v. 10); (4) the obligation to love (v. 11); (5) the rewards of love (v. 12).

Hymn Suggestions

1. "Give Praise to the Lord," The Psalter (1912); LAUDATE DOMINUM, C. Hubert H. Parry (c. 1915)

"God requires a new song delivered with enthusiasm to the accompaniment of instruments, for his people shall prevail over kingdoms and nations, bringing glory and praise to God's name." Thus is the burden of Psalm 149 faithfully paraphrased in this excellent metrical version. It could be sung in place of the Psalter reading.

2. "Draw Us in the Spirit's Tether," Percy Dearmer (1931); UNION SEMINARY, Harold Friedell (1957)

Though this twentieth-century hymn is most obviously appropriate for use at the Lord's Supper, its first stanza paraphrases Matthew 18:20, which concludes the Gospel lesson for this day. Just that stanza would be effective as a sung prayer following the New Testament reading.

3. "At the Lamb's High Feast We Sing," seventeenth-century Latin, tr. Robert Campbell (1850); SONNE DER GERECHTIGKEIT, Kirchengesang (1566)

One stanza of this translation makes direct reference to the Passover Feast described in the Old Testament reading. The singing of the entire hymn is appropriate in its celebration of the blood of Christ that affects the Christian's Passover—an every-Sunday-Easter theme.

4. "Hark! A Thrilling Voice Is Sounding!" sixth-century Latin, tr. Edward Caswall (1849); MERTON, William H. Monk (1850)

This hymn full of Advent themes quotes in its first stanza the thought of the apostle Paul in Romans 13:12–13 and therefore would be suitable for use with the Epistle reading appointed for this day.—Hugh T. McElrath

Worship Aids

CALL TO WORSHIP. "Praise the Lord! Sing to the Lord a new song, his praise in the assembly of the faithful" (Ps. 149:1 NRSV).

INVOCATION. Holy God, Creator and Judge, we pause in worship to adore and praise you, to call your name, to seek your face, to ask your forgiveness, to pray and wait. Empower us through this hour of worship to be strong Christians who affect the world for Jesus' sake.—E. Lee Phillips

OFFERTORY SENTENCE. "Those who are taught the Word must share all good things with their teacher" (Gal. 6:6 NRSV).

OFFERTORY PRAYER. O God, we thank you that all of us are in the ministry of teaching and preaching together. It is a common task. Grant that we may be aware of our stewardship in giving, in living, in teaching, and in receiving; and bless our work together, that in love and joy we may truly share.

PRAYER. We bring to thee, O God, our repentances. In the midst of all this that is harmonious, how discordant is much of our life; in the midst of all this that is rhythmic, how much is unrhythmic in our poor existence. We bring much of our poverty to thee because in the great upper places are fountains that shall send their great current of life upon our arid deserts. Wherever the River of thy grace cometh, there everything liveth.

Help us to acknowledge our wrongs; help us this morning courageously to name to our own hearts in the silence of this prayer what we repent of. O for the great forgiveness; O for the great love; O for the power to start again; O for the divine energy that we shall find nowhere else save in our Lord and Saviour, Jesus Christ.—Frank Gunsaulus[175]

Sermon: Who Says You're Not Beautiful?

TEXT: Luke 19:1–10

Have you ever stood before a mirror and wished you had a different face or body? If you haven't, you belong to a very small minority of the human race. Psychologists say that even the most beautiful people in the world often feel ugly or unattractive.

Our preoccupation with attractiveness ought to make us extremely receptive to the plight of poor Zacchaeus in our text today. Aside from those with such obvious problems as blindness or lameness, Zacchaeus is the only person in the entire New Testament noted for having a physical handicap. That is truly exceptional. Zacchaeus must have been very, very short for his size to have drawn attention to him. Israel surely swarmed, as it does now, with short people, people with warts on their noses, people with ears missing, people with deformed bodies, people with no teeth, people in all shapes and conditions. Yet nothing was said about them.

Have you ever stopped to imagine what life must have been like for Zacchaeus? People can be thoughtlessly cruel about handicaps, can't they?

Zacchaeus must have been the butt of many jokes. He was probably always chosen last for games and laughed at by the prettiest girls. Maybe this is why, when he had the opportunity, he took the position as superintendent of taxes for the Roman government occupying his country. Tax collectors were never popular, and in Israel they had the special problem of being thought to be spiritually unclean, because they handled money bearing the Emperor's inscription and therefore were not allowed to observe any of the religious holidays. I can imagine little Zacchaeus saying, "I will show them, I will become the most powerful man in our city." So he made his compact with the Romans, which allowed him to exact extra money for himself, and he rode high and mighty over his fellow citizens. He built himself a great house and gave dinners for important officials who came to Jericho.

It often works that way, doesn't it? It's called the Napoleonic complex. People who are undersized or mistreated or ignored as children vow to become important or noticeable in life, and their determination carries them forward with amazing force.

Thus it was that Zacchaeus was a well-known figure in Jericho when Jesus and his disciples were passing that way, and when Jesus saw a short man sitting on the branch of a sycamore tree and asked who he was, the local rabbi who had come out to escort Jesus and the disciples through town knew him at once and said, "Oh, that's Zacchaeus, our tax collector. He lives in that enormous house we passed back there on the right, the one with all the cypress trees lining the driveway." And Jesus, knowing how it was with Zacchaeus, that he was as bad off as any cripple or deaf person, said, "Come down, Zacchaeus. We are going to your house for dinner."

And that was the day of the miracle in Zacchaeus's life. It was the day he sat at table with the Savior of the world and saw that all his worries about his physical stature and all his ambitions to be important and have people notice him were tawdry and unbecoming concerns in the light of eternity and the Kingdom of God. When Jesus looked him full in the face, something seemed to pass between them that changed Zacchaeus's life. All of the old hurts and indignities faded into nothingness. All the compensatory achievements—the big job, the social prominence, the great house, the financial security—passed into meaninglessness. Only the presence of the Savior mattered.

We do need those old feelings healed so we can put them behind us and get on with the business of living.

That was Zacchaeus's story. His whole life changed as a result of his meeting with Jesus. "I feel so good," he said, "that I want to live differently. I'll begin with my fortune, which I made because I was short and felt inadequate and needed a crutch. Now I can throw away my crutch. I will give half of all I have to the poor, and whoever I have wronged in the course of my triumphal march over my fellow human beings I will repay four times over!" Talk about evidence of a changed life—that's it, isn't it? Zacchaeus didn't need his props any more.

We don't have to be attractive by Holly-

[175]*Prayers*

wood standards to be beautiful. Our noses and eyes don't have to match our faces, our teeth don't have to be straight, our bodies don't have to look great in bathing suits. We only have to be channels of God's love in the world—that's all. And when we are, we're beautiful, just the way Zacchaeus was when he was with Jesus at the table.—John Killinger

Illustrations

A DIFFERENT STANDARD.   When I think back over my life and the people I've known, I realize that some of the most beautiful people are those who might not be judged beautiful by the world's standards. I remember Harry, the crippled man who delivered handbills in our neighborhood when I was a boy. He was always kind and generous to us children as he walked through our yards in his hobbled way. Sometimes he would take me upon his deformed back and give me a ride. I cried when Harry stopped delivering bills and I didn't see him any more. I remember Joe, a man who befriended me during my teen years. Joe was tall and oversized, and he had a bad eye that gave him a slightly menacing appearance. Joe didn't marry until he was in his

forties, because not many women wanted to date Joe. But Joe was one of the kindest, gentlest men I ever met. He encouraged me by buying some of the fledgling drawings I made, though I later realized he sometimes missed a meal because he had given me a dollar. I loved Joe. I still do. He was a beautiful human being.—John Killinger

IN GOOD COMPANY.   You are in good company when you stand there wishing your nose were longer or shorter, or that your ears didn't stick out, or that your chin didn't look like the Spanish Steps in Rome, or that you had Omar Sharif's eyes instead of the ones you were born with. You are not alone when you worry that you are too thin or too fat, or that your hair is too sparse or too coarse, or that you need, as Don Knotts once said he did, a body transplant. It is the millions of persons who feel the same way that have made reducing spas and plastic surgery as common as indoor plumbing. One woman who had made more trips to her surgeon than either he or she would admit was heard to say, "If I have any more face-lifts, the skin from my knees will be halfway up my thighs!" —John Killinger

SUNDAY: SEPTEMBER TWELFTII

LECTIONARY MESSAGE

Topic: With God Nothing Is Impossible
TEXT: Exod. 14:19–31
Other Readings: Ps. 114; Rom. 14:1–12; Matt. 18:21–35
For thousands of years people have been the same when it comes to trusting God: when things go well, there is gratitude and rejoicing; but when we encounter a humanly insurmountable obstacle, our trust in God drains out of us. Look at the people of Israel who had just been freed from Egyptian slavery! For many years it had appeared unlikely that Pharaoh would ever let go of his cheap labor force. As much as Moses and Aaron had pleaded with Pharaoh, the lot of the exiled Jews seemed only to worsen. Pharaoh labeled them lazy (5:8) and ordered, "Make the work harder for the men so that they keep working, and pay no attention to lies" (5:9). The Jews were Pharaoh's

property, thus he never considered their desire for freedom.

When God, in support of Israel's pleading, sent various plagues (blood, frogs, gnats, flies, death of livestock, boils, hail, locusts, and darkness), even then the occasionally badly shaken Pharaoh would not let them leave. It took the death of "all the first-born in the land of Egypt, from the first-born Pharaoh who sat on his throne to the first-born of the captive who was in the dungeon" (12:30) to finally get Pharaoh to give the Israelites permission to leave Egypt.

Then they were on their way. After four hundred and thirty years, they breathed the air of freedom again! "And the Lord was going before them in a pillar of cloud by day to lead them on the way, and in a pillar of fire by night to give them light, that they might travel by day and by night" (13:21). The future looked bright. God was a God to be trusted.

I. *Wandering forward under God's protection* (vv. 19–20). On their wanderings toward the promised land the Israelites had taken it for granted that "the Lord was going before them" just as a good shepherd would do. Now, with the hostile Egyptian army in pursuit of them, "the angel of God, who had been going before the camp of Israel, moved and went behind them," (14:19) as did the pillar of cloud.

Did these freed slaves understand God's move to the rear? Do we? As God's children we want to see our heavenly Father take the lead at all times. When we move toward an unknown destiny, we want God to be there ahead of us, beckoning us to follow him. God knows where the real danger lurks, however; it may be behind us rather than in front.

Yet, in the case of the Israelites, there was just as much danger ahead of them: the Red Sea. Their only escape route was blocked by water. How could six hundred thousand men along with women, children, flocks, and herds get to the other side? Most of the Israelites knew that they had reached a real dead end. Turning to their leader, Moses, they asked in disgust: "Is it because there were no graves in Egypt that you have taken us away to die in the wilderness" (14:11)? Many of them were ready to exchange renewed slavery for freedom that led to a certain death (14:12b). We can feel with them, because we also have come to places in our lives that looked so gloomy that even the utter darkness of our past seemed to contain more light.

Did the Israelites blame Moses for their hopeless fate or did they rebel against God's leading? Often we don't have anybody in particular to blame, so it must be God who has let us down! And we don't realize that God is about to provide a solution to our dilemma.

II. *Walking with God where nobody had walked before* (vv. 21–29). Would you have wanted to walk in Moses' sandals? It must have been a mammoth task to organize the Exodus, but there were no instructions in his leadership manual regarding *this* situation. Yet even though he didn't know *how* God would solve this problem, he told the people not to be afraid, to stand firm and see the deliverance (14:13).

And how did he himself feel? His soul must have been all in knots, beseeching God with constant prayer. "Then the Lord said to Moses, 'Why are you crying out to me? Tell the sons of Israel to go forward'" (14:15).

Can you imagine God getting tired of Moses and of our prayers? All our lives we have thought that prayers will lead us to final victory. And so it is, and so it was. But God already had a strategy for victory. All he needed now was the active cooperation of the people. He had heard the prayers for rescue and he had a plan of salvation. "So, Moses, why are you still praying? I am with you. Lift up your staff and stretch out your hand over the sea and divide it" (14:16).

Had we been there in place of Moses, we would have looked for a hidden Candid Camera. Sure, just stretch out your hand and divide the water! How else would you do it?

But Moses did as the Lord had commanded. He had never heard of this method himself—but he trusted the wisdom of God. And, after a strong east wind, "the sea turned into dry land, so the waters were divided" (14:21). The nation on the move reached the other shore safely, on dried-up ground.

But not so the chariots of the Egyptians. Once they were on the sea bed, the wheels of their chariots got clogged up and made the maneuvering nearly impossible. Upon turning around, they were taken over by the onrushing waters, and they drowned to the last man and horse. Again Moses' outstretched hand had been the improbable instrument, this time to trigger the return of the sea.

Once we realize that God wants us to be his acting agents, we may think that our own tools are totally inferior to the task he wants us to perform. If that should happen, just think of Moses' staff and his hand. It is not the sturdy wood of the staff, not the muscles of your hand; it is God at work in and through you.

III. *Salvation comes from the Lord* (v. 14:31). There is no question who brought about the victory. It was neither Moses nor Aaron. It was neither man, nor woman, nor child, nor animal. All would have fallen prey to the Egyptian pursuers bent on revenge. "Thus the Lord saved Israel that day from the hand of the Egyptians" (14:30). It is no wonder that these hunted refugees now "feared the Lord and they believed in the Lord and in his servant Moses" (14:31).

Does it take a miracle to convince us that

with God nothing is impossible? In spite of this overwhelming event, it didn't take long for the Israelites to start murmuring against God again, and even to rebel openly.

May our faith in God not be built on the desire to see him perform miracles. Rather, may our hearts and minds acknowledge his omnipotent greatness, so that in all situations of life we will not only pray to God but also act upon his will, always trusting that the Lord knows best and that he is about to surprise us if we follow his guidance, day and night.—Reinhold J. Kerstan

Illustrations

PROOF OF THE DIVINE.   We believe in the supernatural not because we can prove that long ago certain extraordinary events took place for which there have been no later parallels, but because we find in the world today events and experiences which irresistibly suggest a mind that plans and a will that acts. Whatever in life calls forth wonder and surprise—the discovery of beauty in nature, the sense of honor in persons, the occurrence of crises in history—all the arresting experiences that have captured the imagination of man and made him feel that he is not the only spirit at work in the universe—all these are just as much a part of the real world as the elements into which science analyzes them, or the uses which industry makes of them. Not to realize this and to make place for it in one's philosophy is to lose sight of the central fact of life. When we are engaged in the work of dissection, we are carried along by our interest in the process we are analyzing. But when the dissection is over, we too often feel that something has dropped out—a perfume, a thrill, a reverence, a loyalty. It is in these, not in any logical argument, that we find our convincing proof of the divine.—William Adams Brown[176]

EVIL AND GOD'S PLAN.   The existence of evil in the world is not part of the eternal Divine order. It is a transient element, and seeing it in the light of the Eternal, faith may say of it what a Father of the Early Church said of the terrible Diocletian persecution, "It is

but a little cloud; it will pass away!"—D. S. Cairns[177]

SERMON SUGGESTIONS

Topic: Religion and Happiness
TEXT: Prov. 3:17
(1) The influence of piety (or religion): (a) upon length of days; (b) upon reputation; (c) upon riches; (d) upon our social relations. (2) The new sources of happiness that piety opens up within us: (a) trust in providence; (b) peace of spirit; (c) the enjoyment of religious experiences, both public and private; (d) self-sacrifice for the good of others; (e) the hope of eternal blessedness.—John A. Broadus

Topic: The Cure for a Divided Church
TEXT: 1 Cor. 13
The church at Corinth was terribly divided. (1) What is the answer to such a situation? (a) Is it eloquent and learned preaching? No (vv. 1–2). (b) Is it self-sacrifice? No (v. 3). (c) Is it dictatorial control? No (vv. 4–6a). (2) Rather, it is love: (a) It lasts forever (v. 8). (b) It is the fundamental truth and character of God that we can come to share (vv. 11–12). (c) It is the greatest and most promising and creative of spiritual qualities (v. 13 and 1 Cor. 12:31).

Hymn Suggestions

1. "We Are the Lord's," Karl J. P. Spitta, tr. C. T. Astley (1843); WE ARE THE LORD'S, Ludwig Lenel (1960)
Echoing the apostle Paul's message to the Romans, this hymn asserts that whether we live or die, we are the Lord's. The four-word theme with which each stanza begins and ends could be highlighted by special reinforcement from a designated group of singers (choir or congregation) as well as with musical instruments (organ and orchestra).
2. "Come, Ye Faithful, Raise the Strain," John of Damascus, tr. John Mason Neale (1859); ST. KEVIN, Arthur S. Sullivan (1872)
This hymn, usually reserved for Easter worship, celebrates (especially in its first stanza)

the delivery of the Israelites at the Red Sea from the Pharaoh's armies, that is, the account in the Old Testament lesson. Making use of this metaphor of the Resurrection of our Lord is not inappropriate for Sunday worship, because in a real sense every Sunday is Resurrection day.

3. "Forgive Our Sins as We Forgive," Rosamund E. Herklots (1966); DETROIT, Supplement to Kentucky Harmony (1820)

This contemporary hymnic expression reflects the teaching that Jesus shared in the parable of the unforgiving lord. Its singing would be an appropriate response to the Gospel lesson for this day.

4. "When Israel Fled from Egypt Land," Ps. 114, vers. Henrietta Ten Harmsel (1985); ANDRE, William B. Bradbury (1853)

This rather close paraphrase of Psalm 114 could be sung in the place of the Psalter reading or in alternation with scripture as follows: vv. 1–2 read, vv. 5–6 read; stanza 1 sung, stanza 3 sung; vv. 3–4 read, vv. 7–8 read; stanza 2 sung, stanza 4 sung.—Hugh T. McElrath

Worship Aids

CALL TO WORSHIP. "Tremble, thou earth, at the presence of the Lord, at the presence of the God of Jacob; which turned the rock into a standing water, the flint into a fountain of waters" (Ps. 114:7–8).

INVOCATION. Almighty God, our heavenly Father, strengthen our faith in what you are able to do. Remind us through your Holy Word of your awesome deeds in the past, and grant us new eyes to see the wonderful things you are doing in our midst. To that end, may this service of worship truly honor and praise your name.

OFFERTORY SENTENCE. "Offer unto God thanksgiving, and pay thy vows unto the most High, and call upon me in the day of trouble: I will deliver thee, and thou shalt glorify me" (Ps. 50:14–15).

OFFERTORY PRAYER. Make our lives your witness, not only by how we live and what we say, but by what we give through our monetary offering.—Henry Fields

PRAYER. Give us, O God, confidence that comes when we put our assurance and trust in the things that are real; grant that we may never be afraid of our sincere desires; give us the courage also to test them by the facts of existence; and then give us that strength of mind and body and spirit to make the leap out into the uncharted areas where the heart has reasons that the mind knows not of.—Theodore Parker Ferris

Sermon: When God Says No

TEXT: 2 Cor. 12:7–10 TEV

I have difficulty identifying with Paul in many of his experiences recorded in the New Testament because he seems to be far more than human in dealing with the challenges that came before him. He is portrayed as a fearless defender of the faith, ready to give his dramatic testimony to kings as well as commoners. His conversion experience is the most outstanding recorded in the New Testament.

He was stoned and left for dead, but he escaped. He was in a storm-tossed sea, but he made it safely to shore. He was bitten by a poisonous reptile, but he survived. His death was plotted, but he found a way to escape. He was imprisoned, but when most people would have been depressed and despairing, he prayed and sang songs, and a miraculous earthquake opened the prison doors for him. He seemed to have had some kind of special relationship with God, where he always got what he asked for. He marched on through experiences that would demoralize most of us, seemingly always riding the crest of the wave. We may assume that it was always that way with Paul.

Somehow Paul let us into his heart in 2 Corinthians 12:7–10 as he said, "I didn't always come out on top. I didn't win every battle, or have my desires granted in every circumstance."

Paul had a problem, which God allowed and refused to remove, although Paul begged him three times to remove it. But God said to Paul, "I will give you my grace, and this problem will not defeat your life." It was most likely just what the *Good News Bible* says—some type of painful physical ailment (v. 7). Paul thought that he had to be rid of this problem to carry on with his work; he couldn't see how this "thorn" fit into God's plan for his life at all. When God does not give us what we feel is the solution, what do we do?

I. *Admitting the problem.* Paul found a tremendous victory for Christian living in facing a problem. That is a tremendous step of courage and faith. He could have gone on smiling bravely, saying that everything was fine, trying to hide it all and press it all down. Instead, he faced it directly and said, "Here's what I'm having to struggle with." He said it to himself, to God, and to his friends and supporters.

When difficulties come to us in life, there's no better path to follow than Paul's. Own up to the difficulty, whether it is a personal problem, marital problem, or a family crisis. We must not go on pretending it's not there but bring it out in the open, talk about it, face it, deal with it, and ask for God's help.

Simon Peter taught us by his denial experience that what we deny about ourselves ends up controlling us. Jesus said to him: "Peter, you're not as brave and strong as you think you are. You can stumble and fall, too."

We may have a surprise in store unless we keep in touch with ourselves and our humanity. I hope we can come to be the kind of people who know that God invites us to own up to our sins and problems and deal with them.

II. *Living with the problem.* Paul's second lesson had to do with living with his "thorn." He came to accept the fact that in this particular case God was not going to take it away. It may have been a nasty kind of physical problem, something repulsive to look at, humiliating, especially to a man who grew up with a background that placed so much importance on an unblemished body. But he owned up to it and accepted the fact that he would have to learn to live with it. God did not ask him to passively throw in the towel, to resign himself to this fate. Instead God said: "I will give you grace to overcome this problem. It will not defeat you!"

If we lose a loved one, become handicapped, or suffer an economic loss, we go through deep and dark despairing waters, and we pray to God that he will answer our prayer the way we desire. Then we hear him saying, "Not this time. It will not be changed. You must adjust your life to live with it. I'll give you the grace to do it."

There is no doubt that there are unacceptable traits in each of us. God knows all about these traits, but he loves us and accepts

us anyway. He says to us, "Can you accept the fact that I've accepted you?" That's the challenge of the gospel. God loves us with all of our weaknesses, all of our sins, all of our frailties. We say to God, "I'll never do that again, I'll never stumble again. I'll never be guilty of that again." But we do, and he goes on loving us, goes on being patient, goes on calling us to new life, new strength, and new hope.

III. *Using the problem creatively.* Paul learned to live with his problem because he found that problems can be a creative power for good. God calls people to the ministry and into other helping professions who have had experiences in their lives that took them through some testing and some deep water. God allows us to go through these times to make us better people, to make us able to help other folks in their time of need.

Paul was mellowed, became understanding, more patient, more loving. There was more of the grace of God in his life because of this trying time. Two young folks get married—beautiful, happy, looking forward to all the good things in life. They get jobs, begin buying their furniture, look for a house, and are filled with dreams. But it isn't just those things that make a happy marriage; genuine marriages are born when couples look beyond those things and find that they need each other.

I want to ask you: Have you ever had times in your life where you had troubles that would not go away? When you prayed to God and asked him to take this thorn away, and he did not answer the prayer the way you wished? This does not mean that God did not hear your prayer, that he does not love you. But it may mean that he had something else for you in that experience. He asks us not to resign ourselves to defeat but to call on his love, power, and grace to face our problems as Paul did, and to find that his "strength is made perfect in our weakness." —Billy J. Harrison[178]

Illustrations

UNDERSTANDING. Paul Tournier never knew his own father because he died when Tournier was a baby. Then, at age six he lost

[178]*Award Winning Sermons*, Vol. 2

his mother. He and his sister were left to face life with no parents. Yet there are few people who have written as he has written, with warm compassion and understanding of the struggles of the inner life. Can it be because he has walked through these struggles himself and knows whereof he speaks?—Billy J. Harrison[179]

SOLIDARITY. Problems bind folks together. I grew up in a family of nine people; and it was not just the times of blessing that bound us to each other, but also the times of testing, the times when we knew we had to lean on each other. So it is in a large family, and thus it is in a new marriage.—Billy J. Harrison[180]

SUNDAY: SEPTEMBER NINETEENTH

LECTIONARY MESSAGE

Topic: Food from Heaven
TEXT: Exod. 16:2–31
Other Readings: Ps. 105:1–6, 27–45; Phil. 1:21–30; Matt. 20:1–1

Have you ever been disappointed by someone whom you have provided with continuous assistance and the assurance that you would look after their needs? It would hurt to see the receiver of all your kindness turn against you in ingratitude, should you for a short time withhold your giving.

Can you imagine the sadness in God's heart upon seeing the Israelites turn against his chosen leaders, Moses and Aaron? Through them he had protected them from the various plagues and had led them through the Red Sea. Yes, for a while there had been singing and rejoicing by Moses, his sister Miriam, and the Israelites (Exod. 15). But then, shortly thereafter, there was the incident with the bitter water, and the grumbling started again. God saw to it that His servant Moses knew how to turn the bitter water into potable sweet water. Three days without water in the wilderness (15:22)* may have been hard on everyone—people and animals. But did they have to complain right away? God had come through before. Where was their faith?

Yet before we point an accusing finger at them, let's try to remember our own ingratitude toward and doubts about God, when the water we had to cross was too deep, or when in the parched desert of our lives we finally reached water, just to discover that we could not drink it, or that it would not take away our thirst.

After a brief "vacation stay" in Elim, a re-

sort rich with springs and shady palm trees (how embarrassing this must have been for the ungrateful Israelites!) (15:27), they were on the move again, entering another desolate desert ("wilderness of Sin"). Here they were to face the greatest test of obedience God had ever put before them.

I. *God provides according to his goodness.* By now we have met the grumbling Israelites over and over again. Each time they encountered hardship they would make their way to Moses' tent and complain bitterly. After the retreat in lovely Elim, the hostile desert Sin seemed worse than their slavery in Egypt, or so they said. They used big words: "If only we had died by the hand of the Lord in the land of Egypt, when we sat by the flesh pots and ate our fill of bread" (16:3)! Have they forgotten their sighs of bitterness and groaning over the hard life in Egypt? There they had been willing to sacrifice everything for freedom; now in freedom they want to give up their liberty to be slaves again?

God overlooks their disrespect and ingratitude and promises them bread from heaven as breakfast provision and fresh quail meat for supper. Not a bad deal for people who thought they would have to die of starvation because their God didn't seem to care!

The food bank is in place. All they have to do is come and get it—everything is free.

II. *God's provision requires obedience.* God is willing to provide graciously. His goodness includes everyone. There is just one little catch, however: they have to harvest their food daily, except on Friday, when they are to gather a double portion in order to avoid labor on the Sabbath, when no work is to be done.

Food as much as they need! A daily all-you-can-eat smorgasbord. What a great idea! But why these six food runs per week? Because God had ordered through Moses, "No one is to keep any of it until morning" (16:19).

Naturally, not all of the Israelites trust this arrangement. Who knows what might happen tomorrow!

So "some of them paid no attention to Moses; they kept part of it until morning, but it was full of maggots and began to smell" (16:20).

Not much has changed in these thousands of years since then. We also read and know of God's promises to sustain us, and we praise him for this—at least on Sundays. But throughout the week we "sober up" and let our business mind dictate our actions. From Monday through Saturday we know of God's promises, but often we act as if our trust were built on insurance policies, money, and clever business arrangements.

Yet another test of obedience waits for the Israelites, however. God has made it clear that he does not want them to harvest on the Sabbath. Some disobey. "Nevertheless, some of the people went out on the seventh day to gather it, but they found none" (16:27)—no breakfast, no supper. What a shock!

God had arranged the food supply in such a way that they would have rest on the seventh day. After all, God must have had an idea how many years they would be meandering through the Sinai desert. But some overanxious and many worried Israelites don't want to leave their food collection to "plain chance," so they don't follow God's instructions.

God, however, wants them to trust him daily, without any reservations. Yet when He discovers their disobedience, he breaks out into lament: "How long will you refuse to keep my commands and my instructions" (16:28)?

Here is "one nation under God," yet with people of various degrees of obedience. Those who follow God's instructions are well supplied even on the days when there is no food in the desert. But those who stock up for several days, to shorten the daily duties of collecting, and those who feel that the Sabbath is a good day to catch up on harvesting chores are met with disaster.

All who have experienced shortness of food, if not outright starvation, know how taxing it can be to have food for the day but to have no idea what you will eat tomorrow, if anything at all. Oh yes, the Bible is full of promises that God will look after his children. But at times these promises seem to be given to others, while we live with the nagging feeling that God has forgotten us. So we start hoarding, when a life-sustaining amount would be sufficient; and we make the Lord's Day another day of harvest attempt, only to discover that the hard labor on that day has not yielded any gain.

When did the disobeying Israelites learn their lesson? After a few weeks, a few months? Or did it take all forty years to convince them that you cannot break God's commands and hope for his blessing? Yes, the Lord will be gracious to us, as he was to the ancient Israelites, and he will supply us with nourishment (physical and spiritual) in spite of our stubbornness. But if we refuse to obey his clear instructions for our lives, we will discover "maggots" in our acquisitions and our achievements will "smell" (16:20); or we will face a barren field (16:27) where there is nothing to harvest.—Reinhold J. Kerstan

Illustrations

BLESSINGS FROM HEAVEN. The pious man of later Old Testament days knows that "God hears him from his holy heaven" (Ps. 20). He thus prays that God will send his goodness and truth from heaven to save him "from the reproach of him that would swallow him up" (Ps. 57). A plastic representation of this divine help which comes right down from heaven to human need and folly is to be found in the narrative of Exodus 16, where God answers the murmuring of the people in the wilderness, and its ridiculous hankering for the fleshpots of Egypt, by causing the bread called "manna" to fall from heaven. It is no accident that this passage is so solemnly taken up and given a new meaning in John 6. Similarly, in Deuteronomy 28 heaven is the rich chamber opened up by the Lord "to give the rain unto thy land in his season, and to bless all the work of thine hand." The fact that the divine benefits are already fixed and ready, as it were, in heaven, and have only to come down to the recipient, is also a distinctive New Testament conception, the meaning being that although the men have to receive the divine benefit, they are already its lawful possessors and have already tasted the heavenly gift (Heb. 6). It is not the end but the beginning of the apostolic proclamation that God has already blessed us with all spiritual blessings (Eph. 1:3)—Karl Barth[181]

GOD'S FAITHFULNESS. From the vision of the holy city, the new Jerusalem, John records having heard "a great voice from the throne saying, 'Behold, the dwelling of God is with men. He will dwell with them, and they shall be his people, and God himself will be with them.'" And then, as though to drive home the force of these immortal words, a further divine utterance is added: "Behold, I make all things new. . . . Write this, for these words are trustworthy and true. . . . It is done! I am the Alpha and the Omega, the beginning and the end" (Rev. 21:3–6). This is the meaning and the grace and the glory of the faithfulness of God.—J. Edward Humphrey[182]

SERMON SUGGESTIONS

Topic: Growing in Wisdom

TEXT: Ps. 90:1–2, 9, 14

(1) The unchanging truth: the eternal God (vv. 1–2). (2) The apparent reality: the anger of God toward us (v. 9). (3) The dawning faith: God's steadfast love (v. 14).

Topic: From Trouble to Triumph

TEXT: 2 Cor. 1:8–10

(1) Sometimes life reaches its outer limits, and the worst seems inevitable. (2) Such experiences work to our benefit if they cause us to trust God more completely.

Hymn Suggestions

1. "Guide Me, O Thou Great Jehovah," William Williams, tr. Peter Williams (1772); CWM RHONDA, John Hughes (1907)

This venerable Welsh hymn derives its imagery from the pilgrimage of the Israelites in the wilderness. The first two stanzas in par-

[181] *Church Dogmatics,* III, p. 3.
[182] *The Form of Godliness*

ticular relate to the Old Testament reading appointed for this day.

2. "Trumpet the Name! Praise Be to Our Lord!" Ps. 105, vers. Calvin Seerveld (1883); GENEVAN 105, The Genevan Psalter (1562)

Stanzas 1 to 2 and 8 to 9 of this metrical paraphrase parallel the verses of Psalm 105 selected for reading. Should there be reluctance to try singing this unfamiliar psalm tune, alternate reading of scripture and paraphrase text would be effective, using two readers.

3. "Wide Open Are Your Hands," Bernard of Clairvaux, tr. C. P. Krauth (1870); LEO-MINSTER, George W. Martin (1862)

Translated from the same Latin original from which the more familiar "O Sacred Head, Now Wounded" came, this hymn climaxes with the apostle Paul's often quoted "For me to live is Christ, and to die is gain" (Phil. 1:21). It naturally could function as a response to the Epistle reading for this day.

4. "For the Fruits of His Creation," Fred Pratt Green (1970); AR HYD Y NOS, trad. Welsh tune, EAST ACKLAM, Francis Jackson (1957)

There is evidence that the author had Matthew 20:1–16 in mind when he penned this excellent hymn on the harvest theme. Stanza 2 in particular makes reference to just compensation for the laborer. Sung to either tune, it is appropriate as a response to the Gospel lesson.—Hugh T. McElrath

Worship Aids

CALL TO WORSHIP. "My people, mark my teaching, listen to the words I am about to speak. I shall tell you a meaningful story; I shall expound the riddle of things past, things that we have heard and know, things our forefathers have recounted to us" (Ps. 78:1–4 REB).

INVOCATION. O God, our loving Father, teach us today what to be thankful for, even if at the present moment our problems, our pain, or our need might lead us to believe that we have no cause for thanksgiving. Let thy Spirit open our eyes to thy unfailing goodness.

OFFERTORY SENTENCE. "Upon the first day of the week let every one of you lay by him in store, as God hath prospered him" (1 Cor. 16:2).

OFFERTORY PRAYER.   Lord, as we give, help us to remember from whom all blessings flow and share those blessings with others because we care.—E. Lee Phillips

PRAYER.   O Most Merciful, whose love to us is mighty, long suffering, and infinitely tender; lead us beyond all idols and imaginations of our minds to contact with Thee, the real and abiding; past all barriers of fear and beyond all paralysis of failure to that furnace of flaming purity where falsehood, sin, and cowardice are all consumed away. It may be that we know not what we ask; yet we dare not ask for less.

Our aspirations are hindered because we do not know ourselves. We have tried to slake our burning thirst at broken cisterns, to comfort the crying of our spirits with baubles and trinkets, to assuage the pain of our deep unrest by drugging an accusing conscience, believing a lie, and veiling the naked flame that burns within. But now we know Thou makest us never to be content with aught save thy self, in earth, or heaven, or hell.

Sometimes we have sought Thee in agony and tears, scanned the clouds and watched the ways of men, considered the stars and studied the moral law, and returned from all our search no surer and no nearer. Yet now we know that the impulse to seek Thee came from Thyself alone, and what we sought for was the image Thou hadst first planted in our hearts.

We may not yet hold Thee fast or feel Thee near, but we know Thou holdest us, and all is well.—W. E. Orchard[183]

Sermon: So, What's in This for Me?

TEXT: Matt. 19:27–20:16

Matthew finds himself discouraged. His little messianic community, conceived in openness and servanthood, begins to fall apart at the seams. As he looks around, Matthew sees his friends scrambling for status. Some of the old timers in the community throw their weight around; they try to cash in on their seniority; they build their subtle and impreg-

[183] *The Temple*

nable hierarchies. Clearly Matthew's friends have been around for a while. They have served as the committee chairs, the moderators, the presidents of the boards. They hold offices in the Denominational Conference, they attend national church synods, and they politic to retain their grip on the power positions. After all, they have paid their dues: the organization owes them something for loyalty and overtime.

Matthew tackles this ticklish issue of what loyal church people really deserve. What rewards can we expect? What satisfaction can we claim? If Christianity is so great, what's in it for me, for you, for us? What is the big payoff? And as we will observe, Peter, as usual, plays the clown.

Jesus describes the realm of heaven as being like a landowner who goes early in the morning to hire laborers for his vineyard. The landowner agrees to pay them a denarius for the day and sends them out to work. At about nine o'clock he hires another batch and promises them a fair deal; and perhaps at noon he hires another batch, and at three another group. And then as the sun begins to set, he finds some yet unemployed laborers hanging around, makes a deal with them, and brings them on board. At the close of the day he calls all the workers from the vineyard and pays them their wages, beginning with payment to the last hired, backward through those hired at sunrise. And he pays the last hired, those who had worked the shortest time, what he promised to pay those who began at daybreak. Now, of course, knowing this, those who had worked all day in the heat of the scorching sun smugly expect to be rewarded handsomely for their extra effort. They stand in that line anticipating not simply their promised denarius, but overtime, double-time, a big fat bonus.

But what happens? What does that landowner do? He pays them all the same. The folk who put in fifteen hours get the same amount as those who put in one hour. Each one gets the landowner's daily wage. And those who started at daybreak—Are they furious! They organize. They send an aggrieved contingent to the landowner. They state their case. It's unfair, a rotten deal, a rank injustice. The landowner listens and answers simply: "I made an arrangement with you. I honored it. Take it and go home. I choose to pay the latecomers the same as I pay you early risers. I can do what I want with what I own. And do you begrudge my generosity to these latecomers? So the last will be first and the first last"—meaning that there would be no distinctions among them.

I. Now what odd notion of justice is Matthew promoting? Is this the first salvo in regulating the market, in experimenting with socialism, in instituting "workfare"? Where lies the key to unlocking this shocking and unfair perspective of life? The key, friend, the key to this passage, lies in the ownership and control of the vineyard. This passage sounds unfair, and it is, unless we reposition ourselves, unless we orient ourselves, our loyalties, and our day-to-day perceptions to the one overriding truth behind this parable: the vineyard belongs to Christ. The loving, suffering, reconciling Christ owns this vineyard and pays the wages.

This parable is not about statistics, cash flows, time clocks, career achievements, or union contracts. Here we deal with life and love in a vineyard owned and ruled by Jesus Christ.

And what does that mean? It means, simply, that we live in a community founded and existing only to exercise Christ's healing, restorative, transforming love amid the human family. This healing community and its restorative mission alone are what counts.

In this community, Christ's vineyard, nothing—not race, not class, not gender, not age, not experience, not high elective office—nothing but the quality and intensity of our service on behalf of others cuts any ice.

The major issue of working in Christ's vineyard, as Matthew sees it, cannot be defined in consumer terms: So what's in this for me? What do I get out of it? Rather, it can be defined in terms of joy: What a rich opportunity! With the needs of my neighbor, the challenges of my city, the crises in the lives of my best friends and worst enemies; with an election saturated with cheap shots, half-truths, and shameless hypocrisy; with disparities in income and wealth on a national and worldwide basis growing by leaps and bounds—what a rich opportunity to throw my life away for Christ's sake, and with Christ share, succor, mend, restore, and heal the despair, the futility of striving for success, the hustling for rewards, the fighting for turf and carving out

of its little niches in human life. You see, enlisting in the effort to bind and reconcile humankind is to be a laborer in Christ's vineyard. And the wage, the bonus, the payoff is working side by side, stride for stride with the crucified and Risen Christ in that healing ministry.

II. But for many of us, that wage—that payoff—is hardly enough. Just like Peter. Remember? Peter puts in his time with Jesus. He takes the brunt of three years in the Galilean countryside. Peter lives with the resistance, the threats, the mockery, the failure of Jesus' mission. And finally he asks, "Hey, Lord, anything in this crusade for us?"

Do you see what's happening? For all of his being near Christ's vineyard, Peter spends energy finagling for perks. He hooks his identity, his security to the bonuses, the salary grids, the power slots, the heavy committees, the proper clubs, the key pulpits. You know Peter; he's got his eye on a vanity plate, the embossed letterhead, the clergy discount.

It's terrible, isn't it, this incessant scramble for privilege and payoff outside Christ's vineyard—in the world Peter and you and I live in most of the time?

III. So, enter Matthew and his shocking parable. He offers an alternative. He describes a different kind of world, dissolving merit systems, pecking orders, hierarchies, golden parachutes. He says that to spend ourselves in turning the human race into the human family for Christ's sake engenders a unique but marvelous reward. To commit our lives—yours and mine and this church's—to Christ's new creation right here in Boston is to be engaged in a work of such nobility and grace we can describe it only as St. Matthew does: "a realm we dare call heaven."

When someone comes late in the day to join us in the vineyard, they receive the same wages we do. And what is that wage? It is the enabling presence of the living Christ by his or her side, sharing, sustaining, offering encouragement and support. The solidarity of Christ with us in a reconciling ministry to a troubled individual, family, neighborhood, city, or world—who can begrudge that wage to anyone? On the contrary, we can only rejoice in a latecomer's arrival! "My gosh, where have you been? What took you so long to get here? We've been waiting for you! Thank heaven you've made it!"

Love's generosity comes whenever we stumble into that vineyard where the only work that counts is serving and saving humanity. And the wage paid is the peace and joy, the strength and power, release and friendship—hear that, friends, *the friendship*—of the Risen Christ: encouraging, sustaining, supporting, standing shoulder to shoulder with us through the heat of the day. Talk about generosity! What a reward: the solidarity, the comraderie, the joy of working for the peace and reconciliation of Jesus Christ in this, Christ's vineyard. Frankly, now; who could ask for more?—James W. Crawford

Illustrations

DISTINCTIONS DISSOLVED.   In Christ's vineyard, in contrast to every other vineyard we know, our degrees and seniority, our years of distinguished service, our titles—vice president, chairperson, dean, doctor, professor, honorable, reverend, whatever—are irrelevant to the overriding question: Are you immersed in and compelled by love? Are you saving, serving, and seeking creative community among others? Is your discipleship exercised from a community founded to heal the wounds caused by the conceit of birthrights, the arrogance of racial identities, the disparities of privilege rooted in gender—indeed, all of our pathetic definitions of success reflected in status, income, residence, and luck? These distinctions dissolve in the vineyard of Christ.—James W. Crawford

LATECOMER'S BLESSINGS.   Those latecomers do not mock those who labored since dawn. On the contrary, they ask: "Where has this been all my life? Why didn't I come sooner? How could I have learned so late of this joyous, exhilarating intimacy and service with the loving, compassionate Christ which makes working in the midday heat feel like coasting in the cool of the dawn? Indeed, show me the needs. Where can I help? Who cries for justice? Where's the leaky dike, the empty trench, the deserted outpost? Where lies the toughest task? Oh Lord, just be with me as I take it on; that's all I ask!"

That is the truth, friends. You know, as well as I that "when you work with someone you love and who loves you, you cannot get enough of it." In the words of St. Catherine, "All the way to heaven is heaven."—James W. Crawford

SUNDAY: SEPTEMBER TWENTY-SIXTH

LECTIONARY MESSAGE

Topic: Imitating Christ
TEXT: Phil. 2:1–13
Other Readings: Exod. 17:1–7; Ps. 78:1–4, 12–16; Matt. 21:23–32

For more than two thousand years the Church of Jesus Christ has been the most unique organization in the world. It is composed of the most diverse "material" with regard to race, economic standing, education, and philosophical background.

The apostle Paul knew of this diversity, and he was concerned that the Church would experience both the joy of existing together and the joy of serving in unity. He was convinced that unity with Christ would make them Christ's imitators, while unity among them would bring about harmony.

A church congregation that had among its members the wealthy business woman Lydia (Acts 16:14), the former fortune-telling slave girl who had been freed from an evil spirit (Acts 16:16ff), and the jailer (a Roman?) who had experienced a dramatic conversion needed to make a special effort to safeguard its unity.

In his letter to the believers in Philippi, Paul listed several resources that would enable them to live in unity (2:1 NIV):

- Encouragement stemming from being united with Christ
- Comfort from his love
- Fellowship with the Spirit
- Tenderness and compassion

Let us look at these resources and discover how they can help us become true imitators of Christ.

I. *Applying Christ's resources.*

a. *Encouragement/consolation.* All Christians belong to the same body, whose head is Jesus Christ. Any damage inflicted by one upon another is self-destructive. Thus, instead of fighting each other, the members of the body of Christ are to encourage and uphold each other.

b. *Comfort of love.* Christ's love "generated" the world and wants to "regenerate" humankind. As followers of Jesus Christ, who have been reconciled with God through his sacrifice, we now live by God's grace—which makes loving others so much easier for us. Our existence as a church is dependent upon love. At the beginning of his Epistle, Paul has given the Philippians the following admonition: "And this is my prayer: that your love may abound more and more in knowledge and depth of insight" (1:9).

c. *Fellowship with the Spirit (NRSV), or sharing in the Spirit.* Fellowship among believers is great, but fellowship with the Spirit is divine and God's gift. Note Romans 8:9b: "And if anyone does not have the Spirit of Christ, he does not belong to Christ." The Holy Spirit binds us to God and enables us to live a life of love, which is the life of God.

d. *Treating others with tenderness and compassion.* Jesus would treat us that way, and he has done so. Standing by the gallows, John Whitefield exclaimed compassionately, "There but for the grace of God go I!" Remembering our salvation, we will develop the mind (that is, the attitude) of the Savior.

When we apply the resources listed in verse 1 to our church life, we will be "like-minded," having the same love, being one in spirit and purpose (2:2). This will not mean doing everything in unison, but rather in harmony. Just as an orchestra is composed of different instruments of various sizes and tone qualities but all players have the same music scores and the same conductor, so the Church of Jesus Christ is to follow his leading/conducting in order to produce harmony and beauty.

II. *Fighting fragmentation.* In spite of noble intentions, any local church can end up in multifragmented ministries that either compete with or fight one another. How can that happen?

a. *Through selfish ambitions* (2:3) (NEB and Phillips: "rivalry"; KJV: "strife"). Each church congregation has workers who want to be involved but on their own terms. Then, when they have to face criticism, they start complaining and fall into self-pity. The body of Christ is not the place for self-advancement and self-interest.

b. *Vain conceit* (v. 3) (NEB and Phillips: "personal vanity"). Today we would call this "a cheap desire to boast" or empty pride.

The Church is no place for prima donnas (in choirs, on deacon boards, in youth leadership) who pout and sulkingly walk away when they don't get enough recognition! William Barclay warns: "Prestige is for many people an even greater temptation than wealth." Vain conceit leads to the desire to be admired, elevated, famous—the opposite of community, which is building love. We need to remember that Jesus expects from his disciples self-denial rather than self-display. Christ's humility glorified his Father and laid the foundation for the early Church.

III. *Being true imitators* (v. 3b): "In humility consider others better than yourselves." Such an attitude will lead you to "look not only to your own interests, but also to the interests of others" (v. 4).

Our Scripture passage (vv. 5–8) gives us a vivid picture of the sheer indescribable humility of Christ, who gave up his divine splendor and "made himself nothing, taking the very nature of a servant, being made in human likeness" (v. 7). What did he try to achieve? Jesus came to do the will of God and to honor him through his humble obedience. This is something to ponder, if we want to be Christ's imitators. Let us also remember Solomon's admonition: "God mocks proud mockers but gives grace to the humble." Even Christ's disciples discussed heatedly who would be the greatest in heaven, while Jesus taught, "Whosoever wants to become great among you must be your servant" (cf. Mark 10:44–45).

When we "consider others better than ourselves," humility will be within reach, and the next steps will be genuine unselfishness and generosity. Even "like-mindedness, some love, and a united spirit and purpose" (v. 2) will become the mark of our church congregations.

He exchanged his throne for a stable and his crown for a cross to give us access to God's throne and to being crowned by him—to him be glory and honor. He who was the personification and perfect image of humility, "God [has] exalted to the highest place and has given him the name, that at the name of Jesus every tongue confess that Jesus Christ is Lord, to the glory of God the Father" (2:9–11).

What a privilege to imitate Him!—Reinhold J. Kerstan

Illustrations

FOLLOWING CHRIST.   He that followeth me walketh not in darkness, saith the Lord [John 8:12]. These are the words of Christ, by which we are taught to imitate his life and manners, if we would be truly enlightened, and be delivered from all blindness of heart. Let therefore our chief endeavor be to meditate upon the life of Jesus Christ.

The doctrine of Christ exceedeth all the doctrines of holy men; and he that hath the Spirit will find therein the hidden manna.

But it falleth out that many, albeit they often hear the gospel of Christ, are yet but little affected, because they have not the Spirit of Christ.—Thomas á Kempis[184]

From "The Chambered Nautilus":

Build thee more stately mansions, O my soul,
as the swift seasons roll!
Leave thy low-vaulted past!
Let each new temple, nobler than the last,
Shut thee from heaven with a dome more vast,
Till thou at length art free,
Leaving thine outgrown shell by life's unresting sea.

—Oliver Wendell Holmes[185]

SERMON SUGGESTIONS

Topic: The Value of Faith

TEXT: Gen. 15:1–6; Rom. 4:1–8; Jer. 2:18–24

(1) A life of good works can be a life of true value. (2) However, such a life is lacking what is even more important if it lacks faith. (3) True faith and good works belong together.

TOPIC: THE TESTING OF FAITH

Text: James 1:2–5, 12

(1) Surprisingly, the testing of our faith in

---

[184] *Of the Imitation of Christ*
[185] "The Chambered Nautilus"

---

various kinds of trials can be an occasion of joy. (2) Specifically, such testing develops perseverance. (3) Any efforts we make in this venture of faith will not go unrewarded (v. 12).

Hymn Suggestions

1. "At the Name of Jesus," Caroline M. Noel (1870); KING'S WESTON, Ralph Vaughan Williams (1925)

This hymn would be an effective response to the Epistle reading (Phil. 2:5–11), on which it is based.

2. "All Hail the Power of Jesus' Name," Edward Perronet (1789); CORONATION, Oliver Holden (1792)

For the "name above every name" to whom "every knee should bow," this great hymn, when sung fervently and sincerely, does just that. The writer could have had the Philippian passage in mind (Phil. 2:9–11), along with other scriptures, when creating this hymn on the coronation of our Lord in the hearts of sinners and saints. The hymn also relates to the authority of Jesus, about which the priests and elders raised doubting questions (Matt. 21:23–32).

3. "Rock of Ages, Cleft for Me," Augustus Toplady (1776); TOPLADY, Thomas Hastings (1830)

This once-popular hymn could well introduce the Old Testament reading, drawing attention to the symbolic meaning of Moses' striking the rock to cause water to flow out for the people to drink.

4. "Let Children Hear the Mighty Deeds," Ps. 78:1–7, vers. Isaac Watts (1719); WEYMOUTH, Theodore P. Ferris (1941)

A children's choir could sing this simple psalm paraphrase based on the first part of Psalm 78 as an introduction to the Psalter reading for the day.—Hugh T. McElrath

Worship Aids

CALL TO WORSHIP.   "Whatever happens, let your conduct be worthy of the gospel of Christ" (Phil. 1:27a REB).

INVOCATION.   We come to you, O Lord, asking you to make us by your grace what you want us to be. To that end, teach us, lead us by your Spirit, and give us comrades along the way to encourage us, pray for us, and set before us a worthy example, and may we do the same for them.

OFFERTORY SENTENCE.   "By love serve one another. For all the law is fulfilled in one word, even in this; thou shalt love thy neighbor as thyself" (Gal. 5:13b–14).

OFFERTORY PRAYER.   Lord, may the law of love woo us into every good work, every kind word, and every gracious thought. Let this and every other offering of our lives be guided by that pure grace.

PRAYER.   Standing in the midst of time's quick-flowing flood, we reach out toward thee, O God, who art the Lord of eternity. Our days are as grass, and our years as a tale that is told; yet our hearts hold dreams that time cannot quench, and cherish in the fading flesh treasures beyond change and decay. Although our life is but a span and our understanding limited on all sides, yet we have felt the intimations of a vaster world than any we have seen with mortal eyes. Even these days so rounded with a little darkness, these frail souls embarked on so great a sea of mystery, shine with the splendor of distant destinations. In the daring of our humblest yearning we set our sails across these tumbling seas of time for a port we shall not reach except through death's darkness and the light of thy guiding love.—Samuel H. Miller[186]

Sermon: C. S. Lewis Was the Most Converted Person I Ever Met—A Biographical Sermon
TEXT: Isa. 55:6–9; Phil. 2:12–13 (REB)

C. S. Lewis's life really was a sermon, if we define a sermon as an invitation to be open to all that God has for us. I hope this morning is that—that when we hear this story we will be receptive to what God can teach us through the life of a great Christian. I'm only going to give you *some* of the high points, and believe me, there are many.

C. S. Lewis died on the same day as President Kennedy's assassination in Dallas; if he had lived a week longer he would have celebrated his sixty-fifth birthday. He was buried four days later in the parish cemetery of his

[186]*Prayers for Daily Use*

"home" church, Holy Trinity, in the Oxford suburb of Headington. *The events of that day are well worth remembering.*

Lewis's former student and biographer George Sayer wrote this account of that day: "We clustered around to see the coffin lowered into the grave. It was the sort of day Jack (as his friends knew him) would have appreciated: cold, sunlit, and still. A lighted church candle was placed on the coffin, and its flame did not flicker. For more than one of us, that clear, bright candle flame seemed to symbolize Jack. He had been the light of our lives, ever steadfast in friendship. Yet, most of all, the candle symbolized his unflagging *pursuit of [light]*."

Later, a few of the other close friends and relatives went over to the Lewis home, "the Kilns," for the reading of the will. One person there was Fred Paxford, Lewis's long-time gardener and friend (and the model for Puddleglum the Marsh-wiggle in *The Silver Chair*). Paxford said this [in his Welsh brogue]: "Mr. Jack, 'e never 'ad no idea of money, 'is mind was always set on 'igher things."

That same day, a local reporter who had been at the funeral asked one of the friends (as only a reporter could!) "to sum up C. S. Lewis in one sentence." How could one possibly do that! The friend thought for a while and said: *"C. S. Lewis was the most converted person I ever met."* What a way to sum up a person!

The next story I have to paraphrase. You may have heard of Bob Jones University in South Carolina. In the fifties the president of the school, Bob Jones Jr., had a chance to meet C. S. Lewis in Oxford. Jones is the man who once called Billy Graham a liberal! Someone asked Jones what he thought of Lewis, and as the story goes a look of great pain and severity came over Bob Jones's face. He thought for a while, then said (weighing every syllable), "That man smokes a pipe, and that man drinks in the pubs . . . but I *do* believe he is a Christian."

The candle on the coffin symbolized his unflagging pursuit of the light of God. His mind was always set on higher things. He was the most converted person any of his friends had ever met. Even an arch fundamentalist like Bob Jones said, "I do believe Lewis is a Christian." And there are other testimonies: Many people have called Lewis "*the* modern hero of the faith." Many have said that "Lewis is the greatest Christian of the twentieth century." And it is my personal opinion that C. S. Lewis has helped lead more people to the cause of Christ and his church than anyone of our time.

Some people have made the mistake of thinking that it was always this way for Lewis. But it wasn't. Many have forgotten that he was a "hard" atheist for about eighteen years or so—and that it was a very difficult pilgrimage for him, first to faith in God, *then* to faith in Christ. Some have also forgotten that although Lewis was "raised in the church," he left that church while he was a teenager. And *everyone* has forgotten that Lewis wasn't a very nice person for much of his early life; in fact, he was an "arrogant prig" (as he called himself). This is illustrated in a tribute he wrote to his boyhood friend Arthur Greeves: "He was the most faithful of friends [but] he was not a clever boy. . . . *I* was a scholar. He had no ideas. *I* bubbled over with them. *I* could give concepts, logic, facts, arguments. . . . He was always very inarticulate. I learned charity from him and failed, for all my efforts, to teach him arrogance in return."

Lewis's attitude toward God in those days is best summed up in a letter he wrote to Greeves: "The trouble about God is that he is like a person who never acknowledges your letters and so, in time, you come to the conclusion either that he does not exist or that you have got his address wrong." He also said that religion was a human invention and Jesus was a mythological being "converted by popular imagination."

His beliefs slowly started to change after he served and was wounded in World War I. At Oxford, Lewis graduated from University College in 1923 with the highest honors, and he was on the faculty of Magdalen College by 1925, as a tutor in the English Department. He met and became friends with a group of men who were both Christians *and* intellectuals. He came to notice what he later called "holiness" in friends such as J.R.R. Tolkien, Nevill Coghill, Hugo Dyson, and Owen Barfield. More and more he turned to the reading of distinctively Christian writers, such as George MacDonald and G. K. Chesterton. He soon came to feel that "Christianity was very sensible apart from its Christianity."

An event that pushed Lewis along toward conversion was a conversation he had with the "most hard-boiled atheist in Oxford." T. D. "Harry" Weldon was a philosopher at Magdalen College. He was Lewis's age and very cynical and pessimistic about religion of any kind.

The two were talking about history after dinner one night, and Lewis was stunned when this "hard-boiled atheist" said: "Rum thing, all that stuff about [a] dying god. . . . It almost looks as if it really had happened once." Lewis almost fell out of his chair. An atheist admitting there was good evidence for the truth of the gospel accounts!

Lewis later called it "the checkmate," and it started to happen one day as he was perched on the top of one of those wonderful English double-decker buses going east from his college to Headington. He felt, as he said, "the deeply quiet experience of decision." "I felt myself, being, there and then, given a free choice. I could open the door or keep it shut. . . . Neither choice was presented as duty, no threat or promise was attached to either." After this experience on the bus, he said he felt like a snowman "at last beginning to melt."

Lewis describes what finally happened to him in *Surprised by Joy,* and these are some of the most famous and inspiring words he ever wrote:

You must picture me alone in that room at Magdalen, night after night, feeling, whenever my mind lifted even for a second from my work, the steady, unrelenting approach of Him whom I so earnestly desired not to meet. That which I greatly feared had at last come upon me. In the Trinity Term of 1929 I gave in, and admitted that God was God, and knelt and prayed: perhaps that night the most dejected and reluctant convert in all England. I did not see then what was the most obvious and shining thing; the Divine humility which will accept a convert even on such terms. . . . The hardness of God is kinder than the softness of men, and His compulsion is our liberation.

This conversation to *theism* took about thirteen or fourteen years, but he did not yet believe in Christ. His conversion to Christianity took another five years. Lewis kept on remembering Chesterton's words in his great book, *The Everlasting Man,* that in claiming to be the son of God, "Jesus Christ was either a lunatic or a dishonest fraud or he was speaking the truth." He started reading the Bible again, particularly the Gospel of Mark and especially the Psalms.

Another big influence on Lewis was his friend and lawyer Owen Barfield, who is still alive today, ninety-five years old. Lewis admitted that Barfield made short work of his chronological snobbery, the assumption that whatever is "out of date" (or old) is of no use and is not valid. This freed Lewis to take seriously the biblical and early Christian writings. This also caused him to reexamine the supernatural world and to consider it seriously. Barfield also convinced Lewis that "the world of the senses" did not go far enough to explain ethics and moral behavior. Only God did.

Several other factors pushed Lewis down the path toward Christianity. His father Albert died in the autumn of 1929. Lewis had never gotten along with his father, and Albert's death affected him greatly. For about a week after the funeral, Lewis had a strong feeling of his father's presence; this caused him to meditate on the possibility of an afterlife and to investigate the Scriptures.

In mid-September of that year, a monumental event happened in Lewis's life. His friends Hugo Dyson and J.R.R. Tolkien had visited for dinner; afterwards the three took a long walk around Addison's Walk, that beautiful and secluded path around the deer park where Lewis lived (during the week) at Magdalen. It was a *very* long walk and talk. Tolkien went home at three o'clock in the morning; Dyson stayed on until about six. A few days later Lewis wrote to a friend, "I have just passed on from believing in God to definitely believing in Christ." During that long walk, Dyson and Tolkien had helped Lewis see that the Christ story in the Gospels was true, and that it had really happened. Furthermore they convinced Lewis that Christianity works; a believer can have peace and freedom from sin *and* receive help in overcoming faults; a Christian can be a new person.

A few days later Lewis was sitting in the sidecar of his brother Warren's motorcycle; they were going to visit the Whipsnade Safari Zoo in London. After the trip, Lewis wrote:

"When we set out I did not believe that Jesus Christ is the Son of God, and when we reached the zoo I did. . . . It was more like when a man, after long sleep, still lying motionless in bed, becomes aware that he is now awake."

After Lewis became a Christian, he then set out to find the total implications of his faith. He discovered "ludicrous and terrible things" about himself, the worst being a great depth of pride. He describes his self-inspection this way in *Surprised by Joy,* and these are some of the most chilling words ever written by a Christian: "For the first time I examined myself with a seriously practical purpose. And there I found what appalled me; a zoo of lusts, a bedlam of ambitions, a nursery of fears, a harem of fondled hatreds. My name was legion." When he looked at his sins one by one, and painfully confessed them, he said that "pride arose and congratulated him" on how well he had done. Pride was something he was to wrestle with personally and write about for the rest of his life.

For many years it was very tough for him. In another letter to a friend, he wrote: "I am appalled to see how much of the change I thought I had undergone lately was only imaginary. The real work still seems to be done." He looked back on his life and remembered and reevaluated his personal relationships. In particular, he tried very hard to forgive his father Albert, with whom he had had an often very shaky and bitter relationship. And he found that even writing was "spiritually dangerous." He said to a friend, "One must reach the point of not caring two straws about his own status before he can wish wholly for God's kingdom, *not his own,* to be established." Lewis learned that his new life as a Christian must start with the "death of ambition and pride." He was later to give his "credo" in *Mere Christianity:* "that part of a person which puts success first must be humiliated if that person is to ever be free."

Lewis came to understand that everything that was of "self" must be renounced in favor of the will of God. He wrote: "It is not your business to succeed, but to do right; when you have done so, the rest lies with God." From then on, that was his attitude as a writer, as a teacher, as a husband, and as a private citizen: *to do right.*

I want to close with three stories that illustrate just how far Lewis traveled after his conversion; one has to do with forgiveness, and two have to do with the sin of pride. When he was a boy, Lewis had many traumatic and terrifying experiences at his early schools. At one school the headmaster had beaten the boys (including Lewis), and later the school closed because the man was declared insane. For more than fifty years Lewis felt anger and resentment toward this man. Once he became a Christian, he tried hard to forgive, to heal the memory and free himself from this almost obsessive resentment. On July 9, 1963, he was able to write a friend this: "Do you know, only a few weeks ago I realized suddenly that I at last had forgiven the cruel schoolmaster who so darkened my childhood. I'd been trying to do it for years. . . . One is safe as long as one keeps on trying."

In that same summer of 1963, just before he died, a friend of his was talking to some of the dons at University College, where Lewis had been an undergraduate. When the friend told some of the professors that he knew Lewis, one of them shook his head and said, "Lewis is too proud." The friend said later that this reaction surprised him as much as if the man had said, "Mother Teresa is too selfish!" He thought, how on earth could he think that of the man who is the most humble person I have ever met? The next time the friend saw Lewis, he told him, "I met the strangest man in the world last night [at the college]. He described you as proud . . . and it was really comical to me." Lewis was very hurt (for a moment) and replied, "Oh, I was trying so hard to get over that! Apparently I haven't come as far as I thought." When the friend then apologized for telling him, Lewis insisted that he had done him an important service.

The third story comes from an unexpected source: a taxi driver. Lewis never learned to drive a car. He either walked, rode buses, taxis, and trains, or was chauffeured by friends and family. He came to rely on Clifford Morris of the Oxford Taxi Company as his good companion and driver for much of his later life.

In a radio talk over the Oxford BBC, Clifford Morris said this about his friend (after Lewis's death): "It always seemed to me a great pity that he did not preach more often, until I learned the reason for his reluctance to do this. He told me one day after he had delivered a sermon and had received the kind words and the congratulations of all and sundry—as always happened when he spoke in public—he began to think what a jolly fine and clever fellow Jack Lewis was, and said he, 'I had to get on my knees pretty quickly to kill the deadly sin of pride!'"

For about twenty years C. S. Lewis had been an atheist and an arrogant intellectual. After his conversion, he dropped his idea of Jesus as a "man-made myth." He totally rejected his former "sophisticated" assurance that "educated and thinking people" could not believe in Christ as Savior. He also learned that overcoming sin is very difficult and sometimes takes a lifetime. But in that long process, he started becoming a little like Christ himself.

I mentioned at the first that C. S. Lewis's life was really a sermon, if we can define a sermon as an invitation to be open to all that God has for us. I believe that his last sentences from *Mere Christianity* are a specific invitation for this morning, and I ask that you hear them now:

Give up yourself, and you will find your real self. Lose your life and you will find it. Submit to the death of your ambitions and favorite wishes every day; submit with every fibre of your being, and you will find eternal life. Keep back nothing. . . . Look for Christ and you will find Him, and with Him everything else thrown in."

—Perry Bramlett

Illustrations

Several illustrations are included in the sermon.—James W. Cox

SUNDAY: OCTOBER THIRD

LECTIONARY MESSAGE

Topic: The Tragedy of the Tenants
TEXT: Matt. 21:33–46
Other Readings: Exod. 20:1–4, 7–9, 12–20;
Ps. 17; Phil. 3:4b–14

Preaching from Matthew 21:33–46 (the same story is also found in Mark 12:1–8, Luke 20:9–15a, and Thomas 65:1–7) places one in a strange world. It is the world of the allegory, something that preachers have long been warned about. This text has a parable at its root, but Matthew, Mark, and Luke have thoroughly allegorized it—and not in a comfortable way at all. What is created (in fact, most elaborately by Matthew) can only be described, from a contemporary perspective, as an anti-Semitic allegory. Its repetition throughout the canonical Gospels suggests that it was a favorite among early Christian communities. How to preach it, though, is a dilemma at best.

I. In the Matthean account, a landlord planted a vineyard and put it in the hands of tenant farmers. He then sent servants to collect the crops for him from the tenants. But the tenant farmers abused the servants, beating one, killing another, all the while refusing to turn over the crops that belonged to the landowners. Finally, the landlord sent his son and heir to the land to collect the crops. From the tenants' point of view, if they killed the heir to the land, they had a chance to take over the land for themselves and the crops would finally all be theirs.

In Matthew's allegory, God is the landlord, the Jews are the tenant farmers, the servants of God are the prophets, and Jesus is the heir whom the tenants killed when he arrived to claim the crops. Matthew actually has Jesus telling the allegory about himself, and the Jewish leaders recognizing clearly that he is talking about them. What are we to do with this story, we who hear it today? Of course we do not want to preach it, or even approach it, as the anti-Jewish story that it is. It would be easy for us to bypass this text, but the lectionary does not want us to do that. So what to do?

II. One answer may be found in knowing that there's another version of the parable in the Gospel of Thomas, that remarkable text

discovered in 1945 with the Nag Hammadi writings. Thomas's Gospel appears to be a very early collection of Jesus' sayings, with striking parallels to the Synoptic Gospels. Thomas contains this parable, but remarkably without the allegorization added. We may well have in Thomas the story that Matthew, along with Mark and Luke, embellished with anti-Jewish theology.

In Thomas the story is bare. A landlord owned a vineyard and rented it to some tenant farmers. When the owner sent servants to collect the crops from the tenants, they beat the servants and sent them away (no servant was killed). Then the landlord sent his son, the heir, believing that the tenants would at least respect him. Because they knew the son to be the heir to the land, Thomas says, they grabbed him and killed him. Thomas concludes, "Let one who has ears to hear, hear." The story ends with the crime committed. There is in fact no explicitly stated moral in the original story.

The story appears originally to have been about the problems of inequity, poverty, and suffering in the relationship between wealthy landowners and tenant farmers or peasants. It is a tragic story, but one that in its original form—the form, we can suggest, in which Jesus originally told it—included no punishment of the tenants for their crimes. Instead, it communicated only a profound concern about their plight, their treatment, and particularly their reaction. The story in this form may be said to reflect Jesus' deep social concerns, his insights into the economic order and what it did to common people. How strange that later writers turned it into a polarizing religious tale.

III. A sermon on this text may in fact discuss these matters. The preacher may properly set aside the allegory as profoundly detrimental to Christian-Jewish relationships—just as, no doubt, it was detrimental to them in the early centuries. He or she may use the resources of the Gospel of Thomas to provide listeners with rudimentary instruction about the story, while at the same time indicating this Gospel's importance in working through this Synoptic text. A preacher may properly ask in the sermon what Jesus might have had in mind in telling the original story, which he either devised himself or picked up elsewhere and made his own.

The sermon that evolves, then, works toward addressing one of the unrelenting problems of human living, troublesome now as it was then: the landlord-tenant relationship, with all of its implications for esteem. The landlord-tenant arrangement caught Jesus' interest and he spoke boldly about it. As he tells the story in the Thomas version, he makes an unmistakable effort to call attention to the plight of the farmers. There is a strong sense that he "understands" them, that he grasps how they see the world, that he is trying to identify with the depth of oppression and dehumanization that would cause them to rebel violently against the absentee landlord and the landlord's family. Would those tenants know the consequences of their behavior? Of course they would. But the commission of the crime in the story only intensifies the depth of the despair that they experience. Can't we, with insight, research, and even restraint, still bring this message to the pulpit? Can't we raise the issues again that plague all of the great, decaying cities of the world, the issues of tenancy and absentee ownership that result in poverty and hopelessness for countless peoples? Can't we call people again to understand and to try, however it may be done, to stand with struggling, poverty-stricken people whose backs are literally against the wall and who see no way out except through "senseless" violence?—Joseph Webb

Illustrations

MATTHEW'S INTERPRETATION. Some scholars object . . . that the sending of the son is an allegorical touch, but this is not necessary. Jesus may use an actual incident to illustrate Israel's rejection of the last and most decisive offer of salvation. Matthew has no other source than Mark 12:1–12. Such additions as vs. 43 are his own interpretation.—Sherman E. Johnson[187]

A LAST WARNING. The tenants, like Joseph's brothers (Gen. 37:18–20), see in his

coming only an opportunity to get their rival out of the way; they falsely assume that the owner will not come and punish them. So they kill him. The story does not mean that the Jewish leaders clearly know Jesus to be the Son of God. But it makes a tremendous claim for Jesus and may imply that the leaders, in opposing him, are suppressing inner awareness that God's power is really working in him. The climactic murder of the only son is a pointed challenge to the leaders to stop before they commit the greatest possible sin. The parable offers a last warning, with little hope that they will accept it.—Floyd V. Filson[188]

SERMON SUGGESTIONS

Topic: Believing the Impossible
TEXT: Jer. 32:15
(1) *Then:* as a prophetic act of faith, Jeremiah bought a field in territory doomed to be conquered by enemies. (2) *Always:* throughout biblical history, the most unpromising conditions have not prevented positive outcomes, such as the Crucifixion. (3) *Now:* (a) It is good if we can deny ourselves today for the expectation of blessing tomorrow. (2) It is better if we can work for God without recognition or earthly reward, assured that others will be blessed and that God will be glorified. (c) It is best when we can simply trust God and leave the shape of the future in his good hands.

Topic: A Pattern for Spiritual Progress
TEXT: 1 Pet. 5:6–11
(1) Humility. (2) Trust. (3) Self-discipline. (4) Perseverance. (5) Patience.

Hymn Suggestions

1. "The Spacious Firmament on High," Joseph Addison (1712); CREATION, Franz Joseph Haydn (1798)
Written as a paraphrase to Psalm 19:1–6, this majestic hymn is ideal for the beginning of worship or for use in connection with the Psalter reading.
2. "My Soul, Recall with Reverent Won-

---

[187] *The Interpreter's Bible,* Vol. 7 (New York: Abingdon-Cokesbury Press, 1951), 511.

[188] *The Gospel According to St. Matthew* (New York: HarperCollins, 1960), 229.

der," Exod. 20:1–1, vers. Dewey Westra (1987); LES COMMANDEMENS, Genevan Psalter (1547)

Among metrical psalm singers of the Calvinism orbit (Presbyterian, Reformed Church, and so on), a few biblical passages other than the psalms were metricized and set to congregational tunes. These included the Ten Commandments, set to its own tune, which can be sung in place of the Old Testament reading from Exodus 20.

3. "When I Survey the Wondrous Cross," Isaac Watts (1707); ROCKINGHAM, adapt. Edward Miller (1790); HAMBURG, Lowell Mason (1824)

Though Watts was inspired to write this masterpiece primarily by Galatians 6:4, his first stanza is clearly based on Philippians 3:7–8. No hymn more appropriate than this could be selected to accompany the reading of the Epistle lesson.

4. "And Can It Be," Charles Wesley (1738); SAGINA, Thomas Campbell (1825)

This Wesleyan hymn, with its fervent personal expression of faith in Christ's power to resurrect the soul that trusts in him, echoes the apostle Paul's thoughts in this day's Epistle reading.—Hugh T. McElrath.

Worship Aids

CALL TO WORSHIP.   "The heavens declare the glory of God; and the firmament showeth his handiwork" (Ps. 19:1).

INVOCATION.   Sometimes, Father, we feel like wanderers and strangers in this world. We wonder if we are just making a journey to we know not where and if we have come from some unknown place which we can never find again. Then, in a rare moment, we catch glimpses of purpose for our lives, or we feel akin to something majestic and eternal, and for that brief moment we understand that we are a part of a family whose heritage is grounded in eternity. This morning, give us the perception and sure knowledge that we are children, one and all. Deliver us from being like sons and daughters who have gone into the far country and forgotten home and father and family. In this sacred hour of worship, recall us to you, that our assurance of belonging may be personal and that we may be given the courage to live bravely in the family unit we love as well as in the larger family of humankind. Thus will we become more like those first followers of Jesus whom he taught to pray [recite the Lord's Prayer]. —Henry Fields

OFFERTORY SENTENCE.   "God so loved the world that he gave his only Son, that everyone who has faith in him may not perish but have eternal life" (John 3:16 REB).

OFFERTORY PRAYER.   Joyfully we bring our offerings this morning, Father. Accept them as love gifts given to the world for the glory of your Kingdom, as lives are saved and situations changed through the power of Christ, in whose name we pray.—Henry Fields

PRAYER.   This morning as we come into this place of worship, we bring with us the gifts we have received for use in your service, Father. Some come bringing the ability to make music. Some come with the gift of administration. Others come with the gift of listening, while still others come with the ability to do charitable acts. There are among us those gifted with the ability to teach, others with the ability to weave words together into a picture of thoughts that bless and challenge us. There are those who come with the gift of intercession, and some who bring simply the gift of their steadfast presence. Some come not realizing what wonderful gifts they possess and how meaningful those gifts are to others. Here in this place enable us to be thankful for the gifts we possess, and lead us to dedicate them to higher use in your service.

Let them be used to comfort the sorrowing among us and in the larger world, where we journey in our pilgrimage week by week. Let them be used to enlighten the minds of those who are struggling with truth. Let them be used to lift the spirits of those who are downhearted. Let them be used to befriend the lonely and carry the burden of those who are overloaded. In moments that we cannot plan, lead us to use our special gifts to help others and open the road that leads to you. Above all, let our use of your special gift to us always be dedicated to telling the wonderful news of Christ's love and salvation so that his Kingdom may come to every person.

Now enable us to worship completely and

wholly as we wait together in your presence for a world of grace, a note of hope, and a song of joy.—Henry Fields

Sermon: How We Can Experience God's Grace

TEXT: Matt. 11:15

Why is it that two people leaving a Sunday morning worship service during which two other people had accepted Christ as Savior and Lord would say to me, "We didn't hear the gospel today. We didn't worship." As they angrily walked out in their punk-rock-styled hair and clothing, I again realized the truth that "it's not given unto any minister nor any church to ring everyone's bell."

Worship, the holy experience of encountering God, is extremely simple and yet extremely complex. It is simple because God's presence is freely offered to us all. But experiencing God requires our thoughts, feelings, and actions to be engaged, and as human beings we tend to make this process complicated.

Jesus promised that "wherever two or three are gathered together in my name, there am I in the midst of them." But it has also been said that wherever two or three Baptists gather, there are four to six different opinions.

God doesn't leave us alone to muddle in uncertainty. Clear directions are given to us so we can experience the worship that heals our aching souls. The Bible describes worship experiences for when we are alone, in small groups, or in a packed church building. Clarity happens as we praise God's trinitarian splendor, confess our human frailty, sing our gratitude, and search the scripture for guidance.

The questions we ask reveal the desires of our soul and set the context for our experience of God. Kenneth Scott Latourette, a church historian who taught at Yale and pioneered studies in church growth principles, uncovered six essential questions asked by the fifty to sixty million people who lived in the Mediterranean world during Christianity's first three hundred years. By successfully answering these questions, Christianity became the prevailing religion of the Roman Empire. Interestingly, these are also the essential questions of our present age. For the Christian movement to continue growing,

churches must effectively answer these questions, because people are experimenting with any possible source to find their answers. Americans join the world's other 5.25 billion people in wanting to know:

Where can I find a guiding force for my society?

How can God give effective guidance in my personal life?

Who can heal my pain?

How can I have immediate contact and union with God?

Where can I find a guiding way through my life passages and accompanying temptations?

Which road to God will assure me of personal immortality?

How do we find answers to these questions? By experiencing God. How do we experience God? Through worship. It seems simple enough, but there is a problem called fallen pride, or *hubris*. This fallen pride is woven into the fabric of our human condition and it wreaks tragedy upon our desire to experience real answers to our spiritual questions.

This fallen pride is acted out in many ways, but in each expression it leads us into worshiping gods rather than God. It blinds and deafens us from having "eyes to see with and ears to hear with." This pride condition causes damnation unless we are willing to be worshiped out of it, to be reconditioned through God's amazing grace.

The hymn "Amazing Grace" is a case study. The author of this hymn, John Newton, was an eighteenth-century former slave-ship captain. He knew about amazing grace from his own life: *Amazing Grace! How sweet the sound, that saved a wretch like me! I once was lost, but now am found, was blind but now I see.* Newton was the prodigal come home. He had found God's answers to the six essential questions of his aching soul. In this first stanza, he describes the joy of God healing his pain.

An answer to the question of how to have immediate contact with God is in the theme of the second stanza: *'Twas grace that taught my heart to fear, and grace my fears relieved. How precious did that grace appear the hour I first believed.*

Knitted into our soul is a desire to be in

union with God, and "our hearts are restless until we find rest in Thee," said another discoverer of God's amazing grace thirteen hundred years before Newton: Augustine of North Africa.

When we understand heartache and what people will do to ease their heartache, we know why millions of Americans from all walks of life are hooked on drugs. They want an immediate experience to take them out of their painful loneliness. In this sense, drugs are being used as a religious experience. But when the chemical high subsides, the spiritual low is despairing. America's drug epidemic is an indictment of our failure as churches to demonstrate the healing joy of worshiping the splendor of God.

The answer to the question about searching for a guiding force through life's passages and temptations resonates from the third stanza of "Amazing Grace": *Thro' many dangers, toils, and snares I have already come. 'Tis grace that bro't me safe thus far and grace will lead me home.*

Our quaking desire for eternal salvation in the stage of a worshiper's life in heaven: *When we've been there ten thousand years, bright shining as the sun, we've no less days to sing God's praise than when we first begun.*

Or as King David penned in Psalm 23:6, "Surely goodness and mercy will follow me all the days of my life and I will dwell in the house of the Lord forever."

Our need to have spiritual guidance in national affairs and personal issues is satisfied when we practice the worship art of leaving the sanctuary under the power of the final stanza: *The Lord has promised good to me; his word my hope secures. He will my shield and portion be as long as life endures.*

This is why "Amazing Grace" is America's favorite hymn. In these 123 words, the ones, twos, and threes of Christian experience are explained. These simple words are one person's testimony being given as an offering for all people. Believers sing the words, knowing them to be true. Seekers sing them hoping that they can become true for them. Church worship services need to follow the hint given by America's response to this hymn. The questions are being asked, and the answers can be had if we are willing to sing the good news of God's grace.

God's grace gave Newton the experience of regeneration, sanctification, and glorification, which are "salvation in its broadest sense."[189] This salvation liberates us to experience God's worshipful presence as the healing source for our spiritual wounds.

In regeneration our sins are forgiven and our fallen pride is submitted to the power of Christ Jesus. This is why Christianity's oldest confession—"Jesus Christ is Lord"—is the most basic. Those who are seeking Christian answers to their soul questions are worshiping to experience regeneration. Consequently, every public worship service needs to be empowered by the vision God has for those who are blind but want to see. Worship at the regeneration level shows that Christian life begins through the redeeming love of God as expressed through the life, death, and Resurrection of Christ Jesus (or justification).

Worship at the sanctification level is engaging God so that we will mature in Christ. Here, Christians' quest for meaning and fulfillment comes by seeking "moral and spiritual perfecting through the presence and power of the Holy Spirit dwelling" in believers.[190] Worshiping Christians are set apart for God's purposes and mobilized for action. Growth in this amazing grace is a lifelong process. Though converts sing, *When the roll is called up yonder, I'll be there,* faith still must be lived on earth, and worship services must include power to stir spiritual growth.

Glorification, the culminating stage, which begins at physical death, unfolds for an eternity of worship in the universe of God's heaven. It is when the things of this earth grow strangely dim and we worship face-to-face with God. Every worship gathering should climax with the promise of Christ's Resurrection becoming our own. Though we are on different timetables, we are all marching to the call of death. For those to whom Christ Jesus is Lord, there is a roll called up yonder and every worshiper will be there to sing.

The two people who years ago angrily left the worship service claiming that they hadn't experienced worship, well, I guess maybe they didn't, or maybe they did and their stirred souls became angry because they too needed to come forward but chose not to.

[189] *The Baptist Faith and Message*
[190] *The Baptist Faith and Message*

But if it was our worship style that turned them off while turning others on, I am glad to know that among the varied styles of Baptist worship there is a sister church that would perfectly frame the old, old story of Christ's redeeming blood in a way in which they could receive their six answers and experience God's amazing grace. The worship story can and must be styled in different ways so that all worshipping personalities can know that there is a way for the worshiping bell to be rung for them.—D. Leslie Hollon

Illustrations

THE KEY.   "This world can be saved from political chaos and collapse by one thing only, and that is worship." So said William Temple, then the Archbishop of Canterbury. Temple acknowledged that this sounds outrageous, but clarified his assertion as he continued: "[Men] are to find their fellowship with one another as their hearts are given to God in response to that divine love which Christ showed to men in His life and in His death."[191]

SEEING THE INVISIBLE.   Raymond Abba relates this story. An English colonel billeted in a French village during the First World War delighted in badgering the old village priest for one reason or another. One Sunday morning, as a mere handful of worshipers were leaving Mass, the colonel said to the priest at the door, "Good morning, Father. Not very many at Mass this morning, Father—not very many!" The priest replied, "No, my son, you're wrong. Thousands and thousands and tens of thousands!"[192] He had in mind the words of the Sanctus: "Therefore with angels and archangels, and with all the company of heaven, we laud and magnify thy glorious Name; evermore praising thee, and saying: Holy, holy, holy, Lord God of hosts, heaven and earth are full of thy glory: Glory be to thee, O Lord most high.

SUNDAY: OCTOBER TENTH

LECTIONARY MESSAGE

Topic: Getting Dressed for Dinner?
  TEXT: Matt. 22:1–14
  Other Readings: Exod. 32:1–14; Ps. 106:1–6, 19–23; Phil. 4:1–9

This parable, like the one that precedes it in Matthew's Gospel, is also an extended allegory and as such it presents enormous problems for the preacher. Like the preceding parable, it is strongly anti-Semitic; this time, however, it is an allegory of Christian salvation. Whether this parable is actually the one told in Luke 14:16–24 is questionable, because their differences are striking. Again, the preacher must be willing to look outside the Synoptic Gospels for help on these problematic texts, and I suggest that the Gospel of Thomas is often a useful guide. It is likely that this is the parable told in Thomas 64:1–12.

  I. In the Synoptic allegory, a king—God—gives a wedding celebration for his son—Jesus—and sends out invitations for the great feast. But those who receive the invitations—the Jews—want nothing to do with the celebration; so they not only reject the invitations, but they also kill those who carried them throughout the city. So the angry king sends out his armies to destroy the murderers and their city—most likely a reference to the Romans (God's armies?) and the destruction of Jerusalem *circa* 70. Again servants are sent out, this time with invitations to anyone who will come to the dinner—and the Christians this time are seen as the respondents. Now *they* sit at the king's table.

  But that is only the first part of the story. The second part has the king coming in to review the guests and finding one who is not, as Matthew puts it, properly attired for dinner. Because the guest cannot give a reason for his improper dress, the king orders him bound hand and foot and thrown into outer darkness, where there is weeping and grinding of teeth.

[191]William Temple, *The Hope of a New World,* quoted in James W. Cox, *Preaching* (San Francisco: HarperCollins, 1993), 36.
[192]Raymond Abba, *Principles of Christian Worship,* quoted in James W. Cox, *Preaching* (San Francisco: HarperCollins, 1993), 36.

What is unusual about this allegory is that the first part is about Christian-Jewish relations, and the second part is about the situation among Christians themselves. Ironically, the first half is much easier to comprehend than the second half. Christian preachers, in my judgment, should stay away from the anti-Jewish theology of the first half of this allegory—except perhaps to explain that that is the gist of what it says. To try to "spiritualize" the Jewish-Christian relationship or draw some lesson from it about rejecting Jesus today does nothing but offer legitimacy to notions and texts (like this one) that have caused tremendous damage to Christian-Jewish understanding over the centuries. It is not surprising that in what is clearly an earlier version of this parable in the Gospel of Thomas no such destruction elements are present. What is also important, however, is that in Thomas's version, the "Christian" section of the parable is also missing, which tells us that it was most likely added by the writer of Matthew.

II. Two things may be suggested about preaching from this Matthean text. First, the Thomas version—and Luke is much closer to the Thomas story than is Matthew—is not about Christians and Jews; it is instead about the wealthy and the poor. A man prepares a dinner and invites his well-to-do friends to share it (their wealth is emphasized in their excuses), but each friend refuses because of something associated with his wealth. So the man sends his servants out again, this time with the instruction, "Go out into the streets and bring back whomever you find to have dinner." The poor people replace the rich at the dinner. This, of course, is one of the abiding themes of Jesus' ministry, as best as we can construct it.

It is always a question how to preach about wealth and poverty most effectively. One useful way to approach the subject is to think about it in terms of an "other"—that other person who is wealthy and that other person who is poor. It is indirect method, but it works; we can all feel both distanced and implicated in the "overhearing." How should the layperson, the normal Christian, define these others? This approach provides a middle ground for thinking (and preaching) between a generic stereotype of each person and the necessity of naming each one. The key word for the sermon preparation is *definition:* How should one define the rich and the poor "other" whom one encounters in a variety of real-life places?

III. There is another important dimension for preaching here, though it is not for the faint-hearted. It is to tackle the ambiguity involved in the "Christian" section of Matthew's allegory. The king sees the improperly dressed guest and decides to throw him or her out. The suggestion would be that all who think they are "at the table" are not. There are weeds among the good plants, to use one of Matthew's parallel metaphors. But nothing is said here about how one gets properly dressed, or what proper dress is. Can we assume that we know? Matthew might suggest that it means to accept Jesus as the Son of God, but that only begs the question further. We live in a time when religious things that once might have been self-evident are no longer that way. We also live in a time when the old theological categories themselves must be rethought. Such work cannot be left to the theologians. It is preachers who are asked to be frontline thinkers in their sermons. Here is a place, and a text, where the most troubling questions about "coming to the table" can be posed. Who may come? And how? The answers are neither obvious nor easy.—Joseph Webb

Illustrations

FRUIT BEARERS.   The message of the parable is stated explicitly: God's Kingdom will be taken from Israel and given to a people that "produces the proper fruits." This represents a typically Matthean extension of the term *give* (literally "deliver") in verse 41, which is more appropriate to the parable. There is more at stake than recognition of the owner and his claim to his harvest; what matters is that the fruits of the harvest be "produced" (3:8, 10; 7:19; 13:26; cf. the discussion of 22:11–13). Matthew has the listeners themselves pronounce the verdict (v. 41).

The new people comprises all nations, as 28:19 shows. Therefore Matthew does not use the word, hallowed by Biblical tradition, that designates Israel as the people of God (for example, 21:21), but one that usually refers to the Gentile nations. The community is therefore not simply the new Israel, but a new people of a special sort. After such a clear statement as verse 43, which rejects *all* who have failed to do God's will, verse 45 is not really appropriate—it implies that Jesus is speaking only of the chief priests and the Pharisees. This verse was borrowed (and altered) from Mark, and was probably taken by Matthew to mean that the leaders of the people "know" that Jesus is rebuking not just Israel in general but them in particular. . . .

Much as Matthew is thinking of the transfer of the Kingdom from Israel to the new people of God, his emphasis on the production of fruits always confronts this new people with the question, Are they really bearing fruit?—Edward Schweizer[193]

AN ELECT REMNANT.   Matthew does not use *call* in the sense of "effective call," as does Paul, but in the sense of initial invitation to become a disciple. Whether one is actually "chosen" ("elected," that is, accepted in the last judgment) depends on manifesting authentic Christian faith in deeds of love and justice. For the first time Matthew explicitly appropriates the term rendered *elect*, referring not to a specific group (Jews, Christians) but to those who will finally be accepted in the last judgment (see also 24:22, 24, 31). The focus of an elect people of God has shifted from the Old Testament understanding of the people of Israel as a whole to that of the righteous "remnant," a shift already made in some streams of Judaism. The dispute between Matthew and the pharisaic leaders of his own time concerned who constituted this elect remnant, the continuing people of God. —*The New Interpreter's Bible*

SERMON SUGGESTIONS

Topic: The Image of God
TEXT: Ps. 8:4–5

"And what is man? . . . Thou hast made him little less than divine . . ." (Moffatt). (1) Both Old and New Testaments say he is a person created in the image of God and crowned with glory and honor, the supreme concern of God, the supremely worthwhile value in the universe. (2) Consider how God

dignified man by weaving into his nature the mysterious gift of freedom. "Thou madest him to have dominion." (3) Now we must move to the highest point of vision—the Incarnation. God has supremely dignified man by clothing himself in the likeness of our nature.—J. Wallace Hamilton[194]

Topic: A Model Conversion
TEXT: Acts 16:25–34

(1) *The Narrative:* A jailer's Christian experience. (2) *The Essential Elements:* (a) a sense of spiritual need; (b) acceptance of the Lord Jesus Christ as the way of salvation and true knowledge of God; (c) baptism as the defining act of public commitment to Christ.

Hymn Suggestions

1. "Rejoice, Ye Pure in Heart," Edward H. Plumptre (1865); VINEYARD HAVEN, Richard W. Dirksen (1974); MARION, Arthur H. Messiter (1883)

This exuberant hymn gathers up the exhortation of the apostle Paul (Phil. 4:4) with quotations from the psalms to offer a joyous opportunity for opening worship.

2. "Where Cross the Crowded Ways of Life," Frank Mason North (1903); GERMANY, Gardiner's Sacred Melodies (1815)

The kingdom parable in today's Gospel reading (Matt. 22:1–14) brings to mind this noble hymn written with the teeming masses of the modern city in mind. As a response to the Gospel lesson, the stanzas of North's hymn could be alternately sung and read.

3. "O Praise Our Lord, for He Is Good," Ps. 106, vers. Marie J. Post (1985); SEDGWICK, Lee Hastings Bristol (1951)

The stanzas of this metrical paraphrase of Psalm 106 that parallel the selected verses for reading are 1, 2, and 4. Antiphonal singing between choir and congregation would make this long psalm more meaningful.

4. "Rejoice, the Lord Is King," Charles Wesley (1746); DARWALL, John Darwall (1770)

Also quite appropriate for beginning worship would be this Wesleyan hymn with its refrain—a direct quotation from Philippians 4:4.—Hugh T. McElrath

---

[193] *The Good News According to Matthew*

[194] *Who Goes There?*

Worship Aids

CALL TO WORSHIP. "Praise ye the Lord. O give thanks unto the Lord; for he is good: for his mercy endureth forever" (Ps. 106:1).

INVOCATION. Gracious Lord, we cannot truly worship you without being changed in the experience. Help us to worship you in spirit and in truth, and so to be changed by your grace more and more into your likeness.

OFFERTORY SENTENCE. "Give unto the Lord the glory due unto his name; bring an offering, and come before him; worship the Lord in the beauty of holiness" (1 Chron. 16:29).

OFFERTORY PRAYER. Before you we bring gifts of tithes and offerings—hard currency. Pray, Father, turn it into bread, housing, words of eternal life, and salvation, that it may be used to bless the world in Jesus name.—Henry Fields

PRAYER. Lord, you have been our resting place through all the years of our life. Before we knew about the big world that we inhabit, we learned about you. From our earliest memory we have known that you are everlasting. Sometimes we get worried about what is happening in life. We think that we have to handle every detail and make things come out as we want them to. Yet we know so little. Our knowledge is small and our vision is limited. We can see only what is right before us. The future for us is undisclosed. In our few years of wandering this earth we struggle with so many issues and think that these moments in our time are all that there is. Yet a thousand ages in your sight are no more than an evening gone—just like a few hours are to us. We face death and are petrified because of the mystery of the unknown and the seeming length of its lasting. Then we hear someone telling us that it is only a movement into something more, something worthwhile, something that is eternal. And he promises that everything will be prepared for us when we make the journey from life as we know it here. So this morning we would ask that you

teach us to make high use of every day, that we might gain a heart of wisdom and be set free from the frustration of fearing the future. Here in these moments, as we wait before you, strengthen us inwardly with the true satisfaction of your unfailing love. Thus we will be enabled to sing joyfully with the rhythms of life, making for gladness in the world all the days we live.

As feeble followers we come, Father, to have our weakness changed to strength, our fear to faith, our hate to love, and to have our sinful souls cleansed in the fountain of your salvation. Pray, let it happen even now as we wait together in your holy presence.—Henry Fields

Sermon: The Story of the Golden Calf
TEXT: Exod. 32

The story of the golden calf concerns us in the twentieth century. We find in that story highly polished surfaces that reflect our own image; it reveals to us things about ourselves as human individuals that we may be the better for knowing.

I. Let us look at the calf first from the point of view of the people who wanted it. They were ordinary people like us; they had had a very difficult time of it; they had been under oppression and tyranny in Egypt, and now they were liberated. They wanted a god. They said to Aaron, whom Moses had left in charge of them, "Make us a god which shall go before us." They wanted something infinitely great to bow down before, and something of supreme excellence to look up to, something to trust, something in which they could place their ultimate hopes and fears and loyalties; something they could live for and die for. It is the deepest desire in human beings.

They wanted a god they could see, for they were not satisfied with abstractions, with invisible, intangible ideas about God. Aaron knew that from the start. They wanted a figure that they could see before them.

The only trouble was that they, so characteristically human, forgot something: they forgot Moses! They forgot Moses who had given his very life to them, who had risked himself, exposed himself to every conceivable danger, and by the sheer power of his genius for leadership had liberated them from their bondage in Egypt.

Not only did they forget about Moses, but they forgot also the fact that through all those long months of trial and danger he had stood between them and the Lord. They forgot that through Moses they had seen God. He showed them something about God that they had never dreamed of before: God was at work in the affairs of men, in justice among men and women, in righteousness in people's dealings with one another. They knew, through Moses, that it was that very God of nature and of man that had saved them from their oppression, and made it possible for them to escape from Egypt. But they forgot that!

We are here because of the principles and the ideals that are incarnate in Christ Jesus: the dignity of individuals, the right of every person to certain things in life. But in these few centuries our people have forgotten God and are asking for a golden calf. Only three centuries from the Pilgrim Fathers to the prodigal sons!

So, these people yielded to the greatest of all temptations: they worshipped something less than God. We see ourselves reflected so clearly that it is impossible to mistake our own image, and I hope that you will have enough objectivity about yourselves to find yourselves in this picture.

So, we set up these little golden images, little half-gods, and bow down before them and worship them because in our humanity we want a god that can go before us.

II. Then, look at the calf from the point of view of the man who made it. He is an interesting person, Aaron; by name, he is Moses' brother. He was a capable man, a good man; Moses saw fit to leave him in charge while he was away. He is the kind of leader who plays down to the people. You can almost hear him say to himself, "Well, if these people want a golden calf and that will make them feel better and give them something they can see to represent the God that they are worshiping, why not let them have it?" In other words, he played down to the people.

We see people like that, don't we, all around, all the time. I see parents like that—parents who play down to their children. Preachers are inclined sometimes to do that. If we are smart, we know the things that stir people's emotions and rouse them in a way that is sometimes very satisfying and pleasing to us to see.

All sorts of people do that in their dealing with other people. And of course, Aaron, when he realized what he had done, did something else that we all do: he blamed it on somebody else. When Moses came back to the camp and confronted Aaron with what had happened, Aaron said, "Why, you know these people. They are set on mischief. I couldn't do anything about it." He blamed it on the people first, and then you almost feel his personal shame; he himself heard the hollow ring of the words as he spoke them. So he tried again. "When I asked them," he said, "to bring me their gold, I cast it into the fire and out came this calf! I didn't have anything to do with it." First he blamed it on the people; then he blamed it on the fire.

We often talk about passing the buck; how often we pass the blame in life. How many times have you perhaps said, or heard somebody else, someone who has made a rather sorry mess of his life, say, "Well, what could you expect of me, with the kind of childhood I had?"

Once people begin to play down to life, they usually go down themselves. If you don't stand up to circumstances, you will succumb to them. So much for Aaron.

III. There is just a moment left for the key figure in this story. Let us look at the calf from the point of view of the man who destroyed it—Moses. When all this took place, Moses was up on the mountain, a place associated with the deity. We do not know what he was doing there, but he came back from there with the Law.

We watch him coming down the side of the mountain with the tablets of the Law in his arms—one of the most dramatic moments in the Old Testament. Joshua was with him, and while they were still far off, Moses could hear the sound of voices in the camp. Joshua, less quick-witted, less discerning, less perceiving than Moses, said, "It is the sound of war in the camp." Moses said, "Not at all." And then when he came down from the side of the hill he could see them. He saw the calf, and his people dancing around it. You can almost feel the disappointment in the leader's heart—the disappointment of a man who had worked with and trusted the people, who had expected great things of them, and who in the end was forsaken by them.

Moses went down into their midst, took the calf, burned it, ground it to powder, cast it into the water, and made the people drink it. Moses did not play down to the people, you see.

So stands this old story of the golden calf. We see ourselves so clearly outlined in it; we see dangers, our temptations, and our possibilities, and as we read it we think of the words of an old hymn, and we say them as a prayer, perhaps in a new spirit:

The dearest idol I have known
What'er that idol be,
Help me to tear it from thy throne,
And worship only thee.
—Theodore P. Ferris[195]

Illustrations

OUR DEEPEST DESIRE. "My soul is athirst for God; my heart and my flesh cry out for the living God," sang the psalmist for every man. There isn't a soul alive who does not in some way want a god, something he can bow down before, something he can look up to, something he can count on, something he can die for.—Theodore P. Ferris[196]

MONEY. I was speaking to a man the other day who has traveled extensively. When he arrived in New York, the customs officer, observing his Bible in his bag, said to him, "Say, brother, you'll have no time to read this in the States. We are all too busy making dollars. Guess the almighty dollar is our god."— Ronald K. Ross[197]

SUNDAY: OCTOBER SEVENTEENTH

LECTIONARY MESSAGE

Topic: The Question Left Unanswered
TEXT: Matt. 22:15–22
Other Readings: Exod. 33:12–23; Ps. 99; 1 Thess. 1:1–10

At the heart of this text is one of those remarkable lines, well-known by every Christian. It is repeated in virtually the same form in every Synoptic Gospel, in the Gospel of Thomas, and even in other fragments of biblical text that we have. It is the aphorism, "Pay to the emperor what belongs to the emperor, and to God what belongs to God." To preach this message, we must find a way to set it into the various contexts within which it falls, and then we will be pressed to see behind it and around it.

I. In the Synoptic versions of this statement, a story is constructed so that the statement is placed within a particular context. The Pharisees and the Herodians set out to mock Jesus, hoping to trip him up in some kind of theological double-talk. "Teacher," they say, "we know that you are honest and impartial and that you pay no attention to appearances. So, should we pay the poll tax to the Roman emperor or not?" Jesus, we are

told, reacts angrily, asking them for a coin used for the tax. They produce one and he asks about the picture on it. It is Caesar's, they say. He then directs them to pay to Caesar what belongs to him and to God what belongs to God. They go away, Matthew's story says, dumbfounded. The Gospel of Thomas— the "sayings" Gospel—on the other hand, does not have all of that story setup, but only the simple words: "They showed Jesus a gold coin and said to him, 'The Roman emperor's people demand taxes from us.' He replied, 'Give to the emperor what belongs to the emperor and give God what belongs to God.'" Thomas adds, strikingly, "And give me what is mine." Thomas's account has no trick, no trap; it has only what appears to be an honest question posed by someone who wanted to know what to do about the money with Caesar's picture on it.

In neither case does Jesus respond directly to what he is asked. If it was a trick, an effort at entrapment by the Judean leaders, Jesus refused to fall for it; his retort was bound to be puzzling to them, if not unnerving. In the narrative, the crowds around him certainly loved to see the underdog get the

[195] *Selected Sermons,* Vol. 1

[196] *Selected Sermons,* Vol. 1
[197] *Treasury of the Christian World*

best of the religious high hats. If the question was an honest one, posed by a potential follower, then Jesus may be said to have reflected his own struggle with the question. He does not give a direct answer, perhaps because he does not have one—and that is not a reflection on divinity or ultimate knowledge or anything like that. The question may simply be too complex and thorny to have some easy answer.

II. This is in fact where we find ourselves as we confront this particular text from the pulpit. We can handle the matter of the context as either Matthew or Thomas does, or we can acknowledge both, making clear that the story may have two very different perspectives underlying it. No matter: what Jesus said is still there, still a haunting statement. But it is not the statement itself that we should preach; to do that is to miss the point. The statement contains within it the problem— the problem that Jesus raised but to which he gave no answer. Give to government what is government's, and to God what is God's. *But how do we decide what belongs to whom?* How do we know what belongs to government? Do we just look for the picture on whatever it is? On some things, yes; but that approach is deceptive, too. We can think in terms of democracy, even, rather than dictatorship, as in the symbol of Caesar. What Jesus posed is a profound dilemma—one might call it the central riddle of religious faith itself. Whether Jesus spoke to confuse, as Matthew suggests, or to call attention to a haunting enigma, as Thomas suggests, does not matter. Jesus framed the ultimate ethical question, but remarkably he left it to us to work out the answer. Here, in fact, is not where our preaching ends, but where it begins: with Jesus' questions.

III. The sermon can work at three things. First, it can try to clarify and legitimize the nature of the two worlds in which we all live, the two worlds exemplified by Jesus' statement. In virtually every Christian theological tradition there are ample guidelines, as it were, for setting these two worlds into historical perspective. Second, the sermon can explore the usually overlooked fact that most of our pressing ethical problems are found not in one world or the other but straddling both worlds. This is what, in the final analysis, makes virtually every ethical choice such an agonizing one for the thinking Christian. Honest Christians can disagree over virtually every ethical quandary, whether abortion, euthanasia, or responsibility for education. Such questions require our accountability both to God and to each other in community, exemplified, at least in part, by representative government. Ultimately, it is not an either/or question, but a both/and one.

Finally, the sermon would do well to raise the larger issues, even of peace and justice in a torn-apart world. Individuals acting before God must be part of the healing, but one is foolish not to realize that governments, too, must be a part of bringing peace and justice on earth. The sermon should call people to think—and to think deeply and courageously—about these things. There is a reason that Jesus did not give a glib answer to the question he was asked.—Joseph Webb

Illustrations

TENSION. The tension between the call to the desert and the call to the marketplace arises not from the greater presence of God in one or the other, but from our varying psychological needs to apprehend him in different ways.—Sheila Cassidy[198]

SAINT OR POLITICIAN? This is what distinguished Gandhi from other politicians. The argument—Was Gandhi a saint or a politician?—is endless yet barren. Polak quotes Gandhi as having said in South Africa, "Men say I am a saint losing myself in politics. The fact is that I am a politician trying my hardest to be a saint." The important fact is that in politics Gandhi always cleaved to religious and moral considerations, and as a saint he never thought his place was in a cave or cloister but rather in the hurly-burly of the popular struggle for rights and right. Gandhi's religion cannot be divorced from his politics. His religion made him political. His politics were religious.—Louis Fischer[199]

[198]*Prayers for Peace*
[199]*The Life of Mahatma Gandhi*

SERMON SUGGESTIONS

Topic: When God Speaks
TEXT: 1 Sam. 3:1–10 (11–20)
(1) We may not at first recognize his voice.
(2) We may receive an unwelcome message.
(3) We may be charged with a crucial responsibility.

Topic: The Scope of Christian Unity
TEXT: John 17:20–26
(1) It is modeled in the unity of the Father and the Son. (2) It is a gift to the believing church. (3) It reaches out to the unbelieving world.

Hymn Suggestions

1. "Holy, Holy, Holy," Reginald Heber (1827); NICAEA, John Bacchus Dykes (1861)
This hymn, ideal for the beginning of morning worship, makes specific reference to a verse from the Old Testament lesson (Exod. 33:20) in its third stanza: mortal worshipers are not allowed to see the glory of a holy God.
2. "The Lord God Reigns in Majesty," Ps. 99, vers. from Psalter; ELLACOMBE, Gesangbuch, Wittenberg (1784, 1912)
This free paraphrase of Psalm 99 can be sung effectively in alternation with the reading of the psalm as follows: verses 1–3, read; verses 4–6, read; stanza 1, sung; stanza 2, sung; verses 7–9, read; stanza 3, sung.
3. "Baited, the Question Rose," Carl P. Daw Jr. (1996); MERCER STREET, Malcolm Williamson (1975)
This very recently written hymn[200] is the only one known to this writer that sets forth the story of Jesus' encounter with the Pharisees concerning the proper payment of taxes. In its third stanza it applies the Gospel lesson prayerfully to the devotion and behavior of the singing worshiper.
4. "We, Thy People, Praise Thee," Kate S. Page (1932); ST. ANTHONY'S CHORALE, Franz J. Haydn (c. 1780)
A vibrant expression of general praise, this hymn appropriately reflects the general spirit of the apostle Paul in his appreciation for

[200]Carol P. Daw Jr., *New Psalms and Hymns and Spiritual Songs* (Carol Stream, IL: Hope, 1996).

the joyful spirit and faithful service of the Thessalonian church (1 Thess. 1:1–10).—Hugh T. McElrath

Worship Aids

CALL TO WORSHIP. "Exalt ye the Lord our God, and worship at his footstool; for he is holy" (Ps. 99:5).

INVOCATION. God of mercy, in this hour, in this sacred place, have mercy on us. God of light, shine into our hearts with searching radiance. God of power, be our refuge and our strength, that we may ably manage the hours of life within your will and purpose for us. God of love, let love flow through us, enabling us to meet others in the same spirit of love as does the Lord Christ, God of life, who lives within us, making us aware of the eternal dimensions of life.—Henry Fields

OFFERTORY SENTENCE. "Be ye steadfast, unmovable, always abounding in the work of the Lord, for as much as ye know that your labor is not in vain in the Lord" (1 Cor. 15:58).

OFFERTORY PRAYER. Father, generate in us a giving spirit and attitude so that we can willingly do our part to meet the many needs of those we meet on this highway of life.—Henry Fields

PRAYER. Father, in Christ we come into your presence this morning, seeking to lay all that we are and have into your hands, that our bodies and souls may become fair temples in which your Holy Spirit may dwell. This morning, breathe into us a desire for our wills to become your will, that we may look upon this world and see it as you see it. Fill us with a Christlikeness, that through our feeble hearts may beat the pulse of your eternal love. This morning, let our eternal souls possess something of your eternal joy.

We do not ask that you come to us this morning as an external possession for us to hold, though such would be a wonderful gift. We do not ask that you come in condescension from above, though such an arrival would definitely grasp our attention. We do not desire that you come with glory and power from without, for such coming would not inwardly effect lasting change in our hearts. We do not ask that you come this morning, or any morning, as a set of beliefs to be comprehended, for such a coming would not touch the chords calling for our repentance and renewal, which are so sorely needed; ours would be head knowledge with no heart involvement. Nor do we ask that you come as a wave of emotion to be felt and forgotten. We long for you to come as an indwelling Spirit within our souls, transforming us into your divine nature and will, creating within us your joyful and loving spirit.

Enable us to know beyond a doubt that in you we live and move and have our being. Then may we so live before others in daily practice and devotion that life-changing examples of peace and joy and patience, and fortitude and humility and love, may be available to you for your work in building your Kingdom among us.—Henry Fields

Sermon: Worship—A Way of Discovering True Happiness

TEXT: Gen. 4:2–16; 2 Cor. 3:4, 18

Worship isn't a Christian's escape route from life's challenges. It is the opportunity to be empowered by God and to greet those challenges with a ready attitude (Matt. 5:1–11). Through the holy experience of encountering God we are shown the strategies by which to be successful.

Worship is the key to success if we use biblical standards to shape our definition of success. Success is being who God made us to be and doing what God called us to do. Faith is the strategy. Hope is the vision. Love is the power (1 Cor. 13). The heart's comprehension of biblical success comes by worship.

I. *Knowing God.* In worship—whether in private, with a small group, or with the full church—we still our hearts to know God. Knowing in the biblical way is a personal relationship. It is knowing God's character as our Creator, Redeemer, and Comforter. It is knowing God's attributes: all-knowing, all-powerful, and all-present. It is knowing God's desire to give us treasures: love, joy, peace, patience, kindness, goodness, faithfulness, gentleness, and self-control.

Successful knowing flows from the worship rhythm of waiting and acting: waiting on God's vision to show the way, and acting on the vision received from our waiting. To act

when we should wait forfeits the promise; to wait when we should act forfeits success (Prov. 29:18).

The worship rhythm is found by praise, confession, gratitude, and submission. This rhythm can be as obvious to worshipers as the seasons of the year are to farmers. In each season farmers know what to do, and in each worship dimension worshipers also know the direction in which they are to pursue knowing. *Wanting* to know is essential.

One morning after the close of an annual meeting of the Missouri Baptist Convention, I was standing in a hotel checkout line with Calvin Miller. The day's sun had not yet risen and I was sharing my gratitude for his stirring sermon given the night before. Then I asked Dr. Miller what he most hoped for from his recently announced move, in which he would be leaving behind a successful long-term pastorate to become a seminary professor. His answer? "To know God better!"

Although a nationally respected author, teacher, and pastor, he realized that there is always more to know from God. He knew that his key to success was in direct proportion to his knowledge of God.

Dietrich Bonhoeffer, a powerful World War II Christian martyr, wrote in *Creation and Fall* that Adam's and Eve's first sin was not eating the forbidden fruit. Instead, it was talking *about* God rather than *to* God. There in creation's most beautiful sanctuary—the Garden of Eden—the father and mother of all humanity made the fundamental mistake of not seeking God's counsel.

Thinking that they knew all there was to know from God, Adam and Eve failed miserably when confronted with the temptation to find success through forbidden knowledge. Their fallen pride (*hubris*) shut them off from worshiping God at the very moment when worship was what they needed most. What a price they paid to discover that the key to success is the waiting and acting rhythm of worship.

When they needed to be silent before God, they spoke. When they needed to wait upon God, they acted. When they needed to trust the truth of God, they let themselves be misled by fallen pride.

Sound familiar? It does for all of us who are "like sheep gone astray, turning each unto his or her own way" (Isa. 53:6). But the most amazing thing happened to Adam and Eve. What God did to them after their sin was even more incredible than making the stars, the oceans, the land, and the animals. The Lord God, Creator of all the universe, forgave the sinners. Adam and Eve were then able to walk into the future—east of Eden— because they were forgiven.

Forgiveness brings hope, and hope is a worship cornerstone. Because of God, Adam and Eve felt confident, and they gave birth to Cain and Abel. As parents, they taught their sons the importance of worship. Abel learned from his parents' mistake and worshiped God without arrogance. But Cain, filled with fallen pride, worshiped himself, causing his work to become his god. Success for Cain was what he could produce by the sweat of his brow. Master of his own fate, he would tease God by his pretentious acts of worship.

II. *God-given understanding.* Success for Abel came from knowing God and knowing that all of life was a God-given gift. By knowing God, Abel could know himself, and from this God-given self-knowledge, Abel's spirit was enabled to worship. He understood that without God there isn't spiritual life, and that without spiritual life there isn't success, and that absent success there isn't happiness, and minus happiness it's hard to live.

Consequently, Cain killed Abel. Without true worship, life was agony for Cain, and except for anger he had no reason to live. Like his parents before him, filled with conceit, he blamed others for his failed spiritual life. Cain had to accept responsibility for his own failure, and from this confession he was free to live again.

The story of Genesis 1–4 is the story of all people, even those who have never heard the names Adam, Eve, Cain, and Abel. Deep within the recesses of each human soul is the spirit of our being, made in God's likeness, and this presence of God prompts us to worship (Rom. 1:18–32).

The stakes are high, eternally high. If we worship ourselves or our work or our idols, the chain effect of hell-on-earth is set loose: no true worship to no spiritual life to no real success to no "shalom" happiness to no reason to live.

Only by the holy experiences of knowing God—true worship—are we set free to live (Luke 8:9–14).

III. *Worship's bigness.* What happens in worship is bigger than any one of us. The size of the happening fits God. God's presence breaks through for worshipers when we don't play games. If we are merely posturing our bodies in traditional worship position while our inner thoughts worship human-made gods, we are kept from reaching our God-given potential.

Worship requires change, and change usually makes us feel uncomfortable. When presented with God's bigness and the accompanying growth opportunities, we are tempted to shrivel God to our size and relieve ourselves from growth responsibility. Through a combination of bold and subtle efforts, the resistance to let God be God comes through our attempts to limit him to our own set of experiences, our own way of reasoning and feeling, our own realm of ambitions. It approximates our wanting to make God over in our own image—to make God into a god or idol we can control.

Christians stand in the earthly place of God's Kingdom while knowing that only in heaven can perfect bliss be found. As one Presbyterian friend who has been a minister for forty-five years says, "Walk with your head in heaven and your feet on earth."

We are to live in the tension between the "already" and the "not yet." Through worshiping God we learn how not to get enslaved by mortgage payments, food consumption, sexuality, book learning, spectator sports, or materialism. We are to be converted and discipled by following what God promises (Heb. 12:28–29). By accepting this eternal truth we are set free to experience God's bigness in our lives.

As Paul said, "We all, with unveiled faces, beholding the glory of the Lord, are being changed into his likeness from one degree of glory to another, for this comes from the Lord who is the Spirit" (2 Cor. 3:18). The Christ in us shines through in proportion to our allowing his likeness to shape our character (Matt. 5:14–16, 48; John 13:34–35).

Our character is the consummation of our decisions and experiences. Because what we do with our heads, hands, and hearts shapes us and reveals us, we are not to conform to idols of this world but to be transformed by Christ's renewal of our minds (Rom. 12:2). As people redeemed in Christ, we stand in a

Kingdom that is both present and future, earthly and heavenly. We are as Jesus was, between baptism and crucifixion-resurrection. Living at the in-between puts us on life's cutting edge and keeps us from being dulled by the forms of the world. Paul warned that "the god of this world blinds unbelieving minds and keeps them from seeing the light of the gospel of the glory of Christ, who is the likeness of God" (2 Cor. 3:4).

IV. *Discover your treasure.* Coincidence isn't the reason that the first four of the Ten Commandments focus on worship. The principle of first things first is true of God's expressed priorities for our happiness. God knows that who or what we worship determines the content of our character. Our worship focus is determined by what we think will bring us happiness. As Jesus said, "Where your treasure is, there is your heart also" (Matt. 6:21).

The heart, biblically understood, deposits and directs our desires. Therefore, the key to successfully worshiping the one true God comes by our treasuring God. This means that we trust God to be the source of real happiness—the *shalom* kind of happiness. Where our treasure is in the true worship, God's presence and our heart's delight come together. The treasury of God is opened in our very midst.—D. Leslie Hollon

Illustrations

THE IMAGE OF CHRIST. We all, reflecting as a mirror the character of Christ, are transformed into the same Image from character to character—from a poor character to a better one, from a better one to one a little better still, from that to one still more complete, until by slow degrees the Perfect Image is attained. Here the solution of the problem of sanctification is compressed into a sentence: Reflect the character of Christ and you will become like Christ.—Henry Drummond[201]

SURVIVAL THROUGH WORSHIP. What matters . . . is not whether God can be God without our worship. What is crucial is whether humans can survive as humans without worshiping. To withhold acknowledgment, to avoid celebration, to stifle gratitude, may prove as unnatural as holding one's breath. Martin Luther took the story of the ten lepers (Luke 17:11–19) as an example of "true worship." The one leper who was grateful praised God. The event for which he was grateful became an occasion to honor God.—John E. Burkhart[202]

SUNDAY: OCTOBER TWENTY-FOURTH

LECTIONARY MESSAGE

Topic: The Unrelenting Universal
TEXT: Matt. 22:34–46
Other Readings: Deut. 34:1–12; Ps. 90:1–6, 13–17; 1 Thess. 2:1–8

The lectionary sometimes asks us to do the impossible, as it may do with this Matthean reading. There are two short texts here, divided between verses 40 and 41. One is the "greatest commandment" text, and the other is a strange bit of sophistry that has Jesus asking the Pharisees to do some logical hairsplitting. It is a long shot as to whether the latter piece even came from Jesus, and the preacher would be well-advised not to get too deeply involved with it. The commandment text, however, deserves the best effort that we can give it. Three suggestions may be made about preaching this text, not as a single sermon but as multiple sermons over time.

I. The commandment mentioned here may be considered the greatest because it is one of the few religious "universals." Virtually every religion contains such a statement at or near its core: love and honor God, honor the Supreme Being, however that being is conceived, and then love one another; love your neighbor as yourself. As numerous scholars have pointed out, this dual commandment is at the heart of Judaism, and this particular formulation is even credited to the great rabbi Hillel, with whom Jesus was no doubt familiar. The statement echoes as well in both Buddhist and Muslim teachings, as it

[201] *The Changed Life*
[202] *Worship*

does in different ways in many African and Native American religions. When he was asked about the greatest commandment, or the greatest two, inseparable commandments, Jesus, it appears, had no difficulty repeating a central lesson from his youth. And on these two commandments, he added, hangs everything in the Law and the Prophets—and, presumably, everything in his own life and teachings.

II. In our pluralistic times, understanding this commandment becomes critical. While we adhere intensely to our own Christian faith and its theological tenets, we are profoundly aware that we share planet earth with peoples of many faiths. Whereas once Christians treated those "others" as heathen who must at all costs be Christianized or be damned, we are finally beginning to appreciate, at least, the integrity with which other faiths are embraced. We are starting to appreciate, in other words, our commonality with human beings of other religions, rather than seeing them as in conflict with our "true" faith.

Now, we ask, what might we possibly have in common with the people or teachings of other religious perspectives? We are confronted with such an idea here, in this text. Love your Maker with all your soul and mind, and love your neighbor as yourself. There is not a lot of theological baggage as that line stands; there is not a lot of exclusivity in it either. There is, however, a lot of bridge-building material here. It is the universal call that spans the theological and the ethical, that ties the two together. Love the Creator Deity—there stands the theological pillar. It is not tied to this religion or that one; it is, in fact, the core of "religion" itself. And "love each other as you love yourself"—in these words is summed up the core of every human ethic, regardless of its cultural soil. This commandment is from Jesus, not from some interpreter or theologian of the faith. It is as straightforward a statement of the commonality of humankind as one can make.

III. What, then, is the preacher to do? It is not so much that one is to preach this text as it is. The lines are deeply clichéd, so much so that we are all inclined to pass over them, not finding here much homiletical appeal. But that is a mistake. What the lines most lend

themselves to—in fact, what they call out for—is *exploration*. It is not so much what they mean that is questionable; that seems patently clear. Even in the text, the scholar of the law who asked the question of Jesus was looking for a theological discussion or debate of some sort, and what he got instead was this crystal-clear response. It was as though the statement had no retort, no debating potential—which is true. What the statement lacks, however, is a sense of its implications—and that is where the preaching of this text is to begin. It is as though Jesus were saying: There, now figure out what to do with that. In fact, the questions that ring out from his statement are unrelenting and provocative. For example: How do different people understand the Lord their God? All of the evidence suggests that God goes by very different names in different settings, situations, and cultures? How are we to think about God as "ground" and "process" and "ultimate?" What does it mean to love God, however we conceptualize that being? If people express their love for God in ways that I do not understand, what am I to make of that? Are there "right ways" and "wrong ways" to love God—and if so, how does one distinguish between or among them? How is the connection between loving God and loving one's neighbor to be understood? Does one issue from the other? And if it does, how? There is nothing about that in the text. And if I love my neighbor as myself, how am I supposed to treat my neighbor? It depends on the situation, does it not? Or does it? And while we are on the subject, who is my neighbor anyway? That must be another story for another time, right?

Significantly, these questions must always be at the heart of our preaching. And in a small and shrinking world, a world of many religions and constantly "new neighbors," the pulpit must keep these matters central. People are desperate for help. As Rodney King asked, Can't we learn to live together? It is not clear that we know how; but this text does not want us to stray very far from the implications of that question.—Joseph Webb

Illustrations

KOINONIA.   Only the passing of years has brought home to me the deep significance of the Church as a fellowship and its influence upon my own spiritual development. My youth was filled with experiences, good and clean and idealistic, among friends within a working-class congregation of an industrial city. My deepest friendships grew there. The Church was the backdrop before which other like-minded youths and I strutted with all the vanity and certainty and desolating shyness known only to the adolescent. Sunday afternoons after church we walked by the river through the park, vehemently arguing about the big questions of the Christian faith—the miracles, the divinity of Our Lord, the existence of God, relativism in the moral life. Summer Saturday afternoons we played tennis. . . . Nor have I anywhere encountered more searching debate than among these young craftsmen of industrial Glasgow, though I confess I recall those days through the gossamer of love's prejudice, undimmed and unforgotten.

Subsequent New Testament studies quite vividly revealed this fellowship to be New Testament Christianity. The Church was the family of God, the beloved community, *Koinonia,* to which I also belonged. Here was friendship that could forgive and restore the faults and failings of youth and age, and big enough to be all-embracing of every class. Within the pages of the New Testament there is no such person as a solitary Christian.— George M. Docherty[203]

THE HEART OF IT ALL.   All the doctrines of Christianity are more and more seen to be bonds of close, spiritual, reverential union between man and man, and this is the most cheering view of our time. Christianity is a revelation of the infinite, universal, parental love of God towards his human family, comprehending the most sinful, descending to the most fallen, and its aim is to breathe the same love into its disciples. It shows us Christ tasting death, for every man, and it summons us to take his cross, or to participate of his sufferings in the same cause.—William Ellery Channing[204]

---

[203] *One Way of Living*
[204] *Selected Writings*

SERMON SUGGESTIONS

Topic: You Can Depend on God
TEXT: Isa. 46, esp. vv. 3 and 4
(1) We would like to believe that we are secure in God from infancy to old age—and beyond. (2) But many events in our lives cast doubt upon such a faith. (3) Nevertheless, we can be confident: (a) because of God's purpose, (b) because of God's promise, (c) because of God's power.

Topic: Temptation to Idolatry
TEXT: Rom. 1:18–25
(1) What is idolatry? It is putting any thing or person ahead of God in our commitments and affections. (2) What are the consequences? (a) self-deception, (b) addiction, (c) self-destruction. (3) What is the remedy? (a) facing the facts (vv. 19–20), (b) honoring God as God (v. 21 and 1 Cor. 6:19–20).

Hymn Suggestions

1. "O God, Our Help in Ages Past," Isaac Watts (1719); ST. ANNE, William Croft (1708)
One of the greatest of Watts's paraphrases of the Psalms, this noble hymn based on Psalm 90 could be sung at the beginning of worship as well as in response to the Psalter reading.
2. "Jesus Calls Us, O'er the Tumult," Cecil F. Alexander (1852); GALILEE, William H. Jude (1974)
This hymn of commitment constitutes a fitting response to the great commandment of Jesus to love God and to love neighbor (Matt. 22:37–39).
3. "Christian Hearts, in Love United," Nicolaus Ludwig von Zinzendorf (1725); CASSELL, trad. German melody (1735)
This beloved Moravian hymn reflects the spirit of the apostle Paul's letter to the Thessalonians in this day's Epistle lesson.
4. "Sweet Hour of Prayer," William Walford (1845); SWEET HOUR, William B. Bradbury (1861)
If its original fourth stanza referring to Mt. Pisgah is used, this familiar hymn on the theme of prayer could acquire fresh meaning when sung in connection with this day's Old Testament reading. When connected with its biblical base in the singers' minds,

Mt. Pisgah takes on a symbolic significance that can prompt meaningful identification with Moses' experience.—Hugh T. McElrath

Worship Aids

CALL TO WORSHIP. "Lord, thou hast been our dwelling place in all generations. Before the mountains were brought forth, or ever thou hadst formed the earth and the world, even from everlasting to everlasting, thou art God" (Ps. 90:1–2).

INVOCATION. Today, O Lord, we call upon you for a clearer understanding of who you are and of what you would have us be and do. Open our hearts to your truth and to one another.

OFFERTORY SENTENCE. "He that taketh not his cross, and followeth after me, is not worthy of me" (Matt. 10:38).

OFFERTORY PRAYER. Lord Jesus Christ, you, for the joy set before you, endured the cross, despising the shame. Give us the faith and the vision to see beyond our difficulties and self-denials and contemplate the joy that service and sacrifice can bring.

PRAYER. This is a beautiful day that you have made, Father. How can we but rejoice and be glad in it? The changing season bathed in autumn beauty, freedom to choose to be present in worship, challenges calling out the best we have to give, music lifting us above the humdrum of life. . . . It is indeed a day of thanksgiving and celebration and anticipation.

Yet, we too often do not come together in joy and anticipation. We come many times burdened with cares that blot out the sunshine of your presence and cloud the joy of anticipation. Often we move into place like well-trained soldiers falling into ranks out of habit; we do not gather simply because we long to express heartfelt thanks to the giver of every good and perfect gift. Too many times we enter your courts thinking that you cannot get along without our deluding ourselves that you should be grateful for our time and energies, forgetting that in reality we are nothing without you. Forgive us, Father, for our arrogance, our foolishness in thinking that the Kingdom cannot thrive apart from us. Deliver us from doing what we do from a self-seeking spirit or from a sense of others' expectations of us. You know our motives, Father. You know the truth about us. You see into the inner chambers of our hearts and souls. This morning, help us to see the truth about ourselves and to admit our need for a new beginning with you, a new beginning with a new sense of values, even about our worship.

Let today be a turning point for us. Let it be a time when we see you more clearly and come to love you more dearly. In powerful ways, reveal yourself to us and change us. Change us so that our hearts may be filled with your kind of love, and let that love flow through us like a tide rushing to the shores of eternity, meeting needs and enabling change in others all along the way of its flow.—Henry Fields

Sermon: Saved—From What?
TEXT: Acts 2:47 (RSV)
Other Readings: Zeph. 3:14–17; 1 Tim. 2:1–7; Luke 7:36–50

The greatest and most lasting revolution in human behavior happened like this: "The Lord added to their number daily those who were being saved." And it's still going on.

I. I can't find in the New Testament this rigid classification of the "saved" and the "unsaved." The word *unsaved* is totally unscriptural, and the word *saved* is seldom used; we read rather of disciples, believers, saints, and followers, and there is no suggestion that we are entitled to judge who is genuinely one of them and who is not. On the contrary, Jesus condemned all such judgments, and his apostles never played that particular kind of numbers game. John Calvin, based as he was in Scripture, contended that it is God alone who can make judgments as to who is saved and who isn't.

There is no evidence in the New Testament that the decisive question is whether or not we have experienced one overwhelming moment of conversion in which we pass from darkness to light, unbelief to belief, being unsaved to being saved. St. Paul himself was an example of cataclysmic conversion, but he never referred to that moment as the basis of his salvation, as the experience, with all its drama and emotion, on which his salvation rested. No, what happened, he said, was that the God "who had set me apart from birth, and called me through his grace, chose to reveal his Son to me. . . ." The people we find in the Gospel and in the Epistles became believers in an astonishing variety of ways. There is never any suggestion that there was a standard way of responding to Christ. To proclaim that there is one particular way to become a Christian is being unfaithful to the Scriptures, and to assert that our salvation rests upon *our* choice at one emotional moment is heresy.

II. The next point to note is that this kind of evangelism has a very limited conception of the answer to a question that is equally important. We must ask, not only "Saved from what?" but also "Saved for what?" As I read the New Testament the answer comes through clearly: For a life of devotion to God and service to others, for a life increasingly conformed to Christ himself. The impression one gets from hearing some of today's televangelists is that we "get saved" (a totally unscriptural expression) in order to become exactly like all others who accept this view of the gospel. Great emphasis is laid on certain sins that must be eliminated—mostly, unlike our Lord's emphasis, notorious sins of the flesh, and the Christian life is portrayed as an abstention from a list of specific activities that most normal people find harmless. Little is said about arrogance, intolerance, jealousy, bitterness, divisiveness, and insensitivity to the needs of others—all the sins on which the New Testament lays the greatest stress.

The only criterion that Jesus gave us for estimating the character of a professed disciple is: "By their fruits you shall know them." In his eyes, salvation is not something you claim as a once-and-for-all transaction—a ticket for heaven in your pocket—but a new way of life, to be discerned in the practice, not the theory, of love. What did he say when Zacchaeus, the chiseling tax collector, came down from his tree to dine with him and declared that he was going to give half his fortune to the poor and restore fourfold all money he had gotten by cheating? "This day is salvation come to this house." Our Lord clearly had a different conception of what is meant by salvation than that of those who use the word most often today.

III. This leads me to examine the use of the word *saved*. In the Bible it is not attached to a specific religious experience, but to a whole way of life—the deliverance that God has brought into our world, culminating in the gift of Christ. "Being saved" in Scripture doesn't refer to a religious upheaval you can date, but to the direction in which you are going. Note the words of our text: "And the Lord added to their number day by day those who *were being saved*." There's not a trace here of the notion that these new Christians had passed some kind of test to prove that they were saved. They had accepted the gospel and were on the new way of life—being saved. It was a process, not a once-and-for-all experience.

The question then that we should ask ourselves is not "Am I saved?" but "Am I being saved?" Am I on the right road? Am I responding more and more to the love of God, to the grace of our Lord Jesus Christ, and to that supporting environment of fellow believers in the communion of the Holy Spirit? That is what matters—not searching our souls to see if we have ever had some specific moment of conversion. Some have; some haven't. It's not the past that matters but whether right now we are being saved—or being lost.

We are invited to come and be one of those whom the Lord keeps adding to his Church. We are invited to get onto, or back onto, the Christian road on which we are being saved. The Christ who blazed the way for us on the heavenward road still stands at the door and knocks, and the voice comes to each one of us, whatever our temperament, position, or status in the eyes of the world, saying, "If anyone hears my voice and opens the door I will come." To answer "Yes, I hear" is not to claim that we are saved, secure, and holier than thou. It is to respond to the day-by-day grace that is freely offered to those who are being saved, and to know in which direction we are headed.—David H. C. Read

Illustrations

FROM AND FOR. A recent biography of Martin Luther King, who was raised in a strongly evangelical home and church, has this to say about his early experience of the

Church. "Conversion for him was never an abrupt religious experience, never a 'crisis moment.' It was simply a gradual assimilation of religious ideals from his church and family environment." When we think what flowed from his convictions, from his interpretation of "being saved," we can have some idea of what that expression really means. He was saved *from* a life of frustration—and *for* a life of courageous, sacrificial, and liberating service unto death.—David H. C. Read

A SERIOUS QUESTION.   We may congratulate ourselves that we don't use high-pressure tactics in confronting people with the gospel: no altar calls, no instant demands for decision, no sawdust trail. But I sometimes wonder if we are so afraid of emotion, so anxious not to offend, that we never present the gospel as requiring a decision, an acceptance. "Come unto me," said Jesus, and we so often choose to ignore the RSVP.—David H. C. Read

SUNDAY: OCTOBER THIRTY-FIRST

LECTIONARY MESSAGE

Topic: Where Are the Simple, Honest People?
    TEXT: Matt. 23: 1–12
    Other Readings: Josh. 3:7–17; Ps. 107:1–7, 33–37; 1 Thess. 2:9–13

Pity the poor Pharisees, even though they probably brought it on themselves. It is hard to get a clear fix on them. Until the destruction of Jerusalem and the Temple by the Romans in about 70 A.D. they were only one of several groups of powerful Jewish religious leaders; after the destruction, they emerged virtually alone as the "rulers" of the Jews. They are singled out in this text in Matthew as occupying (along with the "scholars") the seat of Moses. And over the next few chapters in Matthew they are castigated again and again, with most of the words put into the mouth of Jesus. Here, at the beginning of chapter 23, they are charged with being all talk and no action—so we are warned, don't do what they do. Yet later they are charged with being all action and no heart. One gets the feeling that no matter what the Pharisees do, they are not going to win.

There is a sense in which the Pharisees in the Gospels are the Christian foil. Many, if not most, scholars believe that such overt confrontationalism probably does not reflect Jesus' style, despite the sense that his behavior probably provoked religious authorities. The language of this text most likely represents the later Church's battles with synagogue rulers. Again and again, the lines resound in the Synoptic Gospels. Don't be like the Pharisees: all talk and no action, or too much action—meaning that they observe the "letter" of every law—without any feeling

behind it; laying burdens on people that they have no intention of carrying themselves; behaving to be seen, without any corresponding measure of devotion. The charges against the Pharisees seem endless. So what is going on? To what are writers like this one in Matthew trying to call attention? This is not an easy question to answer. Two themes, however, seem to be involved in it, and although these can probably be incorporated into a single sermon, my judgment is that they would work best as two distinct though related sermons.

I. When one tries to take the issue apart, it seems that what early Christians find the Pharisees guilty of is good old-fashioned duplicity: the outside and the inside of the person do not match. Even though one can say such a thing in many ways (and Matthew seems to get them all said), it boils down to a call—a Christian call—to what we might describe as a "wholistic character." Call it honesty. Call it "what you see is what you get." Call it "being genuine." Call it integrity—whatever one wishes. Its appeal seems to be universal. It is the opposite of what the New Testament refers to as the "hypocrite," and the poor Pharisee has forever (it seems) come to symbolize that blighted spirit.

I have puzzled for years over the Acts story of Ananias and Sapphira, two new converts struck dead as they brought money to the disciples, each one lying about the amount. I have concluded that the legend of their instant deaths was designed to signal the Church's adamant refusal to tolerate duplicity, lying. Ironically, one can argue that in the Christian frame of reference one can place a higher value on a scoundrel who is a scoundrel through and through, with no duplicity and no deception, than on a person whose outward actions are good but who is motivated by deceit.

This is, granted, a difficult subject to preach, for several reasons. For one, it needs to be preached without further maligning the Pharisees; the Gospel writers have turned them into cardboard figures in order to make a point. Make the point, but let the Pharisees be. Another reason this is a difficult matter to preach is because the preacher usually is only too aware of his or her own failures at precisely this point. What to do? Preach using "we"; preach with gentleness and not stridency; preach in a way that emphasizes the joys of the wholistic, harmonious life, frailties and all.

II. The second part of the text comes into play as well, whether in the same sermon or another. Ironically, it also represents another overarching theme of the New Testament, which is the beauty of humility. Again and again it is said: the first shall be last, the last shall be first; the one who would be great shall be the least among you. This theme is in this text as well, but in different ways: don't worry about what you are called; leave the titles and honors alone; those who demote themselves shall be promoted. It is not just that duplicity is seen as the problem here; it is that the roots of a particular ethic are planted and seem to be growing. One can see already how well it will fit with an ethic of the cross, an ethic of suffering, an ethic of self-giving, an ethic of communitarianism. Pride and self-aggrandizement still characterize the human condition; maybe they always will. Sin is still self-puffery and vanity, raised to new and original heights in these technological times. So, to preach the gentle, unrelenting ethic of humanity is still to preach the gospel; yet the two ingredients of this text are inextricably linked. Humility is not humility if it is not singular and whole in the one who lives such an ethic. To find such a person is to find both the image and the shadow of Christ.—Joseph Webb

Illustrations

BELONGING. The most elementary ethical principle, when understood by the heart, means that out of reverence for the unfath-

omable, infinite, and living reality we call God, we must never consider ourselves strangers toward any human being. Rather, we must bind ourselves to the task of sharing his experiences and try being of help to him.—Albert Schweitzer[205]

TO WORSHIP RIGHTLY. O brother man, fold to thy heart thy brother! Where pity dwells, the peace of God is there; to worship rightly is to love each other, each smile a hymn, each kindly deed a prayer.—John Greenleaf Whittier[206]

SERMON SUGGESTIONS

Topic: The God Who Hides Himself
TEXT: Isa. 45:15; also 8:17 and 28:21
(1) When? (a) In our times of philosophical probings and doubt; (b) during our experiences of personal suffering. (2) Why? (a) It is the expression of God's freedom and sovereignty; (b) it is his purposeful and temporary withdrawal while pursuing our ultimate good and his glory.

Topic: Something to Be Proud of
TEXT: Rom. 1:16–17
(1) The gospel is the power of God. (2) The gospel is effective for the salvation of all who have faith. (3) The gospel is revealing God's kind of justice: (a) love reaching out to us; (b) faith in our hearts receiving what God offers.

Hymn Suggestions

1. "Now Thank We All Our God," Martin Rinkart (c. 1636); NUN DANKET ALLE GOTT, Johann Cruger (1648)
Reflecting the spirit of Psalm 107, this great thanksgiving hymn could be sung either as an introduction or as a response to the Psalter reading. Its German provenance would make it also appropriate for a Reformation Day emphasis.

2. "Guide Me, O Thou Great Jehovah," William Williams (1745); CWM RHONDDA, John Hughes (1907)
Stanza 3 of this powerful Welsh hymn

---

[205] *Reverence for Life*
[206] *Worship*

makes direct reference to the experience of Joshua and the Israelites (Josh. 3:7–17), who by God's intervention crossed over the Jordan River as if on dry land.

3. "We Are Travelers on a Journey," Richard Gillard (1974); BEACH SPRING, The Sacred Harp (1844)

The theme of this recently written hymn on service to others could well have been based on the scriptural teaching of Christ in this day's Gospel lesson, that he or she who would be greatest must be the servant of all.

4. "The Word of God Is Alive," L. W. Terley (1990); PARKS, Paul Yeary (1991)

This contemporary hymn elaborates on the eternal truth set forth in the Epistle reading, in which the Word of God is asserted by the apostle to be at work in the lives of the Thessalonian believers (1 Thess. 2:13).—Hugh T. McElrath

Worship Aids

CALL TO WORSHIP.   "O give thanks unto the Lord, for he is good: for his mercy endureth forever" (Ps. 107:1).

INVOCATION.   How lovely are your dwellings, O Lord of hosts! This morning as we gather in this sacred place we pray that we will be filled with a sense of your presence and love. Visit us with the challenge of speaking your truth, loving others in your fashion, and following your purpose for our lives. Through what we experience here in this special hour, may each of us become more dedicated followers of Christ.—Henry Fields

OFFERTORY SENTENCE.   "Therefore, as opportunity offers, let us work for the good of all, especially for members of the household of faith" (Gal. 6:10 REB).

OFFERTORY PRAYER.   Our faith in Christ's mission is seen in our gifts to his church. May our faith be strong and our gifts large.—E. Lee Phillips

PRAYER.   That in the beginning your Word was present, creating a cosmos out of chaos; that at the dawn of history your Word of covenant was spoken to your people Israel, calling them to be bearers of the Light that was to shine on all people and nations; that

in these latter days you called Jesus of Nazareth at his baptism to be your Word, your Light, the Light of the world; that through him—his life, ministry, passion, and living again—you established the Church to be and to be prophetic of the community that your Word proclaims for all; that through the ages you have called Luthers and Calvins to reform and renew the Church in mission; that in this time and place we should be called to be your Church; that on this occasion we are privileged to be together celebrating Word and Sacrament—we praise you and give you thanks.

We pray for those who have heard your call through our life together and have come today in commitment and recommitment to your love-purpose in Christ. With them, may we be faithful to the gospel of reconciliation to which we all are called. Take the diversities of our membership and enrich our whole life together. In the power of your love to heal, may we embrace those among us who are ill, those facing the loneliness of bereavement, those discouraged with failure, those made anxious with difficult decisions.

We pray for the family of faith; we pray, too, for our families, in which our lives are most intimately set. To these we bear an urgent responsibility to share the gospel, but often we are hesitant, even reluctant. Increase your love in us, strengthen our faith, empower us with your Spirit to do what we know.

We pray, too, for the family of humankind. How can we worship you except when our brother and sister is with us? We thank you for all who affirm and celebrate your Word, your intention from the beginning—one world, one people. We pray for the United Nations, where this dream is precariously and painfully nurtured. We pray for leaders and field-workers and soldiers who persevere in seeking to bring order out of chaos—seeking to pass bread to those who are starving. With them may we all give and labor with the confidence that there is a grace at work that can fashion wholeness even in the face of all of man's brokenness—the grace of our Lord Jesus Christ.—John Thompson

Sermon: What Do You Mean, Good Works?

TEXT: Matt. 5:16 (13–20)

If it was not uttered when Jesus said these amazing words in his zesty Sermon on the

Mount, it was certainly a question of the people of the Renaissance. It was Martin Luther who elicited from Scripture the concept that humanity is saved by grace, not by works. It was an era in which people thought they could buy their way into heaven, but we know better now. Yet here Jesus himself declares that we are to "let [our] light shine before others, so they may see [our] good works. . . ."

The point is not that the reformers opposed good works but that they rejected the idea that a person is saved by good works. God saves us through Christ. It is a gift, a magnificent gift. It is not something earned. It is not a do-it-yourself project. It is light for our darkness, grace for our sins. But just as God loves us and demonstrates that love most avidly in the sacrifice of his Son upon the cross, so he seeks for us to live in the spirit of that love, glorifying him. We earn nothing by it—for we have already been given the gifts of forgiveness and eternity; but we gain joy by living lives that are pleasing to God and useful to the community in which we live. Here is true satisfaction of the heart: praising God by living lives that radiate his love.

"What do you mean, good works?" is an apt question, because it helps us put the emphasis where it needs to be. It is not to be on what we earn by such a lifestyle, but on the joy we receive when our righteousness is a happy response to God's great and loving gift in Christ.

Good works are meant to glorify God, not our egos. They are intended to enrich our community, not our wallets. They are meant to share Christ, not to display our goodness for the purpose of public adulation.

Jesus tells the parable of the Pharisee and the tax collector (Luke 18:9–14). The Pharisee was among the most respected of the religious Jews, whereas the tax collector was loathed as a rascal. Jesus told the story because he was aware, Luke says, of "some who trusted in themselves that they were righteous and regarded others with contempt." The story is familiar to most of us. The Pharisee enters the Temple to pray. He stands by himself and prays boastfully, "God, I thank you that I am not like other people: thieves, rogues, adulterers, or even like this tax collector. I fast twice a week; I give a tenth of all my income."

By contrast, the tax collector, seemingly nervous in the awesome surroundings of the Temple, where others would, with accusing eyes and fingers, show their contempt for him, stood "afar off." He "would not even look up to heaven, but . . . beat . . . his breast saying, 'God be merciful to me, a sinner!'" Chances are the Savior actually observed two men at prayer in the Temple one time and noted the contrast—and more than that: the fault-finding "goodness" of the one, and the humility but abiding faith of the other, the sinner.

Jesus says that this rejected man of Jewish society was accepted by God rather than the Pharisee. And the simple reason was not his good works or lack of them, but his sincere, trusting faith. George Buttrick writes that "self-righteous pride is as noxious a sin as penitent humility is an essential grace."[207] The Pharisee brought no light to the Temple, but clouded it with the darkness of his own petty accomplishments. The tax collector, on the other hand, let his light, the light of humble faith, shine in the shadowy darkness of his corner. Jesus urges us to let the flame of the tax collector's faith illumine us also, so that others may see not us but Jesus through us.

Richard Dunagin tells about a family situation. His kids attended a school carnival and won four goldfish. On Saturday morning, Dunagin went madly searching for a fish tank in which to house the family newcomers. He was appalled at the prices. They ranged from $40 to $70. In the middle of the store aisle he saw what he needed: a discarded ten-gallon display tank, complete with gravel and filter, but nasty, dirty. They wanted $5 for it. He bought it and the cleanup was quickly done. He felt good about his money-saving accomplishment. The fish looked great in their new home.

On Sunday morning, however, they found one gold fish dead, and Monday morning revealed a second one floating belly-up. By that night there was a third causality, so they called in an expert friend. It wasn't long before he knew the answer to the problem. Dunagin had washed the tank with soap,

[207] The Parables of Jesus (New York: HarperCollins, 1928), 87.

which is absolutely forbidden for fish tanks. "My uninformed efforts," he wrote, "had destroyed the very lives I was trying to protect."

What has this got to do with good works and self-righteousness? A lot. In our zeal to make ourselves look good or to improve the spiritual appearance of our family or friends, we sometimes use what Dunagin calls "killer soaps." Like the Pharisee, we condemn, criticize, nag, or go into fits of temper. In our attempt to do right, we become abrasive and harsh, and fail to let our light shine. We emphasize what we must do rather than what Christ already has done for us. We slip into deep darkness rather than allowing the flame of hope to illumine either ourselves or others.

Jesus sends us out to let our lights shine so that others may see not how wonderful we are but how great God is. That's the point. We are to let our light shine before others so that in our good efforts they may see God a little more clearly.

But it is not only major, earth-shaking actions that Jesus talks about in wanting us to let our lights shine. It is the simple things as well as the profound.

Forgiveness is the application of love. That's the basic need. If there is no forgiveness, there is no love. Love is the salt that preserves and flavors. Light is the faith that chases darkness and brightens the horizon. To be salt and light is to do more than good works; it is to share the God of greater works, the Christ of the gospel, the Lord of love, the one who triumphed over sin and death.

Married couples would stay married if they did less talking about their love's situation and more living it out by forgiveness. Families would have fewer rivalries if forgiveness rather than resentment illumined their darkened relationships. Neighbors would get along successfully if they let love be lived by forgiveness, for that is the way to glorify God—and to keep the neighbor as a friend.

Good works? Jesus commends us to do them, but so that the light of his love will glow in the light of our faith, rather than as a means to earn the Kingdom that has already been given to us.—Richard Andersen

Illustrations

FROM CHRIST WITHIN.   Our whole relation to the law has to be considered in terms of Christ. What is most essential for the Christian disciple is that Christ does not command him from outside, as does a human lawgiver, and as did the law of Moses, to the extent it was viewed in terms of the letter rather than of the spirit. But Christ commands from within, through our living in corporation in him.—Bernhard Häring[208]

HOPING IN GOD ALONE.   In the Bible, however, it is said that you cannot satisfy God, but God satisfies Himself and you. You are not to rely on what you do, but solely, alone, on what God does. We must say even more than that. You cannot know what the word "God" means until you are at the end of your strength, and can hope only in God. The man who has not yet discovered this "God only" has not yet discovered God. The gods of the heathen are not truly God. The true God is the God a man finds when he can no longer help himself, and he puts his hope in Him alone. To hope in God alone, not in the power of self, one's ability or knowledge, means faith, means being God's own.—Emil Brunner[209]

SUNDAY: NOVEMBER SEVENTH

LECTIONARY MESSAGE

Topic: Prepare for Nothing
TEXT: Matt. 25:1–13.
Other Readings: Josh. 24:1–3, 14–25; 1 Thess. 4:13–18

"Where is your God?" This is a question asked not only by enemies of believers but also by believers ourselves. "How long, O Lord?" is another. Who among us has not wondered in times of distress or discouragement why the Lord does not step in and end this thing right now?

I. Can you see the ten bridesmaids in the story Jesus told just a few days before his

---

[208]Quoted by John Macquarrie, *Principles of Christian Theology*
[209]*Our Faith*

death? They were all ready for the coming of the bridegroom—all ten of them. They all did what they were expected to do: they took their lamps, filled with oil, and went to the appointed place and waited. All ten were following directions, even the five whom Jesus later calls "foolish."

What distinguishes the wise women from the foolish ones in the story is that the wise ones took extra oil. Then, when the bridegroom was delayed in coming, those five had enough oil to keep their lamps burning, while the others had to go in search of more oil and thus missed the entrance of the bridegroom. All ten were prepared for his coming; only five were prepared for his *not* coming. Ten had prepared for the event; only five had prepared for the nonevent. Ten prepared for something; five also prepared for nothing.

II. Apparently the church in Thessalonica had this same problem. They all seem to have been prepared for the return of Christ, but many became confused when that return was delayed. God's people in former times had also faced this problem. Over and again in the Hebrew Bible we read of the concerns aroused in people by a God who appeared not to be doing anything. The prophets ask, "How long?" The psalmists echo the taunt of Israel's enemies, "Where is your God?" Psalm 22 begins, "My God, my God, why have you forsaken me? Why are you so far from helping me, from the words of my groaning? O my God, I cry by day, but you do not answer me; and by night, but find no rest."

III. Can any of us claim not to have felt such despair in some challenging situation of our lives? As we face the beginning of the third millennium after the first coming of Christ, this problem rears up again. Why is he absent so long? When will he finally come? The delay has been so long that many believers have trouble taking his return seriously at all. Our end-time lamps are out, and we don't even see the need to get more fuel.

All around us we see the results of living only in and for the present. Many of our contemporaries are interested only in the immediate pleasure they can find. Power, knowledge, status, wealth—these things and more like them define the purpose of those people whose horizons are marked by their span of life on earth.

We also see the sad cases of people living in the past. It is not only people in retirement centers who dote on their past accomplishments. All around us are men reliving their athletic glories, women pretending to hang on to their teenage beauty.

Others are living only for the future. How often do we hear people say, "When I am older" or "When this or that circumstance changes, everything will be better." It seems that they just never get on with their lives; they are constantly waiting for better days.

IV. Christian faith roots us in the past— not just in our personal history, but more important, in God's history in Christ Jesus. Without that past we have no foundation for the present and no assurance for the future. We are rooted in the past. Remember your baptism and be glad! We are rooted in the past, but not buried there.

The love of God thrusts us into the present to work the works of him who has redeemed us. For God so loved the world that he gave not only his Son but also his Church to work redemptively in and for the world. There is nothing wrong with paying attention to the challenges of the present, unless we do it selfishly. Because we are rooted in the past we can take the present seriously.

But it is our hope that makes the primary difference in the Christian life. As Paul wrote to the Christians in Corinth, "If for this life only we have hoped in Christ, we are of all people most to be pitied" (1 Cor. 15:19). The present moment is gone as soon as it is noticed. We really cannot live in the present, because it is always passing away. We live on the border between now and not yet, between present and future. It is our hope in Christ that draws us inexorably into the future, that keeps us from living in the past or living for the present. That hope, in other words, keeps us alive.

V. Now back to our initial problem: Are we prepared for nothing? Are we ready to be leaning into the future trusting that our Lord will be there even when we lose the sense of his presence? We can be ready for his arrival only if we live in expectation during his absence. To be ready for something we must prepare for nothing. We prepare for his coming by preparing for his absence.—Bruce E. Shields

Illustrations

A TIMELY APPROACH.   To discuss the questions raised in section III, the preacher might describe groups or individuals in the news who are setting dates for the second coming or trying to rush the return of Christ.

A CLASSIC EXAMPLE.   To address the issues presented in Section IV, one could describe the apostle Paul as a good example of the balance of faith, love, and hope—one who referred in faith to the past, lived actively and lovingly in the present, and looked forward to God's future appearance.—Bruce E. Shields

SERMON SUGGESTIONS

Topic: God's Care for His Own
TEXT: Ps. 121:1–8 (NRSV)
(1) The universal quest for an ultimate answer (v. 1). (2) The bold answer of faith (v. 2). (3) The areas of God's protection: all circumstances of life (vv. 3–8).

Topic: Why Center on Christ Crucified?
TEXT: 1 Cor. 2:1–5
(1) The "mystery of God" breaks the bounds of popular oratory and conventional logic. (2) God is not limited by the human frailties of the messenger of the gospel. (3) Those who hear can be lifted from their deep need only by the power of the one who raised the crucified Christ from the dead.

Hymn Suggestions

1. "Wake, Awake, for Night Is Flying," Philipp Nicolai (1599), tr. Catherine Winkworth (1858); WACHET AUF, Nicolai (1599), harm. J. S. Bach (1731)
    Known as "the King of Chorales," this great hymn is based on the parable in Matthew 25:1–13, of the wise and foolish maidens. Its message—to be ever watchful for the Lord's coming. Its singing would be appropriate at any point in a worship service on this day.
2. "When Peace, Like a River," Horatio G. Spafford (1873); VILLE DU HAVRE, Philip P. Bliss (1876)
    The last stanza of this poignant gospel hymn makes clear reference to the coming of the Lord at the sound of the trumpet on the last day. The singing of this song would constitute a suitable Christian response to this truth set forth in the Epistle reading (1 Thess. 4:13–18).
3. "Let Children Hear the Mighty Deeds," Isaac Watts (1719); WEYMOUTH, Theodore P. Ferris (1941)
    This delightful hymn written for children by the "Father of the English Hymn" is ideal to accompany the Psalter reading for this day (Ps. 78:1–7).
4. "Oh, Blest the House," Christoph C. L. Von Pfeil (1746), tr. Catherine Winkworth (1863); WO GOTT ZUM HAUS, Klug's Geistliche Lieder (1533)
    This fine hymn of commitment, especially in a family context, harks back to the declaration of Joshua that although others may choose otherwise he and his house would serve the Lord. It is thus suitable for use with the Old Testament reading (Josh. 23:14–25).
    —Hugh T. McElrath

Worship Aids

CALL TO WORSHIP.   "Listen! I am standing at the door, knocking; if you hear my voice and open the door, I will come in to you and eat with you, and you with me" (Rev. 3:20 NRSV).

INVOCATION.   Gracious Lord, the urgency of our times and of our need makes it imperative that we receive all the help you offer us. Therefore, we would have you come among us and bless us in this service and in our day-to-day lives with your presence and your answers. Enter, Lord Jesus!

OFFERTORY SENTENCE.   "It is God who is at work within you, giving you the will and the power to achieve his purpose" (Phil. 2:13 Phillips).

OFFERTORY PRAYER.   We thank you, O God, for putting into our hearts the desire to see your work grow and prosper, and we thank you as well for the opportunities to have a part in that work through our tithes and offerings.

PRAYER.   We have come here this morning as worshipers from varied backgrounds and needs, Father. We know that Christ died for our sins. But often we forget that he has entrusted us with the responsibility of declaring his reconciliation to all people everywhere. Prepare us today to be sent forth as laborers in the harvest, free from reluctance and shame, to tell others of the faith we have found in Christ. To all who have been at war with themselves and you, enable us to speak a word of peace. To dying folks, help us to bring your word of life eternal. To hate-filled people, lead us to utter your word of love. To despairing souls, help us to say words of hope. To those weeping tears of sorrow, may we bring glad tidings of comfort and joy. To those drowning in the captivity of sin, may we extend the life-raft words of salvation, so that our fellow pilgrims lost to Christ may be won by his truth and power and by our compassionate hearts.—Henry Fields

Sermon: Partakers of Grace

TEXT: Phil. 1:1–11

The church people at Philippi had remained loyal to Paul; that could not be said of other congregations he had established. Knowing of the Philippians' "partnership in the gospel" (as Paul called it), he felt he could address them with appreciation and affection, and that he did. The apostle even envisioned these friends as his companions in prison, with both him and them being, as he said, "partakers of grace."

Someone has said that partaking of grace means living in style. "Grace involves style at its best," this person noted, "a style of living that is never out-of-date, a style that finds expression on various levels of our existence." When we allow the love of God to fill us—which is what it means to partake of grace—we think and act in ways the apostle Paul itemized in his Philippian letter. Wrote Paul: "Direct your thoughts to all that is true, all that deserves respect, all that is honest, pure, decent, admirable, virtuous, and worthy of praise." That list can be lengthened— it is not exhaustive—the point being that these qualities represent a timeless style of life. Participating in the grace of God enables us to live in style, to live in the noble, heady atmosphere of divine love.

I. *Counting our blessings.* Characteristic of this way of life is a spirit of gratitude. Paul spoke of gratitude and thankfulness in several of his letters. For Christians, such an outlook is normative and natural. Gratitude becomes second nature when we are partakers of grace—gratitude to God, which, wherever it is expressed, makes better people of us. When some unexpected blessing comes our way, we react out of that dominant spirit of gratitude that belongs to a Christian's lifestyle.

We could say it this way: grace makes us glad. Receiving the love of God moves us to praise and thanksgiving.

W. E. Sangster described the evidences of God's love in a threefold pattern. He said, there are "common blessings"—the innumerable gifts of everyday that too often are taken for granted. Then there are "special blessings"—particular enrichments unique to us and to our personal experience. Finally, there is the "greatest blessing" of all—the incredible gift of God's presence in Jesus Christ. For all of these things, we have abundant cause to be grateful.

In his letter to the Philippians, Paul implied as much when he told his friends that he was praying for them that they would "learn to value the things that really matter." Valuing our blessings—the common ones, the special ones, and the greatest and supreme one—issues in words and deeds of thankfulness.

II. *The rainbow in the rain.* The surrounding and embracing love of God, that grace of which we partake, does not deliver us from the jolts and stresses of daily life. Christians no less than others face problems, perhaps hardships and trials. We scarcely are exempt from sorrow, even tragedy. What grace provides is not deliverance from these things but a sure and sturdy anchor in the midst of them. It is a divine love that will not let us go, as poet George Matheson said. Even in the face of overwhelming odds, that gracious love abides— which Matheson compares to a rainbow traced through the rain. And let it not be forgotten: the apostle Paul wrote his encouraging letter to the Philippians from a prison cell. His life was in the hands of his enemies, yet he wrote to church friends, "Grace and peace be yours from our Father God and from Jesus Christ, our Savior." Then he spoke of how the Philippians were all "partakers of grace," persons sharing a blessed privilege along with him, even in the face of an unknown future.—John H. Townsend

Illustrations

NO ONE TO THANK?   A certain woman who was not known for having personal faith exclaimed one bright spring day, "I'm so grateful!" Her more believing friend responded, "Grateful to whom, my dear?" In a similar vein the English poet Christina Rossetti identified as the crowning horror a scenario in which God did not exist. That circumstance, she said, would place us in this glorious world with grateful hearts and no one to thank. Clearly, a Christian's style of living is founded upon a gracious God to whom thanksgiving and grateful praise everlastingly belong.—John H. Townsend

LEARNING TO THANK.   A restless child in an airport was given some candy by a friend, also a waiting passenger. The child's mother urged him to say thank you. "That's alright," said the passenger, "He doesn't have to say thanks." To that the mother replied, "But if he learns to, he will be a better person."—John H. Townsend

SUNDAY: NOVEMBER FOURTEENTH

LECTIONARY MESSAGE

Topic: Faith in Reverse
  TEXT: Matt. 25:14–30
  Other Readings: Judges 4:1–7; 1 Thess. 5:1–11
  I. The Parable of the Talents, which is our text for today, has been familiar to me for many years, as is probably true for you. We hear it referred to at times of stewardship emphasis—not only because it deals with money but also because it is a good reminder that if we don't use our talents we are likely to lose them. In fact, the word *talent*, which to Jesus' audience meant a coin, means ability to us.

As I looked closely at the story this time, however, it surprised me. As often as I had read it and heard it taught and preached, I didn't recall much emphasis on the master. Most of my memories of this text had to do with the maxim, "Use it or lose it."

But take a look: the master "entrusted his property to them." Then he returned and called them to account. The first two servants are dealt with rather quickly, even though they are the good examples for us. The third is in trouble because the master trusted him and he betrayed that trust by taking himself too seriously. He practiced what psychologists call "self-protective behavior."

But the master was anything but self-protective. Some today would question his sanity, or at least his judgment. He left his entire estate in the hands of servants without sensible checks and balances! He trusted them. In our "get it in writing" age, we are urged not to trust anybody without an ironclad contract.

II. We preach, as we should, on the importance of trusting God; rarely do we hear anything about God trusting us. Yet the Bible often refers to the faithfulness of God. In fact, the Bible talks about God's faithfulness toward us much more often than it mentions our faith in God. Exodus 34:6 refers to the God who is "abounding in steadfast love and faithfulness." Deuteronomy 32:4 calls the Lord "a faithful God without deceit." Psalm 89 uses the word *faithfulness* eight times. In the New Testament the Greek word that can be translated as either "faith" or "faithfulness" is most often translated as referring to a human being's faith in God. In many instances, however, the reference could just as easily be made to God or Christ, which would correspond much better with the usage in the Hebrew Bible. (See for example Rom. 3:22 and Gal. 3:22.)

Theologians usually define God's faithfulness with reference to God's own integrity, as well they should. But that divine faithfulness ever since the creation of the first human pair has entrusted much to us. The mandate in Genesis 1:28, to "be fruitful and multiply, and fill the earth and subdue it; and have dominion over the fish of the sea and over the birds of the air and over every living thing that moves upon the earth," is a great responsibility for us human beings. But it is an even more astounding statement of God's willingness to trust us.

III. We have betrayed that trust time and again, and yet God has redeemed us and given us new responsibilities over and over. Deborah and the other leaders of ancient Israel were entrusted with the good of their people. Jesus returned to his God, leaving in the hands of that ragtag group of followers the responsibility of telling the world. The apostle Paul caught this vision and communicated it to the Ephesians when he wrote, "Of this gospel I have become a servant according to the gift of God's grace that was given to me by the working of his power" (Eph. 3:7). In that chapter Paul consistently refers to his work of proclamation as a gift of God's grace. It was not a chore, not just a duty; it was a great privilege to be entrusted with the work of communicating the gospel of Christ. In much the same way, Paul tells the Thessalonians, "Therefore encourage one another and build up each other, as indeed you are doing."

IV. God does not just save us helpless humans by his matchless power. He entrusts us with the property that rightly is an extension of heaven until the time of his return to call us to account. Oh, there will be an accounting; but today, let us celebrate the trust that God shows us when he charges us with the divine business. What a privilege is ours, to be entrusted with the gospel! What a privilege to have the wealth and the freedom to take it all over God's world! What a privilege to have access to the means of transportation and communication afforded us as we enter the twenty-first century! What a privilege to look forward to the opportunities of service awaiting us in the next millennium! What a God we serve! God not only calls us to trust him, he also trusts us with everything important to him in this world.

And with that trust comes the power to accomplish whatever God wants us to do. The parable of the talents indicates that the master assigned responsibilities according to the servants' abilities. God knows what we can do, and he assures us that we can accomplish what he assigns us to do. Fear of failure must not impede God's work in the world. If we are working for God, God is working with us. That does not spell failure. That spells success, in capital letters and bold type.

God has demonstrated faith in reverse. He believes in us, as strange as that may seem. He trusts us with the creation and with the gospel. And as God entrusts all of that to us,

He also empowers us with the means and abilities we need to accomplish the divine purpose. The primary flow of faith is from God to us! The appropriate response to that faith is our trust in God as we work for him in the world.—Bruce E. Shields

Illustrations

CREATED EQUAL? Shakespeare has five talents in literature, Michelangelo five in art, Savonarola five in preaching, and Edison five in invention. These are the bright particular stars in the human firmament. The vast majority have two talents. They are the useful hosts of mediocrity. Then there are those who seem limited and handicapped—the one-talent people. "All men are created equal" in the sense that God intends that every man shall have an equal chance to prove himself, but the historic statement when taken at its face value is not defensible. For we are unequal in native gift—one man a Shakespeare and another always a hack-writer. We are unequal in opportunity—one man moving in that "fierce light which beats upon a throne," and another living out his lonely days as a trapper in far woods. We are unequal in advantages—one born in poverty and another given an education as a matter of course. All men are created unequal.—George A. Buttrick[210]

HOARDERS OF THE LIGHT. In parables with three characters, like this one, the spotlight falls, by the rule of "end stress," on the third character in the story—that is, on the servant who did nothing with his money. Who did this "barren rascal" signify in the mind of Jesus? (The successful two, be it noted, are only there as foils to him.) Who was this "slothful and wicked servant" whose caution amounted to a breach of trust? The answer is that he typified the pious Pharisee who hoarded the light that God gave him (the Law) and kept for himself what was meant for mankind. Such a policy of selfish exclusivism yields God no interest on his capital; it is tantamount to defrauding him and must incur his judgment. And the time for

[210] *The Parables of Jesus*

settling accounts is approaching.—Archibald M. Hunter[211]

SERMON SUGGESTIONS

Topic: The Blessing We Need and Can Enjoy
TEXT: Num. 6:24–26
(1) God's protection. (2) God's undeserved favor. (3) God's abundance (*shalom*).

Topic: Is Anger Wrong?
TEXT: Eph. 4:25–5:2
(1) Anger is inevitable—it is a factor of our God-given humanity. (2) Anger can be sinful—it can be excessive, prolonged, demonic, destructive. (3) Anger can be useful: (a) when it leads to action for justice, (b) when it leads to efforts for reconciliation, (c) when it reminds us of what God has done in Christ for us who have sinned against him.

Hymn Suggestions

1. "Come, All Christians, Be Committed," Eva B. Lloyd (1963); BEACH SPRING, The Sacred Harp (1844), harm. James H. Wood (1958)
   In connection with the Gospel reading on the parable of the talents, this contemporary hymn of stewardship and service could be appropriately sung.
2. "To You, O Lord, I Lift My Eyes," Ps. 123, vers. from Psalter (1912); SARAH, Hughes M. Huffman (1976)
   This modern paraphrase of Psalm 123 could well be sung as the Psalter reading for the day.
3. "Canta, Deborá, Canta!" Luiza Cruz (1973); tr. Gertrude Suppe (1987); DEBORA, Luiga Cruz (1973)
   This song, originally from the Portuguese, incorporates the spirit of the Song of Deborah recorded in the Old Testament lesson. Deborah, a "Mother in Israel" and leader of armies, sings to the Lord, who gives the victory. Among hymnic expression coming recently from Latin America, this is one of the most popular.
4. "My Lord, What a Morning," African

American Spiritual (nineteenth century); BURLEIGH, African American Spiritual
   This slave song of hope concerning the coming of the "Day of the Lord" could well accompany the Epistle reading for this day. It is a song of those who remain sober and awake, watching for that great day of deliverance that will come "as a thief in the night."
—Hugh T. McElrath

Worship Aids

CALL TO WORSHIP.   "Unto thee lift I up mine eyes, O thou that dwellest in the heavens" (Ps. 123:1).

INVOCATION.   God of every place, meet us in this sacred place to which we come to be found by you, we pray. Inspire us to worship fully in spirit and in truth. In this holy hour let us come face to face with your eternal glory, your everlasting strength, your merciful love, your healing touch, and your forgiving grace.—Henry Fields

OFFERTORY SENTENCE.   "He also said to them, 'Take note of what you hear; the measure you give is the measure you will receive, with something more besides'" (Mark 4:24 REB).

OFFERTORY PRAYER.   You have given us power over a few things, Father, and for such a gift we are grateful. This morning, lead us to use the power you have given to provide for the needs of others so that all may have enough. Through our gifts save people from their sins, as well as from the sins of others, we pray in Jesus' name.—Henry Fields

PRAYER.   Living Father! We thank Thee for our life with its unspeakable privilege and dread responsibility. Thou hast given it to us that through it may throb the mighty tide of Thy love, that in it may be revealed some aspect of Thy being and beauty. Thou hast beset us behind and before. Thou makest us to sorrow for our sins. Thou dost stir us with a divine discontent, and we forget the things that are behind and reach forth unto the things that are before. We rejoice that Thou hast set our life amid gracious opportunities,

[211] *Interpreting the Parables*

whereby Thou wouldst train us to truer vision and larger understanding of Thee and of ourselves.—Samuel McComb[212]

Sermon: Oh, Loneliness!

TEXT: 1 Kings 19:1–18

"Oh, loneliness," the poet T. S. Eliot wrote. "Oh, loneliness. Everyone knows what that's like." And Eliot is right, you know. You and I do know what loneliness is like. And nobody likes loneliness. For some of us, loneliness is a reality this morning. For many of us, loneliness is one of our biggest fears.

The psychological truth is that loneliness is a normal part of human existence. But it doesn't help much to know that when you're crying and shouting inside like Elijah and feeling completely alone. What does help is knowing what to do. And interestingly enough Elijah's story gives us some pretty good ideas about things you and I can do to cope with loneliness.

I. First, you can do something positive for yourself. Loneliness says, "I'm not wanted. I'm not loved. What point is there in going on?" So Elijah ran out into the desert to get away from Jezebel, who had told him she didn't appreciate him, and when he'd been going a whole day with nothing to eat and nothing to drink, he lay down, exhausted, to give up. And the angel said, "Get up and eat."

The trouble with loneliness, you see, is that it eats away (I seem to be stuck in the same imagery here) at our self-respect. You and I translate "Nobody loves me" into "I don't deserve to have anybody love me." We start to believe that we're worthless or that life is over for us. And if we're not careful we start to act toward ourselves in the way we feel. You may even lose your health altogether. Statistics say that divorced nonsmokers have about the same death rate in this country as married smokers.

So the first thing to do when you and I feel lonely is to look around for something positive you can do for yourself—something that makes you feel good, besides eating. Something that makes you feel good about you. Take a walk in Bernheim Forest. Get a haircut. Read the book you've been waiting to read. Go for a workout. Write a letter. Try to

see this time alone differently. Take it as a gift and use it to your own advantage. Paul Tillich said, "It's easy to be lonely but it's difficult to be alone." Part of what he meant, I think, is that it's easy for you and me to feel sorry for ourselves when we feel lonely. Remember that little children's chant? "Nobody loves me. Everybody hates me. Guess I'll go eat worms." It's easy to let loneliness be destructive. It's harder to take that aloneness and make something good out of it. But it can be done. First, do something positive for yourself.

II. Second, do something positive for someone else. Elijah's loneliness came in the first place because he chose to stand up for Israel's God against Ahab and Jezebel's plot to worship Baal. Elijah defeated the false prophets and defied Ahab and Jezebel, and that got him into hot sand. But even later he took it on himself at God's instruction to anoint new kings for Aram and Israel and a successor for himself. His crisis became the impetus to new service.

The problem, of course, is that very often when we're lonely you and I are concentrating on our own need. What if the next time you're feeling lonely, instead of waiting around, you got on the phone and called up someone you think might be lonely, too? Call them up. Suggest dinner or a movie. Listen to their problems. Elijah had to come back from the desert to do what needed to be done. But there were two results, not one. The first was that he helped his country. The second was that he found his way out of his own personal wilderness. Second, do something positive for someone else.

III. Third, seek fellowship for yourself. Now we get to the heart of the matter. "I alone am left!" Elijah cries out to God. "Nobody else is doing what's right. Nobody else is worshiping you. I'm the only one, God, and one is the loneliest number." In the end God tells Elijah that he's miscounted by seven thousand. But what makes this story so poignant in the first place is Elijah's despair, his sense of abandonment. Oh, loneliness. Elijah knows what that's like. And what he really needs is somebody to talk to.

Ray Oldenberg, in his book *The Great Good Place*, says in effect that for many of us church becomes home: home in the Bible study classes; home in the ministry projects; home in prayer and in the conversations at Wednesday night suppers. Here we share our lives with one another. And that can take care of our social loneliness, if we will let it. I hope that every one of us will do our very best to get better still at being welcoming and inclusive and warm. My friends, the lonely have a right to come to you and me looking for fellowship. By becoming home for them we not only help them, we also make our home stronger for ourselves.

But there is a more intense level of loneliness that Robert Weiss talks about in his book on loneliness. Emotional loneliness is what happens when you lack or lose a truly intimate relationship. Emotional loneliness is what happens to those who don't have a really close friend or to those who lose a spouse. In the short run, there's not much we can do about emotional loneliness. The trusting fellowship of the Church is the best place in all the world where emotional intimacy can grow. Still, you can't create real intimacy quickly or easily. That's what frustrates people who try to fight their loneliness by jumping quickly into bed with somebody. Sex and intimacy just aren't the same thing. Sex without intimacy can be the loneliest act in the world. Authentic intimacy takes time and work. It takes choosing someone new. You can't replace a loved one you've lost. No one ever takes the place of anyone else. The best we can hope for is that someday a new place can be created in our hearts. The best the Church can do is provide a place where that can happen. Third, seek fellowship with others.

IV. And finally, above all, seek fellowship with the Lord. Did you notice where Elijah found God? Elijah found God out in the wilderness; after his own personal hurricane, after his firestorm, after his earthquake, Elijah found God in the still small voice that came to him out of the sound of sheer silence. Do you hear what that means?

It means that even when you and I are at our loneliest, when everyone has abandoned us and everything has gone wrong, even in the midst of absolute desolation, if we seek him, God is there. In the Gospel according to John, there is a painful, painful moment at the last supper. The disciples have just told Jesus they believe in him. And Jesus says, "Oh, do you really? Let me tell you how it's going to be. Very soon now every one of you will desert me utterly and scurry off to your homes to hide. You will leave me alone. But I won't be lonely, even then. God my father will be with me." So he said. And then he walked down the most difficult road any human being has ever walked. He walked it alone. Even he felt abandoned. But God was with Jesus every step of the way. God proved it by raising him from the dead. And in doing that, Jesus proved that God wants to be with you and with me, even in the most frightened moments of our lives. Jesus didn't give up on the disciples any more than God gave up on Elijah out there in the wilderness. Christ came back to them. And even more than that, Christ made them, and through them Christ made you and me, a promise: "I will be with you always."—Ronald D. Sisk

Illustrations

SELF-GIVING.   I've always admired Jimmy Carter's mother, Miss Lillian, for one special reason. When Miss Lillian was already an elderly widow, she went to India in the Peace Corps. At a time in life when most people would have either been resting on their laurels or sitting at home expecting friends and family to come to them, Miss Lillian stirred herself and went out and gave away part of what she had left. At her age, it could easily have been everything.—Ronald D. Sisk

GOD'S PRESENCE.   Roy Honeycutt tells the story of visiting American missionaries who were the only Christian family in a large city in Japan. Their children attended Japanese school, but the teacher complained to the parents that she had no way to discipline them. When they asked why, she said, "When one of our Japanese children misbehaves we put them in the spirit room. It is totally dark with no lights and no windows. The children are terrified and they soon behave. But your children aren't afraid when we put them in the spirit room. They just tell us their God is everywhere."—Ronald D. Sisk

SUNDAY: NOVEMBER TWENTY-FIRST

LECTIONARY MESSAGE

Topic: Surprise, Surprise!

TEXT: Matt. 25:31–46

Other Readings: Ezek. 34:11–16; Eph. 1:15–23

I. *The day of judgment.* Can you imagine it? In different texts of the Bible it is described in different ways, which indicates that we can't imagine it—that it's really beyond our capacity to describe. When Jesus described it he did not try to depict the details of the scene. In today's text he is presented as dealing with the scene briefly: "When the Son of man comes in his glory, and all the angels with him, then he will sit on the throne of his glory." That's it. We are left to try to imagine the glory. Jesus seems to be more concerned with what happens when "all the nations will be gathered before him."

Even the process of judgment is briefly stated: Jesus will separate people into two groups. What gets emphasized here is the conversations between the Son of Man and the sheep on one side and the goats on the other. The Lord explains his judgment; that might be the most surprising thing of all. The Lord doesn't owe an explanation to anybody, but he gives it. The Lord has the right to do with the creation whatever is the divine will. The prophets and the apostle Paul used the metaphor of the potter and the clay to show that humans have no right to demand explanations from God. But here Jesus indicates that the Judge is ready to explain.

And what is the explanation? The judgment has already been made by the people, when they chose to do or not to do certain acts of kindness for those who had needs. The Judge says, "You saw me . . ." and people in both groups reply, "When was it that we saw you . . . ?" Total surprise is the reaction of both those who served the Lord and those who did not. Surprise, surprise!

II. *Human service is unself-conscious or else it is self-serving.* And what is self-serving cannot be service to Christ. We feed people because they are hungry, not because it will win us points in heaven. We serve water because people are thirsty, not because it will win us points with the Judge. We welcome strangers because they need to be included, not because it will win us

points with Jesus. We clothe the poor, we care for the sick, and we visit those in prison because they need it, not because it will win us points with God.

"We love," writes John, "because [God] first loved us" (1 John 4:19). No matter how hard we work, we cannot win God's love, because God already loves us and was working on our behalf long before we were conscious of it. When we discover that divine love flowing into us, then the most natural thing in the world is to act lovingly toward others—to feed the hungry, clothe the poor, care for the sick, and visit prisoners. And if we live this way, the most natural thing "out of this world" will be to "inherit the Kingdom prepared for [us] from the foundation of the world."

But what about those who will be sent "away into eternal punishment?" They are people who have been so caught up in themselves that they have failed to notice the hungry, the poor, the sick, or the prisoners. They might have been looking for the Son of man, but they never found him, because he was to be found in his lowly brothers and sisters.

III. If you have never had the privilege of serving a meal to people who really need it, or of caring for sick people at home or in the hospital, or of visiting in a prison, I recommend that you arrange to do one of these as soon as possible. You will likely be afraid as you prepare for such service, but those who do such things regularly will testify to the great feeling of satisfaction that comes with forgetting ourselves for a while and helping those who really need our help. In fact, we usually return from such activities feeling that we have gained much more than we have given.

If you live a life full of such unself-conscious service, I expect that you will be as surprised as the self-absorbed person when you hear Jesus say, "You saw me. . . ." For we shall all reply, "When was it that we saw you . . . ?" Surprise, surprise!—Bruce E. Shields

Illustrations

A SURPRISING REVERSAL.   In discussing Section III, the preacher might describe (without betraying a confidence) a visit in the hospital that he or she faced with great hesitation but which turned out to be a blessing for the preacher.—Bruce E. Shields

MADE FOR GOD.　　Would a duck have the instinct to swim if there were no water? Would a baby cry for nourishment if there were no such thing as food? Would there be an eye unless there were beauty to see? Would there be ears unless there were harmonies to hear? And would there be in you a craving for unending life, perfect truth, and ecstatic love unless Perfect Life and Truth and Love existed?

In other words, you were made for God. Nothing short of the Infinite satisfies you, and to ask you to be satisfied with less would be to destroy your nature. As great vessels, when launched, move easily on the shallow waters between the narrow banks of the rivers, so you are restless within the confines of space and time and at peace only on the sea of infinity.—Fulton J. Sheen[213]

SERMON SUGGESTIONS

Topic: Holy Ground
TEXT: Exod. 3:1–12, esp. v. 5
(1) Wherever God chooses to meet us is "holy ground." (2) Our spiritual blindness and certain preoccupations may cause us to miss the special wonder and potential glory of God's presence. (3) However, when we do recognize and listen to God, the experience comes with a challenging call to duty.

Topic: When Our Eyes Really See
TEXT: Eph. 1:17–19
(1) We can know the hope to which God has called us. (2) We can know how rich and glorious is our share among God's people in their inheritance. (3) We can know the greatness of God's power at work for us.

Hymn Suggestions

1. "All People That on Earth Do Dwell," William Kethe (1561); OLD HUNDREDTH, Louis Bourgeois (1551)
No more appropriate beginning of worship than this venerable psalm paraphrase

[213]*Preface to Religion*

can be found for this day. The singing of this version of Psalm 100 to the oldest tune in continuous use in all Christian hymnic history could well take the place of the Psalter reading.

2. "Christ Is Made the Sure Foundation," Latin (seventh century), tr. John M. Neale (1851); WESTMINSTER ABBEY, Henry Purcell (1680)
This majestic hymn on Christ, the head of the Church, would make a suitable response to the Epistle reading (Eph. 1:15–23). It would also function well as a processional hymn.

3. "Open My Eyes That I May See," Clara H. Scott (1895); OPEN MY EYES, Scott (1895)
The Ephesian passage (Eph. 1:18) also speaks of "having the eyes of your heart enlightened," making this song appropriate to introduce the Epistle reading. Indeed, one stanza softly sung would be a meaningful prayer before any scripture lesson to be read.

4. "Crown Him with Many Crowns," Matthew Bridges (1851); DIADEMATA, George J. Elvey (1868)
This coronation hymn depicting Christ in glory on his heavenly throne could well accompany the Gospel reading describing the King's judgment at the end of time.—Hugh T. McElrath

Worship Aids

CALL TO WORSHIP.　　"Enter into his gates with thanksgiving, and into his courts with praise: be thankful unto him, and bless his name. For the Lord is good; his mercy is everlasting; and his truth endureth to all generations" (Ps. 100:4–5).

INVOCATION.　　God of grace and glory, so bless us with wisdom and understanding that as we worship you in humility and adoration we may behold the glory and know the joy that faith imparts, through Christ our Lord.—E. Lee Phillips

OFFERTORY SENTENCE.　　"With a free-will offering I will sacrifice to you; I will give thanks to your name, O Lord, for it is good" (Ps. 54:6).

OFFERTORY PRAYER.　　Almighty God, you have taught us that "to whom much is given, much is required." Grant that we will be generous with all that is ours, always remembering the poor in possessions and the poor in spirit. Let giving be our habit and sharing our joy because we would be like our Savior, who gave his life as a ransom for all, rich or poor.—E. Lee Phillips

PRAYER.   O you who are the great God and the great King above all gods, how can we appear before you except that you draw near to us. You draw near in the greatest way that you can, in the fullness of your love and grace manifested in the person of Jesus. In him you invite us—you plead with us—to come home, to receive our true estate as your children, your sons and daughters. "Once we were no people, but now we are your people; once we had not received mercy, but now we have received mercy so that we may declare the wonderful deeds of him who called us out of darkness into your marvelous light."

The light that shines more and more onto the perfect day is the light of your love—the light of the star that shone at Bethlehem and seemed eclipsed at Calvary but then burst forth on the Resurrection morning in a blazing light of hope, so that whatever the darkness of our night, the light of your presence is sure to bring the dawning of a glorious new day.

That we are party to a fellowship not limited by time and space, the communion of saints, we praise you. That Jesus' words in establishing the church, that "the gates of death shall not prevail against it," are verily true, we rejoice. What a succession through the ages of prophets, apostles, reformers, preachers, and teachers, that in this time and place we should be heirs of your promise. We are your children now, but it does not yet appear what we shall be. When the swollen waters of some Jordan come sweeping down upon us, may we establish our feet on the rock of your Word lest we be swept away by the torrents of the time.

May the word of promise—of hope—declared and celebrated on this occasion find a home in our minds and hearts and yield a rich harvest of joy and gladness in all the days and nights to come.

May the community of your love be present in and among us as in prayer and helpfulness we reach out to one another.—John Thompson

Sermon: The Divine Mirror

TEXT: Ps. 119:17–24; James 1:22–25; 2 Cor. 3:18 NRSV

When we get up in the morning, one of the first things most of us do is look in the mirror. It seems to be the natural thing to do. We look to see what kind of shape our hair is in; we check to see if we have changed any overnight; we may check for any new traces of gray hair and jerk out the most obvious ones; we shave or fix our face; in short, we try to get ourselves presentable for the world. What would we do without mirrors?

I. *The Bible is a mirror, the Divine Mirror, we might say.* It is the most natural thing in the world for us to look in the Bible as we look in the mirror. For as we look in the Bible, the Divine Mirror, we see ourselves. The Bible is the one universal book. It matters not who you are, what country you were born in, or what religion your parents taught you. All who take time to look in the Bible will see themselves there. As the Russian novelist Fyodor Dostoevsky put it, "What a book the Bible is, what a miracle, what strength is given with it to man. It is like a mold cast of the world and man and human nature; everything is there. . . ."[214]

Though the Bible is old and the accounts are ancient, the stories of the biblical characters become our stories. With Adam and Eve we have felt estranged from God; with the Israelites we have longed to be set free from that which has oppressed us; with David we have struggled with temptation and then paid for the folly of our sins; with the psalmist we have both rejoiced when we have been happy and lamented when we have been sad; with Job we have suffered and asked "Why?"; with Jonah we have found ourselves running from God; with Jeremiah we have found new cause for hope; with the prodigal son we have found ourselves separated from the comforts of home and family; and on and on we could go. The Bible is the book of every man and woman. It is a constant unfolding of humankind's quest to know God, to know ourselves, to know the best way to live, and to know what lies beyond this present life.

II. *As we look into the Bible, the Divine Mirror,*

---

[214]*The Brothers Karamazov* (Originally published 1879.)

we see ourselves as we really are. Sometimes when we pass before the mirror at home and look at ourselves, we like what we see. If we are feeling good that day, if we are all spruced up in our best suit or finest dress, we may look in the mirror and say to ourselves, "You handsome specimen of a man," or "You gorgeous creature." And then other days, when we first get up in the morning with our hair standing straight up, or when we are feeling really low, or when we have on the slouchiest outfit we own, we may look at ourselves in the mirror and be repulsed; we may not like what we see at all. We may want to crawl back into bed and forget about the day.

So it is when we look in the Bible: we see ourselves as we really are. We read some passages (like Psalm 8, for instance) that make us feel pretty good about ourselves. And then when we read other passages in which we do not like what we see. The Divine Mirror exposes our imperfections. As the writer of Hebrews puts it, "Indeed, the word of God is living and active. . . . It is able to judge the thoughts and intentions of the heart" (Heb. 4:12). The mirror of God points out to us our less-than-Christian habits. It calls into judgment our thoughts, our words, our actions, and our motives. The Divine Mirror convicts us of our sin, and exposes our human weaknesses and prejudices. But that is all right. That's the way it should be.

III. *Because as we look into the Bible the good news is the Divine Mirror, we see ourselves as we can be.* The Bible is the inspirational book *par excellence.* As we look into the Bible we see ourselves as we really are, but also as we can be; it inspires us to aspire to great things, it urges us to correct our faults, and it encourages us to perfect our character. This is precisely what James is talking about when he compares looking into a mirror to looking into the living Word. Those who look into the Divine Mirror, the law of God, and then decide to act on what they see, are, James says, the ones who will be changed and whose lives will be blessed. They will become more beautiful on the inside.

And Paul says, in writing to the Corinthians, "All of us . . . seeing the glory of the Lord as though reflected in a mirror, are being transformed" (2 Cor. 3:18). That's what Bible reading, looking into the Divine Mirror, is really all about: transformation, being changed, becoming more Christlike, conforming to the image of God within us. In the Bible, the Divine Mirror, we see reflected the image of Christ, who bore the image of God, the image that we are destined to become.

The belief that the Bible has the ability to transform lives and impart hope has been the impetus behind the American Bible Society's work since its founding in 1806. Story after story has been shared with American Bible Society workers and translators about how a copy—or even a few pages—of the Bible drastically changed someone's life. It is the Bible Society's goal to translate the Scriptures into every language and dialect on the globe. To repeat what I said in the beginning, it matters not what country of the world one comes from or what language one speaks: when one looks into the Bible, the Divine Mirror, one will see oneself.

The character Samuel Hamilton in John Steinbeck's novel *East of Eden* observes, "Give me a used Bible and I will, I think, be able to tell you about a man by the places that are edged with the dirt of seeking fingers."[215] What does our Bible reading, or lack of it, say about us, who we are, how we are being changed, and how we are growing spiritually each week? We would not even consider going all day without looking at our physical selves in the mirror and trying to improve our outward appearance. Why would we want to go week after week without looking at ourselves in the Divine Mirror and without trying to improve our inward appearance?

Charlton Heston, the movie star who played the part of Moses in *The Ten Commandments,* has written a coffee-table book about the Bible, the *King James Bible* to be exact. The book is a collection of the actor's favorite Bible stories and includes his own short commentaries. Heston describes the Bible as the "best writing this side of Shakespeare." He laments the fact that people aren't exposed to the Bible stories the way they used to be.

Have you looked in the mirror lately—the Divine Mirror, that is? When you do, you are bound to see yourself there, including all the God-given beauty and all the human imperfections. But you will also see yourself in the

---

[215]*East of Eden* (New York: Penguin Books, 1992), 267. (Originally published 1952.)

Bible as you can be—if you're willing to be a doer of the word and to act on what you see there.—Randy Hammer

Illustrations

RENEWAL. By reading the Scriptures I am so renewed that all nature seems renewed around me and with me. The sky seems to be a pure, a cooler blue, the trees a deeper green. . . . The whole world is charged with the glory of God and I feel fire and music . . . under my feet.—Thomas Merton [216]

PERSONAL RESPONSIBILITY. Light does not fail. Because men have blinded themselves, it remains, with its own properties, while the blinded are plunged in darkness through their own fault. The light does not force itself on any man against his will; nor does God constrain a man, if he refuses to accept God's working. Therefore all who revolt from the Father's light, and who transgress the law of liberty, have removed themselves through their own fault, since they were created free and self-determining.—Irenaeus[217]

SUNDAY: NOVEMBER TWENTY-EIGHTH

LECTIONARY MESSAGE

Topic: You Never Know
TEXT: Mark 13:24–37
Other Readings: Isa. 64:1–9; 1 Cor. 1:3–9

I. If you are disappointed that Jesus didn't give us a vivid description of judgment day in Matthew 25, you should be happy with today's text. This so-called "little apocalypse" in Mark 13 offers us some words of Jesus that do get graphic. Here we have suffering, darkened sun and moon, stars falling, heavenly powers shaking, and the Son of man coming in clouds. That's enough to get our imaginations going—enough to give Hollywood's special effects experts a challenge.

There is an interesting dynamic to this text, however. It begins with that bombastic description, but then it immediately turns to the fig tree. The quiet growth of a tree through the calm passing of the seasons tells us about the course of time. And then in verses 32–37 we are brought back to an actual life situation—a man going on a journey giving advice to the servants to be watchful.

A musician would mark verses 24–27 *ff* (very loud), verses 28–31 *mp* (medium soft), and verses 32–37 *mf* (medium loud), with perhaps a two-note accent at the end of verse 37. This seems to be the opposite of how most of us would chart a course of music dealing with the second coming of Christ. We would want to begin more softly and work up to the fortissimo at the end. But the

master musician often does the unexpected, as does the master communicator. Jesus shakes us with the picture of the judgment day and then brings us back to present reality with the assurance that the day will come but we have some living to do in the meantime. His refrain is, "Keep awake." You never know, so keep awake.

II. A question we need to be asking ourselves is, Am I awake—really awake? Am I really aware of what is going on around me? If I do not "tune into" the people and events that confront me every day, how shall I be paying attention to the coming of Christ? It would be easy if we were given a complete schedule. With our computers, daily calendars, and timepieces, we manage our use of time rather well. We can register each appointment and schedule each task, and then check them off as they are completed. But God, with whom a thousand years is as a day and a day as a thousand years, offers us no such schedule. Jesus tells us, "You do not know when the time will come."

So the Christian life becomes a continuous vigil. We Christians are to be watching all the time. We are to be watching for the Lord. That does not mean that we are to stand around with our faces pointed upward. According to Acts 1:10 and 11, when the disciples stood "gazing up toward heaven" after Jesus ascended into heaven, two angels came and asked them why they were standing

---

[216] *Thoughts in Solitude*

[217] Ireaneus (Second Century), quoted in *Affirmations of God and Man,* ed. by Edmund Fuller

there. Even though the Christian life is a life of constant vigilance, it is not a life of stargazing. Watching for the Lord as a Christian means seeking to serve him.

III. So, have you seen the Lord lately? Have you noticed him in the face of a person needing a good meal? Have you seen him in the worker who needs a glass of cold water? Have you spied him in a hospital room or in a prison? Might he be hanging out on your neighborhood playground or ball field? Is he visiting one of your elderly neighbors? Might you visit him on some far-flung mission field? Are you watching? You never know when the Lord will show up.

Or are you for all intents and purposes asleep? Have you become unaware of the people around you every day who have great needs? Do you go through your daily routine with very little thought beyond your own circumstances? Are you in danger of sleeping through the second coming—or at least of slipping through life so oblivious to others that you miss serving the Lord? "Keep awake—or else he may find you asleep when he comes suddenly."

IV. Today is the first Sunday of Advent. We are reminded that it is time to prepare for the coming of the Christ. In one month we shall be celebrating the birth of Jesus. But for the Church through the ages, this time of year has meant more than just a nice memory of a romantic birth in a stable. It has meant that the Lord has come and that he has promised that he will come again. It means that as God prepared the world for the first advent, so he wants to prepare us for the second advent. That final coming will be accompanied by cosmic upheaval; but until then God's people are to "keep awake" by staying active in service to others, so that having seen the Lord in "the least of these, his sisters and brothers," we shall recognize him for who he really is—the one who said, "And what I say to you I say to all: keep awake."—Bruce E. Shields

Illustrations

CHRISTIAN VIGILANCE.   It is important to notice that in nearly all Christ's sayings the object towards which we are to direct our watchfulness is not His future appearing but our present state and present task. The crisis may come at any time, yet the way to prepare for it is not to be all the time on the lookout for it, but rather at each time so to attend to the work we have in hand that our Lord, when He comes, will find us doing His will. The true state of Christian readiness does not consist in being constantly keyed up to a nervous expectation, either of our own last hour or of the end of the world. It consists rather in a calm fulfillment of each duty as it comes to us; and the best preparation for the next demand that may be made on us is the punctual and conscientious fulfillment of the demand that is being made on us now.—John Baillie[218]

TAKE HEART!   Many a time might our Lord say to each one of us, "I have redeemed thee." Out of six, yea, six thousand trials He has brought us forth by the right hand of His power. He has released us from our afflictions, and brought us forth into a wealthy place. In the remembrance of all these redemptions the Lord seems to say to us, "What I have done before, I will do again. I have redeemed thee, and I will still redeem thee. I have brought thee from under the hand of the oppressor; I have delivered thee from the tongue of the slanderer; I have borne thee up under the load of poverty, and sustained thee under the pains of sickness; and I am able still to do the same: wherefore, then, dost thou fear? Why shouldest thou be afraid, since already I have again and again redeemed thee? Take heart, and be confident, for even to old age and to death itself I will continue to be thy strong Redeemer."—Charles H. Spurgeon[219]

SERMON SUGGESTIONS

Topic: God's Victory in Our Troubles
    TEXT: Gen. 50:19–20
    (1) God has a plan for every life. (2) Different factors often hinder the fulfillment of that plan: (a) the fallen condition of the world in general, (b) the sin of other people, (c) our own sin. (3) Nevertheless, God is infinitely resourceful and can make the things

[218]*Christian Devotion*
[219]"Redeemed Souls Freed from Fear"

SUNDAY: NOVEMBER TWENTY-EIGHTH

that handicap us actually enrich our lives and the lives of others, and glorify himself as well.

Topic: An Angel in the Sun

TEXT: Rev. 19:17

We do not know what the original idea underlying this phrase may have been. And yet we are justified, it seems to me, in taking this symbol and considering what it means to us. (1) The symbol of an angel standing in the sun suggests that we should always try to see the spiritual in the material. (2) This symbol suggests that we look for the divine in the human. (3) This symbol suggests that we should look for the constructive elements in every destructive experience.—Harold Cooke Phillips[220]

Hymn Suggestions

1. "This Is the Threefold Truth," Fred Pratt Green (1980); ACCLAMATIONS, Jack Shrader (1981); THREEFOLD TRUTH, William P. Rowan (1987)

The ancient formula used by the early Christians in worship, which constitutes the refrain of this contemporary hymn, climaxes with "Christ will come again"—a declaration, in keeping with the Gospel reading, on the signs of the times and the second coming of the Lord—a central Advent theme.

2. "O Hear Our Cry, O Lord," Ps. 80, vers. Fred B. Anderson, (1986); VINEYARD HAVEN, Richard W. Dirksen (1974)

With its refrain, "O come, Lord, come, restore and save us now," this paraphrase of Psalm 80 is eminently appropriate for an Advent emphasis, as well for use as a replacement for the Psalter reading of the day.

3. "Have Thine Own Way, Lord," Adelaide A. Pollard (1901); ADELAIDE, George C. Stebbins (1907)

The reference in the Old Testament reading (Isa. 64:8) to the Lord as a potter and the people of God as clay makes appropriate the use of this song of consecration built upon this metaphor.

4. "Great Is Thy Faithfulness," Thomas O. Chisholm (1923); FAITHFULNESS, William M. Runyan (1923)

This popular song on the theme of God's

[220] *The American Pulpit Series,* Book I

faithfulness could be sung in response to the Epistle reading in which the apostle Paul (1 Cor. 1:8–9) declares that God is faithful and that he will sustain his people to the end. The refrain lends itself to antiphonal singing.— Hugh T. McElrath

Worship Aids

CALL TO WORSHIP. "Turn us again, O God, and cause thy face to shine, and we shall be saved" (Ps. 80:3).

INVOCATION. Lord, how can we praise you unless you place the desire in our souls? How can we worship you without a longing born of holy initiatives? How can we find the way of life except that you lead us? Lead us now, Lord, as in stillness and prayer we wait before you and open ourselves to the mystery.— E. Lee Phillips

OFFERTORY SENTENCE. "Do not forget to do good and to help one another, because these are the sacrifices that please God" (Heb. 13:16 TEV).

OFFERTORY PRAYER. Our Father, we confess that often we have sought everything but your Kingdom and your righteousness. Guide us and strengthen us as we attempt to establish our true priorities, assured that if we attend to what is most important, the less important things will fall into their proper places.

PRAYER. For your Word in song, in Scripture, in sermon, we are grateful. We praise you for those who in every generation have been faithful in transmitting your Word so that we might know the fullness of the gospel in our time—your Word mighty to save.

With what self-giving you are present to our every need. But sometimes we are insensitive to your coming—we are blind to all the signs of your presence. The gospel proclaims that you are always present to each one of us in the greatest way that you can be—you so love the world that you have given your only Son. If there is any reticence—any insensitivity—it is in us. You are always giving, but sometimes we are unwilling to receive. We are well aware of the blessedness in giving, but let us not miss the blessedness in receiving.—John Thompson

Sermon: Getting Ready for Christmas—The Ax and the Tree

TEXT: Luke 1:13–15, 3:1–18

One of my favorite Christmas memories is of going for the tree. I don't recall precisely how old I was when my father began letting me accompany him on this sacred quest, but I remember the excitement of it. If I ever felt like Caesar marching into Rome or Charles Lindbergh riding down the avenues of New York in a shower of confetti, it was on these occasions when we drove home with the Christmas tree on top of the car.

The ax and the tree. There's a different allusion to the ax and the tree in our text today, isn't there? "Even now the ax is laid to the roots of the trees; every tree, therefore, that does not bear good fruit is cut down and thrown into the fire."

I. *John the Baptist and the judgment that goes along with Christmas.* Did you know that, that there's a judgment that goes along with Christmas?

a. Think about how it was a judgment. A gang of teenage hoodlums roams the streets of a certain city. One day a beautiful young man walks into their midst. He is kind and good. His speech is trustworthy, and he befriends everyone he meets. His very presence is a judgment on them, isn't it? It makes obvious the low and treacherous level of their existence.

b. This is what John the Baptist saw in the coming of Jesus: it made obvious the deficiencies of others. It reminded people of the corruption, materialism, and hostility into which the world had fallen—even the world of religion.

II. Now Christmas is coming and we are thinking once again of John and Jesus. Shouldn't we consider John's message about corruption and materialism and hostility, and measure our own times against it? We are always willing to remember the little baby born in a stable in Bethlehem; it is a beautiful, warm picture of God's goodwill toward all humanity. But can we honestly come to that lovely scene without remembering what led up to it—without reflecting on God's judgment against the world?

Maybe we don't want to think about judg-

ment because we know how bad the situation is.

a. *Corruption.* We more or less expect it in Rome and Moscow and New York, don't we? But we don't like to think that it exists in schools and churches and nonprofit institutions. We don't like to remember that the seeds of corruption are in all of us, and that this is why the federal government must monitor *our* IRS returns and why the shop owners and movie houses must check *our* children's IDs and why the police must set up speed checks in *our* neighborhoods. As much as we dislike him for it, John Calvin was right to insist that there is depravity in all of us, and that we are all kin to the criminal and the pervert, despite the way we like to represent ourselves.

b. *Materialism.* If you don't think we're materialistic, watch the way we observe Christmas, with the biggest buying spree of the year. I heard of a child who got mad at his parents last Christmas because the three pairs of jeans he received were not designer jeans, and of another child who didn't speak to her parents for four days because she didn't like the color of the seat covers in the new sports car they gave her.

c. *Hostility.* Has there ever been a time when there was more anger and resentment in the world than there is right now? I mean the sense of powerlessness that workers feel before management, and that management feels before competition. I mean the fear and reaction that people on fixed incomes experience in the face of inflationary medical and banking and housing costs. People are insecure and pressured and put upon, and when people are insecure and pressured and put upon they become hostile and angry and resentful.

III. Christ's coming *is* a judgment, isn't it? Christmas *ought* to make us think about all these things. Our world is in need of redemption. *We* are in need of redemption. Oh, we can draw our robes of self-righteousness around us and pretend that everything is all right with us, the way some of the Pharisees did under the preaching of John the Baptist. But that doesn't make it so in the eyes of God, and if it isn't so in the eyes of God, it just isn't so.

a. How much better and richer we will be if we can hear the word of judgment and then ask, as many did of John, "What then shall we do?" And John said, "Collect no more than is appointed you." Be honest with people. The soldiers asked, "And we, what shall we do?" And John said, "Rob no one by violence or by false accusation, and be content with your wages." Treat people decently and don't take what belongs to others in order to improve your own financial situation.

b. John had the same message for all of them: Straighten up and obey the laws of God, and then you will be ready for the coming of the Messiah. Get your life in order. Stop thinking of yourselves so much and start thinking of others. Learn to be thankful for what you already have, and stop worrying all the time about what you don't have. Let God be God in your life, and stop worshiping idols.

IV. *The ax and the tree.* The ax is *always* at the root of the tree that is diseased and nonproductive, isn't it? God's judgment is forever present in life. One can no more avoid it than one can avoid breathing or feeling. It is how we respond that matters. The tree can be saved. That is the good news of Christmas. God doesn't want to destroy; God wants to save. But we have to receive the judgment before we can understand the grace.—John Killinger

Illustrations

CHRISTMAS MEMORIES. My father was an agricultural agent, and I am sure he had scouted out the right tree while visiting farmers throughout the year. But he always gave it the air of a great search, as if we might look for hours before finding the perfect tree. Then, when we finally came upon it, we carefully surveyed it from all sides, being certain that any bare spot might be easily hidden by turning it to the wall, and assessed its height, to be sure that once it was fastened in its stand it would just touch the ceiling, not an inch too little or an inch too much. At last, when all the qualifications were satisfied and there was no doubt in our minds that this was the tree that had waited for us since the day of its planting, we bared the ax from the gunnysack in which we had carried it, felled the tree, and lashed it to the top of the car for the trip home.—John Killinger

THE CHRISTIAN PARADOX. We wait in hope. *There* is the Christian paradox, the Christian tension: he is here, and still we wait in hope.

Christianity is indeed a historical religion: Christ did come; but we do not survive on nostalgia. Christianity is indeed a present fact: Christ is here, now; but we are not imprisoned in the present. The risk in being a Christian is that you open yourself to a future, and that future is God's future. The first Letter of John is so insightful: "Beloved, we are God's children now; it does not yet appear what we shall be . . ." (1 John 3:2). I do not know what tomorrow will bring—only that tomorrow Christ will be there. I do not even know if I will experience his presence—only that my life, like my liturgy, must relive the Jesus who was and celebrate the Jesus who is. Only thus is every risk-laden tomorrow an act of hope in God's future: "Into your hands. . . ."

And the day will dawn when that sentence of John's will be completed: ". . . It does not yet appear what we shall be, but we know that when He appears we shall be like Him, for we shall see Him as He is."—Walter J. Burghardt, S.J.[221]

SUNDAY: DECEMBER FIFTH

LECTIONARY MESSAGE

Topic: Living in the Meantime
TEXT: 2 Peter 3:8–15
Other Readings: Ps. 85:1–2, 8–13; Isa. 40:1–11; Mark 1:1–8

The apostle Peter, within thirty to forty years of Jesus' death and Resurrection, was faced with questions and doubts about the promised return of Jesus to establish God's reign and deliver the saints. While reminding his readers that God is always faithful to his promises, he warns them about being distracted from living appropriately in the meantime. He encourages the Church to continue

[221] *Tell the Next Generation*

faithful living during that undetermined stretch of history between the first and second advents of Jesus Christ.

If Christians in the first generation of the Church had doubts and questions about the promised return of Jesus, we should not be afraid to face our own uncertainty some fifty generations later.

For many of us, the stories of Jesus' first advent are closer to myth or ancient history than living reality. The promise Jesus made of a second advent seems more like fantasy or a distant prospect than a valid truth. We will profit by hearing Peter's counsel about living in the meantime.

I. *We have had a taste of that which is to come.* At the beginning of his second Epistle, Peter reminds us that "[God's] divine power has given us everything needed for life and godliness, through the knowledge of him who called us. . . . Thus he has given us, through these things, his precious and very great promises" (2 Pet. 1:3–4a). In God's gracious gift of Jesus Christ, fellowship with God has been restored. Our sin has been forgiven. Our hearts have been cleansed. "Salvation is at hand. . . . His glory [dwells] in our land. . . . Righteousness and peace [have kissed] each other" (compare Ps. 85:9–10). In Jesus Christ, the Kingdom of God comes near, and we anticipate that time when "the kingdom of the world has become the Kingdom of our Lord . . ." (Rev.11:15). Yet for his own reasons God has not brought the promise to final fulfillment. So we live in the meantime. We live between promises.

II. Like those first-generation Christians, we can respond to living between the already and the not yet in one of three unacceptable ways.

a. *Like the Zealots of the first century, we can try to force God's hand.* True, not many of us advocate armed rebellion. However, the millennial obsession with signs, wonders, and predictions of Armageddon can be a way of saying, "See, God, you promised. You gave us clues. We've figured it out. Now, pay up!" Jesus warns against wasting time trying to discern what only God knows.

b. *We can become anxious and fall prey to despair.* The meantime is not an easy time. Jesus warns that violence, war, famine, injustice, persecution, and natural disasters are facts of life lived in the meantime.

Peter cautions us to be on guard against scoffers who will use the tragedies and misery against us. He exhorts us not to give in to the temptation to surrender the hope of the gospel.

c. *We can act as if the meantime is the only time.* We can ignore the promise of the future and place all our hope in the now. Peter is most concerned about this course of action. A large portion of 2 Peter 2 addresses this issue. Carnal Christians, those who try to profess faith in Jesus Christ while satisfying every desire and want, have always been a concern for the Church. However, spirituality can become self-indulgent when disconnected from the apocalypse. When the meantime becomes the only time, the basic spiritual question becomes, "What has God done for me lately?"

III. In contrast to these three unacceptable ways of living in the meantime, Peter advises us on how to conduct ourselves as we await the fulfillment of God's promised Kingdom.

a. *The meantime is not a time for passivity.* It is a time for action. Peter chooses strong words to define the type of action called for: "strive to be found." What is called for is the believer's best effort to use the time wisely. The *Revised English Bible* renders this phrase as "do your utmost." Former President Jimmy Carter, writing in *Living Faith,* captures Peter's spirit when he writes, "when we accept the free gift of salvation . . . , it imposes an obligation—a pleasant one—to serve by striving to live in harmony with his teachings."[222] Throughout his book, Carter gives testimony to his desire not to waste time pursuing activities that do not give witness to his relationship with Jesus Christ and his hope for God's Kingdom.

b. *Striving by itself has no intrinsic value.* Peter is not counseling frenetic, exhausting motion. Our effort is to be purposeful. We are to labor to be found at peace. At first blush this admonition may seem oxymoronic. Peace is often associated with rest, or with the absence of strife. Yet Peter encourages us to strive toward peace. What could he have in mind?

Again we turn to President Carter: "Christ

---

[222]Jimmy Carter, *Living Faith* (New York: Times Books, 1996), 179.

wants us today to follow his example by expanding the meaning of forgiveness, service, and love—all in a practical way. And he goes on to teach that this is the avenue toward personal peace and freedom. . . . The essence of Christ's teaching is to liberate us and give us peace."[223]

"To be found by Him at peace" describes not a relaxed, leisurely state. If Carter's description of Christian discipleship is accurate, Peter may be encouraging us to strive, so that when the promise is fulfilled we will be so lost in working to extend Christ's forgiveness, love, and service that we will be surprised but not unprepared.

IV. Ours is a challenging age. We who are Christians live between the first advent of Jesus, when the angels proclaimed "peace on earth," and the promised second advent, when all our hopes will be fulfilled. In the meantime, we are called to a life of love and service in Jesus' name.—Jim Holladay

Illustrations

NO SUBSTITUTE FOR AN ACT.   There is no substitute for an act. For instance, our churchyard was a nondescript half-city lot. We didn't make any big announcement; three of us just started to clean it up and set in some plantings. Then other people said, "I'll come over next Saturday to help you." Or they said, "I admire you heartily, but I'm too weak to dig; here's ten bucks."—Joseph A. Sittler[224]

THE DAY OF THE LORD.   All lives are purposeful because they are part of the eternal world; and the Day of the Lord, though future as far as history is concerned, is an eternal reality, a present experience, as well as a future consummation of the victory of God. Though we must still work for it, pray for it, and indeed fight for it, in the eternal world the victory of God has happened already, and the proof of that happening is the life, words, acts, death, and resurrection of Christ. God's own purpose and grace were given to us in Christ Jesus, as Paul said to Timothy, "before the world began, but is now made manifest

by the appearing of our Savior Jesus Christ, who hath abolished death, and hath brought life and immortality to light through the gospel."—Leslie D. Weatherhead[225]

SERMON SUGGESTIONS

Topic: There Is a River
TEXT: Ps. 46:4
(1) The river of God is life-giving (Rev. 22:1). (2) The river of God is gladdening: (a) it strengthens obedience and diminishes sin; (b) it strengthens courage and diminishes fear; (c) it strengthens joy and diminishes dullness. (3) The river of God is adequate (John 7:37–38; Zech. 14:8).

Topic: How People Find God
TEXT: Job. 11:7–9; Jer. 29:11–13; Matt. 7:7; John 14:8–10
(1) Finding God is difficult, because we look for him so anxiously. If we trusted as we should, we would know God. Every experience of life would confirm his reality.
(2) But for many of us, simple faith, that awed innocence of childhood, is not possible. The nature of early training has exaggerated the importance of the question mark. We take beliefs apart like clocks to see what makes them go. But like clumsy, inept children we do not find it easy to put them back together.
(3) We need God—how desperately we need him! We have scrutinized and dissected so many experiences of life that the romance and glow are gone. Pleasure has ceased to please. Money no longer can buy happiness. Youth marches toward decrepitude. No warm love of earth is beyond the chill of grief.
(4) Thus, our skepticism at last brings us back to God. At first, our skepticism seems to devour God, but succeeds actually in destroying our idols and setting us before God for life or death. We capitulate before our heavenly Father, find life's ultimate meaning in him, and start from there to put the wheels of life in place again.
(5) It is Jesus Christ—the Way, the Truth, and the Life—who gives the clues, the directions, and the evidence we need.

[223]Carter, *Living Faith*, p. 179.
[224]*Grace Notes and Other Fragments*
[225]*The Significance of Silence*

Hymn Suggestions

1. "Rejoice, the Lord Is King," Charles Wesley (1746); DARWALL, John Darwall (1770)

Appropriate for the beginning of worship, this vibrant hymn, in its fourth stanza—"Rejoice in glorious hope"—refers to the Second Advent of Christ, who shall come to judge the world and take his servants to their eternal reward.

2. "Comfort, Comfort Ye My People," Isa. 40:1–5, Philip Doddridge (1755); CHESTERFIELD (RICHMOND), Thomas Haweis (1792)

A comforting advent prophecy, this metrical version of Isaiah 40:1–5 could well be substituted for the Old Testament reading. It can be sung antiphonally between choir and congregation with good effect.

3. "On Jordan's Bank the Baptist's Cry," Charles Coffin (1736); WINCHESTER NEW, Musikalisches Handbuch (1736)

Based clearly on Mark's passage concerning John the Baptist, this hymn, appropriate for Advent, could be sung before the Gospel reading.

4. "Hark, the Glad Sound," Philip Doddridge (1755); CHESTERFIELD (RICHMOND), Thomas Haweis (1792)

A clarion call to prepare for the coming of the Savior, this Advent hymn can be used as a response to any of the day's readings—Old Testament prophecy, New Testament Gospel, or Epistle.—Hugh T. McElrath

Worship Aids

CALL TO WORSHIP.   "Deliverance is near to those who worship him, so that glory may dwell in our land. Love and faithfulness have come together; justice and peace have embraced" (Ps. 85:9–10 REB).

INVOCATION.   Into this sacred place we come at this advent season, Father, bringing our sins that they may be confessed and forgiven. We come bringing our minds to you, that we may be given deeper insight into the meanings of the birth of the Lord Jesus. We bring our hearts to you, that they may be filled with your love and thus become instruments through which that love may flow out to the world. Like followers through the ages, we bring our wills to you this morning, that

you may guide us in all we do and say.— Henry Fields

OFFERTORY SENTENCE.   "Now the whole group of those who believed were of one heart and soul, and no one claimed private ownership of any possessions, but everything they owned was held in common" (Acts 4:32 NRSV).

OFFERTORY PRAYER.   How can we not give, Father, when we remember how much you gave? Here is our offering this morning. May it increase as we learn to love you more and understand our purpose more clearly.— Henry Fields

PRAYER.   Our hearts beat faster and our adrenalin flows at this time of the year, O Lord. We respond to the lights and decorations; to the cheerful, beautiful music; to the prospects of gifts and brightly decked houses and parties and friends and relatives coming to call. But let us not forget, O Lord, that the origin of all joy is in your love and self-giving, which were made known most completely in Jesus Christ. Teach us to be still and get in touch with that joy. Let it flow through us like some eternal medicine, healing our hurts and wounds and illnesses. Let it perfume the air we breathe, filling us with its sweetness. Let it ring through the corridors of our minds like heavenly bells, tolling happiness and fellowship and a peace we have never really known. And when we have felt it, when it has flowed through us and perfumed the air around us and rung in our minds like bells, let it move from us to everyone we meet and know. Let the true spirit of Christmas begin in us and gradually take over the world, converting hate to love, and greed to generosity, and ignorance to enlightenment, and strife to peace. Touch the sick with healing. Grant mercy to the self-driven. Open the arms of the shy and retiring. Give blessedness to the broken in heart. And let the song of the angels be our song, as we are drawn together in the name of him who was born and died in Judaea to save the world from its sin.—John Killinger

Sermon: Amid Everything Else: Hope!

TEXT: Ps. 85

I. The psalmist finds himself in a trying, frustrating, nearly hopeless situation. He and his people have made it back home from a terrible exile. All those years under the thumb of a cruel and bloodthirsty tyrant generated dreams of what it would be like to get back home, to return to Israel, to nestle again in their dream city, Jerusalem. And now here he is. He is home. And what does he discover? The city is a wreck. It is leveled. The houses are in shambles, public order is nonexistent. Chaos reigns. The streets are under the control of thugs, muggers, bullies, the protection rackets. The psalmist's hopes and dreams, projected from the years in exile and slavery, are null and void; the promises of God are an apparent illusion. "Will you not revive us again," he pleads, "that we may rejoice in you? Why do we, even as we arrive home, feel damned, rejected, isolated, cursed? When will you restore us?"

But wait a minute. This psalm is more than an exercise in despair, more than a lament arising from divine abandonment. The psalmist opens with testimony to a past deliverance. He offers thanksgiving for the intentions and activity of a divine savior, who brought the psalmist's slavery to an end. He praises a God who defeats the oppressing empire. The psalmist and his people, for all of their current troubles and frustration, for all of the wreckage surrounding them, remember one whose purpose operates to release them from bondage, directs them toward freedom, liberates them to return to their homes, and enables them to consider the possibility of restoring their fragmented people and ruined city.

And more! The psalmist not only evokes this memory of deliverance. He also includes a creative and empowering hope. The psalmist surveys the destruction about him, as he broods over the chaos and suffering afflicting his people, his city, and his nation. The memory of the God who initiated deliverance compels him to celebrate a God whose liberating promises will transform and ultimately overcome the current discouraging devastation that is tearing him apart. The psalmist envisions a community grounded, as one commentator suggests, in the very character of God. The psalmist's vision includes literal flesh and blood images of love and faithfulness meeting, righteousness and peace kissing. He depicts unblemished trust rising up from the earth to be greeted by the em-

brace and ebullient forgiveness and welcome of the God who wishes only our welfare and happiness. You see, amid these troubled and desolate circumstances the psalmist trusts in one who saved him once before from oppression and despair and whose very character promises to do the same again.

Friends, the psalmist's vision expresses the Advent promise. Amid everything else that is getting us down, eating us up, and stressing us out, hope against hope, as the psalmist asserts, is "at hand." And the question lurking in our hearts is simple: Can we believe it?

You could make your own catalog of threatening and troubled circumstances: family collapse, chronic illness, job catastrophe, financial wipeout, friends' betrayal, a loved one's protracted or sudden death—circumstances flying in the face of divine hope, which often seems like no more than wishful thinking.

II. Well, God bless the psalmist! For amid everything else, he remembers the goodness of God. Amid the tangle of life, he trusts the love of God. Amid everything denying it, he hopes in the future of God. The psalmist speaks uniquely to us who wait for that healing, reconciling, compassionate world he describes from the ruins of his own city, a world that we Christians on the one hand wait for and on the other hand confess to be borne among us by this man Jesus, compelling us to call him Christ. The psalmist's memory and hope is embodied in the person of Jesus.

Look at it this way. We do not worship this morning as the psalmist did, in a ruined and devastated city. But we do meet under the cross. The cross talks about devastating, catastrophic circumstances. Like the psalmist amid his ruined city, asking furious questions about the faithfulness of God, we might ask of the cross: If the forces of this world can mutilate and kill the likes of Jesus, then where is our hope? If goodness like that can be put on the gibbet by political and religious coalitions who think they do it for good, then where is our hope? You know where: because of our faith, hope is right there amid the ruined city, at the foot of the cross all the time. Hope emerges not necessarily in the devastating circumstances but through them. Hope does not necessarily change tragic circumstances, but it bears us through them. Hope may burst from a new vision of the future, radically changing our perception of the situation in which we find ourselves.

Like the psalmist's wasted city, the cross, if anything, can be understood as the final sign of cynicism and despair, the vivid signal that evil really does bear the last word, that goodness is up for grabs, that love is a fraud and hope a pathetic joke. The cross can be seen as the concentrated symbol of that abyss between our troubled everyday reality and our Advent hope.

But the cross is not the symbol of the abyss. It is anything but. We worship here this morning the very God who through the toughest, most unfair, troubled, and inhumane circumstances bears us hope. This empty cross represents a new reality, a new community, a new creation that we might describe as the psalmist does: as love and faithfulness meeting, grace and peace kissing each other, trust and forgiveness reaching toward one another from the ends of the universe—promises assured by a power that is able to take a bloody cross and turn it into the visible fact of love that will never let us go, and into a hope that will, in God's good time, recreate and transform us all. Hope, you see, from a ravaged city; hope through a ravaging cross. Hard to believe! Where hope is lost, hope is also at work. Where circumstances say no, the transforming power of God, even there, says yes to life and love.—James W. Crawford

Illustrations

MATURE HOPE.   To have mature hope is to rejoice in the whole drama of human history, including the terrible anxieties of a nuclear age.—Reinhold Niebuhr[226]

THE GLORY OF THE CROSS.   Man was so limited: he hadn't even the ingenuity to invent a new vice, the animals knew as much. It was for this world that Christ died: the more evil you saw and heard about you, the greater glory lay around the death: it was too easy to die for what was good or beautiful, for home or a civilization—it needed God to die for the half-hearted and the corrupt.—Graham Greene[227]

Illustrations

GOD'S RELATIONSHIP TO THE WORLD.   The nature of God is so august that we find when we emphasize one aspect of it we almost deny another. But it may help some to think of a man in relation to his own hand. (1) He is greater than it, transcendent above it, and would exist if he lost it. So is God in relation to his world. (2) A man uses his hand, works with it, expresses himself by it. So does God in relation to his world. (3) A man suffers if his hand is injured, feels by means of it, is sensitive to anything which wounds it. So is God in relation to his world of men and women.—Leslie D. Weatherhead[228]

FORGETTING.   In the life and letters of T. E. Brown, the poet in the Isle of Man, there occurs a notable instance of this. He is writing to a friend about the poems of his youth. One would think that a poem, the expression of a mood of passionate feeling, which had been dwelt upon with keen intellectual interest, whose words had been chosen and polished with care, would not be forgotten. Yet Brown writes: "They seem, many of them, to be strangers to me, in no way expressing a mood that is now even possible, and quite startling either in being foreign to my mind or inadequate to its conceptions." So also the man in us, sin-stained, sin-haunted, may cease to be. God restores the years that the locust has eaten. As we throw ourselves into Christ's service, and as His wisdom works into the veins of our thinking, and His life beats within our will, the past dies within us. It cannot be recalled even with an effort. It has been blotted out as completely from our minds as from the mind of God. There is a depth of forgetfulness out of which a forgiven and never-recalled sin cannot emerge.—W. M. Clow[229]

---

[226] *Justice and Mercy*

[227] *The Labyrinthine Ways*
[228] *This Is the Victory*
[229] *The Cross in Christian Experience*

SUNDAY: DECEMBER TWELFTH

LECTIONARY MESSAGE

Topic: A Prescription for Renewal
TEXT: Isa. 6:1–11
Other Readings: Ps. 126:1–16; 1 Thess. 5:16–24; John 1:6–8, 19–28

Renewal is on the minds of many in the Christian community these days. Many are praying for another "Great Awakening," in which multitudes of persons will make or renew their commitment to Jesus Christ. Others hope for a "national return to the Lord," in which the institutions of society will mirror Judeo-Christian values. Still others long for new starts in their churches, which will result in full church houses. Regardless of the desired outcome, few doubt that a fresh movement of God's Spirit would be a welcome experience.

During this season of the year, when we prepare to celebrate the advent of God's ultimate act of rebirth, the incarnation of the eternal Word, a look at God's pattern for renewal is in order. Although most commonly used to illustrate the call of God, today's Old Testament lesson furnishes an outline for experiencing renewal. Isaiah's call experience provides an answer to the question, What is the basis for genuine renewal?

I. *Renewal begins with a breathtaking encounter with God* (vv. 1–4). In a time of intense personal and societal crisis, Isaiah encountered the Lord in an unexpected way. Much has been made of the fact that Isaiah was in the Temple seeking direction and guidance from God. However, that is not at all clear from the context. What is clear is that wherever he was, God appeared to Isaiah as one who is holy and wholly other. The vision God presented to Isaiah conveyed in sight, sound, and symbol that he had encountered the "mysterium tremendum."[230]

In Isaiah's vision God was seated on a throne. In keeping with the Temple imagery of the passage, this could well be the Ark of the Covenant, whose lid was commonly understood to be the throne of God. The Ark was housed within the Holy of Holies, where none but the High Priest was allowed. Be-

cause it is unlikely that Isaiah was actually in the Holy of Holies, what he described is an encounter in which he was brought face-to-face with the living Lord, whose presence enveloped him and all the space around him. He witnessed an awesome sight: angels flying to and fro around the throne, attending to every need of God. As they did their work, they cried to one another, "Holy, holy, holy is the Lord of hosts; the whole earth is full of his glory." So powerful were their voices that everything around Isaiah trembled at their speaking. By their speaking they reminded Isaiah that not only was God holy in this place, and not only did God's presence envelop Isaiah, but God is holy in every place, and his presence fills every place on earth. For Isaiah, whose vision of God's presence may have been limited to the Temple in Jerusalem, this encounter was not only an eye-opener, it was also frightening. The core of Isaiah's beliefs and identity was shaken by this overpowering experience with the holiness of God. This encounter altered the path of Isaiah's life. The beginning of any life-changing renewal experience begins with being encountered by God.

II. *Renewal continues with the confession of sin* (v. 5). Being encountered by God usually results in the ability to assess the human situation with brutal honesty. Isaiah recognized that any pretense he held about his own integrity or the virtue of his community was clearly a sham. Not only had he seen the face of God, but he had done so with sin on his lips. The King James translation of this passage, "Woe is me for I am undone," captures Isaiah's dilemma most accurately. Before God, all his self-righteousness was stripped away. His only authentic choice was to confess his condition.

One writer has described confession as agreeing with God about who we are and where we are going. It is being willing to drop our claims to worthiness and to acknowledge the truth of God's perspective. Unless we are willing to agree with God about who we are, renewal will not happen.

III. *Beyond the confession of sin, renewal depends on our willingness to submit to the cleansing grace of God* (vv. 7–8). If we are unwilling to submit to the cleansing power of God's grace,

---

[230]See Rudolph Otto, *The Idea of the Holy*

then our confession amounts to little more than a child saying "I'm sorry" when caught with a hand in the cookie jar only to put a hand back in as soon as the parent's back is turned. Submitting to God's grace is not as easy as some preachers of cheap grace would make it sound, because God's grace not only forgives sin, it also releases its grip and purges it from our lives. This experience is both exhilarating and frightening, joyful and painful. No doubt Isaiah felt the searing of the live coal on his lips, but he also felt the cleansing release of this purifying act. Authentic renewal involves allowing God to free and purge us from sin.

IV. *The prescription for renewal is complete when we commit our lives to doing God's work no matter what the cost* (vv. 8–11). Immediately after the angel purified Isaiah's lips, he overheard God asking, "Whom shall I send, and who will go for us?" Without hesitation, Isaiah volunteers, and God sends him on "mission impossible." Isaiah does not back away once God explains the difficult details. Unless we are willing to commit our lives to the Lord without reservation, the process of renewal is short-circuited. God's renewing activity is always purposive.

During this Advent Season, as we struggle with keeping Christ in our preparations and celebrations of Christmas, hear the voice of God inviting you to an experience of renewal and rebirth. Know that the process is not always easy or painless. To find life we must face honestly the truth about who God is and how we look before him.

To satisfy the deepest longings of our heart we must submit our lives to God for cleansing and service. For self-sufficient, individualistic people such as ourselves this is not easy. But it is the only way to life.—Jim Holladay

Illustrations

ELECTION. The Jews were "chosen" not for special privileges but rather to bear special responsibilities. They did not have an easier time because they were God's chosen people. They had a tougher time. The pagans could in a sense be excused for their wrongdoing, but the Jews had no excuse—they knew better! So we must rule out any notion of "favoritism" in the sense that election made things easier for the elected.

Furthermore we must see the election of the Jews in terms of its ultimate purpose, which was that through them God's love and concern could be expressed to *all* people: "I will give you as a light to the nations, that my salvation may reach to the end of the earth" (Isa. 49:6). And it is a matter of sober fact that it *was* through the events of Jewish history that the nations did come to see God at work, and were prepared for his final manifestation in Jesus Christ.—Robert McAfee Brown [231]

EVANGELISM OF YOUTH. On the occasion when the late D. L. Moody was conducting meetings in England, he returned home one night to his friend's house, where he was staying. His friend said to him, "Well, how many were converted tonight in the meeting?" "Two and a half," replied Moody. "Why, what do you mean?" asked his friend. "Was it two adults and a child?" "No," replied the evangelist, "it was two children and an adult. The children have given their lives to Christ in their youth, while the adult has come with half of his life."—Benjamin P. Browne[232]

SERMON SUGGESTIONS

Topic: When God's Spirit Prevails
TEXT: Isa. 11:1–9
(1) It can come to expression in a human sovereign (vv. 1–3a). (2) It will be characterized by justice (vv. 3b–5). (3) Peace will be the product (vv. 6–9a). (4) Would this not be a fair picture of the triumphant reign of the Messiah (v. 9b)?

Topic: Something Important to Talk About
TEXT: Titus 2:11–15
(1) The appearing of the healing grace of God (v. 11). (2) The discipline that this event makes possible (v. 12). (3) The fulfillment of the hope this salvation promises (v. 13). (4) The Savior who gave himself to this glorious end (v. 14).

Hymn Suggestions

1. "O Come, O Come, Emmanuel," ninth-century Latin, tr. J. M. Neale (1851); VENI

[231] *The Bible Speaks to You*
[232] *Illustrations for Preaching*

EMMANUEL, plainsong, adapt. T. Helmore (1854)

This traditional ancient chant, indispensable for Advent worship, in its refrain echoes the Pauline exhortation in 1 Thessalonians 5:16: "Rejoice always!"

2. "What a Friend We Have in Jesus," Joseph Scriven (c. 1855); CONVERSE, Charles C. Converse (1868)

Exemplifying the exhortation of 1 Thessalonians 5:17 to "pray constantly," this familiar hymn can effectively be sung unaccompanied and antiphonally between two sections of the congregation.

3. "When God Delivered Israel," Michael A. Saward (1973); SHEAVES, Norman Warren (1973)

This modern free paraphrase of Psalm 126 can be quickly learned and sung as a response to the Psalter reading. It places appropriate emphasis on the spirit of joy and gladness that permeates the psalm.

4. "Live in Hope," Jane Parker Huber (1980); TRURO, Thomas Williams (1789)

This hymn, based on the first two verses of Isaiah 61, which Jesus read in the Nazareth synagogue (Luke 4:18–19) at the beginning of his ministry, was the first attempt made by the accomplished contemporary writer Jane Parker Huber. Set to the familiar TRURO tune, it beautifully expresses the principal theme of Isaiah's prophecy.—Hugh T. McElrath

Worship Aids

CALL TO WORSHIP. "The Lord hath done great things for us; whereof we are glad" (Ps. 126:3).

INVOCATION. Help us to see ever more clearly, O Lord, that the great things you have done for us equip us to do helpful things for others, for members of our own families, and for people wherever there is need. To that end bless this service of worship to instruct us, challenge us, and inspire us.

OFFERTORY SENTENCE. "And everyone who was willing and whose heart moved him came and brought an offering to the Lord" (Exod. 35:21 NIV).

OFFERTORY PRAYER. Lord, as we bring our offerings this day, help us to see as we

have never seen before the potential of a gift made in God's name and the value of a heart on fire for God.—E. Lee Phillips

PRAYER. Our Father, wilt thou bless the word of truth spoken, and grant that it may come home to the hearts of those that have heard it with efficacious power. We thank thee for the revelation of thyself, and for all thy helpfulness to us. We thank thee for the inspiration which we have had in times past; for the promises which stretch out over the future, multitudinous—endless.

Thou, O Lord Jesus! art the chief among ten thousand, altogether lovely. We follow thee. We adore thee. Thou art precious now, and shalt be yet more precious. And living or dying we are thine. Grant, we pray thee, that all may be participators in this thy treasure. May those whom we love, love thee. Bound together by these cords and ties, may we walk together along the same pilgrim road, that we may sit down together in the kingdom of our dear Lord. We ask it for Christ's sake.— Henry Ward Beecher[233]

Sermon: The First Disciple—And Us

TEXT: Luke 1—Annunciation with Reference to the Magnificat

We Protestant Christians over the years include in all of our lessons, in all of our models of the creche, certainly on our Christmas cards, and in our mental pictures of what transpired on that first Christmas Eve the presence of a vulnerable child and his mother cradling him in her arms. But in our piety, in our spiritual experience and exercises, in our commitments to mission and ministry, Mary plays a very small role, if any at all. Yet for tens of millions of Christians around the world Mary plays a central part in religious identity and devotion.

I. Indeed, what is it about Mary? Jaroslav Pelikan, a preeminent contemporary church historian at Yale, has assembled a remarkable book entitled *Mary Through the Centuries: Her Place in the History of Culture*. Pelikan catalogs sixteen perceptions of Mary and her spiritual impact over the years, from Miriam of the New Testament to the second Eve, from the

[233]*Plymouth Pulpit*

mother of God to the Woman Clothed with the Sun. This morning, however, I want to touch on that little response Mary offers to the angel who announces her pending pregnancy. At the close of the encounter, with all of its beauty and mystery, its imagery and affirmation of the breaking forth in human shape of the love of God, with all of Mary's surprise and awe, she responds to the encounter with these wondrous words: "Here am I, the servant of the Lord: let it be according to your Word."

Do you see what is happening here? Luke paints a rich and vivid picture that expresses his faith in the meaning of Jesus' life and ministry—all those references to David, to a virginal conception, to the Son of David—this is the poet's articulation of a truth that can come to us in no other way. Mary's reception of that truth, her acceptance of it, her response—"Here, then, am I, your servant; let it be done according to your Word"—this response marks her as the first one who hears the gospel, the first one who says yes to it, the first one who surrenders her life to serving it.

Oh, to be sure, the major affirmation in Luke's passage this morning centers on the bearer of salvation, that anticipated Christ child. But there, buried in the heart of Luke's testimony, is the teenage girl who hears the promise of the new world of grace and peace, that young woman who embraces it, that soul, open in mind and heart, who surrenders in service to it. For Luke, Mary is the first disciple.

II. And what does this first disciple's faith, hope, and service look like? What effect does the announcement of the Christ in her womb and the promise of a new age, a new era, a new world ruled by love grounded in the compassion and justice this Christ represents and manifests have? What kind of witness does this first disciple offer? At what point is her service engaged?

Do you remember the Magnificat? The great composers have set it to music. The sensitive poets have recast it. The preeminent artists have painted it. In our Western culture, the Magnificat comes to us as an aesthetic masterwork. We have seen and heard it so many times it lulls us to complacency. But be careful. The Magnificat packs a wallop. It is revolutionary. It is world-changing.

Mary sings of bringing down the powerful from their thrones. She envisions lifting up the lowly. She speaks of filling the hungry with good things and sending the rich away empty. Not your friendly little Christmas carol.

Oh, friends, this first disciple—this Mary—is hardly that benign, sentimental Madonna loved by the Renaissance painters, the Baroque composers, the producers of Christmas greeting cards. Not really. That first disciple and her chosen vocation turns out to be a willing receiver, a clear proclaimer, and a radiant servant of a world turned upside down.

III. And you? And I? And is this, our church? As the promised Christmas child approaches, can our own discipleship model itself on Mary's? Can we understand that Christmas begins with the promise of a new and different world—a new and different you and me—breaking in among us with this angelically announced child born of and bearing divine love? Can we, in faith and hope, surrender our lives, as Mary does, to Christ's spectacular promise?

Let me tell you of one who did. We are vividly reminded of her every Christmastime. We can see—and hear—the consequences of her life up and down our streets this very day. You may have encountered her legacy already this morning; you surely will as you leave: men and women, their bells tinkling; some in uniform; some dressed as Santa, some not; black, white, Asian—as diverse as the city itself. You guessed it: they are the soldiers of the Salvation Army. And they are children, if you will, of the Mother of the Salvation Army, Catherine Booth. Talk about disciples!

Catherine Mumford Booth began, with her husband, William, in London's East End in 1865, that army whose "purpose," she said, "was to carry salvation through the land and whose commander-in-chief was God." In Catherine Booth we find a woman born with curvature of the spine, in later years afflicted with tuberculine spots, suffering from angina pectoris, remembering scarcely a day in her life free from pain. Nothing could stop her! Catherine and William believed that in Christ there was neither male nor female, and as a suffragette she sought the political and economic equality of women. Her case: "Jesus Christ's principle was to put woman on the same platform as man, although I am sorry to say His apostles did not always act up to it." She designed the army uniform, including that inimitable Hallelujah Bonnet, devised, as she wrote, "to show everyone with whom I came in contact that I have renounced the pomp and vanities of the world and that I belonged to Christ." She dedicated her eight children to the cause of Christ, and they, engaged in works of compassion and justice, lived by her insistence that "we are made for larger ends than the earth can compass." Reflecting on the significant achievements of those eight children, she chose the words Luke put on Mary's lips, "My soul doth magnify the Lord for his grace and truth shown to my children. He hath given me the desire of my heart." Catherine Booth: she flexed the muscle behind one of the most committed and service-based movements inaugurated in Christ's name, with millions in uniform girdling the earth, speaking scores of languages. And as she celebrated the twenty-fifth anniversary of the founding of the Salvation Army, herself near death from cancer, speaking to fifty thousand people, she sounded the watchword of her life: "Love one another. Help your comrades in dark hours. I am dying under the army flag: it is yours to live and fight under. God is my salvation and refuge in the storm."

Oh, friends, ours is not necessarily to be a Catherine Booth in this world. But Christmas, beneath everything else, makes a claim on our loyal, grateful, and committed discipleship. "Here am I, the servant of the Lord: let it be with me according to your Word."—James W. Crawford

Illustrations

OUR SALVATION.   The individual within the society can do no great harm in these days of efficiently organized states, but we have controlled the individual only by creating a super-individual, the state, whose sover-

eign rights are regarded as paramount, and which is, so to speak, an individual without being a person. It has always been man's tragedy that he himself destroys the beauty and the goodness he creates. Now we have committed everything to a corporate Frankenstein that is without morals and religion, and knows no law except its own interest. This is as true of the democracies as it is true of the totalitarian states. All hopes now that man can work out his own salvation must of necessity end in disillusion and failure. If man is ever to be saved, he must be saved from himself and from the modern state-system into which he has surrendered his all. This is why it is not silly in these days to talk about salvation. Here is where Christianity comes in. It offers a solution to this problem which otherwise is incapable of solution.—Norman Snaith[234]

THE GOSPEL ACCORDING TO MARY.   "And Mary said. . . ." Are we listening? She is telling of a gospel that offers to all who are humble enough to receive it, and all who are obedient enough to act upon it, a Savior who will free us from the burden of our sins, inspire us by his Spirit, and give to us and our world the meaning and sense of purpose that we desperately need. It is a gospel offered to all—at ground level or at 30,000 feet—whatever our wealth, or status, or job. It is offered to those who know they need what God alone can supply. This blessed girl who brought our Lord into the world had no pretensions. Nor did she place her hopes in any human deliverer. It is the mighty and merciful God alone whom she celebrates. From beginning to end her song speaks of his revolutionary work in the fulfillment of the promise given "to our fathers, to Abraham, and to his seed for ever." If we can catch its confidence and respond to its challenge, then we too may be able to say with her: "He that is mighty hath done to me great things, and holy is his name."—David H. C. Read[235]

---

[234] *I Believe In . . .*
[235] James W. Cox (ed.), *The Twentieth Century Pulpit*

SUNDAY: DECEMBER NINETEENTH

LECTIONARY MESSAGE

Topic: Where Does God Live?
TEXT: 2 Sam. 7:1–11, 16; Rom. 16:25–27; Luke 1:47–55

Other Readings: Luke 1:26–38

On this fourth Sunday of Advent, we are within days of celebrating Christmas. By the time we gather on the next Lord's Day, we will be in the season of Christmas, that time of the Church year when we proclaim the fulfillment of Isaiah's prophecy, "Behold a virgin shall conceive and bear a son, and they shall name him Emmanuel, which means, 'God with us'" (Matt. 1:23). The Incarnation, the Word becoming flesh, is truly the miracle of Christmas, and the unique message of the Christian faith. Although the Christmas message breaks new ground in God's redemptive activity, it is solidly rooted in the rhythm of God's dealings with his people. The lectionary texts today speak to the continuity and discontinuity of God's self-revelation in Jesus Christ. In these texts we discover both affirmation and expansion of the assertion that "salvation comes through the presence of God."

I. *2 Samuel 7:1–11, 16.* David has completed the conquest of Palestine. The tribes of Israel have been consolidated into one united political kingdom. A time of intense military and political activity has come to an end. Like so many political leaders with nothing else to do, David turns his attention to religious matters. He decides that God needs a better place to live than a well-traveled, somewhat shabby tent. No doubt like any good politician, he reasons that a beautiful temple in the center of the capital city would not only be a boon to the cult of Yahweh, but it would also have the benefit of cementing the rather tenuous bonds of the newly formed state. When he shares his idea with Nathan, the chief spokesman for God, Nathan heartily endorses the plan.

But God has other ideas. He appears to Nathan in a dream and gives him a message for the king. The Lord reminds David that from the time of the Exodus until the present, he has been content with a mobile home. Its existence reminds the nation that salvation comes through the active presence of God in their midst. Its very mobility is a reminder that God is free to move at will among his people to accomplish his purposes. God does not need a "house made with hands" to establish his presence. In fact, God seems to suggest that such a dwelling might get in the way. His place is with his people. Salvation comes by God's hand as he works to deliver and procure his people. Where does God live? God does not live in any structure, temporary or permanent. God lives in the midst of his people.

As powerful an affirmation as that may be, it is a limited one. God was understood to live only among a certain group of people—the children of Israel. God's saving acts were designed to benefit only the children of Abraham. Where does God live? God lives in the midst of his people—a people originally defined by their embrace of the covenant but later by birth.

II. *Luke 1:26–38.* After the Babylonian conquest of Judah, the people of Israel lost a sense of God's presence in their midst. The people of God were convinced that God had withdrawn his presence. Messianic expectations began to grow as people longed for a day when God would once again live and move in their midst to deliver and procure his people.

Into this time of heightened expectation an angel appeared to Mary. He announced that God was about to execute an unheard-of plan. Through the Holy Spirit, she would give birth to the Son of God, whose name was to be Jeshua (Jesus). Within this annunciation, the angel disclosed that God was coming back to live among his people. The activity of the Holy Spirit in the birth of the child, and the child's name ("the salvation of God"), spoke to the saving presence of God. But the angel's message also contained a shocking revelation: God was not coming through a law or a cult; nor was God going to use a mere human agent like a king or a prophet. No! God was coming in the person of his Son. The promise was being fulfilled, but in a more dramatic way than anyone expected. God was coming to live among his people as the "Word made flesh," to deliver and procure his people.

III. *Romans 16:25–27.* At the end of his letter to the church in Rome, Paul pronounces an amazing benediction. Throughout this Epistle, he has struggled with God's promise to redeem his people, and with their rejection of God's presence in Jesus Christ. Over the course of the letter, he offers a remarkable insight. In Jesus Christ, God has extended salvation to "all the Gentiles." Not only is God's presence no longer confined to a particular cult, law, or building, but God's presence is also no longer confined to a particular people. For ages, the God of creation has been a mystery to people outside the covenant community of Israel. God now intends to dwell with all people, everywhere. In Jesus Christ, God has fixed the boundaries of the people of God to include all humanity. In Jesus Christ, God is coming to live among the Gentiles, to deliver and procure his people.

IV. The miracle of Christmas is not simply that God has come to live with his people, offering salvation by his presence. Throughout the history of Israel, God's presence has delivered the Jews from the hands of their enemies, secured their existence as his people, and led them in a new way of living. The true miracle of Christmas is that God has promised his saving presence to everyone. Without that miracle, you and I, as members of the Gentile race, would still be "strangers to the covenants of promise, having no hope and without God" (Eph. 2:12). "But thanks be to God, who gives us the victory through our Lord Jesus Christ" (1 Cor. 15:57), God has come to live with us to deliver us and procure us as his people.—Jim Holladay

Illustrations

AGAINST THE STREAM. In the so-called Western countries where Christianity takes a majority position, there is a temptation for men and women to become Christians too easily. When a baby is born, he receives baptism as if receiving a vaccination. In this technological age, automation is going on even in the process of becoming Christian. You accept the Christian religion because this nation traditionally was founded on Christian principles. You go to a church because others in the community go to that church.

But in Asia, the reasons are reversed. Christians attend church not because of the external social and cultural influences, but in spite of the oppositions, indifference, or even persecution of the society about them. Men and women commit themselves to accept the truth in love, revealed in the drama of redemption in Jesus Christ. Something happens within them.—Masao Takenaka[236]

THE LIGHT OF THE WORLD. Let me tell you about a very famous picture. It is inspired by those words I have just quoted: "I stand at the door and knock." Jesus stands outside a door, which is all overgrown with ivy and weeds, and there is no knocker or handle on the outside. He is waiting, having knocked, to enter. That picture is in St. Paul's Cathedral in London, and it is called "The Light of the World." No reproduction of it can ever do it justice. Now because it has been for many years in St. Paul's, right in the heart of London, at a juncture of many busy roads, it began to lose its color through the accumulation of dust. So the cathedral authorities decided to have it cleaned. It was sent to an art specialist who does that sort of thing. When the men who were assigned to do the job took the picture out of its frame, they saw words . . . that no man was ever intended to read. They were written by the artist and this is what he wrote: "Forgive me, Lord Jesus, that I kept you waiting so long." He had known about Jesus and his readiness to share life with him, but it was evidently a long, long time before he responded to the invitation of the Lord. But in the end he did, and by his picture he sent the message to unknown thousands who have gazed upon it.—George Beasley-Murray[237]

SERMON SUGGESTIONS

Topic: Great Things for Us
TEXT: Ps. 126

God acts for his people, and that means: (1) rejoicing in God's blessings, (2) confidence for the future, (3) willingness to face difficulty to allow the promised future to happen.

[236]Donavan E. Smucker (ed.), *Rockefeller Chapel Sermons*
[237]James W. Cox (ed.), *Best Sermons 4*

Topic: The Great Mystery of Our Religion
TEXT: 1 Tim. 3:16 NRSV

(1) Jesus Christ: (a) revealed in flesh, (b) proclaimed among Gentiles, (c) believed in throughout the world. (2) But this one so presented to us: (a) was vindicated in spirit by his Resurrection and Exaltation, (b) was seen by angels in the heavenly court, (c) was taken up in glory when he ascended to the Father.

Hymn Suggestions

1. "Come, Thou Long-Expected Jesus," Charles Wesley (1744); STUTTGART, Witt's Psalmodia Sacra (1715), HYFRYDOL, Rowland Hugh Prichard (1831)

This fine hymn on the coming of Christ makes an excellent congregational call to worship for any of the four Sundays in Advent.

2. "Tell Out, My Soul," Timothy Dudley-Smith (1961); WOODLANDS, Walter Greatorex (1916)

A contemporary version of the Song of Mary, this hymn would logically either precede or follow the reading from Luke 1:47–55—the Magnificat.

3. "To a Maid Engaged to Joseph," Gracia Grindal (1983); ANNUNCIATION, Rusty Edwards (1983)

In narrative fashion, this modern carol recounts the visit of the angel Gabriel to the Virgin Mary in such detail that it can easily replace the Gospel reading in Luke 1:26–38. The first two lines of each stanza may be sung in alternation by choir, congregation, and soloists, with everyone singing on the final stanza.

4. "The Angel Gabriel from Heaven Came," Luke 1:26–38, para. Sabine Baring-Gould (1891); GABRIEL'S MESSAGE, Basque carol

This is another musical narrative account of Gabriel's visit to Mary, with its appropriate refrain: "Most highly favored lady, Gloria!" Simple folk instruments, both melody and percussion, would enhance the medieval style of this carol from Southern Europe.— Hugh T. McElrath

Worship Aids

CALL TO WORSHIP.   "He that is mighty hath done to me great things, and holy is his name. And his mercy is on them that fear him from generation to generation" (Luke 1:49–50).

INVOCATION.   O Lord of bright light shining on humble shepherds, shine on us this day and lead us to the Christ child again, that we may behold the mystery and bow in wonder. Break in on every doubt with incarnational hope and bring every seeker to salvation through the Prince of Peace.—E. Lee Phillips

OFFERTORY SENTENCE.   "For ye know the grace of our Lord Jesus Christ, that, though he was rich, yet for your sakes he became poor, that ye through his poverty might be rich" (2 Cor. 8:9).

OFFERTORY PRAYER.   Lord, as the gift of life begins in small ways and can grow to mighty heights, bless this Christmas offering, small though it be, that it might do mighty deeds, proclaiming the Jesus of the manger, Son of the living God.—E. Lee Phillips

PRAYER.   We wait upon you, O God, as those who wait for the morning. We wait in faith, knowing that you are the God who comes. Your coming to this planet is such an advent that earth cannot contain the goodness of it—but the heavens break forth with music and singing, "Glory to God in the highest."

Something has happened that has never happened before, for almost every home has some symbol of your coming—a candle, a wreath, a tree, bright lights. We praise you for your coming: in the meaning that enlightens us, in the mystery that fascinates us, in the beauty that inspires us, in the love that grasps us and does not let us go.

We praise you for your coming just now in the Word, music, song, and fellowship of this time and place. Our hearts have been strangely warmed; our minds have been challenged to new heights and depths of the meaning of your coming; our imaginations have been dared to let go of "that is" to perceive the "not yet."

For your coming in the many blessings of this joyous season—the reunion of families, the joy of friendships, the blessedness of giving and receiving—we give you thanks.

May your coming this Christmas be heralded in and through us as we seek out the homeless, the powerless, the hopeless, to be loving and caring and giving according to their need. Grant us the commitment to live out what we know—that hospitality to the highest is to embrace the least of those among us.

We pray for the land of your appearing on that first Christmas: for the peace of Bethlehem, of Jerusalem, of Jericho, of Gaza. May the handshake to symbolize the turning of the tide from war to peace, from provocation to reconciliation, from fear to trust, be fulfilled in a just and enduring order for the Middle East, and that right soon.

We pray, too, for the peace of Somalia, Bosnia, Haiti.

To celebrate your coming on that first Christmas and to herald your coming in every Christmas is to live by the faith that there is a grace now present—in the Word becoming flesh and dwelling among us—that can reconcile all nations, peoples, and persons. May we faithfully pray and wisely work for that day when all creation will echo back the angels' song and, as the prophet declared, all peoples "shall go out in joy and be led forth in peace, and the mountains and the hills shall break forth into singing, and all the trees shall clap their hands."

Through him who is the "joy of man's desiring," we pray.—John Thompson

Sermon: A Savior for You!

TEXT: John 1:1–11

Nineteen centuries of Christian history have seen Jesus Christ, the Son of God, conquer the hearts of men and women. Nations have trembled at their foundations because of him. People have felt him touch and strangely influence their lives, whether they wished it or not. The centuries have not been able to lose sight of this Jesus Christ. Can we dismiss him now? Let me put to you three pertinent questions.

I. *Can you handle the past?*

a. No recording angel could be more accurate in cataloging the wrong things we have done than our own subconscious mind. The sordid thoughts we have fondled, the foul and harsh words we have spoken, the bad things we have done—all of these things, even though we charge them up to experience, have gone down into the storehouse of memory, and they are there. Psychological analysis may give us new labels for old sins, but we may know better than anyone else that this is not quite enough.

b. If our sins of thought and word and deed were only against our own self or even against a fellow human being, then we might forgive ourselves or make amends and get the forgiveness of our neighbor. But what if, in the last analysis, sin is against God? What if, when we sin against our wife or husband, children or friends, employer or society at large, we sin against God? The psalmist had wronged himself and other people, yet he declared in sorrow: "Against thee, thee only, have I sinned, and done this evil in thy sight" (Ps. 51:4). Sin is against God, for he is hurt when we hurt ourselves and when we hurt other people.

c. So I ask the question, can you handle the past—your past, with its sin, its guilt, its failure—without Jesus Christ, the Savior?

II. *Can you, on your own, overcome the sin in your heart?* I am not talking about sins, but about sin! It is clear that some habits can be broken with one's own strength. But sin itself—can we conquer that with our own strength? We cannot do that alone!

a. Nevertheless, we try. With spurts of determination to do better and with a flamethrower of indignation at the failings of others, we kid ourselves into believing that we are headed for sainthood. How easy it is to add up the faults of our neighbors and to consider our moral arithmetic some kind of redeeming virtue in ourselves! We can do that, and all the while within our own hearts may be the unresolved problem of sin, such as pride or selfishness, which in the end may be far worse than the sins of the flesh that are so easy to see in others and condemn.

b. Simon Peter does not impress me as being one who would ordinarily think he was better than others, yet he boasted that he would stick with Jesus even if everyone else denied him. In the time of testing, he failed. Paul the apostle confessed that his own struggle with sin was useless. The more he struggled with the sin in his heart, the more he got into it (Rom. 7:21 TEV).

c. New Year's Day is noted for the fine resolutions that we make; the days that follow are notorious for the resolutions that we break. It ought to be clear to every one of us, through personal experience as well as from observation, that in our own strength we cannot transform a heart of stone into a heart of flesh, that in our own strength we cannot shatter the shell of selfishness that in many ways separates us from even those closest to us, and from God himself.

III. *Can you be fully satisfied with an earthbound view of life?* This is a question to be answered early, because it will sometime be too late to return a misused life for a refund.

a. It is true that many people have gotten beyond the idea of just living for the day. They have hope; they live for tomorrow or for the next generation; they seek immortality in their children or in some of the noble institutions or worthy causes they have served. These sentiments are fine, but they do not go far enough. They never quite get out of this world. And then there are those who seem to be satisfied to eat, drink, and be merry in the cultural lag and call it heaven.

b. Is this world—this world that you can see and foresee—are these activities enough? Do you not hope for more beyond this life than the triumph of your influence or the proud remembrance of your name? Surely you want to get behind all that you can see and feel and know of this earth to the one who made it, and who made us for his purposes as well as for our enjoyment.

c. The fourth Gospel tells us of a fine, upstanding man of the first century whose name was Nicodemus. The community regarded him highly; he was a member of the powerful and prestigious Jewish court called the Sanhedrin. But Jesus confronted him with a startling truth: this world and its ways of thinking, even if the thinking is done by intelligent, respectable, religious people, is not good enough. What Jesus was saying to a splendid, pious Jew he is saying to you and to me: You will find out what life was meant to be only if your life has a new beginning—this time from above, from God, from beyond this earth!

d. Jesus Christ came into the world to give us a new birth, to put us in touch with God in such a way that life is made new on a different basis. Jesus Christ comes to us today. Not once did he even hint that the passing centuries would make him harder to know as Savior than when he lived in the flesh. There is a Savior for you! Receive him today and enter into all the riches of the blessings of God!—James W. Cox[238]

Illustrations

WHAT KIND OF GOD?   Even God, as some of us come to him, is no answer. It may be easier to believe that God is a consuming fire than that he is a forgiving Father. When I was in college, I read from *Life with Father* Clarence Day's comment on his mother's faith, and I have not forgotten it. "She loved God," he said, "as much as she dared to." We may see God only as an avenging judge, eager to exact a penalty for every violation of his law.—James W. Cox[239]

SPLINTERS AND LOGS.   Carl Jung, the renowned Swiss psychologist, noted with keen perception, "When we dare not acknowledge some great sin, we deplore some small sin with greater emphasis." This applies to the small sins of others as well as to our own.—James W. Cox

SUNDAY: DECEMBER TWENTY-SIXTH

LECTIONARY MESSAGE

Topic: Are You Coming Home for Christmas?
TEXT: Gal. 4:4–7
Other Readings: Ps. 148:1–14; Isa. 61:10–62:3; Luke 2:22–40

One of the most often repeated phrases around this time of the year is, "Christmas is for children." A close runner-up is, "Christmastime is family time." To some extent, the apostle Paul would agree with the sentiments expressed in those clichés. Today's Epistle lesson is filled with references to family and children in order to speak of God's redemptive activity in Jesus Christ.

I. *"God sent his Son, born of a woman."* A re-

---

[238] *Surprised by God,* p. 12.
[239] *Surprised by God,* p. 13.

markable facet of God's redemptive story is borne by the Christmas story. Rather than a prophet, king, philosopher, military leader, or other prominent personage, God chose the image of a son to carry the weight of his self-revelation. It was in the person of his offspring that God chose to redeem the world. By adding the classic Christian affirmation that Jesus was Mary's child, born under the law, Paul affirms that Jesus was not a divine being, dropped from heaven into human history. He was born into and was nurtured in a human family. His story and ours travel similar paths.

One can almost hear echoes of Luke's birth narrative: "While they were there, the time came for her to deliver her child. And she gave birth to her firstborn son and wrapped him in bands of cloth, and laid him in a manger" (Luke 2:6–7). Or perhaps, the testimony of the writer of Hebrews comes to mind: "We have a great high priest who has passed through the heavens, Jesus the Son of God. . . . For we do not have a high priest who is unable to sympathize with our weakness, but we have one who in every respect has been tested as we are, yet without sin" (Heb. 4:14–15).

Christmas is indeed family time, because God has lashed his eternal Son to the human family in order to accomplish his redemptive plan.

II. *"So that we might receive adoption as children."* At this point in the passage, Paul builds an extraordinary argument. God's purpose in Christ is "to redeem, to liberate those who are under the law." All of us are being crushed by the demands of the law. That is, God's holiness requires more of us than we are able to fulfill with our own strength and by our own wisdom. On our own, we are condemned. Only God can save us.

And the way God chooses to deliver us from our predicament is not through another religious system or cult, nor through another set of moral guidelines. Rather, he chooses to reestablish that which is broken—the relationship destroyed by sin. Of all the possible relational patterns God could have chosen, he decided on the intimacy of the parent-child relationship. No cold transaction here. We are to be brought into the family. Christmas is indeed family time. We will be invited to the family table to be fed and nourished, to have a place called home from

which we can face the uncertainties of everyday life.

III. "God has sent the Spirit of his Son into our hearts, crying, 'Abba! Father!'" Just when we think that Paul's description of God's redemptive activity on our behalf could go no further, Paul pushes the imagery even further. Just in case we have no idea how to act as children of God, as members of God's family—and this is not an uncommon experience for adopted children—the Spirit of God's true and only begotten Son is sent to take up residence at the core of our personhood. From that driving center of our being he models true sonship. No, he does more than that; he lives for us and in us the life of a child of God. Christmas is indeed family time. Not only are we adopted into God's family, but we are also conformed to the role of child of God by the Spirit of the eternal Son who comes to live in us.

IV. *"So you are no longer a slave but a child, . . . an heir."* The consequence of God's adopting us into his family is that we are set free and given a secure future. Paul turns to an unexpected mental picture. In God's scheme of things we have moved from the status of slaves to positions around the table as family. We are granted freedom by being made children and given access to all the resources the family owns.

Slaves have always had the option of being freed. Sometimes the master, in an unusual act of gratitude or generosity, may decide to release a slave from his obligation. At other times another person may pay the price to emancipate the slave. On other occasions the slave may gain freedom by escape or by purchasing his own freedom. In all these scenarios, the slave is only a freedman who must now make his own way in the world. In those cases in which the slave has gained freedom on his own, he must continue to defend and guard that newfound status lest someone take it from him.

In contrast, Paul describes the indescribable. The one who used to work in the master's house taking care of the master's things is now one of the master's children and an heir to all the master's holdings. The one who used to wait on the master's table and observe the family celebrations from the outside now eats at the family table and joins the family celebrations as a full participant.

V. *Before the advent of Jesus Christ, Jew and Gentile alike toiled under the heavy burden of the law.* Being created in God's image, made for communion with God, we nonetheless find ourselves separated from God. We are cut off from the very relationship that gives life. Because of this separation, a large hole exists in our souls—a hunger that we struggle to satisfy. Our dilemma is that we find ourselves with some idea of what God wants, but totally unable to do what it takes to reestablish the relationship in order to fill the hunger.

But thanks be to God, Christmas is family time, because "when the fullness of time had come, God sent his Son, . . . in order to redeem those who are under the law, so that we might receive adoption as children . . . no longer a slave, but a child, . . . and . . . also an heir." Come and celebrate Christmas with the family of God.—Jim Holladay

Illustrations

THE FAMILY.   God is the author of the family, as he is the author of society; but in the Christian family, he is the prototype of the master, the father and the husband, while the servant, the son, and the wife find their symbol and model in the Church. Christianity does not break marriages; it consolidates them by sanctifying them. It does not loosen the natural ties between fathers and children; it sanctions and strengthens them. It respects the legitimate relations between masters and slaves, but it supernaturalizes them. The great principle inculcated in his converts by St. Paul is to change nothing in the external conditions of their life, provided that these [conditions] agree with the precepts of the Gospel. To put off vice and to put on Christ, but to remain in the post assigned to them by Providence, such is his word of command and countersign.

This recommendation referred above all to slaves, who pressed forward in crowds to the Church's open arms. You need not be troubled any more about your condition, the apostle said to them. In Christ you are all brethren and the equals of free men; serve them for the love of Jesus Christ, but without enslaving yourself to them morally.—Fernand Prat, S.J.[240]

BECOME LIKE CHILDREN.   And Jesus tells us again, "Become like children." Yet we know that this is impossible. In the very effort of trying to become like children, if the effort can so much as be imagined, we put our goal still farther out of reach. But it is precisely here, perhaps, that we come as near to the heart of the mystery as we are able. It is just when we realize that it is impossible by any effort of our own to make ourselves children and thus to enter the Kingdom of Heaven that we become children. We are children, perhaps, at the very moment when we know that it is as children that God loves us—not because we have deserved his love and not in spite of our undeserving; not because we try and not because we recognize the futility of our trying; but simply because he has chosen to love us.—Frederick Buechner[241]

SERMON SUGGESTIONS

Topic: The Secret of Strength
    TEXT: Zech. 12:8
    The text in the fullness of its meaning is a prediction of the greatness of the Sons of God in the then Kingdom of the future (Pss. 18:36, 8:5). (1) A spiritual faith is preeminently calculated to fashion great character. (2) The age in which we live is one in which we may expect eminent character. (a) In Christ we have the most exalted conception of God. (b) In Christ we have the noblest ideal of humanity. (c) In the gift of the Spirit we have the largest measure of moral force.—W. L. Watkinson[242]

Topic: The Untidiness of the Kingdom
    TEXT: 1 Cor. 4:1–13; Matt. 13:24–43
    The untidiness of the Kingdom comes as a grace to us. (1) That the Kingdom is untidy frees us from an awful compulsion to neatness and orderliness. (2) That the Kingdom is untidy frees us from having to maintain our purity by isolating ourselves from "the corrupt." (3) That the Kingdom is untidy saves us from having to make the judgments that are beyond our competence. (4) That the Kingdom is untidy lets us know that

[240] *The Theology of St. Paul*, Vol. 2

[241] *The Magnificant Defeat*
[242] *The Blind Spot*

the Kingdom somehow is for us.—Harry B. Adams[243]

Hymn Suggestions

1. "Joy to the World," Isaac Watts (1719); ANTIOCH, Lowell Mason (1848)

This premier Christmas hymn is ideal for the beginning of worship during Christmastide. Based on Psalm 98, it is a Christianization of the Hebrew psalmist's invitation to joyful praise of the Lord who comes to rule the earth.

2. "Praise the Lord, Ye (O) Heavens Adore Him," Foundling Hospital, stanza 3, Edward Osler (1836) Collection (1796); HYFRYDOL, Rowland H. Prichard (1831), AUSTRIA, Franz J. Haydn (1797)

This free paraphrase of Psalm 148 could be sung in response to its reading.

3. "Now May Your Servant, Lord," Luke 2:29–32; vers. Dewey Westra (1931); NUNC DIMITTIS, L. Bourgeois (1551)

This simple setting of the canticle of the priest Simeon fits its tune found in the Genevan Psalter. In the Gospel reading, when verse 29 is reached, this song could be sung by all. Then, at verse 33, the reading could continue to the end of the lesson.

4. "Good Christian Men (Friends), Rejoice," fourteenth-century Latin carol, tr. J. M. Neale (1855); IN DULCI JUBILO, German trad. carol (fourteenth century)

This true carol that comes from the folk of medieval Germany captures the unbridled joy as well as the profound truths attending Christ's birth. Simple accompanying instruments such as finger cymbals, triangle, and recorder (or flute) would reinforce its folklike character.—Hugh T. McElrath

Worship Aids

CALL TO WORSHIP. "Young men and women alike, old and young together! Let them praise the name of the Lord, for his name alone is exalted; his glory is above earth and heaven" (Ps. 148:12–13 NRSV).

INVOCATION. Only in you, Father, do we find that light and wisdom fully dwells. This morning, by the presence and power of your Holy Spirit, illumine our minds with the true understanding of your Word. Give us the grace to receive that truth with reverence and humility. May your truth lead us to put our complete trust in you and you alone. May our trust bring us to serve you, give you the honor that is yours, and in all our efforts glorify your name as we become good and honorable witnesses to our neighbors.—Henry Fields

OFFERTORY SENTENCE. "Jesus looked around and saw rich men dropping their gifts in the temple treasury, and he also saw a very poor widow dropping in two little copper coins. He said, 'I tell you that this poor widow put in more than all the others. For the others offered their gifts from what they had to spare of their riches; but she, poor as she is, gave all she had to live on'" (Luke 21:1–4 TEV).

OFFERTORY PRAYER. Help us this morning, Father, to envision our tithes and offerings feeding the hungry, speaking salvation to the lost, comforting the sorrowing, instructing the learner, housing the homeless, visiting the sick, and doing the work of Jesus across the world. May such a vision bring us to be more than generous as we give now in Jesus name.—Henry Fields

PRAYER. Lord of all being, whose throne is in the heavens yet who by our response in faith can make our hearts a house of prayer, may our constant devotion lead us into the deeper discoveries of faith. Support us in our leap of faith, and may its risk turn into certainty as we learn the meaning of the gospel, the joy and finality of its truth, and the victory of its cross in unveiling your purpose for all creation. Restore us this day in soul and spirit, and save us from allowing our faith to burn low. May the wonders and glories of the Christian faith in every age inspire our zeal to work and win and sacrifice for you, and in doing your holy will may we see your new name written forever upon our hearts. Abide with us always, dear God, in faith, and in your Kingdom may every child of earth find an appointed place. Through the same Jesus

---

[243]James W. Cox (ed.), *Best Sermons 5*

Christ our Lord, we kneel and ask these things.—Donald Macleod[244]

Sermon: Facing Fear of the Future

TEXT: Jer. 29:1–7, 11–13

You and I are afraid. Like the exiles so long ago, we are afraid of what the future will bring us. You and I fear what will happen that's beyond our control. Perhaps even more we fear how we will respond to the challenges ahead. Fear is more a part of our lives than most of us would like to admit. It's hard to be thankful for your past when you're spending so much energy being afraid of your future.

The first way to deal with our fears is to name them. The exiles in Babylon knew exactly what they were afraid of. They were afraid that their future as a people was gone. As professor Andrew Lester writes, they had lost their future story. They had been ripped from their homes and families and were in the grip of a hostile power, feeling helpless, not knowing what the enemy would do to them next.

Very often, of course, you and I just don't want to talk about our fears. We think if we don't talk about them, if we ignore them long enough, they will somehow go away. It is true that something like 90 percent of the things you and I are afraid of never happen. But ignoring our fears is not the way to deal with them. The remarkable thing about Jeremiah's letter is that through Jeremiah the Lord spoke directly to the exiles, his diagnosis going straight to the heart of the problem.

I. *So, the first thing some of us need to do this morning is admit that it is the future we're afraid of.* Some of us are afraid for the future of our church; you just know we'll never raise the extra dollars we need for the next four years. Some of us are afraid of growing old or ill. Some fear being alone. Some of us are afraid for our jobs. Some of us are afraid of being poor. And Jeremiah says, when you are afraid of the future, first know what it is you're afraid of, then. . . ?

II. *Do the next thing.* "Build houses and live in them. Plant gardens and eat what they produce." Work on your relationships where you are. The exile's world was shattered, re-

member. As far as any of them could tell, their future was gone. And Jeremiah knew that the real danger was that they would sit down there in the desert and give up, either die or focus on the past or assimilate with the Babylonians and lose their identity as a people; that they would let the loss of their future story destroy them. So he brought them back to what they could do right now.

The trouble with many of us, you see, is that we get so bogged down worrying about some possible problem out there in the distance that we forget to pay attention to what's next.

The way not to be afraid of the future is to concentrate on what you can do in the present. The best recommendation anybody ever gave a terrified student at the beginning of a semester was to do the first assignment first and then do the second and then the third. Start at the beginning and work your way through until you get to the end.

III. *Third, "seek the welfare of the city where I have sent you."* Think with me for a moment what this Word from the Lord must have meant to the exiles. Here they were, in a foreign capital, hundreds of miles from home, brought here by force, angry, bitter, surrounded by their enemies. Psalm 137 gives us the mood of the captives when Jeremiah wrote. It says, "By the rivers of Babylon we sat down and wept when we remembered Zion," and it ends, "O Babylon, happy shall they be who pay you back what you have done to us. Happy shall they be who take your little ones and dash them against the rock." Anger at what you've lost is a natural part of the grief process. These were not happy Thanksgiving pilgrims in the school play in Babylon, my friends. The last thing in the world they wanted to do was start a newcomer's Babylon booster club.

You and I may not control every aspect of our future, you see, any more than we can control every aspect of our present; but there is one thing you and I can control. We can control our attitude toward our present. We can do more than that: we can build our future one positive act at a time in our present.

IV. *Fourth, seek the Lord of tomorrow.* "For I know the plans I have for you, says the Lord: plans for welfare and not for harm, to give you a future with hope." You can't read the history of Israel without learning that their crises came because again and again they turned away from the Lord and tried to build their future without him. And the result of their failures was always the same. Again and again they ended up in exile of their own making. Sometimes you and I end up in exile of our own making, you see.

It's simply the exile you and I choose whenever we go our own way, whenever we look to our own solutions. That's why it's so hard for some of us to be thankful to God this week. We haven't really given God much chance this year. The truth, you see, is that any future but God's future is exile. If you're here today and you're afraid for your future, my friend, whatever you think that future might be, then hear with me the good news.

It is the answer to my fear of the future and yours, my friend. The answer is that God holds the future. God offers you and me the future he has for us. God will give us a future with hope, if you and I will turn to Christ. The promise of Jesus Christ is that from the moment you and I give God our lives, God will take care of us. If we follow Christ wherever he leads, the Spirit will see that no harm comes to us. Even if you feel yourself in exile this morning, even if you got there on your own, even if you cannot begin to see your way ahead, if you will just follow Jesus he will lead you around the next turn and the next until almost before you know it you will find yourself home again. "For I have plans for you," writes the Lord, "plans for your welfare and not for harm, to give you a future with hope." Well, what about it this weekend? Would you like something to be truly thankful for next year? Will you take the future Christ offers? Will you follow Jesus home today?—Ronald D. Sisk

Illustrations

FAITHING.   Jesus said that if one has the faith of a mustard seed, one can move a mountain. What is the faith of a mustard seed? A mustard seed is a very small seed, but when it's planted it grows into a great tree, producing millions of mustard seeds.

The mustard seed doesn't have to *think,* "Oh, I'm really a tree and I know I can be one." The mustard seed has the faith of *action.* Contained within it is all that is necessary to grow a tree. Once planted—if properly nurtured—it will just do it.—John Rogers and Peter McWilliams[245]

POTENTIAL.   Before his death Rabbi Zusya wept as he said: "In the coming world God will not ask me: 'Why were you not as Moses?' because I am not Moses. God will not ask me: 'Why were you not as Isaiah?' because I am not Isaiah." "Why then do you weep?" queried his disciples. Rabbi Zusya sighed as he answered: "It is because God will ask me: 'Why were you not Zusya?' Have I lived up to the best that is in me? What shall I answer?"—William B. Silverman[246]

[245] *You Can't Afford the Luxury of a Negative Thought*
[246] *Rabbinic Stories for Christian Ministers and Teachers*

SECTION III.
Messages for Communion Services

SERMON SUGGESTIONS

Topic: True Vine

TEXT: John 15:1–8

Here is Jesus at the Passover meal with his disciples, talking with them about his life and ministry, his mission and his purpose, and one of the ways he expresses these ideas is to tell his disciples, "I am the true vine, and my Father is the vinedresser." Jesus is not trying to get poetic or creative. He is not grasping for new images. He is trying to build upon what his disciples know to explain to them who and what he is.

The vine has been used often and consistently as a symbol of God's relationship with Israel. "Thou didst bring a vine out of Egypt, thou didst drive out the other nations and plant it. Thou didst clear the ground for it; it took deep root and filled the land." God was the vinedresser even then. The prophet Isaiah writes the lament of the vinedresser: "He digged it and cleared it of stones, and planted it with choice vines; he built a watchtower in the midst of it, and hewed out a wine vat; and he looked for it to yield grapes, but it yielded wild grapes. What else can the vinedresser do? I will make it a waste and trample it under foot." The vines that do not produce fruit will be used for wood for a fire. God is the vinedresser, the people of God are the vine that is cared for and loved.

Jesus has built upon this image of the vineyard and God's care in the many parables and stories he has told. The story of the day laborers who are hired at various times throughout the day is a story of God the vinedresser's generosity and faithfulness. The religious authorities are stung by the stories Jesus tells about the wicked tenants who will not give to the servants of the vinedresser the rent in kind, who will not yield the share of the harvest, who kill the son when he comes to collect the vineyard owner's share.

Jesus takes this image of the vine—which has stood throughout tradition for the people of God, for God's chosen ones, for Israel, for the community—and applies it to himself. Jesus is saying that he is the reality of that divine-human relationship that is the true life and witness of the people of God. All hopes and visions and dreams of what the vine of God's choice should do are fulfilled in Jesus' life and in what he is doing. Israel has been a barren, wild vine. It has not been productive, it has not brought forth fruit. The witness of the people of God should have been a light on a hill to the Gentiles, but the people of God have been selfish and elitist and have hoarded the spiritual gifts and produced no fruit. Jesus says, "I am the true vine." He says that what he is doing and how he is living is how the people of God are called to live, witness, evangelize, and bear fruit.

"I am the true vine." Jesus says that this is God's intended relationship between humanity and his love.

It is not just something that Jesus has because of who he is, for he immediately suggests to his disciples that they are his branches. They are part of the vine as they abide in him, as he abides in them, and as they bear fruit. The image of the branches and the vine has the same kind of power and purpose as St. Paul's image of Christ as the head of the body and each of us as part of the body, and important, but each needing to be obedient to the head, the mind and will, of Christ. The community of disciples, the Church of Jesus Christ, is always marked and judged by these twin dimensions of our intimacy and relationship with Jesus Christ as his people and the production of fruits.

Those are the two dynamic pulses of this passage: abide in me as I abide in you, and bear fruit. "I am the vine, you are the branches; he who abides in me, and I in him, he it is that bears much fruit. . . . If you abide in me, and my words abide in you, ask whatever you will, and it shall be done for you. By this my Father is glorified, that you bear much fruit."

When we abide in Christ and Christ abides in us, his life and love move through us and we seek and pray for what Christ seeks and prays for, we live and love as Jesus lived and loved, and our approach to the darkness and evil is not to flee from it but to live in it and redeem it by God's gracious love.

The more we abide in Christ and Christ abides in us, the more fruit we bear. The more faithful we are to Christ, the more impact we have within our community. This is not a demand that we do more and work harder; it is simply that in such faithful obedience we will be *able* to do more. God the vinedresser will be the one who prunes and cares for us, and thus we will be prepared and equipped to be more and more productive. That is the promise throughout the Gospel. The faithful stewards were praised for their faithfulness over little, then told that their master would now make them responsible for more. If we bear good fruits, God will prune us so that we might bear even more fruit.

Jesus said, "I am the true vine. And my Father is the vinedresser." Jesus doesn't say these things to make it tough on us or to put some burden on our shoulders. He goes on to say, "These things I have spoken to you that my joy may be in you and that your joy may be full."—Rick Brand

Topic: The Power of Blessing

TEXT: Gen. 32:24–28, 33:4–11

Ethicist James Gustafson declares that gratitude "is at the heart of religious morality in the Western world. . . . God has been good to human persons and communities; in thank-

fulness to him we have reason enough to seek the well-being of others, to honor their rights, to fulfill our natural duties and obligations to them. In thankfulness we are moved to do so."[1] Historically, the Judeo-Christian thanksgiving is much older and deeper than our national civil observance. Christian gratitude is centered in the Eucharist—the prayer of blessing at the Lord's Supper—"When he had given thanks. . . ." The Jewish tradition of gratitude proceeds from the covenant blessing of Israel developed through the Patriarchs.

Of all the stories of the Patriarchs, the story of Jacob seems to fit best with contemporary literature and drama in the struggle to be brutally realistic. The character of Jacob might well have been created by Hemingway, Faulkner, or perhaps Mickey Spillane. If I were giving it a movie rating, I would have to suggest a PG. It may be suitable for young audiences, but parental guidance is needed. When you read the text with your children, be certain to note that Jacob is not the best model for brotherly love. Perhaps the story of Jacob should be viewed as interesting reading but a poor ethical model. Maybe the only redeeming quality in Jacob is as an example to avoid. Daniel Defoe justified writing the obscene story of *Moll Flanders* by saying he wrote it so "that others might avoid the error of her ways."[2] So, Jacob is an example of a bad example. Jacob/Israel gave his name to a nation. Nationalism is one explanation for his shenanigans. As Jacob was superior to his brother Esau, the nation Israel is superior to Esau's descendants the Edomites. This story may also be a prime example of biblical realism—telling the truth. I have always been impressed with the way the Old Testament portrays its heroes warts and all. They are usually dressed in the shabby apparel of real life, including all of the tears and patches we find in ourselves.

I. *We dare not underestimate the power of cursing.* Jacob's story is about his name—trickster, supplanter, con artist, crook. His name was like a curse; one tends to live up to or down to what people expect. Jacob was the victim of parental favoritism and the system of pri-

---

[1] James Gustafson
[2] Daniel Defoe

mogeniture that preferred the elder brother on the basis of age, without any consideration of ability, personal achievement, or justice. The word to Rebekah during her pregnancy was *ultimogeniture:* "Two nations are in your womb, and two people born of you shall be divided; the one shall be stronger than the other, the elder shall serve the younger." A family pattern is developing. Isaac had received the blessing which by age should have gone to Ishmael, and Jacob's son Joseph would be a younger son preferred over his elder brothers. From the beginning, family problems were brewing: "Isaac loved Esau, but Rebekah loved Jacob." There is no place in the home for parental preference and favoritism, but this seemed to be common to the age. Like Avis, Jacob was second best; he had to try harder. Unfortunately, "trying harder" meant for Jacob that "people are for profit." He would have made a good companion to Ivan Boeske on Wall Street. Some folks are looking for Jacob to coach the football team of their alma mater. He was willing to do anything to win. The Robin Hood type always has an appeal, even if he is a bit unscrupulous. To see Uncle Laban get the tables turned is poetic justice—even if it is not ethical justice.

II. *Blessing is worth the quest.* Let's give a half-cheer for Jacob for his sense of value. In contrast with Esau, Jacob prized the blessing of God through his father and valued the birthright more than his own physical appetites. We are prone to undervalue the meaning of words passed from one generation to another. Either we are more sophisticated in our word-weary world, or we share Esau's crass materialism. Henri Nouwen tells of driving down a Los Angeles freeway feeling like he was on the inside of a dictionary.[3] We live in a society in which words are cheapened by their abundance. What's a father's blessing? Jacob came out of a religious culture that valued blessings and found power in the words of which they were composed. God spoke the world into being. John reflected on the power of the Word in creation when he wrote, "The word became flesh and dwelt among us." Esau's vision was always limited to an immediate crisis. He was too shortsighted and materialistic to appreciate the power of blessing. He sold out too cheaply—something that Jacob would never have done.

Yet we have to wonder if Jacob's insatiable appetite for blessing was terribly misdirected. Can a blessing ever be stolen? Do we receive the blessing of God by forcing the hand of God or by deceiving the mind of our father? Is not the blessing of God somewhat related to the means by which it is attained?

III. *Blessing is completed in giving.* Jacob's story is about learning to bless. Encounters with God are notably lacking in Jacob's biography. When they occurred, Jacob was in true form, seeking his own profit, looking out for number one. But something happened at the Jabbok River. This was prelude to meeting Esau. Jacob rightly feared for his life, and perhaps the fear had driven the Patriarch to seek God in ways that had never before occurred to him. A conversion seemed to take place. For the first time in his life, Jacob learned the power of blessing beyond his own self-serving hunger for position and possession. The tears and gifts that he presented to his brother may well have been an extension of a life of deception, but I choose to believe that Jacob had learned the most important value of blessing: that the power of blessing is in giving.

A significant dimension of the covenant blessing that God had bestowed on Abraham and Isaac went far beyond Jacob's self-service. God not only blessed the Patriarchs, he also blessed the world through them and their children. The blessing of God must always be fulfilled in giving rather than merely in receiving. Jesus is quoted in Acts: "It is more blessed to give than to receive."

Have you learned to appreciate the power of blessing? The ancient world placed more stock in the potency of words than we do, yet real change does take place in people when they are blessed or cursed. Gratitude and praise go a long way toward healing broken covenants and dysfunctional families. I wonder how Jacob would have lived had his name been Israel from the beginning? Accusation and curses are powerful tools for the total destruction of children. Children who are called stupid or mean have a tendency to think that they are.

Of all the people in history who deserve to be blessed by God, Jacob is the least deserv-

[3] Henri Nouwen

ing, but that is the way of God. Blessing is not a favor that is earned. It is sheer grace. The basis is *hesid* or *charis*—the steadfast love, the unmerited favor of God. Blessing is never a birthright; it is a gift. It is the dynamic for the redemption of lost souls, regardless of the source of condemnation—whether by social status, family dysfunction, self-image, or sinful deeds and thoughts.—Larry Dipboye

Topic: When God Gets Angry
TEXT: Jer. 2:4–13; Heb. 10:11–18
What do we do about the anger of God? It's probably the biggest stumbling block to understanding the Old Testament. We resonate with God's compassion, which we see in Christ. That is very appealing to us, and explains why most of us gravitate toward the New Testament instead of the Old Testament.

But what about God's anger that we see so vividly in books like Jeremiah, in passages like the one we read today?

We try to be selective in our reading of the Scriptures and avoid the passages that speak of the wrath of God, assuming that God doesn't get angry anymore. For almost two thousand years Christians have been trying to explain away the anger of God. The earliest heresy in the Christian church, in the year 140 A.D., was the teaching by a man named Marcion that the God of the Old Testament is different from the God of the New.

You can sympathize with Marcion and his followers, many of whom are still around today, although they may not have ever heard his name.

God's anger is such a problem for us because the anger we see most often is associated with malice.

But there's another side to anger. Have you ever noticed that the people with whom you get the angriest are often those you love the most? Anger can be a sign that a relationship is alive. I know plenty of couples who have had the divorce papers signed for years, but emotionally they're still connected by the anger they have for each other.

Anger in and of itself isn't necessarily a bad thing. What's bad is what we do with our anger. Anger can be helpful if it makes you notice something that isn't right, if it motivates you to take steps to correct a relationship that has gotten off kilter. There are times when anger is the most appropriate response to a situation, when not being angry is a sign of a hardness of heart that's almost inhuman. Sometimes anger can motivate people to make the world a better place. Several years ago a group of mothers was furious at how many kids were being killed by drunk drivers. Their anger is what led them to begin Mothers Against Drunk Driving (MADD).

It's important to understand that the anger of God we read about in the Old Testament is a sign of God's deep love for his people. In the Old Testament, God used his anger as a way to bring his people back to him. And it's important to understand that the Bible is very clear that God's anger is always a passing thing, like a summer afternoon thunderstorm. The psalmist says that God's anger does not last forever, but his mercy is everlasting.

It may be that God still uses wars and famines and natural disasters as ways to express his anger, but we're left with the problem of how to explain the suffering that innocent people have to endure. What happened to Jesus on the cross and what happened to those early Christians in the Roman coliseum is proof that sometimes suffering comes to those who deserve it least. But that doesn't mean that God is any less involved with us than he was with the people in the Old Testament. Sometimes people went through the motions of trying to appease God without really being sorry for what they'd done or really wanting to change. And the price of a bull or a goat offered on the altar was not nearly great enough to be an adequate offering to God, who made the whole creation and demanded total commitment.

So God, in an amazing act of love, sent his son Jesus to come between his anger and his people. Jesus died on the cross to pay the penalty of whatever any of us ever did to anger God. For those who believe in Jesus, who accept him as Lord and Savior, Jesus takes away whatever judgment God has and changes us from the inside out so that we are acceptable before God.

We still have to live with the consequences of our actions. Christians still do things that are wrong, and God can use those things we do to teach us and help us grow in our faith in him. But in Christ we're assured that we're forgiven, and we know that nothing, not even God's anger, will separate us from God's love.

At this Communion table we are reminded of the deep love God has for us, that he would send Christ to die for our sins. Although we deserve the brunt of God's anger perhaps as much as the people of Judah did in Jeremiah's time, God has come to us in Christ to reclaim us. He has washed us clean of our failures by the blood of the New Covenant. He has strengthened us to do good by feeding us the Bread of Life. This feast is for you. Our host is one who cares deeply enough about us to be angry with us, one who loves us enough to die on our behalf.—Stephens G. Lytch

Topic: Power to Live by

TEXT: John 14:8–17, 25–27; Acts 2:1–4, 43–47

Is your life more like a dictionary or a novel? Somebody once defined a dictionary as a book with an excellent vocabulary whose plot leaves something to be desired.

A novel is different. In a novel, words are carefully selected and arranged to weave a tale that in the hands of a skilled author can keep you up into the wee hours of the night. Like a dictionary, a novel is a book full of words. But its words have a purpose and a goal.

Life can be like a dictionary. Each event, each phase of life, standing on its own, is interesting enough. But most of us want life to be more than just a collection of random experiences. We want our lives to have a plot, to be moving toward a goal that's larger than ourselves. And we want to know what our triumphs mean in the vastness of eternity.

Just as the words of a dictionary need an author to fashion them into a novel, to give them a purpose, a plot, the experiences of life need an author if they're going to be more than a jumble of loosely connected events.

We've gathered at this table this morning because we know the author of our lives. We're not here just because we've heard his story. Many people have heard it, but it hasn't changed their lives.

For those of us who believe, something has changed that story, from an event that happened long ago into the reality of the Son of God who is being born every day into the hearts of women and men, showing them that God is as intimate and as real today as he was when Jesus was lying in that manger.

The power that makes those stories in the Bible our story is the Holy Spirit, who takes the stories we read in the Bible and burns them on our hearts so that they're no longer quaint tales from long ago but stories that live in us, that guide us, that interpret all we do.

People often think that it must have been easier for Jesus' disciples to be good Christians. He was right there with them all the time. Doesn't it seem strange that as they all sat around that upper room, Jesus told them they would be better off because he was going away?

But his disciples *were* better off once he left them. For all their love of Jesus and their dedication, they never really caught on to who he was and what he meant for their lives until after he had left them. Now that Jesus has gone to be with the Father, the Holy Spirit brings him right into our hearts. He becomes a part of us, inside us. The Holy Spirit is like a chemical that binds two elements together.

One reason we need the Holy Spirit is that Jesus didn't specifically address every situation we encounter in our lives. It's the Holy Spirit at work in us today that makes Christianity something that's current and alive. It's what gives the Church authority to address situations that the Gospel writers never conceived of. The Holy Spirit is the power of God working in us to guide us in the way of Jesus. It's what makes Jesus' love and wisdom our own. It's what makes faith more than a mastery of facts. It's what makes faith a way of life, always ready to meet new situations, to bring the Scriptures to bear on what happens from day to day.

The Holy Spirit is the power of God guiding this congregation as we reach out into the community, as we look for ways to serve those in need and to live together as God's people. We're guided not only by our knowledge and our decisions, but also by a faith that there's a power working among us to give us a vision of who we should be as a church.

And the Holy Spirit shows us how we have a part in the story of the whole creation. It keeps us from thinking that our own individual stories are disconnected from the story of the world. The Holy Spirit, God alive and active today, is what guides us as we work for peace and justice and harmony around the world. The Spirit keeps reminding us that we're part of the whole story of creation. You can't isolate parts of a novel from one another and still have the whole work make sense.

The Holy Spirit is the author who is writing the novel of our lives. If you're reading an author you trust, you know that eventually you'll see how the puzzling incident fits in—perhaps even changes the whole outcome of the book. The Holy Spirit connects our story with God's story and gives us glimpses of meaning behind life's mysteries.—Stephens G. Lytch

Topic: Healing Waters

TEXT: John 5:2–16

As we enter the chapel, for some of us our first prayer comes with the dipping of our fingers into the holy water font. The opening verse of the Genesis account tells of the divine wind sweeping over the waters even before light appeared. To bring home to the Hebrew people the life-giving power of God, Ezechiel used the image of water flowing throughout the land, from the threshold of the Temple to the Dead Sea, stirring the lifeless salt water so that fish could abound and trees branch forth. Jesus himself waded into the waters of the Jordan to be baptized by John the Baptist; he sent the blind man to the pool of Siloam. From Jesus we learn that the offering of a glass of water indicates hospitality. The first Benedictine monks made sure that their monasteries were close to living streams, medieval towns sprang up on the banks of rivers, and factory cities along our East Coast were located along the fall line. Electric power continuously stirs Easter water in the baptismal font of our chapel.

At our initiation into life with Christ, water was poured on our forehead; now the rite of immersion in a pool at baptism is being revived. The many gifts that water signifies—cleanliness, refreshment, purification, and power—are symbols for us of the love of God so freely given, so unrestricted by formalities or propriety. Yet in today's Gospel the line that struck me most was, "The man who had been restored to health had no idea who it was [who healed him]." How many at this moment are being healed without comprehending the waters, the source, of their renewed life? At each Eucharist, may we be thankful that the offering to us of the cup, of transformed wine and water, isn't dependent on our worthiness.—Grace Donovan, S.U.S.C.

Topic: Peter and Judas

TEXT: John 13:21–33, 36–38

At Stonehill, like other colleges, we reward excellence in studies with placement on the dean's list and with graduation honors: cum laude, magna cum laude, and summa cum laude. We also present awards for outstanding service in other aspects of the student's lives. Thus far, campus ministry has refrained from handing out such distinctions. It is not that we frown upon the recognition of achievement. It is simply that we do not consider ourselves the ones to evaluate the expression of giftedness of students and others in the college community who, like Isaiah, like faithful Israelites, like the disciple whom Jesus loved, like Peter, like responsive Christians, have been called by the Lord even before their birth. Their reward is with the Lord, their recompense is with God.

There is the mystery of the use each of us makes of our commission to be a light to the nations. At the table with Jesus on that fateful Passover almost two thousand years ago, two disciples were recorded for us by name, and one was described by his closeness to Jesus. Jesus loved all the disciples. Yet we usually recall and contrast the two who were named. Judas and Peter both failed Jesus' trust—Judas by betrayal, Peter by denial. Peter, like the psalmist, came to Christ for forgiveness, rejoined the disciples, and proceeded to proclaim Jesus' wondrous deeds to Jews and Gentiles. Judas, by his own will, left Jesus and the other disciples, appealed to his tempters rather than to Jesus, and failed to turn to God for forgiveness and strength. The unnamed disciple was constant in his faithful love and puzzled that anyone could turn from Jesus.

Today's Gospel leaves out two middle verses from the text. Those two verses tell how we disciples of Jesus are to be recognized, renowned, and honored. How? "It is by our love for one another, that everyone will recognize you as my disciples."—Grace Donovan, S.U.S.C.

Illustrations

THE FOCAL POINT. The Eucharist has been and remains *the central service of Chris-*

tianity. It was given by Jesus and was the focal point of Christian community and worship during those glorious years when the Church was most alive. Most of the Christians who were thrown into the arena were apprehended worshiping at Eucharist. They knew the risks they were taking, and still they continued to come. In the Eucharist they met their risen Lord, and this was worth risking their lives for.

Eucharist provides a model for all Christian prayer; it is complete prayer. . . . Eucharist is a unique combination of praise for the love of God so clearly pictured in Jesus' death and resurrection and in the giving of the Holy Spirit, adoration of this love, contrition and confession before God, absolution from God, listening and learning through Scripture, intercession, fellowship through the passing of the peace, communion and blessing.—Morton Kelsey[4]

KEY TO THE FUTURE.   In the upper room Christ taught his disciples that the key to the future would be to remember the past with him through the institution of his holy supper. Christ left them with bread and wine, simple elements to serve as an ongoing memorial to his life together with and sacrifice for them. In the remembrance of Christ's death and resurrection for us, we receive grace and strength to carry on, yes, and even to remember with thankfulness for what was with loved ones and hope for what will be in the eternal joyous presence of our Lord.—Gary L. Ziccardi[5]

SACRIFICIAL LOVE.   As the Lord's Supper places us in the presence of the self-giving of divine love, the celebration of the Supper implies a consecration to a life in sacrificial love. The Lord's Supper tells us that the sacrificial act of self-giving love must never depart from the Christian life. The Lord's Supper serves in this respect as the conscience of the Christian life. Participation in the Lord's Supper is a consecration to Christ, and therefore also a consecration to self-giving love; it is true of our lives also that they

are to be broken and given in the service of love (Rom. 12:1).—Gustaf Aulen[6]

REMEMBER ME.   Hanging on the cross, one thief mocked Jesus. The other said, "Man, don't you fear God? We're getting what we deserved. This man has done nothing wrong."

And then he said, "Jesus, remember me. . . ."

Remember not the sins; remember me. It's our last, deepest prayer.

Two psalms later (27:10), the poet recalls, "If my father or mother forsake me, Lord, you will take me."

"Remember not the sins of my youth, or my transgressions; according to thy steadfast love remember *me*!"—William H. Willimon[7]

WORD AND SACRAMENT.   The eucharistic mode of presence is inseparable from the "sacrament" of the Word, for this is the conclusion of the story: "They told what had happened on the way and how they had recognized him at the breaking of the bread." Instruction on the meaning of the cross, which made Jesus someone other than the prophet who would redeem Israel from political slavery, preceded the breaking of the bread. The preaching of the Word leads to the acting of the Word, which is the offering of the self. Both of them together open the eyes of the Church. The presence remains elusive, for sight is temporary, but faith takes over, fills in, and holds on.—Samuel Terrien[8]

ALWAYS WITH US.   "I am with you always" introduces a mode of psychological communion which goes beyond the patriarchal or prophetic promises. The doubt of the disciples stresses the elusive character of all modes of presence, even that of an "appearance," and *a fortiori* that of a psychological awareness of companionship. A poetic *inclusio* on a grand scale embraces the entire gospel, since the affirmation of comfort, "I am with you always," constitutes a closing response to the Isaianic motif of the name *Immanuel*, "God is with us," with which the gospel began (Matt. 1:23).—Samuel Terrien[9]

---

[4] *Resurrection*
[5] James W. Cox (ed.), *Best Sermons*, Vol. 2

[6] *The Faith of the Christian Church*
[7] James W. Cox (ed.), *Best Sermons*, Vol. 1
[8] *The Elusive Presence*
[9] *The Elusive Presence*

SECTION IV.
Messages for Funeral Services

SERMON SUGGESTIONS

Topic: What Happens After We Die?

TEXT: 1 Cor. 15:12–20

What happens when we die? That's a question everyone wants to know the answer to but most people are reluctant to talk about. On the one hand, we are repulsed by death—by its finality, by the way it ends our relationships with those we love, by its inevitability. On the other hand, we're attracted by the hope of what might be beyond—escape, new beginnings, freedom from pain. The boxer Joe Louis said it best: "Everybody wants to go to heaven, but nobody wants to die."

I want to talk with you about what happens after we die. I can't answer all the questions. I can't even answer most of them. In the end, we're still going to be faced with a mystery. What we do know, we know through Jesus Christ. Just as he is our model for this life, he is also our model for the life to come.

Now, there are many people who believe that nothing happens after we die—that's it, the end, period. They believe that after death we cease to exist, that there's a total void. Our senses support that understanding. The way we know another person is by what we see them do, what we hear them say, the way they touch us, either gently in love or harshly in anger. Death brings an end to all that. Our senses cease to know the person. We have precious memories, and the things they have taught us continue to affect us deeply. But at the moment of death, all communication, the lifeblood of human relationships, stops.

There is biblical support for that understanding. The Old Testament talks about the dead going to a place called Sheol, a place of darkness and emptiness, a place separated from the life-giving presence of God. The New Testament also understands the finality of death. If death were not such a formidable thing, then Jesus' Resurrection wouldn't be such a big deal. If death were just an automatic passageway from this life into a better one, Jesus' return from death would be a regression. Instead of rejoicing that he returned from the dead, we would feel sorry for him. But the Scriptures say that for three days Jesus was dead, and that he was in that vast, empty place the Old Testament calls Sheol, what we call hell.

Yet there is something in the human spirit that knows we are intended to exist beyond our death. From the dawn of time, human beings have been straining to break the boundaries of life that death puts on us. The ancient Egyptians built pyramids to shelter their pharaohs as they journeyed to the afterlife. The Confucians of China built altars in their homes to provide a place for the spirits of their ancestors. We know there must be something about us that was meant to live beyond death; that's why 1 Corinthians 15:26 calls death "the last enemy." It's something that works against what we were created to be.

I think that *Embraced by the Light* was a bestseller because it affirms what so many of us want to believe: that death is really no big deal. But that is not what the Bible teaches. The Bible affirms that death is a big deal, and the only one who can keep us from being destroyed by it is God himself, who sent Jesus Christ to face it head on. It wasn't something he looked forward to. On the night before he died, Jesus prayed in the Garden of Gethsemane that he would be delivered from death. He prayed so hard that he sweat blood. It's only because Jesus Christ himself died and suffered the full power of death and then was raised from its abyss on Easter that there is any hope for us beyond the grave.

Eternal life isn't something that's programmed into us. It's not an automatic event. The Bible calls death our enemy because it has robbed us of eternal life. The power of Christ is that he has reclaimed life for us and that he gives it back to us as a gift. If Jesus had not conquered the power of death by his Resurrection, we would think of him as only another great teacher, perhaps sent by God to enlighten us but not having the power of God to create and restore life. It is through his Resurrection that Jesus is our Savior, and his life and teachings show us how we are to live now that we have been saved from the destruction of death.

So what are those whom we love who have died doing right now? Are they watching over us? Are they enjoying God's presence? Do they know how much we miss them? The Bible doesn't give a detailed account of what we do in those years between our death and the return of Christ. I suspect that's because we would not be capable of understanding such an account if it was provided.

When we think about where the dead are or what they're doing, the only way we can think about them is in ways that we who are alive can conceive. But I suspect that when we die, all the categories of time and knowledge that we use to order our lives will be changed.

My friend George Sweazey once wrote about death, saying that death is not a collapse of the soul but an expansion. He compared the experience of dying to that of a little boy walking through a dark vale full of fears and uncertainties after being away from home. In the darkest and most frightening part of the journey his father goes out to meet him and takes his hand and leads him the rest of the way until they reach home.

I like George's description. Dying is the scariest part of life's journey, something none of us has ever done before. It's at the moment of our death that God takes us by the hand and holds us until we reach our final destination. We don't reach it the moment

we die. It's not until Christ comes again that God will gather all God's children into God's home. But when we die, we are with God, free from pain and worry as we wait for the resurrection of our bodies at the end of time.

We know that there are a lot of things we don't understand, but we also know the one who provides for us. We have many fears about death and questions about resurrection, but we know that whatever is in the future, our Savior Christ is there waiting for us, and that the love and acceptance we know here are but a foretaste of what is to come.— Stephens G. Lytch

Topic: Funeral Message for Mrs. Stewart (Ella) Cannon Sr.

When Patty and I first moved to Johnson City, young and with a new challenge before us, we enjoyed the gift of a gracious and warm welcome. Among those who made us feel a wonderful sense of belonging were Mr. and Mrs. Cannon—Stewart Sr. and Ella. They became like parents to us, with their caring, their exemplary lives, and their wise counsel.

After Mr. Cannon's sudden, unexpected passing, Mrs. Cannon continued her faithful role as caregiver with her new granddaughter Connie, and much more recently, of course, with her great grandsons, Christopher and Wesley. During those significant years, she was also a housemother at the university. I recall the glowing appreciation of her expressed to me by one of my seminary students who had lived in Mrs. Cannon's dormitory—appreciation of her love, her listening, and her counsel.

These qualities in her that so many people have admired and that were a special blessing to them were qualities nurtured in the church and in the Holy Scriptures. But this love that I have described was not one-directional: *she* has been loved and tenderly cared for, too. Stewart and Norma Jean, Connie and John, Christopher and Wesley have given her the kind of devotion and attention that she gave to them. And today, you—by sharing in these solemn moments—show your appreciation and love for her, too, for she has in many ways blessed us all.

In times such as this, we turn to the 23rd Psalm and to the 14th chapter of John perhaps more often than to any other parts of the Bible. In recent days I have reflected on the reasons for this: Why do these passages speak to us with special meaning at these times?

Well, the 23rd Psalm sings to us of God's total care, sounding the deep throbbing notes that assure us that the foundation of our life is secure in the Lord God, the Maker of Heaven and Earth, the exalted ruler of the universe who is also our caring Shepherd, who keeps the stars in place but who also provides for our human needs so that we look to him for daily sustenance. That psalm also sings to us of our pilgrimage through this world, when we confess that as we travel we are weak while God is mighty, when we pray, "Bread of heaven, feed me till I want no more," and say with confidence, "The Lord is my shepherd; I shall not want"—whether we walk through the many valleys of the shadow of death before we come to the end of our pilgrimage, when our "way is dark with a nameless dread and fear"; or even when we might stand surrounded by enemies of every kind. I can imagine that this psalm made it easier for the apostle Paul to declare: "We are more than conquerors through him that loved us. For I am persuaded that neither death nor life, nor angels, nor principalities, nor powers, nor things present, nor things to come, nor height, nor depth, nor any other creature, shall be able to separate us from the love of God, which is in Christ Jesus our Lord" (Rom. 8:37–39).

The fourteenth chapter of John tells us of our eternal home. How welcome are those words when our "sad heart aches till it nearly breaks"!

Heaven is a roomy place, a place of many dwelling. Jesus said, "In my Father's house are many mansions" (v. 2). There is a place for you, a place for me, a place for everyone, for "whosoever will may come." The wonderful thing is that it begins right here on earth, in the midst of crime, injustice, and suffering; sometimes it is almost invisible, but it is nonetheless real. We pass from death to life here.

We speak of death even for the very best of God's people. But in a sense, there is no death—what we call death is only moving from one room, one dwelling place in the Father's house into a larger, a better, a more beautiful room. Jesus said, "I am the resurrection and the life. Those who believe in me, even though they die, will live, and every-one who lives and believes in me will never die" (John 11:25–26 NRSV).

Heaven is where Jesus is—here and hereafter. Only a thin veil separates us from those we have "loved long since, and lost awhile." Sometimes we may even be strangely aware of their presence, like guardian angels, helping us on our way, the living Christ chief among them. "Wherefore seeing we also are compassed about with so great a cloud of witnesses, let us lay aside every weight, and the sin which doth so easily beset us, and let us run with patience the race that is set before us, looking unto Jesus the author and finisher of our faith" (Heb. 12:1–2a).

We remember and are comforted by our Lord's words: "I go to prepare a place for you. And if I go and prepare a place for you, I will come again, and receive you unto myself; that where I am, there ye may be also" (v. 3).—James W. Cox

Topic: Homily for the Funeral of Christopher

I must confess my own inadequacy in the face of today's task.[1] No amount of seminary training is adequate to lead a funeral for a child. But my job today is simple and easy compared to that of Chris's parents and brothers. No amount of living with him and loving him would have been enough for his family to feel like it was time to let go. There is no way to rehearse for today—no way for any of us to be prepared for what we must do. We come with our feelings tender and our hearts aching, and with not a little fear and uncertainty. Nevertheless, we persevere because the only way out is through the pain. We pluck up our courage and go through the pain of saying good-bye because we know that on the other side of grief, life will be

---

[1]This little boy was born on Christmas Eve. On Christmas Day ten years later, he came down with bacterial meningitis. In the afternoon his mother and stepfather rushed him to the hospital, but the infection was too far advanced. He died the next morning. His parents were not members of our church, but as the "community minister" I was asked to conduct the funeral in our sanctuary. An overflowing crowd (nearly two hundred adults and children in a town of six hundred) of relatives and friends came out to mourn and express their concern for the family.

good again. It will never be the same as it was, but there will again be laughter and hope.

I have a few thoughts to share with you. I offer no glib answers or pious platitudes. There are no words magical enough to take away the pain, or profound enough to explain Christopher's death in simple terms. But I believe there is a source of comfort and strength that can make this time bearable. I want to speak first to the family, but I invite you all to listen in.

It is never easy to say the last good-bye to a loved one. When an elderly parent or grandparent dies we at least have the consolation that they lived long and died full of years. We expect to attend the funerals of our parents. We never anticipate burying our children. It is almost too difficult, and yet we must do it.

This is a heart-wrenching distortion of our expectations in life. It breaks the pattern we think is normal and ours by right. To see a life cut so short is difficult to understand. Why should a healthy boy die at Christmas, so soon after his tenth birthday? It doesn't seem fair. There is so much he never had a chance to do, to learn, to experience. Why should this sometimes loud and exuberant little person be silent and still at his age? Why should the world be deprived of his artistry, his fearlessness, his skill at sports?

Right now you are probably still numb. As the numbness wears off there will be strong feelings. You may feel cheated because you will never see him doing, learning, and experiencing the possibilities in life. You may be frustrated that this one whose daredevil exploits often put him in such danger should survive them only to die from a silent and stealthy disease—and angry that modern medicine couldn't prevent an illness from taking even a "tough little guy" like Chris.

There is a big why question that hides behind our lesser questions and our anger and disappointment. The biggest why of all is, Why would a good and loving and all-powerful God allow something like this to happen? We don't often say it out loud, for fear of being sacrilegious.

I'm not here to defend God against charges of injustice. I believe that God is big enough to hear your questions, your anger, even your accusations. The Psalms are full of angry prayers. I believe also that God is the only one big enough to help you shoulder your burden. The presence of family and friends will be indispensable in the weeks ahead. But there will be times when no one is around to hold your hand, to talk with you and keep you busy. In the silence, you will need someone larger than life to lean on.

We are just passing through the season of Christmas. I believe there is comfort and hope we can take from the Christmas story and the life of Jesus. The miracle of Christmas is that God chose to enter our world of uncertainty, disappointment, and pain in a personal way. The writer of Hebrews puts it this way: "Since the children have flesh and blood, he, too, shared in their humanity so that by his death he might destroy him who holds the power of death—that is, the devil—and free those who all their lives were held in slavery by their fear of death. For surely it is not angels he helps, but Abraham's descendants. For this reason he had to be made like his brothers in every way . . ." (Heb. 2:14–17). I believe that because Jesus himself suffered and was tempted just as we are, he is able to help us.

There is comfort, too, in the way Jesus related to children. He showed a special interest in them and demonstrated the constant care of God. One day some people brought their little children to Jesus so he could touch them, but his followers told them to stop. When Jesus saw this, he was upset and said to them, "Let the little children come to me. Don't stop them, because the Kingdom of God belongs to people who are like these children." Jesus took the children in his arms, put his hands on them, and blessed them (Mark 10:13–16).

In the end, the child of the manger in Bethlehem who blessed other children died a cruel death on a Roman cross. His Heavenly Father could have saved him but did not, in order to show at the apex of humanity's wickedness that the forgiveness of God would prevail. Those who watched him die thought that his death was senseless and useless. His mother stood grieving at the foot of the cross, helpless to stop his death. His disciples couldn't understand why he had been taken from them at the height of his life. Three days later they began to understand. The Resurrection gave meaning to Jesus' death. And his Resurrection gives hope to all who have sat grieving since then. Death is no longer the end of life, but a new beginning. Death no longer has the sting it once held. Death has been swallowed up in victory. Victory for Christopher. Victory for all who dare to believe.

I know that you don't feel victorious now. It is too soon. For now your comfort comes from knowing that God walks with us in our pain. The angel that announced the birth of the Christ child said he would be called Emmanuel, which means "God with Us"—not far away in heaven and out of touch with humanity, but here and now, in our pain and sorrow. The Word became flesh and dwelt among us because God loved the world that much. God loves not only the world in general but you and me and Chris.

It is in times like these that faith is so important. Faith doesn't always answer why, but it allows us to continue in the face of unanswered questions. It allows us to go on living in the emptiness that surrounds such a death as this, until life begins to take on meaning again. I encourage you to draw on your spiritual resources of the present and to rediscover those from your past. Don't let helplessness lead to hopelessness. Rather, lean on the everlasting arms of God, who walks with us to strengthen us and lead us into the future.

I have just a word to say to Christopher's friends, and I invite the family to listen in.

We are reminded today just how precious and fragile is the fabric of our lives. Death reminds us that life cannot be taken for granted. We may not have tomorrow to enjoy. We may not have next week to get around to those things we have been putting off in hope of a better time. The past trails behind us like a shadow, the future is but a light over the horizon. All we really have is today. All we really have is now. Although the chances of a death like Christopher's taking us by surprise is very small, we never know when we will draw our last breath. We do not know for sure how long our parents, our children, our friends and loved ones will be with us. We don't know for sure if there will be another chance to settle an argument, to give a hug or say "I love you."

Christopher's life was unfinished by all the measures we usually make of life. Your relationship with him was unfinished, too. Perhaps there was something you meant to do, something that you intended to say: a word of praise, a word of friendship, a thank you or "I'm sorry." I suggest to you that it's not entirely too late. Go ahead and say those words in the privacy of your heart. Or write him a note. Compose a poem to celebrate what he meant to you. Draw him a picture. In your own way, tell him what he meant to you and that you will miss him.

To everyone here I say, Chris is gone from sight but not from memory. His voice is silent, but you will hear him still. His life will echo in your thoughts the rest of your lives. At first the echoes will be painful. They will remind you of your loss and you will feel the emptiness acutely. In time they will be treasured memories. Until then, be gentle with one another. Time alone will not heal this wound, but time and love surely will.—Alan Hoskins

Topic: Remembrance Service for Members Who Have Died This Past Year
TEXT: Rev. 7:9–17

We most likely do not consider ourselves prophets, yet each of us probably holds a vision of what will come, of the so-called dead experience. This evening we are called to move beyond the sobering Lenten reminder of dust and ashes to imagine what follows that physical decomposition. We have just listened to a dream that contains positive, hopeful images: an innumerable, united, inclusive assembly, all wearing white as a symbol of cleansing having taken place; all holding fast to fresh branches of palm, signifying the thrill of completion; all miraculously singing a harmonious song of praise; all beyond wrangling as to ways of worshiping the Lord.

After several readings of these few verses from the liturgy of November first, I found myself most encouraged by the concept of an ever-increasing membership being enfolded under the boundless tent of God. At different times of the year, iron stakes secure tents of varying sizes and usages throughout our campus. For athletic contests, the modest covering protects the servers and the food. During commencement, a tent for the musicians is helpful for acoustics. Probably the largest tent is that set up on the quad for orientation of new Stonehill students and their parents.

It may be difficult for us to liken a chapel

to a tent with canvas flaps—especially a sacred space with a splendid floor of marble tiles, not ground dirt; a resonant baroque organ instead of a primitive gong; striking bronzes, seasoned wood, and mellow brick; and iridescent stained glass banners recalling Genesis and Revelation. Yet, in gathering around the altar of the one who to Christians is God expressed in love, we are called to reflect on the beauty, the awesomeness, of God's unlimited protection. We are reminded of our own genesis, of the beginning of our relationship with those inscribed on our scroll.

For some of us, the pain of a loved one's illness, of slow or sudden death, is still too strong to let us move on to anticipation of revelation, to prophecy of a future filled with joy and constant peace. Yet our God of salvation, unless we reject this gift, wills that we too join the circle of members, parents, brothers, sisters, students, in-laws, friends, husbands, wives, and grandparents who have moved on from a foreshadowing of Easter-raising to a fullness of living beyond our finite understanding. Others among us who have endured near-death moments or witnessed a peaceful, faith-filled passage, a passing on, assure us that we do continue in communion, however mysterious and undefinable, with these chosen people, the spiritual family of which we also are members.

Recently the media, both religious and secular, have been transmitters of hope, of peace, in their concentration on the way in which Cardinal Joseph Bernardin lived and suffered, rather than just existed, in those final days of his time among the people of Chicago, before he was called to join that apocalyptic multitude. In what may have been his last public visitation, he asked the members of a parish whose prosperity had been made possible by the sacrifice of Irish and Italian immigrants to ensure that the tent of their love and concern expand to include newer Latino and African American sons and daughters.

The first bishop of the diocese of Fall River, William Stang, in his final testament written a few days before an unsuccessful operation, pleaded with the people of that diocese—laity, priests, religious, whatever their national heritage, race, tribe, or language—to resist divisiveness and narrowness of spirit.

In our own personal loss we are comforted by the compassion of those who, like us, are remembering their loved ones, and perhaps the way they were treated. Yet this is also the time between our own genesis, our baptism, and our common revelation, the ultimate Holy Union, that is beyond our power to anticipate. As we continue with our lives, we can also strengthen one another in courageous solidarity as faithful and faith-filled daughters and sons of God.

Physically erected tents are transitory; strong gusts cause the sturdiest, the largest of tents, to collapse. A tornado could uproot chapel or cathedral. For secure shelter let us be thankful, that each one we name at this service is enfolded in the embrace of God. In communion with them, may we too pray, *praise and glory and wisdom, thanksgiving and honor and power and strength to our God for ever and ever.* May the Lord give us the gift of peace. Amen.—Grace Donovan, S.U.S.C.

Illustrations

LIFE IN THE SCALES.   Death is the common denominator of life. By it we are reduced to exactly what we are: no more, no less. The grave is the portal through which everyone must pass to enter into the timeless eons of eternity. One's view of death will depend upon his view of life. While the nature of man is to pass from life into death, the nature of the "new creature in Christ" is to pass from death into life. It is this principle and pattern which Jesus came to reveal. At death, man's worth is not increased one iota by his silver and his gold. Every life must be weighed upon the same balance, and the scale is tipped by one thing only, faith in the risen Lord. Passing from death into life begins with renunciation of self and a turning to the Lord of life. The life that weighs the most is the life that has lost itself in the greater, eternal life of God.—Richard Bennett Sims[2]

DEATH IS A DISORDER.   The Bible makes this crystal clear. The death of human beings points to an ultimate disorder. It should *not* be; the grim boundary markers should *not*

---

[2] *The Righteousness of God*

stand between us and the eternal life of God. And precisely for that reason this whole un-natural state, this disorder, this "brokenness" of the world, gives way when Jesus Christ comes and lays his ordering and healing hand on his fellow humans.—Helmut Thielicke[3]

FROM SUFFERING TO SONG.   Says Dr. Luc-cock: "Christianity made its way throughout the Roman world by the communication of wonder!" I believe it did. For men had had enough of household deities, and gods of small utility. This new faith caught hold of their farthest-flung imagination, for He took His time by such surprise that it could only sputter, as it staggered back from Him: "Why, we have seen strange things today!"

He scandalized society!

He ruffled every tradition that they knew! See! God on earth: an intimate divinity.

Death on a Cross: a loving Saviour! And an open tomb: eternal life!

They stood enchanted, and at last when breath broke through, they sang, *Gloria in Excelsis!*—Wyn Blair Sutphin[4]

A MIGHTY GOD AND A GLORIOUS SAVIOR. "Who died for us, that whether we wake or sleep, we shall live together with him" (1 Thess. 5:10). God has honored and crowned His creation, dressed him with dignity, given him the opportunity to make choices, and enabled him to reason and think. He gave His Son that we might have a way to the Almighty. Without God life would be an end-less vacuum with no incentive or purpose. Life without God would be a cheat. God has made life a challenge, a thrill of conquest. He gives strength far beyond ourselves. He encourages the downcast heart.

Isaiah, the mighty statesman of the Old Testament, said: "Thou wilt keep him in per-fect peace whose mind is stayed on thee: because he trusteth in thee" (Isa. 26:3). —W. E. Thorne[5]

THIS VERY MOMENT.   St. Francis of Assisi, hoeing his garden, was asked what he would do if he were suddenly to learn that he was to die at sunset that very day. He replied: "I would finish hoeing my garden."

If we were to live nobly, then we must redeem this present moment, this present hour, this present day. The unknown author of the following lines, originally in Sanskrit, knew this:

This Is the Day!
Listen to the Exhortation of the Dawn!
Look to this Day, for it is Life—
The very Life of Life!
In its brief course lie all the Verities
And Realities of your Existence:
The Bliss of Growth,
The Glory of Action,
The Splendor of Beauty;
For Yesterday is but a Dream,
And To morrow is only a Vision;
But To day well lived
Makes every Yesterday a Dream of
    Happiness,
And every To morrow a Vision of Hope,
Look well, therefore, to this day!
Such is the Salutation of the Dawn.
                    —Luther Joe Thompson[6]

---

[3] *Being a Christian When the Chips Are Down*
[4] *Thine the Glory*

[5] *A Bit of Honey*
[6] *Monday Morning Religion*

SECTION V.
Lenten and Easter Preaching

SERMON SUGGESTIONS

Topic: Setting the Record Straight

TEXT: Ps. 51:1–17

On Wednesday many Christians around the world began a pilgrimage to Easter. Ash Wednesday marked the opening of the Lenten season, a time traditionally dedicated to spiritual self-evaluation, confession, and new resolve. Lent is meant to be a period of personal growth resulting in a deepened knowledge of who we are and where we are going.

Lent is that focused period of time when Christians probe their spiritual identity, endeavoring to discover who they are and where they are going. It really wouldn't hurt for someone to get us started on this pursuit by shouting, "Hey man—or woman! Do you know who you are?" It is from first knowing who we are that we may proceed, under God, to become what we ought to be.

I. Discovery of himself is what lay behind King David's moving prayer of contrition recorded as Psalm 51 in our Bibles. David may not have written this lament, but it fairly represents the plight in which he found himself. This is the psalm that begins by pleading, "Have mercy on me, O God, according to your steadfast love; according to your abundant mercy blot out my transgressions. Wash me thoroughly from my iniquity, and cleanse me from my sin."

David had abundant reason to pray like this. King of Israel that he was, possessing the power to get what he wanted and seemingly to do as he pleased, he had sinned grievously. He had arranged for the death in battle of one of his brave warriors, a man named Uriah.

David wanted to be rid of Uriah so that he might claim Bathsheba, Uriah's wife, as his own. Already he had committed adultery with her, and she was going to bear his child. It was a simple thing for the king to order Uriah to the forefront of the hardest fighting against Israel's enemies. When Uriah was slain and his death reported, David passed it off by saying, "The sword devours now one and now another," as though such things were inevitable. He then quickly moved to take Bathsheba as his wife.

In this instance it took an outsider to call David to accountability, to show his soul. The Scriptures tell us that "the Lord sent Nathan to David." Nathan was a prophet and, actually, the chaplain in the king's court. Gaining the king's ear, Nathan told a parable about a rich man who possessed everything imaginable and a poor man who owned only a single small lamb. As Nathan told the story, a traveler came to the rich man's house. Rather than prepare food for the visitor from his own ample flock, the rich man seized the poor man's only lamb, killed it, and offered it to the guest.

Hearing of such cruel and insensitive behavior, David grew angry and declared to Nathan, "As the Lord lives, the man who has done this deserves to die." He went on to say that this loss should be restored fourfold. When the King's words ceased, Nathan said to David, "You are the man." It took little additional explanation for David to realize that he had betrayed not only other people, not only himself, but also God. Within moments the proud ruler was confessing to Nathan, "I have sinned against the Lord."

277

Subsequently, the penitential psalm from which I quoted was ascribed to David and then preserved as a lasting witness to self-discovery, confession, and new resolve. That psalm includes these lines: "Create in me a clean heart, O God, and put a new and right spirit within me. Do not cast me away from your presence, and do not take your holy spirit from me. Restore to me the joy of your salvation, and sustain me with a willing spirit."

It is a fitting prayer for Ash Wednesday, and for the weeks of Lent which follow. Properly called the "most sacred lyric" of Scripture, Psalm 51 searches the human soul and then lifts life to God for purification. It says this: "The sacrifice acceptable to God is a broken spirit; a broken and contrite heart, O God, you will not despise." Grateful we can be for such an insight, and for the message of this psalm. Born out of crisis—whether that of David or someone else—it gives us voice to say, "Hide your face from my sins, O God, and blot out all my iniquities."

II. When we know who we are at the point of our failure and sin, we can then turn to renewal—and that is what the days leading up to Easter are all about. A Latin phrase associated with the Lenten Season—*Vacare Deo*—describes our initial step in this process. It means, "to empty oneself for God." The emptying has to do with pride and willfulness, as well as with those small or large betrayals of others, ourselves, and God, which mar our days. Draining away those negatives, we then are ready for positive experiences of growth and fresh resolve. *Vacare Deo* became King David's action when the prophet Nathan confronted him with his sin. David emptied his soul before God and confessed what kind of man he had been. The time had come for him to try to set the record straight.

Symbolically, that is the meaning of the ashes used to mark the foreheads of Christians who gather for worship on Ash Wednesday in liturgical churches. Individuals are marked with a smudge of ash by a priest (or perhaps they do it themselves) as an outward sign of our humble beginnings and our common end. Dust we are and to dust we shall return. The point of this ritual is not to create morbid feelings about human existence but to accept responsibility for the lives God has given us. It is a way of calling us to atten-

tion, a way of acknowledging who we are and where we are going. Wearing ashes at the beginning of Lent thus is not so much a statement that we are "nothing but" ashes as it is a gesture made to bring us down to earth. It is a way for us to start setting the record straight.

The Danish theologian Sören Kierkegaard was troubled by the fact, as he said, that "man comes to himself only once in a while, as it were on a visit, to see whether a change has not occurred." Lent, once again, is a specific time for getting us to come to ourselves, not just for a visit to see if changes have occurred, but for true self-discovery. But notice this: self-discovery, with its attendant acts of confession and new direction, does not leave us ever-after introspective and self-absorbed. Our willingness before God to arrive at greater levels of self-knowledge simultaneously removes inward preoccupation with ourselves. We grow content to be known as well as to know. More than that, as we move beyond subjective introversion, a vaster preoccupation becomes ours. St. Paul declared it when he said, "I want to know Christ and the power of his Resurrection." Paul continued by seeking personal identification with Christ's sufferings, becoming like him in his death and in his Resurrection. This is to say that knowing who we are leads us to who we ought to be. The goal is to be persons who reflect and reveal Jesus Christ, even as Paul did.

This becomes a personal objective, but it is a corporate one as well. As a community of people, as the Church, we also are meant to have a sense of identity and mission. The world's criticism of the Church is not that it clearly and boldly reflects and reveals Jesus Christ, but that it so often fails to do this. Preacher Dick Sheppard once said, "Men do not blame us . . . for being like Christ; they worry about us and complain because we are so unlike." It is a criticism worth taking seriously. It may alert us to doing whatever is necessary to set the record straight.

This can be the moment of turning to God anew, even as King David did, and saying as he said, "Teach me wisdom in my secret heart. . . . Wash me, and I shall be whiter than snow. . . . O God of my salvation, my tongue will sing aloud of your deliverance."—John H. Townsend

Topic: Naming Our Insanity
TEXT: Mark 5:1–13

I was a small child when I was first introduced to the world of microbes. My sister, with great delight, informed me that everything I touched and ate was covered with bugs so small that I could not see them. You can imagine what the thought of invisible bugs on food will do to a small child's appetite, but obviously I have not suffered any lasting effect. I learned to eat without giving a second thought to the invisible world on my plate, until I contract a cold or the flu, or when I spent five days in the hospital a few years ago with the possibility of a bacterial infection. Then I begin to think about where I have been to ingest the little buggers. As a teenager I was allowed to look through a microscope at slides of an amoeba and other one-celled beings. My sister was right: another world, buzzing with activity, is living inside my world. Some microbes are helpful, even necessary, to sustain my life. Others are destructive, causing all kinds of illness, even death.

I. Demons explained illness in primitive eras. In the world of the New Testament, most of the ills of humanity were explained by the existence of an invisible world much like our world of bacteria and viruses. Some physical ills that we might identify with infection, and almost all diseases of the mind, were explained by the invasion of demons. Demons were spiritual evil. To be physically effective, they required the possession of a body. People lived in fear of demon possession much as your child might be terrorized by the world of bacteria. Although the details are a bit fuzzy, demons appear to require cooperation, either from the host or from the social environment, to establish an incarnation. The antibiotic for demon possession was a ritual of "casting out," or exorcism, of the unwelcome parasite.

A large part of the ministry of Jesus was devoted to the healing of people who were thought to be infested with demons. When Jesus sent out the Twelve, he instructed: "Cure the sick, raise the dead, cleanse the lepers, cast out demons" (Matt. 10:8a). As we have become better informed about the causes of disease, we have become less comfortable with the accepted diagnoses of Jesus' time. My generation tends to be embarrassed by talk of demons. We would just as soon raise the dead as center our ministry in the exorcism of demons. Besides, so many of the cases of demon possession in the Gospels are obviously cases of epilepsy or mental illness. The man of Decapolis who lived among the tombs and broke chains with his bare hands is often identified with the psychotic illness we call schizophrenia. "My name is Legion" is the tip-off. His head was full of conflicting voices that had driven him to madness. Our age can easily dismiss the incident with a nod of the head: "Too bad he could not have access to some of our drugs that help us to restore self-control"; and we stand in danger of ignoring a major part of the ministry of Jesus.

II. Evil is a spiritual reality. Walter Wink calls the demonic "the drunk uncle of our age," whom we prefer to keep hidden in a closet to avoid acknowledging his existence. Instead of ducking the embarrassment of exorcism, perhaps we ought to ask, What is the evil here? The name of the man's insanity is Legion. Is this a classic case of the highly debated multiple personality disorder? The man is not an "I." He is a "we." Small towns have a way of assigning roles to misfits and eccentrics. I still remember with horror the cruelty heaped on a kid in my school who was assigned the role of being the scapegoat for homosexuality. I don't claim to have the answers for the cause or condition of homosexuality, but I do know that the behavior toward this kid was the worst kind of evil. I think we needed Bobby to make the rest of us feel normal. I also remember Willie, a Down's syndrome man who hung around the school yard. Willie carried the burden of retardation for us. Then there was a deaf mute who lived down the street from my family. A local church would invite him in annually to be healed. The town drunk also lived on my street. When he died, the funeral sermon (thankfully not from my church) began, "This man is burning in hell today."

A strange phenomenon of alcoholics and drug addicts has become something of a cliché in pop psychology. The family of the addict or alcoholic gets itself organized around the addiction in a state of codependency. When the addicted person begins to gain control of the problem with alcohol or drugs, the rest of the family goes into chaos. Spouses, siblings, and children have become so dominated by the family problem that they cannot function normally without someone to rescue.

Why did the town want Jesus to leave them alone? One would think that transforming the town spook would make this a more peaceful place to live. To a Jewish reader, the evil is compounded: (1) this is a Gentile situation; (2) the man has an army, a Roman legion, of demons that have taken up residency in his mind; (3) he is living among the tombs (contact with the dead rendered a Jew unfit to associate with the faithful in worship); (4) the demons are transferred to a herd of swine, the classic symbol of an unclean animal; and (5) the swine rush over the cliff into the chaos of the sea of Galilee, where Jesus had just rebuked the destructive power of the storm. Everything about this situation speaks of pure evil, yet the community does not want to see change. Have they become, to use the contemporary word, codependent on the behavior of the wild man who lives in the cemetery? Walter Wink observes that a Roman legion was stationed in this area at the time and that the people of this community had been a political soccer ball, kicked around by Jews and Romans. Maybe the man got his name from the Roman army and he acted out the insane violence that the rest of the people could only dream about. Maybe he just made everyone else feel normal.

Mark alludes to the suspicion of Jesus' own family that he had drifted away from the norm. Perhaps in telling this story Jesus was experiencing more than sympathy. He knew what it is like to be thought mad. Have you been there? Don't dare laugh at the crazies. First you need to name your own demons. The demons of self-destruction leave when the Spirit of God takes up residency in our lives. The man named his demon and was made whole. Unfortunately, the community was left in a state of self-denial, and he may have been the only member of the community with demons in check.—Larry Dipboye

Topic: The Danger of Spiritual Illusion
TEXT: Rev. 3:14–22

Are you as amazed as I am at the ability of illusionists to mystify and entertain us? Being a rational, logical creature by nature and nurture, I watch them closely to see if I can discover exactly how they do what they do. It is all to no avail, however—indeed, their hand is quicker than my eye. Some call these people magicians, but in reality they are illusionists. Whether it is David Copperfield or the Amazing Kreskin or some lesser-known person, what they thrive on is their ability to make us think that what we see is real even when we know that it is not.

I. Although illusion is wonderful in entertainment, it is a disaster in real life. Too many people live under an illusion as they try to be someone or something they are not. Life, unfortunately, is filled with illusion. We eat poorly, exercise little, use tobacco products, and then wonder why we have so many heart attacks and strokes. We live with the illusion that coronary artery disease and cancer will happen to someone else, never to us. We live in illusion about our intellectual prowess, often thinking that we are smarter than we are. We cut this corner, cheat on that tax return, tell a white lie—and when it catches up to us we are amazed, for we thought we were smart enough not to get caught.

Although these are grave and serious dangers, the greatest danger is that of spiritual illusion. Spiritual illusion has eternal rather than temporal consequences. Although ignoring our physical, intellectual, relational, or financial conditions may cause us and others deep pain, ignoring our spiritual condition will bring about eternal pain. Let's look closer at Laodicea so we can understand spiritual illusion.

II. Laodicea was in an important geographical location: it was right on the road from Ephesus to Syria, which was the most important route in Asia. With the coming of Roman power and the stability that followed, Laodicea was given the opportunity to become distinguished, and the town made the most of it. It became a great banking and financial center, one of the wealthiest cities in the world. Like some of the other communities of Asia Minor, it was severely damaged by occasional earthquakes. But Laodicea had accumulated such wealth that it needed no outside assistance to recover. It was a center of clothing manufacture. A famous medical center that gained its reputation for its eye salve and ear ointments was located there. To sum it up, life was good. The citizens of Laodicea had it all, and that feeling was as obvious in the church as anywhere else.

The Christians there were not under the persecution that other congregations experienced. There was a large and influential Jewish population in town, but they apparently were willing to live and let live. There were centers for emperor worship there, but no one was too zealous about making demands. These Christians had a relatively easy time of it.[1]

The situation of the Laodicean church sounds like that of the modern church in America. They were living under the illusion that they were all right when in reality they brought on themselves the most severe rebuke of any church from our Lord Jesus Christ.

III. What were the illusions of the church in Laodicea? The foundational illusion was that material wealth equaled spiritual health. As a wealthy church, Laodicea thought they needed nothing, but in reality they were the worst of all the churches in Asia Minor. Jesus sought to counter head-on the idea that material wealth indicated spiritual blessing. We are so susceptible to the lure of the material, and it is so dangerous because if not put in its proper perspective material wealth will destroy our soul. Understand, Jesus and Holy Scripture do not condemn wealth, but they warn of its dangers and especially of the danger of pride, which wealth can bring.

As wealthy people, the Laodiceans took great pride in their dress. In their illusion the Laodiceans were proud of their clothes, while in reality they were naked before our Lord.

Another illusion was that physical sight was equated with spiritual sight. Because of their medical center with its eye ointments, they were proud of their eyesight. Jesus looked at this church, saw that it was spiritually blind, and called them to get his "salve to put on your eyes so you can see." Can you not hear this church? "We're doing rather well: the budget is met, the bills are paid; the church facilities are up-to-date; the staff function

well. Isn't God lucky to have us out of all these churches in Asia Minor?"

The illusion of sight will destroy our impact on our world, for illusion looks outward but God looks upon the heart. Illusion looks to see what we did; spiritual sight looks to see what God did. Illusion is proud of its accomplishments; spiritual sight is humbled by the presence of Almighty God.

IV. What is the reaction of Jesus? Total disgust. Jesus says to the Laodiceans, "You are lukewarm—I am going to vomit you out of my mouth. . . ." Jesus is referring here to water that has traveled far from its source and that is therefore not worth being used for its original purpose—healing baths. We become lukewarm when we accept second or third best in our walk with Jesus Christ. If we are cold, we know it—and the Spirit can work in our life. If we are lukewarm, then we live with the illusion that everything is alright and we are usually closed to the movement of the Spirit in our lives.

Jesus not only reacts with disgust, he also reacts with compassion and affirmation. "Those whom I love I rebuke and discipline." Jesus loves this church and wants it to be a beacon of the gospel to the world, but he knows that as long as they live under their illusions they will never be acceptable. Jesus wants his people to persevere and overcome so that they might celebrate with him in the Kingdom of God.

Because he loves us, Jesus gives what we know as the Great Invitation: "Behold I stand at the door and knock. If anyone hears my voice and opens the door, I will come in and eat with him and he with me." Based on the first-century Palestinian understanding that eating with another was the most intimate relationship outside of marriage, these words of Jesus mean that if we will open the door of our hearts to him, he will come in and dwell in our lives.

Jesus stands at the door of the heart of any church and knocks, waiting to come in if they will let him. What? A church without Jesus? Yes, we can become so captive to our illusions that even Jesus becomes an illusion rather than the Lord of the universe. We can make Jesus into our own little paragon of virtue and mystic hero, so that we never understand the radical grace and the radical call that are his gifts to us.—Robert U. Ferguson

---

[1]Description taken from David Leininger, *When the Lord Gets Disgusted with His Church*

Topic: Remember How He Told You

TEXT: Isa. 65:17–25; Luke 24:1–12

Sometimes, just when we think we have life figured out, the rug gets pulled out from under us. That must have been how those women from Galilee were feeling that Sunday morning as they walked to the tomb. Only a week before, everything was coming together for them. They had left their homes and their families in Galilee and followed Jesus to Jerusalem because they were convinced that he was the Messiah, the long-awaited king of Israel. On Palm Sunday their convictions had been confirmed when he rode into the city to a royal welcome. They must have had that wonderful feeling that comes when you see something to which you've dedicated your life finally acknowledged by the crowds.

But now, only one week later, they were lost. They had that emptiness and despair that comes when everything you've staked your life on collapses under you. It must have been like that feeling you have when you lose your job, or your marriage falls apart, or a child dies.

So the women were on their way to do the only thing they could think of doing under the circumstances. Jesus had been buried hastily as the sun was going down on Friday afternoon. The Jewish law required that he be entombed before the sunset that began the Sabbath. There had been no time to prepare his body for burial, to anoint it with spices and give it the dignity it deserved. So they went to the tomb at first light, the earliest opportunity the law allowed them to touch the corpse. I suspect they hadn't been able to sleep that night anyway.

When they got there, they found that the stone that had sealed the door to death had been rolled away. Standing inside the tomb were two men in dazzling clothes—angels. What strikes me every time I read this story is the tone with which the angels addressed the women. You would expect them to be bursting with excitement, to say something like, "We've got incredible news! You'll never believe it! He's risen! It's unbelievable!" But that's not the way the angels spoke to the women. They sounded like they were impatient with them, the way a teacher might be with a student who just doesn't catch on. I can see the angels shaking their heads with a look of disbelief in their eyes. "Why are you looking for the living among the dead?" they asked the women. Then, as if they were reporting the most obvious thing you could imagine, they said, "He is not here. He is risen. Remember how he told you, while he was still in Galilee, that the Son of man must be handed over to sinners and be crucified, and on the third day rise again." Jesus had told them all this would happen. All they had to do was remember.

I think we often underestimate the power of remembering. We like to think that we can put the past behind us, that once something is finished we can forget about it and go on.

Our memories shape us and almost dictate the way we approach the future. The happy memories of her childhood Easters motivate a mother to recreate those joys for her children. The memories of happier times together motivate a young couple to work through their problems to save a marriage. The memories of friendship and acceptance in Sunday School lead a man back to church after many years away. The great tragedy of Alzheimer's disease is the way it robs its victims of memory. Without memories, we lose touch with who we are. We have nothing on which to build our relationships with those we love.

But not all our memories affect us positively. We remember the hurts and the hatreds of those who we feel have betrayed us, and those memories make us angry and on the alert for more affronts to our dignity. Memories of a harsh pastor or a harmful experience in church can keep people away for the rest of their lives. Memories of abuse can cause a person to do tragic things. Susan Smith's lawyers are going to build her defense on the destructive memories she has of her stepfather's abuse when she was a teenager.

Memory is powerful, one of the most powerful things about our human experience. But not all memories lead us to life. Not all memories are healing. It's a certain kind of memory that the Bible recalls to our minds—the memory that allows us to overcome everything that holds us down or harms us. The memory that gives life is the memory the angels recalled for the women at the tomb. "Remember how he told you," they said. Remember the promise Jesus has given. It's that promise that gives us hope. And hope is what leads us into the future.

You see, remembering what Jesus told us makes the difference between optimism and hope. Most of us want to be optimistic. Optimism is that positive outlook that's based on how things are going. Economists are optimistic because all the leading economic indicators are looking good. Optimism is the belief that a positive trend will continue. But it may not. Jesus' friends were optimistic on Palm Sunday. But things changed drastically during the week.

Hope is different from optimism. Hope isn't based on what is going on at the moment or on the direction in which things are headed. Some of the most hopeful people I've ever met were the Christians I met in Sudan last year. They're living in a situation where the prospects for peace are slim. The trend appears to be toward continuing famine and bloodshed. Yet they have a spirit about them that is hopeful. They don't despair. They look for blessings in each day, not because things are going well at the moment but because they have hope that something is going on that transcends the war and famine they see every day. They have hope that God is at work in ways they cannot even see.

Hope isn't based on how things are going. Hope is based on something from outside ourselves. Hope is based on a promise that something is going to break in from the outside and change the course of events. It's not based on the latest experience we've had, or on how optimistic or pessimistic we feel at the moment. It was hope, not optimism, that led the civil rights workers of the sixties and seventies to face fire hoses and police dogs and firebombs—hope that went beyond the way things were, hope that even if they themselves didn't see a day when people were treated right without regard to race, at least their children or their grandchildren would see that day. Hope keeps on going when optimism fails.[2]

Hope is remembering the promises of God, remembering how he has broken into human events in the past, and the promise that he will do it again. That's why the Bible is filled with commands to remember. God knew the power of our memories when he gave the fourth commandment, "You shall remember the Sabbath day and keep it holy." Christ knew how important our memories are when he commanded us to take bread and a cup and "do this in remembrance of me." God knew how easy it is, in the press of life's agendas, to forget who God is and what God has done. God knew that unless we remember who God is and all he has done, we start to take at face value all the messages we hear bombarding us.

That's why we keep telling this story over and over again—so we won't forget. We bring our children to Sunday School to hear the same stories we heard as children. We bring them even if they protest and squirm, because even if those stories don't strike a chord when they're first heard, there will come a time when they'll remember, and remembering those stories will mean life. There will come a time, as it did for the women at the tomb, when the words they had heard but hadn't understood finally made sense. Standing before the door of death, when everything seemed lost and they couldn't figure out which way to go next, they remembered. And when they remembered, they believed, and believing, they were filled with joy and ran to tell the others.

We're here this morning to remember, to remember the glorious victory Jesus won for us on Easter. We're not here to commemorate a momentous event of the past. We're here to remember the statement that's as true today as it was two thousand years ago in Jerusalem. We are here to remember that Christ is alive, that he gives us hope to carry us through every hardship life can sling at us. We are here to remember how Christ kept his promise that he would be raised, and to remember that he will keep his promise that we share his victory. Remember how he told you. Christ is risen. He is risen indeed.— Stephens G. Lytch

Topic: What Makes Jesus Angry?

TEXT: John 2:12–24

Chaos—that's what it was: chaos. Tables flipping, money flying everywhere, animals in a stampede as man and beast fled from the Court of the Gentiles. Then the figure of Jesus emerged, standing with whip in hand. "Get out of here! How dare you turn my Father's house into a market."

This is not the Jesus meek and mild that is so often portrayed, is it? This is not the nice, gentle, pastoral shepherd who leads us into green pastures and beside still waters. This is the angry Jesus, the passionate Jesus, the Jesus who scares us to the core. What's going on here? Why is Jesus so angry, so passionate about what is transpiring in the Temple?

I. The scene that greets Jesus at the Temple during this high holiday is not unexpected. Merchants offered sacrificial animals for sale to Diaspora Jews who had traveled long distances to make their annual pilgrimage. Being able to purchase animals at the Temple instead of bringing them on a long trek was a convenience for the observant. Likewise, the money changers accepted coinage from any number of distant places and replaced them with the Tyrian coin required to pay the temple tax.

Jesus' reaction to this typical scene is shockingly aggressive. John's Gospel increases the physicality of Jesus' reaction by "whip of cords," used to drive the crowd from the outer courtyard. Some grammatical imprecision in verse 15 makes it unclear whether Jesus uses this whip to drive out only the animals (the sheep and the cattle) or if he plies this whip against the backs of the sellers and money changers as well. In the same way that the animal stables are opened, so too are the financial stables. First the coins are poured out; then the tables themselves, heaped with spilled riches, are overturned completely.[3]

It is difficult to understand the anger of Jesus. After all, these merchants were not doing anything illegal or immoral. In fact, they were providing a service that helped people to worship. As much as we want to understand this story as an indictment of commerce at the Temple, I think it is much more than that. Jesus is angry not just with the merchants but with the entire Jewish religious system that had desacralized God and worship.

II. The real problem here is not just that Jesus is mad, but that he is at the Temple mad, that he is at the Passover mad. Hundreds of worshipers would have been at the Temple at any given time during the Passover. This was one of the holiest of feasts for the Jews, because through it they remembered that the death angel had "passed over" their homes that last night in Egypt. This is when they paused to remember their deliverance from slavery in Egypt. This is when they were coalesced as a people by God. Now, of all times, Jesus shows up and really lets them have it.

Why? Simply put, worship had become a "market enterprise" rather than a spiritual enterprise. Worship had become a matter of ritual, of doing the proper thing at the proper time, rather than a matter of the heart and soul. Religion and worship had become matters of transaction rather than relationship: you pay your money and you get forgiveness. Or as in our modern church, you just say a few words and accept Jesus as your Savior and all will be forgiven and you will go to heaven when you die. Before you revolt, hear me clearly: there is nothing wrong with the previous sentence, except when that is all there is to one's faith. There was nothing wrong with the Jews buying doves, goats, lambs, and cattle for sacrifice, except when that was all there was to their faith.

When our faith is determined more by what we want or need than by what God wants for us, then we are destined to become more like Walmart than the Church of Jesus Christ. We have so prostituted the nature of the Church that often people go "church shopping" with the attitude of seeing which church offers the most bang for their buck, rather than spending time in prayer seeking God's will.

III. The problem with this type of Christianity is that it can be both superficial and artificial. Jesus is striking out at a loss of sacredness, at a loss of a sense of holy places and holy times, which is revealing of a loss of relationship with the Holy One, God. When worship becomes duty rather than love, obligation rather than opportunity, it is not long before it becomes optional altogether. When we lose worship, when we lose the sense of the Holy God among us, we have lost what makes us special creatures of Holy God. Whenever I have seen a person drop out of church and worship, except for medical reasons, I know it will not be long before God will be a distant memory. When God becomes a distant memory, then we have opened up our lives to all manner of chaos. For without

[3]Leonard Sweet, *Homiletics*, 1997, 9(1).

the Spirit, creation always returns to chaos— every time.

To regain a sense of the awesomeness of God, we need to begin with regaining a sense of the Sabbath. The Sabbath was to be a separate time, a holy time, in which we consciously pause to nurture our soul. The Sabbath was to be a reminder that life is not all about who we are or what we do, but that it is more about who God is and what God does. Through a genuine Sabbath of rest, of deep worship composed of heartfelt prayers and serious wrestling with the Scriptures, we can regain that sense of God's presence and renew our souls. When was the last time you let your mind rest and your soul soak in the presence of God? In our overactive and spiritually undernourished Christianity we are in danger of losing our very souls. It takes a long time for a soul to heal from starvation— much longer than we could ever dream. Much as those with anorexia learn to live on very little if no food at all, so we learn to live on just enough spiritual food to get by. And our soul slowly dies—and we do not even notice.—Robert U. Ferguson Jr.

Topic: Ordinary People
TEXT: Matt. 21:1–11; Phil. 2:5–11

Who are the people God chooses to use? Most of us would answer: great people, gifted people, talented people, holy people. We answer this way because the people in the Bible have been held up to us as icons of virtue—and we know that we are anything but that. The thought remains that if God uses someone, then they must be radically different from the normal person, and therefore God cannot use me. Nothing is further from the truth. God is in the business of using normal, ordinary people to do normal, ordinary things that become extraordinary in their impact through his love and power.

I. Two unnamed disciples are sent to get a donkey from an unnamed owner. The faces in the crowd are nameless, insignificant people just going about whatever it is they are supposed to be doing. If they are disciples, then they are following Jesus, something they have done for up to three years, and other than a few miracles nothing earth-shattering has occurred. The crowd—those anonymous souls going about their daily work of buying and selling, doing whatever their livelihood

requires—sees a parade coming their way, so they stop for a few moments to see what the commotion is about. The people ask who this is and the reply comes: Jesus of Nazareth. They were somewhat accustomed to kooks showing up every so often and proclaiming themselves to be the Messiah, so this is nothing new. Though it may bother us to think that our Lord was perceived as insignificant, is this not the way God works? Hasn't God always worked through insignificant people at insignificant places in insignificant times doing insignificant things to accomplish the significant? God always works through the insignificant and unimportant—and does so in ways that are mysterious and wonderful.

II. Our lives are like that, are they not? We are neither the famous nor the important—at least as far as the world is concerned—and yet Jesus continues to show up in our lives at the oddest moments to work his miracle of grace. Every once in a while, every so often, something dramatic happens, but most of the time we live in the ordinary. I believe, as strange as it may sound, that this is a message we need to hear amid the pomp and pageantry of Palm Sunday: Jesus is most often found among the ordinary, among the normal, among the humdrum experiences of life.

Look where people found Jesus in the New Testament: by the Sea of Galilee, walking along a dusty road, at a well at noontime in Samaria, or on a hillside teaching. We find Jesus most when we look for him in the everyday aspects of life. Someone has said that the secret to life is doing the ordinary in an extraordinary way. When we know the love of God, when we have been touched and transformed at the core of our being, then the ordinary becomes extraordinary.

III. How could Jesus have accepted those accolades that day while knowing that by Friday the hallelujahs would turn to "Crucify him?" He knew that he was coming to Jerusalem to die. He had made no secret of that to his disciples. Could it be that Jesus accepted this because he knew of the ordinariness of life? Could it be that Jesus saw that for these people this moment would be one that, after the Resurrection, they would look back on and know that God had been with them?

God shows up in the most unexpected ways and at the most unexpected times—and in so doing he graces our ordinary lives with the extraordinary. A simple meal with family or friends becomes a special moment as we share together the stuff of our lives—and God is present. A gesture by a neighbor, a visit to a shut-in friend, a helping hand to one who needs it—and before we know it God has been present and our lives have been transformed. How did those disciples on that road to Emmaus put it when they realized that they had been walking with the Risen Christ? "Did not our hearts burn within us?" Ordinary moments made extraordinary by the presence of Christ.

IV. Some of you are saying, "Wait just a minute. I'll agree that my life is ordinary, but don't give me any of that 'extraordinary' stuff. My life is just plain boring. I've never had anything extraordinary happen to me." That is the problem. Ordinary and boring are not synonyms. When we speak of ourselves and our lives as ordinary, we mean that we are just normal human people. When we pause and look at our lives, we can see moments pregnant with all sorts of possibilities that we overlooked at the time. It is in the eyes of the seer that the ordinary becomes the extraordinary, as we perceive the presence of God.

There are two inherent dangers in being a person who wants to accomplish something: one is that we will think that the "big event" is what life is about and so will ignore all else in trying to achieve that moment. The other danger is that we will develop "routine" lives that have no hills or valleys—everything is the same: flat. When we ignore the presence of God in the ordinary of life, then it becomes flat, boring, and routine.

Thomas Carlyle wrote: "The tragedy of life is not so much what men suffer, but rather what they miss." When we fail to see the importance of the ordinary and of what God is doing in the ordinary stuff of our lives, then we are missing the presence of the Almighty and the essence of life is gone, vanished like a vapor on the breeze of the moment.

In the passage from Philippians, Paul writes of the humility of Jesus. Humility comes not from a "poor me, down in the mouth" attitude, but from an understanding that the God of the universe, the Holy One, loves me enough to be involved in my life. This fact ought not just bring us to our knees occasionally; rather, it ought to open our eyes to see the presence of Christ in our lives. When I see that God is working—even in ways I never dreamed—then I can and will have open eyes and a humble heart.—Robert U. Ferguson

Illustrations

THE RIGHT PATH. The *Chicago Daily News* once ran a series of articles about young, self-made millionaires. It told about one man who had made his millions and become a great success in the commercial world, but who had lost his wife and children along the way under the pressure of the drive for the top. "If I could start over," he said, "I wouldn't do it again."—Robert Howard Clausen[4]

LEAD US NOT INTO TEMPTATION. When a sin is forgiven, the matter may be settled between the sinner and the one sinned against, but that is not all there is to it. For instance, I may tell a lie about you, and you may forgive it, saying, "Let bygones be bygones." But if I think the matter is settled as easily as that, I may be tempted to presume on your repeated magnanimity and mercy. In families we sometimes see children who come to presume on their parents' unfailing forgiveness. Likewise, the temptation to presume on God's forgiving grace is also very real. The thought, "Well, I got away with it again," may lurk in the mind of the forgiven sinner and make him prone to repeat. Therefore, after we have prayed for forgiveness and received it, we should go on to pray, Lead us not into the temptation to presume on the repetition of that forgiving grace.—Ralph W. Sockman[5]

CHRIST IN OTHERS. A few years before his death I spent several hours in conversation with one of the most alive and single-minded Christians I have ever met, Richard Cardinal Cushing of Boston. Coming to know him just a little through those hours gave breath and life to these words of his: "It cannot be enough that the church should merely proclaim her faith in Christ with the hope that those who hear will turn at once and confess their faith in him. To engage

[4] *The Cross and the Cries of Human Need*
[5] *Now to Live!*

men of our age, the church cannot begin from the point of authority and revelation but rather from experience and relationships. The men of our time are not very much different from those of the Lord's own day. They must find Christ in others before they are ready to see him in the Church's teachings."—Floyd Thatcher[6]

THE SERVANT.   Does St. John ever reach such heights in his Gospel as he does in the passage which I have chosen for my text (John 13:3–5)? "Jesus, knowing that . . . He was come from God and went to God . . . laid aside His garments, and took a towel, and girded himself, and poured water into a basin, and began to wash the disciples' feet, and to wipe them with the towel wherewith He was girded." Here is the divine condescension incarnate. Here is the Son who is also the Servant, doing the dirty work and doing it with infinite grace and love. You look at the Cross where He bore the heaviest load of all and cried, as they drove the nails in, "Father, forgive them, for they know not what they do." You look at the empty tomb, symbol of victory, of battle hard fought and well won. You look at it all—the divine condescension, the standing in with us of the Son of Man who is Son of God, and you say: "Jesus is what God has to say to men. Thanks be to God."—Frederick Donald Coggan[7]

DON'T STRIKE OUT HERE!   I know of a student who attended a high school with an enrollment of over 2,000 students who lived such a winsome Christian life that he molded the thinking and conduct of the entire student body of that large high school. In a stenographers' pool of a large concern there was a young woman who lived the teachings and spirit of Jesus in such a radiant and convincing way that the fifty girls in that particular group came to her for counsel and inspiration. Many men in military service have so lived the teachings and spirit of Christ that the spirit and attitudes in entire barracks have been changed—not because of what the men said but because they dared to live their Christianity daily.—Chester E. Swor[8]

THE IMPOSSIBLE POSSIBILITY.   When Jesus Christ hung on the cross, when he no longer had anyone or anything, when his disciples were scattered to the four winds and even his robe had fallen into the hands of the gambling and drinking soldiery, then he was nearest to his Father. Then there was nothing else that stood between him and his Father. And he bowed his head and committed himself to the eternal hands. Here he had nothing left, and therefore the Father could be everything to him. Everyone who wants to have eternal life must pass through this "death and resurrection." We certainly can't do it ourselves. We are not able to pry open those fists of ours with which we hold on tightly to what is ours. "With men it is impossible." God knows, it is impossible. But with God all things are possible.—Helmut Thielicke[9]

[6] *The Miracle of Easter*
[7] "Divine Condescension" in G. Paul Butler (ed.), *Best Sermons*, Vol. 4

[8] *The Best of Chester Swor*
[9] *How to Believe Again*

SECTION VI.
Messages for Advent and Christmas

SERMON SUGGESTIONS

Topic: Angel's Song

TEXT: Luke 2:8–20

Isn't it significant that the announcement of the birth of Christ came to shepherds, hard workers, those who society needed but didn't consider important? They were next to the last on the scale of occupational work, just above the tanners.

They were the insignificant, but to them— and not to the king, to those in power, nor to the rich or famous—the angel came. What was the Christmas Word given to the strugglers of the world? What is that Christmas Word to us?

I. *We matter; each of us is loved.* God came to the world in a baby to show that he is love. The announcement of this birth came to those who were considered unlovely shepherds, lonely people who carried out their difficult work in relative obscurity. I'm sure they wondered whether anybody really noticed them, whether anybody cared about them, whether anyone worried over them. For the most part, it seemed they had no one. But the angel came to them and tried to let them know that God cared, that God noticed, that God worried over them, that they mattered to him. "I bring you good tidings of great joy. Unto you is born, a Savior, Christ the Lord" (vv. 10–11 AT).

Do you ever wonder if anybody notices you? Do you matter to anyone? Does anybody care about you? Listen to the angel's song: "Unto you is born this day a Savior." Unto *you!* For God loved you so much that he came down to this Earth in the form of Christ ulti- mately to climb a cross to die for your sins. That's how much you matter to God. The angel's song is an announcement that you are known by God, noticed by God—that you matter to God. Although no one else may see or hear or care for you, the God who made it all does notice and does care.

II. *The angel's song: life has meaning because God is in it.* I'm sure these shepherds won- dered a lot about life. They had a lot of time to sit around the fire and meditate. I'm sure they wondered what they were here for, and what was the purpose of their lives. Were their lives headed anywhere? What was going to happen in the end?

Suddenly, the angel came and sang a song that God had come into life itself. What a dif- ference that made! Not only did these shep- herds learn that they mattered, they also learned that life mattered. It was God's life and God cared about it. God was working out his purposes. There was much they didn't understand, but this they did. Life was sacred because it was God's, and because it was God's, life was not just headed nowhere. Life was headed somewhere, and everything they did was important if offered to God. Even a task that seemed unimportant to the eyes of the world, like tending sheep, could be used by God to work out his purposes. God was no longer distant; he was immersed in the mid- dle of life, trying to bring out of it what he wanted. Purpose had come to the world.

Life is not insane. It has meaning and pur- pose. If we unite ourselves with God, we will find the hope of it. We will be able to laugh a little bit more because we will see that whatever we do, if done in service to Christ, is worthwhile. It will not be in vain. That is what the angel said. We matter, what we do matters.[1]

III. *The angel's song said that faith matters, it is not in vain.* The shepherds were Jewish folk with a rich religious heritage. They had worshiped. They had carried out the sacrifices and rituals. I'm sure that they longed for the coming of the Messiah. They were God's chosen people, but they were oppressed. They were God's chosen people, but they were suffering. They were God's chosen people, but their faith didn't seem to do them any good. What good was it to believe and have to go through all that they did?

The angel came to tell them that their faith was right, that the values they were living by—honesty and integrity and justice and righteousness and love—were the right values. They were the values that one day would triumph. They were the values that would bring them life, abundant and eternal. The shepherds had their faith affirmed in the song of the angel.

This is what Christmas tries to tell us. "Today Christ is born." He still is and always will be. In all that we have to deal with, we have the truth walking alongside us. Christ is born, and our faith is not in vain.

So hear the angel's song, a song that told the shepherds that they mattered, that what they did mattered, that faith mattered. That was God's word to those strugglers, and it is his word for all the strugglers in our world today. It is God's word to us. We matter to God. What we do matters to God. Our faith matters. God is with us. We can listen to the angel's song with new hope.

Christ has been born. He has come for you and for me. Therefore, for us there is always laughter, laughter born of hope because Christ is born forever.—Hugh Litchfield[2]

Topic: What Then Shall We Do?
TEXT: Luke 3:7–18
Everybody has a definition of what is appropriate for this time of year. The *Daily Dis-*

patch runs a happy story about a couple who fills their yard with hundreds and hundreds of lights. More and more and more lights. The number grows each year. It brings such joy. It is such stories like these that are the essence of Christmas.

The *Life's Little Instruction Calendar* on my desk knows what is appropriate behavior. It tells me: Christmas is the only time of the year when bigger is always better and the gaudy is beautiful.

So perhaps it is not really surprising that we find such a strange combination of expectations even in the preaching of John the Baptist in preparation for the coming of God's revelation. "John was an austere man with a religion of high moral earnestness, and he could not conceive of greatness except in terms of a severity excelling his own. The coming crisis would see the mighty overthrow of ancient wrong, the settling of accounts on the basis of strict justice. Before such a prospect the Jews must not claim preferential treatment on the grounds of their ancestry. Trees are not judged by their roots but by their fruits." A harsh and frightening time of judgment was coming. John had come to warn them. And yet when the people who heard his preaching were convicted, convinced, converted, baptized, and redeemed and had asked John, "What then shall we do?" John seemed so unconcerned and so unprepared to give an answer. Just as Robert Capon brought us to the farm with God—with the father inviting the elder brother to come inside and enjoy the party, and the younger brother already welcomed home and celebrating with the servants— and left us there, with no hint of how life on the farm would go the next day, with no suggestions as to how younger brother is to treat the older brother, with no discussion about whether the elder brother gives the younger brother a job to do, so John seems unprepared to talk ethics and morality with those who are repentant. When the multitude comes and asks John, "Now that we have repented and been baptized, what are we to do?" John's answer seems so spur-of-the-moment, so pathetic in comparison to his demands, so anticlimactic, as if he had not taken much time to think through the ethical consequences of his preaching. "What are we to do? Huh? Well, if you have two coats,

---

[1]John Killinger, "Priorities in Preaching," in *Priorities,* proceedings of the Christian Life Commission, Southern Baptist Convention, Jackson, Mississippi, Mar. 21–23, 1977, p. 54.
[2]*Preaching the Christmas Story*

you could give one to someone who has none. And he who has food, let him do likewise." When the hated tax collectors ask what they are to do, he says, "Well, you could collect no more than is appropriate." When the Roman soldiers get converted, they ask for instructions and John says, "Rob no one by violence or by false accusation. Be content with your wages."

Advent is our time of waiting and preparing for the coming of the revelation of God; we are baptized, converted, and waiting. What then shall we do?

"He who has two coats, let him share with him who has none." It seems so innocent and simple. But like drops of water on sandy ground, the water just keeps penetrating the ground. What if John is suggesting that we need to give away all that we have that is more than we need? Surely there are more than two coats in my closet. Am I supposed to give away all but one of them? What about the cars? The TV, radios, tools? He who has two, give one to him who has none? Is John suggesting that somehow our possessions keep growing in importance in our lives, clogging up our time and our energy, somehow getting all tied up in our identity; that we think we are somebody because we have so much; that our sense of self-worth and our meaning and motive for living are becoming what we have and what we can acquire? The one who has the most toys wins. To the ordinary people who have become so blinded by their own concern for their own stuff that they cannot see the needs of others, John says, you need to get rid of the stuff. Only by stripping ourselves back to what is really required for living—by looking at the needs of others in the community, by focusing on the deep reality of God, that we do live in one small, global village, that the second, third, and fourth coat I have is really the coat of my brother and sister in the family of God—only by such a chopping away of the branches can we prepare for the coming encounter with the presence of God.

When the tax collectors ask the same question, they are given the simple answer: do not take more than you are supposed to. The tax law and enforcement of tax laws were oppressive at that time, and according to lots of people they are still confusing, and oppressive and intimidating. The law is being misused

and misinterpreted, and the power of the laws is being twisted and extended, to rob those who do not know the law and who do not have the power to make interpretations of the law. John points us to the age-old temptation of those who make the laws to make them in their favor. The tax collectors made the rulings and benefited from them. The *News and Observer* keeps asking the question, Why do those who have so many real estate and development interests always end up on the Department of Transportation board, where they make the decisions about highways and roads that will affect their interests? John says to those who have the power to make and interpret the rules of taxation: Do not abuse that power by making the rules in your favor.

A woman came into the office needing help with her electricity bill. It was more than $600 and she said that she had gotten it down to $600.00 during the winter by doing what the power company had suggested and putting plastic over the windows. But she rented the house, which was old and lacked any insulation; the windows all leaked, and the doorways had major gaps between the door and the frame. The furnace was old and very inefficient, and the landlord did not care how big the woman's bill for electricity was. She was legally responsible for the utilities. It wasn't the landlord's problem! Is this the use of the law to rob from another person?

To the tax collectors John said, do not use the law and the interpretation of the law to rob others. Author Sue Grafton made the subject of one of her alphabet mysteries the growing problem of staging automobile accidents for the purpose of using the law and the rules to defraud the insurance companies and other people. People are pulling in front of others, stopping suddenly, and being rear-ended, and because the law tends to blame the one in the rear for hitting the one in the front, people are using the law and its interpretation to rob and to steal. John says that in order to get ready for the coming of God, renounce the exploitation of the law for your own benefit. Give justice.

Even the Roman soldiers come wanting to be advised on what they are to do now that they are converted and baptized. John says to renounce the use of fear and intimidation as weapons. Live within your means. John says that those who are preparing for the coming of God are not interested in winning by intimidation. Those who are preparing for the new Kingdom do not seek to keep order by fear and force, to rule by coercion, to gain obedience by force. Parents may keep discipline by physical abuse. People may attempt to impose their will upon another by threat and fear, by child abuse, and by sexual harassment. People in athletics may talk trash and taunt. The whole notion of might makes right, John says to the soldiers, is to be turned loose, let go. Give up that special clout you swagger around town with because of your military authority.

Because what is coming, for John, is like a toothache being fixed. It is a hurting that will heal. It is the ending of a long friendship with "good old drinking buddies." It may leave you lonely and friendless for a while, but to continue the friendship would lead to your death. The coming day of judgment is like the day of retirement from the rat race; for a long time it is tough because you do not know what you are supposed to do, but slowly you find yourself no longer a rat but a human being, and there are lots of places you can go, lots of places that need you, lots of opportunities for joy and friendship. And you wonder how you ever had time to work. It is the emptying of your life of all the things that clutter it up that you might indeed discover that which is of eternal importance to you. It is the choosing of the right and the fair and discovering that deep sense of satisfaction that comes in not having to be embarrassed to look in the mirror.

What, then, should we do? Give a coat to one who has none? Collect what is appropriate and fair? Treat with dignity and respect those over whom you have authority? These instructions sound so simple, and like such a letdown after all John's ranting and threatening. But John doesn't want to spoil our excitement, to take all the fun out of the season; he isn't pouring the cold water of Scrooge on our parties. John says that the best way to get ready for the great joy to come is to throw away everything else that in the past we have expected to save us, and make ready for the coming of the Lord's anointed.—Rick Brand

Topic: The Purification of Mary and the Presentation of Jesus

TEXT: Luke 2:22–40

When we reflect on Scripture, we are responding to the intent of the evangelists. Luke, for example, was not trying to present us with exact details of the rite of purification. If we want to know details about the age of the child, about the presence or nonpresence of both mother and father, about the variety of offerings, we should study temple manuals. In his second chapter the inspired writer gifts us with another message from the Lord.

The Christian Church, in continuing this custom, extends its significance. We speak of the presentation of Jesus, the purification of Mary, and in some traditions, of the blessing of candles marking Candlemas day. Some of us may remember watching a young mother approach the front of a church after Sunday worship, where she was joined by the pastor, and the two prayed together. We learned that that was considered "churching," that it was the first time since the birth of her child that the mother was in the assembly. Younger people today would say, "Where was the father? Wasn't the mother at the baptism of her child?" Also, adolescents would say, "Aha, the church does look on sexual action, even in marriage, as somehow impure." So, for many reasons, the church, families, and mothers have discontinued such a misinterpreted tradition.

So, also, the calendar we now use celebrates February 2 as the Presentation of Jesus, with encouragement in some traditions for the blessing of candles. Instead of harking back to Mary's pregnancy and childbirth, we anticipate the lasting favor of God, her continuing as full of grace.

Seniors in our midst are probably more appreciative of the salutation of elderly Simeon, "Now you can dismiss your servant in peace," than are younger people, who are looking forward to decades upon decades of life. Most of them are still at the point of believing themselves invulnerable. Yet even elders may find it difficult to identify with a prophet of a people who had experienced centuries of expectation. We have been nurtured not in the time before Christ, B.C., the era of prophecy, but in A.D., the year of our

Lord, the era of revelation, of the fulfillment of God's promise.

Our experience is so different from that of Simeon and of Anna, who both are described as "of great age." They were certainly educated in the description of the anticipated Messiah. None of those images pictured Emmanuel as a diapered infant. Nonetheless, both Simeon and Anna moved beyond literal interpretations and, inspired by the Spirit of God, recognized their Savior and Redeemer. Let us pause and pray together the hymn of Simeon (Luke 2:29–32):

Master, now you are dismissing
your servant in peace,
according to your word:
for my eyes have seen your salvation,
which you have prepared in the
presence of all peoples,
a light for revelation to the Gentiles
and for glory to your people Israel.

Despite all forecasts of a mighty Messiah, a glorious Avenger of his people, a Protector of a limited chosen people, Simeon and Anna recognized God in this infant. Are there times when, like them, we have found the Lord, known God in unexpected ways, through an encounter with someone weak, dependent, abused, or battered?

On the way to the temple Mary and Joseph must have passed many others, probably parents; evidently these preoccupied worshipers were not stirred to praise God present in this little child. Simeon and Anna had passed the stage of concentrating on their own ambitions, fulfilling their personal dreams. They had reached a level of contemplation that focused their devotion on God and yet included concern for those of younger generations.

Simeon recognized Jesus as the glory of his people, yet he was still in the line of Jewish prophets. So he cautioned Mary about the suffering her son would endure, and about the pain that would pierce her heart also, because Jesus and Mary were ever in holy union. Let us pause another moment and listen to Simeon's words (Luke 2:34–35):

This child is destined for the falling
and the rising of many in Israel,
and to be a sign that will be opposed

so that the inner thoughts of many
will be revealed—and a sword will pierce
your own soul also.

We do not have a record of Anna's prophecy. Meticulous scholars still study texts of the time to find if Anna is an actual person or a symbol of faith-filled widows, freed from the care of spouse and children yet sometimes deprived not only of the love of husband but also that of children, due to plagues or distance. Such a search is not our concern; suffice it to say that Anna represents a senior citizen of her day. Simeon came to the Temple regularly and was fortunate to be at the right place at the right time when Mary and Joseph approached with their son. Anna practically resided in the temple. No matter at what hour the young parents came, she would have been there to welcome them. Simeon expressed his personal thankfulness for God's favor; Anna spread the word to other worshipers.

We can certainly recall times in our lives when we received a special grace, became unexpectedly enlightened. Were we more inclined, like Simeon, to thank God and warn others nearby that joy and sorrow are combined in one life? Or were we more like the extrovert Anna, concentrating on the revelation of glory and wishing all our friends to share our happiness and insight?

This was a moment of revelation for Simeon and Anna. Mary and Joseph had already undergone their test of faith and trust. It must have been consoling for them to listen to a righteous man and a holy woman. The foreboding message, in light of what they had already faced, did not daunt them. Joseph remained quietly by the side of Mary as she listened to the prophecy. The parents would continue to be attentive, loving, responsible, and unassuming—qualities that ensure peace in a family. Neither husband nor wife could anticipate the events of Jesus' childhood, adulthood, passion, death, and Resurrection, or the Pentecostal advent of the Holy Spirit.

Probably we find it difficult to imagine ourselves in the situation of Simeon, Anna, Mary, or Joseph. At least we can conjecture how we would have responded to Simeon and Anna's song of thanksgiving. Would we have joined them? Would we have shushed them for speaking on holy ground? Would we have been annoyed at this distraction from our concentration on personal prayer?

Perhaps the greatest benefit from today's Scripture will be the renewal of our faith that God can make the divine presence known to the aged, the young, men, women, the widowed, the single, the consecrated. We are reminded to keep ourselves open to recognizing God revealed in others around us. The time of public revelation was when the Scriptures were composed; the time of individual coming to the knowledge, love, and service of God is always *now*.—Grace Donovan, S.U.S.C.

Topic: Wanting a Place in the Great Purpose of God

TEXT: Luke 1:26–45

The ability to be surprised: pray God that we never shall lose it! Wisdom was evident when a writer counseled people to "look for the wonderful surprises." Nowhere is this more appropriate than in our search for meaning and significance in personal life. It is important that we be attuned to the possibility of surprise. It has been well said that "God is reliable—but unpredictable." This tells us that in spiritual matters the unexpected may be the norm. The unpredictable may be the one thing we can depend on.

I. The young woman named Mary who gave birth to the child Jesus thankfully allowed herself to be surprised, even astonished and overwhelmed, by the will and action of God. Because of her capacity to accept the unexpected and unpredictable, Mary has been esteemed to be foremost in the affection and devotion of Christians through the ages. The words she spoke—that God "has looked with favor on the lowliness of his servant. Surely, from now on all generations will call me blessed"—have been fulfilled. All generations have stood in awe of Mary's place in the great purpose of God. She gave birth to the Savior, to the Son of the Most High God. She allowed herself to be the servant, the "handmaid" of the Lord. No surprise could have been greater, no surrender to that surprise could have had more far-reaching consequences. In the history of the world, Mary's willing response to God's design gave to humankind, through Jesus' blessing and hope,

meaning and powerful direction. All of us stand forever in her debt.

Concisely and beautifully the New Testament Gospel records her story. It begins by explaining, "In the sixth month the angel Gabriel was sent by God to a town in Galilee called Nazareth, to a virgin engaged to a man whose name was Joseph, of the house of David. The virgin's name was Mary." In brief compass, the sender—God—and the messenger—Gabriel—are said to communicate with Mary, a teenage girl engaged to the village carpenter. Gabriel announced, "Greetings, favored one! The Lord is with you." Mary was taken aback, bewildered and perplexed. "Do not be afraid, Mary, for you have found favor with God." Twice Gabriel spoke of God's favor, reassuring Mary and then preparing her for an incredible announcement: "And now, you will conceive in your womb and bear a son, and you will name him Jesus." The angel then proceeded to describe the greatness of Jesus, this child whom Mary would bear.

Still numb with surprise, Mary did not object or refute Gabriel's words; she simply confessed bafflement as to how this could be. In response she was told, "The Holy Spirit will come upon you, and the power of the Most High will overshadow you; therefore the child to be born will be holy; he will be called Son of God." Commentator Robert Brownrigg says of this account, "Momentarily, the divine plan for the redemption of [humankind] waited upon the consent of this little Jewish girl." Humbly, but apparently not hesitantly, Mary answered, saying, "Here am I, the servant of the Lord; let it be done to me according to your word." With that, the encounter ended.

What happened? Taken off guard, unprepared for the totally unusual, Mary nevertheless allowed herself to be receptive to a message she realized came from God. Hardly fathoming its implications, she nevertheless yielded to its promise. She did that because in her heart she wanted a place in the great purpose of God. No goal for her was higher, no desire stronger. She became the personification of all who stand ready to "hear the Word of the Lord and do it." Mary's surrender literally made a home for God—in the person of Jesus—first within her body and then in the village of Nazareth.

II. It is unthinkable to us that Mary might have refused God's purpose for her life. On the other hand, we probably would have understood if she had protested just a little, saying she was unworthy or only a young woman or not spiritual enough. Had Mary reacted in such fashion she would have been in good company among her own people. Remember how Moses initially tried to dodge God's call by saying he was not eloquent enough to be a leader and spokesperson for his race? Then there was Jeremiah, who became a prophet and shrewd interpreter of events concerning his nation. But Jeremiah also demurred when the word of the Lord came to him. "Ah, Lord God!" he exclaimed, "Truly I do not know how to speak, for I am only a boy." Isaiah, another of the revered Hebrew prophets, also felt inadequate in response to God's claim upon his life. Said Isaiah, "Woe is me! I am lost, for I am a man of unclean lips, and I live among a people of unclean lips; yet my eyes have seen the King, the Lord of hosts!" In every case, after their initial reluctance these individuals accepted their roles and became mighty servants of God. Mary, however, was different: perplexed, yes, but seeking excuses, no. Hers became a reverent and unquestioned act of willing surrender. She found her place in the great purpose of God.

I believe that wanting a place in the great purpose of God is a latent yearning in all of our lives. It is recorded by Bernard of Clairvaux, the saintly Christian monastic, that he placed over the door of his room the inscription, "Bernard, why are you here?" This question, which he confronted every time he entered his room, reminded him to face anew the great purpose of his life. While you and I may never put such a sign over our doorways, that question is vital to our daily existence. Why are we here? To serve ourselves? Or like Mary, are we here to take our unique place in God's plan? Thomas Carlyle said that "in every generation God puts an unfinished task on the workbench of the world." Taking up that task is what life is meant to be about.

We who believe in the God revealed in Jesus Christ are confident that such personal calls come. They came to Moses, Isaiah, Jeremiah, Mary, and many others of biblical tradition. Yet a number of us can testify that we, too, have heard what perhaps was only a "still small voice," but one that defined our futures. Author George Eliot insisted, "There are dealings, dealings with us." That is a way of saying that each one of us is dealt with by God, sought after to fulfill a divine purpose through the expenditure of our human lives. We are here for a purpose; we are meant to play a part in the great purpose of God.

While those who are young have, because of their youth, special reason to heed God's call, every person, regardless of age, has a responsibility here. As has been well-said, "One of the most glorious thoughts in the world is that God depends on us to get his will done. . . . There are some things God literally cannot do apart from ourselves." Think about it. Repeatedly, when God wants something done in the world, he does not mobilize the hosts of heaven. No, God beckons a person— a Mary to become the mother of Jesus; a youth or adult of our time to offer deeds of love and service to hurting and needy souls on every hand. "It is amazing how the eternal, omnipotent God has so condescended to cooperate with [human beings] that apart from us God is helpless to reveal his nature or accomplish his purpose." These words by Leslie Weatherhead direct us again to open our spirits to all that God has in store. And we need to be prepared—for by opening ourselves we may be taken by surprise.

Although this surely is the season of giving and receiving, the time of sharing and being blessed, it also is the right time, the fitting time, for something else. Reflecting on the experience of Mary, it becomes obvious that this above all is a season for *surrender*. It is a moment for saying, "Speak, Lord, your servant hears." Blessed was Mary, the Scripture says, for she "believed that there would be a fulfillment of what was spoken to her by the Lord" (Luke 1:45). Blessed are we if we also believe, having first given our yes, our affirmation of surrender, thus signifying that we, too, desire a place in the great purpose of God.—John H. Townsend

Topic: All in the Family
TEXT: Matt. 13:54–58

With Archie Bunker, Americans were introduced to a different kind of TV family. We had grown accustomed to the almost perfect world of *Ozzie and Harriet, Father Knows Best,* and *Leave It to Beaver*. The Bunkers introduced us to the dysfunctional family, which more nearly approximated the reality of the generational wars of the sixties. Father Archie was a racist bigot who viewed the world through the distorted lens of the conventional wisdom of the working class American. Daughter Gloria and her university-student husband Michael functioned as resident critics of the American culture, while mother Edith was the naive peacemaker who navigated the demilitarized zone between the generations with a simplicity beyond belief. This was an intentional caricature of the "normal" family, with just enough reality to make us laugh at ourselves. Of course the Bunkers were not the typical American family any more than Ozzie and Harriet were, but they succeeded in adjusting our view of the typical and the ideal. Most of us could see something of ourselves in the exaggerated personalities of Archie's world.

I. *Nothing good comes from home.* A few years ago, my church decided to stage a living nativity for the community. We were located on a busy, four-lane road with a large parking lot adjacent to the front lawn. It was a perfect setting. Our associate pastor was determined to do it right. We wired the area for lights and installed a sound system for appropriate music. One of our members had a donkey, and somewhere we acquired sheep. If the zoo had been willing, we would have had camels and elephants. We rotated the roles of shepherds and wise men, Mary and Joseph. Seeing our folks cast in biblical roles and wearing first-century costumes was amusing and a bit sacrilegious. The newest member of our church family was Amy. The young parents were more than willing to allow her to play baby Jesus to their Mary and Joseph. We still chuckle at the memory of breaking the gender line in the living nativity. We still have difficulty casting biblical roles with people like us.

Have you ever wondered about the real picture of Jesus' family? My earliest mental image of the holy family emerged at Christmas. I was impressed by the nativity creche, which introduced me to a totally foreign image of the family. In my world, normal people did not have halos of light around their heads. Add to that picture the children's carol, "Away in the Manger," in which the "little Lord Jesus, no crying he made"

and the distortion is complete. I had a baby brother at home. In our house the baby had a healthy set of lungs and used them appropriately to report discomforts or just to make his presence known. Nothing in the stereotype of the holy family corresponded with my experience of family. My childhood picture of the birth of Jesus was from a totally foreign world—foreign not only to my culture but to any normal family in my time and space. I am still amazed at how much the child's-eye view of the birth of Christ dominates our adult understanding. Our flight from adult reality leaves us with at least two problems: we are left with a misunderstanding of the Scriptures and a distorted view of God.

II. *The Christ was one of us.* The biblical picture of Jesus is closer to our reality than we have allowed. When the adult Jesus dropped by Nazareth, his hometown, to extend his teaching mission to neighbors and friends of the family, he was rejected as "one of us." Somehow we tend to prefer imported heroes. The story is told by Mark and retold by Matthew and Luke. John simply declared that he came to his own and that "his own people did not accept him." Why not? He did not meet their criteria of a prophet. You are not an expert unless you come from a hundred miles away and cost at least $100.

The people were "offended"—actually, "scandalized." They stumbled over familiarity like they would later stumble over the cross. Mark identified Jesus as "the carpenter, the son of Mary." The townspeople were familiar with his parents and his siblings—sufficient proof to dismiss him as an impostor; and Luke reported that they wanted to throw Jesus over a cliff.

About ten years into retirement, my parents moved back to the community where I grew up. Although much has changed, enough remains of the old community to feed my nostalgia on visits to the old church. On one visit, a former teacher located a speaker stand that I had made for our ninth grade class in our school shop. I specifically recall a conversation about one of my peers who had gone on to a university and had finished a doctorate. "Can you imagine calling him Dr.?" I was asked. I fully agreed as I wondered about myself and several other kids who had gone off to acquire degrees and titles. Hometown kids never really qualify as prophets.

If we are faithful to the Gospel, we have to toss out the halo. Luke approaches reality in the story of the boy Jesus in the Temple, and we are reminded again that Jesus did not float down from heaven on a cloud or pop into the world full grown one lazy summer afternoon. Some folks knew him when he was a normal kid playing in the fields around Nazareth, or as a young man working in Joseph's shop. Someone remembered a childhood story. Another had a house with furniture that he had made.

III. *The Christ was sent from God.* God seems to specialize in doing the supernatural through the natural, the extraordinary through the ordinary. The failure in Nazareth was not about what the folks did to the image of Jesus. They did us a favor in identifying him as one of us, even when they closed their eyes to the presence of God. "Because of their unbelief," the power of God was not evident in Nazareth. Faith involves looking and listening for God. As the ministry of Jesus was limited by the myopia of his neighbors, so now we can be blind to the work of God in our presence. Jesus repeated the statement in his preaching. "Let those who have ears, hear." The perception of God in our time has less to do with the divine mystery than with human prejudice. The responsibility falls on us.—Larry Dipboye

Topic: Opening Blind Eyes

TEXT: John 9:24–39

At this time of the year, our Jewish friends celebrate Hanukkah, an eight-day festival that commemorates the cleansing and rededication of the Temple following the victories of Judas Maccabeus on December 25, 164 B.C. The Maccabees made a new sacrificial altar and holy vessels, burned incense on the incense altar, lit the lampstands to give light to the Temple, placed bread on the table, and hung new curtains. The celebration involves lighting one candle each day for eight days; thus Hanukkah, "dedication," is also known as the Feast of Lights.

It was hardly a coincidence in John that Jesus was approaching Hanukkah when he came upon the man born blind and declared to his disciples, "I am the light of the world." The drama of healing was complete when the man, who had regained his physical sight, came to spiritual vision by faith in Christ.

Finally, Jesus interpreted the healing event: "I came into this world for judgment so that those who do not see may see, and so that those who do see may become blind." Of the four Gospel writers, John is the artist. He tells the story of Jesus in circular fashion, identifying central themes, which he repeats and illustrates with events. In the prologue, John announces, "The true light, which enlightens everyone, was coming into the world," and we begin to get the message. But the revelation of this light is more than words. Jesus is the Word become flesh, whose message is visible to those who are willing to see. Jesus is the Word in action who opens blind eyes.

I. *Is destiny determined by birth?* In our time, Rabbi Harold Kushner's book *When Bad Things Happen to Good People* reaches beyond the traditional answers to suffering, much as Jesus did. The question of the disciples, "Who sinned?" was as irrelevant in the first century as it is in the twenty-first century, and as it had been in the story of Job. The question will always be inconsistent with the nature of the God of creation, but for some reason we keep on asking it. The cause of suffering is one of those who-done-it-detective stories, which has to have a villain. To identify the parents as the sinners who caused this poor man to be born blind was about as creative as pointing to the butler, except that the disciples had expanded their vision to allow for the possibility that others, perhaps a sibling or grandparent, had brought down the wrath of God on a helpless newborn. Jesus ignored the cause and got to the opportunity that human suffering presents to do the work of God.

It may be the missions story of the century. Missionaries James and Robbi Francovich visited a remote Indian village of sixty Hindu "untouchables." Birth determines destiny in this culture. There is no way out of the bottom caste of scavengers and servants. They are called untouchables for good reason. But the missionaries did not accept the cultural and religious limits. They visited the small village and embraced the people. They invited them to a Good Friday service and a meal. They told them about the God who had sent Jesus Christ to love them, and on Easter the entire village committed to faith in Christ. They accepted that they were accepted by God. Of course the story is far from over, but who can fail to see the miracle of grace at work here? Ramadu, the village elder, said it best: never before had anyone helped or loved them, much less touched them. People who had long lived in darkness had come to see the great light of God coming into our world.

Don't come down too hard on the Indian Hindu culture. We make the same judgments daily. Where is the hope for someone born poor in our culture? Blame the parents and attribute human suffering to the will of God. Why bother with lighting candles if we attribute the darkness to God? The Gospels seem to be aware that the baby Jesus was as vulnerable to mad kings and unjust public policy as were the other infants of Bethlehem. He too was born poor and deprived. Babies have to be protected, and sometimes rescued. Blaming may help us to duck responsibility for the little ones, but it seldom solves the mystery of evil.

The man was born blind. John repeats the conventional wisdom of the day. Never before had anyone regained sight who had been born blind. Birth had always explained the situation as a divine imperative, and religious folks had always been free to walk away clicking their tongues about how awful it is that someone had sinned and blinded this poor fellow for life.

II. *We choose our destiny.* A story that begins in the darkness of one born blind becomes a celebration of the power of God to open blind eyes. A story that begins with issues of sight finally comes down to a question of vision. Just because your eyes work does not mean that you envision God's redemptive grace. Sometimes blind people envision what sighted people refuse to see.

Helen was born without sight, but her husband, "Park," had been blinded as the result of an accident as a teenager. Carolyn met Helen at a writers conference. Helen needed a ride to Birmingham, and they eventually became regular travel companions and good friends. The Parkers lived near the Louisville School for the Blind, where Helen had sometimes worked translating books into Braille and where her husband caned chairs. The ladies were having a missions lunch at our house, and Park and I were invited to join them. I escorted Park to the car and we drove the ten miles to our house. Park asked a few questions about where we were going, and then began to envision where we were at each turn. He literally saw with his mind's eye. I was fascinated by his knowledge of the streets and his memory of the area. He told me about the days when my subdivision was a cultivated field. He talked freely about compensating for his handicap. He told of a grocer who had bagged spoiled fruit thinking that Park would not know the difference and about how he had confronted the man and demanded direct access to the produce. Helen and Park lacked sight but had tremendous vision. They could not see the world around them, but they lived by the vision of God's grace. They had become models of productive, giving Christians, although they were poor by any standards. They had become beacons of light in a world surrounded by darkness. Helen's biography was appropriately named *Light on Life's Pathway.* We still grieve our loss and the world's loss at her death.

I think of the Parkers when I read John's story. Restored sight is a wonderful miracle, but the real miracle here is a redeemed life, and that is exactly what John wants you to see. Jesus not only healed a blind man, he opened a door to the power of a committed faith. The real vision is revealed in our worship. Jesus was not just born into this world, he came with a mission. He came to expose our blindness and to open our vision to the power of his love. The same Jesus who declared, "I am the light of the world," also has commissioned us, "You are the light of the world."—Larry Dipboye

Illustrations

A WAKE-UP CALL.   As we crossed the threshold of the final decade of the twentieth century, we found ourselves inundated with images of dramatic change and flickering hope. . . . I strongly affirm that these flickers of hope are neither random nor isolated. The jubilant dancing on the Berlin Wall is the dance of God. The songs of freedom sung exuberantly by South African children are the songs of God. The ardent prayers of East European young people are the prayers of God. And the longings for peace in the Middle East are the longings of God. Our God is alive and well—and not found only in the songs of celebration. Our God can also be heard in the cries of pain in the prisons of El Salvador, the scenes of desperation in the urban wastelands of the United States, and the mounting famine in the Horn of Africa. Our God fully participates in both the pain and the hope that fills our world.—Tom Sine[3]

SEEING GOD.   God would have us know him and meet him in Jesus Christ. It is by no rarefied speculative flights of reason, nor by the intuitions of any light within us, that we are to find God; but God comes to us in Jesus, in a real person who lived, loved, and suffered and who is now alive in the unseen world and very near to all who seek to know God. Our hearts have often cried out at all times: "Show us the Father"; and the answer is still given to us: "He that hath seen Me hath seen the Father."—W. D. Davies[4]

WHAT GOD GAVE US.   What God gave us was neither His portrait nor His principle; He gave us Himself—His presence, His life, His action. He did more than show us Himself, more than teach us about Himself—He gave us Himself, He sacrificed Himself. It is ourselves He seeks, therefore it was Himself He gave, life for life and soul for soul. He asks us for life-committal, because it was His life He committed to us. He gave us love by giving us Himself to love.—P. T. Forsyth[5]

THE NEWS IS FOR YOU.   The news of the birth of the child in Bethlehem is not to be likened to a statement made in a textbook. A professor would perhaps have said: "To mankind is born a Savior." So what? We are apt to deduce that mankind in general does not include me, is only meant for others. It is like in a movie or a play where we are confronted with people who are not ourselves. In contrast, the angel of the Lord points to the shepherds and points to *us*. His news is directly addressed to us: "*To you* is born this day a Savior!" You, regardless of who you are, whether or not you understand the message, whether or not you are good and pious people. The news is meant for you. For your

benefit the Christmas story happened.—Karl Barth[6]

A GIFT MONEY CAN'T BUY.   A missionary tried desperately to teach her young African students about the real meaning of Christmas and why Christians often exchange gifts in celebration of the Savior's birth. She wasn't sure that her students understood. But then one day, one of the boys brought her the most beautiful seashell that she had ever seen. "It's absolutely gorgeous!" she said. "It's wonderful! Fantastic! Where did you ever find such an unusual shell?"

The boy explained that sea shells could only be found on a remote beach about twenty miles away. He had walked there and back a few days earlier to find just the right gift for her.

"You shouldn't have gone all that way just to get a gift for me," she said almost apologetically. But the boy explained, "But the long walk is part of the gift."

Then the teacher realized that perhaps her students understood the lesson better than she ever imagined.—Gary C. Redding[7]

EARS TO HEAR.   "Behold I stand at the door and knock!" A strong, large hand reaches out after us. What does it want of us? What will become of us in its grip? That is none of our business. We need only know that we are in this hand. He, who knows this, understands the Bible, the heart of the Bible—Jesus Christ. One may live without knowing this, for Jesus Christ does not thrust himself upon anyone. We must again and again remind ourselves that we have forgotten this fact. We may call to Him: "Come, Lord Jesus, be our guest!" but He will not become once for all a member of any household. The announcement is and always will be a question addressed to each of us. For Jesus Christ is and always will be the living word of God; and his thoughts are not our thoughts and our ways are not his ways. We may or may not hear; Jesus Christ speaks to those who have ears to hear.—Karl Barth[8]

---

[3] *Wild Hope*
[4] *The New Creation*
[5] *Revelation Old and New*

[6] *Deliverance to the Captives*
[7] *I Love to Tell the Stories*
[8] *Come Holy Spirit*

SECTION VII.
Evangelism and World Missions

SERMON SUGGESTIONS

Topic: Risky Business
TEXT: John 3:1–21

Someone once said that there are three types of people in the world:

Risktakers: those who are willing to gamble everything

Caretakers: those who watch out for others and themselves, playing it close to the vest

Undertakers: those who do so little they bury everyone and everything around them

We meet all of these types in the New Testament, and there is no doubt as to which group Nicodemus belongs: the risktakers. It is highly risky for Nicodemus to come to Jesus—even under the cover of night. He must talk to Jesus himself to get answers to his questions, so he dares to risk his reputation, his position, and his standing in society in order to talk with Jesus.

If we would follow Jesus, then we must also be willing to take risks, to step out onto ground that is both unsure and uncharted. Quite honestly, the Church is known for anything but risk taking, is it not? We plan our course of action and set our goals, financial and otherwise, based on the predictable, that is, on what we did last year. We discover the direction of the societal or cultural wind, and then we follow that breeze, regardless of where the Spirit blows. Because we view our church as an institution rather than as a mission outpost, as an organized society rather than as a guer-

rilla camp, we become more concerned with institutional survival than with impact.

Fortunately—or unfortunately, depending on your point of view—Jesus has not called us to be caretakers or undertakers, but to be risktakers. Jesus calls us to drop all that we consider valuable and important and follow him.

I. What are the risks inherent in following Jesus, the risks we cannot avoid if we would be true followers and not distant admirers. The first risk is that *we will never fully comprehend where the Spirit is leading or what God is about in our lives and our world.* Our knowledge of God's will is always after the fact, never before. Paul expressed it this way: "We gaze through a dark, shady glass."

Nicodemus wants a completely rational belief, and God will not let him have it. Jesus says to Nicodemus, "You must be born from above," and this is incomprehensible for Nicodemus.

Some of us have never experienced that spiritual birth, that birth from above. Ours was a rational, intellectual decision, prompted by parents or by the decisions of friends; it was not a life-transforming experience in the depths of our soul. We're like Nicodemus—religious but separated from God—and we need to let the Spirit blow through our lives.

II. If we would follow Jesus, then there is another risk: *we will never be in control of our lives.* Jesus said to Nicodemus, "The wind blows wherever it pleases. You hear its sound, but you cannot tell where it comes from or where it is going. So it is with everyone born of the Spirit." As one who has been trying to follow the Spirit, let me share one word: *unpredictable.* We can never predict what the

301

Spirit will do or how the Spirit will lead or act in a given situation. The Spirit will lead us into some of the most difficult situations we have ever faced.

III. This following Jesus is risky business because *it begins with a leap of faith and is a roller coaster ride from there on out.* Jesus said to Nicodemus "For God so loved the world that he gave his one and only Son, that whosoever believes in him shall not perish but have eternal life." We have taken the verb *believe* and have made it into a noun, *belief,* and in so doing we have exchanged trust in Jesus for intellectual assent. The phrase would be better translated (because of our usage), "whoever faiths in him." Jesus is not referring here to intellectual assent to doctrinal statements—although these are important as road signs on our faith journey—but to a surrender of

our lives to him in an act of trust that through Jesus we will find forgiveness and a quality of life that is so drastically different as to exist forever—eternal life.

Almost two thousand years ago a man walked on this earth who was more than a man. He said that if we are willing to risk our lives on the belief that he is the Messiah, then the Spirit will come and blow through our lives and we will be radically different. He said that our lives, though dead and lifeless because of our sin and evil, will be radically born from above through the power of the Spirit. Are you willing to risk your life that Jesus was right? Am I? Is our church? God will that we might listen to the Spirit and follow, no matter what the risk, Yes, following Jesus is risky business.—Robert U. Ferguson Jr.

The Call to Evangelism: A Series of Three Sermons

by William Powell Tuck

Topic: The Call to Evangelism

TEXT: Gen. 12:1–2; Mark 1:17; Matt. 28:19

Who among us has not encountered some evangelist, professional or lay, who has assaulted us with his or her approach to religion? In their pushy, offensive, arrogant way they have demanded that we believe what they want us to believe or we can't be Christian. Unfortunately, a lot of people have seen this negative approach as evangelism, and they have been clearly, and maybe rightfully so, turned off by it. A beautiful word has been twisted and distorted into a negative image.

I. *The drift away from evangelism.* Many contemporary churches have shifted away from the early Church's commitment to evangelism. What has caused this to happen?

a. The first reason I would suggest is that many people in our churches have a vague sort of naive assumption that everybody in American society is already a Christian. But this "civil" religion is a far cry from the authentic New Testament version of the faith.

Look around you and you will notice quickly that few people have any real sense of sin today. *Sin* is a word that is foreign to many people. They attach no meaning to the word

sin, and they seldom worry about what they have done that is wrong, unless they get caught. We assume that as long as people are wealthy and successful they have no spiritual needs. This would imply that they have no need of God or Christ. They have money! Often we are unaware of their deeper needs for meaning, purpose, understanding, forgiveness, hope, and love. Sometimes they are lonely, frustrated, depressed, and confused. They, too, long for wholeness and faith. We have a word of hope that they need to hear.

b. Second, *evangelism* has become a bad word today because of the distorted images we often see in society. Who among us has not been the victim of some preacher who has tried to browbeat us, twist our arms, and make us feel guilty? The recent scandals of several television evangelists have marred the image of evangelism. Many people cannot see beyond these images.

We are usually turned off by these distortions of evangelism. Tragically, the corruption of something that was once good has caused many to reject evangelism. My wife was recently reading a book dealing with the faith of some of our country's founding fathers and she came across a line from Thomas Jefferson, who had been reading a lengthy work by Joseph Priestly dealing with corruption in religion. Jefferson said, "I thought I had rejected Christianity but I had rejected only a corruption of Christianity." Don't reject evangelism; reject the corruption of evangelism.

c. Third, evangelism has also waned in our day because many Christians are ignorant of the real content of the Christian faith they claim. They cling to fuzzy notions of Christianity and have never ventured into a pilgrimage to understand or grow into a more mature faith.

d. Fourth, I think that evangelism has fallen on hard times because of the claims by some that everything the Church does is evangelistic. The assertion that everything we do is evangelism is often an excuse that keeps a church from being evangelistic. Yes, everything we do as a church should point persons to the ultimate source of why we do ministry. But most of these ministries are not evangelism per se. They point to Christ and prepare persons to hear the good news. Everything prepares or leads the way, but the good news has to be shared at some point.

e. Fifth, another hindrance to evangelism is our timidity. We are often too embarrassed and timid to share our faith. Some are embarrassed because they do not want to appear as fanatics. If our faith is shared naturally and without pressure, we will not have to worry about this kind of label.

f. Sixth, one of the major reasons that evangelism has fallen on such hard times is that many churches have lost their sense of mission. Many churches have become community centers or family clubs. Apathy has overtaken the church members, and few seem concerned with sharing the message of salvation with others. The church cannot—must not—be preoccupied with itself and forget those outside its walls who need to hear the message of salvation.

Without evangelism the Church will die. The Church is always one generation away from extinction. As important as all our other ministries are, if the Church is not careful, we may let everything else we do keep us from doing the work of evangelism.

The word *evangelism* is a beautiful New Testament word. The prefix on the word, means "good." The main body of the word, means "angel." An angel is a messenger who brings good news about God. Evangelism is bringing good news—good news about what God has done for us in Jesus Christ! You and I need to remember that evangelism is the marvelous message of the good news of God's grace in Christ. Our responsibility as evangelists is to share that good news with others.

II. *The call to evangelize.* You and I, as members of the Church of Christ, should respond positively to the call to be evangelists, for many reasons. Let me suggest a few of these.

a. First, because it is the command of God. In Genesis we read that God commanded Abraham to leave his country and go searching for a new land that God would give him, and he promised that Abraham would be a blessing to all nations. When the people of Israel turned inward and became consumed with their own nationalism, they corrupted the call of Abraham.

Jesus called his disciples to be fishers of men. He summoned Peter and Andrew with the words, "Come after me, and I will make you fishers of men." Jesus commanded his followers, in the great commission, to "go into all the world and preach the gospel," to "go and make disciples of all nations," and to "be my witnesses unto the uttermost part of the earth."

b. Second, we notice in the New Testament, in the example of the early Christians, that evangelism was the responsibility of every Christian. Evangelism was not left to a few preachers.

c. Third, we should be evangelists not only because of the command of Christ and the example of the early church, but out of our own concern for other people.

d. Fourth, we should want to be evangelists because we should want to speak out of the love that we have experienced in Christ. Paul says, "For the love of Christ constrains us" (2 Cor. 5:14).

e. Fifth, I also want to share the good news of Christ with others out of the joy that I have experienced in God's love. When the joy of Christ beats in our hearts, we will radiate a light that will enable us to be "epistles known and read by all persons" (2 Cor. 3:2).

Topic: The Church's Mandate for Evangelism
    TEXT: Mark 1:14–15; Luke 4:18–19; Phil. 2:5–8

I want to begin with the declaration that the evangelism of the Church originated from our Lord himself. Jesus modeled authentic evangelism for us. The man from Nazareth is the one who has given us the ideal pattern of how to be evangelists in the world.

Theologians and New Testament scholars have written thick books in which they have tried to explain the meaning of the word *gospel*. Mark summarized in two verses the gospel that Jesus preached. He wrote that Jesus came into Galilee preaching the good news about God. He noted that the time was fulfilled, and that the Kingdom of God was now present; repent and believe the good news. Jesus came announcing that the time for God's reign was imminent. The Roman roadways and culture, the Greek universal language and philosophy, and the dispersal of the Jews around the world made the time ripe for God's Son to come. Paul expressed it this way: "When the time had fully come, God sent forth his Son" (Gal. 4:4). The Kingdom of God—the reign, the rule, the sovereignty of God, the new order—was about to be instituted by Jesus.

Following his announcement that the new order was at hand, Jesus issued an appeal: *repent*. He did not hesitate to call persons to repentance. He called them to turn around, to change their minds, and to go in a new direction. "Look, the new order is present. Believe the good news. Believe, commit yourself to the way of God, and follow that truth." Jesus made his bold announcement and then delivered his appeal to respond. He called his hearers to respond to the proclamation of the good news that the new order had broken into time.

I. *Jesus' concern for persons.* As Jesus went throughout Galilee preaching the good news about God's Kingdom, the Master Teacher demonstrated through his words and life the model for evangelism. The basic principle he taught was his concern for persons. Wherever Jesus traveled he responded to the people who reached out to him.

To Jesus, persons are more important than institutions, public meetings, personal success, traditions, laws, or anything else. His priority was with persons.

The Gospels record that Jesus showed his concern for persons by associating with people from every walk of life. He did not hesitate to associate with persons who were classified as sinners and outcasts.

II. *Those who are lost.* Jesus favorite word for describing those who had not responded to the gospel was *lost*. Jesus said, "I have come to seek and to save that which is lost." We live in a world filled with all kinds of lostness and brokenness. Men and women are estranged from God. They are fragmented in their relationships with one another and do not understand their authentic personhood. Jesus told various parables to describe different ways that individuals could be lost.

III. *Concern for the whole person.* The concern that Jesus had for persons was not limited to their souls; he was concerned with the whole person. Before you can give the Bread of Life to a person who is starving, you must first feed him or her physical bread. Before you can give the good news of salvation to one who is drowning, you must first rescue that individual from the waves. In his sermon at Nazareth, Jesus stated that the Spirit of the Lord was upon him and that he had come to preach the good news to the poor, to heal the brokenhearted, to deliver those in captivity, to open the eyes of the blind, and to set free the oppressed. He was the herald of the good news of God's Kingdom. He proclaimed that the acceptable year of the Lord had arrived.

True evangelism—the saving message of God's grace for all persons—will also be concerned with the social conditions in which people live. Authentic evangelism will confront racism, sexism, drugs, alcoholism, war, famine, disease, child abuse, exploitation of persons, and AIDS. All of these great social issues are concerns for the evangelists. Before we can bring the good news to persons, we have to be concerned with their problems, and we have to work to overcome these problems as well as to carry to people the words of salvation.

IV. *Jesus' response to people.* As we study the life of Jesus, we observe that he had no set method of evangelism but responded to persons where he found them and to whatever their need was. He had no rigid pattern, no Roman Road to salvation, and no thought that there was only one way you could proclaim salvation to somebody. In his concern for persons, he responded to each one individually.

V. *Jesus' method of teaching.* Just as Jesus used variety in his response to persons, so we notice the varied methods he used to teach the good news. When you read the Gospels, you discover that Jesus used simple, everyday experiences and stories about life to convey the good news of God. He drew analogies, illustrations, and many of his thoughts from people's home lives.

Sometimes Jesus gave his listeners a short, memorable sentence: "If a person strikes you on one cheek, turn to him the other." "Seek first the Kingdom of God." "Do unto others as you would have them do unto you." The beatitudes and the Lord's Prayer hung in the listener's mind and heart. The Gospels are filled with simple statements of truth that Jesus used to convey his message about God.

Jesus often used pointed questions to communicate his gospel message. He raised questions with his listeners to arouse their interest. "Which of you, being anxious, can add a cubic to his span of life" (Luke 12:25)? "Can a blind man lead a blind man" (Luke 6:39)?

Jesus often drew upon the Scriptures in his ministry. In his temptation experience with Satan in the wilderness, he quoted passages of Scripture (Luke 4:1–12). Frequently Jesus asked his listeners, "Have you not read where it is written" (Matt. 21:40)? He was thoroughly grounded in the Scriptures, and often began or ended his discussion with a person with a quote from the Scriptures.

Jesus also devoted himself to long hours of prayer. His concern and compassion for those who were lost took him to his knees. Jesus continually prayed for those who had not responded to his Kingdom message. He prayed before he chose his disciples, and before he sent them out, entered a city, taught, preached or made an important decision. He prayed for those who were like sheep without a shepherd.

On other occasions Jesus used humor to communicate his message. "Why are you concerned about that tiny speck in your brother's eye when you have a log sticking out of your own" (Luke 6:41)?

VI. *What methods should we follow today?* Churches may spend so much time with methods and procedures that we never get on with the plan to rescue those who are lost. Following the example of our Lord, we need to be about the business of meeting people, responding to their needs, and carrying the good news to them.

When you read the Gospel records, you will notice that Jesus Christ lived and died the gospel that he preached. He didn't simply talk about religion and God; his whole life demonstrated what he taught. As John said, "The word became flesh."

Jesus not only talked about ministry and lived it, but he also was willing to lay down his life so that persons might know God. "I have come," he declared, "to give my life as a ransom for many" (Mark 10:45).

Topic: A Guide from the Biblical Evangelists
TEXT: Exod. 4:10–16; John 20:30–31; Acts 2:14–16, 22–24, 37–38

Jesus gave his disciples a commission: "Go into all the world and preach the gospel" (Matt. 28:19). "You shall be my witnesses beginning in Jerusalem . . . to the uttermost parts of the world" (Acts 1:8). The apostle Paul later wrote: "Woe is me if I preach not the gospel of Christ" (1 Cor. 9:16). The early disciples had a dramatic sense of compulsion to share the good news of Jesus Christ.

I. *How the disciples shared their witness.* Let us look now into the New Testament and learn from the biblical evangelists something about how they witnessed for Christ. In what ways did they share the good news?

a. One way the disciples bore witness for Christ was by *preaching.* The first disciples didn't have church buildings like we do today, to which they could invite people, saying: "Come to our church. There is going to be preaching at eleven o'clock on Sunday morning." No, they had to preach wherever they could. Sometimes the disciples preached outdoors. There are many occasions in Acts where Paul, Peter, and others preached in Jerusalem, Samaria, Lystra, and many other places.

If you look carefully at Peter's first sermon, and at most of the rest of the sermons in Acts, you will notice that there are five basic points—not three, but five! An outline for Peter's sermon and the others might be the following:

Look at what Jesus did. The disciples pointed to the wonders, signs, and messages of Jesus.

Look at what you did to Jesus. This was their point if they were talking to the Jewish people. They would declare, "You rejected him, crucified him, and put him to death." If speaking to Gentiles, they would point out how Jesus was put to death by the Jews.

Look at what God did. God raised Jesus up from the grave.

Look at what we are doing. We are bearing witness to the power and glory of God. We are the witnesses to what God has done in Christ.

Look at what you need to do. Repent and be baptized.

b. Another method the disciples used was *personal witnessing.* When Andrew talked with Jesus and came to believe that Jesus was the Messiah, he brought his brother Simon Peter to meet Jesus (John 1:41). After Philip met Jesus, he in turn told Nathaniel about Jesus (John 1:45). The disciples always seemed to be busy telling others about Jesus.

c. The Book of Acts shows the apostles engaging in *house-to-house visitation.* Paul stated, "I did not shrink from declaring to you anything that was profitable, and from teaching you in public and from house to house" (Acts 20:20). Paul spoke wherever he had opportunity: in the synagogue and from house to house.

d. The apostles also *shared their personal experience with Jesus Christ.* John wrote in his Epistle, "That which we have heard, which we have seen with our eyes, which we have looked upon and touched with our hands, concerning the word of life—we proclaim also to you" (1 John 1:1–3). They were witnesses to an event, and they shared this experience with others.

e. A fifth way in which the early disciples spread the good news about Christ was a completely new approach that we can describe as *literary evangelism.* The verses in the Gospel of John 20:30–31 were originally meant, most likely, to be where he planned to end his Gospel. The rest might be a long footnote to the ending. What was the purpose of the writing? He declared: "But these are written that you may believe that Jesus is the Christ, and that believing you may have life in his name."

The Gospels were a completely new way of writing in that day. As far as scholars can tell, no other groups had constructed this way of proclaiming the truth about their religious leader. This approach was radically new. The

Gospel writers did not try to write a historical biography about Jesus. No one of the Gospels contains all the truth about Jesus Christ. In fact, John wrote, "Now, Jesus did many other signs in the presence of his disciples which are not written in this book (John 20:30) but there are also many other things which Jesus did; were everyone of them to be written I suppose that the world could not contain the books that could be written" (John 21:25).

Most of us first came to Christ through the work of an individual. But following the work of that person, we began to read and study the Scriptures. The Gospels, the other portions of the Bible, and other Christian writings continue to point persons to Christ and to guide them into a deeper, richer faith.

II. *A closer look at the way the disciples shared their faith.*

a. How did the biblical evangelists bear witness to Christ? The first thing I would mention is this: *they shared their faith wherever they met people and in whatever opportunities they had.*

b. Second, the apostles *shared their faith with enthusiasm.* Peter and other Christians were accused of being drunk (Acts 2:13). Why? Because they were excited about their faith. Festus said to Paul, "Why, you are beside yourself. Too much learning has made you mad" (Acts 26:24).

c. Third, the apostles were *courageous* in their witness. Even while Stephen was being stoned by the religious authorities, he bore witness to what he had experienced in Jesus Christ (Acts 6:5–7, 60). While Paul held the garments of those who had stoned Stephen, the blood of the first martyr began, somehow, I believe, to penetrate Paul's mind and heart. Later, when Jesus Christ confronted him on the Damascus Road, his life was changed forever. But the blood of Stephen was the seed that produced fruit later. The one who had been persecuting the Christians now became persecuted. Paul was stoned, whipped, imprisoned, beaten, shipwrecked, and ridiculed. Paul, Peter, Stephen, and Barnabas witnessed with boldness for Christ. Legend says that Peter was crucified upside down in Rome. Most likely Paul, after he was imprisoned, was put to death for his witness to Christ.

Beginning with the first disciples, who were courageous enough to stand up and proclaim the good news of what God had done in Christ, others have joined their ranks through the centuries. The presence of their living Lord sustained them and gave them courage.

d. Fourth, they *drew on the Scriptures* as their source of authority. On almost every occasion when they preached, Peter, Paul, Stephen, and others quoted from the Old Testament Scriptures. They attempted to help their listeners understand by these references how Jesus Christ was the fulfillment of their long-awaited expectations. They declared that Jesus was the Messiah. They opened the Scriptures and pointed their hearers to Christ.

e. Finally, note that the disciples *always pointed people to Jesus Christ*. They never tried to call attention to themselves. Their goal was to lead persons to belief in Jesus Christ as Lord. As Paul declared, "For it is not ourselves that we preach" (2 Cor. 4:5).

Every witness—preacher, layperson, spokesperson—needs to remember that in evangelism we don't call attention to ourselves. We point people to Jesus Christ so that they might find in him redemption and eternal life. Now it is your turn and mine to be witnesses.

Illustrations

LED BY THE SPIRIT.   The Spirit led Jesus into the desert to be tempted by Satan. Later, the Spirit led Jesus to Jerusalem to be crucified.

The Spirit led Stephen to preach about Jesus—and he was murdered for following the Spirit.

The Spirit led Paul to preach the gospel—and to get kicked out of just about every major city from Jerusalem to Rome.

The Spirit led St. Augustine, John Wesley, Martin Luther, John Calvin, Roger Williams, and Martin Luther King, and in our day the Spirit continues to lead those who will follow.—Robert U. Ferguson Jr.

PERSONS OR PROCEDURES?   In Mark Twain's *Huckleberry Finn,* Huck and his friend Tom Sawyer are depicted in the last chapter trying to figure out a plan to help free old Jim, a runaway slave who has been captured and imprisoned in a cabin by Tom's uncle. Tom comes up with the most elaborate plan you have ever seen to try to free Jim. His imagination runs wild. It would take years to implement the elaborate rescue that they wanted to perfect to set Jim free. All the time they are talking and dreaming about their plan to set him free, Jim is chained to his bed in a dark cabin without food and water and his life is threatened. The procedure to free Jim has become more significant than the person who needs to be rescued.—William Powell Tuck

THE JOY OF GOD.   Joseph Haydn, the famous composer, was asked one day why his music was always so animated and cheerful. He replied, "I cannot make it otherwise. I write according to the thoughts I feel; when I think of God, my heart is so full of joy that the notes leap and dance as they leave my pen; and since God has given me a cheerful heart ... I serve him with a cheerful spirit."—William Powell Tuck

FEELINGS OF INADEQUACY.   I can remember that on several occasions when I was a young minister and went to call at a certain home, I would pause before I knocked on the door and pray silently, "Oh, Lord, don't let them be at home." Many are timid because they do not know what to say or how to approach another person with the message of good news. Training and experience can help us overcome these feelings of inadequacy and fear of failure.—William Powell Tuck

GETTING IN THE WAY.   A magazine carried a cartoon that showed a minister preaching a sermon about Jesus and the cross. Along with his sermon, he showed some slides of Jesus on the cross. But the minister was standing down front and his shadow was cast across the picture of Jesus and the cross. The line in the cartoon read: "Down in front, please."—William Powell Tuck

SECTION VIII.
Bible Studies

BY EDUARD SCHWEIZER

Bible Study I: God

TEXT: Exod. 3:1–14; Phil. 2:6–11

God? There are so very many people to whom God means nothing. For them, God is but a word, and even an old-fashioned one. For them, God is not a reality. But is he a reality for us? Are we his people, a band of disciples from whom power and joy and peace go out to the world, contaminating it, changing it, giving it new hope and courage? God? Is God a word for us, and perhaps even an old-fashioned one? Is he reality for us? Is he merely a concept preserved within credal formulas and religious hymns? God? Does he mean anything in the laboratories where they prepare ever new kinds of devilish bombs, in the parlors of diplomats where new aggressions are planned, in the offices of captains of industry where they decide about the wages of thousands of workers, in the schools where they teach us how to cultivate our land? Does God mean anything in this, our modern world? Or is he perhaps living in some hearts but imprisoned there so that he cannot enter into our real, modern world to change structures of authority and subjection, to bridge deep clefts, to give new directions. There have been and there are men who kill one another in the name of God, who hate men of other races in the name of God, who suppress weaker peoples in the name of God, who sweat their laborers in the name of God. Is God but a word, and even an old-fashioned one, in our world that has come of age?

V. 1a. *"Now Moses was keeping the flock of his father-in-law, Jethro."* Where is God? Oh, there was a time when one could believe in God.

Moses had been saved from an almost certain death. He had been brought up in luxurious surroundings. He had been educated in the best schools. A brilliant career was lying before him. And suddenly, at the age of forty, he had to flee, out of Egypt, out of the glamour of a royal palace, out of the learned discussion of the scholars, out of the diplomatic center of a world empire. And for another forty years (Deut. 34:7) nothing happened. He got married and a son was born to him and his wife; otherwise he was simply keeping the flock of his father-in-law. Nothing happened. Everything seemed to be lost: his miraculous salvation from death, his education, his preparation at the palace of the king. And much more than that. Nothing happened with Israel, with the oppressed people who still had to slave under the floggings of their oppressors. Where was God?

V. 1b. *"And he led his flock to the west side of the wilderness, and he came to Horeb, the mountain of God."* Sometimes, we come to the mountain of God just in the course of our boring everyday duties. Sometimes we are on top of the mountain of God, only we do not realize it. We are still thinking that God is but a word, and even an old-fashioned one. We are still thinking that he means nothing at all for the real world, as it is. Sometimes God is on his way to his people from the mountain of God, only his people do not realize it. They are still suffering and tired and hopeless. They are still thinking that God might have been alive in the past, but in the last forty years nothing has happened that could show his hand.

V. 2.a. *"And the angel of the Lord appeared to*

309

him in a flame of fire out of the midst of a bush."
Moses has not the slightest inkling that God
is now entering his life. He has learned at
school that God is almighty and eternal, sitting on a heavenly throne and speaking only
in scriptures of a faraway past. The real God
is always quite different, however, from what
we imagine him to be. He comes to Moses in
the form of the fire. So full of life, so utterly
full of life, is God as the fire flaring up in the
bush. And so dangerous is God to those who
come near him, as the fire licking out of the
bush. When God comes over us, something
has to get moving, and we do not know where
he will lead us. He might burn down many
things that we have clung to up to now. He
might even burn us and our way of life, and it
might really hurt. He might change his appearance, as fire changes it, so that we are
never quite sure what the next morning will
bring and what God will expect us to do for
him. He will certainly never let himself be
captivated by us and give himself into our
hands so that we should become master over
him, knowing all of him, explaining all his
ways, just as the fire cannot be caught by
Moses' hands.

V. 3. *"And Moses said, 'I will turn aside and
see this great sight, why the bush is not burnt.'"*
Moses still does not understand. He has no
idea of God being on his way to him. He just
wonders. Often when we are wondering, no
longer understanding what is going on—perhaps without even thinking of God—is the
time of God's approach. Moses could have
shrugged his shoulders and trotted on with
his flock, and he would have missed God,
perhaps for his whole life. Sometimes we just
jog along on old beaten tracks, although there
are so many things to wonder about, and
God waits for us in vain. Sometimes a whole
nation just trots along and is not awakened to
its new course, although there are so many
things to wonder about, and God waits in
vain. There are perhaps new ideas flaring up,
new hopes licking out of the bush, and who
knows whether God is waiting for us; but we
are so often too lazy and too lame, too comfortable in our old way of life. Thus we go on
and leave God behind, still waiting for us. But
Moses has turned aside.

V. 4. *"When the Lord saw that he turned aside
to see, God called to him out of the bush, 'Moses,
Moses!' And he said, 'Here am I.'"* This is the
decisive moment, when God ceases to be a
mere word in old-fashioned liturgies or hymns
and starts to call us by our personal name.
We may not hear a voice that could be tape-
recorded, but we know that it is we who are
meant, who are to go on a new road, who will
no longer be able to go on living in the old
way that is, despite this or that difficulty, so
comfortable. The question is only whether
we respond, "Here I am."

V. 5. *"Then he said, 'Do not come near; put off
your shoes from your feet, for the place on which
you are standing is holy ground.'"* The way with
God is no easy way. He keeps Moses at a distance. He does not give himself into the
hands of Moses. The place where God dwells
is holy ground, and man cannot simply penetrate into his plans. This is probably one of
the main differences between ideologies and
the gospel: Christians are never so dead sure
of their view that nothing could shake them.
You can take over an ideology, you can swallow it and fight for it, being blind and deaf to
all the suffering it brings and to all the cries
of those who are run over by it. But you can
never swallow God. We may perhaps, therefore, go along quite a long way with a party or
an idea, but suddenly God bars our way and
says, "Stop!"

V. 6a. *"And Moses hid his face, for he was
afraid to look at God."* We are crying: "Where is
God? Why does God not step in and take
action?" But when God really does what we
were crying for, we are afraid of him and hide
our faces. Moses is afraid of God because he
has an inkling of what God plans to do. It
seems to be not as simple as God just killing
the Egyptian oppressors with lightning from
heaven. It looks as if God would want men like
Moses to fight for him. And this is not an allur-
ing prospect for Moses: to leave his peaceful
flock of sheep and go get entangled in the
intrigues of politics and social fights. In Egypt
it is so much more probable that one might be
killed than here with a peaceful flock. But
God seems to be not at all impressed by this
aspect of danger and risk, and to have decided
to send Moses into the very center of all trouble. Moses is afraid of this God and wants to
draw back and get disengaged, to keep his
face, and as quickly as possible.

V. 6b. *"And God said, 'I am the God of your
father, the God of Abraham, the God of Isaac, and
the God of Jacob.'"* And how does this help

Moses? This is what he learned at school; this is nothing new. However, sometimes the old truth becomes surprisingly new in a new situation, so new that suddenly it begins to mean something. For Moses it begins to mean something that there are men who long ago experienced God; men who are signposts to the reality of God; men who with the experiences of their lives testify to him. And all at once Moses is no longer totally alone; he is among the men of the Bible who have wandered with God and realized that he was leading them in a good way.

To be sure, what God has to say to Moses seems to contradict all reality and to be rather incredible.

V. 9. *"And now, behold, the cry of the people of Israel has come to me, and I have seen the oppression with which the Egyptians oppress them."* It is easy to say that God sees all oppression and hears all the cries of oppressed people. But what we see in the world looks different. What does God do about it?

V. 10. *"Come, I will send you to Pharaoh that you may bring forth my people, the sons of Israel, out of Egypt."* This is what God does do—he sends us. And this is exactly what we are afraid of.

V. 11. *"But Moses said to God, "Who am I that I should go to Pharaoh and bring the sons of Israel out of Egypt?""* Oh, Moses is so undeniably right. Who am I? Certainly this is the question that we can always put to God, with which we are able to destroy all God's attempts to help us. Who am I? Up to now, Moses has not shown any extraordinary performance, perhaps even less than we. He had been rather spoiled in his youth by the luxury of a royal palace, and he has succeeded in destroying everything he gained by a violent fit of wrath, in which he killed a man. And now he is eighty and nothing but a refugee with a foreign wife and a son and doing nothing but keeping some sheep that do not even belong to him. And all this is not merely a tragic fate; he himself has brought it about. Who am I? Indeed, Moses has every reason to ask this, as much as or even more than we do. I know, we are Presbyterians or Congregationalists, and we have been trained for four centuries to ask, Who am I? and to answer, I am a poor sinner, and we even know that this is quite true. However, the question remains open whether there is not

a truth that is infinitely more true than that—namely, that God wants to do his work, to perform his actions, to change the world with us.

Some of the Pharisees in the time of Jesus were wont to investigate their lives every evening and to state with some complacency how perfectly they had fulfilled all the commandments of God. In this way they were spinning around like those poor animals who are running like mad in a revolving cage and remaining all the time at exactly the same place. God therefore had no use for them. We have been trained not to be complacent. We are therefore spinning all the time around our sins, and perhaps even our would-be sins. And whenever God wants to enter our life and send us somewhere, we say, Who am I? God therefore has no place for us. All the time we even think—exactly like the Pharisees—how very pious we are, how much we feel our sin and God's forgiving grace. And all the time God is asking us to go and do his work, to act for him, and to liberate his oppressed children, but we remain seated on our cushions and believe quite honestly that we are sinners and that God will forgive us and even use us for his purpose. The only difficulty is that whenever he wants to do that, we start again from the first step and ask, Who am I? And then the whole liturgy begins again, and it never ends in action. It is a very strange fact that in the whole New Testament, with the exception of one passage in the letter of James, there is not a single confession of sins spoken by a believer after his baptism. Of course they knew that they were sinners, and they said it, by implication, when they prayed the Our Father; but there was no need for them to repeat a confession of sins every morning and every Sunday, because they knew that God had accepted them, justified them, made them his children. And now there was work to do, there were roads to go upon. They would realize where they failed to do God's mighty works, where people had to suffer because they were not obedient enough. They would admonish one another, they would help one another to do what was necessary, and they would therefore point out to themselves and to their fellow Christians where their disobedience might endanger God's good work. But they would never have expressed this in a general confession of sins, as if they had to start every morning from zero, as if God had done nothing up to now. It is so utterly easy to say Who am I? and to do nothing at all. And in the meantime, until we have completed the whole course of thinking about our sins and about God's grace, God's promises fall flat, because we are still sitting on our cushions or squatting on our heels like Moses, saying all the time, Who am I? but not entering into the adventure with God.

V. 12. *"God said, 'But I will be with you; and this shall be a sign for you, that I have sent you: when you have brought forth the people out of Egypt, you shall serve God upon this mountain.'"* Again God's answer is most unexpected. He promises his presence, but he gives no guarantee whatsoever. He tells Moses that after he has obeyed God's order and has liberated his oppressed people, they will adore God and pray to him thankfully. That means, the only guarantee God offers us is that we shall experience him, if and when we have dared to follow him and to go our way with him. The proof of God's promise, which shall move us to dare to trust in it and to serve him, will be the fact that we shall trust in it and serve him. This seems rather strange to our logic, but this is indeed the logic of God. For if he gave us all the guarantees we postulate, he would no longer be God. He would be in our hand; no longer would he be able to await us behind every bend of our way and point us in new and ever surprising directions. He would cease to be our leader and would become a magic power that we would use as we would want. This is exactly the way in which the name of God has been used many times, for the aims and purposes of men and nations. But God had not been with them; he has been with those who have been oppressed in his name. God himself may bar us from repeating the history of violating and twisting his name. Let us beware of the devilish temptation to use him for our own dreams and ideas and wishes. If the name of God becomes an instrument in our hands, if it no longer happens that his name stands time and time again in opposition to our program, we may be certain that the living God lives no longer in his name, that he has left us and is far away, perhaps with our foes, and that we have nothing in our hand except three letters that mean nothing: G. O. D.

Vv. 13–14. *"Then Moses said to God, 'If I come to the people of Israel and say to them, "The God of your fathers has sent me to you," and they ask me, "What is his name?" what shall I say to them?' God said to Moses, 'I AM WHO I AM.' And he said, 'Say this to the people of Israel, "I AM has sent me to you."'"* This is the name that God gives us. He is who he is. When we get a dollar, we can pocket it. Then we have got it, and we can take it out and use it whenever we want to do so. We can never pocket God. He can use us, but we cannot use him for our wishes. There are people who hang a good-luck charm, perhaps an emerald scarab, on a necklace because they believe that this scarab will protect them and save them from all mishaps. If we try to use God in this way, as a guarantee for the fulfillment of all our wishes and a protection against all uncomfortable experiences, he may well turn out to be a kind of scarab that bites and that does not let us go our own way. "I am who I am." At every moment God remains God—the one who goes before us, deciding where to go, and not simply behind us in order to be at our service whenever we want it.

And yet this is not the last word of God. The first Christians used to sing in their services a hymn that has been handed down to us in the letter to the Philippians. They sang: "Therefore God has highly exalted him and bestowed on him the name which is above every name, that at the name of Jesus every knee should bow, in heaven and on earth and under the earth, and every tongue confess that Jesus Christ is Lord, to the glory of God the Father" (Phil. 2:9–11). This is no different from what we have heard in the Old Testament. Jesus is the one who "humbled himself and became obedient unto death, even death on a cross." A crucified man—we should think that this is certainly the place in which *not* to find God. An executed Jesus, dead, definitely dead—we should think that this is the end of all illusions about a mighty God, eager to help. A cross with nobody under it except mockers and laughers—we should think that this is the proof of the death of God, even more than Israel's slavery under Pharaoh. Everybody thought so, including Jesus' own disciples. For we disapprove of a God who is unsuccessful. We want gods according to our images and wishes.

But the cross cuts across our images and wishes. The cross has a vertical line, which often bars our way so that we have to stop, unable to go on, as we wanted to go, and be forced to listen anew to God's will. The cross also has a horizontal line, which often strikes out our ideas and slogans so that we suddenly have to say no and search for new directions. But this Jesus, who seemed to be so definitely dead, was raised from death, and his name became the name that is conquering the world. For his name is the name of God's love, which humbles itself unto death, which is free from the coercion to succeed and to overcome, and therefore free to love and to help. And every knee that bows, and every tongue that confesses that Jesus Christ is the Lord belongs to the band of his disciples who conquer the world, because they no longer use God's name for their own ideas, aims, and purposes, but let God make use of them and send them to his oppressed people wherever they are on earth.

Bible Study II: God Reconciles

TEXT: Jer. 7:1–15; Mark 11:15–19

V. 1. *"The word that came to Jeremiah from the Lord."* There are times in which God remains silent, in which his word seems of no importance at all for the course of the world, its political problems, its economic progress, or even its religious activities. There are other times in which the word of God comes to people. It came to Jeremiah at that time. It might come to us.

V. 2. *"Stand in the gate of the Lord's house, and proclaim there this Word, and say, Hear the Word of the Lord, all you men of Judah who enter these gates to worship the Lord."* So God wants to speak to his Church—not to those who believe nothing, not to the ungodly oppressors of his people, not to the enemies beyond the border of the Holy Land. He wants to speak to those who enter the gates of the house of God to worship the Lord. He wants to speak to us—precisely and definitely to us. This Word of God comes along in strange dress. It is not the priest within the gates of the holy house of God who utters this Word; it is not one of the recognized prophets; it is not even one of the elders. It is a man without any title, post, or authority. He is the son of a priest; but what does this mean? He himself did not care for the ministry. He is simply

someone without any status. We do not know in what profession this Jeremiah earned his living. He might have been a farmer or a student or a newspaperman. Indeed, the Word of God might come to us through a farmer, a student, or a newspaperman. Oh, no, the Word of God does not always put on a robe and hang a silver cross around its neck so that everybody will realize that it is in fact the Word of God that shall be spoken here. Oh, no, it comes so often in such unexpected dress—a farmer or a student or a newspaperman—that nobody realizes it is God who speaks through farmers, students, and newspapermen. They did not recognize the voice of God in that strange person of Jeremiah, whom everybody considered a bit odd or even crazy. They acted as people usually act when somebody becomes inconvenient and when his words create some trouble for the official government or the official church: they tried to chase him away, out of the house of God, and when this did not work they threatened him with prison and even with execution. And all the priests and recognized prophets of the official God were leading the mob in its effort to reduce the Word of God, of the real, living God, to silence. And then they preached on and on, and nothing was unexpected or even different from what one had heard for generations. And the walls of the temple were still standing there—strong and high and beautiful walls. And the cult of the church went on within these walls, as it had gone on for generations, and everything was as it had always been. Only the Word of God, the living Word of the living God, who had tried to reach his people through a farmer or a student or a newspaperman, had been driven out. It was no longer inside the walls of stone that surrounded the house of God. The official priests preached and the official prophets prophesied and the elders kept good order in the service, and the welcoming people at the gate were very hospitable and friendly to those who entered the gates. Only God, who wanted to speak to those who entered those gates, was absent, very absent. He was somewhere in the city trying to speak through a man who was neither a priest nor an official prophet nor an elder.

Within the walls of the house of God they still go on, crying, "This is the temple of the Lord, the temple of the Lord, the temple of the Lord," and nobody can doubt this. This is undoubtedly true as it is true that this is the Reformed Church of the Lord. Yet the Word of God, of the real, living God says (v. 4), "Do not trust in these deceptive words: 'This is the temple of the Lord, the temple of the Lord, the temple of the Lord.'" Why should these words be deceptive? Are they not correct? Is it not the temple that God himself has chosen as his dwelling place, the true house of God in Jerusalem? Is it not true what we confess: "I believe in one holy apostolic and catholic church?" Why does God call this deception? Is it not the church into which we invite people? Is it not the church that tries to be obedient to God and to praise him, whereas the world does not care for him and his Kingdom?

God is not impressed at all by our long pleading. He is still speaking through exactly this world outside of the walls of his house, through the man who has been driven out of this church (v. 3): "Behold, you trust in deceptive words to no avail. Amend your ways and your doings, and I will let you dwell in this place." How often do we speak words and sentences that are correct and yet not really true? We say with all the solemnity and all the emphasis we consider appropriate: "Jesus Christ has died for our sins," and this is doubtlessly correct, very correct. But we live on as if nothing had happened, and we go on sinning as if Jesus had not had to die for us. We go on bullying others as if Jesus had not died for them; or we go on living depressed and suffering, because we are not so perfect or so beautiful or so powerful as others, as if Jesus had not died for us. We go on separating the races, as if Jesus had not died for both black and white people, or we go on excommunicating brothers of countries that have to face insoluble problems, as if Jesus had not died for those who are in such difficult situations that sometimes they cannot avoid sin, such as the centurion who had to execute Jesus yet was to be the first man on Earth to confess that this was the Son of God. And then all these correct words do not become true in our lives, nor in the lives of those who are living with us.

It is the same as with music. We may be listening to some music. We have good ears and are not hard-of-hearing; we hear it as well as those beside us. But we do not under-stand it; it does not move us; we do not become more joyful or more serious; it does not give us enthusiasm or bemuse us. In this case, the music remains but a noise; we have heard the noise, but not really the music. In exactly the same way we may hear the noise of all the good and correct words of the minister or the elder who reads the Scriptures; we may even understand them in our heads; but they do not reach our hearts, they do not change us. Then nothing has happened, except that some noises have hit our eardrums and have made them vibrate a little bit—as if someone tried to blow a trumpet with all the strength he had in order to wake up his people, but everyone around him was stone-deaf and the only thing that happened was that a few leaves on a tree nearby began to tremble because the man blew so mightily into his trumpet. So often this is what happens to God; he blows into his trumpet, into Jeremiah, for instance, or a farmer or a student or a newspaperman, in order to wake us up. But nothing happens, except that a few leaves begin to tremble, because God tries so hard and with all his might to raise up his stone-deaf Church through a man of the world.

To be sure, this Word of God is not very comfortable (vv. 5–7a): "For if you truly amend your ways and your doings, if you truly execute justice one with another, if you do not oppress the alien, the fatherless, or the widow, or shed innocent blood in this place, and if you do not go after other gods to your own hurt, then I will let you dwell in this place." This looks not like a reconciling but rather like a very aggressive Word. It puts questions to us, very hard and uncomfortable questions. And it is obvious that it cannot reach our hearts if we do not listen to these questions, and listen very carefully.

V. 5b. *"If you truly execute justice one with another."* God is asking: Are there people in your country who are continually living in fear of the police because some who are of the "right" race, or party or belief, can easily call in the police, and some who are of the "wrong" race, or party or belief, can equally easily be arrested by this police? God is asking: Are you creating justice in your country, or are you even adding to a feeling of injustice by your whole way of life?

God goes on, "If you do not oppress the

alien. . . ," and asks: Does the alien feel at home in your country, even without speaking your language and knowing your customs? Or is he oppressed by your otherness? "The fatherless or the widow" have come even nearer to us than in the days of Jeremiah. In that time they lived in the neighbor's house; today they enter our living room through the television set, even though they are actually living in Indonesia or Siberia. And what do we do for them? There was a time in which it was not so awfully difficult to avoid "stealing and murdering," because we were living within the borders and under the protection of our tribe. Our neighbor's property and life were sacred; if one stole the fruit of the enemy and took his life, it was a heroic act. Today the world has become one, whether we like it or not, and God is no longer the god of our tribe only; he is also the god of the other tribe or country or race. And he keeps asking us: "Will you steal and murder and then come and stand before me in this house, which is called by my name, and say, 'We are delivered!'—only to go on doing all these abominations?" To be sure, we are progressive; we not only steal and murder in riots or war against one another, but we also have invented laws and systems of commerce and expropriations, shares that can be made worthless and party books that can be annulled. And God goes on and on, asking questions. He speaks about adultery and asks us why our young people are so skeptical about marriage and family or why our systems make all real family life impossible— because father and mother are no longer father and mother but merely male and female workers. God speaks about "swearing falsely" and asks us why we write our newspapers so it is always the other nation or the other party or the other race that is wrong; why we twist whatever they try to say or do; and why we never read their newspapers.

It will not be easy to answer God. Oh, certainly, we are the Church, even the Reformed Church. Oh, certainly, we do want to worship God. The only difficulty is that we "go after the gods to our own hurt," as Jeremiah puts it. We want a god who helps us to reach what our own hearts desire. We want a god who is always pro-white or pro-black or pro-Eastern or pro-Western. To be sure, we add that there is but one God, our white or our black God,

our Eastern or our Western God. And this is exactly what he, the real, living God, calls "to go after other gods to our own hurt." We preach about him, and we pray to him, and we praise his reconciliation, but there is no reconciliation, because the god whose reconciliation we are seeking is simply our self-made black or white, Western or Eastern god, but not God himself.

V. 11. *"Has this house, which is called by my name, become a den of robbers in your eyes? Behold, I myself have seen it, says the Lord."* It is not so easy to recognize ministers of the Church today. In old times they wore clerical collars or even robes. Today, they may come along in shorts and gym shoes. God sees the difficulty in the opposite direction, however. It is not easy to recognize the robbers. They may assemble to listen to a sermon, to pray and sing hymns, and they might be robbers nonetheless. Preaching and praying and singing robbers, very churchly robbers, but robbers nevertheless. And the Church becomes a den of robbers; its walls of stone are still there, but God has emigrated, and very soon it will be but walls of stone, a ruin with nothing in it except some thistles and rats (vv. 12–15): "Go now to my place that was in Shiloh, where I made my name dwell at first, and see what I did to it for the wickedness of my people Israel. And now, because you have done all these things, says the Lord, and when I spoke to you persistently you did not listen, and when I called you, you did not answer, therefore I will do to the house which is called by my name, and in which you trust, and to the place which I gave to you and to your fathers, as I did to Shiloh. And I will cast you out of my sight, as I cast out all your kinsmen, all the offspring of Ephraim."

God's reconciliation is no cheap reconciliation; it is a costly one. No doubt it is God who reconciles, and it is we who are reconciled. But how shall he reconcile us if we are not able to hear his reconciling words so that they reach our hearts? How shall he play the tune of reconciliation if we hear only a noise that is unable to move our hearts? God may play with drums and trumpets, but his Church says merely, "What a noise!" as long as it confesses the reconciliation of God in Jesus Christ without letting God reconcile it with people of other nations, other races, other colors, or other social levels. Therefore, the same God who let David build his Temple as a place of reconciliation for his people destroys this same Temple in order to reconcile his people through his judgment. "Then," he says, "when you will listen to my words so that they move your hearts and change your ways of life [v. 7], then I will let you dwell in this place, in the land that I gave of old to your fathers for ever." Long before we were even born, he has loved us and done for us whatever he could, and long after we shall be buried he will love us and do for us whatever he can. This is the God who calls us today with his hard words of judgment, because he knows that we are unable to let him love us, as long as hatred toward and incomprehension of others occupy our hearts.

Centuries later, there was again a time in which the Word of God came to people. It was the same Word: "You have made my house a den of robbers" (Mark 11:17). This time, it was not Jeremiah, it was Jesus who said it. He did not merely say it; he "began to drive out those who sold and those who bought in the temple, and he overturned the tables of the money changers and the seats of those who sold pigeons" (v. 15). The money changers and the pigeon sellers were at that time as necessary for the worship service as are the ministers and choirmasters of today, and their tables are as necessary as are our communion tables. Might it be that God's wrath shall drive out our robed ministers and choirmasters and turn over our communion tables so that the wine will be spilled on the floor and all the pieces of bread will be scattered around? Might it not be?

There is an even more subtle way of robbery than in the Jerusalem of Jeremiah's time. We try to rob God's grace and salvation without being forced to change our attitudes toward other people. We try to rob reconciliation on a religious level—whatever this may mean—without letting anybody, even God himself, reconcile us with people of the other, hated race or nation or party. We are conscientiously giving our church taxes or our weekly offerings to the tables of the cultic money changers; we are even zealous in bringing additional sacrifices—sheep and pigeons and checks and tithes. And we think that we are able to rob God in this way and to get his reconciliation out of him, without being driven out into the world of social misery and political hatred. But who knows

whether God's reconciliation is there waiting for his people?

"And when evening came Jesus went out of the city" (v. 19). They are still standing within the walls of the house of God, and it is as true as it was in the time of Jeremiah that this is the Temple of the Lord, the Temple of the Lord, the Temple of the Lord. Only Jesus had left it, and with him God and his reconciliation. And there was nothing left but walls of stone with a lot of very religious men inside, going on with their worship services, on and on and on, without God. God was out there in Bethany, where a strange and perhaps a bit crazy woman of not quite commendable morals wasted an extremely expensive flask of ointment on his head. The walls of stone of the house of God stood and stood for another forty years, until they became ruins. There are walls of stone of Christian churches in ruins everywhere around the Mediterranean Sea, and there are churches that are nothing but walls of stone in ruins even if the cult is still going on and on inside.

But God is still waiting, still waiting for his people. "And Jesus taught, and said to them, 'Is it not written, "My house shall be called a house of prayer for all the Gentiles?" But you have made it a den of robbers'" (v. 17). His house a house of prayer—without prayer it is but a few walls of stone in ruins. Prayer is the life of the Church; for a praying Church knows that it is God alone who can reconcile it. When we pray we must empty our hands. We cannot keep a gun or a bundle of shares or a lampoon in our hands when we raise them. A praying Church raises empty hands to God and expects everything from him. It is therefore totally impossible to pray boasting: "I am white, I am black, I am bourgeois, I am a communist, I am a millionaire, I am a member of the party, I am a devoted Christian, I have the right faith, I am. . . ."

"Whoever I am, I need you, O God; without you and without your reconciliation I am lost." A church that is praying has ceased to boast and is, by necessity, reconciled not only with God but also with all other people. God's house is therefore a house "for all the Gentiles," for all those who are living outside, who have been unable to find their way into the house of God. Where are the Gentiles today, those who could not find their way into the Church because it has been a white church or a nationalistic church or a wealthy church or a traditionalistic church or a godless church, a church with full hands expecting everything from its own ideology and its own white or black, conservative or revolutionary, eastern or western programs? Where are the Gentiles to whom we have barred the entrance doors?

And yet, is this not too simple? Are there not people with whom we cannot become reconciled? Is reconciliation possible with those who oppress God's people, who kill the innocent, who exert ruthless pressure on the poor? The chief priests and the scribes heard the way and sought to destroy him. This is the way of Jesus, this is the way of his Church. There was no reconciliation with the thinking and acting, with the doctrine and program, of, for instance, those chief priests and scribes. And yet Jesus was reconciled even with those chief priests and scribes—so much so that he did not leave them alone; he met them, attacked them, and did all this for their sake, not in opposition to them. It cost him his life that he did not avoid them, that he searched them out right up to his Crucifixion. Among the disciples of Jesus there were zealots and publicans, men who fought against the Roman occupation power and men who worked with them, revolutionary and appeasing groups. For all of them he went to his death.

Impossible? But Jesus is still living in this world, and his power of love and reconciliation is still among us—so much so that no tyrant reigns without protesting that he is socially minded and fighting for the poor. Even if it is nothing but lies and deception, Jesus still forces him to play this role. Jesus

came to power by dying for the truth of God's all-embracing reconciliation. A church that is not ready to die will die without resurrection, will become a ruin that is nothing more than a few walls of stone open to sightseeing tourist groups for not much more than a tip; and the guide may still cry, "This is the temple of the Lord, who was worshiped here in 100, or 1900, A.D.; this is the temple of the Lord, this is the temple of the Lord." The Lord, however, is not to be found in the ruins; he is going just now, step by step, beside his disciple who refuses to hate; who attacks all churchly or worldly self-conceitedness; who opens the doors for all the Gentiles.

The death of a church is not the death of God. It might be God's judgment, it might be God's direction; it might die unwillingly or willingly. But God will go his way and create new life out of his dying church. When in the fourth century the church of North Africa was dying, God raised Augustine out of this dying church and in this way gave to the world a leader for centuries, who even a thousand years later gave the decisive impulse for the Reformation—thus creating again new life in God's Church.

When God sent Jeremiah to pronounce his judgment over God's Church, frozen in its tradition and its cult, God was on his way to reconcile it. God' reconciliation will never be cheap, a reconciliation that costs nothing, because a band of reconciled disciples of Christ can no longer go on hating other races or parties or nations or classes. They will be ready to die, in order that God may become the living power of reconciliation in a world that knows no reconciliation.

SECTION IX.
Preaching on Faith

BY CLAYTON K. HARROP

Topic: The Faith That Saves

TEXT: Acts 16:25–34

Other Readings: Gal. 2:15–21; Rom. 10:9–13

People often ask questions that relate to their eternal destiny. The questions may be like that of the young man who asked Jesus, "What must I do to inherit eternal life?" (Mark 10:17) People responded to the preaching of Peter on the day of Pentecost by asking, "What should we do?" (Acts 2:37) The Philippian jailer asked, "What must I do to be saved?" (Acts 16:30) However the question may be worded, there is a deep hunger for something solid on which life may be based in the present and that will give hope for tomorrow.

I. *The nature of faith (v. 25–31a).* The words *faith* and *believe* are religious words in our day. The world's understanding of these words is quite different from what we mean when we use them in the context of our Christian life. For the world, these words express an intellectual understanding. People accept with their minds certain facts in any area of life. This carries over into the religious sphere as people say, "I believe in God." All they may mean is that they accept that there is some supreme being or force. But such intellectual affirmations fall far short of the biblical understanding of faith.

It is true that there must be some understanding with the mind. One cannot believe in God without having evidence of his existence. One cannot believe in Christ without knowing something about him. But one may be a diligent student of Scripture and believe the evidence provided in it about God and about Christ without having what the Scrip-

ture speaks of as faith. Faith centers on the aspect of trust and commitment. When Jesus encouraged his disciples to "believe in God, believe also in me" (John 14:1), he was not encouraging them simply to have head knowledge. Rather, he was calling on them to trust God even in the face of the most impossible situations, such as the crisis that lay before them.

So it was with the Philippian jailer. Paul and Silas called upon him to believe. How much did the jailer know about Jesus? Perhaps he had heard Paul preach in the streets of the city. Perhaps he had heard Paul and Silas singing and praying in the jail. But his knowledge was limited. Paul was not calling upon him to have head knowledge. Rather, he was calling him to trust, to commit, and this is what saving faith always involves.

II. *The focus of faith (v. 31b).* If faith is trust or commitment, then it must be directed toward a specific person or thing. People may trust in a great variety of things to gain what they desire. It may be their own ability, the political system, or power—the list could go on. Paul made it clear that the only adequate focus of faith is "the Lord Jesus." He knew from his own experience that Jesus Christ was the only one who could save. On the road to Damascus he had been confronted by the Risen Christ, and this experience had shown him that salvation could come in no other way.

Paul used two significant terms or names in his appeal to the jailer. First, he used the title *Lord.* This was a common title for God in the Old Testament. It expressed his deity. Paul, along with other early Christians, did not hesitate to use this same title for the Risen Lord. Jesus was not just another man. He was Lord, with all that the title implied: authority, power, and majesty. The second title was the human name, *Jesus*. The Risen Lord is identified with Jesus of Nazareth, who lived among men and gave his life on the Roman cross for human sin. Elsewhere Paul used a third term, *Christ*. He was the Messiah, the one who fulfilled all of the promises of God in the Old Testament, promises that related to the forgiveness of sin and a right relation with God.

Thus faith is trust in a person: Jesus Christ the Lord. Faith is the commitment of life to this person in order that he may be absolute ruler and master of one's life. He is Lord; we are his slaves, his servants.

III. *The results of faith (vv. 31c–34).* Paul promised the jailer that if he would exercise faith in Jesus he would be saved. Faith in Christ results in salvation. The term *salvation* can be used in a variety of ways. It may refer to being saved from danger or the threat of some deadly illness. But Paul was referring to something more important. Salvation meant a new relationship with God that would exist today and endure forever. Salvation does not mean that one gets everything he or she wants right now, but it does mean that one gets the most important thing: a new relationship with God. And in this new relationship, everything else falls into place.

This promise of salvation was made not only to the jailer but also to his whole household. There are no limits on God's mercy. His salvation is not limited to a select few. It is available to everyone who will place trust in and make a commitment to Christ. So after Paul and Silas spoke to all the jailer's household, they were all baptized. This was evidence of their faith in Christ, and it was their testimony to others that they had made this commitment to Christ. Faith had worked its wonderful purpose in their lives: they had been brought from death to life. They had heard of what God had done for mankind in his Son, and when they heard, they committed their lives, their all, to him. This is the faith that saves.

Topic: The Testing of Faith
TEXT: Gen. 22:1–18
Other Readings: Job 2:9–10; 2 Kings 5:8–14; Acts 4:13–22

Often we dream of living in a world where there are no difficulties, no trials. Reality is not like that. Trials come; and while they may be unpleasant, we know that God can and does bring good out of such experiences. This was the situation with Abraham.

I. *The summons of God (vv. 1–2).* Abraham's life was filled with the activity and blessing of God. He was called to leave his home and journey to a land that God promised to give to him and his descendants. Famine drove him to Egypt. Conflicts arose with his neighbors over water and grass for his cattle. Yet in all of this he knew that the hand of God was upon him, and he lived his life on the basis of the promise that God would give him a son and that his descendants would become as numerous as the dust of the earth (Gen. 13:16).

Abraham had to wait many years before the promise of God was fulfilled. But Isaac was born, the one through whom the promises of God were to be brought to fulfillment. Abraham had shown his faith in God by believing that God would give a son to him and Sarah. Now his faith was put to its most severe test. God called upon Abraham to take Isaac and offer him as a burnt offering to God. The son through whom the promises were to be fulfilled was to be killed as a sacrifice.

What thoughts must have gone through the mind of Abraham! He was undoubtedly familiar with the idea of human sacrifice. It was an all-too-common occurrence in his world. But he never believed that his God would call upon anyone to make such a sacrifice. Nor would God accept such a sacrifice if it were to be offered. Besides, Isaac was the one through whom his descendants were to come. How could this happen if he were dead? Certainly this was a crucial test of faith. It is one thing to say one believes in God. It is quite another matter to act on that faith when it appears to go against everything one sees.

II. *The response to God (vv. 3–14).* Abraham's faith led him to do what God commanded. He immediately began to carry out God's instructions. He did not delay but "rose early in the morning." He set out with his son and two other men. They took along the wood, the fire, and the knife. It was a long journey to the place where the sacrifice was to be made. Only on the third day did they reach the site. There was much time for thinking—about God, about Isaac, about faith. If Abraham's faith had been weak, there would have been ample opportunity for him to turn back.

Abraham left the men and went on ahead with Isaac. He told the young men, "The boy and I will go over there; we will worship, and then we will come back to you." Could Abraham really believe that Isaac would come back with him?

Even Isaac became puzzled. He knew what was involved in a sacrifice. He had the wood; his father had the fire and the knife. But "where is the lamb for a burnt offering?" One could not sacrifice without a lamb. And Abraham had not brought one. Abraham affirmed his faith that God would provide a lamb for the offering. He had faith that God would do what was right. Abraham built an altar, placed the wood on it, bound his son, and laid him on the wood. He took the knife and was prepared to kill his son in obedience to the command of God. And only when he had demonstrated his faith in this way did God intervene. He called out to Abraham not to kill his son and then showed him a ram caught by its horns in a thicket. He was told to take this animal and offer it in place of his son. The faith of Abraham was vindicated. He had passed the greatest test. The author of Hebrews caught something of the depth of Abraham's faith when he wrote, "He considered the fact that God is able even to raise someone from the dead—and figuratively speaking, he did receive him back" (Heb. 11:10). Faith accepted the impossible because it was based on complete trust in God. Our times of testing may not be as severe as Abraham's. Yet such tests come. And our faith is measured by how we respond. Only faith that obeys God's commands is adequate to meet the struggles of life and emerge victorious.

III. *The blessings from God (vv. 15–18)*. Strong faith is honored by God. Because Abraham had shown that his was not simply a faith of word but a faith of action, God fulfilled his promise: "I will indeed bless you, and I will make your offspring as numerous as the stars of heaven and as the sand on the seashore." What had seemed an impossibility many years earlier was to become reality. It must have seemed difficult to Abraham to believe that he could become the father of a son and that his descendants could become

so numerous. But Abraham knew that with God nothing is impossible. He trusted God, and even in the most severe test of life he continued to trust God. His willingness to obey God showed that his faith was real. And faith that is real always brings blessings from God. This is our assurance along with Abraham's. Life is hard. Trials are great. But the man or woman of faith who endures trials can rejoice because faith is shown to be genuine and receives rich blessings from God. James wrote, "Whenever you face trials of any kind, consider it nothing but joy" (1:2). This is not because trials are enjoyable, but because the outcome is so rich.

Topic: The Power of Faith
   TEXT: Mark 11:12–14, 20–24
   Other Readings: Matt. 14:28–33, 17:14–21
People worship power, whether it be a powerful engine in a car or a powerful computer. They want to exercise power over other people. Power is sought with such intensity that any action can seemingly be justified in order to achieve it. Jesus reminds us that true power comes through the exercise of faith.

I. *A fig tree cursed (vv. 12–14)*. One of the most unusual events in the ministry of Jesus occurred during the final period of his work in Jerusalem. He and his disciples were walking from Bethany to Jerusalem. Along the road stood a fig tree. Because he was hungry, Jesus went to the tree seeking some figs to eat, but he did not find any. He thereby pronounced a curse upon the tree, that it should never again produce fruit.

This fig tree is a picture of a part of God's creation that was not producing as its creator had desired and hoped. It serves as a reminder to each of us that we are here only because of God's mercy. And that he has expectations of what our lives are to produce. If we fail, we should not expect any better treatment than the fig tree.

Of course, God's mercy at times overrules the judgment that is deserved. In Luke's Gospel we have a parable that Jesus told about another fig tree that failed to produce fruit. For three years the owner had come seeking fruit without success. He commanded the gardener to cut the tree down. But the gardener appealed for the tree to be given one more chance. Although it is not clearly stated, it is implied that the owner granted the request and the tree was spared for one more year (Luke 13:6–9). This is the way God often treats us. Although we deserve to stand under his curse, he gives us another chance.

II. *A fig tree withered (vv. 20–21)*. Jesus' curse upon the fig tree may have made little impression on the disciples. Other seemingly more important things occupied their minds. Jesus had driven animals out of the Temple; he had overturned the tables of the money changers. Perhaps the disciples were aware of how this action had aroused the wrath of the religious leaders and fueled their desire to be rid of Jesus. Something so trivial as the curse on a tree may have slipped from their memory. But the next day, Peter saw that the tree had withered to its roots. Such a sudden change attracted their attention. It might not have seemed so strange if a few of the leaves had begun to turn brown, or if some of them had fallen to the ground. Such a gradual death of a tree would have seemed quite normal. But this tree was completely dead. The previous day it had been alive, with green leaves. Today it was dead, with no sign of life at all.

Peter expressed his amazement and called Jesus' attention to the tree. This was something beyond Peter's understanding. How could it have happened this way? No man could do anything like this. And although Peter had heard Jesus' words the previous day, he had not thought that the tree would immediately die. Peter's lack of understanding and of faith reminds us of ourselves. Often our perception of reality is determined by human standards rather than by God's. We think of things being possible only from a human perspective, rather than considering what God may be able to do. So when God acts with his special power, we share the amazement of Peter. "Look!" What God has promised has taken place.

III. *A call to faith (vv. 22–24)*. There was only one answer to Peter's question. Jesus said, "Have faith in God." Only faith could explain what had happened to the tree. Jesus had called on his heavenly Father to act, with full confidence that God would hear and respond. His faith was answered—the tree withered away. Jesus knew from his own experience that faith had power. But it was a difficult lesson for the disciples to learn, as it is

for us. Jesus told Peter that what from a human point of view seemed impossible could happen. One could call on a mountain to be lifted up and thrown into the sea, and it would happen if the individual had sufficient faith. Of course this was not a promise that whatever we want may happen. Our requests must honor God and conform to his will. But when they do, there are no limitations on what faith can accomplish.

Peter had experienced this earlier. The disciples were rowing across the Sea of Galilee one night. Jesus was not with them. Early in the morning he came toward them, walking on the sea. All were terrified, thinking he was a ghost. Jesus calmed their fear (Matt. 14:22–27). This was not enough for Peter. He asked Jesus to command him to walk on the water also. Jesus did so, and Peter began to walk. His faith was great; but when his faith wavered, he began to sink and Jesus had to reach out and rescue him (Matt. 14:28–33).

On another occasion, while Jesus and three of his disciples were on the Mount of Transfiguration, a man brought his ill son to the other disciples to be healed. They were unable to heal him. Only when Jesus returned and spoke to the demon did the boy become well. The disciples wanted to know why they could not heal the boy. Jesus' answer was, "Because of your little faith." He had demonstrated the power of faith, and he promised that if their faith was no larger than a grain of mustard seed it could move mountains (Matt. 17:14–21). Although God's power is unlimited, we may limit it by our lack of faith. Jesus said, "So I tell you, whatever you ask for in prayer, believe that you have received it, and it will be yours" (Mark 11:24). All things are possible through faith.

Topic: The Obedience of Faith
TEXT: Rom. 1:1–7

Other Readings: Matt. 7:21–27

Faith receives a bad name because some people claim to have faith in God and yet live in such a way that they bring dishonor to the name of God. Their lives do not differ from the lives of the unbelievers around them. People question whether faith can mean much if it does not bring change in life. Paul would have had the same question, for he firmly believed that to have faith in Christ meant that one sought to obey Christ in every aspect of life.

I. *The good news received (vv. 1–2).* Paul was writing to a church community who, for the most part, knew little about him. Some in the church had previously had contact with him, but they were a small minority. Paul therefore wrote many things that would not have been necessary in a letter to close friends.

Paul's understanding of himself and his role was based on the person of God. It was founded upon faith in the promises that God had made in ages past. Paul knew that he belonged completely to Christ and that his one responsibility was to please him. He had been made an apostle, not by his own choosing but by the grace of God. And this role had one purpose: to make known the gospel of God.

After his meeting with the Risen Lord on the road to Damascus, Paul realized that all the promises of God had been brought to fulfillment in Jesus of Nazareth. God had given the assurance that at the right time he would deal with the issue of human sin. Most people had not understood how this was to be done. Even in Jesus' day, most people did not perceive that God was working through Jesus in this special way. But Paul, and others, understood that God had kept his promises, and they based their entire destiny on their faith that this was so.

II. *The good news fulfilled (vv. 3–4).* The promises of God were fulfilled in a person, Jesus of Nazareth. Early Christians knew that in a unique way he is God's Son. He had a relationship with God that no one else had ever or would ever have. His physical descent was from David. And he was God's special Son, conceived through the Holy Spirit. He was Son of God in his very nature. He was one with the Father.

This understanding came about only through Jesus' Resurrection from the dead. Up to the time of his death on the cross, Jesus might have been seen as an unusual man, one who obeyed God completely. He could even have been seen as the Messiah, fulfilling God's promises. But these promises were often understood in earthly, physical terms. At his death, his followers were devastated; they gave up hope. All they had envisioned fled before their eyes. Only the act of God in raising Jesus from the dead and presenting him alive before these men and women could convince them who Jesus really was. True faith was born. He was seen as Jesus, the man born in Bethlehem, but also as the Christ, the Messiah. He was the anointed one of God, with a mission to redeem the world. And he was Lord. This title was given to the Risen Christ as his followers recognized that he was indeed God's Son and that he had absolute authority, given to him by his Father. Faith blossomed as God's Spirit led these people to a deeper understanding of the person and work of Christ.

III. *The purpose of the good news (vv. 5–7).* Jesus chose a select group of men, called apostles, to accompany him and to be sent out to preach and heal. But others also received this title, including Paul. Thus Paul could write about receiving grace and apostleship. He was aware that there was nothing in himself about which he could boast. What he was was due entirely to the grace of God, and he never tired of affirming that.

Paul's purpose as an apostle was "to bring about the obedience of faith among all the Gentiles." Paul knew that he had received a special call to the Gentile world. This dominated his life. It led him to proclaim the gospel and to plant churches in the major cities of the Roman Empire. This mission to the Gentiles was not always popular. Paul faced much opposition because of his faithfulness to his call. But he believed that God had called Gentiles to salvation in the same way in which he had called Jews, through faith.

Perhaps one reason for concern about preaching to Gentiles was the fear that they would bring their immoral lifestyle into the Church. Thus Paul emphasized that faith was intended to bring about obedience. This was true for Gentile and Jew alike. Faith in Christ led one to become a different person. The old person was put off, the new person was put on (Eph. 4:22–24). Paul devoted major sections of his letters to moral and ethical matters. He firmly believed that there were certain things that a Christian must do and other things that a Christian must not do. And these issues were based on faith in Christ. Paul could not conceive of one who had faith in Christ continuing on in the former manner of life. Faith brought change. We are created in Christ Jesus for good works (Eph. 2:10).

Our world today calls any moral standard into question. People like to believe that there are no rules to be followed. Paul insisted that to be a believer, a person of faith, means that one must seek to obey Christ, to imitate him. True faith leads to obedience.

Topic: Faith That Endures

TEXT: Phil. 1:18b–26

Other Readings: 2 Cor. 11:22–33

Faith seems simple and easy when all goes right. It may even stand up against some drastic event that would seem to shake the foundations. Like the Colorado River carving the Grand Canyon, it is constant wear and tear that brings danger to faith. Can it endure over time and in the face of constant pressure?

I. *Assurance of deliverance (vv. 18b–19).* Paul had served Christ for many years before he wrote this letter to the church in Philippi. He had experienced joys and sorrows. In 2 Corinthians 11 he listed many of the things he had suffered in his ministry for Christ. We shudder as we read this list because we realize how hard it must have been for Paul to endure. Only faith gave him the strength and courage to keep on in the face of these circumstances.

Paul loved these friends in Philippi. He had founded the church, and these people seemed to give him fewer problems and more joy than many of the other churches. He was now in prison because of his faithfulness to Christ. His fate was uncertain. He could have complained. The Philippians could have lost heart because they saw their beloved apostle suffering. But the result was quite different.

Paul's imprisonment had resulted in a wider spread of the gospel. He preached to some in his prison. Other believers in the city had become more bold in preaching about Christ. Some did it from improper motives, but Paul rejoiced that Christ was being preached. Even in prison Paul could rejoice. Faith gave him assurance. He knew he was not alone. His friends were praying for him. The Spirit of Christ was present. Thus he was certain that "this will turn out for my deliverance." He was probably not thinking about whether he would be released from prison. That was still uncertain. Rather, like Job, he asserted his assurance of God's vindication

(Job. 13:16). Paul was confident that whatever might happen to him in this world, he would be vindicated when he stood before the judgment throne of God. Only faith could give such assurance.

II. *Avoidance of shame (vv. 20–21).* It is easy to say "I will be faithful to death" when there are no clouds on the horizon. None of us knows how we would react in the face of dying for our faith unless we have faced that threat. We know how we hope we would act, but there is no certainty. Paul realized this about himself. Perhaps he had never faced the threat of execution because of his faith in Christ. But now this was a definite possibility. And he was not sure how he would respond. If the verdict was that he be put to death, would his faith be sufficient in that crisis as it had been in all previous events? Paul hoped this would be true. He did not want to do or say anything that would bring shame to Christ. This had been his goal in living. Now he wanted to be certain that this would continue to be true in dying.

As Paul thought about the possibility of dying, he saw it as another opportunity to bear witness for Christ. He wanted to speak with boldness, with the freedom that comes from knowing he was where God wanted him to be and that he was doing what God wanted him to do. It was a freedom that came only from the presence of God's Spirit in his life and from knowing that God was in control of the situation. Paul's own fate was not important. All that mattered was that Christ be exalted. It made no difference to him whether he lived or died. He could see advantages to both. To live meant that Christ was living and working in him, for even in his earthly life he was not apart from Christ. But death was gain. The trials of earthly life would be gone. Fellowship with Christ would be richer and more wonderful beyond the grave. Faith gave Paul confidence to face the possibility of death with courage.

III. *Continuing service (vv. 22–26).* Paul faced a difficult decision. Was it better to die and go to be with Christ, or was it better to continue to live and serve the Philippians and others? Both choices were appealing. Nothing was more attractive than going to spend eternity with Christ. From a selfish perspective, to die would be better. But Paul saw there was more to the issue than his own personal desires. Which was better for the believers in Philippi? When he thought of this, Paul concluded that it was to their advantage for him to remain alive and come to see them again. For him, faith meant continued service for Christ. There would probably be more trials and difficulties. There could be other imprisonments and eventually execution. But all that was important was to follow Christ. Faith endures regardless of outward circumstances. So Paul looked forward to coming to Philippi again and sharing their joy in Christ.

Our faith may not enable us to see as clearly into the future as Paul seemed to see. Yet our faith has the same quality of endurance. For faith is commitment to God and to his Son, Jesus Christ. And faith knows that God is in control of all things and is in the process of bringing to pass his eternal purpose. Thus there is no reason for faith to falter. It has stood the tests of the past. It can face the unknown challenges of the future, because the nature of faith is endurance.

Topic: Faith in Action

Text: James 2:14–26

Other Readings: Heb. 11:4–7, 22–31

How do we convince the world that we are people of God? People are skeptical of our claims. Do our words and our church activities convince them of our faith? People are more convinced by what they see than by what they hear. Although this attitude may be enhanced by our television mentality, it has always been true. People are going to be convinced of our faith only when they see it in action.

I. *Dead faith (vv. 14–20)*. James sensed a lack of vitality in the faith of some people in the churches. It was of sufficient concern for him to devote a major section of his brief letter to it. His problem was different from the one Paul faced. Paul had to deal with the issue of how one became a Christian. For James, the problem was this: How does one give evidence that he or she is truly a saved person?

James asked whether faith divorced from works has any value. Can such faith really save one? James asked the question with the expectation that the answer would be, "No, it cannot." He then gave an example. Poverty and need were great in the early churches, as

they sometimes are today. James pictured a person coming to a Christian seeking clothing and food. It is easy to express sympathy and give our best wishes to such a person, then send him or her off to continue cold and hungry. Words alone do no good. James was writing about assistance to fellow Christians. His words apply in our day, and perhaps even to meeting the needs of those other than Christians. James was quite blunt. He stated that such faith by itself is dead. It has no life. It cannot give life to others. He claimed that true faith will seek to meet the needs of other people.

Evidently there were some who said that faith and works were separate gifts. If God therefore chose to give the gift of faith to one and the gift of works to another, who should complain? James was skeptical of such an argument. How can one demonstrate the gift of faith except through works? Only works show the presence of faith. For James, works that please God grow out of a faith relationship with him. They are clear evidence of true faith.

Others equated faith with correct doctrine, with accepting a creed or statement of beliefs. James pointed out that even demons have such faith. The great Jewish affirmation was that God is one (Deut. 6:4–5). This was repeatedly affirmed by the people. The demons accepted this, but it did not change their relation to God. No amount of correct doctrine can suffice unless faith shows itself in works. Faith apart from works is barren; it does not produce any fruits; it is useless.

II. *Examples of living faith (vv. 21–26)*. It was not enough for James to point out the deficiencies of faulty faith. He needed to show what saving faith involved. He cited two examples from the Old Testament. The first was Abraham, the father of the Hebrew people. His faith was shown in many ways. He obeyed God's command to leave his homeland and go to a distant country. He built altars where he might worship God. He fought against the kings from the east who had carried his nephew away as a prisoner. But James cited the time when Abraham "offered his son Isaac on the altar." Although Isaac was not actually sacrificed, Abraham was prepared to carry through with this action. Only God's intervention at the last moment saved Isaac's life. For Abraham, faith meant full obedience to God, whatever the cost. His faith was demonstrated in action. He did things that showed that he had absolute trust in God. "Abraham believed God, and it was reckoned to him as righteousness." He was called "the friend of God" (Isa. 41:8). Abraham was an ideal example of one who was justified by faith joined with works.

The second example James used may have surprised his readers, much as it surprises us. Rahab was as far removed from Abraham as one could be. He was a man; she was a woman. He was the father of the Hebrew race; she was a Gentile. He was an honorable man; she was a prostitute. Yet she demonstrated her faith by her works. The account in Joshua 2 says nothing about her faith, but it is not hard to see why James felt she had faith. Why else would she have risked her life for the two spies unless she believed that their God was in control and that he would accomplish that which he had promised? She entrusted herself into his hands and she showed her faith by protecting the two men.

The author of Hebrews gives many examples of faith shown in works. Abel offered a sacrifice pleasing to God. Noah built an ark. Moses chose to share with his people the ill-treatment to which they were being subjected. The Israelites crossed the Red Sea on dry land. Hebrews lists many other people who accomplished great things through their faith. None of these had faith in word only. Always it was shown in their works, in what they did.

James did not assume that works by themselves saved anyone. Only works can be evidence of faith. They have no saving power in themselves, but they are a necessary part of saving faith. Faith must be shown in action, for "faith by itself, if it has no works, is dead" (v. 17).

SECTION X.
Children's Sermons

January 3: Keeping On Keeping On

We are already three days into the new year. Many people think that New Year's Day is a fine time to begin something new, to start practicing a good habit, to quit doing something that is not good. But a lot of the same people who had a wonderful plan give up after a few days or a few months. It isn't easy to keep on doing the good things we decide to do.

What are some of the good things you would like to do and keep on doing?

Most of the time we need help to keep up our good habits. One thing that might help is to write down what you make up your mind to do. Another thing is to ask God to help you keep on doing the good things you have decided to do. Really, God put these good things in our hearts, and God wants us to win. The apostle Paul long ago wrote to the people in a church telling them, "God is the one who began this good work in you, and I am certain that he won't stop before it is complete" (Phil. 1:6a CEV).

Sometimes we don't do exactly what we meant to do. We may feel ashamed, even discouraged; we may want to quit trying. But God loves us and wants to keep on helping us. So, what does God do? He forgives us and helps us to keep trying.

Prayer: Thank you God for giving us good things to do. Thank you for helping us do them and for forgiving us when we make mistakes or forget or feel like quitting. Amen.— James W. Cox

January 10: The Lasso

Preparation: Using a clothes line or a heavy cord, make a lasso.

Do you know what this is? It is called a lasso or lariat. It is a special kind of rope that enables you to extend the holding power of your arm as you reach out with the loop and catch something and then pull it back toward you. You can use it to force someone to come to you when they do not want to do so. Some people think that this is what God should do with all the people of the world. They ask, "Why doesn't God force people to do what is right? God is all powerful, so why doesn't he make everyone follow him?"

Suppose you saw a person that you would like to have as a friend. Do you think it would be all right to take this rope and force that person to come with you wherever you go? Can you force a person to be your friend?

God who made us knows that when we are physically forced to do something our first reaction is to rebel, to pull away and to run away if we get a chance to do so. God could use force on us and make us do what he wants us to do, but God loves us and he wants us to respond to his love. He wants us to go with him because we want to do so, not because we are forced to do so.

So, remember that the lasso has no place in our relationship with God and it has no place in our relationships with other people. You cannot force someone to be your friend. There is an old saying that goes, "To have a friend you must be a friend." Jesus said the same thing when he taught us to do unto others as we would have them do unto us (see Matt. 7:12). We call that the Golden Rule.—Kenneth Mortonson

January 17: People Are Different and the Same

TEXT: Acts 4:12

Object: Wooden shoes (or any ethnic object)

This is a pair of wooden shoes. People in Holland, a country overseas, used to wear these all the time. When a person walked down the sidewalk in wooden shoes, there was quite a noise. These days most people in Holland wear shoes that are similar to ours. But years ago wooden shoes were a distinctive mark of Holland's culture.

Travelers going from country to country discover many things that make people different. Languages are different, eating customs, and manners are just some of the things that vary from nation to nation. In Japan, it is polite to burp at the table. The Japanese do that to show they enjoyed the meal. At home here in the United States, we get scolded when we burp at the table and we have to say, "Excuse me."

There is one thing that is the same for all people everywhere. There is only one way to be saved, and that is through Jesus Christ. Listen to this verse. [Read Acts 4:12.]

We shouldn't be afraid of people who are different than us. Those differences are on the surface, like the kind of shoes or clothing that is worn. Deep down inside, people's feelings are very much the same. People in different countries love their families, they shiver in the cold, and they love to have fun just like us. Part of our human nature makes us want to stay away from people who speak or act differently than we do. We shouldn't feel that way.

God has told us in the Great Commission to go into all the world and tell about Jesus. We have been given that commandment because, though they seem different, people around the world are like us. They need salvation in Jesus.—Ken Cox

January 24: Praising God

TEXT: Ps. 92:1

Song: "Praise Him, Praise Him"

Good morning, boys and girls. This morning I enjoyed good food for breakfast. Would one of you like to tell me what you ate? [Pause for response.] I slept in a comfortable bed last night. Did you? In my home I felt safe and secure. Yes, God is so good to us. He provides for our needs.

Because God is so good to us, we should praise him. It should be part of living each day. But how can boys and girls praise the name of Jesus in church? [Pause for response.] We can sing hymns during the worship service. When we lift our voices in song, we show others that we love Jesus. When someone is praying aloud, what should we do? Yes, we should bow our heads and close our eyes. This shows reverence for God. What can we do during the sermon? Yes, we can be good listeners. What happens if we talk to someone nearby? Or we make noise when the minister is speaking? [Pause for response.] First, it shows that you are not being a good listener to God's word. Then, when you are noisy, you may keep someone else from paying attention. This might be someone who would make a decision at the close of the sermon.

Let us ask God to help us praise him in everything we do. Let us be good listeners while attending a church service. Through our actions, we show our love for Jesus.

Psalm 92:1 says, "It is good to praise the Lord and make music to your name, O Most High." [The pianist plays softly, "Praise Him, Praise Him," as the children return to their seats.]—Carolyn R. Tomlin

January 31: Do You See People as People?

TEXT: Mark 8:22, 24–25

Object: A poster with stickpeople and a group photo

I have drawn fifty stickpeople on this poster. It's hard to get concerned about these fifty stickpeople because they don't project any reality. This is a group picture of some real people. By looking at this photograph we can actually get concerned about their personalities and needs.

Jesus healed a blind man one day. There was a point when the man could see a little, and then, after another healing touch by Jesus, he could see perfectly. Listen to these verses. The man briefly saw people as trees, and then he viewed them just as they were, as people.

We need the same touch of Jesus today to help us grasp the true needs of people. When we talk about mission needs, and about the millions of people who have not heard about Jesus, we may think of them as stickpeople. Statistics don't project any personality or feelings.

We have discovered that a good way to see people as people is through mission trips. When a person goes on a short mission trip, either to the inner city or to a foreign country, he or she has the opportunity to talk to and help needy people. After a missions trip, the participants are always excited about helping again. Their attitudes are different because they have experienced statistics as real people.

We must remember the real folks behind the numbers that we mention in church. For each statistic, there is a person we can witness to or pray for. Let's pray that Jesus will help us to see them not as stickpeople but as real folks.—Ken Cox

February 7: The Mirror

Object: a mirror

Today I would like you to look at something that is very useful and that almost every home has. It's a mirror. What do we use mirrors for? I would like each one of you to look at yourself in the mirror and then pass it on. While you are doing that, let me remind you that with a mirror you are able to see things that you could not possibly see without it. And the most important thing you can see in the mirror is your face. If I had something on my chin, the only way I could see it would be with a mirror.

Now, you have all seen yourself in the mirror. What you saw was a very special person. You know, there is not another person in the world just like you. In fact, you are not only special, you are also precious, for there never has been and never will be another person just like you.

Because you are special and precious, I would like the people out there to have an opportunity to get to know you a little better. So, what I would like you to do is line up and then, one at a time, take this microphone and tell us your name and how old you are and then tell us one thing you enjoyed doing this past week.

Thank you for letting us see you in a new way this morning. You have helped us to know that person you saw in the mirror.—Kenneth Mortonson

February 14: Where Is Your Treasure?

TEXT: Matt. 6:19, 21

Object: A small chest or jewelry box and a paper heart

This is a treasure box. Valuable possessions are stored inside boxes like this. The thing we enjoy more than anything else is our treasure. Inside this treasure chest is a red paper heart. [Open box and remove heart.] This cutout illustrates a truth from the Bible: our hearts will be located wherever our treasures are.

Our treasures may not be valuable watches or jewelry. We may highly value running faster then the rest of the kids our age. We may prize having special athletic shoes or an expensive bicycle. But as we set our hearts on these earthly things, we are going to be constantly disappointed. Listen to these verses.

Jesus said that earthly things can be taken from us. The Bible says that moths eat and destroy the finest clothes. Rust ruins the neatest bicycle and thieves steal other valuables. There will always be someone faster or with a newer bike. Knowing that we can lose what is most important to us at any moment makes us fearful, suspicious, and stingy. Smiles leave our faces, and frowns display our unhappiness.

Jesus said that we are to put our treasures in heaven. We store treasures in heaven by acts of kindness and by sharing with people who need us. Jesus taught that heavenly prizes can never be taken away from us. When we are convinced that we cannot lose our riches of obedience, our hearts become confident, loving, and trusting. People with hearts that are full of joy make the world a very happy place.

Let's be careful about what we treasure. Our most prized possession can make us very unhappy if that joy is not from our relationship with God.—Ken Cox

February 21: Jesus Loves All People

TEXT: Gal. 5:14

Song: "Jesus Loves the Little Children"

Object: Mission picture with several races represented (if available)

Boys and girls, you are beautiful people. You have eyes that see, ears that hear, a nose that smells, hands that touch, and a mouth that tastes good food. Isn't it great that God made us this way?

[Hold up the picture of different races.] Look at this picture with me. God gave these boys and girls the same gifts he gave you. They have ears, eyes, a nose, mouth, and hands that touch. They are like us in other ways, too. They need loving parents who care for them. When they are sick, they need medical care. These children need an education, just like you. They like to run, jump, and skip, just like you.

Perhaps as you look at this picture you see some way in which you are different. Can anyone compare themselves with a child in this picture? [Pause for response.] I hear you saying: a different color hair and skin, curly hair, straight hair, eyes shaped a little different, some are tall, others are short. Yes, we see these things. But these are the physical characteristics. The things that are inside a person are more important. We all have the same needs. Who would agree with this statement? Boys and girls all over the world are more alike than different.

God made these boys and girls and he made you. He loves everyone. God is happy when we love others, regardless of their race or culture.

In Galatians 5:14, Jesus commands us to "Love your neighbor as yourself." Who are our neighbors? Are they people who live next door? Not only that; your neighbors are people all over the world. When we obey this commandment, we please God. [As the children return to their seats, the pianist plays "Jesus Loves the Little Children."]—Carolyn R. Tomlin

February 28: Don't Go It Alone

TEXT: Mark 6:7

Object: Two pieces of string

Jesus had a group of twelve followers, called apostles, who were with him all the time. Jesus sent these men out to teach and work for the Kingdom of God. It is important to see how Jesus sent them out. Listen to this verse. [Read Mark 6:7.]

Jesus sent these apostles out two by two. Alone they might not have been strong enough to complete their mission. Where one person can become lonesome and discouraged, two persons working as a team are very strong.

This piece of string by itself is not very strong. But if we take another strand just like it and weave them together like this, the pieces combine to become strong like a rope. When two pieces of string are put together, the resulting cord can hold three times as much weight as a single length of twine.

The Bible has other verses that stress the importance of teamwork. Listen to Ecclesiastes 4:10, 12.

Jesus knew that the apostles going two by two would be able to finish the work he needed them to do. In the same way, the church in great numbers is powerful and effective. We are here together today to emphasize our strength and determination. Let's remember the lesson of the two pieces of string and work together to complete God's calling.—Ken Cox

March 7: We Are All Both Rich and Poor

When the weather starts to get warm, what do we think of? [Spring.] When spring comes, what happens? [Things start to grow again.] There is an old saying that reminds us what we look for in the spring. It goes: "April showers bring May flowers." In the spring there are flowers everywhere. We see them on the ground, on bushes, and even some trees have beautiful flowers on their branches. In the spring, we are all so rich. There are so many beautiful things around us.

But what else happens in the spring? [Baseball.] Springtime means that baseball teams are busy practicing. One of the things they practice is hitting the ball. I want you to remember something very important about baseball. I can't remember ever hearing of a baseball player that batted .500. That means that even the best baseball hitter misses the ball more times than he hits it.

We are all limited in what we can do, and in that sense we are all poor. Nobody is perfect in anything. And even if we were, there would still be many things that other people can do better than we can.

This is an important lesson for us all. Wise is the person who can see how rich he or she is with what she or he has in life, and who can also accept his or her limitations in life, at any age.—Kenneth Mortonson

March 14: A Little Yeast Goes a Long Way

TEXT: 1 Cor. 5:6

Object: A slice of bread and a cracker

This slice of bread and cracker don't look alike, but they are. Bread and crackers are both made from flour and baked in an oven. The different ingredient in the bread is yeast. Yeast makes the lump of dough swell or rise, as little air holes are formed in the dough.

Those holes, and some can be big enough to stick your finger through, are from the yeast, and they cause the bread to enlarge and be light and fluffy.

In Jesus' day, before a loaf of bread was baked a little pinch of the risen dough was saved. On the next day, that little pinch of dough that contained yeast was added to a new lump of flour. The little bit of yeast remaining in that pinch of risen dough would work its way through the whole new lump of dough, causing it to rise. Another pinch would be saved for the next day, and so on, and so forth. From just one pinch of dough thousands of loaves would be created!

Because of how it acted, yeast became a symbol for sin. Just a little sin would change the whole life of a person and community, spreading continuously. Listen to this verse. [Read 1 Cor. 5:6.]

This verse identifies a little boasting or bragging as being capable of changing all of a person's life. The stretching of the truth was to be avoided because of it's powerful influence.

We are to be careful because trouble is likely to start in small doses. We may not commit a big sin, like stealing an automobile, but we will think about snitching a piece of gum. The Bible warns us that bad actions will spread in our thinking and deeds until our whole life is affected.

There is also a positive side to this image: the powerful influence of good. The Bible promises that if the correct and fair thing is done with the little things in life, we will soon be able to handle big jobs, doing them honestly and properly (Luke 16:10).

So, we should never think that little things are unimportant. Small deeds turn into big actions. With God's strength and truth guiding our consciences, we will always know the right thing to do.—Ken Cox

March 21: A Day of Rest

TEXT: Exod. 20:8–10a

Song: "Jesus Loves Me"

Object: Chalkboard or poster paper

Boys and girls, today you are here because you made a choice. This was a choice between attending church and staying home. Sunday is a day to honor God. But it is also a day of allowing our bodies to rest from school or work.

The Bible tells us that God created the heavens, the earth, and the sea, and all that is within them. Then what did he do on the seventh day? [Pause for response.] That's right: he rested.

After we come with our families to church each Sunday, we have the afternoon for relaxation. That's a big word. Can anyone tell me what *relaxation* means? [Pause for response.] The dictionary defines the word as "to relieve something from effort or strain; to become less formal." Maybe you return home and take off your Sunday clothes. You put on play or outdoor clothes, depending on choices you've made for the day. Let's think of activities boys and girls could enjoy on Sunday and still make it a day of rest? Will you raise your hands and help me as I write your answers on the board? [Pause, giving several children an opportunity to answer.] Yes, these are good answers. Did we include a time to take a nap? Read from a favorite book? Take a walk with a friend or family member? Visit a relative? Go for a pleasant drive? Sundays are different from other days. Yet we still have many choices.

God told his people in Exodus 20:8–10a, "Remember the Sabbath day by keeping it holy. Six days you shall labor and do all your work, but the seventh day is a Sabbath to the Lord your God." [As the children return to their seats, have the pianist softly play "Jesus Loves Me."]—Carolyn R. Tomlin

March 28: The Thief on the Cross

TEXT: Luke 23:42–43

Object: A model or picture of three crosses

This is a model of three crosses. The Bible states that when Jesus was crucified there were two men on crosses on either side of him. One of the men was angry and said unkind things to Jesus. The other, while admitting that he was guilty of criminal wrongdoing, had a meaningful discussion with Jesus. Listen to these verses.

This criminal was asking for forgiveness. Jesus' words of comfort to the man indicated that very soon the man would be with Jesus in heaven. Thus the Bible records that Jesus accepted the criminal as one of his children and ensured that he would have eternal life in heaven.

It would have been impossible for the man on the cross to be baptized or join a church. It was the faith of the man that saved him on that day of his death.

The thief on the cross, as he is sometimes called, shows that it is never too late to make things right with God. Some folks think that they have gone too far and that it is too late for them to follow the will of God for their lives. That is not true. Whenever and wherever we are in life's journey, we can come to God in simple belief. When we accept him as savior, our lives will be transformed and make a mighty difference.

It is never too early to make a decision to live for Jesus. As soon as we clearly understand that God loves us and has a special plan for our lives, we should come to him and seek that plan; we should come to him and seek that special pathway. It is good to be saved just before we die. It is even better to give our hearts to Jesus at a young age and spend all of our lives in devotion to Him.—Ken Cox

April 4: Learning from Color

Every day we have a lot of people around us. There are people at school who we see every day. There are people in your family who are there every day to help you. There are other children who you do things with at play or in special groups. People are all around us and we need to be concerned about what is happening to them.

One way we have of thinking about what is happening to others is to learn from certain colors. Do you know what it means when someone says, "I feel blue?" It means they are sad. Something is missing or is wrong in their life and that is probably why they say, "I feel blue." If heat is missing from a person's body, if they are exposed to extreme cold, they may turn blue. If a person cannot breathe, if they are missing air, they may turn blue. So, a blue person is one who needs something to cheer him or her up, to make him or her smile.

What that person may need is the color yellow. Yellow is the color of sunshine, and the sun brings us warmth and its light helps things to grow. The sun, as the light of the world, is essential for our well-being. Remember, we also speak of Jesus as the light of the world, and he also brings warmth into our lives and with him we grow into the kind of person God wants us to be.

Now, what happens when you put blue and yellow together? You get green. And what is the color of growth? How do we know

that something is growing? By the color green. For example, when spring returns, we see that the trees are alive when they send out green leaves; and we know the grass is alive as it turns into a new rich color of green.

So, remember the lesson of these colors. A person without God is spiritually dead. Color that person blue. Jesus is the light of life. Color him yellow. Now, when a person who is blue accepts Jesus into his life, the new color is green and that shows us that he or she is alive and growing. And by our example we can help others to find that new, abundant life that Jesus wants us all to have.—Kenneth Mortonson

April 11: Hold up Your Candle

TEXT: Matt. 5:14–15

Object: A candle and a bowl

Jesus said that his life shines through us like a candle. One candle may not seem to possess much power, but as the lights are lowered in the sanctuary [have someone appointed to dim the lights] it is easy to see the candle. When a candle is burning like this in the darkness, all attention is drawn to it as the source of light.

Our candle can be dimmed by putting a bowl or cover over it. Look what happens as I cover my candle; the whole room grows dark. When I remove the bowl the light burns brightly again. Jesus said to allow our candles to burn brightly. Listen to this verse. [Read Matt. 5:14–15.]

Jesus commands us to put our candle on a stand, not under a bowl. The Lord wants us to allow his life in us to be clearly seen, not covered up.

We allow the light of Jesus in our lives to be seen as we identify ourselves as followers of Jesus. We don't have to be obnoxious about it. We don't have to preach to people or point our fingers in their face when they do something wrong. We simply confess that we are Christians.

When we are prepared at any moment to tell others about the light in our lives, we begin to live in a way that is very pleasing to God. If we know that we may be called upon to tell others about Jesus at any moment, we stay obedient and prayerful. No one who is planning to say something good about Jesus will allow their lives to be a bad testimony about their Savior.

One little candle has a tremendous impact

on the darkness of this room. The candle in your life, burning with the power of Jesus, can dispel the darkness of this world. Lift up your candle; don't cover it up.—Ken Cox

April 18: God Made the Sun

TEXT: Jer. 31:35
Song: "Sunshine in My Soul"
Object: Picture or drawing of a sun

Boys and girls, will you focus your attention on this picture [or drawing]? We all know what it is, right? Yes, it is an image of the sun. It's a picture of something wonderful that God created in the universe. Without the sun our earth would be cold. Plants would not grow. Plants need sun to produce food for us to eat. I would say that the sun is necessary for survival.

Have you ever had a plant indoors and the sun pulled it toward the source of light? Perhaps the plant was placed in a window. Then one day you noticed that the plant was curved. That's because the stem was bending toward the light. If an indoor plant is too far away from the light source, which is the sun, it will whither and die.

Have you ever played outside on a winter day? The cold wind blew and whistled around you, but you found a sunny spot protected against the wind. Here you were much warmer.

God made the sun, which all living things need to survive. Only he can make the sunshine. We cannot change a cloudy day. But there's something boys and girls can do. We can have sunshine in our hearts. When we have this joy that comes from loving God and serving others, we have a heart filled with gladness.

Listen as I read about God's universe in Jeremiah 31:35. "This is what the Lord says, he who appoints the sun to shine by day, who decrees the moon and stars to shine by night, who stirs up the sea so that its waves roar—the Lord Almighty is his name." [The children return to their seats as the pianist plays "Sunshine in My Soul."]—Carolyn R. Tomlin

April 25: Fruit Stains

Object: You will need a stained wooden strawberry box. If a wooden box is not available, use a plastic box and put a fruit stain on a cloth.

I imagine that some of you boys and girls have seen a box like this lately. This is the kind of box that may be used to collect strawberries from a garden. And if the picker or the buyer are not careful, a strawberry might be damaged and it will leave a stain like this. [Show box or cloth.] Fruit stains can be very difficult to remove. The next time you have some grape juice in your house, take a little rag and put some juice on it. Let it dry and see if you can rinse it out.

Now, Jesus taught us that a Christian should be known by the fruit he or she bears. [See Luke 6:43–45.] That is, when we do good things, we show other people what kind of person we are. On the other hand, when we do bad things, we show that we are not trying to do what God wants us to do. Now, the fact that fruit can produce a long-lasting stain reminds us of something else we need to remember about our good or bad deeds: very often the effect of what we do lasts longer than the actual deed itself. A small, kind deed can make a whole day happier. A word of praise or guidance, given at the right time, can change a person's life forever. A word spoken in anger can scar another person for a long time. As a Christian you are known not only by what you do but also by what effect your deed has on the people around you. That is an important lesson for all of us to remember.—Kenneth Mortonson

May 2: The Family of God

TEXT: Mark 3:35
Object: A picture of a family of God

Families are very important. In our families we are protected, we learn, and we grow up. This is a picture of a family.

The Bible informs us about the "family of God." The Bible states that we become a part of the family of God when we accept Jesus as our Savior. When Jesus taught his disciples to pray, he told them to address God as Father.

One day Jesus spoke about his family and said that all who did his will were his family. Listen to this verse.

Doing Jesus' will means being obedient to him. This includes speaking the truth, being honest, and being kind to others. Being obedient also includes praying and telling others about Jesus.

Each week in America some children run away from home. When they do, they lose the protection, learning, and love of their families. Runaways will be unhappy and may get into serious trouble. When we are disobedient to Jesus' commandments, it's like we have run away from the family of God. When we are spiritual runaways, we lose the blessings that come from being at home with Jesus. Sometimes we sing the chorus, "I'm so glad I'm a part of the family of God." Let's do God's will so we can be glad we are safe at home with Jesus.—Ken Cox

May 9: Homes for Families

TEXT: 1 John 4:7

Song: "God, Give Us Christian Homes"

People live in different kinds of homes. In the early days of our country, natural resources usually determined the kind of house that was built. Pioneers built houses of logs. Native Americans used animal skins. Eskimos cut hunks of ice and formed it into a dwelling. Those settlers who conquered the West relied on sun-dried clay, called adobe.

Today, our houses are very different. Can some of you tell me the building material used in your homes? [Pause for response.] Yes, I hear you saying: bricks, wood, vinyl, and other materials. And some of us live in houses, apartments, trailers—some even on boats. Isn't it great that God has given us homes with families to care for us!

Let's talk together about how a home offers protection. Can you name something a home protects us from? [Pause for response.] A home offers protection from the weather. When it's too cold to play outside, we return to a warm house. And when the temperature rises, many of our homes are air-conditioned or have fans. Aren't you glad your home has a roof when it rains?

Yes, a home offers protection in many ways. But there is something else about a home. A home is shared by a group of people called a "family," who love and support one another. Your family may be different than other families. You may have one parent or two. Or you may live with relatives. You may have foster parents. But God has provided for someone to love and care for you.

I like the Scripture verse from 1 John 4:7, which talks about love. "Dear friends, let us love one another, for love comes from God." Let us thank God for giving us Christian homes in which family members love one another. [The pianist softly plays "God, Give

Us Christian Homes" as the children return to their seats.]—Carolyn R. Tomlin

May 16: We Are to Be Fishers of Men

TEXT: Mark 1:17

Object: A fishing pole, net, and so on

These are pieces of fishing equipment. The line and hook from this pole are used to catch the fish. This net is used to "land" the fish. It keeps the fish from getting away when we are pulling them into the boat.

Fishing can be compared to reaching people for Jesus in at least two ways. First, fishing is like telling others about Jesus because both fish and prospective Christians have to be looked for. The fish will not come swimming to the boat; they have to be located. People without Jesus will not come to the church; we have to invite them. We are commanded to "go and tell."

Second, fish are hungry when they go for the bait. If the fish are not hungry, they just won't bite. People without Jesus are hungry, too, but not for food. People are hungry for answers to life's questions. They want to know how to be happy, and how to solve their problems. Jesus can satisfy that hunger because he is the way to abundant life.

Catching fish is a most enjoyable hobby. It is even more satisfying to become successful fishers of men. We should all be willing to tell others about Jesus.—Ken Cox

May 23: Jesus Calls Us

TEXT: Matt. 4:19–20

Song: "God Is So Good"

Object: A fish hook

Boys and girls, I'm holding something in my hand that has a specific purpose. Do you know the name of this object? [Show fish hook.] This is called a fish hook. Fishermen use this piece of bent wire to catch fish. Look at its shape. Do you see the small hole where the line is tied? This line then connects with the pole or rod and reel. Notice the sharp point on the end. It also has a barb. The barb hangs in the fish's mouth when he grabs the hook.

But in order for the fish to be attracted to this hook, it needs something else. Do you know what that is? [Pause for response.] That's right: the hook must have bait. Many fishermen use artificial lures that resemble a bug. Some fish like that. Other fish are more interested in the bait if it's a minnow or a cricket. It depends on the kind of fish you are fishing for.

Sometimes the devil tempts us, just like a hook tempts a fish. First, he shows us the hook. Then, if we aren't interested, he tries to make it more attractive. This is when bait is used. When we fail to live by God's rules, we often reach out for that attractive bait. And just like the fish, we are caught.

Jesus says for us to follow him. "Come, follow me," Jesus said, "and I will make you fishers of men." At once the men left their nets and followed him (Matt. 4:19–20). Let us ask God to make us strong and to avoid temptation. [As the children return to their seats, the pianist plays "God Is So Good."]—Carolyn R. Tomlin

May 30: Missionaries Meet Spiritual Needs
TEXT: John 20:21

Object: Some purchased items in a sack

When we need things around the house we may have to go to several different stores to make purchases. [Pull items from the sack.] To get this video, I had to go to a department store. To get these metal brackets, I had to shop at a hardware store. To get my favorite food, peanut butter, I had to drive to the grocery store. Some stores seem to have almost everything, but we may still have to make several stops to get everything we need.

A song that we all enjoy singing is "Jesus Loves Me." We all know that song by memory, but for millions of people in the world it is an unknown song. There is a missions area called "the last frontier" where 1.7 billion people live who have never accepted Jesus as their Savior. If we were to sing "Jesus Loves Me" in that area, not only would the children not know the song, they would have to ask us who Jesus is.

When we have a need around the house, we go and purchase what we lack. It is sad that in the last frontier the millions of people without Jesus don't even know they have a spiritual need. Missionaries are believers that travel into areas that have never heard the name of Jesus. Missionaries have been sent to tell others what they have learned. Listen to this verse.

Being a witness involves telling what we know to be the truth. Missionaries are witnesses sent around the world so that "Jesus Loves Me" can be sung in another language.—Ken Cox

June 6: Sunglasses
[Put on a pair of sunglasses.] If I had entered the sanctuary this morning wearing these sunglasses, you would have assumed that something was wrong with my eyes. People usually wear sunglasses only when they are outside in the bright light of the sun. One reason for wearing sunglasses is to cut down on the glare so that we can more clearly see the things around us. When the light is too bright and our eyes are unprotected, we have trouble seeing. Sometimes in the movies we see a person getting what is called "the third degree," and they have a bright light shining in their eyes so they cannot see the person on the other side of that light.

Perhaps this condition gives us a clue as to why the Bible tells us that no one has ever seen God [see John 1:18]. God is too wonderful, too majestic, too brilliant for our eyes to see him and understand what we see. So it is that God, in his wisdom and love, comes to us in his Son Jesus, who people are able to see and understand. In a sense, Jesus is our spiritual sunglasses. Through him we see God. In John we read, "No one has ever seen God, but God the only Son, who is at the Father's side, has made him known" (John 1:18 NIV). It is our faith, therefore, that if we want to know the one true God we must find him in Jesus.—Kenneth Mortonson

June 13: Where Are the Children?
This morning, I would like you to help me remind all these people out there of something very important. But first, we need to help them to think about what it means to be a child. How many of you can drive a car? You have to be older to do that. How many of you can cook a meal? Some of you have learned how to do that, but others of you have not yet learned about cooking. How many of you know how to write a check? Let me tell you a secret. Even some of the adults out there have trouble with that, especially when it comes to balancing the checkbook.

Now, we do not expect you to know how to do all those things, because you are children. You still have a lot to learn. You know that and they know that. But you are not the only children in this room. When Jesus came to his disciples, after his Resurrection, when they were fishing, he called to them, "Children, have you any fish?" (John 21:5 RSV). Why do you think he called those grown men children? It was because they still had a great deal to learn about their new life with Jesus. We are all children of God and that means we will always have a lot to learn about what it means to be a Christian. Now, that is exciting, because no matter how much we know, there is still more to learn as we live with God our Father. And the more we learn, the more we will be able to do in God's Kingdom on earth.

Thank you for helping me to remind all of us of something that is very important.—Kenneth Mortonson

June 20: Role of a Plant

TEXT: Gen. 1:11

Song: "For the Beauty of the Earth"

Object: A plant containing leaves, stem, and roots

What am I holding in my hand? [Pause for response.] Yes, this is a plant. Have you ever seen all the parts of a plant such as this? See, this one has everything necessary to make it survive and grow. Right? Here are the leaves, which catch moisture or rain. Sun and light are brought to the plant through the leaves. The stem of this small plant serves the same purpose as the trunk of a large tree. The stem supports the plant in the soil and links the roots with the leaves. And last, the roots. Who knows what they do? [Pause for response.] Yes, they absorb moisture and nutrients or food from the soil and send it to the part of the plant that is above ground. The stem, leaves, and roots are all important. They each have a role in making the plant grow.

As boys and girls in our church, you also have a role. This is a very important one. Perhaps you aren't old enough to teach a class, or to preach a sermon. Yet there's something only you can do. Can anyone guess what it is? [Pause for response.] You can wear a smile. You can greet visitors. You can show others you are glad to be in God's house.

Just like each part of a plant serves a purpose, every boy and girl in our church has a job to do. Will you do your part? Raise your hand if you will help. We can't be the kind of congregation we should be without boys and girls like you.

In Genesis 1:11 the writer says: "Then God said, 'Let the land produce vegetation: seed-bearing plants and trees on the land that bear fruit with seed in it, according to their various kinds.' And it was so." [The pianist plays softly "For the Beauty of the Earth" as the children return to their seats.]—Carolyn R. Tomlin

June 27: We Should Visit with God Every Day

TEXT: Dan. 6:10

Object: A toothbrush

This is a brand new toothbrush. Dentists tell us that regular brushing is the key to taking care of our teeth. They instruct us to brush after each meal. To have healthy teeth and gums we must dedicate each day to brushing.

Wouldn't it be awful if we didn't believe the dentists? If we only brushed our teeth once a month or so, we would really have trouble with our teeth, not to mention bad breath. Yuck. If we neglected our teeth by not brushing regularly, soon we would have cavities and pain, and before long our teeth would start to fall out.

The Bible tells us that we are to visit with the Lord regularly. A man named Daniel has set a good example of visiting with the Lord regularly. Listen to this verse. Daniel prayed three times a day. Those regular visits with God had a tremendous impact on his life and the world.

The way we visit the Lord regularly is through daily prayer, Bible reading, and worship. We would not think of going several days without hearing from our best friends. In the same way, we need to hear from God regularly. We hear from God through his Word. We talk to God through prayer, and we join our Christian friends through fellowship and praise by worshiping together.

If we fail to visit with God on a regular basis we will lose touch with our heavenly Father. Let us learn to worship and visit with the Lord Jesus every day.—Ken Cox

July 4: The Mousetrap

Object: A mousetrap

There is a special chapter in the Bible that is called "the Proverbs." Does anyone know what a proverb is? It is a wise saying, a short sentence that we can use to guide us. In the first chapter of the Proverbs we read, "If sinners entice you, do not consent" (Prov. 1:10). Now, a sinner is someone who rebels against God, who seeks to completely ignore God and what he wants. Such a person lives only for himself; and he likes to have other people support his way of life by getting them to do what he does. So he tries to get others to follow him. That is what *entice* means.

The mousetrap gives us a good illustration of what is involved. The enticement is the bait that is set out in full view. The mouse likes cheese, so when he sees a piece of cheese all he thinks about is how good it tastes. Why should he not take what he likes? So he enters the trap and pulls on the bait. Do you know what happens then? [If you have set the trap, use a pencil to set it off.] BANG! The mouse is caught.

Now, the mouse is not very smart. All he can do is react to the things he sees around him. He can't look at the trap and figure out what will happen to him if he tries to take the bait. But God has given you a mind so you can think about the consequences of what you do. God expects you to use your mind and avoid those things that can hurt you, even when they look good and offer something that you really want to do. Be careful not to be misled by people who live by a different standard than what you follow. "If sinners entice you, do not consent."—Kenneth Mortonson

July 11: The Barter System

Object: A long tree limb and a saw in a sack

Have you ever heard of the barter system? Before people had a lot of money, the barter system was used to enable them to get the things they needed. Let me show you how it works. [Give someone a two- or three-foot piece of a tree. Pull a saw out of your sack.] You have a piece of wood and I have a saw. Neither of us has any money, but we both could use a piece of wood to put in a stove to cook a meal. I offer to use my saw to cut the wood in half, and for the use of my saw I will get a piece of the wood. Then you will have wood that will fit into your stove and so will I. That is the barter system.

Now, today we also have the money system. People go to work and use their time and talents and they get money for what they do. Then they take that money and go to someplace where they can buy what they need. In

a sense, they are still using the barter system, only what we call money is added so that everyone is able to get what they need when they need it.

Now, every Sunday, as we shall see in a few minutes, the people in the church give money to the church, and they expect something in return. They want you to have the things you need in your Sunday School class. They want the sanctuary to be warm in winter and cool in the summer. They want to help other people in what we call our mission program. They want to have a minister in the church to help teach and lead them. They want to have a church home—this beautiful building in which we gather—and they want it to be maintained. They want to help the church be what it is supposed to be, and when they give their money, which they have earned, they are really giving of themselves, just like in the barter system.—Kenneth Mortonson

July 18: Everything God Made Is Good

TEXT: Gen. 1:31a

Song: "All Things Bright and Beautiful"

How many of you boys and girls have heard of the kudzu vine? [Pause for response.] The kudzu is a fast-growing plant that is native to Asia. This vine was introduced into the United States to control erosion and as food for farm animals. In some countries, the roots are ground to provide both food and medicine.

In many places, however, this wild vine has taken over trees, houses, telephone lines—even entire farms. It is said that the tendrils may grow one foot daily during the growing season. The vine is almost impossible to destroy. Just looking at the vine one sees beautiful green leaves. Long shoots climb trees, giving it a healthy appearance. Yet the vine is deceptive. It chokes and kills weaker plants by blocking the sunlight.

Boys and girls, sin is a lot like the kudzu vine. Oh, it may appear harmless when we first see it, but it destroys lives. The longer we allow sin to control us, the harder it is to get rid of it. God hates sin. This is because it separates us from the loving fellowship he wants us to enjoy.

Let me ask you: How can boys and girls avoid things that are wrong or harmful? How can we make the right choice when faced with decisions? [Pause for response.] God is the answer. We are made in his image. When we pray and ask God to help us, he helps us with everyday problems.

We must remember that everything God made is good. Even the kudzu. The abuse of a certain object or pastime makes it harmful. "God saw all that he had made, and it was very good" (Gen. 1:31). [The pianist softly plays "All Things Bright and Beautiful" as the children return to their seats.]—Carolyn R. Tomlin

July 25: Crowds Followed Jesus

TEXT: Mark 2:4

Object: Picture of Jesus and a crowd

Jesus had a tremendous challenge when he ministered on Earth. Crowds of people followed him. Zaccheus went to see Jesus and had to climb a tree to see him because of the multitude. This is a drawing of what it was like when Jesus moved through a village. Jesus was surrounded by people wanting to hear him teach and desiring his healing touch.

On one occasion some men wanted to take their friend to Jesus so he would be well again. Because of the swarm of people, the men carried the man up onto the roof, dug a hole through the ceiling, and lowered the man right in front of Jesus! Listen to this verse. [Read Mark 2:4.]

Because of their faith, Jesus healed the man. The healed man picked up the mat they had carried him on and walked triumphantly through the crowd.

The crowds came to Jesus because he did so much for them. Jesus met the people's needs and told them the truth so they would know how to live. Our churches should be full to overflowing today because we help people with their needs. When we have a positive impact on people's lives, the word spreads rapidly and others come, too.

God has given us the ability to help people. We help them with what we own and what we know. By sharing with people from our material wealth, we are able to make an impact on practical needs. By telling others the truth of the Bible, we are able to help them with spiritual needs.

Jesus faced crowds wherever he went because he did something very special. We are to continue that same special work today, through our fellowship.—Ken Cox

August 1: The Danger of an Empty Room

Object: A soda straw

I am sure you all know how to drink something with a straw. You put the straw into the liquid you want to drink and then you make it flow through the straw into your mouth. Have you ever wondered why you can do that? The reason is simple. When you suck on the straw you remove the air inside it and the liquid flows up into the straw to take the place of the air that you have removed. You can see how this works when I put a piece of paper over the end of the straw and remove the air from the straw. When the air is removed, it forms what we call a vacuum. And when I remove the straw from my mouth, the air rushes back into the tube and the paper falls off.

This reminds us of an important rule about life: if you remove something from your life, something else will take its place. Jesus pointed this out in a story he told. [See Luke 11:24–26.] There was a spirit that was having a bad influence on a man. But one day the spirit left the man and wandered over the desert looking for a place to rest. Finding none, it said, "I will go back to the home I left." So it returned and found the house swept clean and empty. Off the bad spirit went and collected seven friends, more evil than itself, and they all entered the empty place and lived there, and the condition of the homeowner was worse than before.

You see, it is not good enough to simply say, "I'm not going to do this bad thing any more." Bad habits have to be replaced by good habits. For example, you cannot say, "I will not let my room become a mess." Having said that to yourself, you must also say, "I will put my things away when I am finished with them." We improve life by what we say we will do as well as by what we say we will not do.—Kenneth Mortonson

August 8: Jesus Prayed First

TEXT: Mark 1:35

Object: A candy bar

This is a delicious candy bar. Candy is so tasty that it's tempting to eat dessert before we eat our meal. It's difficult to put the wholesome and healthy foods first when we know that a candy bar is coming up. But if we eat candy first, we are not hungry for the foods that will help us grow strong.

In our spiritual lives we have to put some things first, too. It is easy to get so busy in life that important spiritual matters, such as prayer, are forgotten.

Jesus was very busy during his earthly ministry. Crowds surrounded him wherever he went, and he spent hours teaching and working with the people who needed him. Jesus never got so busy that he forgot to pray. Listen to this verse.

Jesus prayed at the beginning of the day because of its utmost importance. Through prayer we show our dependence on God and garner his strength for the busy day ahead. God answers our prayers. Through prayer God provides our daily food. Because we pray, we are protected and receive help in knowing how to live.

We know better than to eat a candy bar before we sit down to have supper. We should also follow Jesus' example of putting spiritual preparation before busy days filled with practical things. Prayer in the morning is the key that unlocks the remainder of the day.—Ken Cox

August 15: The Big Heart

Object: A cup and a balloon

This morning I am going to try and pick up this cup without touching it with my hand. All I'm going to use is a balloon. Let's see if it works. [Put the end of a round balloon into the cup and blow it up until the balloon fills the cup. Hold the air in the balloon by closing the stem with your fingers. Slowly raise up the cup. Be sure to practice first at home.]

Many people around us are like this empty cup. No one seems to care for them. They don't have any friends, and they are very sad. What they need is someone who has a big heart to come along and enter into their life and give their spirit a lift. [Lift up the cup again.]

I have often noticed that when there is a large group of people standing around talking, one or two people seem to be left out of the conversation. The friends have gathered together, but the stranger, or the person with no friends there, is left standing alone, and he or she usually looks rather sad. The person with a big heart will sense the emptiness, the loneliness of the person standing alone

and will reach out to that person to draw them into a friendly situation.

Jesus taught us that if we only greet our friends then we are just like everyone else (Matt. 5:47). Jesus wants our relationship with him to make us different from everyone else. The spirit of Christianity should give a person a warm and friendly spirit that we call a big heart, which will lift up the lives of the people around them.—Kenneth Mortonson

August 22: God Does Not Change

TEXT: Ps. 100:3

Song: "Jesus Loves Me"

Object: A picture of a chameleon

[Hold picture so children cannot see.] Boys and girls, I want you to guess what's on the opposite side of this picture. Let me give you some clues. Raise your hand when you think you know the answer. First, this is a small animal. It crawls on the ground. Scales cover its body. It can climb the bark of a tree. Does anyone have an answer? [Pause for response.] Listen to another clue. It's color depends on the object on which it rests. Now, many of you know the answer. That's right, it's a chameleon, from the reptile family. This unique trait offers the chameleon protection from an enemy by making the chameleon difficult for the enemy to see.

This important characteristic makes the chameleon a most unusual animal. Could any of you change the color of your skin by standing next to something? Could your skin become greenish by lying on the grass? Of course not!

We are not like the chameleon. We cannot change our appearance in this way. Boys and girls are often try to be like the chameleon. They may do something that displeases God, then they try to hide their wrongdoings. But you know something? We cannot hide from God. Oh, you may do something wrong and your parents or friends might not find out. But God knows. He is a loving God, and he hopes we will return his love.

God has a purpose for each boy and girl here today. We are his. Psalm 100:3 says, "Know that the Lord is God. It is he who made us, and we are his, we are his people, the sheep of his pasture." Let's thank God for making each one of you unique. [The pianist plays "Jesus Loves Me" as the children return to their seats.]—Carolyn R. Tomlin

August 29: It Takes Time

Object: For this sermonette, you will need two jars filled with muddy water. Let one jar sit so that the mud drops to the bottom and the clearer water is seen. Stir up the second jar just before you talk to the children.

This morning I would like to try and show you one of life's most important rules. This jar seems to be full of a gray liquid, and as long as it is stirred up by moving the jar around, you will have difficulty telling what is really in the jar. Now, look at this second jar. It contains the same material we saw in the other jar, but this jar has been sitting still for more than twenty-four hours. Now we can see the heavier mud that has settled to the bottom and the water above is beginning to get clear.

Many times in life, while we are living through some event, we wonder why it is happening to us. Often when things are all stirred up, we cannot see all of the parts of a situation and therefore we cannot understand it. But as time passes and we look back on that event, we begin to see the total situation. For example, there are times when your parents tell you what to do and you cannot see why this must be so. But as you grow older, your understanding of a situation will change and you will see all the parts and understand the reason why your parents guided you in that special way.

Patience is one of life's most important qualities, for it helps us to wait and see, and with the passing of time we find wisdom and understanding, and wounds are healed.

This also applies to our living with God. God rules his world and our lives, if we let him. But it takes a lifetime to see the way God works.—Kenneth Mortonson

September 5: What Makes a Cup Clean?

TEXT: Matt. 23:25–26

Object: A coffee cup, dirty on the inside

Would you drink hot chocolate out of this cup? As I hold it up and prevent you from looking inside the cup, you might answer, "Yes, I would drink from that cup." But as we look closer, we discover that the inside of the cup is filthy. The outside of the cup is nice and clean, but we certainly would desire the cup to be clean inside, too.

Jesus used a dirty cup like this to give a lesson on life. He told a group of leaders that if they were acting good on the outside but had bad thoughts and feelings in their hearts and minds, they were useless like this dirty cup. Listen to this verse. [Read Matt. 23:25–26.]

When we follow Jesus as Lord, we should desire to be clean from the inside out. This is done by asking Jesus for forgiveness of our sins. Each day we should confess to the Lord our failures and admit our need of his special help. When we have bad thoughts and feelings, we should ask the Lord to help us put them aside.

It's tempting to make ourselves look good on the outside and allow bad thoughts and feelings to remain in our hearts. Jesus tells us to make sure we are okay in our thoughts and feelings, and then we will be clean in our outward actions, too.

Jesus provides strength to live for him. If we are honest with God about our problems, he will help us. Furthermore, we won't have to worry so much about doing good deeds. When we feel good on the inside, because God is our strength we will naturally be inclined to help those who need us.—Ken Cox

September 12: The Soldering Gun

Object: Electric soldering gun

For those of you who are not familiar with this tool, it is called a soldering gun. When I squeeze the trigger, electricity is allowed to heat up the metal tip, as is evident when I place the tip against this piece of paper. As long as the cord is plugged into an electrical outlet and as long as the switch is on, the tip will remain hot. You cannot tell that it is hot just by looking at it, but when it comes in contact with something, the presence of the heat becomes evident.

God's Spirit is like the electricity in this soldering gun. When you come to church and learn about God, we hope that what you learn here will make a difference in your life. But that special quality that is in you will not be seen by others if you do not have contact with them. When you are in school, for example, and someone begins to tease one of your friends, you can do one of two things. You can join the person who is doing the teasing and be like him or her; or you can try to find a way to help your friend who is being teased by showing concern for the one in need.

The other thing to remember is that our coming to church on a regular basis is one way we have of keeping that spiritual electricity, that sense of the presence of God, flowing through our life. It is what helps us to be prepared to do the right thing when we have contact with other people.—Kenneth Mortonson

September 19: Show Kindness to Others

TEXT: Eph. 4:32
Song: "Something for Thee"
Object: Brightly wrapped present

Boys and girls, I'm holding something everyone likes to receive. What do we call this brightly wrapped box? [Pause for response.] Yes, this is a present, or some might say a surprise, or a gift. It is all these things. A present is something we enjoy receiving. Have any of you ever received a present? [Ask children to raise their hands.] What was in the container that held your present? [Wait for response.]

Birthdays are a special day for receiving presents. Christmas is another. And many of you may receive surprises for no special occasion, just because someone loves you and wants to make you happy.

Yes, we all agree that gifts are fun to receive. But you know something? Giving a present to others is also very rewarding. In our mission programs at church, we bring supplies for missionaries. We may save our allowance and purchase a gift for a family member. Or we may work for a neighbor and make extra money. But what happens when we don't have any money? What could boys and girls do for others? How could we show kindness to friends? [Pause for response.]

When we show kindness to others, we are making Jesus happy. The other person feels good too. And you have this special glow because you gave something only you could give—yourself.

Ephesians 4:32 commands us to "be kind and compassionate to one another, forgiving each other, just as in Christ God forgave you." [As the children return to their seats, the pianist plays softly "Something for Thee."]—Carolyn R. Tomlin

September 26: Sunday Is for Us

TEXT: Mark 2:27
Object: A calendar

Each day on this calendar has the same-size square. But every day of the week is not the same, and we should not treat them alike. Sunday is to be a special day of worship.

In Jesus' time, the Sabbath had become an unhappy day. There were hundreds of laws describing what could and could not be done. No work was ever to be done, people couldn't even take a long walk. The Sabbath became a troublesome day for people; they didn't look forward to it and they were glad when it was over.

Jesus wanted the Sabbath day to be a joyful time full of blessings. Listen to this verse. [Read Mark 2:27.] In other words, the special day of worship was to help, not discourage or frustrate God's people.

We should look forward to Sundays because it is a time to worship and be in fellowship with God. The Lord is our shepherd and good friend. He loves us and takes care of us. We should look forward to spending time with him. When we look forward to Sundays, the day is always a blessing to us.

I hope that your calendar doesn't treat every day the same. Sundays are special days to be enjoyed in God's house with God's people.—Ken Cox

October 3: Beware of Habits

This morning I want to try an experiment with you. Fold your hands. Now unfold them and then fold them again. Notice which thumb is on top. Is it the thumb from your right hand or from your left hand? When I fold my hands, they are always folded the same way, with my right [or left] thumb on top. Do you do the same? Now unfold your hands and refold them with the other thumb on top. I find that it is harder to fold my hands that way, and it feels different.

You see, I have the habit of folding my hands a certain way and I always do it the same way, without even thinking about it. When I do it a different way, it feels strange.

Now, it doesn't make any difference which way you fold you hands, but this does show us why we need to be careful of the habits we have. When we form a habit it means that we will usually do that particular thing without much thought; and whether it is right or wrong, because it is a habit, it will feel right to us. That is why some people use what we call swear words when they speak. They have gotten into such a habit of saying those words that they use them without thinking about it. But for a person who does not swear all the time, hearing those words from another is very distracting.

If you remember the nature of a habit, you will take time now and then to check up on your habits and see if they are good, and to make sure that they are helping you to do things in the best way.

As you learn more things and get new wisdom over the years, it will help you to learn new and better ways of doing the important things in life—that is, if you are smart enough to learn new and better habits. Unfortunately, some people learn bad habits as a child that they carry over into adulthood. I hope that won't happen to you.—Kenneth Mortonson

October 10: We Contain the Treasure of God
TEXT: 2 Cor. 4:7

Object: Various jars

We can tell what was in some jars by their distinctive looks. This jar held honey. It has a wide mouth for pouring the thick, gooey honey. This little bottle held perfume. Even though the bottle is tiny, the superb smelling liquid was very valuable, not to mention expensive. This bottle held ketchup. Ketchup bottles are easy to spot. The ketchup goes from the broad base of the bottle down to a funnel-type opening to help it flow out smoothly.

A man named Paul described God's presence in the world as being in special containers. When we accept Jesus as our Savior, the presence of God comes into our lives. Thus each of us becomes a container of the goodness and presence of God. Listen to this verse. [Read 2 Cor. 4:7.]

The Lord puts his power and presence in all types of containers. The containers are always human beings. Those jars may speak different languages. Some will be poor and others rich. But we all contain the same presence of God.

Even if we are different, the presence of God in our lives is a treasure. Now, no manufacturer of expensive perfume would put their product in a crude or common container, but God has chosen to put the miraculous presence of his Spirit in ordinary folks like you and me.

We ought to be grateful that God has put

his presence and power in our lives. Furthermore, we ought to be sure that his grace flows smoothly out of our lives in a beneficial way, just as he planned.—Ken Cox

October 17: Addition and Subtraction
Object: A glass of water and a stone

This glass on the tray is filled to the top with water. Now, if I place a stone in the glass, I am sure you know what will happen. Let's see if you are right. The lesson from this simple event is this: when something is added, something is taken away. The glass has only so much room within it. The added stone takes up some of that room and that pushes some of the water out of the glass.

This is an important lesson to apply to life, for there are so many things that we can let enter into our daily living. Some things are essential. You need to eat and sleep. Maybe you have to go to school, and your parents may have to go to work. But there are also a lot of things that you can choose to do. Each day is like the glass. There are only twenty-four hours in a day and you can only do so much in each day. If you watch television a lot, you may not have any time left for reading. If you ride in a car all the time, then you may miss out on the enjoyment and exercise that comes from walking. Because everything we may need to know can be found in books or on the computer, so many people have lost the art of memorizing. When something is added, something else is taken away.

Therefore, as responsible people we need to be more selective and think not only about what we want to add to life but also about what we will lose when that something is added. To be a disciple means to live a disciplined life and to be disciplined means you are in control of your life.

So, do not let the world place rocks in your glass of living water. Remove the rocks, and the living water of God within you will fill the glass again. Remember, the twenty-third Psalm tells us about life with God, where we have a cup that overflows. And Jesus said, "I have come that you might have abundant life" (see John 10:10).—Kenneth Mortonson

October 24: Jesus Is Always Present
TEXT: Ps. 107:1

Song: "My Best Friend Is Jesus"

Have you ever been driving with your parents and suddenly the rain started falling? It began as a light shower. Then the rain came so fast you couldn't see the road. Perhaps you saw images, but not clearly. Or objects right in front of your car were visible, but not those in the distance.

Is there something on a car that makes it easier to drive when it's raining? [Pause for response.] Yes, they are called windshield wipers. They move from side to side, sweeping the rain off the front glass. Without them the driver could not see objects ahead. Without them, there would be more accidents. Aren't you glad that the manufacturers of automobiles decided to include a windshield wiper. Today's vehicles have them as standard equipment.

But have you ever been driving when the wipers didn't work? That really makes a difference. When we turn something on, we expect to get results.

Isn't it great that when we need Jesus, he is always there. During the day and into the night, he's there. When thunder rolls across the sky and lightning flashes, he's there. When we are lonely, he's there. When illness comes, he's there. I would say that Jesus is a friend we can depend on throughout life.

Today as we study God's word, listen as I read from Psalm 107:1: "Give thanks to the Lord, for he is good; his love endures forever." Bow your heads and repeat this prayer with me: Father, please help me place my trust in you. I know you will be present in all my life. Amen." [The pianist plays softly "My Best Friend Is Jesus" as the children return to their seats.]—Carolyn R. Tomlin

October 31: The Mask of Our Mouths

TEXT: Mark 7:6

Object: A mask

A person wearing a mask like this can pretend to be someone or something else. Of course the person wearing the mask knows better, but a good mask can completely fool others about our true identity.

There are different ways that we can conceal who we really are. One method is to try to control what others think about us by what we say. With our words we attempt to make persons think that we are superb ballplayers, experts in computer programming, or faithful Christians.

Jesus called people who put on a disguise

of words "hypocrites." The term *hypocrite* means "actor." Jesus saw people putting on a show for the world around them. It's bad enough that one of these hypocrites would deceive another human. But these actors were attempting to deceive God by what their lips said. Listen to this verse. [Read Mark 7:6.]

God knows our deeds and thoughts. The Lord grasps who we are beneath any masks we might wear. God created us and has given each of us special abilities. Our happiness begins when we admit that God knows everything, even our secrets, and we begin to live truthfully for him. When we are truthful with God, we admit our mistakes and receive forgiveness. Through our honesty we gain a clean conscience and a good feeling inside. Our spiritual lives then become a strength to us, and we no longer feel guilty about the improper things we have said and done.

After we have learned to be truthful with God, we learn to be honest in all our dealings with our friends. It's a relief when we accept ourselves just like we are, and we no longer have to brag or tell stories to try to impress others. Then we discover who God really intended us to be, and that true identity is very special indeed.—Ken Cox

November 7: The Cricket and the Coin

Object: A pocket comb. (To make the sound of a cricket, hold the comb in your hand and draw your thumb rapidly across the comb's teeth.)

Two men were walking along a street in a busy city. One man was very interested in the things of nature. As they walked along, the naturalist said, "Did you hear that?" [Make the sound of a cricket.]

"All I hear are the cars and the people," said the friend.

"Listen, don't you hear it?" [Make the sound again.]

"No," came the answer again. The first man looked around and nearby he found the little cricket that was making the noise he heard. After finding his little friend from nature, the man reached into his pocket and took out a quarter and let it drop on the cement sidewalk. Immediately, some of the people around him felt their pockets to see if they had lost any change, while others looked around for the lost money. The noises of the city smothered the sound of nature, but the sound of a coin was heard immediately.

You see, we hear the sounds we want to hear, the sounds of the things that are important to us, and we turn a deaf ear to all other things. In a like manner, many people hear only the teachings they want to hear and put up a mental block to any new and different instructions. To receive truth, even God's truth, you must be tuned in, you must want to hear. So Jesus said, "He who has ears to hear, let him hear" (Mark 4:9). Jesus also said, "Seek and you will find" (Matt. 7:7). When you believe that what the Bible teaches about life is important, then you will take those teachings into your life and live by them.—Kenneth Mortonson

November 14: Ears

This morning I'd like to take a moment to illustrate something rather important. First, close your eyes. [Hold a book parallel to the floor and drop it so that when the flat surface hits the floor it makes a loud noise.] Open your eyes. How many of you saw the book falling? No one. How many of you heard the noise made by the book falling to the floor? Everyone. God has made us so that we can close our eyes, but we cannot close our ears. I wonder why? There are times when we need to close our eyes so that we can go to sleep. But even when we are sleeping our ears are open, and if a smoke alarm goes off in the house during the night, we will hear it.

This is an important lesson we all need to remember. We all hear what is happening around us, and when what is heard is not what we *want* to hear it disturbs us. Maybe you are watching a special television show and suddenly your brother or sister comes in and starts to talk to you. That talking makes it hard for you to enjoy your show and you probably tell your brother or sister to be quiet. The same thing can happen here in church. When people are trying to listen to something in the worship service and someone else is whispering to a friend, that is heard and it is disturbing. So I hope that you boys and girls will always remember that you are a part of our worship service and when anyone makes a noise, big or little, that is not a part of what we are all doing together, it destroys that sense of togetherness that is so important for us all. I know we can count on you boys and girls to do your part in making each worship service a meaningful experience.—Kenneth Mortonson

November 21: We Are Thankful

TEXT: Ps. 105:1

Song: This Is My Father's World"

Boys and girls, let us talk about things for which you are thankful. Would anyone like to say something that they thank God for? You may want to call out a word or phrase. [Pause for response.] I hear you saying so many things for which we offer thanks.

You have loving parents and caregivers who provide food, clothing, and shelter. What happens when you are sick? You visit a doctor, who helps you get well. Teachers at church tell you about Jesus. At school, you learn to read—plus so many other things.

How many have brothers or sisters? [Pause for response.] Aren't you glad you always have someone to play with? Oh, I know you may not always agree, but your siblings are important to you.

God has given you a good mind. He wants you to use this to make the right decisions. These are choices that make God happy. When we ask God to help us in our daily life, he helps us.

Also we thank God for our senses. Our eyes allow us to see his beautiful earth. Our ears hear our parents and friends talking. Our sense of smell provides the aroma of food cooking, yet warns us of the danger of fire. What sense tells you if you like a particular food? That's right, it's the sense of taste. Our hands allow touching. All our senses are important to our well-being. They keep us safe. And they enrich our lives.

God has given us so much. We are thankful. The psalmist said, "Give thanks to the Lord, call on his name" (Psalm 105:1). [The children return to their seats as the pianist plays "This is My Father's World."]—Carolyn R. Tomlin

November 28: God Sends His Word to Us

TEXT: Isa. 40:8

Object: A scroll, Bible, and computer Bible

God has always given his Word to us. The form of his Word has changed down through the years. In Jesus' day, scrolls like this were used instead of books. The word of God would be written in columns, and the scroll would be unrolled and read to the people. Specially trained and dedicated men, called scribes, would copy the word of God onto scrolls.

About nineteen hundred years ago the book, or *codex*, began to replace the scroll. Binding the pages together in a book like this made it easier to use the Word of God. In those early days of bookmaking, every page was still handwritten by scribes. It took a long time to make a copy of the whole Bible when the copying was done by hand. In those days most people did not have their own copy of the Bible. They had to go to church and hear it read. Next came the invention of the printing press. This technological advance allowed many copies of the Bible to be made and more people could afford their own copy of the Scriptures.

Just recently the Bible has been put on computer. [Show an electronic Bible, CD ROM disk, or floppy disk.] The whole Bible is on this little computer [or disk]. All sorts of Bible study can be done using the Bible on computer. It is even possible to get the Bible on cassette and listen to God's Word while driving or jogging.

God is intent on revealing himself through the Bible. The Lord has used many methods to get his truth into our lives. Whether the Bible is on a scroll, in a book, or in computer form, it is all from him, and the perfect truth for our lives. The Word of God will continue to be passed down through the years. The Bible will last forever. Listen to this verse. [Read Isa. 40:8.]—Ken Cox

December 5: A Sad Story of Foolish Pride
TEXT: Mark 6:26
Object: A picture, toy, or puppet of a crow

This is a picture of a crow. When cooked, crow tastes awful, so it is not a favorite food. When we are wrong and admit it, we say that we have "eaten crow," because we have swallowed our pride, which doesn't taste good either.

One of the saddest stories in the Bible is about the foolish pride of King Herod. One night King Herod held a party for his friends. His stepdaughter, Salome, danced, and Herod was so impressed that he promised to reward her with anything she asked for. Salome's mother had been angry with John the Baptist, and they asked that he be exe-

cuted. Herod was shocked by their outrageous request and seemed to want to get out of his promise. But Herod wouldn't take back what he had said in front of all his party guests. So John the Baptist, a great prophet from the time of Jesus, was wrongfully put to death that very night.

King Herod got into trouble by making promises that he shouldn't have. He wanted to impress everybody, so he said big things. Then he didn't have enough courage to back down from what he had said, even though it was wrong. Listen to this verse. [Read Mark 6:26.]

When we put ourselves in a trap that we have made with our own mistakes, true bravery must be shown by admitting that we're wrong. King Herod should have said, "I have made a very foolish promise; I can't have John the Baptist executed." Sometimes we must say, "I have said that I would go along, but now I realize that I cannot do what you want me to do." It is easy to get swept along in some very bad business just because we won't swallow our foolish pride.

It's hard to eat crow and admit that we're wrong, but in the long run we will be much happier with ourselves. And God will be proud of us too.—Ken Cox

December 12: Nothing Can Separate Us
TEXT: Rom. 8:28
Object: A metal cookie box and an assortment of refrigerator door magnets

Good morning! Do you know what I have in my hands this morning? That's right; it is a box, and it is a special kind of box that you see in many places this time of year. It is sometimes called a cookie tin, and people make a gift of cookies or candy and put the goodies in this kind of decorated box. But even after Christmas is over and all the goodies have been eaten, you can still use this box in a special way.

What do we keep in boxes like this one? Treasures! That's right, Ben. I'll bet you would keep Civil War patches in yours. Some of you would have stickers or trading cards. Treasures! I'll remove the lid so you can see what is in my treasure box. What does that look like? Yes, it is a cinnamon roll. Well, it's not real but it looks just like what we call "sticky buns." See this one. It is a small plaque that was given to me when I taught a course last summer on the Ten Commandments. It says "The Ten Commandments are not multiple choice." Do you know what this treasure is? You remember when we looked at it on another Sunday? It is a sand dollar. You do remember.

Now let's put them back in the box. What would happen now if we shook the box up? Would all the treasures smash into each other? Yes, they would! [Shake the box and then open the box and show the children what happened.] Why haven't they moved or crashed into each other? Yes, there are magnets on the side of these treasures that you couldn't see. We can't always see God's love that holds us secure, like a magnet. That love is stronger than anything else in the whole universe. All the treasures were kept safe. They didn't go flying away from the box or crashing into each other. Keep that picture in your mind and this thought from God's word: "Nothing will be able to separate us from the love of God in Christ Jesus our Lord." Amen.—Gary D. Stratman

December 19: It's Jesus' Birthday

TEXT: Luke 2:11

Object: A birthday card

Christmas is one of the most exciting times of the year. I can tell that each of you is looking forward to Christmas. I can tell by the eager looks on your faces.

This is a birthday card. By mailing one of these to a family member or friend, we convey to them that we have remembered their birthday. When we receive birthday cards we feel very special. Our hearts are warmed with the knowledge of the loving thoughts of others toward us.

Christmas is the time set aside to celebrate Jesus' birthday. When Jesus was born in the city of Bethlehem there was no room for his family in the inn, so Jesus was born in a stable. That night the angels sang the message to shepherds in the fields near Bethlehem. Listen to this verse. [Read Luke 2:11.] Those shepherds dropped everything and immediately went to see the baby Jesus.

We remember Jesus' birthday by observing the special nature of this day. This is a challenge because Christmas has become so busy. We are careful not to overlook giving presents to one another. We are occupied with traveling to visit relatives and eating. Oh, how we eat at Christmas!

We remember Jesus in simple ways. We sing carols about the story of Jesus' birth. We take time to remember the less fortunate. And like the shepherds, we take time to consider and be amazed at the fact that God became human just like us.

I believe that Jesus is happy when we have a great time opening presents at Christmas. Jesus is honored when his birthday celebration is one of the happiest moments of the year for children. However, let's remember the true meaning of Jesus' birthday. Christmas means that God loves us so much that he came to earth to live among us and save us.—Ken Cox

December 26: Complete the Circuit

Object: You will need a working flashlight and another battery and light bulb and a piece of wire that is formed to hook onto the light bulb and bent to go around the battery and touch the bottom.

When I turn on this flashlight, we have light. That light is produced by two batteries and a light bulb, like these. What do you think will happen if I touch this bulb to the battery? Will it light? Let's see. It didn't work. Something is missing. Does anyone know what we need? In the battery we have electricity. The light bulb will light when that electricity flows *through* the bulb, not just *to* the bulb. So, what we need is a complete circuit. If I attach a wire to the light bulb and touch the base of the bulb to the top of the battery and then touch the bottom of the battery with the wire, we will have light. [Do this.]

Love is like electricity. When someone loves you, when they do kind things for you, you can feel their love coming to you. But what really makes a difference in life, what brings a glow to life, is when you receive love from someone *and* you share that love with others. When you both receive and give love, life is beautiful. So, to be happy in life, look for ways in which you can be kind and helpful and loving to others. Jesus taught us, saying, "Let your light so shine before others that they may see your good works and give glory to God the Father" (Matt. 5:16). And John wrote, "We love because he first loved us" (1 John 4:19).—Kenneth Mortonson

ABOUT THE EDITOR

JAMES W. COX, a leading authority on preaching and one of the most influential teachers in the field of homiletics, is a senior professor of Christian preaching at the Southern Baptist Theological Seminary in Louisville, Kentucky. He has been editor of the last sixteen editions of *The Ministers Manual.* He has published extensively in the area of Christian preaching and has preached in churches from Singapore to Louisville. He received his M.Div. and Ph.D. degrees from the Southern Baptist Theological Seminary. He and his wife live in Louisville.

ACKNOWLEDGMENTS

Acknowledgment and gratitude are hereby expressed for kind permission to reprint material from the publications listed below. Each of these selections is used by permission.

Excerpts from Lowell M. Atkinson, *Apples of Gold* (Lima, OH: Fairway Press, 1986), pp. 155–158

Excerpts from a sermon by David Feddes, "Under the Influence," from The Back to God Hour of the Christian Reformed Church in North America, 6555 West College Drive, Palos Heights, IL 60463

Excerpts from Greg Clements in James C. Barry, ed., *Award Winning Sermons,* Vol. 4, pp. 125–132, © 1980, Broadman Press

Excerpts from H. Gordon Clinard in H. C. Brown, ed., *South-western Sermons,* pp. 60–65, © 1960, Broadman Press

Excerpts from William R. Shunk in James C. Barry, ed., *Award Winning Sermons,* Vol. 4, pp. 52–58, © 1980, Broadman Press

Excerpts from James E. Lamkin in James C. Barry, ed., *Award Winning Sermons,* Vol. 2, pp. 19–26, © 1978, Broadman Press

Excerpts from John B. Fowler Jr., in James C. Barry, ed., *Award Winning Sermons,* Vol. 3, pp. 61–66, © 1979, Broadman Press

One page by Bessie Kennedy in *Open Windows,* Jan. 25, 1994, Jan.–Mar. issue, © 1993, The Sunday School Board of the Southern Baptist Convention

Excerpts from Bill J. Harrison in James C. Barry, ed., *Award Winning Sermons,* Vol. 2, pp. 71–77, © 1978, Broadman Press

Excerpts from Hugh Litchfield, *Preaching the Christmas Story,* pp. 107–113, © 1984, Broadman Press

Excerpts from Jerry Hayner, *Yes, God Can,* pp. 36–47, © 1985, Broadman Press

The 1999 edition includes two special sections on "Preaching on Faith," by Clayton K. Harrop, former professor of New Testament and Dean at the Golden Gate Baptist Theological Seminary, and on "Bible Studies," by Eduard Schweizer, former professor of New Testament and Rektor (president) of the University of Zurich.

INDEX OF CONTRIBUTORS

SERMON TITLE INDEX

Children's stories and sermons are identified as (cs); sermon suggestions as (ss)

SCRIPTURAL INDEX

Malachi **3:6,** 54

Wisdom of Solomon
11:24–12:1, 117

Matthew **2:1–12,** 18; **2:11,**
20; **4:1–11,** 45; **4:12–23,**
28; **4:19–20,** 334; **5:1–12,**
33; **5:14–15,** 332; **5:16,**
163, 220; **6:19–21,** 50,
329; **6:33,** 29; **7:7,** 241;
8:23–27, 51; **10:38,** 216;
11:15, 201; **11:27–30,**
144; **13:24–43,** 256;
13:31–35, 118; **13:36–43,**
150; **13:54–58,** 295;
14:22–33, 161; **15:21–28,**
165; **19:27–20:16,** 189;
21:1–11, 67, 285;
21:33–46, 198; **22:1–14,**
203; **22:15–22,** 208;
22:34–46, 213; **23:1–12,**
218; **23:25–26,** 340;
25:1–13, 222; **25:14–30,**
226; **25:31–46,** 231;
25:40, 51; **26:8,** 38;
28:16–20, 115; **28:19,** 302

Mark **1:14–15,** 303; **1:17,**
302; **1:35,** 338; **1:40–45,**
34; **2:1–12,** 39; **2:4,** 338;
2:27, 341; **3:35,** 333; **4:24,**
228; **4:31–32,** 108; **5:1–13,**
279; **5:19,** 87; **6:26,** 345;
6:7, 330; **7:6,** 343; **8:22,**
24–25, 328; **9:2–9,** 43;
11:12–14, 20–24, 321;
11:15–19, 313; **12:1–12,**
199; **12:31,** 83; **13:24–37,**
235; **14:29,** 43

Luke 1, 247; **1:13–15,** 238;
1:26–45, 294; **1:47–55,** 250;
1:49–50, 252; **2:8–20,** 289;
2:11, 346; **2:22–40,** 292;
3:1–18, 238; **3:7–18,** 290;
4:18–19, 303; **5:27–28,** 15;
12:15, 70; **14:30,** 59; **15:20,**
55; **19:1–10,** 180; **21:1–4,**
257; **22:39–46,** 47;
23:42–43, 331; **24:1–12,**
282; **24:13–35,** 85

John **1:1–11,** 253; **1:1–18,** 13;
1:16–17, 170; **1:29,** 24;
1:43–51, 25; **2:12–24,** 283;
3:1–17, 49; **3:1–21,** 301;
3:16, 14, 200; **4:5–42,** 53;
5:2–16, 266; **7:17,** 123; **9,**
92; **9:1–41,** 57; **9:24–39,**
297; **10:1–18,** 90; **11:1–45,**
62; **12:20–26,** 65; **13:3–5,**
162; **13:21–33, 36–38,** 266;
14:1–10, 96; **14:8–10,** 241;
14:8–17, 25–27, 265;
14:15–21, 101; **15:1–8,** 132,
261; **17:20–26,** 210;
20:10–18, 73; **20:19–31,** 80;
20:21, 335; **20:30–31,** 305

Acts **1:6–14,** 105; **1:8,** 107;
1:14, 112; **2:1–4, 43–47,**
265; **2:1–21,** 110; **2:14–16,**
22–24, 37–38, 305;
2:14–21, 145; **2:14,** 36–42,
112; **2:42,** 93; **2:47,** 216;
4:12, 328; **4:32,** 242;
10:42–43, 83; **16:25–34,**
205, 319

Romans **1:1–7,** 322;
1:16–17, 219; **1:18–25;**
4:1–8, 193; **5:2,** 150;
5:12–19, 128; **7:24–25,**
140; **8:26–39,** 155; **8:28,**
345; **12,** 127; **12:3–8,** 174;
12:1–2, 98; **12:11,** 167;
12:14–21, 175; **13:8–14,**
177; **14:12,** 24; **15:1,** 167;
15:5–6, 13, 33, 10;
16:25–27, 10, 250

1 Corinthians **1:1–9,** 22;
1:27, 145; **1:3,** 10;
1:10–18, 27; **1:18–31,** 31;
1:23–24, 46; **2:1–5,** 224;
2:1–12, 36; **4:1–5,** 25;
4:1–13, 256; **5:6,** 330; **13,**
183; **15:1–28,** 77;
15:12–20, 269; **15:58,**
210; **16:2,** 189

2 Corinthians **1:8–10,** 188;
3:4, 18; **3:18,** 233; **4:7,**
342; **4:16–18,** 98; **5:19,** 98;
8:7, 88; **8:9,** 252; **8:12,** 43;

9:7, 47; **9:8,** 159; **9:12,**
140; **9:15,** 136; **12:7–10,**
184; **13:14,** 10

Galatians **1:13–24,** 159;
2:20, 55; **4:4–7,** 254;
5:13–14, 194; **5:13–26,**
131; **5:14,** 329; **6:6,** 179;
6:10, 220

Ephesians **1:17–19,** 232; **2:8–**
10, 149; **3:8–12,** 19; **3:20,**
140; **4:25–5:2,** 228; **4:32,**
341; **5:2,** 131; **5:18,** 114;
6:10–17, 64; **6:23–24,** 11

Philippians **1:1–11,** 225;
1:18–26, 324; **1:27,** 193;
2:1–13, 191; **2:5–8,** 303;
2:5–11, 285; **2:6–11,** 309;
2:12–13, 194; **2:13,** 224;
3:7–21, 140; **4:7–9,** 11

Colossians **3:17,** 65;
3:23–24, 155

2 Thessalonians **1:11–12,**
11

1 Timothy **1:2,** 11; **3:16,** 252;
5:1–8, 103

2 Timothy **1:1–12,** 20; **2:8,**
75

Titus **2:11–15,** 246

Hebrews **6:10,** 123;
10:11–18, 264; **12:6,** 158;
13:16, 237; **13:20–21,**
11

James **1:2–5, 12,** 193; **1:5–8,**
107; **1:12–15,** 158; **1:17,**
171; **1:22–25,** 233;
2:14–26, 325

1 Peter **2:24–25,** 42;
3:10–14, 11; **4:10,** 60;
5:6–11, 199

2 Peter **3:8–15,** 239

INDEX OF PRAYERS

INDEX OF MATERIALS USEFUL AS CHILDREN'S STORIES AND SERMONS NOT INCLUDED IN SECTION X

INDEX OF MATERIALS USEFUL FOR SMALL GROUPS

TOPICAL INDEX